Managing People

A Pearson Custom Publication

Managing People

Compiled from:

Organising and Managing Work
Second Edition
by Tony Watson

Human Resource Management: A Contemporary Approach
Fifth Edition
by Julie Beardwell and Tim Claydon

Essentials of Organisational Behaviour
Second Edition
by Laurie J. Mullins

Contemporary Human Resource Management:
Text and Cases
Second Edition
by Tom Redman and Adrian Wilkinson

Human Resource Management
Seventh Edition
by Derek Torrington, Laura Hall and Stephen Taylor

Introducing Human Resource Management
Fifth Edition
by Margaret Foot and Caroline Hook

PEARSON
Custom
Publishing

Pearson Education Limited
Edinburgh Gate
Harlow
Essex CM20 2JE

And associated companies throughout the world

Visit us on the World Wide Web at:
www.pearsoned.co.uk

First published 2009

This Custom Book Edition © 2009 Published by Pearson Education Limited

Compiled from:

Organising and Managing Work
Second Edition
by Tony Watson
ISBN 978 0 273 70480 5
Copyright © Pearson Education Limited 2002, 2006

Human Resource Management: a Contemporary Approach
Fifth Edition
by Julie Beardwell and Tim Claydon
ISBN 978 0 273 70763 9
Copyright © Longman Group Limited 1994
Copyright © Financial Times Professional Limited 1997
Copyright © Pearson Education Limited 2001, 2007

Essentials of Organisational Behaviour
Second Edition
by Laurie J. Mullins
ISBN 978 0 273 71646 4
Copyright © Laurie J. Mullins, 2006, 2008

Contemporary Human Resource Management: Text and Cases
Second Edition
by Tom Redman and Adrian Wilkinson
ISBN 978 0 273 68663 7
Copyright © Tom Redman and Adrian Wilkinson 2001, 2006

Human Resource Management
Seventh Edition
by Derek Torrington, Laura Hall and Stephen Taylor
ISBN 978 0 273 71075 2
Copyright © Prentice Hall Europe 1987, 1991, 1995, 1997
Copyright © Pearson Education Limited 2002, 2005, 2008

Introducing Human Resource Management
Fifth Edition
by Margaret Foot and Caroline Hook
ISBN 978 0 273 71200 8
Copyright © Pearson Education Limited, 1996, 2005, 2008

ISBN 978 1 84776 397 6

Printed and bound in Great Britain by Ashford Colour Press, Gosport, Hampshire.

Contents

Semester 1
CONCEPTS AND CONTEXTS

Managing work and managing people in the workplace

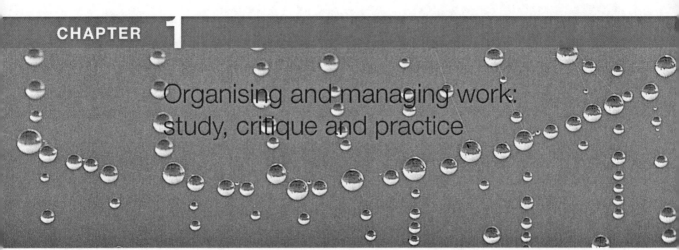

CHAPTER 1

Organising and managing work: study, critique and practice

Objectives Having read this chapter and completed its associated activities, readers should be able to:

- Appreciate the value of a 'management of work', rather than a 'management of people' or a 'management of systems' approach as a starting point for thinking about work organisations and their management.

- Understand the contribution which various social science disciplines make to the academic study of the organising and managing of work.

- See how the study of work organisation and management relates to associated studies like those of strategy, human resource management, organisation theory, management learning and critical management studies.

- Recognise continuity between social science thinking and a critical form of common sense.

- Understand the value of studying the organising and managing of work in a critical way.

- Discriminate between frameworks, perspectives, theories and research findings in terms of how useful (or 'true') they are when it comes to relating theory and practice.

- Use concepts in a social scientific way in the analysis of organisational and managerial practices.

- Distinguish between two broad ways of 'framing' human behaviours and organisational patterns: the systems-control and the process-relational.

The management of work

To create the goods, services and quality of life that people look for in the modern world, rather complex patterns of cooperative human behaviour have to be orchestrated or 'managed'. The academic study of the organising and managing of work involves taking a step back from our day-to-day involvement in these patterns of behaviour and trying systematically to understand how they come about. Such a study can also help us achieve a better quality of productive cooperation than we typically manage in contemporary work organisations.

We study work organisation and its management because we are interested in the various individual human motivations, interests, values and meanings which play a part in bringing about the patterns of behaviour we see in work-places ranging from shops, offices and factories to schools, hospitals and universities. But the study also has to concern itself with the ways in which these human activities and meanings themselves come to be an influence on the people that are involved in them. Once human beings create institutions and structures, like work organisations and managerial practices, their lives become significantly shaped by them. One of the things which makes the study of the organising and managing of work so challenging is that it has to under-stand how individual choices and initiatives, on the one hand, and already existing and *emerging* organisational and societal structures and patterns, on the other, both play their parts in social life. And these two influences – of human action and structural context – do not work separately. They are inextricably intertwined. This means that we must be careful not to overemphasise either the 'people' side of work organising and managing or the 'organisational systems' aspect of work patterning. The intention of *Organising and Managing Work* is to go beyond the tendency, seen in both academic programmes and the everyday thinking of organisational practitioners, to oversimplify these issues by treating organising in a one-sided manner as primarily a matter of, to put it very simply, either 'managing people' or 'managing systems'.

The notion of 'managing people' is widely and popularly used in the organ-isational world. There are, however, three major problems of thinking about organising and managing work in such terms. First, there is the problem of whether it is realistic even to contemplate the possibility of managing people. Is it at all reasonable, especially in a modern democratic society, to assume that there are people about who are willing to be 'managed' – to subjugate them-selves to the wills of 'bosses' at work? Surely not. In fact, it can be argued that one of the main ways that members of the human species differ from other animals is that they are active agents in the shaping of their lives. However meek or submissive particular individuals might be, each human being is nevertheless always the owner and shaper of their own identity, to some degree. As far as the historical record can tell us, no human group in the history of the human species has yet found another group over which it could exert complete control. And this applies even in the extreme conditions of slave societies or extermina-tion camps, where human beings have still demonstrated what looks like an

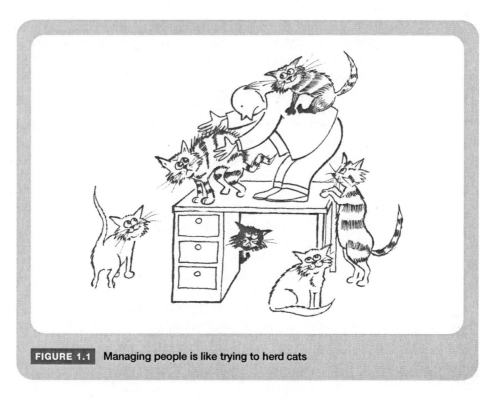

FIGURE 1.1   Managing people is like trying to herd cats

inherent tendency of the species: to be recalcitrant; to resist being managed. There is a very popular cliché that one hears day after day in work organisations to the effect that 'managing people is like trying to herd cats'.

One hears engineering managers say that 'managing engineers is like trying to herd cats'; health service managers saying 'managing medical workers is like trying to herd cats'; retail managers saying 'managing shop workers is like trying to herd cats' and university faculty deans saying 'managing academics is like trying to herd cats'. There is probably no sphere of work where this cliché has not been applied (it is nearly as common as 'You need to be mad to work here'!). But there is an important insight behind the cat herding cliché: human beings are indeed inherently 'unmanageable' in the same way that cats are inherently 'un-herdable'.

A second problem with the idea of managing people is a rather important ethical one. It can be argued that a manager does not have the moral right to direct, manage or 'boss' any individual in their area of responsibility *as a whole person* or in *the totality of their workplace behaviour*. Instead, they have a limited authority to give instructions to employees in tightly prescribed and limited areas of activity. The moral basis of that authority lies in its purpose – to fulfil those work tasks in which the employees have contractually agreed to participate. Employees in modern democratic societies do not sign a contract of employment on the assumption that managers appointed by their employer will have the right to manage them as a person. The manager is appointed to manage the work tasks – and as part of this has limited rights to instruct people.

But these rights only exist as means to specific organisational ends and not because of any 'right to command' over the person as a whole. It is thus morally improper to encourage a view of managerial and organisational work based on a principle of 'managing people'.

The third problem with the people management idea is that a focus on people or indeed on 'organisational *behaviour*' tends to leave blurred the part played by structures, systems, cultures, processes and the rest. It is, in effect, to focus on human behaviours at the expense of paying attention to the performance of the systems within which those behaviours occur.

It has perhaps been in recognition of the problems inherent in shaping work activities by directly focusing on people, rather than structures and processes, that we see an alternative emphasis in managerial thinking and organisation theory existing alongside the people management emphasis. This is what is often called 'systems thinking'; a way of looking at patterns of activity which has some significant virtues, but which has some considerable weaknesses too. Identifying those weaknesses, and going beyond them, is to be a key theme of Chapter 2. But what we can say, for the moment, is that replacing the idea of 'managing people' with the idea of 'managing systems' is rather problematic. Just as with the 'management of people' approach, the 'management of systems' approach founders on a fundamental problem with one of its key assumptions. This is the assumption that once a sensible and coherent system of operating has been devised by systems designers, the people who are to be employed to operate those systems will unquestioningly fulfil the roles in the systems allocated to them. Once again the issues of human self-expression and the universal tendency of people to resist the power of others arises. Of course, people will go along *up to a point* with the instructions of 'people managers' and, of course, people will go along *up to a point* with the requirements of the working systems within which they undertake employment. But their willingness to 'go along' with the requirements of others or fit into the demands of systems is tightly bounded. Recognition of the extent of that boundedness is vital to any realistic understanding of how work organisation and management can realistically be achieved – especially in societies whose cultures emphasise concepts of political freedom, personal expression and social and economic choice.

How do we get away from these two rather limited ways of thinking about the organising and managing of work? The suggestion is that we turn away from a focus on both the management of people and the management of systems and adopt a focus on the management of work itself. The most helpful starting point for any consideration of organisational and managerial behaviour is neither the 'people' nor the 'systems'. It is, instead, the work tasks that are to be carried out and the working relationships associated with those tasks that are managed. It is tasks and relationships which are organised and 'managed', not the people who carry out the tasks. It is the tasks and relationships which have to be shaped, in a relatively predictable and therefore relatively systematic way, not systems as such. And an important insight which follows from the adoption of this management of work focus is the recognition that work tasks are always *to an extent managed by everyone involved in those tasks*. Work management is not simply what people formally designated as 'managers' do. To say this is not, however, to play down the significance of the work done by people holding managerial posts. This immensely important type of work is closely examined in Chapter 3. And careful examination of what managers actually do makes it clear that effective managers recognise that much of the shaping or managing of work tasks is done by those nominally under the control of designated managers – albeit to different degrees in different circumstances.

Studying the organisation and management of work

The field of study covered in *Organising and Managing Work* is broader than that which is typically covered by traditional 'Organisational Behaviour' programmes taught in schools of business and management and, as was explained earlier, it is very different in its emphasis from courses in 'people management'. It can usefully be labelled 'work organisation and management studies' – an activity which is treated here as a social scientific form of activity.

Work organisation and management studies   *Concept*

The analysis of the human aspects of work organisation and its management which draws on the social sciences to develop insights, theories and research findings with a view to informing the choices, decisions and actions of people who have a practical involvement with organisations.

We need to note several things about this way of characterising our field of study.

- What is studied is the 'human aspects of work organisation and its management'. This language is not meant to imply that attention is only paid to 'human aspects' at the level of the human individual. The focus is on work *organisation* and management, which means that patterns of human activity and thinking going beyond the level of the individual are as important as thinking about the human individual. The concern is with the interplay of factors at the level of human initiative and choice and factors at the level of social, political and economic context, or structure.

- The subject *informs* the choices, decisions and actions of people involved in practices in organisations. There is no question of developing an academic study which can tell people what they should do in the complex area of work management. The area is far too complex for there to be any basic rules or even sets of guidelines about 'how to do management'. Not only this but, given the moral factors which must come into every human situation where power and authority are involved, it would be quite wrong for a textbook to attempt to provide guidance in this way. What it can do, however, is to provide insights into the range of factors and issues which are relevant to any particular choice (of, say, job design or planning an organisational change programme). The actual choice or decision that is made is a matter for those involved in the particular organisational situation – with all the political, moral and specific local considerations coming into play alongside the insights which can be derived from academic study of the managing and organisation of work.

- Reference is made to 'organisational practitioners' rather than 'managers' as the potential 'users' of the subject. This is done in recognition of the fact that people other than those formally designated as managers are closely involved in the way work tasks are managed. If there are social scientific ideas which would be helpful to a manager in an organisational situation wishing to have their understanding enhanced by academic thinking then surely those ideas are going to be equally relevant to anyone else concerned with that situation. This would be the case regardless of the person's formal authority in the organisation or, for that matter, their degree of commitment to official organisational policies.

- The social sciences are 'drawn on' in the study. 'Organising and managing work' is not seen as a social science in its own right. A variety of social science disciplines can be turned to to provide research findings, theoretical resources or insights that might be helpful in understanding organisational issues. This does not mean, however, that we simply turn in a random or *promiscuous* manner to the vast bank of social science materials every time we wish to analyse a particular situation. Each individual is likely to build up their set of preferred social science concepts as their learning proceeds. They then turn to the books and journals for further insight, as the need arises, and incorporate the new learning into their ever-developing personal framework of understanding.

The social scientific study of the organising and managing of work has tended to draw primarily on the social science disciplines of sociology, psychology and social psychology. And it supports the contributions of the main disciplines with insights from economics, political science and anthropology. The key concerns of each of these are outlined in Table 1.1.

All of these disciplines can be seen as providing resources which can be drawn upon when wishing to understand the organising and managing of work in general or any particular organisational situation or problem in particular. Many of the human issues that can arise in the organisational context do not fall into any one obvious disciplinary territory and many of them might use ideas from more than one discipline. Bearing this in mind, see how you get on with Activity 1.1.

Activity 1.1

Read the story about Rose Markey taking over as the manager of The Canalazzo restaurant (Case 1.1), thinking about the issues which Rose is going to have to deal with to satisfy her employers. Following the characterisations of the six social sciences set out in Table 1.1, note the factors or issues that you think might be identified as, respectively, psychological, social–psychological, sociological, economic, political and anthropological.

Table 1.1 Focal and supporting social science disciplines for studying the organising and managing of work	
Focal social science disciplines	**Supporting social science disciplines**
Psychology focuses on individual characteristics and behaviour and on such matters as learning, motivation and individual ('personality') differences	**Economics** supports the sociological concern with the economic context and, also, the psychological concern with decision making (through its attention to 'rational' decisions made by economic actors)
Social psychology focuses on group characteristics and behaviour, on roles, attitudes, values, communication, decision making and so on	**Political science** supports the sociological concern with power and conflict and the social–psychological concern with decision making (through its concern with the state and other institutions handling matters of power and difference of interest)
Sociology focuses on structures, arrangements or patterns and how these both influence and are influenced by individual and group behaviour. It is concerned with the structure of the social and economic system as well as with the organisational structure and issues of technology, conflict, power and culture	**Anthropology** supports the social–psychological concern with norms, values and attitudes and the sociological concern with cultures (both organisational and societal) with insights taken from the study of non-industrial or 'less advanced' societies about such things as rites, rituals, customs and symbols

Rose takes over The Canalazzo restaurant

Case 1.1

Rose Markey had been working for a national chain of restaurants for only a couple of years when they asked her to take over a restaurant which they had recently acquired. They had bought The Canalazzo restaurant from the Italian family which had established the business some 20 or so years previously. The family had decided to return to Italy and to warmer summers. The company had originally put in one of their older managers to run the newly acquired restaurant. However, they were very disappointed with what was being achieved. Their Director of Finance argued that the turnover of the business simply did not justify the investment that had been made in the purchase of the business and in the redecoration of the premises. When they challenged the first manager they had put in, he talked of his resentment at being asked to move to a new part of the country at the age of 55. He persuaded the company to give him an early retirement settlement so that he could return to the part of the country he had lived in for most of his life. They were pleased to do this because it was clear, the human resources manager told Rose, that this man's poor motivation and attitude to customers was increasingly being reflected in the way the staff of the restaurant went about their work.

When Rose arrived at the restaurant she soon learned that her predecessor had clashed on several occasions with local police officers about serving late drinks. This was likely to get back to the magistrates and the restaurant would be in danger of failing to have its drinks licence renewed when it was next due for review. The manager's defence was that he was simply following local customs in the town whereby customers would have a night out that would bring them into the restaurant only after spending most of the evening in a public house. It was not his fault, he said, that the police officers and the magistrates all lived outside of the town and did not know about this.

When it came to the problems with the staff, Rose found that her predecessor had set up a strongly hierarchical set of relationships among them. This seemed to be accepted, albeit grudgingly, by the people who worked in the kitchen. But it was resented by the waiting staff who were largely part-time workers studying at the local university. Not only this, but the group of waiters – who all knew each other from the university – and the kitchen workers, all of whom had left school at 16, tended only to speak to members of their own group.

The chef, who was a middle-aged Italian, regularly fell out with the headwaiter – a woman a dozen years younger than him. Their respective ideas about how young female staff should be treated were poles apart and these differences led to frequent arguments. Overall there was very little coordination between the kitchen and the restaurant. All of this, Rose decided, seriously affected the quality of service the customers received.

Perhaps psychological factors will be the first to suggest themselves here, ranging from issues of differences of personality and temperament among different employees of the restaurant to ones of motivation and personal commitment. The varying sets of attitude in the restaurant are clearly a matter of social–psychological interest, as are the problematic patterns of communication and the way the two groups of kitchen and restaurant staff have developed to create a division among the junior staff as a whole. All of this feeds into the sociological factors and issues. There is a power structure within the restaurant and this has elements which relate to sociological variables such as age, gender and ethnicity – all of which relate to the way society as a whole is organised. But there are also sociological factors about the way the restaurant fits into the local economy and community, both as a provider of services and a source of employment. Here there is a clear overlap with economic issues of market organisation and this, in turn, relates to the most obvious economic issues of financial performance, turnover (and, by implication, profitability) and investment. Issues of a formal political nature (i.e. relating to issues of the role of the state) are present with regard to the police and magistrates, and there are obvious informal 'political' issues running right through the whole set of relationships in the restaurant. This is in addition to whatever the 'informal' politics of the relationship between local police officers and restaurant managers might be. Anthropological issues of informal customs might also be involved but, more obviously, the anthropological notions of custom and ritual are highly relevant to the patterns of restaurant use which influence the pattern of work that has to be managed by Rose Markey and the rest of the staff of The Canalazzo.

Work organisation and management studies and associated fields of study

We have now distinguished between, on the one hand, social science disciplines like sociology, social psychology, economics and anthropology and, on the other hand, the field of study that we are calling the organising and managing of work. But there are other fields of study which draw on the social science disciplines to study aspects of work organisation and its management. In fact, the field of study with which *Organising and Managing Work* is concerned brings together material and ideas from several of these. In the traditional curricula of business and management schools we will come across the subjects of Strategy (or 'strategic management'), HRM (Human Resource Management),

Organisational Behaviour (OB), Organisation Theory (OT, or Organisation Studies, OS), Critical Management Studies (CMS) and Management Learning. There are courses or modules in all of these, there are academic journals focusing on each of them and there are textbooks dealing with each one of them.

The field of study covered by the present text incorporates elements of all of these. But this is not done in a spirit of scholarly imperialism. It is done in order to provide a broader base for subsequent study than OB courses have tended to do. OB programmes often form part of the foundational level of business and management studies programmes. And they should thus provide ideas that can be built upon later than in broad strategic management or HRM modules or in more focused modules in such areas as management learning or critical management studies. But they typically do little bridging over into these areas. *Organising and Managing Work* tries to provide precisely this kind of bridging. It does this by actually incorporating into itself as a field of study some of the ideas and materials of strategy, HRM, OT, CMS and management learning.

Figure 1.2 shows the relationship between the 'organising and managing of work' field of study and the fairly standard business school subjects of OB, Strategic Management and HRM and the other fields of Organisation Theory/ Organisation Studies, Management Learning, and Critical Management Studies. OB tends to focus on the human behaviours associated with the internal functioning of organisations, with an eye on what will be helpful to managerial practitioners in this area. Organisation Studies (or 'Organisation Theory') looks at some of the same issues but with greater attention to how organisations relate to their societal contexts. It also has a primarily academic focus – concerning itself first and foremost with scholarly understanding rather than with the

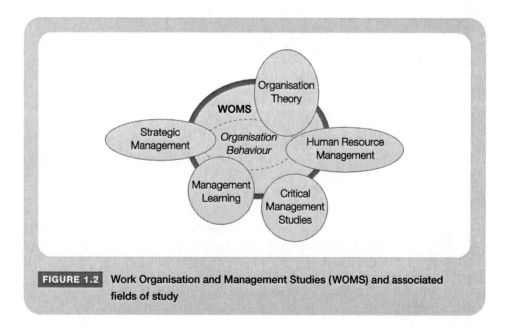

FIGURE 1.2   Work Organisation and Management Studies (WOMS) and associated fields of study

implications of such understandings for practice. The OS and OT materials are to be found in journals such as *Organisation Studies* and books like Tsoukas and Knudsen (2003), Vibert (2004) and Hatch (2006). Organisation Studies/Theory has also been more concerned with taking a critical stance than OB, something which has also informed the emergence of Critical Management Studies – in effect an application of the more critical ideas of Organisation Theory directly to issues of managerial activity (see the Further Reading on critical approaches in organisation and management studies p. 32).

Management Learning is another emergent field of specialist study with its own academic journal, *Management Learning*, and a concern to bring together theoretical developments in the understanding of human learning processes with issues of both educating and 'developing' managerial practitioners. *Organising and Managing Work* is informed by this development in its recognition of the central importance of issues of learning to all aspects of the organisation and management of work. And this is learning which, it is argued, needs to go beyond simple or 'everyday' common sense.

Common sense and social science in the study of work organisation

One of the first thoughts occurring to anyone trying to make sense of the problems we saw earlier arising with regard to The Canalazzo restaurant might be that 'common sense' is likely to be just as helpful as ideas from psychology, sociology or anthropology. It has, nevertheless, been a tradition of social science teachers to contrast social science thinking with common-sense thinking and to argue that social science analysis is to be preferred to common sense. But an alternative response might be to say, 'It all depends on what you mean by common sense.' This is necessary, in fact, because there are two quite different usages of the term 'common sense' that often get muddled up. It is useful to distinguish between *everyday common sense* and *critical common sense*.

Everyday common sense   *Concept*

Analysis based on unthought-out, taken-for-granted, immediately 'obvious', everyday assumptions about the world and human activity within it.

Everyday common sense is necessary for 'getting by' in our daily lives. We all make quick assumptions about what is going on around us, drawing on all kinds of stereotypes, half-remembered experiences and simplistic cause–effect connections. This is necessary to cope with our daily lives. We would not cope with life if we stopped, sat back and deeply pondered on every eventuality that faced us between getting up in the morning and going to bed at night. But perhaps we can see why social scientists claim that their more analytical style of thinking has advantages over this. In the work context, for example, individuals frequently offer woefully simplistic generalisations such as 'People only go to work for the money' – typically adding, 'It stands to reason' or, 'It's obvious' or, 'It's common sense isn't it?' This is a good example of everyday common sense, based as it is on easy, unthought-out, taken-for-granted assumptions. Assumptions like these make life simpler – at first sight, anyway. But such assumptions are often dangerous guides to action on matters of any importance or complexity such as designing a pay system or 'reward structure', for example.

We therefore turn to critical common sense as a style of thinking which involves being deliberately logical or rational about things in the way that is common to all human beings when they are alertly and critically putting their mind to whatever matter is in hand.

Critical common sense   *Concept*

Analysis based on the basic logic, rationality, hard-headedness to be found in human beings whenever they step back from the immediate situation and critically put their minds to an issue or problem.

This is the kind of common sense that we can more reliably use as a guide to action when more complex matters of work organisation and management arise. It is an activity of the same order as that in which the scientist engages. Science, in this view, is essentially a formalised version of critical common sense. Scientific thinking – in principle if not always in practice – is the more formal, systematic and painstakingly analytical application of critical common sense.

Critical common sense analysis tends to start from a consideration of the most obvious or likely explanation of what is going on; the everyday common sense explanation in fact. But it then goes on to ask whether things are really as they seem at first. Alternative explanations are considered and attention is paid to available evidence in judging the various rival explanations. We can see the two types of common sense compared in Table 1.2 and the managerial implications of applying each of them, in this case in deciding for or against a performance-related pay system.

Table 1.2 Two types of common sense in practice

Everyday common sense and pay	Critical common sense and pay
If you pay employees in proportion to their output they will produce more than if they get the same wage whatever they turn out	Pay for output might work. But employees might prefer the comfort of a steady work rate and the security of a steady wage. They might resent the pressures of a bonus system on group relations
They will clearly work better under a performance-related pay system	It would be wise to find out what particular employees' requirements are before deciding for or against a performance-related pay system

The considerations about performance-related pay connected in Table 1.2 to a critical common sense way of thinking about work behaviour are indeed similar to ones which have emerged from social science research and theorising about the relationship between pay and behaviour. See, in particular, the 'expectancy' theory of work motivation explained in Chapter 8. Similar arguments to these critical common sense ones were developed in the light of one of the famous Hawthorne experiments – the Bank Wiring Observation Room experiment – by Roethlisberger and Dickson (1939).

The critical study of organising and managing

A critical common sense frame of mind is obviously relevant to any kind of practical human endeavour. But it has particular relevance to academic work – and especially to studies that claim to be scientific. Scientific analysis, as has already been suggested, can be understood as an especially rigorous or systematic application of critical common sense. And this would suggest that we could not do social science at all without being critical in the sense of constantly questioning taken-for-granted ideas and practices. However, there has been a growing trend of questioning the extent to which social science study of work behaviour and managerial practice has been sufficiently critical.

The crux of the problem that all writers and researchers interested in managerial issues have to face up to is the fact that managerial activities are always and inevitably implicated in issues of power and relative advantage and disadvantage between human groups and human individuals. Everyone engaged in management research and management education is therefore faced with a dilemma. How do they reconcile providing knowledge that might help improve the effectiveness of work activities with the fact that in doing so they might help some people ('managers' and the employers of managers, say) more than others ('the managed', for example)? Helping make work organisations more efficient or more effective is not a politically neutral matter.

In a world where valued resources tend to be scarce and there is continuous competition for the goods, services and rewards provided by work organisations, any intervention can involve one in taking sides between the relatively advantaged and the relatively disadvantaged. The social scientist is in danger of becoming a 'servant of power', as an early polemic on such matters put it (Baritz, 1960, p. 39). A desire to avoid this problem is something shared by all of those associated with the emergent 'critical management studies' movement (see the Further Reading on critical approaches in organisation and management studies p. 32). A radical strategy adopted by some critical management thinkers amounts, in effect, to 'going on the attack' against managerial ideologies and activities that are felt by the critical scholar to be 'wrong' or 'harmful'. Critical research and writing would, for example, offer its students 'an appreciation of the pressures that lead managerial work to become so deeply implicated in the unremitting exploitation of nature and human beings, national and international extremes of wealth and poverty, the creation of global pollution, the promotion of "needs" for consumer products etc.' (Alvesson and Willmott, 1996, p. 39). Such a critical management study is committed to exposing the political implications of managerial work with an ambition of helping achieve 'emancipatory transformation' – the transformation of both people and society. And, in the workplace itself, a 'critical' version of the concept of empowerment is called for, 'empowering employees to make more choices and to act more effectively to transform workplace relations' (Thompson and McHugh, 2002, p. 18).

These advocates of critical management studies, critical management education and critical organisation studies want their work to help change the balance of power in the worlds of work and employment. But they are not just critical of the existing patterns of power prevailing in organisations and society at large. They also aim their critical fire at the type of writing and teaching which constitutes the orthodoxy in contemporary business and management schools. And the main thrust of this critique is against the assumption behind much of this orthodoxy that success in managerial and organisational work comes from acquiring, developing and applying *skills* and *techniques* – skills and techniques which are neutral and 'innocent' in a political sense. Issues of power, inequality, conflict (at interpersonal, group and class levels), gender and ethnicity are either ignored or treated as peripheral matters which, from time to time, get in the way of smooth organisational functioning. Sympathy with this latter criticism has been an important inspiration for the writing of the present text and it informs the critique of what is called the *systems-control* orthodoxy and its displacement by a more realistic and politically sensitive *process-relational* frame of reference. But the whole text is underpinned by a particular notion of a critical organisation and management study, which is summarised in Figure 1.3. It is a notion that shares much ground with the work being produced under the flag of 'critical management studies' but its overlap is only partial, as the earlier Figure 1.1 suggested.

The conception of a critical organisation and management study adopted in *Organising and Managing Work* differs from that taken by some of the critical thinkers whose ideas were looked at above. This is primarily with regard to the issue of arguing for 'transformation', at both the personal and the social levels. It is felt that the choices that these transformations would entail are a matter for political and moral debate in society generally and for contestation within organisations themselves. They are not transformations which social science can or should push people towards. What the social sciences can do is to illuminate or inform those debates with information and insights derived from both research investigations and theoretical reflections. And if these insights, research contributions and theories are going to have any real potential to *make a difference* to practices in the world outside the classroom and library, there has to be openness about the fact that all social science analysis is itself value-laden. To contribute to either societal or organisational debates about how work tasks are to be organised and managed as if this were simply a matter of deciding which power-neutral technique or procedure to adopt would be dishonest at the moral level and misleading at the level of informing practice.

FIGURE 1.3 A critical study of work organisation and management

This means that no study of organisations and management can claim to be objective or in some sense 'value-free'. A critical study of organisation and management must keep asking questions of itself – as the words on the right-hand side of Figure 1.3 suggest. This entails recognising that the management and organisational ideas that are dealt with are not matters of technique or neutral principles, devoid of political significance. It also requires a degree of self-awareness in writing and teaching and a commitment to judiciously revealing our own biases and moral inclinations where this is necessary to help the reader or student take one's inevitable partiality into account. This principle was followed early in the present chapter where the notion of 'people management' was *engaged with* as a matter of morality as well as pragmatic realism.

The writing of the early part of this chapter was also relevant to the words on the left-hand side of Figure 1.3. The essence of critique is *questioning* and a critical study has to ask questions about the organisational activities that it is studying as well as constantly questioning what it is producing itself in its 'literature'. Accordingly we raised questions earlier in the chapter about the practice of speaking of organising work in terms of 'the management of people' or 'the managing of systems' as opposed to 'the management of work'. This argument will be built upon as *Organising and Managing Work* develops. And, as we ask questions about how and why work organisation practices are as they are, we will constantly bear in mind that work organisations are only in an extremely limited way a separate phenomenon from the economy and society of which they are part. They did not historically 'evolve' in the working out of some divine or abstract principle of increasing organisational efficiency. The hierarchy of jobs in today's organisations, for example, is both an outcome of and a contributor to the hierarchy of class and status which has developed in society as individuals and groups have competed with each other for advantage over the years. By the same token, markets do not exist 'out there' as part of the 'economic context' of business organisations. They are *made* by organisational initiatives as much as they are served by organisations. A critical perspective also requires us constantly to observe that differences of interest – and the frequent alignment and realignment of interests – are inherent in organisations. They permeate the managerial strata of organisations as well as underlying the basic tensions between employees and employers.

Activity 1.2

Quickly reread Case 1.1 and how Rose Markey 'took over' at The Canalazzo restaurant. Then read the sequel to that story (Case 1.2), 'Rose and The Canalazzo under threat'. Make a note of all the ways in which an understanding of both parts of The Canalazzo story would require attention to factors to which, it is argued above, a critical study of organisation and management draws attention. The wording on the left-hand side of Figure 1.3 is a starting point for your analysis.

Rose and The Canalazzo under threat   Case 1.2

After six months of managing The Canalazzo restaurant, Rose Markey prepared for her annual performance appraisal at the headquarters of the company which owned the restaurant. She was still finding her job quite a struggle. She had begun to adjust to living in the north of the country, having only ever lived in the south previously. She had established good relationships with the local police and the worry about losing the drinks licence had disappeared. However, she was having difficulties with the chef, who resented a woman being in charge of the restaurant. The problems with the chef were exacerbated by the fact that the kitchen staff seemed pleased to see her discomforted whenever she got into an argument with him. And the kitchen staff's uncooperative attitude towards the waiters had got worse. They knew that Rose was a university graduate and frequently mocked her southern middle-class accent in the same way they regularly mimicked what they called the 'posh' accents of the largely student waiting staff. They saw Rose and the waiters as people who were only in their present jobs as a means towards something better later on.

In spite of these difficulties, Rose felt sure she could succeed in improving the restaurant's popularity. She believed she could win over the chef in the long run, by encouraging him to develop some more adventurous menus and attracting a new clientele. This, she thought, would encourage him to discipline his kitchen staff more effectively – especially with regard to their relationships with the waiters.

Rose was excited about explaining all of this to the manager who was to do her appraisal. However, before she could even begin to talk about what she was doing, he told her that the company was considering closing the restaurant. A rival had ousted the chief executive of the company. The new managing director wanted, she said, to take the whole business 'up-market'. A restaurant in a northern town with a declining local economy did not 'fit into the new scheme of things'. Rose was to be offered redundancy – the terms of which she was invited to go and discuss with the human resources manager.

When Rose found the HR manager, he immediately invited her to go to a nearby wine bar for a drink. He explained that as an old friend of the former managing director he had felt it wise to seek a job with another business. He had been successful in this and therefore felt able, he said, to let Rose know that he believed she had been badly treated. He said that the possibility of closing the restaurant had arisen before Rose had been moved there. Rose had been chosen to take the Canalazzo job because one or two of the headquarter's managers felt that her 'face did not fit'. She was not only the one graduate trainee manager they employed. She was the only one with a black face.

The story of Rose and The Canalazzo involves many of the normal problems that someone is likely to face when trying to manage work – in a struggling restaurant or anywhere else. Alongside the obvious problems about the nature of the market for the particular services offered, and the need to achieve better coordination of the restaurant's division of labour, are a whole series of interpersonal and intergroup relationship problems. But most of these relate in some way to the patterns of conflict, inequality and discrimination existing in the wider culture and society. A critical organisation and management study would take all of this into account in an analysis of what was occurring. This would take it well beyond attention to orthodox issues of motivation, leadership and group relations. But it would also recognise the wider pattern of economic ownership which was relevant to issues in The Canalazzo and observe the way in which boardroom politics can affect what happens at a local workplace level in an organisation. There are politics at every level – workplace, organisation and society. A critical work organisation and management study would see these as centrally important matters, not merely as ones providing the 'context' in which the basic day-to-day application of managerial techniques and motivational skills have to be applied.

By now, after twice visiting The Canalazzo restaurant, two things should be apparent about analysing all the complexities of organisational and managerial behaviour as it occurs in 'real life' (as opposed to how it appears in the idealised world of standard management texts). First, as we saw in Activity 1.2, we have to look critically at facets of social, cultural, political and economic life that go way beyond a simple search for efficient management techniques. A whole series of moral issues arise in the Canalazzo story. Second, as we saw in Activity 1.1, we have to turn to a range of social science sources for help in analysing these matters. But each of these social sciences itself has a range of perspectives, models, concepts, theories and research studies on which we might draw when analysing whatever organisational or managerial issues interest or concern us. How do we choose between these?

Good, better and bad theories of organising and managing

One of the distinctive features of the present book (See Introduction, p. xix) is a concern with doing more than simply leaving readers more or less to decide for themselves which models, theories or ways of looking at organisations they prefer. However fair and reasonable this may seem at first, it avoids the issue of advising students of work organisation and management about what broad criteria they might apply to any piece of research or theorising they come across when trying to understand organisational or managerial practices. And this militates against taking a critical stance with regard to the study of work organisation and management itself. How do we make judgements about the relative value of one piece of analysis or knowledge compared with another?

To deal with this question we have to get involved with issues of *epistemology*. This is the branch of philosophy that deals with the relationship between the way the world is and the knowledge we have of that world. And it has a specific concern with the sort of truth claims that can be made for particular propositions or pieces of knowledge. This might seem a rather complex issue for us to get involved in here, something we can leave to philosophers while we get on with looking directly at organisations and their management. However, we really cannot duck the matter. It is vital to any understanding of how we relate 'theory and practice'.

Whether we like it or not, we all make epistemological judgements every day of our lives. We may have to decide, for example, 'how much truth there is' in the story we just read in our newspaper about an imminent business takeover. We might be concerned with 'how much truth there is' in the picture of society painted by the politician whose speech we have just listened to. Or we might be anxious about 'how much truth there is' in stories we have heard about a local school 'failing' and being closed down. Broadly speaking there are three approaches or 'theories' we can apply to such matters – approaches we can also take to the sort of accounts and analyses we come across when studying organisations and management. These are shown in Table 1.3.

In everyday life we apply all three ways of deciding the validity of a piece of knowledge. We do this in organisational contexts as much as we do in the other areas of life used in the examples in Table 1.3. But the approach to making judgements is obviously the most relevant to deciding what practices we are going to follow in any situation, in the light of the knowledge about that situation which is available to us. In the case of deciding which of the two tourist guides to trust, we would clearly be wise to apply the pragmatist 'theory of truth'. We would similarly be wise to apply this principle if we were considering taking a job with a particular organisation and had available to us, say, both the organisation's recruitment brochure and an article written by a researcher who had carried out participant observation research in that organisation. Which of these two 'pieces of knowledge' is the 'truer' one, we would tend to ask. And we would ask ourselves this question because we would be concerned to decide the most appropriate way to behave when entering the organisation. We would, in

Table 1.3 Three ways of deciding the 'truth' of knowledge	
Three ways of deciding the 'truth' of an item of knowledge	**For example . . .**
Correspondence theories of truth judge an item of knowledge in terms of how accurately it paints a picture or gives a report of what actually happened or 'is the case'	A jury is asked to apply this principle (qualified by the notion of 'beyond reasonable doubt') when deciding between the accounts given by the prosecution and the defence. A judgement has to be made as to whether 'x' actually did or did not kill 'y'
Coherence/plausibility theories of truth judge an item of knowledge in terms of how well it 'fits in with' everything else we have learned about this matter previously	We might apply this principle when deciding whether a piece of gossip about somebody we know is true or false. We ask whether or not it fits with everything else we have seen of them and heard about them
Pragmatist theories of truth judge knowledge in terms of how effectively one would fulfil whatever projects one was pursuing in the area of activity covered by the knowledge, if we based our actions on the understanding of those activities which it offers	We might apply this principle when comparing what a promotional tourist brochure says about a foreign city we are going to visit and what is said in a book by an independent author drawing on their first-hand experiences. We have to decide which account of that city we are going to heed when deciding what to wear, how to address local people, how to find food that we like, or avoid being robbed

this respect, be applying a pragmatist theory of truth claims in the same way that we do when we compare the account of a product given in the manufacturer's advertisement and a report on the product published by an independent consumer association.

In the light of these examples, it is clear that a philosophical pragmatist approach to judging the sorts of material one comes across in studying organisations and management is invaluable. The wisdom of such an approach derives from two main things:

- It is impossible when looking at organisational issues to have enough information – free of interpretation, free of biased reporting, free of the tricks of human memory and free of ambiguity – to apply the correspondence theory of truth. This applies to social life in general as well as to organisations specifically. Because everything we are told about the world is mediated by language and interpretation, we can never receive an account which accurately reports or 'mirrors' that world.

- There are no absolute truths or 'final laws' which social scientific analysis can offer with regard to organisations or any other aspect of social life. One proposition, theory or research study can be judged to be truer than another, however. But this is only to the extent that it will tend to be a *more trustworthy, broad guide to practice* in the aspect of life it covers than the other. It cannot be wholly correct, totally true, or completely objective. One piece of knowledge is simply more useful than the other as an account of 'how things work' which we can use to inform our practices.

This pragmatist approach to judging the validity of the sorts of material we are going to study derives from a particular school of philosophy, the pragmatist philosophy of Charles Pierce, William James and James Dewey as well as, in part, the neo-pragmatist thinking of Richard Rorty (see Further Reading on epistemology and philosophical pragmatism, p. 32). It is important here to recognise that we are using the term 'pragmatist' in a more specific way than it tends to be used in everyday conversation, where it tends to mean 'expedient'. We are not using the word in the same way as the manager who says, 'Let's be pragmatic about this and get the job done, never mind what we ought to be doing in theory or according to the company's principles'. That manager was talking about doing something that was expedient or convenient, in the specific circumstances of the moment. This is not what we mean when we talk of philo-sophical pragmatism. What we talking about is something not dissimilar to the relatively straightforward notion of *critical common sense* looked at earlier. Pragmatist thinking leads us to the eminently sensible critical common sense practice of reading management and social science books (or considering any other kind of knowledge for that matter) and asking ourselves, 'To what extent should I take into account this knowledge when deciding what to do in prac-tice?' If one theory, one research study, or even one piece of fictional writing, is thought to be more helpful in informing our practical projects than another, then it is a *better* theory, article or book. It is 'truer' in the philosophical prag-matist sense of 'true'. And note that this truth comes from the capacity to *inform practices*. It is in this that the truth lies. It is not a matter of a piece of knowledge or information being true because it is simply 'useful'. A lie can clearly be useful. To tell lies can be expedient. But where lies tend to fall apart is when one tries to base human practices on them. This is the sense in which lies are 'untrue' in philosophical pragmatist terms.

We also need to recognise that philosophical pragmatism avoids an absolute notion of truth. Instead, to put it simply, it regards some things as truer than others. One cannot produce a piece of academic research which presents the complete truth about an aspect of the world. The logic of science has to be understood as one of constantly looking for theories or explanations which are truer than those which preceded them (cf. Popper, 1963). But no absolute truth is achievable. In pragmatist terms, we will never have a body of knowledge upon which we can base our practices or projects in the world and which will give us complete success every time. However, there are some pieces of know-ledge that will enable us to 'do better' if we take them as guides to action than if we utilise others. Truthfulness to the pragmatist is a relative matter.

To emphasise the relevance of pragmatist criteria for evaluating pieces of organisational and management knowledge is not to argue for completely turn-ing our backs on the other criteria for judging truth. The concept of justice applied in many societies requires us to work with the correspondence theory of truth, for example, in courts of law or other types of judicial or bureaucratic enquiry. Yet even here, as we noted earlier, the ultimate impossibility of this is recognised in the acceptance that a judgement can only achieve a reliability which is 'beyond *reasonable* doubt'. We are therefore much safer, for most purposes, applying the more modest pragmatist criterion for judging truth claims. And we are certainly much safer applying this approach than making too much use of coherence or plausibility theories of truth. We apply these all the time – when, for example, we ask how one statement on some issue 'stacks up against' everything else we have heard on that matter. At the level of ordinary or everyday common sense we have to do this. But it is not good enough when we are engaged in the more rigorous and critical common sense type of thinking which we frequently have to do in the complex area of organising and managing work. Too many poor theories in the organisational and management sphere have an immediate plausibility, one that soon disappears when rigorous and critical common sense is applied to them.

The pragmatist style of thinking is also relevant, in a very basic way, to the arguments set out earlier for the *critical analysis* of work and organisational behaviours. Doing this, it was argued, involved appreciating that work organisation happens in a context of contest, inequality and conflict and that management ideas are more than neutral rules, principles or guides to action; they always have political significance. Knowledge of organisations and management which gives full recognition to these matters, according to the pragmatist principles, would be better – as a set of resources for informing practice – than knowledge which ignored them. This is because an organisational practitioner, managerial or non-managerial, would be better placed to succeed in whatever their purposes might be if they were informed in this way. We might go as far as to say that an individual who tried to undertake any kind of organisational task without a strong awareness of the political dimension of organisational life would be a fool! It follows from this that critical thinking is equally relevant to a manager, a non-managerial worker or someone wishing to challenge and undermine the whole enterprise. To put this another way, there cannot be 'managerially biased' knowledge – other than inadequate or misleading knowledge. If there is work organisation knowledge which helpfully informs the practices, projects and purposes of managers, then it is likely to be equally helpful to anyone else operating in that context – including someone wishing to oppose 'managerial' initiatives. The same principle applies to other spheres of human activity. Knowledge which helps a government rule can also help an opposition to bring it down, for example. Knowledge which helps a police force fight crime can equally help criminals carry out crimes more successfully, for example.

As far as *Organising and Managing Work* is concerned, everything in the book is intended to inform people involved in the management of work – whatever the nature of that involvement might be. The book should be helpful to those designated as 'managers'. But it should be equally relevant to someone whose 'project' is to have a quiet life at work, make an investment or customer decision about a work organisation or set out in some way to oppose the managers of an organisation. And, to put this style of 'active reading' into practice from the start, it can be useful to apply it to one of the most popular items ever taught to students of organisation and management: Maslow's hierarchy of needs theory.

Assessing a popular 'motivation theory' critically and pragmatically

A central place has been given for half a century or so in management education and organisational studies to certain thoughts of one particular mid-twentieth century American writer, Abraham Maslow (1943, 1954, 1968). Indeed, Maslow's 'hierarchy of needs' theory of motivation has come to play an iconic part in the study of organisational behaviour and courses on management. This is in spite of it having emerged from a body of work which is very much at odds with more recent thinking and values in psychological and social science research (Cullen, 1997). Countless teachers and students of areas of human endeavour ranging from organisation behaviour and supervisory management to nursing education and consumer behaviour have drawn and redrawn the triangle shown in Figure 1.4 – this being used to illustrate Maslow's at first sight plausible notion that human beings in their lives and activities generally work *upwards* through a particular sequence of 'needs'. People are said generally to seek to satisfy 'lower order' *physiological* and *safety* needs before moving upwards to satisfy 'higher order' *social* and *esteem* needs. At the top of the hierarchy is an idealised notion of perfect human fulfilment called *'self-actualisation'*. This is something that people allegedly seek to satisfy once they are well fed, safe, socially integrated and 'well thought of' by others.

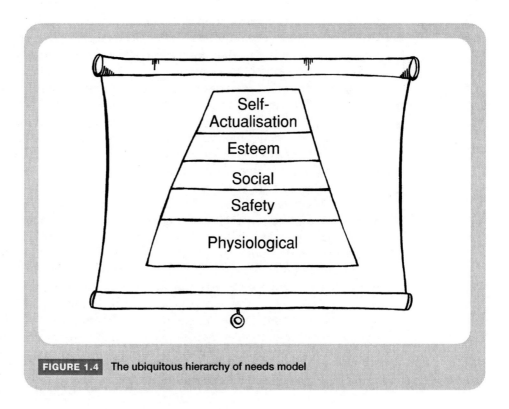

FIGURE 1.4   The ubiquitous hierarchy of needs model

At the level of everyday common sense (p. 10) there is some logic in this. If we wish to 'motivate' a starving worker running away from a hungry lion it is not unreasonable to consider chasing away the lion and giving them a loaf of bread in return for them performing as we require. Once the worker is getting plenty to eat and has had their 'safety needs' met, it seems equally reasonable to expect to have to offer some further incentives to gain worker cooperation: giving them the satisfactions of sociability with other human beings and making them feel esteemed or 'highly thought of'. Perhaps, beyond this, the only incentive that the worker can be offered is an opportunity to self-actualise or somehow to 'become everything that they would most want to be'.

The so-called 'hierarchy of needs' theory has some appeal at the everyday common sense level then. But before we turn to philosophical pragmatist criteria to help us reach a more critically commonsensical evaluation, let us first look at this theory in its social and political context in the way that fits with that requirement shown in Figure 1.2 whereby critical organisational and management studies 'asks why we think about organising and managing the way we do'. To understand why we think about 'motivation' in the hierarchy of needs way we have to note its origins in the particular setting in which Maslow was working. This was one, within the increasingly comfortable middle classes of the USA, where it was plausible to expect people who were 'doing well' to seek to 'get even more out of life'. The message from Maslow's popularisers to employers in the increasingly affluent sections of certain mid-twentieth-century societies was, in effect, 'if you want to get more out of your increasingly comfortable employees you had better think of some extra things to give them'. The ultimate 'extra' that successful industrial capitalism could offer people was the opportunity to achieve the total opposite of the 'alienation' that so many social commentators had worried about as a consequence of industrialism and capitalism. Maslow's message was corporate capitalism's answer to the Marxist fear of work under capitalism leading to dehumanising and the *alienation* of people (p. 448). Instead of people being separated from their essential humanity, as Marxists and other radical critics of capitalism feared, they could be rewarded not just with the material and social rewards of economic success but also with the chance to become everything that a human being could possibly become – the chance to realise their essential humanity, whatever that might be. This was self-actualisation.

Any critical study of organisational and managerial behaviour must pay attention to these ideological implications of what is probably the most frequently taught and most commonly remembered single 'theory' in the business and management studies curriculum.

Having identified the ideological roots of Maslow's thinking, we can move on to apply the normal social scientific critical rigour to the theory itself. Each of the three types of 'truth claim' that can be made for knowledge, set out above (p. 18) can be applied to the hierarchy of needs theory's claim that people only seek to satisfy 'higher order' needs once they have satisfied the lower level ones.

The *correspondence* criterion for judging the 'truth' of a theory might be applied by testing whether the sequence of 'need fulfilment' posited in the theory accords with what we see to 'be the case' if people are systematically studied meeting their needs in a research laboratory. Research psychologists have attempted to do this and found that people simply do not follow the sequence suggested by Maslow (Rauschenberger, Schmitt and Hunter, 1980). On these grounds, then, the theory fails.

On the *plausibility* criterion, which would judge the theory to be true if it fitted with everything else we know, we have already seen that there are some grounds for acceptance. But the plausibility of the theory soon drops away once we move beyond the everyday common sense mode of thinking (p. 10) in which truisms play an important part ('it's obvious isn't it?' we often say when thinking at the unreflective *everyday common sense* level). The *critical common sense* advocated earlier requires us to step back and critically put our minds to what at first seems credible.

So what about the *philosophical pragmatist* principle of judging truth claims? This requires us to ask how helpful the theory would be in informing our practices were we to find ourselves in the situation of trying to 'motivate' people at work. And here we can turn to the case of Campbell Toon, a manager and a management student whom we see in Case 1.3 applying, in effect, both critical common sense thinking and the philosophical pragmatist principle. He does not use these terms himself but the principles they represent are implicit in what he says to the researcher.

Activity 1.3

Read Campbell Toon's conversation with the researcher in Case 1.3 and his experience-based rejection of the Maslow theory of motivation and reflect on:

- why you think so many people seem to remember the 'hierarchy of needs' theory (or the triangular representation of it at least) and not the more complex theories that deal with 'motivation';

- the extent to which the hierarchical sequence of need satisfaction is followed in your own life (following the approach that Campbell takes to analysing the place of different aspects of need satisfaction in his personal life).

Campbell Toon confronts the Maslow triangle   Case 1.3

During a management class the researcher had reported the outcomes of some 'ethnographic experiments' he had done with other management students. During one of these events, a year or more previously, a student had uttered what the researcher took to be the very significant words, 'Motivation, that's Maslow isn't it?' (Watson, 1996a). Most of the current class reacted positively to the researcher's argument that these words perfectly captured the sort of 'surface learning' that can occur in management education when the topic of study becomes 'what this or that American professor wrote years ago' rather than how academic theorising relates to the actual practices of people involved in organising and managing work. Campbell Toon, however, was especially vocal in his attack on what he called 'Maslow's bloody magic triangle', arguing that he had been 'foolish enough to think that what he studied on management courses should be relevant to his practice as a manager'. When he visited the researcher's office after the class to collect a copy of the journal article reporting the study, he agreed to a tape recording of a conversation with the researcher. The researcher speaks first.

I hope, Cam, that I wasn't going too far in the class by asking the course members to be critical of both themselves and the material they have to study.

No, I don't think so. I think that you are right that too many lecturers and too many students simply go through the motions of drawing that dreaded triangle as an alternative to engaging with serious attempts to understand what it really means to have to motivate people at work. I'm not sure, though, whether you are right that people keep reproducing the triangle in their lectures and in their assignments as a magic ritual or a magic charm because they are actually frightened by – what was it you said?

'The frightening realities of managerial work', or some such thing, probably. No, I was just speculating that perhaps the endless drawing of the triangle by teachers and students is equivalent to people crossing themselves when they see a funeral pass by. You know, it's a sort of whistling in the dark when you are frightened because you don't really know what you are doing. But, leaving all that aside, I'm interested in your point that you did try to apply this thinking in your work.

Yes, I was facing some big problems in the packaging business where I work. It was made clear to me that the productivity levels in my part of the factory were not good enough. I knew I had to get more out of people. I had no sticks to beat people with – they were all doing a reasonable job, even if they rarely showed any kind of initiative and hardly ever helped each other out with problems. Generally, people seemed to me to be complacent. The firm was ostensibly doing well and people were reasonably paid and were secure in their jobs. When I tried exhorting people to speed up a bit, to work together a bit more when problems arose and to look for smarter ways of doing things, they just smiled at me and carried on in the same way. So you can see that when it came to the classes on motivation I was dead keen to see what these 'theories of motivation' would have to offer. The Maslow thing clicked with me when we covered it. The lower level needs of my people were all satisfied, I concluded, and therefore to motivate them to do more I had to offer them something at the 'higher order' level. I saw that Herzberg's job enrichment principle ('Herzberg spelled without a "t" ', I remember the lecturer saying) was a way of applying the Maslow theory. I therefore set about rearranging the jobs of my people so that there was more variety in their tasks and, by taking away a level of supervision, they were given more freedom to choose how to do the work. In introducing this I really played up the 'social needs' bit by pointing out that they would need to work more closely together and would find this socially rewarding. I gave even more emphasis to the 'esteem' need by making the point very strongly that I had a high opinion of my staff and that the firm had perhaps been insulting their abilities by supervising them so closely and prescribing every little detail of how to do things.

And did this work?

Did it hell. After only a week and a half I had to get some tight supervision back. The simple truth of the matter is that my people *did not want to have their jobs enriched*. Well, this is not entirely true. Two or three of them were persuaded by my arguments. I had a sort of post mortem talk with two of these. They told me that they agreed that people ought to find some of the fulfilment in their work that they tended to get with their families or in their hobbies. However, I inferred from what they told me that most of their work mates were happier getting their social, esteem and fulfilment needs satisfied outside of work and that they were happy 'cruising along' at work. But when I put it to them that 'money was not a motivator' they just laughed at me and said that had the new system lasted a little longer they were all going to put in a wage claim. When I expressed some shock they said, 'Sod money as a motivator. First, there's no way any factory worker is ever going to feel that they are paid enough. And, second, it would simply be unfair to leave people on the ordinary factory rate when they were now doing some of the old supervisor's job'.

One might argue that you had just been naïve here as a manager and that you can't really blame old Maslow for your naïvety.

I accept that. But your class last week made me think a lot about why, as management students, we often fail to test the material we are offered against our own work experiences, let alone common sense. Somehow, with me though, the confrontation with Maslow's magic triangle had encouraged me to *switch off* my common sense. When you think hard about the so-called hierarchy of needs, it doesn't stack up, does it? I am Jewish and I get a good deal of my self-esteem and an awful lot of the social rewards in my life from belonging to my culture. The meeting of these social and esteem needs, I have to say, comes before I meet my need to eat or my need to make love to whoever I fancy. The rules of my religion and my community define what and when I eat and who I can have sex with. If I was in the Israeli army, like my cousin recently was, I would put the need to belong to my community and my personal prestige needs, as a defender of my community, way before even my need for safety. Yet Maslow's simplistic scheme has us all working up through the satisfaction of the more basic physiological and safety needs towards the higher social or esteem ones. It is nonsense – there is simply no straightforward sequence to how people pursue their needs. And Maslow's whole notion of human beings seems to be one in which people live outside of culture. What I said about being Jewish would apply, in various ways, to members of any other culture of course.

Well, I'm sure he wasn't unaware of all of these things but the 'theory of motivation' that has been extracted from his writings and presented to generations of management students does seem to do just this. It reduces people, with all their choices, preferences, values and cultural influences to need-led little machines.

So this doesn't say a lot for business school education does it?

Well perhaps not. But, to be fair, I am sure that you covered other motivational theories that would be closer to your own commonsensical thinking and would helpfully, in my favourite phrase, 'inform your practice'. Do you not remember coming across something called 'expectancy theory' – an approach which stresses the importance of finding out just what your own particular employees actually want, rather than wasting time reflecting on human 'needs' in general? And did you not look at 'equity theories' and their emphasis on how ideas about fairness influence people's motivation (as happened with your people)? All of that would have been very useful to you as a manager, I suggest. And, of course, I would argue that the ideas about work orientations and implicit contracts that some of us use in this area are even more useful.

I confess that I just didn't take in these other theories – 'process theories' I think they called them. They just seemed to be more complicated – and more difficult to remember.

Well, you're not alone there. In the research paper you will see evidence that the vast majority of the three hundred or so students who took part in the events covered in the project, one year on, could remember practically nothing of the 'process theories' they studied.

For them motivation was Maslow?

Something like that.

On pragmatist grounds, then, it would seem that only very weak truth claims can be made for Maslow's theory. What Campbell Toon has to say, however, has a significance way beyond the hierarchy of needs theory specifically or to motivational theories generally. The conversation raises serious questions about the role that traditional management education plays in the management learning processes of those who take the courses and use the standard textbooks. This connects back to the earlier arguments for applying critical common sense to the questions that surface whenever we really want to understand the complex issues that arise with organising and managing work. Both parties to the conversation reflect on why the particular motivational theory of which they are so critical should be given such massive attention within management education. Cam recognises the relevance of information (and images) being easy to remember. The researcher speculates, at an anthropological level, about a possible symbolic role for the 'magic triangle' as some kind of talisman that helps management tutors and management students alike cope with the ambiguities and anxieties involved in studying something as complex and daunting as managerial practice (see Watson, 1996a). This issue of 'managerial angst' and the 'controlling the uncontrollable' expectations that are put on managers will be returned to in Chapter 6 (pp. 229–34).

Campbell's thoughts about how he does not move through a sequence of need satisfaction that remotely resembles the hierarchical models in his own life are especially significant. As he points out, every one of us lives within a culture. This means that satisfying 'needs' that can be characterised in social, esteem or 'self-actualisation' terms could be seen as having precedence over the satisfaction of so-called lower order ones – contrary to the hierarchical model. Is there anyone who could say that they regularly satisfy their physiological needs for food, drink, sex or to urinate without first considering the norms of the social groups to which they belong or prior to reflecting on what sort of esteem they will be held in if they prioritise their hunger, thirst, lust or full bladder over a need to 'belong' or a need to be admired? Of course not. One's 'motivations', in work or elsewhere, are matters of one's cultural location, personal identity, work orientation, values and life priorities and how these lead to exchanges in particular circumstances – like the exchange that people make through an implicit contract with a particular employer at a particular time.

Furthermore, it is unlikely that any of us would be able to point to any kind of sequential pattern at all in the way we go about managing our lives and handling our 'needs'. Maslow's desire to impose a particular order on people's need satisfaction behaviour is an example of the type of *linearity* in theorising about human behaviour that we will critically examine in Chapter 3. And, as we will also see in Chapter 3, matters of work motivation and orientation simply cannot be reduced to something as simple as 'needs'. While it is reasonable to talk of people 'needing' food and water, it becomes much more difficult to use the language of needs when considering matters like pursuing promotion to a high status position or trying to obtain a company car. 'Wants' would be a more realistic notion here, as would be the concepts of *expectancy* and *equity* that are used in some of the more process-oriented motivational theories that we shall meet in Chapter 8. But what are 'concepts' and how might we most effectively use them in our study of the organising and managing of work.

Concepts, perspectives and two ways of framing reality

Concepts

Concept

Concepts are the working definitions that are chosen or devised to make possible a particular piece of scientific analysis. They are the way scientists define their terms for the purpose of a specific investigation. They therefore differ from dictionary definitions which tend to have a much more general applicability.

In our everyday lives, we often look for *correct definitions* of phenomena, ones that will be generally helpful to us when communicating within a broad public language. If we wish to analyse phenomena with the greater degree of rigour and focus that distinguishes scientific analysis, however, we find ourselves having more carefully to *conceptualise* phenomena. This means devising working definitions which are helpful to us in trying to analyse and understand some aspect of the world. Thus an economist will conceptualise money more rigorously than the person in the street will 'define' it. Psychologists will do similarly with regard to 'intelligence' – working with different concepts of intelligence at different times. What this means is that in engaging in an enterprise like writing *Organising and Managing Work*, one develops concepts that are useful to one's purposes. One does not turn to a dictionary for the universally 'correct' definition. Thus, every time there is a 'defining of terms' in this book (usually using the device of a 'concept box'), it is done to be *helpful* to the purposes of the book – and *useful* to the readers who are interested in improving their understanding of how work is organised and managed. The whole enterprise of the book is based on the notion that some ways of conceptualising, 'management' or 'organisation', say, are more useful than others. The intent is not to find a 'correct' definition of what 'management' or 'organisation' is but to use concepts that help us critically engage with the world.

Although in the subsequent chapters we will be offering conceptualisations of management and of organisations that are helpful in analysing and thinking about work activities and their shaping, it is important to stress that concepts should not be seen as free-standing entities that can be used without being made consistent with other concepts being used in that same analysis. To analyse any area of human life we need 'bundles' or sets of concepts that are all compatible with each other, logically and in terms of the deeper assumptions underlying the concepts (Watson, 1997a). Thus, for any given analysis, one develops a conceptual framework or theoretical perspective that is appropriate to the purpose in hand. Thus a psychologist studying certain types of problem will want a set of linked concepts of, say, intelligence, personality, learning, motivation and so on.

Whilst it is the case that the individual social scientist will choose concepts appropriate to the particular piece of research that they are engaged in at any

particular time, it is nevertheless true that each of us – both in our formal analytical endeavours and in our general thinking about life – tend to build up
bundles of concepts that we find most helpful, these adding up to the personal
analytical frames of reference that we take through life. These are, in the broad-
est sense of the word, 'theories' (systematic ideas about how the world works,
we might say). These schemes are often and very usefully referred to as ways of
'framing reality'.

***

Framings of reality   *Concept*

These are broad ways of looking at the world that people adopt to make sense of various aspects
of human life – work organisation and management being one of these. The framework that we
use with regard to any particular aspect of life will incorporate:

- basic general assumptions about human beings ('people's characters are decided before birth',
  for example);

- conceptualisations of various dimensions of the specific area being considered (concepts of
  organisational culture or work identity, for example);

- broad ideas about how these various dimensions relate to each other (how organisational
  cultures relate to organisational structures, for example).

***

The notion of 'discursive framing' in human life will be examined in Chapter 3
(p. 102). For the moment we need simply to emphasise that the way we 'frame'
reality influences how we both think and act in the world. We might, for
instance, 'frame' *management* as essentially an activity in which intelligent and
trained individuals decide how work should be done and then instruct less able
and knowledgeable individuals to act accordingly. If we do this, we are likely to
act differently when we get into management situations (as either the 'boss' or
the 'worker') than we would if we 'framed' management as a process involving
the bringing together of different types of knowledge, understanding and priorities to get work tasks done.

To help organise the present book, all the time applying the philosophical
pragmatist principle of developing frameworks which better inform human
practices, a basic distinction between *systems-control* and *process-relational* ways
of framing the realities of human life generally and organisational activities
specifically is used. These two framings will be unfolded in the next two chapters. For the moment, however, it is useful to see these two broad ways of
thinking about human beings and about work organisations set out alongside
each other. The first two columns of Table 1.4 (p. 30) derive from the thinking
to be set out in Chapter 2 and the third and fourth columns relate to Chapter 3.
The broad shape of the thinking behind these two chapters is presented here in
part to offer a road map of the terrain over which we are about to travel. But it is
also offered to show the parallels that exist between the issues to be covered at
the organisational level and the issues to be covered at the level of the human

being. This is not to say that organisations can be treated as if they were people. It is, instead, to recognise that there are clear parallels in the way we think about human beings on the one hand and work organisations on the other.

The most important point to stress before we move on is that, whilst it is *not* being argued that the systems-control way of framing is wrong or untrue and the process-relational framework is right or true, it will be argued, in pragmatist terms, that there are real and practical advantages in moving beyond systems-control ways of framing reality towards process-relational ones. This is fully in line with the intention behind *Organising and Managing Work* not to duck the issue of whether some ideas, theories or frames of reference relating to the organising and managing of work might be *better* than others. It is to be argued that all of us will be better placed to cope in the world of work management if we adopt thinking that can be broadly conceived of as part of a process-relational way of framing reality than if we follow the more traditional or ortho-dox systems-control style of thinking.

Table 1.4 is something that can helpfully be referred back to after Chapter 2 and 3 have been read. In the next chapter we will see how the systems-control way of framing organisational and managerial activities derives from modernist and universalistic aspirations to maximise control over human circumstances and does this through encouraging a notion of organisations as large goal-based controllable mechanical systems and individuals as small need-oriented systems. It will be argued that a more useful way of framing organisational realities – and indeed the broader human realities that we will consider in Chapter 3 – is to focus instead on the processes of emergence in the patterning of relations between people, organisations and the wider social world.

Summary

In this chapter, the following key points have been made:

- The most helpful way to think about issues of work organisation and management is not to focus on either the management of people or the management of systems but to focus on the management of work tasks and the relationships involved in fulfilling those tasks. This involves looking at all those activities which contribute to the man-agement of work tasks, only then considering how such activities are divided up between people who have the title of 'manager' and those who do not.

- The field covered in the present text is the study of the human aspects of work organ-isation and its management which draws on the social sciences to develop insights, theories and research findings with a view to informing the choices, decisions and actions of organisational practitioners.

- This field of study is linked to, and incorporates elements of, several other established and developing academic subjects, including management learning, critical manage-ment studies, strategic management and human resource management.

Table 1.4 Systems-control and process-relational ways of framing organisations and people			
Systems-control framing of organisations	**Process-relational framing of organisations**	**Systems-control framing of people**	**Process-relational framing of people**
The organisation is an *entity*: a system of managerially designed rules and roles existing on its own terms	Organisations are *relational phenomena*: sets of relationships and associated understandings	The individual person is an *entity* which exists on its own terms with an essential or 'true' self	People are *relational* beings: their individuality only becomes possible as a result of relating to others
The organisation is based on an *organisation design* with a set of structural and cultural characteristics	Organisations are *emergent patterns* resulting from processes of exchange, negotiation, conflict and compromise	The individual possesses a more or less fixed set of *personality* traits	People are always in a process of 'becoming': they have *emergent identities*
The organisation operates to ensure the completion of the *organisational goals* it was designed to fulfil	Organisations are *strategically oriented* in the sense that those in charge of them strive to ensure that they survive in the long term	People have sets of needs which create *motives* propelling them towards particular behaviours	People are *sense making* and *project oriented* rather than need led: in the light of how they interpret their situation they make *exchanges* with others to deal with their material and emotional circumstances
The organisation is a rational *system of rules and procedures* which ensures the completion of tasks that ensure corporate goal fulfilment	Organisations operate with *both reason and emotion*: the feelings of managers, workers and customers are as relevant to their behaviours as is their rational pursuit of material interests within formal corporate procedures	People at work are capable of suppressing emotions so that their engagement in *rational analysis* and decision making is unaffected by feelings and values	People are *simultaneously rational and emotional*: their feelings about the world and their reasoning capacities mutually influence each other
The organisation is an expression of universally applicable organisational and managerial principles	Organisations all follow modernist bureaucratic principles, but their functioning also reflects the economic, cultural and political circumstances of their societal setting	People, regardless of the society in which they live, play the role of worker, manager or whatever according to the logic of modern systems of employment and work organisation	People are cultural animals: they make sense of the world and their work activities in the light of the culture and values of the society and communities of which they are a part

- The social science disciplines drawn upon by *Organising and Managing Work*, and their analytical styles, are not essentially different from 'common sense' thinking. In fact, they have a close continuity with what can be called 'critical common sense'.

- In the spirit of 'critical common sense', the style of work organisation and management studies adopted here can be identified with certain aspects of the emergent tradition of 'critical management studies'. This entails continually asking, first, why work is organised and managed in the way it is and, second, why we think about and study work and its management in the ways we do. It also involves continuous recognition of the extent to which work organisation happens in a context of human competition, context and patterned antagonism as well as recognising that management ideas are not neutral technical rules and principles but always have political significance.

- To be able to relate what we study to issues of practice in the organisational and managerial world we need some criteria for judging the relative merits of the theories, research studies and other materials that are available to us. The most useful criterion we can apply to judging theories, and the rest, is one derived from pragmatist philosophy. There is no way of judging absolute truth or validity. But some accounts can be seen as 'truer' than others. It is suggested that one piece of material may be judged to be 'truer' than another to the extent to which it better informs human practices or 'projects' in the aspect of human activity with which it deals.

- In spite of a growing interest in processual thinking, an almost fetishistic level of attention is given to 'motivation theories' in business and management education and, especially to Maslow's 'hierarchy of needs' theory. This latter theory has enormous weaknesses and has little value as a guide to human practice. But it nevertheless has an important ideological significance in how employment relationships have been thought about in more affluent societies over the past half century. It may also have a symbolic role in the handling of managerial angst.

- Concepts are vital tools for social scientific analysis and are different from dictionary definitions in that they are devised for the specific purpose of a given analysis. Concepts are drawn together into conceptual or theoretical frameworks. Such frameworks are, again, devised for specific studies. But all of us develop personal ways of looking at the world which are broadly of a similar nature: they help us make sense of the world around us and influence how we act in the world. These perspectives can be understood as ways of 'framing realities'. There are two basic ways of framing the realities of the organising and managing work: a systems-control framing and a process-relational framing. The latter has greater promise as a frame of reference that will inform the practices of anyone involved in organisational situations.

Recommended reading

A stimulating and accessible overview of a critical style of thinking about organising and managing is provided by Chris Grey in his *A Very Short, Fairly Interesting and Reasonably Cheap Book about Studying Organization* (London: Sage, 2005). This book is nicely complemented by the collection of pieces edited by Mats Alvesson and Hugh Willmott, *Studying Management Critically* (London: Sage, 2003). For a coverage of the variety of different theoretical positions on organisations that gives useful background to the systems-control/process-relational scheme used in *Organising and Managing Work* see the book written by Mary Jo Hatch with Ann Cunliffe, *Organization Theory: Modern, symbolic and postmodern perspectives, 2nd edition* (Oxford: Oxford University Press, 2006). And for a fuller explanation of how one can apply pragmatist thinking to research on managing and organising see the Tony Watson article 'Theorising managerial work: a pragmatic pluralist approach to interdisciplinary research' (*British Journal of Management*, 8: 3–8, 1997).

Further reading

Further reading Critical approaches in organisation and management studies

Alvesson, M. and Deetz, S. (1999) *Doing Critical Management Research*, London: Sage

Alvesson, M. and Willmott, H. (1996) *Making Sense of Management: A critical introduction*, London: Sage

Alvesson, M. and Willmott, H. (eds) (2003) *Studying Management Critically*, London: Sage

Fournier, V. and Grey, C. (2000) 'At the critical moment: conditions and prospects of critical management studies', *Human Relations*, 53(1): 7–32

Grey, C., Knights, D. and Willmott, H. (1996) 'Is a critical pedagogy of management possible?' in R. French and C. Grey (eds) *Rethinking Management Education*, London: Sage

O'Connor, E.S. (1999) 'The politics of management thought: a case study of Harvard Business School and the human relations school', *Academy of Management Review*, 24(1): 117–131

Perriton, L. (2000) 'Verandah discourses: critical management education in organizations', *British Journal of Management*, 11(3): 227–237

Prasad, P. and Capruni, P.J. (1997) 'Critical theory in the management classroom: engaging power, ideology, and praxis', *Journal of Management Education*, 21(3): 284–291

Reynolds, M. (1997) 'Towards a critical management pedagogy' in J. Burgoyne and M. Reynolds (eds) *Management Learning: Integrating perspectives in theory and practice*, London: Sage

Reynolds, M. (1998) 'Reflection and critical reflection in management learning', *Management Learning*, 29(2): 183–200

Reynolds, M. (1999) 'Grasping the nettle: possibilities and pitfalls of a critical management pedagogy', *British Journal of Management*, 10(2): 95–184

Sotorin, P. and Tyrell, S. (1998) 'Wondering about critical management studies', *Management Communication Quarterly*, 12(2): 303–336

Steffy, B.D. and Grimes, A.J. (1986) 'A critical theory of organisational science', *Academy of Management Review*, 11(2): 322–336

Watson, T.J. (1994) 'Towards a managerially relevant but non-managerialist organisation theory' in J. Hassard and M. Parker (eds) *Towards a New Theory of Organizations*, London: Routledge

Willmott, H. (1997) 'Critical management learning' in J. Burgoyne and M. Reynolds (eds) *Management Learning: Integrating perspectives in theory and practice*, London: Sage

Wilson, F. (2004) *Organizational Behaviour and Work: A critical introduction, 2nd edition*, Oxford: Oxford University Press

Further reading Epistemology and philosophical pragmatism

Davidson, D. (1986) 'A coherence theory of truth and knowledge' in E. Lepore (ed.) *Truth and Interpretation*, Oxford: Blackwell

Gallie, W.B. (1952) *Pierce and Pragmatism*, Harmondsworth: Penguin

Haack, S. (1996) 'Pragmatism' in N. Bunnin, and E.P. Tsui-James (eds) *The Blackwell Companion to Philosophy*, Oxford: Blackwell

James, W. (ed. D. Olin) (1992) *Pragmatism in Focus*, London: Routledge

Mounce, H.O. (1997) *The Two Pragmatisms*, London: Routledge

Putnam, H. (1995) *Pragmatism*, Oxford: Blackwell

Rorty, R. (1980) *Philosophy and the Mirror of Nature*, Oxford: Blackwell

Rorty, R. (1982) *Consequences of Pragmatism*, Brighton: Harvester

Rorty, R. (1989) *Contingency, Irony, and Solidarity*, Cambridge: Cambridge University Press

Tsoukas, H. (1989) 'The validity of idiographic research explanations', *Academy of Management Review*, 14: 551–561

Tsoukas, H. (1998a) 'Forms of knowledge and forms of life in organized contexts' in R. Chia (ed.) *In the Realm of Organization*, London: Routledge

Tsoukas, H. (1998b) 'The word and the world: a critique of representationalism in management research', *International Journal of Public Administration*, 21(5): 781–817

Urmson, J.O. (1989) 'Truth' in J.O. Urmson and J. Rée (eds) *The Concise Encyclopedia of Western Philosophy and Philosophers*, London: Routledge

Watson, T.J. (1997) 'Theorising managerial work: a pragmatic pluralist approach to interdisciplinary research', *British Journal of Management*, 8 (special issue): 3–8

The wider context of managing people

Chapter 4

Human resource management and the labour market

Tim Claydon and Amanda Thompson

Objectives

- To explain the nature and composition of the UK labour market.
- To identify the major social forces responsible for shaping the nature and extent of people's engagement with paid employment.
- To highlight developments in the nature of work and employment in the late twentieth and early twenty first century and to show how these trends have influenced organisational requirements for labour.
- To present a critical assessment of workers' experiences of employment in contemporary Britain.

Introduction

This chapter is concerned principally with the size, composition and condition of the UK labour market and more specifically with how the labour market shapes employers' choices concerning people management and utilisation. An appreciation of labour markets and how they operate is especially relevant for students of HRM, particularly as HRM claims to offer a strategic approach to managing people. A strategic stance is attractive because it offers organisations the latitude to select an appropriate employment system and a set of complementary HR practices to 'fit' the external operating environment, thus placing the firm in a better position to exploit competitive advantage. From a practical perspective therefore, knowing and understanding labour market issues is likely to be of prime value to the organisation in its bid to formulate a strategic approach to HRM, through which superior business outcomes can, with fortune, be realised.

We divide the chapter into four main sections to draw upon a range of contemporary labour market issues and to consider the significance of each for the practice of HRM. In the first we briefly consider the nature of labour markets and discuss the considerations that influence the employment strategies of firms. In the second we explore recent political and social developments and the implications of these for the supply of labour. The third section explores the changing nature of work and employment and is designed to focus on emergent themes in employers' demand for labour. The final section of the chapter considers key dimensions of job quality and discusses these in relation to workers' experiences of employment in contemporary Britain.

The nature of labour markets

The most general definition of the labour market is that it consists of workers who are looking for paid employment and employers who are seeking to fill vacancies. The amount of labour that is available to firms – *labour supply* – is determined by the number of people of working age who are in employment or seeking employment and the number of hours that they are willing to work. This number will be determined by the size and age structure of the population and by the decisions made by individuals and households about the relative costs and benefits of taking paid employment. These decisions are influenced by various factors, one of which is the level of wages on offer. Generally speaking a higher wage will attract more people into the labour market while a lower wage will attract fewer, as long as other factors, such as the level of welfare benefits and people's attitudes towards work, remain constant.

The number of jobs on offer to workers – *labour demand* – is the sum of people in employment plus the number of vacancies waiting to be filled. The demand for labour is determined by the level of demand for the goods and services produced by firms in the market. When sales and production are rising, firms' demand for labour rises. When sales fall and production is cut back, firms' demand for labour falls.

The simplest view of the labour market is that it is an arena of competition. Workers enter the arena in search of jobs and employers enter it in search of workers. Competition between employers for workers and between workers for jobs results in a 'market wage' that adjusts to relative changes in labour demand and supply. Thus, when labour demand rises relative to labour supply, the market wage rises as firms try to outbid each other for scarce labour. When labour demand falls relative to labour supply, the market wage falls as workers compete with each other for the smaller number of available jobs.

Competition means that no individual firm can set a wage that is out of line with the competitive market wage. Neither can workers demand such a wage. Should a firm try to offer a wage that is below the market rate, it will be unable to hire workers. Should a firm set a wage above the market rate, it will go out of business because its costs of production will be above those of its competitors. For the same reason, workers who demand a wage higher than the market rate will price themselves out of jobs. No firm will hire them because to do so would increase their costs of production relative to those of their competitors.

While it is undeniable that competitive forces operate in the labour market to a degree, few would seriously pretend that this is a wholly accurate description of the real world. There are limits to competition between firms and among workers. Wages do not respond instantly to changes in labour demand. Nor is there a uniform wage in the labour market. Empirical research has shown that rates of pay vary between firms, even in the same industry and operating in the same local labour market (Nolan and Brown, 1983). Other employment policies also vary among firms. For example, some firms employ labour on a hire and fire basis and make heavy use of casualised forms of employment such as temporary work while others offer long-term employment security and career development. The policies that employers adopt are influenced to a great extent by the characteristics they seek in their workforce:

- **The need for a stable workforce.** A stable workforce is advantageous to employers because it reduces the costs of labour turnover, i.e. disruption of production due to the unplanned reductions in the workforce that result from workers leaving, costs of recruitment and selection, such as the financial costs of advertising for recruits and the cost in terms of management time spent in recruiting and selecting replacements, and the cost of training new recruits. These costs may be particularly high where skilled labour is scarce and replacements hard to find, or where employers have invested considerable amounts in training workers. In these situations employers have a strong interest in limiting the extent of labour turnover.

What types of workforce will have low turnover costs and why? What types of workforce will have high turnover costs?

- **The need for worker cooperation in production.** A central issue in managing people at work is how to manage their performance. One way of trying to ensure that workers supply the required level of effort is by subjecting them to direct controls (Friedman, 1977). Traditionally this took the form of direct personal supervision by a superior and externally imposed discipline. Today direct supervision is supplemented with electronic surveillance, 'mystery customers' and customer questionnaire surveys in a managerial effort to make workers' effort levels increasingly visible. However, there are limits to the extent that employers can rely on direct controls. To a great extent employers rely on sufficiently motivated workers using their initiative to ensure efficiency and quality in the production of goods and the delivery of services. The nature of the product or the production process often makes it difficult to define what the appropriate effort levels are for each worker and to measure how hard they are actually working. This makes it difficult for managers to impose effort levels without the workers' agreement. Heavy reliance on supervision and surveillance may also be counterproductive because of the resistance that it can generate among workers. The alternative is to encourage workers to exercise *responsible autonomy* at work (Friedman, 1977). In other words it may be more cost-effective for managers to offer positive incentives to ensure that workers cooperate voluntarily with management and use their job knowledge and their initiative to maintain and improve efficiency and quality.

The greater are employers' needs for a stable, highly cooperative workforce, the more likely they are to introduce policies to retain workers and create a basis for mutual trust and cooperation while also raising the cost to the employee of losing their job should they fall short of the standards demanded by management. These policies, which are associated with the 'best practice HRM' principle of treating employees as valued assets rather than disposable commodities (see Chapter 1), *internalise* employment by fostering long-term employment relationships and giving workers a degree of protection from external labour market pressures. They include guarantees of long-term employment security, opportunities for training and internal promotion, fringe benefits and pay that is higher than the market rate. However these policies are themselves costly. Therefore the extent to which employers seek to internalise employment depends on the cost of labour turnover and the limits to direct control. Where these are low, employers are more likely to treat labour as a disposable commodity, in other words *externalising* the employment relationship.

During 1998 two leading supermarket chains converted two-thirds of their temporary staff onto permanent contracts. Temporary workers had been hired to cope with seasonal peaks in demand or to enable stores to adjust more easily under uncertain trading conditions. However, workers who remained on temporary contracts for too long lost motivation and this had a damaging effect on the quality of customer service. Other problems that managers associated with employing workers on temporary and zero hours contracts were lack of training and difficulty of communication.

Source: People Management, June 1998.

Question

What is it about the nature of customer service work that leads employers to require voluntary cooperation from workers? Why does this set limits to the extent to which management can externalise the employment relationship?

From this we can see that employers make strategic choices concerning the extent to which they internalise or externalise employment. However, these choices are influenced by the specific labour market contexts in which they operate. As we shall see later in this chapter, the overall state of the labour market is one important influence, while another is the way in which the labour market is segmented, giving rise to advantaged and disadvantaged labour market groups. To be able to understand how these influences operate, we first need to examine the two key dimensions of the labour market, labour supply and demand.

The supply of labour

'In being bought and sold in the labour market, labour becomes a commodity' (SCER, 2001: 5). It follows that firms in competition with one another for labour will be interested in the current and future availability of this commodity. Conventionally the process of human resource planning involves forecasting the supply and demand for labour so that suitable plans can be put in place to address situations of labour shortage or surplus (see Chapter 5). Despite the apparent logic of this approach Taylor (2005) suggests there is some evidence of firms rejecting systematic human resource planning as they find it impossible to predict labour supply and demand with any degree of accuracy in a climate of uncertainty. Even so, some understanding of where the future supply of labour can be sourced from and how plentiful that source is expected to be is important in informing employers' actions in the labour market.

The number of people seeking work in the labour market is influenced by factors relating to the size and composition of the population. Within this section of the chapter we consider the main demographic factors affecting total labour supply, namely population and population change, the age structure of the population, gender and ethnicity.

Population

The supply side of the labour market derives from the country's population, specifically men aged between 16 and 65 years and women between the ages of 16 and 60 (working age). Information on the total size of the current population and predictions of future patterns of population growth and decline are thus important in estimating the current and future supply of labour.

Population is affected by birth and death rates. When live births exceed the number of deaths a net natural population increase arises and when mortality rates exceed birth rates a net natural decline in population occurs. Population change is also influenced by net migration; that is the effect caused by people moving into and out of the country. In the 1950s and 1960s population growth was largely attributable to net natural change. Within this period a relatively stable death rate coupled with the baby boom that followed the Second World War triggered net natural growth. Since 1983 net migration has played an increased part in the expansion of the population as the number of people migrating into the United Kingdom continues to surpass the number leaving. In 2004 nearly 222,600 more people migrated to the United Kingdom than left it. This net inflow represents the highest since the present methods of estimation began in 1991. The net effects of migration are forecast to continue to play a major role in population growth alongside net natural change (ONS, 2006a). For illustrative purposes Home Office statistics (ONS, 2006a) show that between 1991 and 2004 the total number of people accepted for permanent settlement in the United Kingdom more than doubled. The biggest increase in acceptances was for people from Europe (excluding EEA nationals) followed by those from Africa.

Latest data from the ONS (2006a) shows that the population of the United Kingdom has been climbing steadily since 1971 and had reached 59.8 million people by 2004. Predictions of population from the 2004 base estimate that by 2011 the population will be 61.9 million, rising to 64.7 million in 2021 and extending still further to 67 million by 2031. Growth is projected to occur most rapidly and over a sustained period in England compared with the rest of the United Kingdom. In line with trends emerging in the 1980s more of the anticipated expansion in the population of the United Kingdom in the period 2004 to 2031 is expected to result from net migration (57 per cent) than from natural increase (43 per cent).

The way in which the country's population expands affects the gender composition, age profile and ethnic diversity of the labour market. Changes to the composition of labour supply arising from fluctuations in birth and death rates and shifting patterns of migration may call into question the appropriateness of established human resource management practices aimed at attracting and retaining suitable labour. Similarly, at a localised level, patterns of regional population density resulting from a combination of natural causes, international migration *and* internal migration (the movement of people between regions within the United Kingdom) lead to variations in the amount and type of labour available in different parts of the country. While labour tends to move to parts of the country where work is more plentiful (ONS, 2001) those organisations reliant on local labour in areas of the country with low population density and/or net population loss are confronted with a different set of labour market circumstances from those operating in areas of higher population density.

Age structure of the population

The age structure of the population is a key determinant of labour supply as firms draw labour from the portion of the total population that is of working age. The age structure is closely associated with past trends in migration; such trends can also be used to explain regional differences in the population's age profile as migrants establish communities in certain areas of the country. ONS (2006a) shows that white ethnic groups, particularly the white Irish population, have an older age structure than other ethnic groups as a consequence of past fertility and immigration patterns. Among non-white ethnic groups younger age profiles are exhibited within groups migrating to the United Kingdom relatively recently whilst, as might be expected, those groups with an earlier history of large-scale migration to the United Kingdom have now begun to display larger proportions of people within older age brackets. For example ONS data (2006a) shows that just 2 per cent of the country's Black African population are aged 65 and over compared with 11 per cent of Black Caribbeans, large-scale migration from countries such as Jamaica and Trinidad having taken place several decades prior to the large-scale arrival of migrants from Nigeria, Ghana and other African countries which began in earnest in the 1980s.

Activity | Examine the information provided in the table below summarising the age structure of the populations of Eastbourne and Leicester at the time of the last census in April 2001.

Age structure of the population	Eastbourne	Leicester
% of the resident population aged 0–4	5.31	6.83
% of the resident population aged 5–15	12.69	15.46
% of the resident population aged 16–19	4.32	5.92
% of the resident population aged 20–44	30.49	38.75
% of the resident population aged 45–64	22.47	19.52
% of the resident population aged 65 or over	24.72	13.52
Average age of the population (years)	43.2	35.5

Source: Census 2001 (ONS, 2001).

Questions

1 Suggest why the proportion of residents over the age of retirement in Eastbourne is almost double the proportion of those aged 65 and over in Leicester.

2 Explain why Leicester has a greater proportion of residents in all age brackets below 65.

3 Consider the possible implications of the above data for the current and future supply of labour in Leicester and Eastbourne.

As well as past trends in migration, the age structure of the total population and of regional populations is affected by births and deaths and past trends in these key indices. Records depict a fairly erratic pattern in the number of live births occurring in the United Kingdom at different phases throughout the twentieth century (ONS, 2006a). Notable decreases in the number of births occurred during the two world wars (1914–1918 and 1939–1945), and apart from a sharp increase in the number of births in the immediate aftermath of the First World War, births fell again and remained relatively subdued for most of the inter-war period. A further baby boom occurred after the Second World War causing another, but this time more modest, increase in the late 1980s and early 1990s as the baby boomer generation produced children of their own. Since this time the number of live births per year has fallen as women average fewer children and delay the age at which they give birth to their first child (ONS, 2005b).

Together with birth rates, the age structure of the population is influenced by the death rate. The ONS (2006a) charts a decline in death rates as the population has grown in size. In the 33-year period between 1971 and 2004 the ONS cites a 9 per cent decline in the death rate for all females and a 21 per cent fall in the death rates for all males (ONS, 2006a). General improvements in living standards and advancements in health and medicine have contributed to an increased life expectancy for both men and women, although women continue to outlive men. Whilst women born in the United Kingdom in 2004 could expect to live to the age of 81, men could expect to live to 77; this contrasts sharply with the life expectancy of men and women born at the start of the last century, a time when boys could expect to live to just 45, and girls to 49 (www.statistics.gov.uk). Projections of life expectancy based on 2004 data (Figure 4.1) foretell an extrapolation of past trends, adding some substance to the claim 'by this time tomorrow you can expect to live for five hours longer!' (Jah, 2006: 6)

Figure 4.1

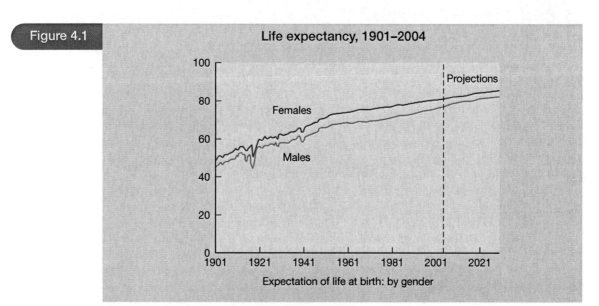

Source: Government Actuary's Department (www.statistics.gov.uk *UK Snapshot 2005*).

We have seen in this section that the age structure of the population is affected by migration, births and deaths. While some non-white ethnic groups display relatively young age profiles, the overall picture is of an ageing population. In short 'there are increasing numbers of people aged 65 and over and decreasing numbers of children under 16' (ONS, 2006a: 11). In recent decades these trends in the age structure of the population can be attributed to lower fertility rates combined with declining mortality rates amongst the elderly. Such trends show little sign of abating; on the contrary it is projected that 'by 2014 the number of people over the age of 65 will *exceed* those under the age of 16 for the first time and the gap will widen' (ONS, 2006a: 12).

In terms of human resource management the implications of changes in the age structure of the population are numerous. The following points indicate some of the challenges presented by an ageing population:

- The prospect of a shrinking pool of people of working age as the 'baby boomers' born in the 1950s and 1960s move into retirement.
- Intensified competition for school leavers/young workers.
- Identifying employment strategies which succeed in attracting and retaining older workers.
- Meeting the needs and aspirations of older workers in work.
- Career management and development.
- Managing sickness absence.
- Growing elder care responsibilities for those in employment.
- Concerns over the adequacy of pension arrangements and the viability of retaining the current State retirement ages. The second report of Lord Turner's Pensions Commission published in November 2005 includes a proposal to increase the state pension age. The Commission also recommends the default retirement age of 65 written into the Age Discrimination Regulations, due to be implemented on 1 October 2006 is removed so that older people can remain in employment beyond 65 if they so choose (CIPD, 2006).
- The need to scrutinise policies and practice to ensure equal opportunities are afforded to workers of all ages to comply with the Employment Equality (Age) Regulations 2006, due to be implemented on 1 October 2006.

How might employees' care responsibilities for elderly relations impact upon their presence and attention to paid work?

Do you think elder care will soon begin to pose a greater challenge to employers and employees than childcare? Why?

What measures, if any, do you think employers should introduce to assist employees with elder care responsibilities?

The gender composition of the population

Although ONS data (ONS, 2006a) shows that more boys are born each year than girls, in overall terms the population of the United Kingdom in 2004 contained more females (30.6 million) than males (29.3 million) (ONS, 2006a: 11). Analysis by gender of the country's population in 2004 shows that the numbers of men and women were broadly in step up to the age of 22 but then began to diverge such that by the age of 30 there were more women than men in the population (ONS, 2006a). In the older age groups (post retirement age) the fissure between the number of men and women in the population broadens, and 'is most pronounced in the very elderly, as women tend to live longer than men' (ONS, 2006a: 11).

As 'the inflow of females has always been higher than the outflow' (ONS, 2006a: 17) net in-migration is one of the key ways in which the female population of the country has expanded. In every year since 1994 the outflow of males *and* females from the United Kingdom has been lower than the inflow of both sexes into the country causing a net in-migration effect to both the male and female population; the more pronounced population gains falling to the female population. In 2003 for example, the net gain for the United Kingdom's female population was more than 15,000 higher than the net gain to the male population (ONS, 2006a: 17). It is highly probable that, at least in numerical terms, the labour market will benefit from net in-migration as migrants (both in and out) are least likely to be over the age of retirement, or children under the age of 15 (ONS, 2006a: 18).

Later in the chapter we consider the ways in which gender shapes people's experiences of work. In particular we explore the interplay of gender and age and look at gendered roles within the family to understand differences in the patterns of male and female participation in the labour market.

Ethnicity and the population

In previous sections we have referred to migration and demonstrated that in the post-war period the United Kingdom has granted residency to people from a variety of different countries including Pakistan, India, Bangladesh, China, parts of Africa and the Caribbean and more recently from countries within Eastern Europe. As a consequence a number of distinct minority ethnic groups have joined the nation's historically white British heritage to form a more multicultural, ethnically and religiously diverse Britain. The census collects ethnicity data by asking people which group they see themselves belonging to. When the census was last conducted in April 2001 it showed England's population to be 87 per cent white British, 3.9 per cent white other, 1.3 per cent mixed, 4.6 per cent Asian, 2.3 per cent Black and 0.9 per cent Chinese and other (ONS, 2001). In terms of religious denomination almost 70 per cent of respondents considered themselves to be of Christian religion and white British ethnicity, other main faiths include Pakistani Muslims, Indian Hindus, black Caribbean Christians, Indian Sikhs and black African Christians.

Whilst in general terms the total population is becoming more ethnically diverse, certain local authority districts contain high concentrations of (non-white) ethnic minority groups, in excess of the national average of 9 per cent non-white (ONS, 2001). The census conducted in 2001 shows that sixteen of the twenty authorities with the highest concentrations of non-white ethnic minority groups are London boroughs (ONS, 2001); of these Newham and Brent both have a majority non-white population (61 per cent and 55 per cent respectively). Outside of London, Leicester, Slough, Birmingham and Luton record the highest concentrations of non-white ethnic minority groups. In some other regions of the country (for example, the south-west and the north-east), non-white ethnic minority groups form a very small percentage of the population, significantly below the national average.

The limited geographic dispersal of non-white ethnic minority groups means that some local labour markets remain practically monocultural whilst others are considerably diverse. As we shall see, men and women from non-white ethnic minority groups tend to experience greater disadvantage in the labour market; they are less likely to be active in the labour market than their white counterparts, more likely to suffer high levels of unemployment and when they are in work, people from ethnic minority groups as a whole have lower levels of occupational attainment and progression than white people (Strategy Unit, 2003). The Strategy Unit report for the Cabinet Office on the position of ethnic minorities in the labour market (2003) suggests that men and women from ethnic minority groups still fare less well in the labour market than their white contemporaries even when factors such as age, gender and qualifications are controlled for and the report concludes that this can partially be explained by the existence of racism and discrimination in the labour market. The role of HRM in combating discrimination at work and embracing diversity is the subject of debate and discussion in Chapter 7.

The workforce

The workforce is conventionally drawn from the segment of the population between the ages of 16 and state retirement age, although some men and women will continue to work beyond the state pension age. Of those aged 16 or older, not everyone will be in employment at any one time. Figure 4.2 is a useful framework within which to define and discuss the activities of people of working age.

A proportion of those over the age of 16 will not be in work or seeking work; this portion of the workforce is classified as *economically inactive*. There are a number of reasons why people might be economically inactive. This group typically includes those with caring responsibilities for children or other dependents, those who have retired from work, students, people who are incapacitated through ill health or disability and those choosing not to work or seek work. People within this group may voluntarily decide to enter (or re-enter) the labour market once their circumstances alter. Others may need to be enticed back to work through incentives and/or government-orchestrated benefit reforms directed at this purpose. For example, the Department for Work and Pensions recently announced plans to radically reform the current system of incapacity benefit in an effort to reduce benefit dependency and get some of the long-term sick back into work (DWP, 2005).

In real terms the amount of labour available to firms at any one time will be influenced by the number of people of working age who are in employment or are seeking employment, in other words those classified as *economically active*. A number of factors affect individuals' propensity to furnish their labour, including the availability and proximity of employment opportunities to meet their personal needs and aspirations, travel links, the levels of pay and benefits offered by organisations, the type of contract offered and so forth. These factors also influence people's decisions to move between jobs within the labour market. The employed segment of the workforce contains those in paid work; this incorporates those working full time or part time, temporarily or permanently as employees (under a contract *of service*), workers (under a contract *for services*) or on a self-employed basis.

Those seeking work are typically registered as unemployed but could also be those who have recently left work but are not eligible to claim unemployment benefit, for example, those who have been made redundant. Job seekers might also include recent school leavers and those completing programmes of study in further and higher education. The term *unemployed* is used to describe those people who are currently not in work but would like to be. To

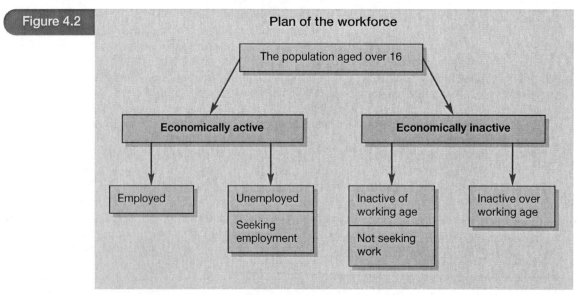

Figure 4.2   Plan of the workforce

Source: Adapted from *SCER Report 1 – Understanding the Labour Market*, 2001.

remain in receipt of unemployment benefit unemployed workers must be able to show that they are actively seeking work. The unemployed group comprises people affected by different types of unemployment:

- *Long-term unemployment or structural unemployment* – those unemployed as a result of the demise of whole industries or distinct occupations, for example mineworkers, ship-builders, textile workers.
- *Frictional unemployment* – those temporarily out of work because they are between jobs.
- *Seasonal unemployment* – those made jobless as a result of seasonal fluctuations in the availability of work. Seasonal unemployment is typically experienced by land workers and those whose work is connected with holiday seasons.

In addition it is also likely that some of those registered unemployed will never work again as they lack the skills and competencies sought by employers. This group of unemployed workers is sometimes referred to as the *residual* unemployed.

The latest ONS data, drawn from the Labour Force Survey (ONS 2006a) shows that over the period 1971 to 2005 the number of both economically active and economically inactive people has increased. The ONS (2006a: 50) attributes much of the climb in the number of those in work or actively seeking work to the increased participation of women in the workforce. By spring 2005 over 30 million people in the United Kingdom were economically active and some 17.6 million economically inactive (if those over the state pension age are included). The employment rate (the proportion of the working age population of the United Kingdom in employment) stood at 75 per cent in the spring of 2005 (ONS, 2006a: 52) although differences in rates exist both within and between different regions of the country.

Unemployment rates also vary across regions of the United Kingdom. In spring 2005 (ONS, 2006a: 60) the lowest rate was recorded in the south-west region (3.4 per cent) and the highest rate in London (7.2 per cent). Nationally the unemployment rate in the United Kingdom stood at 4.7 per cent in spring 2005 (1.4 million people), this compares very favourably with 1984 when unemployment peaked at 3.3 million and more recently 1993 when the number of people out of work again approached the 3 million mark.

Patterns of labour market participation

This subsection of the chapter explores patterns of participation in paid employment by gender, parental/family status, age, and ethnicity.

The operation of the labour market is shaped and constrained by broader societal developments and the behaviour and attitudes of government, employees and employers. In social terms, attitudes to marriage and partnership and men and women's respective responsibilities for childcare and domestic duties shape the labour market decisions made by individuals, couples and families. In so far as government behaviours and attitudes are concerned, the policy direction of government, for example over such issues as the school curriculum and funding for post-compulsory education, affects the skills set and level of educational attainment with which young people join the labour market and influences the age at which young people enter employment. As we saw earlier, the government also acts to stimulate labour supply by implementing policies designed to get the unemployed into work and schemes to encourage the economically inactive to enter into employment.

Further potential constraints on people's participation in employment stem from their inability to understand the labour market and acquire and exploit 'social capital' (SCER, 2001: 17). In other words some people will lack the necessary information and contacts to search for and take advantage of employment opportunities and so tend to be less successful within the labour market. The SCER notes that this is particularly likely to be the case for the unemployed and for new entrants to the labour market. In addition the SCER suggests that 'even with the right information, skills and qualifications, there still exist barriers to full or appropriate labour market participation for some people . . . one such barrier is discrimination, typically race and sex discrimination' (2001: 18). Whilst anti-discrimination legislation exists to help eradicate unfair discrimination in employment, employers' policies and practices may still harbour prejudice and unfairness resulting in patterns of disadvantage in the labour market for certain groups and individuals.

Patterns of male and female participation in employment

Over the last 30 years or so the employment rates of men and women have converged considerably. The period 1971 to spring 2005 saw the employment rate for men fall from 92 per cent to 79 per cent and the employment rate for women rise 14 percentage points from 56 per cent to 70 per cent (ONS, 2006a). A major doorway to the world of work has clearly opened up for women but as we shall see, the career paths and fortunes of men and women in the labour market are often distinctly gendered.

One of the deeper influences attributable to gender that serves to structure women's participation in paid employment is domestic work. Women continue to perform the bulk of housework and to shoulder the primary responsibility for childcare in the majority of households and this shapes the amount of paid work they do. A glimmer of change is offered by Hardill *et al.* (1997) who present evidence of a small move towards more egalitarian relationships in professional/managerial, dual-career households but this is dashed by Laurie and Gurshuny (2000) who find that women continue to do more than 60 per cent of the domestic work even in couples where both partners work full time.

A major element of domestic work is childcare. Table 4.1 below clearly shows the differences in employment rates between those people of working age with and without responsibilities for the care of dependent children. The data illustrates that parenthood affects the employment rates of mothers and fathers in patently different ways; while mothers of working age were *less* likely to be in employment than working age women without any dependent children, fathers were *more* likely to be in employment than men of working age without dependent children. It is noteworthy that mothers of working age in the two elder age brackets had considerably higher employment rates than younger women with dependent children. Within the elder age brackets the employment rates of working age mothers were not remarkably different to the employment rates of women of the same ages without dependent children.

Table 4.1 Employment rates of people[1] with and without dependent children:[2] by age and sex, 2004[3] (percentages)

	16–24	25–34	35–49	50–59/64	All
Mothers with dependent children	35	59	73	68	67
Married/cohabiting mothers	45	63	76	72	71
Lone mothers	25	46	62	55	53
Women without dependent children	62	90	81	68	73
Fathers with dependent children	81	89	92	84	90
Married/cohabiting fathers	82	89	93	85	91
Lone fathers	26	55	72	61	67
Men without dependent children	61	87	85	69	74
All parents with dependent children	45	70	82	78	77
Married/cohabiting parents	57	75	84	80	81
Lone parents	25	47	64	56	54
All people without dependent children	61	88	83	69	74

[1] Men aged 16–64 and women aged 16–59. Excludes people with unknown employment status
[2] Children under 16 and those 16–18 who are never-married and in full-time education
[3] At spring. Data are not seasonally adjusted and have been adjusted in line with population estimates published in spring 2003.

Source: Labour Force Survey, Spring 2004 (ONS)

Why might older mothers of dependent children display higher employment rates than younger women with children?

While parenthood continues to affect women's employment rates disproportionately to men's, the proportion of working age mothers with dependent children who are in employment has risen from 47 per cent in 1973 to 67 per cent in 2004 (EOC, 2006). In 2004 in all but the youngest age category (mothers aged 16–24 with dependent children) the majority of married *and* lone mothers of working age were engaged in paid employment. The speed with which women return to work following maternity leave has also hastened significantly in the period since 1979; according to EOC figures (2006) 70 per cent of mothers are back at work eight months after giving birth, compared with just 15 per cent in 1979. The average amount of time women spend away from waged work for general family care is falling rapidly too (Bradley, 1999).

Further key points to emerge from the data in Table 4.1 are:

- Mothers of dependent children are less likely to work than fathers of dependent children.
- Lone fathers are more likely to be in employment than lone mothers.
- Married and cohabiting parents have higher employment rates than lone parents.

Ethnicity and patterns of labour market participation

Employment participation rates for ethnic minorities are significantly lower than those for the population as a whole. In autumn, 2005 66.2 per cent of ethnic minority people of working age were either in work or seeking work compared with 78.8 per cent among the population as a whole. The employment rate among ethnic minorities was 59.1 per cent as against 74.9 per cent for the population as a whole, while unemployment was higher among ethnic minorities at 10.7 per cent compared with 4.9 per cent of the entire workforce (LFS, 2006). It has been argued that low participation rates among ethnic minorities are related to low levels of educational attainment and low skills, aspects of family structure, poor access to childcare, poor housing and a lack of public transport facilities (Strategy Unit, 2003). However, research by Wadsworth (2003) found that age, region and educational attainment explained hardly any of the difference in employment rates as between ethnic minorities and British-born whites.

There are noticeable variations in activity and employment rates as between different ethnic minority groups. For example, the employment rate among people of Indian origin is 69.8 per cent compared with just 38.5 per cent among Bangladeshis (LFS, 2006). Activity and employment rates also vary within each ethnic group, generally being higher among British-born members of ethnic minorities than among immigrants (Wadsworth 2003). Also, ethnic minority women are less likely to participate in employment than men, with the differential tending to be greater among immigrants rather than British-born ethnic minorities. Nonetheless, British-born Indian women had the same employment rate – 73 per cent – as British born white women in 2002 (Wadsworth, 2003).

Labour demand

Aggregate demand for labour

The aggregate demand for labour consists of total employment plus unfilled vacancies. As the demand for labour is derived from the demand for goods and services it follows the economic cycle, rising in upswings and falling in recessions. Changes in labour demand are reflected in changes in the unemployment rate.

Low levels of unemployment are usually taken as a sign that the economy is growing and is in good shape. For employers however, the combination of record employment, low unemployment and high numbers of economically inactive people exacerbates labour market pressures contributing to what is referred to as a 'tight labour market'. In tight labour markets employers are likely to experience recruitment difficulties and skill shortages (CIPD, 2005). *The CIPD Barometer of HR Tends and Prospects (*2005) suggested further tightening of the labour market had occurred for these reasons during 2004 but problems had partially been off set by firms employing immigrant workers, including those from countries such as Latvia, Poland and Slovenia, which joined the EU on 1 May 2004 (CIPD, 2005).

Tight labour markets mean that employers have to compete more actively for workers and workers have a wider choice of employment opportunities. This will lead to higher rates of labour turnover as workers leave organisations for better jobs elsewhere. In response, firms may be forced to increase pay. They may also adopt other policies aimed at retaining employees, since vacancies arising from labour turnover will be hard to fill. Therefore there will be more internal promotion and redeployment and this may necessitate increased investment in training. While these responses might be seen as moves towards internalising employment they are not driven by the technical and skill requirements of production or a long-term employment strategy but by immediate pressures from the labour market. These pressures may be reinforced by stronger trade union bargaining power as a result of low unemployment and unfilled vacancies. Once established, these employment practices may become embedded, although employers may seek to reverse them should labour demand slacken and unemployment rise.

In addition to changes in aggregate demand for labour, we need to look at how demand conditions for different labour market groups vary as the result of structured patterns of inequality of employment opportunity. We also need to examine the changing pattern of demand for labour and how it affects different labour market groups.

Labour market inequality

The quality of jobs on offer in the labour market varies. Some workers are in 'good jobs' with high earnings, good working conditions, employment security and opportunities for training and career development. Others are in 'bad jobs' with low status and pay, poor working conditions, little access to training and few if any opportunities for promotion. How good and bad jobs get created has been a matter of ongoing debate surrounding the theory of labour market segmentation. One line of explanation, advanced by two economists, Doeringer and Piore (1971), is based on the analysis of employers' labour requirements outlined above. Some firms face strong pressures to internalise the employment relationship in order to train, develop and retain suitably skilled workers and gain their voluntary cooperation in production. Others do not and are able to meet their labour requirements by following the commodity labour approach and externalising the employment relationship.

Another explanation (Gordon, Edwards and Reich, 1982) is that some firms enjoy monopoly power in their product markets and are able to use this power to increase the selling price of the product, thereby increasing profits. Some of these companies are faced by workers who have developed strong trade unions that can use their bargaining power to gain a share of these profits in the form of high wages and other benefits, including job security provisions. At the same time, management seeks to limit union solidarity and bargaining power by dividing the workforce into horizontal segments and offering the prospect of promotion to those who are cooperative and trustworthy. Firms that are unable to use monopoly power to raise their prices do not have surplus profits to share with trade unions, so terms and conditions of employment are less favourable. Since it is more likely that large, rather than small firms are able to exercise monopoly power, primary sector employment is concentrated in large, rather than small firms.

One of the central predictions of the labour segmentation thesis is that there will be little movement of workers between the primary and secondary sectors of the labour market. Workers in the primary sector are unwilling to move to the secondary sector and the high level of employment security that they enjoy means that they are unlikely to be forced to through job loss. Workers who make up the disadvantaged segments of the labour market are unable to move up into the primary sector because employers see them as undesirable candidates for jobs. Primary sector employers want disciplined, cooperative workers with good work habits, so when selecting from among applicants for jobs, primary sector employers will tend to reject those with unstable employment histories that involve frequent unemployment and job changes because they will assume that this indicates a poor quality worker. This will automatically rule out secondary sector workers, regardless of their personal qualities, since by definition secondary workers are in unstable, insecure jobs. It is also the case however, that because of their experience of poor work, some secondary sector workers will tend to develop negative attitudes and poor patterns of work behaviour that reinforce employers' prejudices against secondary sector workers as a whole.

These explanations for labour market segmentation emphasise the way in which firms' employment decisions influence the wider labour market by dividing it into advantaged and disadvantaged groups. However, the question of whether the labour market *is* divided into primary and secondary sectors as a result of employers' labour policies has generated considerable debate. Numerous empirical studies to test the theory have been carried out in Britain and the United States, with mixed results (see Joll, McKenna, McNab and Shorey, 1983; King, 1990 for a discussion of these).

What is not in doubt is that the quality of the jobs that people do is not determined simply by their abilities, educational attainment and skills acquired through training. The chances of someone being in a good or a bad job are also influenced by their membership of particular socio-economic groups. There is clear evidence that the labour market is segmented along lines that reflect 'broader social forces leading to discrimination within the labour market' (Rubery, 1994: 53).

Discrimination in the labour market means that workers' chances of gaining access to 'good' or 'bad' jobs are unfairly influenced by non-work characteristics such as gender, race, class, work-unrelated disability and age. Thus two equally skilled workers will find themselves in different sectors of the labour market because one is a white male from a middle-class social background and the other is a working-class black woman. This reflects deep-seated patterns of discrimination within society in general as well as in the labour market. Here we focus on how gender and ethnicity influence people's experiences in the labour market.

Women and ethnic minority groups occupy a disadvantaged place in the labour market. Women's employment disadvantage reflects deep-seated societal norms concerning the family and the respective roles of women and men in domestic roles and paid work. The domestic roles played by many women mean that their employment opportunities are restricted geographically and contractually. This is particularly true of women with children. In the absence of highly developed systems of state support for childcare, childcare responsibilities mean that many women cannot travel long distances to work and also that they cannot work 'standard' hours. Therefore they are restricted to part-time work in the immediate locality. This means that they have limited choice of employment and therefore little bargaining power and may have to accept secondary sector terms and conditions of employment. Ethnic minority workers, as well as facing racial prejudice and discrimination, may be faced with additional limits to their choice of employment because they live in areas where business activity is low and public transport facilities are poor (Strategy Unit, 2003).

Gender-based inequalities in employment opportunity

The social forces identified above mean there are major differences in the types of work that men and women tend to do and the way in which male and female employment is segregated by time. Patterns of occupational segregation are strongly in evidence in the labour market, creating a division between male and female work. Bradley (1999) suggests that 66 per cent of men and 54 per cent of women work only or mainly with their own sex, with women typically crowded into administrative and secretarial work, catering, cleaning and caring occupations and men in skilled trades, construction and information technology (EOC, 2005). As shown in Table 4.2, patterns of vertical segregation also loom large with men continuing to dominate highly rewarded, senior roles in politics, business, media and culture and the public and voluntary sectors (EOC, 2006).

The work that men and women do in the labour market is also segregated by hours of work. Women are disproportionately represented in part-time work; women hold over 90 per cent of part-time jobs and nearly half of all female employees (44 per cent) work part time compared with just 8 per cent of men (ONS, 2004). Part-time working is most closely associated with women who have dependent children, although students and semi-retired older people are also attracted to working in this way (Hakim, 1998). Part-time working is invariably low-paid and this is reflected in the stubbornly persistent gender pay gap that exists between women working part time and men working full time (EOC, 2005).

Female heterogeneity

The population, and hence the labour market, comprises different sorts of women, fractured by age, class, ethnicity, qualification level, background and experience. So, whilst generalisations about the relative positions of men and women in employment serve some purpose, an understanding of the different experiences of different sorts of people in the labour market is more useful.

While we have seen that women are typically casualties of segregation in employment, some women will be in a more advantageous labour market position than other women (and some men). For example, the spring 2004 Labour Force Study (ONS, 2006a) shows us that a far greater proportion of women with a degree or equivalent qualification were in employment than women without. Some women are making significant strides in training and occupations traditionally dominated by men, for example, women now comprise the majority of medical students, there was also a 24 per cent rise in the number of female law students in the period 1971 to 1990 and a 61 per cent rise in women entering managerial work (Crompton, 1997).

Management is one of the areas in which women have made the most progress. In 2004, 33 per cent of all managers and senior officials were women (ONS, 2004). However, a closer look at the gender composition at different levels of management and at management in different sectors reveals gendered patterns of horizontal and vertical segregation *within* management careers. The dominance of men in the most senior management positions is aptly illustrated by the following findings from the Cranfield Female FTSE Index 2005:

Table 4.2 Women's share of a selection of senior ranked roles in the three consecutive years 2003–2005.

	2003 % women	2004 % women	2005 % women
Members of Parliament	18.1	18.1	19.7
Local Authority Council Leaders	n/a	16.6	16.2
Directors in FTSE 100 companies (executive and non-executive directors)	8.6	9.7	10.5
Small businesses with women the majority of directors	12.3	14.4	n/a
Editors of national newspapers	9.1	9.1	13.0
Directors of major museums and art galleries	21.1	21.1	21.7
Chief executives of national sports bodies	14.3	6.3	6.7
Local authority chief executives	13.1	12.4	17.5
Senior ranks in the armed forces	0.6	0.8	0.8
Senior police officers	7.6	8.3	10.2
University vice chancellors	12.4	15.0	11.1
Health service chief executives	28.6	27.7	28.1

Source: EOC (2006).

- 22 of the FTSE100 companies have all-male boards.
- 6 of the FTSE 100 companies appointed female directors for the first time in 2005.
- Only 11 companies have female executive directors, representing just 3.4 per cent of all executive directorship positions.
- Only one company (Pearson) has a female chief executive.

A similar picture emerges in the professions. Women make up some 40 per cent of those working in the autonomous liberal (traditional) professions, for example law, medicine, veterinary science, accountancy and teaching (EOC, 2001) but there are still some very entrenched areas such as engineering and sciences that are heavily male dominated. Again, even where women formed a sizeable proportion of the profession as a whole, their share of higher-level jobs is low and they tend to be channelled into different branches of the profession to men as the following example illustrates:

- Women made up 34 per cent of hospital medical staff in 1999 (compared with 26 per cent in 1989).
- The number of female general practitioners increased by a similar amount in the same period.

But . . .

- Men made up 79 per cent of consultants (the highest grade) and 95 per cent of consultant surgeons
- Women made up 38 per cent of paediatric consultants, 32 per cent of the psychiatry group and over 20 per cent of gynaecologists.

Source: EOC (2001)

It is evident that higher-level qualifications afford women greater opportunities within the labour market but such credentials do not entirely safeguard against disadvantage. Becoming a member of an esteemed profession is an added advantage to women in the labour market but underpinning their experiences are deeper influences attributable to gender. 'Women can stretch the ties that bind but cannot sever them' (Marlow and Carter, 2004: 16). Moreover, if highly educated women remain at a disadvantage in employment terms, this is even truer of lesser educated women from lower income and lower social class backgrounds (Taylor, 2002b).

Ethnically based labour market inequality

People from ethnic minorities experience disadvantage compared to whites in terms of their access to employment, their level of occupational attainment, and pay. Average unemployment among ethnic minority workers in autumn 2005 was 10.7 per cent compared with 4.9 per cent across the workforce as a whole (LFS, 2006). Ethnic minority men are paid less than white men. Ethnic minority women earn as much or more than white women but this is mainly because they are more likely than white women to take full-time jobs, which are better paid than part-time jobs. Ethnic minorities in general are less likely than whites to be employed in professional and managerial occupations and more likely to be in semi-routine and routine occupations (Heath and Cheung, 2006).

These disadvantages could theoretically reflect differences in education and skills. We know that unemployment is higher and wages are lower among lower educated, unskilled workers. However, these disadvantages remain even when educational qualifications are taken into account. Most ethnic minority workers are paid less than white workers having the same educational qualifications. This means that the return to investments in education, that is the amount that each extra year of education beyond minimum school leaving age adds to lifetime earnings, is lower for most ethnic minority groups than for comparable white workers. While this does not prove conclusively that people from ethnic minorities are being discriminated against unfairly it does make it a distinct possibility.

Stop & think

What are the costs to employers of discriminating against ethnic minority groups? In view of these costs why might employers still engage in unfair discrimination?

Ethnic heterogeneity

Although people from ethnic minorities as a whole are disadvantaged in the labour market, there is noticeable variation in the experience of different ethnic groups and between men and women within ethnic groups. Differences have also been found between members of ethnic minorities born in Britain and more recent immigrants (Wadsworth, 2003).

Unemployment varies considerably between groups; for example in autumn 2005 the unemployment rate among Pakistanis at 14 per cent was twice as high as that for Indians (LFS, 2006). Levels of occupational attainment also vary between different ethnic minority groups, as shown in Table 4.3. Chinese and Indians of both sexes are more likely to be in professional and managerial occupations than whites, as are black African and black Caribbean women. With the exception of Indians and Chinese, ethnic minority workers are more likely to be in semi-routine or routine occupations than whites.

There are also variations in average earnings across ethnic minorities. Thus Indian and Chinese men's average hourly earnings in the period 2001–2004 were 5 per cent higher and 11 per cent higher respectively than British and other white men's earnings. All other ethnic minority men earned less than British and other whites. Black Caribbean workers' average hourly earnings were 90 per cent of whites'; Pakistanis' earnings were 80 per cent and Bangladeshis received just 59 per cent. Ethnic minority women's earnings were as high or higher than those of British and other white women. Chinese earned 16 per cent more than whites while the lowest paid, the black Africans, earned 98 per cent (Heath and Cheung, 2006). At first glance this is surprising but it is explained by the fact that ethnic minority women are less likely to take part-time jobs than white women. Full-time jobs are noticeably better paid than part-time jobs, and it is this that accounts largely for the apparent lack of pay disadvantage among ethnic minority women.

Stop & think

How might you explain the differences in the labour market experiences of ethnic minority groups in the UK?

Table 4.3 Occupational attainment among ethnic groups in the UK 2001–2004

| | Proportion (per cent) of ethnic group in | | | |
| | High and low professional and managerial occupations | | Semi-routine and routine occupations | |
	Men	Women	Men	Women
British/other white	41.8	37	24.5	31.1
Black African	38.8	43	35.6	33.2
Black Caribbean	30.8	39.4	36.5	31.9
Indian	45.3	37	23.7	31.2
Pakistani	27.9	30	29.7	39
Bangladeshi	17.8	20.7	50.2	52.9
Chinese	46	41.6	18.2	26.7

Source: Heath and Cheung (2006: 15).

Heath and Cheung (2006) have found that men and women in most ethnic minority groups face what they call 'ethnic penalties' in the labour market, i.e. disadvantages that cannot be explained by factors such as educational achievement and appear to be related to ethnicity alone. These penalties relate to access to employment, occupational attainment, and pay. All ethnic minorities apart from the Chinese experience ethnic penalties relating to access to employment. Once in employment, most groups – apart from Indians and Chinese – face ethnic penalties in terms of access to professional and managerial jobs and in terms of pay. The highest penalty in this respect is paid by black Africans. From Table 4.3 this group appears quite successful, particularly women, who are more likely to be in professional and managerial roles than whites. However, they remain significantly under-represented when qualifications are taken into account. Black Africans are more highly qualified than whites in the UK. Some 27 per cent have degrees compared with 18 per cent of whites and only 11 per cent have low or no qualifications compared with 13 per cent of whites. On the basis of their qualifications a higher proportion of black Africans should be in professional and managerial occupations and black Africans should also have higher average earnings than whites, rather than lower.

The presence of disadvantaged groups in the labour market increases the range of options open to some employers by allowing them to fulfil their requirements for a stable, cooperative workforce without having to offer the positive incentives associated with internalised employment relationships (Rubery, 1994). This is because, as indicated above, disadvantaged groups have few employment alternatives so they have to take what they can get. The absence of better alternatives makes these jobs more attractive than they would otherwise be and therefore more highly valued by workers. This is reflected in the willingness of many disadvantaged workers to remain with their employer and cooperate with management in order to keep their jobs. This is illustrated in Box 4.1.

Is it rational for an employer to refuse to hire workers on the basis of their ethnicity or nationality? Do employers who hire ethnic minority workers nevertheless benefit from the presence of racism in society as a whole?

Changing patterns of demand

The period since the 1980s has seen significant changes in the pattern of demand for labour and therefore in the types of jobs available to workers. These shifts reflect inter-linked changes in the structure of the economy, government policy for the labour market, and employers' labour requirements.

Box 4.1   ## Advantages to employers of using immigrant labour from Eastern Europe

Recent research carried out for the Joseph Rowntree Foundation into the position of Central and Eastern European immigrant workers in the UK found that immigrant workers from Central and Eastern Europe often had skills and qualifications that were significantly higher than those needed in their jobs. Many of these workers were willing to take low-paid work in the UK because there were even fewer employment opportunities in their home countries. The research also found that employers regarded them as 'high quality workers for low-skilled work' and that employers 'were often trying to balance the requirement for workers who were easy to hire and fire on the one hand but were also reliable and easy to retain'.

Source: Anderson, B., Ruhs, M., Royaly, B. and Spencer, C. (2006).

A shift of employment from manufacturing to services

The proportion of workers employed in manufacturing has declined in the UK, USA and all the major European Union economies since the 1960s. This reflects the effects of economic growth and rising incomes on people's consumption patterns. As people get richer, the proportion of their income that they spend on manufactured goods declines (although people may still spend more money on them in absolute terms) and the proportion spent on services increases. This means that output and hence employment grow faster in the service sector than the manufacturing sector. This trend is reinforced by the fact that the long-run rate of growth of labour productivity is higher in manufacturing than in services. Higher productivity growth plus slower growing demand mean slower growth or even decline of employment in manufacturing.

The decline of manufacturing has been particularly rapid in the UK since 1980. This has reflected additional forces such as the effects of government monetary and exchange rate policy during the 1980s which raised the price of British exports in foreign markets and cheapened foreign imports; the long-term inability of UK manufacturing to respond adequately to foreign competition; and organisational restructuring whereby manufacturing firms have tried to cut costs by hiving off certain 'non-core' and specialist activities, such as security, cleaning and catering to outside suppliers of these services. This has meant that the workers who used to deliver these services are now counted as being in the service sector rather than manufacturing. The trend of employment away from manufacturing towards services is predicted to continue, as shown in Table 4.4.

The growth of service sector employment has been a major factor in the increase in part-time employment in the UK and has therefore expanded employment opportunities for women with dependent children and also, more recently, young people in full-time education.

Stop & think

How specifically has the growth of the service sector boosted part-time and female employment?

Changes in the occupational structure of employment

The occupational structure refers to how employment is apportioned among different jobs in the economy. Changes in the occupational structure of employment reflect changes in the types of skill demanded by employers. The declining relative importance of manufacturing means that, over time, the share of occupations associated with manufacturing has also declined while the share of occupations associated with the delivery of business services, retail services, etc. has increased. Changes in the occupational structure also reflect changes in the demand for skills *within* industries. These changes are generated by new technologies and by organisational changes that alter the way in which goods are produced and services deliv-

Table 4.4 Changes in the distribution of employment by broad sector 1982–2012 (percentage share of total employment)

	1982	1992	2002	2007*	2012*
Primary goods and utilities	5.2	3.5	2.2	2.0	1.8
Manufacturing	22.7	16.6	13.2	11.7	10.5
Construction	6.7	7.0	6.3	6.1	5.9
Distribution, transport, etc.	28.3	29.5.	29.6	29.5	29.6
Business and other services	16.5	21.1	25.6	26.9	28.6
Non-marketed services	20.6	22.7	23.1	23.8	23.6

*Projected figures

Source: Wilson, R., Homenikou, K. and Dickerson, A. (2006: 26).

ered; for example, the introduction of new robotic equipment has reduced the requirement for semi-skilled workers in vehicle manufacture. Over the last twenty-five years the effect of technical change has been to increase demand for skilled workers relative to unskilled workers. A national survey of skills trends for the period 1986–2001 found evidence of an overall increase in the skill requirements of jobs, with the proportion of jobs requiring degree qualifications increasing from 9.7 per cent to 17.3 per cent over the period and the proportion requiring no qualifications falling from 38.4 per cent to 26.5 per cent. (Felstead, Gallie and Green, 2002).

We can see further evidence of this in the way in which the occupational structure has changed since the early 1980s. From Table 4.5 we can see that the most highly skilled groups – managers and senior officials, professionals, and associate professional and technical occupations – increased their overall share of employment from 28.3 per cent in 1982 to 40.2 per cent in 2002. Meanwhile the share accounted for by the remaining categories fell from 71.8 per cent to 59.8 per cent. The projections suggest that by 2012 the three most highly skilled categories will have increased their share to 45.1 per cent while that of the rest will fall to 55 per cent.

We need to be careful in interpreting what these trends mean for actual employment opportunities. They do not mean that there will be no employment opportunities in declining occupations. The figures in Table 4.5 refer to the total number of jobs in each occupation that results from its net expansion or decline – the 'expansion demand' (Wilson *et al.*, 2006). However, we also need to take account of the fact that in addition to net growth or decline, there will be a demand for workers to replace those leaving occupations, mainly for reasons of retirement. Replacement demand means that, although total employment in an occupation may be declining, there will still be a large number of jobs on offer within it at any one time. For example, employment in elementary clerical and service occupations (e.g filing clerks, check-out operators) is predicted to fall by 408,000 over the period 2002–2012 but replacement demand is estimated at 1,108,000. This means that there will be a net labour requirement of an extra 647,000 workers over that period, higher than for most of the professional and associated professional groups, which are predicted to grow (Wilson *et al.*, 2006: 73). It may be for this reason that employers report skill shortages in skilled trades and personal services. These reported shortages do not relate to a dearth of applicants to vacancies

Table 4.5 Changes in the occupational structure (percentage share of total employment)

	1982	1992	2002	2007*	2012*
Managers and senior officials	10.7	12.6	14.9	15.4	16.2
Professional occupations	8.0	9.4	11.3	12.2	12.9
Associate professional and technical occupations	9.6	11.3	14.0	15.1	16.0
Administrative, clerical and secretarial occupations	15.5	15.8	13.2	12.2	11.4
Skilled trades	17.0	14.6	11.4	10.2	9.1
Personal service	3.7	4.9	7.3	8.2	9.4
Sales and customer service	6.1	6.7	7.9	8.5	9.0
Transport and machine operatives	11.8	9.7	8.4	7.7	7.2
Elementary occupations	17.7	15.0	11.6	10.4	8.9

*Projected figures

Source: Wilson, R., Homenikou, K. and Dickerson, A. (2006: 58) .

but to what employers see as a lack of necessary skills among applicants. For example, the 2004 National Employers' Skills Survey reported that 50 per cent of applicants to skill short-age vacancies in skilled trades lacked technical and practical skills (Learning and Skills Council, 2005: 9).

Higgs (2004) observes that in response to a shortage of skills in certain areas, some employers have elected to focus on potential ability rather than current ability when hiring staff, this approach, he suggests 'opens up a larger talent pool and at the same time offers potential employees skill development as part of the 'deal' to attract and retain them' (Higgs, 2004: 20). However, in the light of the evidence of continuing discrimination against women and ethnic minorities in the labour market employers could also put more effort into making fuller use of the skills and abilities of workers from disadvantaged labour market groups.

While employers claim to experience skill shortages in specific areas, there is evidence of a growing mismatch between the qualifications held by workers and those required in their jobs. The supply of workers with intermediate qualifications, i.e. Levels 2 and 3, is outstrip-ping the demand for them and a growing proportion of workers as a whole are in jobs where they are over-qualified. This proportion increased from 30.6 per cent in 1986 to 37 per cent in 2001 (Felstead, Gallie and Green, 2002). This suggests that, in general, the demand for skilled labour has not kept pace with the increased supply of qualified workers, so that more people are experiencing job dissatisfaction as a result of the mismatch between their qualifi-cations and the demands of their jobs.

This growing mismatch may be in part a reflection of a growing polarisation of employ-ment in the UK. While there has been an overall shift in favour of more highly skilled jobs, some of the most rapid growth has been in low skilled jobs such as sales assistants and check-out operators, telephone sales workers and security guards. A recent study found that employment growth was concentrated among the best paying and the worst paying jobs. Those in the top 20 per cent of the pay distribution and those in the bottom 10 per cent increased their share of total employment while the share of the rest declined (Goos and Manning, 2003). This suggests that the labour market is polarising into good jobs and bad jobs as intermediate jobs decline.

Activity   Review the sections of this chapter that discuss differences in employment opportunity between socio-economic groups and then consider the likely consequences of polarisation of employment for these different groups.

Changing forms of employment

During the 1980s and 1990s, senior managers initiated programmes of organisational change aimed at reducing costs and increasing the speed with which their organisations could respond to changes in market conditions. A central feature of organisational change pro-grammes was workforce 'restructuring' that involved large-scale reductions in headcount, achieved partly through redundancies, early retirement and non-replacement of departing workers and partly by contracting out non-core and specialist services. This was accompa-nied by the reorganisation of work and in many cases, wider use of part-time, fixed-term contract and temporary labour and in a minority of cases, highly casualised forms of employment such as zero hours contracts (Cully, Woodland, O'Reilly and Dix, 1999; Millward, Bryson and Forth, 2000). These changes were aimed at increasing managers' ability to achieve greater *numerical labour flexibility*, in other words to be able to adjust the size of the workforce more easily in response to changes in demand.

The result was that, although the total number of jobs grew, there was a net reduction in the number of *full-time* jobs in Britain during the 1990s. All of the growth in employment was accounted for by a growth of part-time jobs, which increased from 22.9 per cent of total employment in 1992 to 24.6 per cent in 1999. The early and mid-1990s also saw an increase in the share of fixed-term and temporary employment from 5.9 per cent in 1992 to 7.6 per cent in 1997. These developments led some to argue that the full-time, permanent job was likely to become the exception rather than the rule (Bayliss, 1998). However, while part-time employment has continued to increase its share of total employment since 1997, reaching 25.8 per cent in 2004, the trend of temporary and fixed-term employment has been downward, with the share falling to 5.9 per cent in 2005 (ONS 2003, 2005).

What factors might explain why the share of employment accounted for by temporary and fixed-term jobs has fallen back in recent years while that of part-time jobs has continued to rise?

Labour market outcomes: the quality of employment

In this section of the chapter we examine how changes in the labour market have affected the quality of employment experience. How should we assess the quality of jobs? What indices should we use? Traditionally economists have used pay as the measure of job quality. Other social scientists have stressed the level of skill as a key measure on the grounds that skilled work not only provides workers with better pay but also more variety, personal autonomy and involvement and ultimately more control over their effort. We have seen that there has been an overall trend towards increased skill requirements in jobs so on the face of things at least it seems plausible that the quality of jobs available in the labour market has, on balance, improved. However, recent research has uncovered unexpected disjunctures between skill and other measures of job quality such as employment security, the ability to control one's level of effort and exercise control over how the job is done. In this section we review evidence relating to these dimensions of job quality to assess whether recent changes in the demand for labour have improved the quality of employment experience in the UK.

Job security

Job security is generally regarded as an important factor determining job quality. Employment security has also been linked positively to skill level, with skilled workers enjoying greater job security than unskilled workers. However, management-led organisational change during the 1980s and 1990s was seen by some to be undermining job security with disproportionately large effects on skilled workers such as managers and professionals.

The erosion of internalised employment systems

As we have seen, in recent years more organisations have restructured their workforces. They have reduced headcount, contracted out non-core and specialist jobs and increased their use of part-time, temporary and fixed-term contracts of employment and self-employed 'freelance' workers. Employers have also reduced their commitment to providing long-term employment security for 'permanent' employees. They have done this in order to achieve greater numerical flexibility of labour and reduce labour costs. However, they have sought to justify it in moral terms by arguing that workers should rely less on employers to provide long-term employment security and planned career paths and take greater responsibility for their own careers and 'employability'.

During the 1990s growing awareness of these changes led to concern at what appeared to be an increase in employment insecurity. It was argued widely in the press and by some academics that changing patterns of labour demand were creating a new era of insecurity for workers and the disappearance of 'jobs for life' (see Heery and Salmon (2000) for a review of these arguments). So have changes in the labour market made jobs more insecure? Before attempting to answer this question we need to define what we mean by employment insecurity. The most commonly used indicators of employment insecurity are the risk of involuntary job loss the costs of job loss, and the subjective feelings of workers.

The risk of job loss

The risk of job loss is affected by movements in the labour market, particularly changes in the rate of unemployment. The risk of job loss is greater when unemployment is rising than when it is constant or falling. However, during the 1990s some observers argued that the risk of job loss was increasing independently of the level of unemployment; in other words for any given level of unemployment the risk of job loss was higher than it used to be. Proponents of this argument pointed to redundancy dismissals and the replacement of permanent, full-time jobs with part-time and temporary jobs among previously secure groups such as managerial and professional workers and public sector workers. These developments were seen by some as marking the end of internalised employment relationships that offered 'jobs for life' and clear career paths linked to length of service.

The costs of job loss

The costs of job loss consist of three main elements. First is the immediate loss of income caused by having to live on social security benefits until a replacement job is found. Second is the likelihood of not being able to find a replacement job as good as the one that was lost. Third, long periods of unemployment lead to psychological and physical deterioration that reduces the chances of re-employment. Supporters of the insecurity thesis argued that the costs of job loss had risen because the level of social security payments had fallen relative to average wages and workers who had lost permanent full-time jobs were less able than previously to find equivalent replacements because of the trend away from full-time, permanent jobs to part-time and temporary jobs.

Subjective feelings of insecurity

These developments were seen as generating heightened feelings of insecurity among workers. However, the argument that workers were entering a new age of employment insecurity was challenged by other observers, who argued that it was largely a media creation that had been fuelled some well-publicised but unrepresentative instances where permanent, full-time employees had been replaced by freelance workers on fixed-term contracts, mostly in the media themselves (Doogan, 2001).

So has job insecurity increased? The evidence is that there has not been a significant increase in employment insecurity in general. While there was a slight increase in the proportion of workers in jobs lasting less than one year, from 18.6 per cent to 19.9 per cent during 1991–1998, there was also an increase in the proportion of people employed in long-term jobs, i.e. those lasting ten years or more, from 29 per cent to just over 32 per cent (Sparrow and Cooper, 2003: 77). Neither, as Table 4.6 shows, was there a long-term increase in people's feelings of employment insecurity.

Table 4.6 shows that workers' perceptions of the risk of job loss moved in line with unemployment, showing a tendency to increase in the early and mid-1990s and decline thereafter. However, the proportion of workers who felt that there was an even chance or greater of losing their jobs rose very little between 1986 and 1997, the period when employment insecurity was supposed to be increasing. Table 4.6 also shows that over the period 1986–2001 workers became more confident of being able to find an equivalent replacement job should they lose their current one. In particular the proportion of male and female workers who thought it would be very difficult to do so halved over the period. Therefore there is no strong evidence that a long-term increase in employment insecurity has led to a decline in the quality of people's employment experience. Significantly too, over the past five years employment insecurity has figured less and less in public discussion.

Although restructuring may not have increased the risks of job loss significantly, it may have contributed to a loss of valued features of jobs, which has led workers to feel less secure

Table 4.6 Workers' perceptions of employment insecurity in the UK 1991–2001

Perceived likelihood of job loss (%)	All employed workers		
	1986	1997	2001
No chance	80.0	77.1	83.4
Very unlikely	1.3	1.3	1.0
Quite unlikely	3.5	5.2	3.7
Evens	6.6	9.2	5.9
Quite unlikely	4.0	3.5	3.1
Very likely	4.6	3.6	2.9

Perceived difficulty of re-employment
How easy do you think it would be to get another job as good as your current one?

% replying:	Men			Women		
	1986	1997	2001	1986	1997	2001
Very easy	4.9	5.5	9.9	4.5	8.5	10.8
Quite easy	14.9	21.8	28.5	18.4	27.2	29.8
Quite difficult	37.2	39.7	39.5	41.8	41.8	42.1
Very difficult	43.0	33.0	22.2	35.3	22.6	17.3

Source: Green, F. (2004) p. 26.

about their long-term futures. One example of this is how organisational restructuring has eroded internal promotion ladders. 'Downsizing' has been accompanied by 'delayering'. Not only have jobs been cut; the number of job levels has also been reduced. The result is that workers have fewer opportunities to gain access to internal promotion ladders. This has been particularly noticeable in the banking and finance sector and in supermarkets, where jobs that used to provide stepping stones from junior to more senior grades have largely been eliminated (Grimshaw, Ward, Rubery and Beynon, 2001; Hudson 2002). This may also be contributing to the polarisation of employment opportunities that has been noted above.

Activity   Discuss with fellow students your perceptions of your own job security or insecurity. What factors influence your assessment?

Effort and work pressure

Feelings of insecurity at work may also result from being under pressure at work and more particularly being unable to control the pressure of work. Since the 1980s many have argued that work pressure has been increasing on two fronts in the UK. First, managers have been putting workers (and each other) under increasing pressure to work long hours. The prevalence of the 'long hours culture' in the UK is indicated by the fact that average working hours are higher than elsewhere in the European Union (EU). The British government has been accused of supporting a long hours culture by seeking to limit the effect of the EU Working Hours Directive in the UK. Second, since the mid-1980s analysts have argued that work is being intensified; in other words, workers are being made to work harder during their working hours.

Green (2006) notes that there is a widespread perception that work is encroaching on other aspects of life, restricting the time available for non-work activities and subjecting people to increased time pressures. This has fuelled recent discussion of 'work–life balance' (see below, p. 148). Statistical evidence, however, shows that there has not been a long-term increase in average hours worked in the UK. Average hours worked per employed person fell from the 1950s to the 1980s. The decline was halted during the 1980s but has resumed since. In 2003 average annual hours worked per employed person were 1673 compared with 1767 in 1990, 1713 in 1983 and 1833 in 1979 (Green, 2006: 46). What have increased are working hours per household as the proportion of households where all the adults are working has grown. The growing proportion of women with dependent children who are in work has been a major influence here. According to Green it is the increase in the total hours worked per household rather than an increase in hours worked per worker that has made it more difficult to balance between work and non-work activities and put people under pressure of time. Even so, there is widespread dissatisfaction over working hours among the UK workforce as a whole. Boheim and Taylor (2004) found that over 40 per cent of male and female full-time workers were dissatisfied with their hours of work, with the majority wanting to work fewer hours.

If the average amount of time that workers spend in work has not increased since the 1980s, people are nevertheless working harder during working time. Workers' self-reports show that the amount of effort required of them has increased, that they have had to work faster to cope with their workload and that they have increasingly been working under a great deal of tension. Thus the proportion of workers reporting that they worked at very high speed all the time or almost all the time rose from 17.3 per cent in 1992 to 25.6 per cent in 2001 and the proportion agreeing or strongly agreeing that they worked under a great deal of tension rose from 48.4 per cent to 58.4 per cent over the same period (Green, 2006: 54). A growing proportion of workers also reported that they found it difficult to unwind after work, that they kept worrying about work problems after work and that they felt 'used up at the end of a workday' (Green 2006: 156).

Work intensification has been driven mainly by the 'effort-biased' nature of technical change (Green, 2006), which enables management to exercise closer control over workers' effort. A clear example of this is the automated call distribution technology that is used in call centres. This ensures that call centre operators receive a continuous stream of incoming and outgoing calls, setting the pace of work in a similar way to the assembly line of an automated manufacturing plant. Another factor contributing to work intensification may be change in the labour market environment, particularly the decline of collective bargaining. This has given employers greater freedom to introduce new pay systems that are designed to extract higher effort from workers (Green, 2006).

 Think about your own workplace. What systems and technologies are in place to regulate your effort? Have you noticed an increase or decrease in the intensity of your work over time?

Worker discretion and autonomy

Worker discretion and autonomy are usually associated with skill. In fact the skill content of a job is partly defined in terms of the extent to which workers are required to exercise their own judgement in deciding how the job should be done, the other elements being task complexity and variety. The fewer the prescribed instructions to workers and the greater the number of decisions that workers have to make in the course of the job, the more skilled it is (Noon and Blyton, 1997). We have already seen that changes in the demand for labour have led to an increase in the average skill requirements of jobs. But does this mean that workers are enjoying increasing influence and control over how they work? The trend towards work intensification noted above suggests that workers have been losing control over effort levels and the pace of work. What has happened to their ability to influence other aspects of their work?

Various studies have cast doubt on how far recent upskilling of jobs has been accompanied by increased discretion and control for workers. Ramsay, Baldry, Connolly and Lockyer

(1991) found that white-collar workers in local government reported increased supervision following the introduction of information technology. Dent (1991) found that doctors and academics were being subject to increased bureaucratic control and a large survey carried out by Gallie *et al.*, (1998) found that skilled workers were subject to increased supervision, particularly when they worked with new technology.

National survey data also shows that the overall increase in skill levels has not been accompanied by increased worker discretion; if anything the reverse has occurred. The proportion of all workers reporting that they had a great deal of choice over the way they did their job fell from 51.8 per cent in 1986 to 38.6 per cent in 2001, a decline of 13.2 percentage points. While all broad occupational categories reported a decline in discretion, it was most marked among professional workers, where the proportion reporting that they had a lot of choice over how they did their work fell from 71.5 per cent to 38.3 per cent, a drop of 33.4 percentage points (Green, 2006: 105).

Rather than the shift in favour of more skilled jobs providing workers with greater control over their work, there has been a marked overall decline in discretion, particularly among professionals, who are among the most highly skilled workers. The reasons for this probably include the effects of new technology, financial pressures in the public sector, the spread of subcontracting and the increased public accountability to which professions have been subjected in the interests of improving public services such as health and education. New technologies allow the implementation of routine processes and the closer monitoring of individual workers. Professional workers are also concentrated in the public sector, where government-imposed financial constraints have encouraged closer managerial control of professional workers. At the same time, political pressure to reform and improve public services has involved criticisms of established standards and practices among professional groups that have led to managerial interventions to limit professional autonomy.

Stop & think

Identify as many examples as you can of politically inspired managerial interventions that have affected public service sector professional workers. Here is one to start you off – the National Curriculum in schools.

Job quality – an assessment

The evidence that we have reviewed in this section suggests that in important respects workers' experience of employment has deteriorated since the 1980s. While there has not been a general, long-term increase in job insecurity, work has become more intense and pressured and workers have less control over how they do their jobs. At the same time, the increase in the number of households where all adults are working has led to difficulties of balancing work and non-work areas of life. These changes have led to a significant decline in job satisfaction among British workers with just over 40 per cent of workers reporting high levels of job satisfaction in 2001 compared with just over 50 per cent in 1992 (Green, 2006: 154).

Dissatisfaction appears to be particularly strong among older workers and women. A comparison of the 1992 and 2000 Employment in Britain surveys by Taylor (2002b) showed that among workers aged 50 and over the proportion who were completely or very satisfied with pay fell from 37 per cent in 1992 to just 12 per cent in 2000 while the proportion expressing satisfaction with hours of work halved from 53 per cent to 25 per cent. Dissatisfaction with work intensification was revealed in drop in the proportion who were satisfied with the amount of work they had to do from 51 per cent to 26 per cent (p. 12).

Among women there was a decline in job satisfaction at all occupational levels. However, the decline was greatest among women in intermediate and routine occupations. While the proportion of women in higher level professional and managerial posts expressing satisfaction with their jobs fell from 38 per cent to 26 per cent between 1992 and 2000, the proportion of lower administrative, clerical and sales workers who did so fell from 61 per cent to 35 per cent and that of skilled manual workers from 44 per cent to 17 per cent (Taylor, 2002b: p. 14)

Responses to work pressure – the quest for 'work–life balance'

One important response to the growing sense of work pressure being experienced by people has been the emergence of demands for an improved balance between work and non–work aspects of life. Taylor (2002a) argues that work–life balance is about how to deal with the conflicting demands of corporate profitability on the one hand and the concerns of workers who are under work pressure and strain on the other. In this sense it is an expression of declining job satisfaction over hours and workload. While the increased employment participation of women with dependent children and an ageing population have raised issues of how to combine work with the care of relatives, dissatisfaction with workload and hours is not directly linked to having caring responsibilities. Therefore we need to take a wider view of work–life balance and not just see it in terms of the 'family friendly' agenda (Taylor 2002a).

What do we mean by work–life balance?

Work–life balance is not an easily defined term. The word 'balance' suggests the search for equilibrium between work and life; a settled point perhaps at which work and the rest of life's activities can comfortably reside side by side. Part of the problem associated with the notion of striking a balance or equilibrium is that work and non-work aspects of life are often entwined rather than entirely separate, compartmentalised spheres. For example, we might read a report for work on the train on the way home, we may look up the cinema show times on the web at work or chat to colleagues about non-work related issues during working hours; in essence what we are doing is seeking to find ways to *integrate* work and other aspects of our lives in ways that are workable and beneficial. Sparrow and Cooper (2003: 219) suggest therefore that 'work–life balance concerns those practices that enhance the flexibility and autonomy of the employee in this process of integration and in the negotiation over the attention and presence required'. They suggest that autonomy can either be guided by the provision of specific organisational arrangements to enable employees to split work and non-work aspects of their lives, for example, options to work part time or full time, to work in school term time only or to job share, or it can be achieved by the organisation making available practices which allow individuals to draw their own lines between and around work and non-work, for example, unpaid leave, career breaks, parental leave, sabbaticals, paid holidays. Work–life balance strategies are thus often associated with the provision of greater flexibility in terms of working arrangements.

Work–life balance and government policy

Legal imperatives for employers to address issues of work–life balance began to emerge at the end of the 1990s. In 1998 we saw the introduction of the Working Time Regulations, aimed at curtailing the working week to a maximum of 48 hours and requiring employers to formally secure an 'opt-out' agreement with those employees willing to contract in excess of the 48-hour cap. On the heels of the Working Time Directive, the Employment Rights Act 1999 contained provisions to bolster the position of working parents and carers within the workplace whilst the Employment Act 2002 propelled the legislative agenda underpinning work–life balance provisions yet further (see Chapter 11 for further details of the legislation). At the time of writing it is anticipated that the government will extend the right to request flexible working to carers of adults with effect from April 2007.

The Government's concern for work–life balance was formally highlighted in Spring 2000 at the launch of the Work–Life Balance Campaign (Hogarth *et al.*, 2000). The objective of the campaign was to alert employers to the business case in favour of introducing practices to help employees strike a better balance between work and other non-work areas of their lives. Importantly the campaign sought to promote the merits of work–life balance *for all* rather than identifying those with caring responsibilities as key beneficiaries of support.

The pattern of employer responses to work–life balance issues

There are potentially strong business reasons why employers should offer arrangements to employees to help achieve a better integration of work and non-work aspects of their lives. Specifically they may aid recruitment and retention at a time when organisations are competing for highly qualified, talented workers. Edwards and Wajcman (2005) refer to international survey evidence that shows that graduates give a higher priority to work–life balance than to pay. Clutterbuck (2004) suggests that creating an enabling culture in which employees can amend and re-apportion the time and attention they pay to work to meet their particular needs and circumstances can be a source of sustainable competitive advantage (Clutterbuck, 2004).

Employers' responses to the work–life balance issue have, however, been mixed. Some appear to welcome and encourage work–life balance initiatives while others are more reticent. Work undertaken by Wood (1999) for the National Centre for Economic Research suggests that employers' motives for introducing work–life balance initiatives can be summarised within a four-fold theoretical classification;

- institutional theory;
- organisational-adaption theory;
- high-commitment theory;
- practical response theory.

Wood explains that whilst some firms will apparently willingly and proactively adopt work–life balance initiatives, others will only do so to respond to pressing and immediate circumstances.

In adopting the classification Wood argues that those organisations whose behaviour shows them to be eager to reflect broader societal values in their practices conform to *Institutional theory*. Typically these firms operate in the public sector and need to be seen to be proactive, or they are large private sector firms in the public gaze for whom there is visible kudos to be earned from setting the lead in developing and implementing work–life balance solutions. Additionally firms with trade union presence are more likely to conform.

Organisational adaption theory relates to those organisations in which societal norms are interpreted in ways that are seen to be consistent with the views and interests of senior management, so alongside the pre-mentioned conditions favourable for the adoption of work–life balance initiatives, firms conforming to organisational adaption theory are likely to be drawn towards work-life balance initiatives because of specific organisational circumstances. Such firms may be especially reliant on a predominantly female workforce or require skill sets that are difficult to secure and retain and employee retention issues therefore critical. Organisational adaption theory also captures the propensity for firms to implement work–life balance initiatives when existing working patterns and systems are conducive to or compatible with them.

Within Wood's framework *high-commitment theory* is used to explain the uptake of work–life balance initiatives among those organisations with developed HRM systems and practices, where it is understood that mechanisms to help employees achieve a better work–life balance may in turn engender greater levels of employee commitment.

Finally, *practical response theory* applies to organisations who display a rather more *ad hoc* approach to the development and introduction of work–life balance initiatives; resorting to implementing work–life balance practices if they are perceived to be beneficial in helping to address particular organisational difficulties.

Stop & think

The following organisations all have in place work–life balance practices:

(a) British Telecom
(b) Asda
(c) Lloyds TSB Plc
(d) The University of Leicester Hospitals Trust

In each case, which of Wood's theories do you think most closely relates to the organisation's particular motives for embracing work–life balance practices?

In commenting on Wood's analysis Clutterbuck (2004) suggests that the primary drivers for work–life balance in the EU differ from those typically forwarded by US organisations. In the US he recognises a model firmly centred upon work–life balance as a source of competitive advantage whilst in the EU motives typically push social responsibility to the fore.

Stop & think

Think of an organisation you have worked for where some work–life balance practices were available. Why do you think this organisation elected to develop and introduce WLB initiatives?

The take-up of work–life balance initiatives by employers

The first findings of the 2004 WERS survey (Kersley *et al.* 2005) reported an increase in the proportion of employers who believe that employees' work–life balance is their responsibility. Latest findings from WERS 2004 (Kersley *et al.*, 2005: 31) show an increase in the availability of parental leave, paid paternity/discretionary leave for fathers and special paid leave in emergencies for at least some non-managerial employees in the period 1998 to 2004. WERS data continues, however, to reflect a chequered picture in terms of employees' access to a range of work–life balance provisions, suggesting that not all employers feel pressured to prioritise provision for work–life balance. The WERS panel survey showed the proportion of workplaces providing access to zero hours contracts, annualised hours, job sharing, home working, term-time only contracts, flexi-time and the facility to switch from full-time to part-time employment to at least some of their non-managerial employees increased during the period 1998 to 2004. However, Kersley *et al.* admit that 'generally these practices were more common in larger workplaces, the public sector and where unions were recognised' (2005: 28). This pattern is illustrative of the sway of institutional theory. In a pattern resonant with organisational adaption theory, Kersley *et al.* (2005) have found that workplaces in which female employees outnumber male employees are more disposed to permit some employees to use all of the practices listed in Table 4.7 apart from homeworking and flexi-time (2005: 28).

In light of this, the trend to smaller workplaces combined with sparse trade union presence suggests that progress in addressing work–life balance issues will continue to be uneven. Moreover, even in those organisations where opportunities for flexible working are offered barriers to their take-up by employees remain. These include the irreducible nature of work tasks in many cases, possible damage to career prospects resulting from taking flexible work options and for low earners, loss of earnings resulting from some options. Workers may also be unwilling to take advantage of work–life balance initiatives because they are worried that it will generate hostile responses from colleagues who are unable or do not wish to do so

Figure 4.7 Availability of flexible working arrangements

Flexible working arrangements	Per cent of workplaces offering the arrangement to some employees
Reduced hours	70
Increased hours	57
Change working pattern	45
Flexi-time	35
Job sharing	31
Homeworking	26
Term-time only	20
Compressed hours	16
Annualised hours	6
Zero-hours contracts	5

Source: Kersley *et al.* (2005: 29), Inside the workplace: first findings from the 2004 Workplace Employment Relations Survey.

(Sparrow and Cooper, 2003). More optimistically, there is evidence that the incidence of long hours working and work intensification is declining. The proportion of workers working long hours peaked at 36 per cent in 1995 and fell to 30 per cent by the end of 2002 (Green, 2003: 140). Also, while work was more intense in 2001 than in 1992, the process of intensification halted in 1997, since when there has been little change (Green, 2003: 144).

Conclusion: labour market developments, job quality and the implications for the employment relationship

The evidence discussed in this chapter suggests that, despite the widespread rhetoric of high commitment and high involvement and the tendency among advocates and practitioners of HRM to present the employment relationship in terms of mutual consent, it continues to be characterised by conflicts of interest. Currently these centre on hours of work, work intensity, lack of discretion and control over how work is performed, and structured inequalities in the labour market.

The main labour market development over the last ten years has been a sustained growth of employment accompanied by increasing inequality in the distribution of pay as a result of the polarised nature of employment growth. While employment and pay have risen for all groups of workers since 1993, the *relative* position of less-skilled workers in terms of unemployment, access to jobs, and pay is worse than it was at the start of the 1980s. This is despite recent government interventions such as the national minimum wage and measures aimed at improving the employability of young school leavers (Goos and Manning, 2003)

In addition, long-standing patterns of inequality and disadvantage remain. The difference in employment rates between women and men has not really changed over the last ten years, the employment rate among women remaining 11 percentage points below that of men. Neither has there been much change in the quality of jobs occupied by women. They are still concentrated in occupations and industries where rates of pay are low and working conditions are poor. While the overall pay gap between women and men has narrowed, it is the minority of women who are working full time in higher-paid occupations who have benefited. This group have also benefited from statutory maternity leave provisions, which have given them the right to return to their jobs after childbirth. The pay gap for the majority of working women, who are in part-time jobs, has not narrowed and may even have increased slightly (Robinson, 2003). Moreover the position of these women, employed mainly in low skill occupations, has deteriorated to an even greater extent than that of low skilled men in relation to unemployment, access to employment, and pay (Gregg and Wadsworth, 2003).

Established patterns of labour market inequality between ethnic minorities and whites have also persisted. There has been an increase in the employment rate and a consequent reduction in the employment gap relative to whites among some, but not all British born ethnic minority groups and a slight reduction in the degree of occupational segregation. However there is less evidence for a reduction in the pay gap. The position of ethnic minority immigrants has shown no sign of improving relative to whites (Wadsworth, 2003).

These features of the contemporary labour market suggest that employers have a number of serious issues to face. First, it is clear that there is a growing mismatch between the way managers are organising work and designing jobs on the one hand and how workers' job aspirations are developing on the other. Widespread job dissatisfaction is weakening employees' commitment to their employers and eroding the goodwill that is necessary for cooperative behaviour in the workplace. Given the particularly steep decline in job satisfaction among the over-50s and women, employers need to take action to address these workers' grievances.

Second, if, as is widely predicted, the ageing of the population means that the future supply of skilled labour is likely to become increasingly tight, government and employers will need to develop and utilise more effectively under-employed skills in the ethnic minority population, among women and older workers as well as making greater use of migrant workers from the expanded EU. This implies a stronger commitment to valuing diversity in the workforce and managing it effectively.

However, employers individually may benefit from the presence of disadvantaged groups who can be exploited because they lack alternative job opportunities. Therefore there is a case for stronger state intervention to combat unfair discrimination in the labour market. There is also a case for strengthening workers' rights to trade union membership and representation.

Finally, the evidence reviewed in this chapter should lead you to think about the nature of HRM and the extent of its adoption in the UK. What do we consider to be HRM? Is it a set of practices aimed at generating high levels of employee commitment or high performance through employee involvement? If so, there would appear to be little evidence that it has spread widely in the UK since the 1980s.

Summary

- Labour markets are often seen as arenas of competition in which forces of supply and demand determine wage and employment levels. In reality however, there are limits to competition in labour markets.

- Employers have some freedom to make a strategic choice between internalising or externalising the employment relationship. Their choices are influenced although not completely determined by the nature of their labour requirements and by features of the labour market context in which they operate.

- The aggregate supply of labour – the size of the workforce – is determined by demographic factors such as the size and age structure of the population and by social and political factors that influence the participation rate of different socio-economic groups within the population. In the UK differential participation rates can be observed between men and women of different age groups and different ethnic groups.

- Aggregate labour demand consists of total employment plus unfilled vacancies. The demand for labour is derived from the demand for goods and services. In conditions of low unemployment – tight labour markets – employers have to compete more actively to attract and retain workers.

- The demand for labour is segmented into jobs offers of varying quality. Unfair discrimination along lines of gender and ethnicity mean that women and ethnic minorities are disadvantaged in terms of access to good jobs.

- There has been a long-term change in labour demand away from manufacturing to services. This has been an important force driving the long-term growth of part-time employment and women's employment.

- Since the 1980s there has been a shift in the occupational structure of labour demand mainly towards highly skilled occupations but also leading to the growth of some low-skilled occupations. There has been a relative decline in intermediate occupations.

- Since the 1980s managers have restructured their organisations and their workforces. This has involved a retreat from internalised employment relationships.

- Contrary to what might have been predicted from the overall trend towards more highly skilled work, the quality of jobs has deteriorated in terms of work pressure and worker autonomy, although not in terms of job stability leading to falling levels of job satisfaction compared with the early 1990s. The demand for better work–life balance is a recent response to growing work pressure.

- Declining job satisfaction and the presence of disadvantaged groups in the labour market indicate the continued presence of conflict in the employment relationship.

1 Explain the factors that influence the differential labour market participation rates of women and men and ethnic minorities and whites.

2 How has the structure of demand for labour changed since the 1980s?

3 Why have levels of job satisfaction declined since the early 1990s?

4 Who have been the man beneficiaries of changes in the labour market since the 1980s and who have been the main losers?

CASE STUDY

Stuck on the 'mummy track' – why having a baby means lower pay and prospects

From the moment they give birth, women get stuck on a 'mummy track' of low pay and low prospects as their wages fall and never fully recover – even when their children have left home, a new study has found.

Far from being a liberating release, the point when their children start school marks another sudden slump in the average growth of women's pay compared with male wages, according to the report by the Institute for Fiscal Studies.

Before they have children, the average hourly wage for female workers is 91 per cent of the male average but declines to 67 per cent for working mothers juggling jobs and childcare.

Their wages relative to men then stagnate for 10 years before showing a modest recovery, reports the study, Newborns and New Schools. But even when children have left home, the average hourly wage for their mothers remained at 72 per cent of the male average.

Rather than facilitate a large-scale return to the workforce for women, the moment their children enter full-time school accelerates relative wage decline. The average wage growth over two years for women before having children was 11 per cent, but fell to 8 per cent for women with newborn children. While it recovered to 9 per cent for those with pre-school children, it fell again to less than 5 per cent when their children entered school. The aggregate proportion of mothers in work before their children began school compared with afterwards only rose slightly from 53 per cent in June to 57 per cent when term began in September.

'There is a huge assumption that suddenly because the child is at school the mother can return to work,' said Gillian Paull, a co-author of the study for the Department for Work and Pensions. 'But school hours are far too short to cover most jobs and school brings with it a new set of responsibilities in terms of children needing input from parents and parents being involved in school life. Finding childcare that fits around school hours and the holidays is difficult unless you pay for expensive full-time care.'

Only a small part of this gender wage gap is because mothers choose to work part time. For full-time workers, the gender wage ratio suffered a similar slump between childless women and working mothers, with a decline from women commanding 94 per cent of male wages before children to just 74 per cent for those with children and 79 per cent for the group after children.

When researchers took account of other factors which might determine the gender wage gap such as gender differences in demographic background, educational attainment and work characteristics and conditions they still found 'a substantial "unexplained" gender wage gap' of 11 per cent for those before children, 30 per cent for those living with children and 23 per cent for those whose children have grown up or left home.

'The million-dollar question is: "Are the wage levels different because working mothers are treated differently or is it that they choose a different way to behave in the labour market?"' Dr Paull said.

Working mothers could be suffering a wide pay gap because of pure discrimination. Or, controversially, some employers claim they do not pay as much because working mothers are not as productive as men. Thirdly, Dr Paull said, it could be that women were choosing jobs that fit in with the demands of motherhood, finding work that was less physically demanding, for instance, so they could devote more energy to their families.

➤

Case study continued

'Too many women get stuck on a "mummy track" of low pay and low prospects. The pay gap for women working part-time, at nearly 40 per cent, has barely improved since the Sex Discrimination Act was introduced 30 years ago,' said Caroline Slocock, the chief executive of the Equal Opportunities Commission.

'Many women choose to work part-time, but they don't choose low pay. Four in five part-time workers – 5.6 million people, most of whom are women – are working in jobs which do not use their potential, because flexible and part-time work is too often low-status and underpaid. This is a colossal waste of talent for employers and the economy as well as individuals.'

The IFS study is published days before the Women and Work Commission reports to Tony Blair after spending 18 months looking at the problem of the gender pay gap. The prime minister is expected to help launch the report next month, which is expected to outline radical proposals to help women return to well-paid work.

Children represent a 'major part' of the gender pay gap, according to Margaret Prosser, who chairs the Women and Work Commission. 'Once women have children, their job choices are hugely constrained, either because they have to choose local work which provides fewer options or choose part-time employment, where there are few jobs at a professional or senior level.'

Lady Prosser said she was not surprised that figures showed women's pay stagnating even years after they have raised young children.

'The majority of women who have children want to spend some time with those children. What they would like is work that is sufficiently flexible but what they do not want is work that is always at the bottom of the ladder.

'There is no silver bullet answer to this. There has to be a whole range of policy proposals around edu-cational choices, encouragement for girls and more widely available childcare facilities.'

Source: Patrick Barkham, 20 January 2006, *The Guardian*

Questions

1 To what extent do you believe that women get stuck on the 'mummy track' because they *choose* to prioritise responsibilities to their children over and above paid work?

2 Are New Labour's promises to improve access to affordable childcare and plans to introduce school 'wrap around time' (the provision of breakfast clubs and after school activities to extend the school day) the 'green light' needed for working mothers to be able to compete on equal terms with men in the workplace?

3 Whilst organisations might not deliberately set out to discriminate against working mothers, consider ways in which norms and expectations in the contemporary workplace may make it difficult for working mothers to gain promotion and hence access to better paid positions. What steps could organisations take to help more women off the 'mummy track'?

Activity

You have been invited to a campus debate to discuss the proposition outlined below:

Given employers' demand for low skill workers to fill low-paid jobs in the service sector, the existence of receptive pockets of labour (for example, working mothers, students, migrant workers) prepared to accept these jobs is beneficial for organisations and the economy at large.

Using the article 'Stuck on the Mummy track' as a starting point, consider positions both *in support of and against* the above statement. You should be able to draw upon several segments of this chapter to inform your arguments.

References and further reading

Adkins, L. (1995) *Gendered Work, Sexuality, Family and the Labour Market.* Buckingham: OUP.

Anderson, B., Ruhs, M., Rogaly, B. and Spencer, C. (2006) *Fair Enough? Central and Eastern European Migrants in Low-Wage Employment.* York: Joseph Rowntree Foundation.

Bayliss, V. (1998) *Redefining Work: An RSA Initiative.* London: Royal Society for the Encouragement of Arts, Manufactures and Commerce.

Boheim, R. and Taylor, M.P. (2004) 'Actual and preferred working hours', *British Journal of Industrial Relations*, 42, 1: 149–166.

Bradley (1999), *Gender and Power in the Workplace: Analysing the Impact of Economic Change.* Basingstoke: Macmillan Press Ltd.

Browning, G. (2005) 'The Search for Meaning', *People Management*, 11, 25: December.

CIPD (2005) *A Barometer of HR Trends and Prospects, Overview of CIPD Surveys.* London: CIPD.

CIPD (2006) 'Jobs blow to women as economic slowdown hits consumer services', Press Release, London, CIPD, 15 March.

CIPD and KPMG (2006) Labour Market Outlook, *Quarterly Survey Report*, London, CIPD Spring.

Clutterbuck, D. (2004) *Managing Work–Life Balance in the 21st Century*. London: CIPD

Connor, H., Tyers, C., Davis, S. and Tackey, N. (2003) *Minority Ethnic Students in Higher Education*. London: DFES

Cooper, C. (2005) 'Another Year Down?' *People Management*, 11, 25: December.

Crompton, R. (1997) *Women and Work in Modern Britain*, Oxford: Oxford University Press Ltd.

Cully, M., Woodland, S., O'Reilly, A. and Dix, G. (1999) *Britain at Work. As depicted by the 1998 Workplace Employee Relations Survey*. London: Routledge.

Dent, M. (1991) 'Autonomy and the medical profession: medical audit and management control', in Smith, C., Knights, D. and Willmott, H. (eds) *White-Collar Work: The Non-Manual Labour Process*. Basingstoke: Macmillan, pp. 65–88.

Doeringer, P.B. and Piore, M.J. (1971) *Internal Labor Markets and Manpower Analysis*. Lexington, Mass.: Heath.

Doogan, K. (2001) 'Insecurity and long term employment', *Work, Employment and Society*, 15, 3: 419–441.

Drucker, P. (2001) 'Beyond the Information Revolution' in Giddens, A. (ed.) *Sociology: Introductory Readings*. Cambridge: Polity Press.

DWP (2005) Speech given by the Rt Hon Alan Johnson MP, Secretary of State for Work and Pensions, 7 February, www.dwp.gov.uk.

Edwards, P. and Wajcman, J. (2005) *The Politics of Working Life*. Oxford: Oxford University Press.

EOC (2001) *Women and Men in Britain: Professional Occupations*.

EOC (2005) Facts about Men and Women in Britain 2005, an EOC Fact Sheet

EOC (2006) Then and Now; 30 years of the Sex Discrimination Act, an EOC Fact Sheet.

Felstead, A., Gallie, D. and Green, F. (2002) *Work Skills in Britain 1986–2001*. Nottingham: DfES publications.

Friedman, A. (1977) *Industry and Labour*. London: Macmillan.

Gallie, D., White, M. and Cheng, Y. (1998) *Restructuring the Employment Relationship*. Oxford: Clarendon Press.

Goos, M. and Manning, A. (2003) 'McJobs and MacJobs: The growing polarisation of jobs in the UK', in Dickens, R., Gregg, P. and Wadsworth, J. (eds) *The Labour Market under New Labour: The State of Working Britain*. Basingstoke: Palgrave, pp. 70–85.

Gordon, D.M., Edwards, R. and Reich, M. (1982) *Segmented Work, Divided Workers: The Historical Transformation of Labor in the United States*. Cambridge: Cambridge University Press.

Green, F. (2003) 'The demands of work', in Dickens, R., Gregg, P. and Wadsworth, J. (eds) *The Labour Market under New Labour: The State of Working Britain*. Basingstoke: Palgrave, pp. 137–149.

Green, F. (2004) 'The rise and decline of job insecurity', Department of Economics Discussion Paper, Kent University.

Green, F. (2006) *Demanding Work: The Paradox of Job Quality in the Affluent Economy*. Oxford: Princeton University Press.

Gregg, P. and Wadsworth, J. (2003) 'Labour market prospects of less skilled workers over the recovery', in Dickens, R., Gregg, P. and Wadsworth, J. (eds) *The Labour Market Under New Labour: The State of Working Britain*. Basingstoke: Palgrave, pp. 87–97.

Grimshaw, D., Ward, K.G., Rubery, J. and Beynon, H. (2001) 'Organisations and the transformation of the internal labour market', *Work, Employment and Society*, 15, 1: 25–54.

Hakim, C. (1998) *Social Change and Innovation in the Labour Market*. Oxford: OUP.

Hardill, I., Duddlestone, A. and Owen, D.W. (1997) 'Who decides what? Decision making in dual career households', *Work, Employment & Society*, 11, 2: 313–326.

Heath, A. and Cheung, S.Y. (2006) *Ethnic Penalties in the Labour Market: Employers and Discrimination*. DWP Research Report 341.

Heery, E. and Salmon, J. (2000) 'The insecurity thesis', in Heery, E. and Salmon, J. (eds) *The Insecure Workforce*. London: Routledge, pp. 1–24.

Higgs, M. (2004) 'Future Trends in HR', in Rees, D. and McBain, R. (eds) *People Management Challenges and Opportunities*. Basingstoke: Palgrave.

Hogarth, T., Hasluck, C., Pierre, G., Winterbotham, M. and Vivian, D. (2000) *Work-life Balance, 2000: Baseline Study of Work-Life Balance Practices in Great Britain*. Warwick: Institute for Employment Research: Warwick University.

Hudson, M. (1999) 'Disappearing pathways and the struggle for a fair day's pay', in Burchell, B., Day, D., Hudson, M., Ladipo, D., Mankelow, R., Nolan, J., Reed, H., Wichert, I. and Wilkinson, F. *Job Insecurity and Work Intensification: Flexibility and the Changing Boundaries of Work*. York: Joseph Rowntree Foundation, pp. 77–93.

Hudson, M. (2002) 'Disappearing pathways and the struggle for a fair day's pay', in Burchill, B., Day, D., Hudson, M., Ladipo, D., Mankelow, R., Nolan, J., Reed, H., Wichert, I. and Wilkinson, F. *Job Insecurity and Work Intensification: Flexibility and the Changing Boundaries of Work*. York: Joseph Rowntree Foundation, pp. 77–93.

Jah, A. (2006) 'The future of old age', *The Guardian*, 8 March 2006, p. 6.

Joll, C., Mckenna, C., McNab, R. and Shorey, J. (1983) *Developments in Labour Market Analysis*. London: George Allen & Unwin.

Kersley, B., Alpin, C., Forth, J., Bryson, A., Bewley, H., Dix, G. and Oxenbridge, S. (2005) *Inside the Workplace: First Findings from the 2004 Workplace Employment Relations Survey*. London: DTi.

King, J.E. (1990) *Labour Economics*, 2nd edition. London: Macmillan.

Laurie, H. and Gershuny, J. (2000) 'Couples, Work and Money' in Berthoud, R. and Gershuny, J. (eds) *Seven Years in the Lives of British Families*. Bristol: Polity Press.

Learning and Skills Council (2005) *National Employer Skills Survey: Key Findings*. Coventry: Learning and Skills Council.

Leonard, D. and Speakman, M.A. (1986) 'Women in the family: companions or caretaker?', in Beechey, V. and Whitelegg, E. (eds) *Women in Britain Today*. Milton Keynes: Open University Press.

LFS (2006) 'Ethnic minorities in the labour market: Autumn 2005', *LFS Update*, www.emetaskforce.gov.uk.

Marlow, S. and Carter, S. (2004) 'Accounting for change: professional status, gender disadvantage and self-employment', *Women in Management Review*, 19, 1: 5–17.

Miller, H. (1991) 'Academics and the labour process', in Smith, C., Knights, D. and Willmott, H. (eds) *White-Collar Work: The Non-Manual Labour Process*. Basingstoke: Macmillan, pp. 109–138.

Millward, N., Bryson, A. and Forth, J. (2000) *All Change at Work? British Employment Relations as Portrayed by the Workplace Industrial Relations Survey Series*. London: Routledge.

Nolan, P. and Brown, W. (1983) 'Competition and workplace wage determination', *Oxford Bulletin of Economics and Statistics*, 45, 269–287.

Noon, M. and Blyton, P. (1997) *The Realities of Work*. Basingstoke: Macmillan.

ONS (2001), Census 2001.

ONS (2003) *Labour Market Trends*, 111, 12.

ONS (2004) *Labour Force Survey*, Spring 2004 dataset.

ONS (2005a) *Labour Market Trends*, 113, 12.

ONS (2005b) *Population Trends*, 121, Autumn 2005.

ONS (2005c) *Annual Earnings Survey*, Office for National Statistics.

ONS (2006a) *Social Trends*, 36th edn, Office for National Statistics.

ONS (2006b) 'Diversity within and between ethnic groups', *Social Trends*, 36th edn, News Release, 21 February.

Ramsay, H., Baldry, C., Connolly, A. and Lockyer, C. (1991) 'Multiple microchips: the computerised labour process in the public service sector', in Smith, C., Knights, D. and Willmott, H. (eds) *White-Collar Work: The Non-Manual Labour Process*. Basingstoke: Macmillan, pp. 35–64.

Robinson, H. (2003) 'Gender and labour market performance in the recovery', in Dickens, R., Gregg, P. and Wadsworth, J. (eds) *The Labour Market Under New Labour*. Basingstoke: Palgrave, pp. 232–247.

Rubery, J. (1994) 'Internal and external labour markets: towards an integrated analysis', in Rubery, J. and Wilkinson, F. (eds) *Employer Strategy and the Labour Market*. Oxford: Oxford University Press, pp. 37–68.

Scottish Centre for Employment Research (2001) *SCER Report 1 – Understanding the Labour Market*, Department of Human Resource Management, University of Strathclyde.

Sparrow, P.R. and Cooper, C.L. (2003) *The Employment Relationship: Key Challenges for HR*. London: Butterworth Heinemann.

Stanworth, C. (2000) 'Flexible working patterns', in Winstanley, D. and Woodall, J. (eds) *Ethical Issues in Contemporary Human Resource Management*. Basingstoke: Palgrave.

Strategy Unit (2003) *Ethnic Minorities and the Labour Market: Final Report*. London: Cabinet Office.

Taylor, R. (2002a) *The Future of Work–Life Balance*. Swindon: Economic and Social Research Council.

Taylor, R. (2002b) *Britain's Diverse Labour Market*. Swindon: Economic and Social Research Council.

Taylor, S. (2005), *People Resourcing*, 3rd edn. London: CIPD.

TUC (2005) 'Challenging Times'. London: TUC

Wadsworth, J. (2003) 'The labour market performance of ethnic minorities in the recovery', in Dickens, R., Gregg, P. and Wadsworth, J. *The Labour Market under New Labour: The State of Working Britain*. Basingstoke: Palgrave, pp. 116–133.

Wilson, R., Homenikou, K. and Dickerson, A. (2006) *Working Futures: New Projections of Occupational Attainment by Sector and Region 2002–2012. Volume 1: National Report*. Coventry: Institute for Employment Research, University of Warwick.

Wood, S. (1999) Family-friendly management; testing the various perspectives, *National Institute for Economic Research*, 168, April 2/99: 99–116.

For multiple-choice questions, exercises and annotated weblinks specific to this chapter visit the book's website at **www.pearsoned.co.uk/beardwell**

Organising people — responses to control

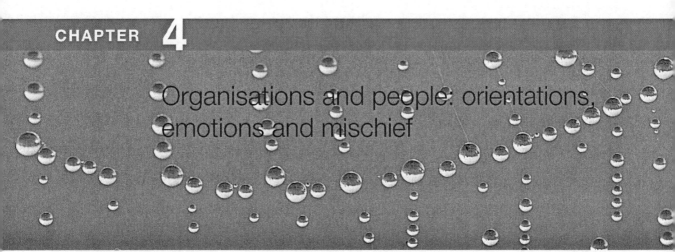

CHAPTER 4

Organisations and people: orientations, emotions and mischief

Objectives	Having read this chapter and completed its associated activities, readers should be able to:

- See how a *strategic exchange* perspective can be developed within a process-relational frame of reference to help us understand particular aspects of the relationship between people and organisations.

- Recognise the importance of the *implicit contract*, which is made between the employee and the employing organisation, to an understanding of work behaviour and organisational relationships.

- Apply the concept of *work orientation* to people's involvement in work organisations, appreciating that organisational employees are better understood not as 'motivated' to work in particular ways but as 'oriented' to their work circumstances by the meanings they both bring to the organisation in the first place and by the way these meanings change as they move on through their life and work careers.

- Understand the importance of matters of *emotion* and *feelings* in the work context and come to terms with the fact that these permeate every aspect of organisational activity.

- Recognise that an emotional dimension is sometimes deliberately built into the design of certain kinds of work and that people in various kinds of work, including management, find themselves engaging in *emotional labour*.

- Appreciate how emotional matters are involved in situations of individual stress and how the experience of stress, or work-related distress, can best be understood in terms of an interplay of factors in the organisational circumstances and factors in the individual's own life – especially their 'personal resources'.

- See how practices that can be characterised as *organisational mischief* – from fiddles and sabotage to sexual, joking and 'play' activities – all relate to matters of power, identity and negotiated order in the workplace.

- Recognise the particular significance of sexuality and humour in both challenges and adjustments to organisational controls.

Shaping lives and shaping organisations: a strategic exchange perspective

Within the process-relational way of framing human and organisational activities that has been unfolded over the previous chapters we can now develop a more tightly focused perspective to help us deal with specific aspects of the relationships between organisations and people who work in them. This is the *strategic exchange* perspective. It is intended to draw our attention to two things. First, attention is drawn to the *parallel* that exists between human beings and organisations: the fact that both people and organisations, albeit in different ways, have to make exchanges of various kinds with the world in order to survive in that world into the future. And, second, attention is drawn to a key *link* that exists between people and organisations: the exchanges that occur between organisations and people as part of their survival processes. The idea of organisations existing without some kind of giving to and taking from 'people' is clearly ridiculous. It is possible, however, to envisage people surviving without trading with organisations. But that would only be possible in a very simple society where there were no bureaucratised state bodies or commercial enterprises with which people have to deal in order to participate in society. In modern societies it is out of the question for anyone to contemplate living without some kind of give-and-take relationship with enterprises, institutions, firms and corporations.

The importance of exchange in human existence generally was stressed in Chapter 3 where it was pointed out that people's physical and psychological survival depends upon give-and-take exchanges with others. People exchange meaning-giving and emotional resources as well as material goods or necessities (p. 95). And a proportion of these exchanges is inevitably with organisations – in activities ranging from the buying goods and services from an organisation to the entering of an employment relationship with one of them. It was also recognised that human beings are 'strategic' in the sense of actively shaping their lives, identities and their biographies. People are 'strategic and situationally sensitive' (pp. 94–5): people always act with regard to their specific context, given their broader projects in life and what they currently regard their identity to be.

Although the lives of all of us are influenced and constrained by the social-structural, cultural and other circumstances in which we find ourselves, none of us can simply lie back and adopt a totally passive stance towards the world. It is true, of course, that people vary considerably in how purposefully active ('proactive') they are in shaping their lives. But human survival, in both the physical and psychological senses of the term, requires of everyone a degree of strategic initiative-taking, a degree of life shaping and the pursuit of survival projects. In Table 1.4 (p. 30), where process-relational thinking is contrasted with systems-control ideas about human beings, it was pointed out that people are not best understood as 'need-led'. Rather, they are sense-making and project-oriented creatures who, in the light of how they interpret their situation, make exchanges with others to deal with their material, psychological and emotional circumstances.

People can be seen, then, always to be striving to come to terms with the circumstances in which they find themselves and to shape their existence. Their 'biography' does not just write itself. People, in part, have to be the authors of their identities and biographies. They therefore pursue their projects in life and manage their continuously emerging identities through exchanging meanings and resources with others and, as we argued in Chapter 3, through a 'dialogue' with their cultures. And, here, there is a parallel with organisations.

Organisations are most certainly not people. But their future existence, just like the future existence of the human individual, depends on their making exchanges with others – in this case with customers, suppliers, employees and so on. Both organisations (as sets of understandings and arrangements), and the people involved in them (as individuals with identities and biographies) are shaped and shape themselves to continue their existence into the future. This shaping may be relatively deliberate ('planned') or it might be very reactive, haphazard even.

Strategic exchange   *Concept*

As both individuals and organisations shape themselves and are shaped to continue their existence into the future, the exchange of material and symbolic resources occurs (a) between individuals and others in their social worlds (including employing organisations) and (b) between organisations and their internal and external constituencies upon which they are resource dependent (including employees).

The concept of strategic exchange draws attention to the interplay that occurs between how people involved with work organisations shape and make sense of their lives and the way organisations themselves are strategically shaped. People make many exchanges, materially and symbolically, with the whole range of people whom they encounter in their lives. The exchange they make with the work organisations in which they become involved, typically in an employment relationship, is an important one for many people. And organisations themselves would be nothing without exchanges made with all of those who become attached to the organisation as owners, workers, managers and so on. The exchange between such individuals and the organisation is represented in Figure 4.1. This exchange is a contractual one – a point we will develop shortly.

This 'interplay' between individual and organisational exchange processes, at the heart of which is a specific contractual exchange, will be seen in many of the cases that we shall encounter in coming chapters. The interplay can be seen in an especially clear way in the story of Peter Brodie in Chapter 5 (Case 5.2, p. 177). We will see there how this chief executive of a charity was simultaneously working to shape his own life and that of the Youth Links organisation which employs him. We will see how the organisation was being shaped, and

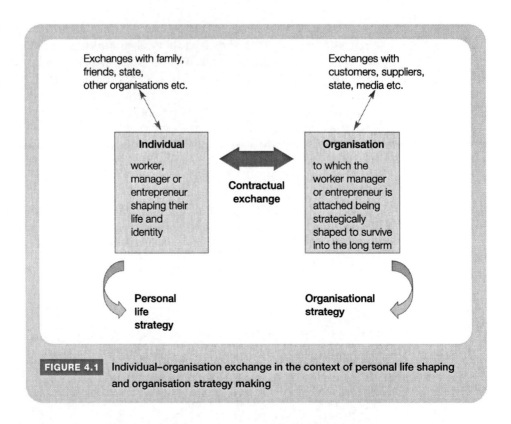

FIGURE 4.1 Individual–organisation exchange in the context of personal life shaping and organisation strategy making

taken forward into the future, through processes of economic, political and social exchange. These exchanges were managed by Peter to ensure that the resources of effort, support, accommodation and so on, needed by the organisation to survive and continue into the long term, were obtained from employees, politicians, police officers, landlords and the rest. He did all this in a way that shaped and expressed his own life and identity at the same time as it shaped the enterprise he was running. And we will see similarly striking evidence of this type of interaction between individual's life-shaping efforts and the strategic managing of a guitar-making firm in Case 9.4 (p. 388) where the entrepreneurial individuals who created a business confront, at the same time, questions about where they are going with their personal lives and questions about the future of the Strath Guitars. In this case the two are very tightly interrelated indeed.

The focus of the present chapter is not so much on the organisational shaping side of the picture presented in Figure 4.1 but on the exchange that occurs between workers and organisations generally. Although we are focusing on one side of the picture, it is vital to recognise that this exchange would not come into being were it not playing a part in the other side of the picture. Organisations, in principle at least, do not pay and otherwise reward people for involvement that has no significance for the strategic shaping of the enterprise as a whole.

Implicit contracts and orientations to work

Our main concern for the present is with the exchange that occurs between organisations and the people working in organisations. This exchange is identified in Figure 4.1 as one of contractual exchange. There is a trade, a 'deal' at the heart of the exchange relationship. And much of this contract is implicit. The normal way for people in a modern society to join a work organisation is to enter into an exchange with that organisation whereby they trade their application of skills and capabilities for a bundle of 'rewards' including cash, security, status, work satisfaction, opportunity for advancement and so on. Certain elements of this exchange are formally agreed and a very limited proportion of it is written in a formal contract of employment or perhaps a more short-term formal contract of engagement. However, the bulk of the 'understanding' that comes about between the employer and the worker is unwritten and is, in large part, unstated. The concept of implicit contract first started to be used (Levinson *et al.*, 1966) at about the same time as the work orientation concept, to which we shall shortly connect it, and is related to the concepts of *effort bargain* (Behrend, 1957, Baldamus, 1961) and *psychological contract* (Schein, 1978). (See also Further Reading on work orientations, implicit and psychological contracts, p. 160.)

Implicit contract   *Concept*

The tacit agreement between an employing organisation and the employed individual about what the employee will 'put in' to the job and the rewards and benefits for which this will be exchanged.

The implicit contract is clearly a relational matter. It is an exchange between an individual who is seeking employment as part of the way they are strategically shaping their lives to take them into the future and an employer who requires their services to shape its activities to take it into the future. It takes the form of a set of understandings negotiated between the employee and the employer, much of which is unlikely to have been explicitly stated, let alone written into a formal contract. There will be unstated understandings about such matters as how long the job is likely to last, what sort of career advancement might be available or how much overtime can be earned. Inferences will be made about how willing the employee will be to take orders from managers and how adaptable the employee will be if organisational circumstances change. What all of this means is that the employment relationship is a highly ambiguous one. It is also a potentially fragile one, given the very different power positions of the employee, on the one hand, and the employer on the other (an observation central to Marx's classic critique of class relations in capitalist societies).

As the individual approaches the organisation to seek work, they take into the potential relationship more than just the skills and working capacities that they possess. As the strategic exchange perspective highlights, the individual also takes with them an identity and a biography as well as various values and feelings or emotions about the world. The human being approaching engagement with the organisation is a whole human being, not just a human resource. But, as they approach an organisation, many of these aspects of their lives and identities will, in the light of their particular life circumstances at the time, inform a particular meaning which they attach to the work and the job they are going into: a *work orientation* (or 'orientation to work').

Work orientation   *Concept*

The meaning individuals attach to their work which predisposes them both to think and act in particular ways with regard to that work. There is an *initial orientation* at the point of entry to work and this is liable to change as circumstances and interests change within the continuing employment relationship.

At the stage of approaching engagement with the organisation we can refer to an initial orientation to work, in recognition of the fact that it is liable to develop and change once they have joined the organisation. The concept of orientation to work has its origins in sociological studies that were carried out in the 1960s in Britain. Goldthorpe, Lockwood and their colleagues (1968) developed the concept as they recognised the inadequacy of need-based motivational analyses for understanding the groups of employees that they studied. The concept of work orientation was seen as a more realistic tool for analysing what employees were seeking when they took certain jobs. The researchers argued that to understand the way different groups of workers behaved one should examine what those workers' jobs meant to them and what calculated choices they were making when entering that particular employment. Some people had an orientation to work that caused them to seek jobs which offered promotional opportunities or the opportunities to apply manual skills, for example, while others sought simply to maximise the money they could earn and *discounted* opportunities, say, for job interest or career advancement. Clearly these choices were made in the light of the abilities and aptitudes which people possessed as well as their value preferences. Most famously the study showed that many of the people working in the car assembly factory had chosen this work to maximise the income they could then spend on their families. And this meant forgoing the potentially more satisfying, but lower paid, work that they could have taken, should they have so chosen.

A way of linking the concepts of work orientation and implicit contract, as well as identifying some of the elements of the employment bargain is suggested in Figure 4.2. This recognises that the individual's 'understood deal' or *perceived implicit contract* is at the centre of their work orientation. It does not exist 'in the head' of the worker in isolation from their relationship with the employer but it does play a key part in how they *enact* their work roles and their

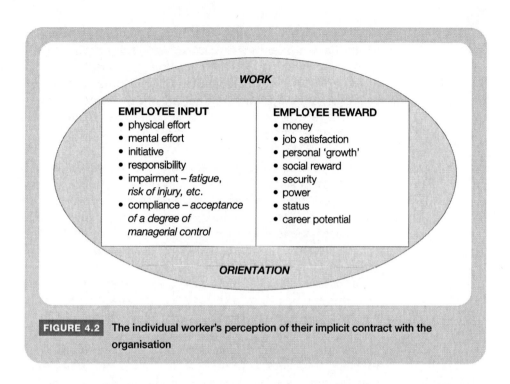

WORK

EMPLOYEE INPUT	**EMPLOYEE REWARD**
• physical effort	• money
• mental effort	• job satisfaction
• initiative	• personal 'growth'
• responsibility	• social reward
• impairment – *fatigue,*	• security
risk of injury, etc.	• power
• compliance – *acceptance*	• status
of a degree of	• career potential
managerial control	

ORIENTATION

FIGURE 4.2   The individual worker's perception of their implicit contract with the organisation

relationships with the managers in the employing organisation. Every employed individual, in the light of their current circumstances, their self-identities, life projects and the rest, has a notion of what they are exchanging with the employer: what mix of *inputs* of physical and mental efforts, the taking of responsibility, willingness to take risks of accident, stress and acceptance of managerial control is being traded with the employer for a particular mix of money, job satisfaction, social reward (satisfaction of serving the community, say), employment security, status, and opportunity to wield power, develop skills and advance a career.

This way of looking at people's work meanings and behaviours takes us a long way from the old-fashioned debates about whether people generally 'go to work mainly for the money' or seek employment for some other reason. Such 'either–or' thinking is simple-minded and of little value in understanding either work behaviour generally or the behaviour of particular groups of worker. In practice, every one of us has our own bundle of expectations and wants that we take into the strategic exchange we make with an employing organisation. There may be times in the life of each of us when we prioritise, say, money over job interest or security over high pay. But such a situation is recognised in this process-relational focus on orientations and implicit contracts as something which is particular to a particular person at a particular time and in particular circumstances. This is not to say that the concept cannot, to a certain extent, also be applied to groups, however.

A pattern of similar orientations may be seen across groups of employees who are similarly placed in the organisation or have come to the organisation from similar situations. It would tend to be the case that highly qualified senior staff would have different orientations, as a group, from unskilled and temporary manual workers, say. And it is possible that a different pattern of orientation might be found amongst people coming from one ethnic grouping, age or gender group rather than another, within the same organisational area of activity. Clearly, the cultural or age-group expectations of different groups of employees will vary, as will the bargaining strength which different types of prospective employee will take into their negotiation of an implicit contract – these varying with the skills, competencies or experiences they have to 'trade'. And, in circumstances where there is a formal trade union or other group representation, the bargaining over some aspects of the contract of employment will actually take place collectively. Nevertheless, even where there are clear patterns of orientation across groups of organisational members, it is necessary to recognise the variations that occur between individuals, albeit within these group patterns.

To understand any individual's or group's work behaviour we have to look at how they are predisposed to act in certain ways in the light of their orientation at that time and their perception of the deal they are making with the employer. We have to consider how they *enact* their role within the organisation, in other words. This, however, has to be set in the context of the employees' lives before they enter the organisation. We can see the importance of this in the case of Ravi Barr and how he came to be in the management job that he now does, by looking at the *initial orientation* which he brought to his present employing organisation. To look at processes of work entry and 'occupational choice', as it has traditionally been called, in the process-relational way, which a focus on work orientation involves, means once again turning away from the kind of *serial thinking* which was criticised in the previous chapter. Orthodox thinking tends to see the process of work entry as one in which we develop our interests, values and aptitudes as we grow up and go through education and then make a *choice* of occupation or career to fit this. Thus 'choice' precedes entry into a job or occupation. But, in practice, it does not work as simply as this, as Ravi Barr's story illustrates. What is the outcome of choice and what is adventitious, or a matter of circumstance and chance, is far from straightforward when we look at how people come into the sort of work we find them in at any point in their lives, in practice.

Activity 4.1

Read the conversation with Ravi Barr in Case 4.1 and consider the following questions:

- To what extent did Ravi 'choose' his career? Did he 'make a choice' of career and then enter it. Or did he 'find himself' in a job and then give this the rationale of a choice? Or was it a combination of these two?

- How has Ravi's work orientation changed over time, from the work he did in the family business, to the part-time jobs he took as a student, to the jobs he has done in the organisation he joined when he left school?

- How has Ravi 'managed' his identity? Because he has lived 'between two cultures', as he puts it, he is especially conscious of how identity is not a 'given' or fixed thing.

Ravi Barr gets oriented
Case 4.1

Tell me how you came to be a human resources manager, Ravi?

It was pure accident really. I was working as a supervisor in one of our shops, a job which I took when I got chucked out of university in my second year. I had always liked playing with computers, would you believe, and when a job came up in the home electrics department, as it was then called, I jumped at the chance. They said they wanted someone to build up that side of the department's business and I thought this would suit me. In fact it built up quite fast and I was soon spending a lot of my time recruiting new staff and training people on the computing side of things. I was training myself as I went along but I persuaded the general store manager that I was much more expert than I really was. The consequence of this was that he promoted me to a store-wide training job, getting managers and supervisors across the departments up to speed with computing. This went so well that when a personnel officer's job came up, I got it and then when the top human resources job become vacant I chose to go for that. I found I enjoyed the status I was building up and I liked the power that went with it. So here I am.

But you said, a moment ago, that it is 'pure accident' that you are in this job. And a few breaths later, you are telling me how you 'chose' to apply for the job. Can you explain this seeming contradiction to me?

Sorry about that. I suppose what was in my mind is that I originally wanted a career in marketing. This is what I hoped to specialise in on my degree course. So it's a sort of accident that I am now firmly in an HR career. I suppose that, on the other hand, there is consistency in that I am in a managerial sort of career. I wanted something that would give me seniority in an organisation – although I never thought of retailing as the industry I would end up in. And it is true that I enjoyed the human resources module I did in the second year at university – even if I failed it like all the others because I was enjoying myself too much pubbing and clubbing to do any academic work.

So why did you take the risk of not getting into a managerial career by not working at university?

Believe me, that is something I thought hard about at the time. In part, it was me sorting out who I was. You see my parents are in retailing and I was brought up to be a 'good hard-working Indian boy' who would eventually run the family business. And through my school years I accepted this. Well I more or less did. I worked enthusiastically in the family business whenever I had got my homework out of the way. I simply fitted into the business, like my older brothers, and did whatever my father asked me, whether it was delivering orders or sorting out the invoices. I didn't think of myself as cheap family labour. At home I was their dutiful Indian boy. At school I played that down and was just 'one of the lads' who were particularly interested in computers and computer games. Some of that group were Asian, others weren't. And it didn't matter. Asian identity was something for home. I was just another of the 'computer boys' at school. I sort of shifted my identity about across the two cultures I lived in. But I didn't really think about it at the time. I only started to think about all of this when I was at university. It was when I came home on the first vacation and found that I was expected to carry on the same as before. I started to see myself then as cheap family labour. I began to resent this and I got more and more awkward with my father and brothers – doing the minimum amount of work and refusing to take any kind of initiative at all. This all ended up in a big row and for the next few vacations I got work near the university, refusing to go home. I resolved never to have anything to do with retailing again. Apart from that, I did any work I could get, my main concern being to earn as much money as I could as fast as possible. I did labouring, worked in bars. I even did some horrible work in a chicken factory.

You just worked for money?

Exactly. The work was a means to an end.

And the end was?

Having a good time. And the money I made enabled me to carry on partying in term time too. I was sort of shaking off all those years of being the quiet conscientious boy. And I was also refusing the plan my parents had for me, as the first one in our family to go to university and, hence, the one who would eventually run the business (something I knew my elder brothers really resented).

But now you are a senior manager in a retailing business.

Funny isn't it? I am very career oriented now. I am making sure that I am learning about every aspect of this business so that I can eventually be a chief executive of a large retailing outfit. My parents have now accepted that I do not want to work in the family business. I think they are proud of what I have achieved and I suppose I want them to be even more proud of me when I really get to the top. My wife, who comes from a similar background, thinks similarly about her career as an accountant. I think my marriage, in fact, has been an important factor in my approach to career. Her family wanted to arrange a marriage for her and she had to fight them to marry me. So we have both had to make our way, and establish who we are, by sort of escaping from our families. So we are both making careers away from the Asian community. But, as we have both realised, we are still very much the products of the community and families that, in part, we turned away from. Yes, funny, isn't it. There are so many reasons for what you do, aren't there?

Ravi Barr's closing words rather neatly summarise the story he has told. But what is really interesting about his story is not just the large number, or even the variety, of the factors that have shaped his life and career. It is also the fascinating way that they interact with each other – home factors with work factors, family pressures with school priorities, ethnic influences with individual assertiveness, and so on. So complex is this interplay, in fact, that Ravi finds himself, rather paradoxically, talking of his career 'choices' since leaving university in terms of 'accident' one minute and 'choice' the next. This is not unusual when one interviews people about their work histories. The work biographies of most of us involve a complex interplay of choice and chance factors and when we report them to others we find ourselves, at certain points, drawing on all those stories in our culture which have the theme, 'Isn't it strange what things happen to people in life?'. And at other points in the narratives or biographies we present to people interviewing us, we draw on the discursive resource of the 'rational man or woman' who carefully plans a career to make the best use of their talents in the labour market. The 'either–or' dualism of choice *or* chance is not in fact helpful to understanding people's biographies. The two aspects of the duality do, however, interact with each other in different ways in different people's biographies. As we shall see in Chapter 10 (p. 442), the way we present that biography to employers or potential employers can have important consequences for recruitment and promotional decisions made by employers.

Ravi Barr's orientation to work is clearly tied up with his family and his ethnic background and with the process of managing his identity. He is making choices about his own life but those choices are very much made in the context of the structural situations in which he has found himself – whether these be the family and community structures into which he was born, or the structure of opportunities he later found himself in within the company for which he is now working. In different work situations in which he has found himself he has made different *implicit contracts* with the people employing him. When he first worked in the family firm he exchanged hard work and a willingness to be flexible for personal security and the social reward of belonging to a family and a community. Once he had left home and he felt that this reward was not what he was seeking, he was less willing to 'put in' so much effort or, as he points out, show so much initiative. The orientation to work and the implicit contract had changed, albeit with the same person and the same work situation. Ravi's changing concept of who he was and what he wanted from life led to a change in his work orientation. And when he sought employment while at university he thought of it in terms of a very simple trade – he wanted to maximise the money he could earn.

After the shock of having to leave university, Ravi approached his employment in the department store with a different kind of orientation. He was clearly willing to put more into that job than he had into the temporary jobs. And one of the rewards which was important in his understanding of the implicit contract with the company was the opportunity to work with computers. We can see then his orientation shifting further as he discovered his abilities in recruiting and training people. The ambition which then developed meant that the 'career potential' element of the reward side of Figure 4.2 was becoming more salient. Undoubtedly it was not replacing an interest in monetary reward, because we can presume that this was increasing at the same time, as were the rewards of status and power. We can see him trading a particular bundle of work inputs for a particular bundle of rewards. And this exchange is not just influenced by his relationship with the employing organisation. His current family life plays an important part in his emergent identity and his shifting work orientations. And this current family situation is itself related to his own and his wife's biographies. They are still working out their pasts as they work on the present and on their futures. Their exchanges with their present employers and with all the other people in their lives are indeed *strategic exchanges*. We each make strategic exchanges in our lives in our own ways.

Activity 4.2

Moving your attention away from Ravi Barr's story to your own, ask yourself the following questions.

- In what ways have both choice and chance played a part in your own unfolding work career or career ambitions?
- What different implicit contracts have you made in different work situations at various stages of your life? Use the employee input/employee reward boxes in Figure 4.2 to chart the

perceived 'trades' you made in different jobs you have done.

- To what extent have you ever changed your orientation to work (and, of course, the way you perceived your implicit contract) within the same job? If you wish to be prompted on this question, you may choose to give a quick initial glance at what Sacha Boath has to say about how 'people change at work' in Case 4.2.

Varying and changing work orientations in a corporate affairs department

Case 4.2

Yes, you will hear several of the managers here refer to me and my department as Sacha and the Seven Dwarves. As Director of Corporate Affairs, I am the only woman in the company's top team and they like to tease me about being tall and fair-haired. That's OK, I can handle the banter and I suppose being compared to the fairy-tale Snow White is not really uncomplimentary. I do get bothered sometimes, though, that they are rather diminishing my team by referring to them as dwarves. Only one of them is really a small person, even if they are all shorter than me. In fact some of them have actually 'grown' in the job you might say. I think it's really interesting how people can change at work. Let me tell you about them; 'Smithy' Smith, 'Biffy' Currie, 'Sniffy' Gerardo, 'Snippy' Spedale, 'Chippy' Bliss, 'Iffy' Humphries and 'Sparky' Learmonth, as the managers call them.

Smithy, Biffy and Sniffy are my three public relations officers. Biffy and Sniffy are amazing cases of people who have changed. When I came here I was told they were simply miserable types. It was also said that they both had 'chips on their shoulders' because they had lost their jobs when the second of the town's papers closed down. They felt they were demeaning themselves by working in public relations. Both were well on the way to becoming alcoholics and they ruined their marriages, largely because of the drink. However, about a year ago there was this amazing change. In part, it was down to my giving them the most almighty shouting at – 'Shape up or ship out' is what I basically said. But it was also to do with some kind of conversion experience they had, as our Managing Director put it. They had both joined Alcoholics Anonymous and, at the same time, they discovered the delights of line dancing. Somehow the smartening up that went on with getting off the booze and their meeting women at the dancing sessions translated into their work. It was amazing. Almost overnight they changed from lazy and uninspired individuals who were in danger of letting the company down to smart and reliable characters who I can happily allow to speak for the company. Smithy, on the other hand, is somebody I increasingly can't trust. In her case, the change seems to have come about after moving in with a new partner, as opposed to losing a partner. She is my languages person and used to be brilliant at dealing with almost any issue where we needed to deal with Europe. It seems that her bloke has been getting resentful about her travelling abroad for us and this has led to her taking it out on all of us in the office. She's managed not to go abroad for six months now and the other day she rushed out of the office screaming, 'Oh, sod the

French'. One of my best people has become a complete liability for reasons which, it seems, have nothing to do with the company.

Changes at work do seem to be the source of the changes we've seen with Snippy, however. Her job is to monitor press coverage. She used to be the life and soul of the office. She would sit over there, snipping away at her press cuttings and joking with everybody who came into the office. But since we've rearranged the office and her desk is less central to what is going on, she seems to have completely dropped her role as the office wit. I shall have to rethink the office layout, I think. But, for some reason, she's recently taken up smoking and keeps disappearing to the smoking room across the road to have a cigarette. In the past, I could have spoken to her about that, but the way she is just now would make that difficult.

In some ways Snippy's social role in the office has been taken on by Iffy. She is my secretary, sorry PA – personal assistant. She used to be a total misery. She was a graduate trainee with the company. She said she didn't mind taking on a 'graduate secretary' role but she resented the fact that it was only female graduates who did that. They called her Iffy because she was always saying things like, 'If a man were asked to do that, he'd refuse.' So what's made the difference? I don't really know. The job title change might be a factor, but I don't think it was that important. And it might be that she became aware that I was never going to ask her to make me coffee or go out to buy flowers for me to give to my mother on Mother's Day (something she says happened to her before I came). Actually, I think it is simply that she and I have become good friends. We do meet socially but, at work, we really enjoy working together. There's no doubt that I am 'the boss', as anyone will tell you ('the blonde Tsarina', Iffy called me the other day, when I stormed into the office generally threatening murder all round). The simple truth is that Iffy enjoys working with someone she gets on with, and that has led her to take on more and more tasks which she then finds she really enjoys.

I wish I could bring about a similar change in Sparky. He runs the computing and IT side of the department – our web site and all that. When he was here first I think he felt that he was a pioneer and that he understood things none of us had a clue about. He was a cheerful chap to have around – a really sparky character in fact. It seems now that everything has settled down and his work is more routine, he is a bit bored. Consequently he is not helping people as much as he should be. He's well paid though and I think that he has got himself locked in here by the salary. He has taken on a mortgage on a new house recently and doesn't want to risk a job change. He's pretty secure too, given the relevance of his skills to our work. I can't see what promotional opportunities we can offer to 'turn him back on'. I'll have to look for some exciting new project.

Chippy is someone for whom everything is a new project. I have rarely seen anyone so positive about his job. He came to us from the maintenance department who 'redeployed' him when that operation was downsized. His resentment of moving into here was palpable. He thought he was simply going to be some sort of odd job man who would only occasionally use his carpentry skills when we needed a display preparing. However, once he realised that he could make the job an important one, by seeking opportunities to make exhibition stands and by being the key person at out-of-company presentations, he really changed. He regularly travels abroad now – which he had never done before, and I often think he has developed better public relations skills than some of the professionals. The job is very much what he has chosen to make it. After that first miserable couple of weeks here he just seemed to decide, 'Right, let's make something of this'. The MD – ever the joker himself – actually asked me the other day, 'Is that Chippy of yours still a chirpy chappy?'. Indeed he is.

These brief portraits painted by one manager of the staff in her department very effectively illustrate the foolishness of looking at the demeanour or the behaviour of any given person at work and concluding, 'Aha, that is the sort of person they are'. Although there will be certain consistencies which could be perceived over time in the lives and identities of each of these individuals, the orthodox psychology categories of 'personality type' hardly seem relevant to the complexities of what is going on in these seven lives and to the work orientations of 'Smithy' Smith, 'Biffy' Currie, 'Sniffy' Gerardo, 'Snippy' Spedale, 'Chippy' Bliss,' Iffy' Humphries and 'Sparky' Learmonth. The concepts of emergent identity, work orientation and implicit contract are far more helpful than any concept of personality type.

Activity 4.3

Carefully examine each of the individuals that Sacha Boath talks about and, using the model in Figure 4.2:

- note what factors appear to have led to their changed orientations;
- given that Sacha has only a partial picture of what has happened in each case, speculate about what other kinds of factor might also have

come into play (i.e. things you might 'look into' if you were trying to do a research project on the orientations of people in this Corporate Affairs – or 'public relations' – department);

- try to think of any examples of people, other than yourself, whose work orientations appear to have changed during their employment within a particular job.

A complex multiplicity of factors seems to be relevant to the workplace identities and the work orientations of each of these people. Numerous factors influence how they see the implicit contract they have with their employer. Sacha Boath has clearly tried hard to understand each of these people and, indeed, she gets close to analysing how they might perceive the implicit contracts they have with her and the company. Notice, for example, the way in which she analyses how Sparky might be thinking about the rewards he is getting from the company: he has got security and good pay but he is not getting any intrinsic rewards or fulfilment from the job itself. He is bored. This might be compensated for by promotional opportunities, but that is not really a possibility. Sacha is therefore considering what she might do to give him more excitement in the job. She is not getting the work 'inputs' she wants, given what rewards she is offering. She therefore needs to act to get a better trade. And this takes us into that area of management often called 'motivation' and which, in Chapter 8 (pp. 315–24), we will be reconceptualising as a process in which managers manipulate the perceived implicit contracts of workers.

For the present, however, we simply want to give full recognition to the extent to which a person's identity is always *emergent*, their work orientation is always liable to change and their involvement at work has to be seen in the context of the strategic exchanges which are going on in their lives and biographies as a whole. And if we are going to look at people in this holistic way, then we have to recognise that they do not simply go to work to act as task-completing biological machines. The 'whole person' goes to work, as we recognised earlier.

And that means that they approach the organisation with feelings, preferences, beliefs and the whole range of human vulnerabilities, as well as the skills, aptitudes and willingness to follow instructions that the employing organisation is buying from them.

Feelings, emotions and the experience of stress

Work organisations are parts of an institutional pattern which has developed at a very recent stage in the overall evolution and history of the human species. This pattern is associated with *modernism* which, as we saw in Chapter 2 (p. 36), involves a concerted attempt to apply rational thinking to human activities and institutions in order to increase humans' control over their circumstances. The principles of *reason* and of *control* are thus central to the work of trying to shape modern organisations and, as we established earlier, the form which this reason takes is that of 'instrumental rationality', whereby calculated choices are made to find the best means for achieving given ends. People in modern organisations are not meant to perform work tasks in the way that they *feel* like doing at a particular moment. They are not meant to carry out tasks in a particular way because they *guess* that this is how to do it. And they are not meant to do a job in a particular way because that is the *traditional* way in which it has always been done. To act in these ways is to go against the principles of carefully, or scientifically, calculating the most efficient way of carrying out work tasks.

Max Weber, the key theorist of these matters, pointed out that this would mean that if modern organisations or 'bureaucracies' were to exist in a pure form, they would have no place for 'love, hatred and all purely personal, irrational and emotional elements which escape calculation' (Weber, 1978, p. 975). The key phrase here is 'which escape calculation'. Weber was identifying here the aspirations of those building and leading the large organisations of the modernising world and, as Albrow (1997) points out (in contradicting a common misreading of Weber), Weber was well aware that they were not seeking to *exclude* an emotional or affective dimension from organisational life. We might say that what they were seeking were ways of *harnessing* the 'humanness' and the emotional involvement of human labour. This was indeed the logic of the attention given to 'informal' aspects of organisational functioning in those classic 1930s studies by Roethlisberger and Dickson and by Barnard, which we looked at in Chapter 2 (pp. 61–2). Managers should pay heed to the 'sentiments' of workers in shaping factory activities, argued the former, while the latter put the management of 'informal activities' at the centre of the executive's job.

In effect, Barnard was recognising the need of organisational managers to appeal to employees' hearts and sentiments as well as to their minds. His social science influenced analysis of all of this, and the advocacy which follows from it, can itself be seen as part of what Weber recognised as a trend not to allow 'emotional elements' to 'escape calculation'. Emotions are all very well in the modern work organisation, in this view, but they must be kept under control and, wherever possible, harnessed to the ends being pursued by the organisation's controllers. Hatred for an enemy would probably be a managerially desirable emotion to be felt by soldiers in a modern army during a war. And passion for the product being sold by a commercial enterprise could be very welcome to those in charge of that enterprise. However, if either of these got 'out of hand' – beyond calculation and control – the soldiers might disastrously run amok and the over-passionate sales person might frighten away some of their customers.

It has been recognised in recent years that the bulk of management and organisational texts attend too little to the emotional side of organisational life and work involvement (see Further Reading on emotions and work, pp. 160–1). Where it is given recognition in standard texts, it is dealt with in an indirect, and often rather 'bloodless' way. Sometimes it is seen as a dimension of gaining employee compliance – rewarding people with *self-actualisation* or overcoming their *resistance to change* for example. At other times it becomes pertinent because of an interest in overcoming tendencies of individuals to break down through *stress* or the inclination of certain groups overenthusiastically to pursue *grievances*.

We can usefully reflect on why there has been little direct attention to the emotional aspects of working lives. The subjective states of the individuals whose feelings and emotions make up the 'emotional side of organisational life' are not easy to understand and, partly as a result of the ambiguity and unpredictability that such matters involve, people can readily become quite uncomfortable when trying to address them. It might also be the case that when we are working as researchers, or as thoughtful managers, in specific organisational situations, we feel uncomfortable about invading the privacy of the people we come across. We might ask whether we have the right to enquire too deeply into the emotional states and the private feelings of the people we meet in work situations. This would be a proper ethical question to ask. Yet if we want to understand the full complexities of organising and managing work, we need to attend to matters of feeling and emotion in the workplace. The ethnographic style of research, in which the researcher gets closely involved with the people living or working in the particular setting being studied, enables such factors to be looked at. An ethnographic episode which demonstrates the type of insight that can be gained in this way is that of Ken Steary's collision with his office desk (Case 4.3). At this stage we have not formally conceptualised the issues that arise in this broad area of the 'emotions and feelings'. This is deliberate. We will look at some events occurring in Ken Steary's hotel and then consider how we might bring some conceptual rigour to bear on them.

Activity 4.4

Read the researcher's conversation with Ken Steary in Case 4.3. Then:

- list all of the ways in which issues of emotion and feeling come into these events;

- identify any way in which those running this hotel organisation – represented in this story by the regional manager – appear to have taken account of the emotional dimension of what goes on in hotels.

Ken Steary laughs, cries and falls over   Case 4.3

You don't look good, Ken.

I don't feel good, mate.

You look altogether stressed.

Stress is supposed to be a mental thing, isn't it? Well, you see this black eye. That's stress for you. It's physical and it hurts. And I know what you think. You think that I am going to tell you that I got so stressed last night trying to manage this bloody hotel that I got into a fight with a customer. Well that isn't what happened.

Did a member of staff thump you, then?

No. I didn't get into a fight with a member of staff. It was my office desk what did it.

I see.

No you don't. I was at the end of my tether last night, stressed up, tired out and on the point of laughing and crying at the same time. But I am the manager and I am meant to be in control. I can neither afford to let the staff see me crack up nor let the hotel guests see me fall apart. So I went up to my office and drank myself stupid. And then I fell over, catching my eye on the corner of the desk. I thought I was doing really well, keeping up the façade of the man who is always in control – dealing with my pathetic grief in private. And now I've got to explain to everybody how I got the black eye. I've already told three different stories to explain it away. I am really losing the plot.

OK, tell me the plot then. What is the real story?

The problems started yesterday with the visit from the Regional Manager. She comes round every month to look at 'the figures' with me and generally to keep me on my toes. I really hate her, the officious cow. She has a go at me for things that she couldn't do. She really likes to wind me up.

How do you mean?

Well, yesterday, I started off in a good mood. I was feeling good because I knew the figures were OK. Our occupancy figures have been really excellent, the bar and restaurant turnovers are on the up and up and the staff turnover figures are slightly down. I've even got the wages tightly under control. But guess what? Did they thank me? Did they congratulate me? Did they hell. No, what I got from madam was, 'Region are perturbed about some complaints they have received.' They had got a couple of complaints about the sullen behaviour of my reception staff. I'd like to see her try to deal with a problem like that.

You recognise that this is a problem, then. I must admit that I was put off earlier by the rather surly manner of one of your barmen. I felt most unwelcome and would have walked out if I hadn't been meeting you.

Don't you start. I thought you were my friend. But, yes, you are right. This is an issue that has been bothering me. I just didn't like the idea of my bosses sitting around their boardroom table tut tutting about poor old Ken Steary not being able to make his staff smile at the punters. And that cow of a regional manager wouldn't be able to make a drunk on his honeymoon smile. So who is she to lecture me?

But you accept that there is a problem?

Oh yes. And I could do with some help handling it. But who do I turn to? I am the boss here. And you can get very lonely, even in a big hotel full of people like this one was last night. I've got to show a smiling face to the world and my staff know damn well that they need to do the same. Even on my way up to my office last night I smiled at a grumpy guest who refused help with his suitcase and then complained that the steps on the stairs were too steep. 'What's wrong with using the lift, you stupid bastard?', I said under my breath as I felt my skin burning and my colour rising. But my expression was a picture of genuine sympathy. And since I've had this black eye, I have smiled a hundred times at one member of staff and one hotel guest after another.

But you can't get all of your staff to act in this way?

Most will, they know their jobs depend on the hotel doing well and that it won't do well if the guests are not treated hospitably. That doesn't seem unreasonable. And they have chosen to work in the hospitality industry, for God's sake. They are paid to be hospitable.

But are they paid to be actors?

Would you like a black eye too?

Matters of feeling and emotion come into this story from the beginning. One of the first things Ken says is that he does not *feel* good. He talks about how his black eye 'hurts' – suggesting that the abstract phenomenon he calls 'stress', itself 'hurts'. His reference to his hotel as 'this bloody hotel' is clearly emotionally loaded, as is his worry that one might infer that he had fought with a customer. He loads his account of his feelings the previous evening with terms like 'the end of my tether', 'tired out', 'crack up', 'fall apart', 'drank myself stupid', 'pathetic grief' and 'losing the plot'. The description of his 'laughing and crying at the same time' involves the use of a discursive resource commonly used in the wider culture to give a picture of somebody who is so out of control that they have gone beyond the cultural norm of crying to express sadness and laughing to express happiness. He talks of hating the Regional Manager and, twice, uses another common discursive resource which is applied to express strong antipathy to a woman, as does his ironic use of the term 'madam'. Positive feelings are expressed when Ken looks back to earlier the previous day when he 'felt good' and was, it seems, feeling that he deserved thanks and congratulations. These are aspects of the sort of reciprocity we referred to in Chapter 3 when discussing culture and social exchange (p. 81). His looking for these endorsements and the manager failing to provide them reveal significant *relational* aspects of the emotional temperature which built up for Ken. Also, the Regional Manager's use of language in saying that the 'region is perturbed' is interesting. She is mystifying exactly who is worried by *personifying* 'Region' (see above p. 50), something which, if Ken is reporting her verbatim, we might take to be slightly provocative. It implies that some power greater than any nameable human individual is looking down upon the insignificant figure of Mr Steary. The formality of the word 'perturbed' rather than the more obvious 'worried' has been taken by Ken, we can infer, as a further attempt to 'wind him up'.

The alleged 'sullenness' of the reception staff, and the researcher's mention of the 'surly manner' of a bar worker, are clearly matters of emotional interpretation made by customers of the apparent emotional state of these hotel employees. The researcher speaks of *feeling* unwelcome and Ken goes on in the conversation to paint a picture of a very emotional state he was in the previous night and the equally emotional state he is in at present with the use of one emotionally loaded expression after the other. He also makes a bitter joke about the Regional Manager's demeanour, one that has all sorts of sexual and sexist undertones (couldn't 'make a drunk on his honeymoon smile') and he even threatens the researcher with violence, even though (as it happened) he says it with a smile on his face, echoing back to the pathos of the earlier 'I thought you were my friend'.

This episode is packed with emotionality and it could be argued that an exaggerated picture of the role that feelings play in organisational life is being painted by the selection of an episode in which there has been a crisis in the life of one particular individual. There is some truth in this. But it can be argued that critical events like this simply reveal factors and issues that are present all the time but only come fully to the surface when circumstances arise in which the normal controls of social life are weakened and conventional courtesies are strained. For example, if the Regional Manager had been polite to Ken and thanked him for his good work before diplomatically raising the question of the customer complaints, there would still be emotional factors in play. The Regional Manager would have been taking Ken's feelings into account and he might have 'felt good' about being thanked and he might have appreciated the senior person's 'sharing' a managerial problem with him. This kind of social exchange process and the maintenance of reciprocity is so common or 'normal' in social and organisational life that we tend not to be consciously aware of it. It is when there is some breakdown in it that the presence of feelings and emotions in the work context become starkly apparent. They are, however, never absent.

The emotional issues raised by Ken Steary's tale go beyond ones of staff relationships. The issue that triggered Ken's distressing experience was one of how the organisation, as a business, relates to its customers. It does not apparently stay in business simply by selling food and renting beds to customers. It provides *hospitality* to its *guests*. The very tasks which are done 'in the organisation's name' (above p. 58) are ones with a strong emotional dimension. Ken is fully aware of this. And one can reasonably infer from his outburst, 'they have chosen to work in the hospitality industry, for God's sake', that a key source of frustration to him is the difficulty he is having in getting some of the staff to *engage emotionally* with their work, by acting in a friendly and smiling way towards 'guests'. We notice that he stresses how the Regional Manager would be unable do this. And we note that he emphasises how he is willing to 'make his face a picture of genuine sympathy', even when he is in a bad mood and is provoked by a 'stupid bastard' and 'grumpy guest'. A concept which we will use to look at the issues that arise here is that of *emotional labour*. But, before we can properly deploy that concept, we need to conceptualise the more general phenomena of emotion and feeling.

It has been possible in the above analysis to refer in a broad way to 'feelings and emotions' as if they were more or less the same thing. This is what we tend to do in everyday life. We talk about 'feeling happy' on one occasion, for example, and refer to the 'emotion' of happiness on another. It has been normal, in the history of human reflection, to link feelings and emotions. So why should we consider splitting them – distinguishing between the two? The only justification for doing this would be the pragmatist's one of developing our conceptual tools to enable us to analyse something more effectively than we would otherwise do, with a view to better informing our subsequent practices. On these grounds, it is useful to conceptualise feelings and emotions as separate, but closely linked, phenomena.

Emotions and feelings	Concept

Feelings are sensations felt bodily which relate to a psychological state. *Emotions* are the way these sensations are made sense of with reference to culture, either privately or socially.

It is helpful to follow Fineman in separating *feelings* – the 'subjective experience' in which 'we are aware "in" ourselves of some bodily state, peturbation, or more diffuse psychological change' (Fineman, 1999, p. 546) from the more culturally mediated *emotions* with which they are associated. Fineman, however, treats emotions as *displays* of these feelings. He does this to enable him to distinguish between, say, the way someone might express the *emotion* of anger in a situation, by shouting and raging, while actually *feeling* pleasure in what they are doing. There is clearly an important distinction to be made here (to understand situations like the one Ken Steary was in when he *felt* angry with the grumpy customer while he *displayed* sympathy). However, it is felt more analytically useful here to say that the *feeling* was the physical sensation Ken describes when he says 'I felt my skin burning and my colour beginning to rise'. And the *emotion* is the cultural label of 'anger' that might be attached to this feeling when we try to make sense of it. The two are closely linked but the 'animal' sensation that Ken experienced does not automatically read across to the cultural interpretation of 'anger'. Ken himself, or somebody else hearing about his experience, might choose to interpret or 'construct' that experience as one of 'going mad', 'being disgusted', 'getting furious' or 'being appalled'.

The distinction between feeling and emotion, then, is a way of taking account of both the 'animal' and the 'cultural' aspects of our natures – our humanity. As we said earlier, with regard to instincts (pp. 81–2), everything in the human being, is culturally mediated. Animal 'things' are 'there in us', as indeed our body is ontologically 'there'. But they are always subject to processes of social construction, to cultural interpretation, to enactment. The situation is not as simple as, say, good *feelings* first being 'there', or being 'experienced', and then being *enacted* in a particular way as happiness, joy, contentment or whatever. To assume this is again to fall into the trap of the 'linear' type of psychology we rejected in the previous chapter (pp. 87–8). It might be possible, for example, for one to start off sad and then, with the cultural notion of happiness in mind, to lie back on a pile of comfortable cushions, smile to oneself and actually experience the sensation we label 'happiness'. It has been widely observed, in fact, that choosing to smile can make one 'feel happier' than one was before the smile appeared on our face.

We are getting ourselves involved here in matters which philosophers and psychologists have agonised over for centuries. Why should we trouble to engage with such matters? It is to sharpen our conceptual tool kit in order to come to terms with the issues that were raised in Ken Steary's story. If we are going to require people like Ken and his staff to perform in ways which involve emotional labour, then we need to understand the relationship between the feelings these people might have and the emotional face they are required to present to the world. What are we asking of people who we require to smile at – and 'make feel good' – hotel guests, airline passengers, hospital patients, shop customers and a multitude of other consumers of services in modern societies?

Emotional labour

Emotions and the way these are presented play a key part in all the exchanges we make with other human beings. We smile at a child to show our approval of its behaviour or we frown at a friend who fails to notice the new clothes we are wearing. This is an exchange, in the sense that we are suggesting certain emotions on our own part in order to elicit certain emotions in the other person, ones that will take the relationship forward in the way we wish it to go. This kind of emotional management, which characterises much of our private lives, is called *emotion work* by Hochschild (1985) and she contrasts it with *emotional labour*.

Emotional labour	Concept
An element of work activity in which the worker is required to display certain emotions in order to complete work tasks in the way required by an employer.	

Here, emotional work on the part of an organisational employee is carried out to further the interests of the employer who is buying their services. There is a close relationship between the emotion work which is a normal part of everybody's lives and emotional labour. In the workplace, one does 'emotion work' all the time, simply in order to relate to the other human beings with whom we come into contact. But this overlaps with those efforts that we feel obliged to make as part of our implicit contract with the employer. In dealing with other people at work we would generally be unaware of any tension between our 'natural' inclination to interact, say, in a warm and friendly way with colleagues or customers and what our employment entails. However, once our 'private self' (our self-identity as we are experiencing it at that moment) finds itself in some tension with our self as an 'organisational representative' (a manifestation of our social identity, as required of us by our employment) we are likely to experience discomfort. We tend, then, to become aware of that which we conceptualise as emotional labour. Such an awareness is reported by Ken Steary when he describes the friendly and sympathetic demeanour he presented to the grumpy guest. He felt obliged to behave in this way because of his understanding of his contract with the hotel company. As a hotel manager and a representative of the organisation he had to behave in this way. His private self, however, was silently addressing the customer as a 'stupid bastard'. He could not show this to the guest because to do so would be to break his implicit contract with the employer. And he believes some of his staff are doing precisely this. The reception staff who were complained of were forgetting, or ignoring, what Ken takes to be implicit in the agreement made between employees and employers in the *hospitality* industry: that employees should act hospitably.

A useful distinction that Hochschild makes when examining emotional labour is that between *surface acting* and *deep acting*. Ken Steary's behaviour was an example of surface acting, because he was aware that he was 'putting on a show'. He might be deceiving the guest, but he was not deceiving himself. With deep acting, the employee either 'works up' a feeling in themselves which fits with the emotion they are expressing in doing their job or, as Hochschild puts it, they train their imaginations to achieve the same effect. We see an example in some of the experiences of Cindy Sutor, a sex worker who is reflecting on her work and what it requires of her 'self'.

Activity 4.5

Cindy Sutor's work (Case 4.4) takes her towards the more extreme end of the 'emotional labour market'. Consider:

- how the concepts of *deep acting* and *surface acting* can be applied to Cindy's experiences;

- how the implicit contract she used to make with the clients or with the employer she now works for contains limits on what can be expected emotionally;

- having looked at this relatively extreme case of emotional labour, how many relatively 'normal' jobs can you think of which involve *emotional labour*;

- what elements of *emotional labour* there have been in any jobs you have done and to what extent (a) this involved deep and surface acting, (b) there were limits built into the implicit contract, as you perceived it, which helped in the managing of the emotional demands of the job.

Cindy sets the limits for emotional engagement in her work   Case 4.4

I have recently stopped working as a prostitute on my own account and I now do just five shifts a week for the sex phone line company. It pays less but it's safer. It's also different because I now just *talk* about what I actually used to have to *do*. But there are lots of similarities. In both kinds of work, you have got to protect your own idea of who you are. You must not sell your whole self. When I was working on the street I knew that I had to show a certain level of interest in the punter – but not too much. I'd say something like 'Come on, big boy', without really implying that I thought that he was a big boy. You train your clients to know what they are paying for. You show a certain amount of interest in the man, especially if you are hoping for repeat business, but what you don't do is show any kind of excitement and, certainly, absolutely no hint of passion. I'd demean myself if I let that happen. And if I felt myself getting interested I'd damn quickly shut that off. The only exception to this was when I got into the posh call girl game for a while. You get paid a lot more then. So you play it just a little more positively.

Working on the telephone line is really an acting job. You sometimes put on a sexy voice and tell the punter that you are dressed in a skimpy nightie. But, as you tell them this, you make sure you keep a blank face and you look down at the dirty old jeans you are wearing.

Sometimes, though, I get bored with this. If I then find myself talking to someone who sounds really nice I let myself imagine that he is someone that I would actually like to go out with. Then I close my eyes and let myself stop pretending. Sometimes I quite enjoy this, get genuinely excited even. It helps the shift go a bit faster. It's only daydreaming, though. But perhaps those punters do get a better deal – something more genuine. I doubt it though – a proportion of our calls are monitored by the management and I would not want that creep in the 'control room' to think I was giving more than I am being paid for.

As Cindy Sutor is engaged in activities which potentially have deep emotional significance yet which occur within a framework of instrumental economic transaction, she has to work hard to manage boundaries and to 'set limits'. The public or temporary social identity she is paid to adopt must not be allowed to take over her private self-identity. Such issues arise for workers in an increasing number and variety of occupations, ranging from the airline workers, to whose work Hochschild first applied the *emotional labour* concept, to sales staff, call centre workers, entertainers, medical workers, and the 'greeters' who welcome customers as they walk through the entrances of some supermarkets. The more work organisations attempt to develop internal cultures which follow the 'quality management' principles of treating fellow workers as 'internal customers', the more we will see a requirement for most employees to go beyond the 'emotion work' which is a normal and spontaneous part of all human exchange and to be monitored for the quality of the *emotional labour* they put in.

It might be argued that issues of this general kind have to be handled by all workers: protecting themselves from what has often been called the *alienation* of self or, in a more recent formulation, the 'corrosion of self' (Sennett, 1998). The notion of alienation is more a philosophical than a social scientific one and it adopts an *essentialist* view of the human individual, instead seeing 'humanness' *processually* as something which people 'work at' and 'achieve'. But the notion has played a major part in critiques of modern work institutions and the effects they have on the integrity of the human individual. It is consistent, however, with the process-relational recognition of the need of each human being to manage their identities. Identity has to be managed and a logic found or created which links people's self-identities and their social identities to keep them sane and capable of competently playing a part in social life.

Alienation	Concept
The destruction of the integrity of the human self – a splitting of one part of a person's 'being' from another.	

Cindy Sutor's management of identity involves a high degree of 'distancing' of her 'self' from her work and this means that much of her 'acting' is of a surface kind. However, she does talk of occasionally moving over into some 'deep acting' when she decides to use her imagination and let herself 'daydream'. But even that is circumscribed by the contractual setting in which she is operating – and by the constant reminder of this in the form of the monitoring manager in the 'control room'. Just as she did not want her prostitution clients to get more than they were paying for, she was not willing to exceed the 'inputs' she was making in her implicit contract with the phone line company. We can well imagine Ken Steary's unsmiling hotel workers in Case 4.3, in the same spirit, arguing that for the money they are paid they cannot be expected to put 'heart and soul' into their jobs. They cannot be expected to treat hotel guests in the way that they would treat guests in their own houses, any more than Cindy would treat her 'punters' as if they were lovers. We might not expect Ken, as a manager, to go along with such an argument. But if Ken were to point out that he always treats customers as if they were his personal guests, we can imagine his reception staff pointing out that Ken is much better rewarded than they are for continuously presenting a positive 'face' to customers. Implicit contracts are not only perceived differently by different parties to them. They are also frequently contested.

Stress, strain and distress

The stressed executive, falling apart under the strains of heavy responsibility, has been one of the clichés of modern life for some time. But this image is coming to be replaced by the one of employees of every kind afflicted with the pathology of *stress* in every corner of the pressured and increasingly competitive organisational world. We hear of people being 'off work with stress', in the same way that they might be off work with mumps or measles. But stress is not something that one 'has' in this way. The notion simply implies that someone is suffering in some way under the strains of their work situation to the extent that they are becoming unable to perform satisfactorily in that work. Stress is a reaction to circumstances and it can arise in situations other than work. A poor single parent with several energetic and demanding children could well find themselves approaching an emotional state where they no longer felt able to act as a parent is expected to act. A husband or wife, oppressed by the nature of their relationship with their spouse, could well find themselves emotionally unable to continue to act as a husband or wife is expected to behave. Similarly a teacher, office cleaner, social worker, factory worker or manager might reach a stage of emotional agitation within their work experiences in which they become incapable of fulfilling the tasks required of them.

Stress   *Concept*

A sense of distress arising because of pressures experienced in certain social or economic circumstances that render the sufferer emotionally, and sometimes physically, incapable of continuing to behave in the ways expected of them in those circumstances.

What characterises the state of being 'stressed', in work or elsewhere, is clearly being in a position where the person *feels* they cannot continue to perform as they are expected (see Further Reading on work and stress, p. 161). It is a subjective state – it is not just a matter of being incapable. Someone who found that they simply did not have the patience to look after children, that they were no longer attracted to their spouse or that they were no longer physically strong enough to continue in their current job could *rationally decide* to abandon their children, leave their spouse or resign from their job. Stress – as the etymology of the word suggests – implies something oppressing, pressurising or 'drawing tight' around one. This leads to a feeling, a subjective state, in which one cannot tolerate these pressures. And that subjective state may be accompanied by one or more physical afflictions in which there is a breakdown of some part of the body. No sense can be made of the many experiences of stress if one persists with the Cartesian dualism which separates body and mind and tries to suggest that suffering has to be *either* in the body *or* 'just in the mind'.

While there is no denying the 'reality' of stress, as something which people experience and which can be manifested in physical symptoms, it is important to recognise that this reality is nevertheless one which involves processes of social construction (see above, pp. 56–8). People are making sense of their situation through the use of discursive resources which are available in their culture (pp. 102–5). In another place and time, a worker suffering from what we would nowadays label stress might simply be dismissed as a 'weak character' and a soldier who would, today, be recognised as undergoing stress might be shot at dawn as a coward. But to recognise the importance of processes of construction, interpretation or enactment in how stress is experienced and handled is not just a matter of how we are socially labelled. The sufferer from 'stress' will make sense of their situation in their own way, albeit in the context of the discursive resources which are available to them. Each individual will also be better or worse placed with regard to personal resources such as experience, physical strength, intelligence, intellectual ingenuity and a self-identity which entails their defining themselves, say, as a relatively robust or vulnerable person. They will also be better or worse placed with regard to friends, relatives or advisers to whom they can turn for advice and emotional support. All of these resources, cultural and personal (not that in the final analysis these can be separated – to decide that one is a 'fighter' rather than a 'quitter' is clearly both a personal and a discursive matter), are drawn upon to deal with whatever pressures, strains or 'stresses' are being experienced. Thus, in any workplace or occupational stress situation we choose to look at, we have to consider the interplay of two sets of factors: the *pressures of the work circumstances* and the psychological, emotional and *social resources of the worker* facing those circumstances.

Activity 4.6

Look at the experiences of Tim Dyke and Con Tessock in Case 4.5 and:

- note the ways in which the personal resources of the two individuals made a difference to the ways they experienced and dealt with the stress of handling the pressures of the work circumstances they faced;

- identify any work or organisational situation you have witnessed, experienced or can envisage in which different individuals react differently to the same potentially stressful situations, noting which factors you think were the most important in leading to these different reactions.

A tale of two deputies   Case 4.5

We were seen as a team over the several years we worked together as classroom teachers – Tim Dyke and Con Tessock, the dedicated teacher twins. Then, when the school got into trouble and they put the new Head Teacher in to sort it all out, it wasn't seen as strange that we were both appointed as deputy heads. I was to look after the lower school and Con the upper school. In some ways mine was the more difficult job because I had a higher proportion of disruptive pupils. By the time you reached the senior classes, which were Con's, the worst troublemakers had left. But we had both been pretty good at classroom control and we both had managed to get reasonable examination results with the sort of pupils which we had to handle. What I am saying is that we both started off the managerial stages of our careers similarly placed, similarly matched – not that there was any competitiveness between us, as far as I could see at the time anyway. So it's really interesting to try to work out why I am now about to become a head teacher and Con is a retired teacher at 48, 'put out to grass' on ill health retirement because he couldn't take the stress.

Because the school had been inspected and deemed by the inspectors to be an officially 'failing school', the local authority got rid of our old head teacher and put in Winnie Knowe with a brief to act as a 'superhead' and 'turn the school around'. So, from Winnie's arrival and the appointment of Con and myself as deputies, we were being constantly watched and monitored. We knew that everything we did was in order to get a clean bill of health when the Ofsted inspectors came back in. Every little success had therefore to be recorded, every little failure had to be explained and we had to write policy documents for every single aspect of school life – from a careers advice policy to a buildings maintenance policy. The workload was enormous, with all these tasks being piled on top of what was thrown at us by daily events in the school. Con and I seemed to cope well with this, not least because, as mates, we were able to work together. We had each other's shoulders to cry on, if we needed it. So far, so good. But, after a while Con started to get bad tempered with me and he increasingly failed to meet the deadlines we agreed to set each other. I first realised that things were really going wrong one day after he'd had a meeting with Winnie. He came into the staff room absolutely fuming. Winnie Knowe had failed to support a decision that Con had made about disciplining a girl who had been found with a pocket full of illegal pills. Not only had she not backed him, but Winnie had apologised to the girl's parents for the school not being 'sympathetic enough' to a girl 'going through a difficult time'. I couldn't blame Con for getting angry. What sort of time did Winnie think we were all having? I had got angry with the Head on a couple of occasions, for exactly the same reasons. She was clearly unwilling to back Con and me in any risks we took. When we were successful she used to take the credit, and when something went wrong, she blamed us.

Having a boss who does not back you when you are doing an already difficult job is a real strain, believe me. And not only was this made worse by her not giving us any kind of reward or thanks for good work done, she was always sneaking around asking the other staff about us. So, all of the time you felt you were being watched and that you would get slapped if you fell short. The stress of all this was made worse by the press, who seemed to be very keen to see us fail again. Anything negative they could get hold of, they would make a fuss about. You began to feel the whole world was against you. The kids in our school always were difficult. Con and I both knew that before we went there. But somehow the parents were now getting even more of a problem than they had been before. They had never been wonderfully supportive but, now, they seemed to take the attitude that we should sort out their kids all on our own. Disciplining these obstreperous teenagers was our job, they seemed to think. When we asked for their help they tended to look at us and say, 'Just because you are useless – a teacher in a failing school – don't expect us to do your job', and all that.

At times I thought the job was too much. At one point I came out in this rash. The doctor just laughed this off and told me that she knew it was just a stress symptom that I should 'shake off' – because she got exactly the same problem when she found her workload beginning to get too much for her. After that visit to the doctor, I decided that there wasn't much else I could do but will the rash to go away. That didn't work exactly, but once I got into the habit of a glass of good malt whisky every night, it slowly disappeared. Poor old Con, on the other hand, was down at the doctor's all the time. He developed an ulcer, which tended to make him even more evil tempered than he had already become. And he started to talk about a blood pressure problem too. With all of this he became more and more unpredictable, failing to turn up to meetings and one day he actually hit a pupil who, he said, had come out of a French lesson and called him 'Con the con'. It was his final downfall. So they got him out: a 'victim of the government, the Head Teacher and of stress' he said at the embarrassing leaving party we held for him.

Why, I ask myself, did I cope and my pal didn't? We were both able and confident teachers. We both had exactly the same stress problems at work. In a sense, I probably just made up my mind I was going to cope and realised that both of us couldn't go under. I sort of took responsibility for him as he started to break down. I needed to do that because I knew he was getting no support from his wife. She's a successful fashion designer who could not see how he couldn't deal with what she saw as the simple problems that face teachers. My wife, on the other hand, was once a teacher and she used to 'talk me down' some nights when I got home. And the kids used to take my mind off things. Con doesn't have kids, just a temperamental dog which is more unpredictable than our worst pupils. I thought at the time that Con had support from his parents, who are both ex-teachers, whereas my parents show no interest in my work. But I rather think, in retrospect, that his parents were just another source of pressure, always telling him what he might do in his job, without realising just how different a school like ours was from the old grammar schools they had taught in.

I also think that Con was starting to be troubled by his association with a notorious and rough school. 'Doesn't it damage your self esteem, having people know you work in such an awful place?', Con asked me one day. 'Self esteem, what's that?', I thought. On reflection I have come to the conclusion that I had no problems in this area. I had convinced myself that the world was a rough old place and that perhaps I was a bit of a hero taking on the challenge of working at the rougher end of the educational service. Con, on the other hand, convinced himself that things shouldn't be the way they are and that the world was somehow against him personally. 'The whole effing world, and this ulcer, is against me' he sobbed one day into his empty coffee mug, the one with the slogan 'A good teacher can make a world of difference' painted on it.

These two individuals involved in managing a large problem school were faced with considerable sources of stress. Not only did they have an enormous amount of work to do, at both the operational and the policy levels, but they also received very little support in the job. Even worse, they tended to get criticised from every quarter – by the head teacher, by journalists and by parents of pupils. Stress, as an emotional and physical reaction to these circumstances was something that Tim and Con both experienced. But Tim was better placed in terms of personal resources to manage the symptoms. Just at the physical level, it would seem that Tim was fortunate in that his body did not react as negatively as Con's did. But, we must be careful not to de-couple the physical and the emotional or mental aspects of human functioning in a Cartesian manner. We cannot assume that there was an initial physical difference between the two men. The mental state of each could itself have been a factor in the physical state that each found himself in, just as the physical state of each of them could have been a factor in their respective emergent mental and emotional states. However, it would seem that Tim was better placed than Con in terms of social and family resources, and the support and opportunity to relax that he could find at home.

On top of all of this, we can see Tim actively adopting a certain orientation towards his work which helped him manage his situation. He opted to define himself by applying a particular culturally available discursive resource to himself: the notion of a 'hero' who takes on a challenge. He also takes his relationship with Con into account in trying to explain his emergent orientation to events – suggesting that taking some responsibility for his friend was a factor in his adopting a positive stance towards the difficulties of their shared circumstances. Notice also that he adopts a positive characterisation of the school, as 'rough' as it was, as part of an educational *service*. And where Tim takes a stoic philosophical view of the world, seeing it as a generally 'rough place' that one has got to make the best of, Con adopts a different view of the world as one which 'ought' to be better than it is. Whereas Tim is willing to try to take control over circumstances, Con seems to be adopting an orientation in which he resigns himself to losing control, because the world is against him.

In looking at this case study in occupational stress and how individuals manage it, we must remember that we cannot read it as if we were actually seeing into the minds of these two individuals. Tim is creating an account of what happened, rather than neutrally 'reporting' it. He is constructing a plausible tale which helps make sense of things both for himself and for the researcher that he is speaking to. The only account we have of Con's experience is that which his old friend gives us, on the basis of what he remembers seeing and hearing. We might also note that Tim Dyke is taking part in the ongoing social construction process, whereby work researchers, and others, analyse the sort of events that happened here in terms of 'stress' factors and personal resources for 'managing stress'. Nevertheless, in pragmatist terms, there is value in using an analysis of this kind. It is invaluable in helping us to understand and, potentially, to manage stressful situations.

We are making use here of a process-relational style of analysis in which exchanges and reciprocities – positive ones and negative ones – are seen to play a part in the way two individuals manage their identities, their work and their lives. We have a framework that we can apply to situations of stress and stress management generally. It suggests that we should not regard stress as something that necessarily results from having either heavy responsibilities in our jobs or being faced with a heavy workload. The emotional and physical difficulties which we label 'stress' arise when the individual does not have the personal and social 'resources' to enable them to define the pressures of this responsibility or workload as *manageable*. Occupational stress, or *distress*, is avoided when the occupational or organisational circumstances are ones over which the individual feels they can assert control, rather than ones which will swamp them or lead to their 'breaking down'.

One of the ways in which stress at work can be handled is by having a home or family life that enables one to balance the stresses of work with the pleasures and recreation of home life. However, the growing problem of a 'long hours culture' in work organisations has made this increasingly unlikely for many professional and managerial employees – even if it were true in the first place that home life is the haven of peace and relaxation that we often would like it to be. In spite of employers claiming to be concerned with helping employees to find a 'work–life balance', organisational restructuring and the associated insecurities have increased the pressures on managers to spend long hours at work (Worrall and Cooper, 1999). For many people the stresses of family life and the stresses of work have come to be mutually reinforcing, leading to a situation when, as Hochschild (1997a and 1997b) has put it, 'work becomes home and home becomes work'.

One of the ways that people handle, or avoid, stress at work is to indulge in practices that we can characterise as acts of workplace mischief.

Workplace mischief and the organisational underlife

There are both 'official' and 'unofficial' aspects to the negotiated order of every organisation. It was shown in Chapter 2 (pp. 61–3) that, in different circumstances, unofficial or 'informal' practices can contribute either positively or negatively to the long-term survival of the organisation – towards officially approved ends, we might say. This applies to what we can call 'organisational mischief'.

Organisational mischief   *Concept*

Activities occurring within the workplace that (a) according to the official structure, culture, rules and procedures of the organisation 'should not happen' and (b) contain an element of challenge to dominant modes of operating or to dominant interests in the organisation.

Although we are now focusing our attention on something explicitly called *mischief*, the same ambiguity arises with regard to its likely corporate effects. *Organisational mischief* is a category of unofficial workplace activity that involves some kind of challenge by organisational members to the dominant order of the enterprise (see Further Reading on deviance and misbehaviour in organisations, pp. 161–2). It clearly has the potential to undermine a dominant order or to thwart dominant interests. However, there are *unintended consequences* of mischievous actions just as there are unintended consequences of formal and official corporate initiatives (Chapter 2, pp. 63–73). This is illustrated by the story of the man who set fire to the premises where he worked as an extreme expression of the contempt he and his workmates felt for the company that employed them. After initial resentment at this act of sabotage, the senior management came to see it as an immense piece of good fortune. The building completely burned down, but it was old, inefficient and awkwardly located. New premises that were much better suited to strategic managerial priorities were built with the insurance money that the company received and a new, much more compliant, workforce was recruited to work on the new site. The challenge had misfired. An act of gross organisational mischief had the unintended consequence of reinforcing the order and the interests that it had been intended to undermine.

Much of the mischief that routinely occurs in the unofficial or informal *underlife* of an organisation challenges the dominant order much less directly, and often less deliberately, than was the case with the aggrieved arsonist. An employee might, for example, falsely claim that they were taking a day off work because they were ill when, in fact, they simply wanted to avoid the pressures of a typical Monday morning in their office. Such behaviour, especially if it becomes widespread or persistent, will have the effect of challenging organisational interests. The worker has prioritised their own interests over those of the employing organisation – in spite of the commitment they have made to the employer through their employment contract.

The *implicit contract* that employees make with employing organisations is the most useful starting point for any attempt to understand what is going on when people go absent from work, engage in sabotage, steal from the workplace, or 'misbehave' at work in any of the variety of other ways we will shortly be considering. A key element of the implicit contract between the employee and the employer is the employee 'input' of *compliance*, the acceptance of a degree of managerial control over the worker. This means that whenever someone joins an organisation as an employee they *surrender a degree of personal autonomy* but, as we have frequently observed, human beings do not readily give up control of their circumstances or their 'selves'. This is especially the case in modern democratic societies, where the concepts of human rights and the autonomy of the 'free citizen' are culturally significant and people are only willing to submit to the control of others to a very limited and closely circumscribed extent. When one takes a job, for a certain level of pay, job security, opportunity for fulfilment, and all the rest, one accepts that certain people, to a certain extent, may tell one what to do. Such an acceptance is typically loaded with reservation, reluctance and caution. Resistance to any attempted control that falls short of total legitimacy in the employee's eyes is to be expected in every workplace circumstance. And where that resistance cannot take the direct form of a straightforward refusal to comply – which often it cannot – we can expect the employee to seek one means or another to maintain their pride or otherwise protect their identity.

To defend their sense of 'self' and, in effect, to restore some balance to a threatened implicit contract, people engage in activities ranging from burning down their workplace to stealing a pencil from their desk; from circulating rude cartoons round an office to playing practical jokes on people. To point to this 'defence of self' aspect of such activity is not, however, to deny that people at work often joke with each other simply for the sake of enjoying a joke or take a pencil home simply because there is no one looking and the pencil from the telephone pad at home has worn out. However, this should not stop us recognising that there is often a further and a deeper significance to many of these acts – a significance that we must always take into account when trying to understand behaviour in organisations.

Many of the studies of workplace resistance to organisational control have focused on manual workers in industrial situations, and deep insights into the importance of acts of defiance and anti-authority cultural gestures have been gained by close studies of the experience of working class employment. It is unfortunate, however, when managerial workers are excluded from analyses of organisational mischief, as is done in the review of what they call 'organisational misbehaviour' by Ackroyd and Thompson (1999). Managers are themselves employees of organisations and the majority of them are subject to controls over their behaviour by more senior managers – controls that may be experienced by a manager as a 'threat to self' no less significant than the threat felt by a non-manager. Indeed the controls to which managers are subject can be far more sophisticated or even insidious than those experienced by more junior employees. Managers frequently invest more of their 'selves' in their work than do ordinary employees. Consequently, 'defence of self' gestures and acts of 'resistance' through mischief are to be seen from the top to the bottom of the organisational hierarchy. This is apparent in the case we will look at in Chapter 6 (Case 6.2, p. 219) where the later arrival and early departure of the senior manager Todd is not essentially different from that of an ordinary worker cutting short their working day. And the suspected discouraging of the visit by the police officer and the security consultant by the security manager is not essentially different from, say, a gym assistant in that organisation persuading a maintenance engineer not to repair an exercise machine that she does not like.

Mischief at any level of the organisation is likely to involve a mixture of the more 'psychological' *defence of self* and the more material pursuit of *self-interest*. A day 'illegally' taken off work may, for example, benefit a worker by giving them the satisfaction of upsetting a supervisor who has been overloading them with work. The worker's pride and sense of autonomy is thus defended and if they use that day to paint a room in their house, they also save the money they might otherwise have had to pay someone else. Their material self-interest has thus been served at the same time as they were protecting their sense of self-integrity and personal autonomy.

Some forms of mischief are relatively individualistic and involve just one person defending their sense of self, engaging in an act of personal resistance or otherwise furthering their personal interests. We might include here:

- *Spontaneous individual acts of absenteeism.* The shop worker staying away from work on the day that it is rumoured the company's 'mystery shopper' will be visiting the store to check up on the quality of service.
- *Inattentiveness through day-dreaming or chatting to work colleagues.* The counter staff in a council office failing to notice someone entering to pay their rent because they are too busy discussing rumours about their manager's private life; the police officer allocated to a particularly boring beat failing to notice a street crime because he is replaying in his mind the football match he watched the night before.
- *Minimal compliance with instructions.* The activities of the 'jobsworths' or 'bureaucratic personalities' we came across in Chapter 2 (p. 72); the warehouse labourer who was told to 'get those boxes moved out of the gangway before you go home' moving a pile of cardboard boxes containing fragile goods out into the yard so that heavy overnight rain destroys their contents.
- *Keeping information to oneself.* The maintaining of a strong sense of indispensability and 'being in control' by a bank's branch manager who gives staff only minimal information about the headquarters' guidelines to which the branch is meant to be working.
- *Bullying.* The regular tormenting of the weakest member of a work team by a supervisor who feels aggrieved at having to take orders from a manager who is 'half my age and barely out of college'.
- *Sexual harassment.* The repeated commenting on the sexual characteristics of women colleagues by a male employee who also pinned photographs of naked women to the wall above his desk and who only modified his behaviour when the women took to decorating another wall of the office with pictures of naked men.
- *Opportunistic pilfering or embezzlement.* The taking of a couple of new books from a library by a library assistant who feels that he is too poorly paid to

afford to buy books and who finds himself left alone to lock up a local library one evening; the regular siphoning-off of amounts of money by an accountant who finds that a particular very rich client rarely checks the figures with which they are provided.

- *The sabotaging or breaking of goods or equipment in a moment of individual frustration.* The throwing of a crate of bottled beer down the cellar stairs by a bar manager whose staff had failed to turn up for work, leaving him to cope with a rush of customers.

- *Using work premises or equipment for private purposes, both within and sometimes out of working hours.* The use of a production machine to make a toy for one's children; the photocopying at work of invitations to an employee's birthday party; the sending of flirtatious or aggressive personal e-mails to other employees.

- *The punishing of an awkward customer who has offended the worker.* The waiter who spits in the third plate of soup to be taken to a customer who has sent back a first plate of soup because it was too cold and a second plate of soup because it was too hot.

- *Leaving the organisation at an especially inconvenient time.* The university professor falling out with the faculty dean and resigning from their post so that their departure coincides with the beginning of the vital and difficult report-writing stage of a major research project which they have led and which only they fully understand.

All of these relatively individualistic pieces of mischief still have a social dimension. They all relate to problems in the employment 'trade' with the employing organisation. And it is likely that individual acts such as going absent from work will develop into a more general pattern of absenteeism, as more and more people see staying away from work as a defence against work overload. This possibility needs to be recognised when we identify some of the more social and group-oriented types of organisational mischief:

- *Acts of absenteeism or inconvenient resignation that accord with unofficial norms which have developed in an organisation or a sub-unit of an organisation.* The standard practice of people claiming to be ill when allocated to the shift in a restaurant when the most difficult customers tend to turn up.

- *The setting of group work-output norms that suit group members but are managerially defined as 'restrictions of output'.* The refusal of a group of machine operators in a garment factory to allow any of the group members to produce more than 15 garments per hour or fewer than 13 garments (because that is deemed a 'reasonable and fair' work rate by most of the group) in spite of the fact that the management want a higher output and indeed operate a bonus system that would give higher pay for higher output.

- *Organised fiddles.* The standard practice among staff in a public house of overcharging customers who are thought unlikely to check their change; shop staff giving extra change to customers to whom they are related.

- *'Dehumanising' or 'putting down' customers or clients – typically behind their backs but sometimes 'to their faces'*. The practice of referring to all customers as 'punters', 'marks' or 'Johns' rather than customers; the norm among motor mechanics in a garage of telling customers that the fault with their car is something different from what the customers say they believe it to be; the labelling by workers in a fish and chip shop of all customers into categories like FOBs (fat overeating slob), TLTCs (too lazy to cook) and SUBs (soaking up the beer).

- *Using work premises for group-sanctioned non-work purposes*. The use of a medical room by nightshift workers taking turns to snatch an illegal hour's sleep during the shift; the playing of competitive computer games involving several workers during office hours.

- *Workplace games*. The weekly competition between senior managers in a company to collect as many as possible management 'buzzwords' used by the managing director, both orally or in documents; the throwing of an item such as a chicken leg from worker to worker in a food factory whenever supervisors or managers are not looking.

- *Practical jokes, organised 'piss-takes' or 'wind-ups'*. The pinning of a large sheet of paper bearing the legend 'pompous bastard' to the back of a manager's jacket, unknown to him, before he shows a group of visitors around a new building; the nursing tutors in a hospital always ensuring that they send at least one member of each new intake of nurses to the medical stores to collect an item such as a 'bronchial tube' or a bottle of 'mild infarction'.

- *Organised bullying and harassment*. The persistent persecuting of black men and women workers in a textile factory, involving name-calling and the damaging of work in progress, by a group of white male maintenance workers whose supervisor not only encourages such behaviour but discriminates against men in his team who do not join in these practices by giving them fewer overtime opportunities and by allocating them to more than their fair share of unpleasant jobs.

- *The organised sabotaging of goods or equipment*. The regular damaging of an assembly line to give all the workers on it a break from machine-pacing; the deliberate overloading of an organisation's e-mail system by people widely and unnecessarily circulating copies of lengthy documents and large attachments.

- *The mobilising of groups to take sanctions against management as a means of resolving a grievance*. The decision of a group of design engineers, after taking a vote, to work on only one design at a time – this sanction to continue until the company brings the department up to its official full staff strength; the agreement by a group of van drivers that their union representative should tell management that no overtime will be worked until the pay is brought up to the level of a rival delivery service company; the refusal, after a brief lunchtime meeting, of all the departmental managers in a large retail store to attend meetings called by the general manager after the 6 p.m. closing time.

In each of these more group-oriented types of organisational mischief, we again see people protecting or advancing the material aspects of their implicit contract with the employer. The van drivers want more pay, for example, and are disrupting the overtime arrangements to achieve this. The cheating of drinkers in the public house is a means of maintaining a higher level of income than the employer provides in the pay packet. A certain level of pay – part legal, part illegal – has become part of the implicit contract associated with their employment, in effect. The machine operators who fix an output norm are also working to shape their implicit contract (as were the workers in the famous Bank Wiring Observation Room study at the Hawthorne plant reported by Roethlisberger and Dickson, 1939). There is, then, a degree of informal bargaining between employers and employees occurring in all of this misbehaviour. Does this mean we should reject the 'mischief' label, then? It does not. All of these behaviours are, to some degree, taken against the dominant order of the organisation. They constitute a refusal simply to accept the roles and rewards laid down for them by the employer. Just as with the more individualistic types of behaviour, these group-oriented actions have a 'defence of self' or protection of autonomy dimension for the members of the groups. This works in conjunction with the pursuit of shared material interests. Each member of the workgroup that has agreed its own definition of a 'fair day's work' can work with a sense that group membership protects them from managerial pressures. The food workers throwing food around the factory are ritually undermining the supervisors' control over their activities. The managers who mock their boss's pretentious language and the managers who refuse to attend their general managers' out-of-hours meetings, are expressing a degree of independence or distance from their senior managers. The strategies of independence that we see in all of these groups are not acts of rebellion or a fight for full autonomy. As part of their implicit contract with their employer, they submit to a certain amount of managerial control but what their collective misbehaviours are in effect saying to those in authority is 'This is who we are. So far and no further.'

Organisational employees who deal directly with customers or clients have an additional need to protect their personal identities and their sense of autonomy. It is not just the manager or supervisor who exerts pressures here on the worker to behave in a certain way. It is also the customer. In many aspects of service and retail work the worker is required to act like a servant. The emotional pressures that this can put on both the worker and the manager alike were looked at earlier and the problems of engaging in *emotional labour* were illustrated both by the hotel manager Ken Steary in Case 4.3 and the sex worker Cindy Sutor in Case 4.4. Some important psychic relief from the pressure to act subserviently is thus achieved by the rude labelling of clients in the chip shop and by the motor mechanics always claiming to know better than the motorists what is wrong with their vehicles. The notion of 'getting one's own back' on people who are put into the master or mistress role, vis-à-vis the service worker's role as servant, can take some very unpleasant forms. The ploy of the waiter who, behind the scenes, spits in the diner's food is a classic example of this, but repulsive as such behaviour may seem, it is far from uncommon in the food and drinks industry, at both the customer service end of the business and at the food processing stage. It is rare to find anybody who has worked in a food processing plant who cannot relate tales of people throwing rat droppings into food mixing machines, urinating into beer vats or tipping floor sweepings into hoppers of cereal. Outside the food industry, one hears similar reports of people chalking obscenities on the insides of the items of furniture they are making or leaving hidden parts of metal products insufficiently protected against rust. One hears of unspeakable things being done to dead bodies in hospitals or undertakers' workshops. All of these are human gestures of defiance and demonstrations of personal or group autonomy, however alienated or degraded a form of human expression we may deem them to be.

In the conversation about some of the examples of workplace mischief that they have come across as managers, Hazel Hopeman and Jenny Elgin recognise that there is 'something deeper' going on in what Jenny calls the 'underlife' of organisations.

Activity 4.7

Read the conversation in Case 4.6 between Hazel Hopeman, a manager in an airline, and Jenny Elgin, the manager of a supermarket, and:

- note down examples arising in this conversation of the various types of organisational mischief that we identified above (recognising that certain activities may straddle more than one category);
- think about any examples of organisational mischief that you have come across or heard about

that you might have thrown into the conversation if you had joined Jenny and Hazel in their discussion;

- consider the extent to which Hazel and Jenny's attempts to make sense of (or 'theorise' about) these activities fit with the attempts to understand organisational mischief that have been made in this chapter so far.

Hazel and Jenny probe the organisational underworld   Case 4.6

What really started me thinking about these things was a strange experience I had one day when I was a victim of a practical joke organised by a couple of my departmental managers. I was walking around the shop doing my usual thing of smiling at everyone and having a friendly word with a customer here and a colleague there. One of the customers made a very strange comment. 'You don't look very sore to me', he said. I was puzzled, but carried on. Then one of the checkout operators said, 'You don't look sore to me Jenny.' Again, I said nothing. But when a customer who I'd helped with a query about Sunday opening hours asked me, with a rather enigmatic smile on her face, 'So what are you sore about, Miss Elgin?' I let my puzzlement show. 'Look at your badge, dear', the customer said. And when I looked at my 'Jenny Elgin, Store Manager' badge, I saw that it had been skilfully doctored to say 'Jenny Elgin, Sore Manager'.

I expect that did make you a 'sore manager'.

I was not pleased, I can tell you, Hazel. But I had been rather short tempered with my management team for more than a week. They knew I was having problems with my car and that I was getting tired of having to drive so far to work at this branch. 'Don't take it out on us', the grocery manager had said to me only the day before. He was very understanding. I don't think the others were. They were getting their message over to me another way.

And they were obviously having a good laugh too.

I am sure they were. But what occurred to me was that you always have to look for deeper meanings in these things. There are all sorts of things bubbling away, seething sometimes, beneath the surface – in the underlife of a business, if you like. I'm sure part of the context of 'the laugh' that my managers were having was the fact that I am the only woman manager in the store and that I am the only graduate manager they have ever had close contact with. They know I will be moving on in my career. But I doubt if any of them will. So they 'brought me down a bit'. I said nothing about what happened. But I've never forgotten about it.

I agree that you have to probe beneath the surface, as a manager, when you come across anything like this. One partly hilarious and partly very serious problem I had to deal with was the case of a cabin crew whose male and female members swapped clothes towards the end of a flight. When the passengers were disembarking, there were the cabin crew as usual, thanking passengers for flying with us and very politely wishing them well. But the women were in the men's trousers, and far more peculiarly, the two chaps were in dresses. As you can imagine, we got some complaints.

What was going on, Hazel?

In a way it didn't surprise me. As a management we are well aware of this issue of 'emotional labour' that researchers write about. The man who was behind the jape told me, 'Sometimes you've just got to burst out and be yourself.' 'Cross-dressing is being yourself?' I came back – incredulous. 'Well it is for me,' he said, winking at me in a very camp manner. I believed him. 'But what about the others?' I asked. 'Oh, they'd never done it before. But, you ask them, they all say that the laugh did them good.'

So who were they having a go at – the airline, the managers, the passengers?

Oh, I think all of these. And none of them at the same time. I don't think it is as direct or as specific as it was with the case of your managers 'having a go' about your irritability. I think it's all got to do with this 'underlife' that you talk about. All sorts of things are going on behind the scenes in every type of organisation, aren't they?

Yes, but I can't imagine that a lot can go on behind the scenes in an airliner. The cabin crew are on display most of the time, aren't they?

Absolutely right – and that's why I was very lenient with them.

And there must be little scope for them to engage in the sort of fiddles that we have to deal with in retailing.

Well, there is just one. The biggest fiddle in the past – one that used to give them a lot of satisfaction as well as being materially rewarding – was the fiddling of time.

Claiming more hours that they actually put in?

Exactly. But that's now gone with computerisation. The only scope they have to line their pockets and 'have one over the airline' at the same time is with regard to complementary alcohol. We can't know how many free drinks passengers have or have not accepted. So a good proportion of those drinks go home with the cabin crew. We are well aware of this. But, as I say, it's the only thing we are aware of. I'm sure it's much more com-plicated in your business?

It certainly is. We get everything from people hiding stock that they know is going to go down in price the next week to check-out staff keeping vouchers they should give to customers. I've caught staff eating food they have taken off the shelves and which will obviously never go past the till. You get people swapping the tickets on items so that they are scanned at a lower price than they should have been and colleagues giving discounts to friends who are not entitled to them. And a scam was recently discovered in which store managers in one region were getting builders retained by the business to build conservatories on their houses, and charge these to the company.

And do you get people deliberately causing damage?

How do you mean?

I was thinking about what goes on with the men who load and unload planes. They are largely young blokes who are young and very strong. You get the impression that they are very conscious of their masculinity. And I think that their very low status in the airport's pecking order is experienced as some kind of threat to this.

So what do they do?

Well, first, they are always fighting with each other. They have time on their hands when there's no plane to work on and, of course, they have quite a mixture of nationalities and ethnic backgrounds. It can be quite explosive. And when they are not knocking each other to pieces, they are prone to smashing up luggage or bits of freight.

Yes, I've only had a couple of fights to sort out in my career so far. But damage to goods is not uncommon. I had a disgruntled bloke regularly leaving stock out of refrigeration last year and we had a spate recently of staff damaging goods in order to get them reduced in price. There was also the time we caught one of the shelf stackers opening jars of peanut butter and scratching little smiley faces into the surface of the product. What amazed me was that we only received a handful of complaints from customers. Yet he must have contaminated scores of jars, from what we understand. It could have been very damaging for the business. But it didn't even get in the press.

You confined it to the store's 'underlife'?

Thank goodness, yes. The young man who did it apparently felt he was 'having a laugh' at the expense of shoppers who, he said, never bother to speak to him or even smile at him when he is filling shelves.

Oh this is something we are very aware of with our cabin crew. In their training we have to prepare them for ungrateful or rude passengers. They know the score and are generally very good.

Generally?

Well I suppose so. A story is told about one of our crews who got really sick of a man who was regularly rude to them. He was also very demanding. So, one day, they laced his coffee with a strong laxative. That really sorted the bloke out.

Do you think that really happened? I mean it sounds unlikely to me – given that the crew who did it would probably end up cleaning up any mess that got made.

True. But if the story is apocryphal, it is rather interesting, isn't it, that people still take pleasure in passing it on. It always gets a good laugh. It sort of helps keep the customer in their place, psychologically speaking.

Yes, that reminds me of a rather different story – a true one that happened here. But it also has that element of the employee putting a distance between themselves and customers. There was this very attractive young woman who used to shop in here. The male colleagues were always looking out for her coming into the store. Well it turned out that she did some modelling for one of those erotic magazines. When the blokes discovered this, they made sure they obtained plenty of copies of the pictures and passed them round all the staff – men and women alike. It meant that a lot of silly and unpleasant giggling went on whenever she came into the shop. It also led to a game among the lads of 'talent spotting', as they named it. I discovered that they were competing to identify likely models that they might contact a particular magazine about. Fortunately, the first woman who was approached, as far as I know, came straight to me. She was very good about it. But two of those young men no longer work for us!

If only we could get these young men – I'm thinking of our baggage handlers again – to leave their sexuality, and their problems with their masculinity, at home.

And women?

Yes, we ought to be fair here. But I think that the women cabin crew who work for us are all very discreet and sophisticated about how they relate to male passengers. There's no way they could – or, to be honest, we would want them to – leave their sexuality at home. But all sorts of trouble follows if sex does rear its beautiful head at work.

How do you mean?

I was thinking of the time that the airport security caught a couple of our employees having sexual intercourse on the altar of the airport chapel. It was after a party and the place was locked. But they had got a key and thought that no one would disturb them in that part of the building. They were both single and I don't think it even occurred to them that the tabletop they were using was meant to be an altar. But none of this stopped my boss from ordering me to sack both of them. I really had to fight him on this and, in the end, I refused to do it. What amazed me was how hot under the collar he got about the whole business. I mean it really upset him. I argued that there were no serious business or managerial implications whatsoever and that, at the most, it was a minor disciplinary matter. But he had a real problem with it.

I think it's the fear some managers feel about having the lid lifted on this 'underlife', as I call it. Some managers just don't want to acknowledge that people are a lot more than little robots. I think it's the idea that employees are flesh and blood that bothers them. I had a similar difficulty when I discovered that one of the office workers occasionally played this game of leaning out of her office window during her lunch break – the window is immediately above the shop entrance – and passing the time of day with customers. What they didn't know was that, while she was doing this, she was getting served from behind by her boyfriend.

What did you do about that?

Nothing. It was me who caught them. And I decided that their embarrassment at being caught 'at it' was punishment enough. I am utterly confident that they won't do it again. No damage was done. Nobody else knew about it. But when I related this story at a corporate training event, ages after the event, I found that several of the managers there were absolutely appalled. Several people regarded as an utter outrage what I thought was quite an amusing, and even touching, piece of mischief. 'It simply shouldn't have happened' one of them kept muttering. 'The workplace is no place for that sort of thing', another spluttered before walking out of the room.

What was their problem?

What indeed? But I always remember that phrase, 'The workplace is no place for that sort of thing'. If only it were that simple!

This conversation represents a good example of managers taking a step back from their everyday practice and reflecting on the significance of some of the activities that they come across, and indeed have to deal with at work. All of the activities about which they are comparing notes fit more or less with the categories of organisational mischief set out earlier. A series of *practical jokes* or 'wind-ups' make up perhaps the most significant category here. Such a joke is played on Jenny herself and Hazel reports jokes played on airline passengers both as a group (with the cross-dressing farewell) and on one particular passenger who was 'punished' with an unwanted laxative drink. These latter two pieces of mischief to some extent also fit into our category of *putting down customers* – something that would also apply to the 'talent-spotting' *workplace game* Jenny talks about. The same might apply to the office worker communicating to customers from her office window and enjoying the irony of the fact that she was taking certain pleasures they knew nothing of. However, this case, and that of the late night use of the airport chapel for lovemaking was an example of *the use of premises or equipment for private purposes* rather than for organisational ones. *Sabotage* occurs in the loading and unloading of aircraft at the airport and in the interfering with the peanut butter in the shop. We hear of *fiddles* occurring in the airline with regard to alcoholic drinks and both money and goods in the case of the shop.

Jenny and Hazel are doing more in their conversation than simply swapping stories about their respective work organisations. They appear to have a shared interest in making sense of the various examples of organisational mischief that they present to each other. They recognise a straightforward role that these activities play *at a surface level* in organisational members' lives. People enjoy the 'laugh' that follows from the practical joking. Service workers feel better for 'having a go' at or 'keeping in their place' both managers and customers. And employees 'line their pockets', as Hazel puts it, by engaging in fiddles at work. However, both women feel that there is something more significant about these activities, something going on *at a deeper level*. Jenny suggests that there are 'deeper meanings' to these activities and that there are all sorts of things 'bubbling away' or even 'seething' below the surface. Hazel seems to agree with this and takes on Jenny's notion of an organisational 'underlife'. And there is some interesting theoretical reflection that fits with this concept in her interpretation of the behaviour of the cross-dressing cabin crew members. She uses a notion of people 'bursting out and being themselves' to make sense of what was occurring here, thus seeing their gesture as a particularly positive form of the 'defence of self' aspect of much organisational mischief. She also connects the fighting and the sabotage that occurs among the young men who load and unload the aircraft with problems that she thinks they have with both their ethnic identities and their masculinity. In thinking about such 'deeper level' factors she is still aware that the behaviour also has a more 'surface level' function of relieving boredom between flights.

Sexuality, humour and the struggle for control

Jenny and Hazel both imply that the area of human sexuality may be one in which clues might be found about the deeper issues that organisational mischief relates to. They both speak of managers who 'had a problem' with the idea of sexual behaviour occurring at work. They were frightened, Jenny suggests, by the prospect of 'having the lid lifted' on the 'underlife' of the organisation. Both sexuality and humour appear to play a major part in the organisational underlife of the organisations that these two managers work in. Can we go more deeply into these matters to explore the full depths of the organisational underlife and what its significance might be in the lives of organisational managers and employees? This is quite a challenging question, and Activity 4.8 is an invitation to take it up.

Reread the conversation between Hazel and Jenny and:

- Consider why it might be that some of the managers that both Hazel and Jenny have come across seem to be especially troubled about sexual behaviour occurring in the workplace. Why do they consider the workplace to be 'no place for that sort of thing' do you think?

- Look back to the discussion of narratives and stories and how they can be seen as elements of human culture that help people to handle existential problems (pp. 99–102) and reflect on whether the 'laughs' that Hazel and Jenny talk about have a significance which fits with this kind of analysis. Does this workplace humour have a function that goes beyond simply providing 'fun at work' or the pleasure of 'getting one's own back' on certain people?

Jenny Elgin offers one explanation of why managers might be troubled by sexuality in the workplace. To lift the lid from the organisational underlife and contemplate its sexual dimension is to come to terms with 'the idea that employees are flesh and blood' (see Further Reading on sexuality in organisations, p. 163). This means accepting, Jenny thinks, the fact that 'people are a lot more than little robots'. Sexuality, this suggests, stands for the basic humanity – and the fundamental 'animality' we might say – of the people that managers might prefer to treat as cogs in the organisational machine. To be reminded that employees are living creatures with bodies, desires and libidinal drives might make some managers uncomfortable. It reminds them of how limited their capacity to control human beings is. For a manager to be reminded that employees are living animals with emotions and desires is to be reminded that one is being required to control the uncontrollable – to 'herd cats' (Chapter 1, p. 3). It is perhaps also discomforting because it reminds the manager of their own desires and the sexuality that they too are required to leave behind when they come to work. But sexuality, desire, and indeed the enjoyment of laughter, are not things that can be left behind when the human being goes to work, whether as a manager or as an ordinary employee. And they are behaviours that defy organisational control.

Work organisations are set up to be places where rational and instrumental behaviour occurs and where attention is to be focused on the completion of formal tasks. If there is to be love, it is to be love of work or love of the company. If there is to be passion, it is to be passion for the product or a passion for customer satisfaction. If there is to be desire, it is to be desire for the success of the organisation and a desire for the formal rewards of pay and security that are offered for contributing to that corporate success. For love, passion and desire to be directed to other than corporate ends is to threaten the managerial controls that are intended to achieve those ends. Any display of passion or desire on the part of organisational members for the bodies of other organisational members or for organisational clients is an especially powerful symbolic challenge to that control. We should not be surprised, therefore, that Jenny Elgin speaks of managers arguing emphatically that the workplace is 'no place for that sort of thing'. Indeed, most of us would see the point of their wanting to discourage shop workers spending time identifying which customers might be potential erotic magazine models or wanting to discourage office workers from having sexual intercourse at the window of their offices. However, Jenny and Hazel seem to be implying that a reasonable and sensitive manager would recognise that, while the sexuality of organisational employees may need to kept discreetly under control within the workplace, it is not something that can be completely suppressed. Sexuality may be expressed directly in the workplace through individuals courting each other or engaging in overtly sexual activities. Equally, it may be expressed indirectly through women expressing their femininity and men expressing their masculinity at work through the way they dress or through their style of relating to others. Either way, it is an aspect of the human spirit that will always present a possible challenge to managerial control.

Joking and humour can be seen, like sexuality, as expressions of the 'human spirit'. But humour, again like sex, is associated with pleasure rather than with work. Work organisations are meant to be serious places and not comedy clubs or sites for the pursuit of bodily pleasures. But both sex and humour are serious matters as well, it can be argued. This is partly because they are expressions of human 'spirit' and often express that spirit in the face of managerial attempts to harness human efforts to corporate ends. The office workers having sexual intercourse at the office window were not just finding an opportunity to express their love and desire for each other. They were also making a gesture of independence towards both their employer and the customers of the shop. The cabin crew cross-dressers can be seen as doing something similar with regard to the airline and to the passengers whom they had served. In each of these cases humour and sexuality were both involved in the expression of human autonomy. There was a serious aspect as well as a fun aspect to each of these two pieces of mischief. But the 'seriousness of humour' goes deeper than this (see Further Reading on humour in organisations, p. 162).

It might seem strange to talk about humour as a serious matter, but it can be understood as playing a seriously important role in the human construction of identities and the handling of existential anxieties. Earlier it was argued that narratives, stories, films, news stories, gossip and jokes all play a role in human culture of reassuring people in the face of the life's anxieties. It was pointed out how often these elements of culture lead us to contemplate the horrors of life – horrors ranging from being murdered or having an accident to a sexual partner's infidelity or the loss of one's job. Our engagement with fiction and non-fiction alike, with 'serious' stories as well as with comedy, frequently involves confronting the breakdown of order in our lives as we engage with the story we are reading or watching on a screen – before being reassuringly returned to order and reality as we close the book or leave the cinema. Humour, comedy and joking operate in a similar way. By making work-related jokes or transmitting funny stories about aspects of the work organisation, for instance, we challenge or question the normal order of the work organisation and its control apparatus – an order that is, however, left more or less intact after we have enjoyed 'the laugh' and returned to 'normal service'.

Activity 4.9

Look at the five 'messages from the underworld' (one picture and four documents) that have been collected from different work organisations and consider what role you think they might be playing in the lives of the employees of the organisations in which they were circulating.

Messages from the organisational underworld   Case 4.7

FIGURE 4.3   Our company was recently in a boat race with two of our competitors. Guess which boat was ours!

If you are unhappy

Once upon a time, there was a non-conforming swallow who decided not to fly south for the winter. However, soon the weather turned so cold that he reluctantly started to fly south. In a short time, ice began to form on his wings and he fell to earth in a barnyard, almost frozen. A cow passed by and crapped on the little swallow. The little bird thought it was the end. But, the manure warmed him and defrosted his wings. Warm and happy, able to breathe, he started to sing. Just then a large cat came by and, hearing the chirping, investigated the sounds. The cat cleared away the manure, found the chirping bird and promptly ate him.

There are three morals to this story. First, everyone who shits on you is not necessarily your enemy, second, everyone who gets you out of the shit is not necessarily your friend and, third, if you're warm and happy in a pile of shit, keep your mouth shut.

Job vacancy: Staffing and administration services sub-assistant

The pay is the market rate less 10% (but with a boredom compensation bonus).

We are a leading financial services company which is creeping into a very long period of unparalleled slow change.

If you are sure, predictable, pedantic and inflexible in your outlook, you could be just what we are looking for. Ideally aged exactly 42.5 years of age, a conservative dresser with at least 22 years' experience as the Personnel lady in a building society (or very similar environment) you are a play-it-safe procedure-follower who relishes plodding through long hours.

You will be administering pay and rations to our Head Office staff along with ensuring all paperwork is completed fully on staff movements.

Career prospects are excellent. Keep your nose clean and an increment each year can be yours. In as little as 15 years you could rise to be a Staff and Administration Services Assistant Officer with additional responsibility for sick pay.

Benefits are excellent: pay every month, holidays every year and your own desk and chair.

Interested applicants should apply in writing for a long application form from Major Gen. Horatio Flash-Blindly DSO (ret'd), Staffing and Administration Assistant Sub-General Manager, Newco Financial Services, Staid House, Oldtown.

We think we are an equal opportunities employer and believe this job would especially suit a nice lady.

In the beginning was the Plan
In the beginning was the Plan.
And then came the assumptions.
And the assumptions were without form.
And the Plan was completely without substance.
And darkness was upon the faces of the workers.
And they spake unto their Supervisors, saying
"It is a crock of crap and it stinketh".
And the Supervisors went unto the Section Heads and sayeth
"It is a pail of dung and none may abide the odour thereof".
And the Section Heads went unto their Managers and sayeth unto them
"It is a container of excrement and none may abide its strength".
And the Managers went unto their Directors and sayeth
"It contains that which aids plant growth and is very strong".
And the Managing Director went unto the Chairman, saying unto him
"It promoteth growth and is very powerful"
And the Chairman considered the Plan and sayeth unto the Board
"This powerful new Plan will actively promote the growth and efficiency of the Company".
And the Board looked upon the Plan.
And saw that it was good.
And the plan became policy.

Memorandum to all staff
From: the Board of Management
Subject: Retirement policy

As a result of the reduction of money budgeting for departmental areas, we are forced to cut down on the number of our personnel. Under the plan, older employees will be asked to go on early retirement, thus permitting the retention of younger people who represent our future.

Those being required to retire early may appeal to upper management. To make this possible there will be a Survey of Capabilities of Retired Early Workers (SCREW). The appeal process will be known as SHAFT (Scream to Higher Authority Following Termination). Under the terms of the new policy employees may be early retired once, SCREWED twice and SHAFTED as many times as the company deems appropriate.

If the employee follows the above procedures, he or she will be entitled to HERPES (Half Earnings for Retired Personnel's Early Severance). As HERPES is considered a benefit plan, any employee who has received HERPES will no long be SCREWED or SHAFTED by the company.

Management wishes to reassure the younger employees who remain on board, that the company will continue to see that they are well trained through our Special High Intensity Training known as SHIT. The company takes pride in the amount of SHIT our employees receive. We have given our employees more SHIT than any other company in the area. If any employee feels he or she does not receive enough SHIT on the job, see your immediate supervisor. Your supervisor is specially trained to make sure that you receive all the SHIT you can stand.

Each of these documents was widely circulated in the large organisations where they were collected by the researcher. The picture was collected in a hospital, the story of a swallow in a manufacturing company, the mock job advertisement in a building society, the 'In the beginning' text in a pharmaceutical company and the staff memorandum about early retirement in a retailing business. However, it is apparent that these same documents, sometimes in identical form, sometimes with local variations, can be found in one organisation after another. They circulate across societies, it would seem, as well as within organisations.

The documents mock or satirise aspects of the organisation and the way it is managed. They induce mirth by challenging the normal order of these organisations. The picture engages with the notion that the hospital has too many people giving orders (directing the boat), in relation to the numbers of people who are doing the real work (rowing the boat). The story of the swallow satirises those activities we have characterised as 'micropolitical' and implies that the workplace is a dangerous place in which it is difficult to know who is your friend and who is your enemy. The job advertisement apparently mocks the excessively bureaucratic nature of the building society and the poor career opportunities that staff are offered. Its satirical swipe at the employer's claim to be an equal opportunity employer suggests ignorance on the employer's part of the principles of equal opportunities (with the choice of the anachronistic and patronising term 'a nice lady'). It also portrays the management as hypocritical. Senior organisational managers seem to be the main target of 'In the beginning' piece and they are portrayed as plainly stupid, out of touch with common sense and prone to go along with any business nonsense as long as it can be dressed up in the language of planning, efficiency and growth. The workers and the section leaders can see that 'the plan' stinks. The managers, directors and the chairman, however, convince themselves that it is something worthwhile. And, with the retirement policy memorandum, another specific aspect of managerial language and discourse is mocked – the use of acronyms to give weight and importance to relatively routine managerial initiatives. But the document is, more seriously, an attack on what it implies are harsh, unfeeling and exploitative human resourcing policies being pursued by the company.

All of these documents, clearly intended to give employees 'a laugh', deal with serious matters that constitute threats both to employees and to the long-term survival of the organisations themselves (and hence, of course, to the job security of all employees). All comedy, as has been recognised by numerous theorists of humour from Aristotle onwards, deals with incongruity. It focuses upon the unexpected. It plays with the inappropriate. It turns normality on its head. The normal order of each of these organisations is made to look abnormal by being stretched and bent in the distorting mirror of the satirical document. This is exactly what was being done by the airline cabin crew exchanging clothes or by Jenny Elgin's colleagues altering her name badge. These documents and practical jokes distort normality so that we can laugh at and enjoy a temporary suspension of that normality before returning to our normal serious workplace demeanour and getting back to our work.

Workplace humour helps people adjust to aspects of work that they dislike or feel threatened by and it is always possible that some of the satirical intentions of comic interventions may be fulfilled. Mockery of individuals and practices can lead to changes in behaviour and procedures. But workplace humour and joking behaviour can be seen as playing a deeper role in people's lives too. It is part of the way we maintain our sanity. We often joke about the things that worry us most. At work for example, it is noticeable that people whose autonomy is most threatened by overbearing customers or managers will tend to make jokes about such customers or managers more often than those who do not experience such pressures. People whose jobs are the least secure tend to joke about 'getting the chop', 'getting the bullet' or receiving the 'little brown envelope' containing a redundancy notice than those who are relatively secure in their jobs. People doing the most dangerous jobs tend to be those who joke most about possible accidents. Those whose work in emergency services, hospitals and mortuaries involves them in matters of life and death, are the most prone to indulge in black humour and 'laugh in the face' of the death and mutilation that their jobs force them to confront. The joking here can be understood as a glimpse into the abyss. A glimpse into the abyss of disorder and madness, we might say, helps us retain our sanity in the light of the dangers that are seething down there and threatening to swallow us up. Much of our engagement with humour and comedy is like the tightrope walker in Figure 4.4 with his quick occasional glimpses down into the abyss over which he is walking.

To get across to the far side of the ravine, the tightrope walker must keep his eyes most of the time on the solid ground that he wants to reach. However, if he too casually or too confidently strides out in this direction, forgetting what horrors are seething beneath his feet, he is likely to slip from his rope. Equally,

FIGURE 4.4   Humour helps us over the existential abyss

though, if he looks down too intently into the cauldron below him, he will lose his balance and fall into the pit of horrors. When we move through our everyday lives, intent on our various life, work and family projects, we are like the tightrope walker looking to the solid ground that we wish to reach. But to remind ourselves of the precariousness of our situations, and to come to terms with everything that actually or potentially troubles us about the world, we glimpse into the abyss from time to time. We therefore laugh at the figure slipping over on the banana skin, we laugh at the stupidity of people from a neighbouring society, we laugh at the managers whose pretentiousness or incompetence threatens the security of our employment. Having laughed at what might otherwise frighten us into a loss of control in our lives (madness even), we return to our serious demeanour and travel onwards. When we bring sexuality and humour into the workplace, and when we indulge in the lavatory talk and sexually 'dirty' language of the 'underworld' documents reviewed earlier, we are reminding ourselves and those around us that we are not cogs in the corporate machine. We are demonstrating that we are also both creative human beings (who create jokes, write satires and make each other laugh) and recalcitrant biological animals (who copulate, excrete and refuse to be herded). Sexuality and humour thus play a part in the way each one of us struggles to control our lives and identity. It also plays its part, when it is mischievously brought into the workplace, in the struggle for control that goes on between people with varying degrees of power in the organisational pecking order.

We have concentrated in this chapter on various aspects of the informal and unofficial aspects of organisational life and looked at various challenges that are constantly being made to managerial efforts to shape and control work organisations. In the next chapter we turn to those aspects of the struggle for managerial control that are concerned with obtaining and maintaining 'human resources'.

Summary

In this chapter the following key points have been made:

- At the heart of the relationship between the employee and the employing organisation is an *implicit contract* whereby it is understood that the employee will make a particular set of contributions, at a particular level, to the organisation's work in return for a particular mix of rewards. This bargain has to be understood in light of both the life situation and projects of the employee and the strategic direction being followed by the organisation – it is thus central to the *strategic exchange* relationship between the individual and the organisation.

- The implicit contract, as it is understood by the employee, forms part of that employee's *orientation to work*, the meaning they attach to their employment and which influences the ways they act within that employment.

- Individuals' entry to work or to an organisation can be understood in terms of their *initial orientation to work*. This, however, is likely to change as both the organisational and the individual's circumstances (inside and outside work) change. The process of change continues as the individual's personal life and projects move on and as their employment career develops.

- Feelings and emotions play a central part in all work and organisational situations. They cannot be seen as incidental and peripheral to the rational task-based activities with which people are involved.

- In various kinds of work, service work and managerial work especially, there is an emotional dimension built into what is required of the worker. This *emotional labour* can be handled in different ways; by the worker choosing to engage in either 'deep' or 'surface' acting, for example.

- *Stress* is an emotionally related phenomenon. It involves an experience of distress which leads to an individual being incapable of performing the tasks that are required of them. It is not something that is inherent in either the individual or the work. It can only be understood by looking at how the circumstances of the individual interrelate with the organisational circumstances and pressures.

- People vary in how they cope with potentially stressing circumstances and the psychological, emotional and social resources that they can draw upon influence how well they cope.

- A variety of activities go on in every organisation which are not officially 'meant to happen' in the organisation. Examples of *organisational mischief* like fiddling, practical joking, sabotage and workplace sexual activity tend to challenge dominant modes of operating in organisations as well as helping people both to further and to defend their interests. They also enable people to protect their personal notions of 'self'. Managers and non-managers alike engage in organisational mischief.

- Sexuality and humour have a particular significance in the 'underlife' of the work organisation as they represent aspects of humanity (including the 'animal' aspects of humanity) that are especially unsusceptible to corporate or managerial control.

- Humour has a very important role in work situations in enabling people both to challenge and adjust to organisational controls and dominant interests. It also helps people control their lives generally and cope with the existential threats to sanity and a sense of order.

Recommended reading

The variety of ways in which matters of emotion arise within organisations is demonstrated by Steve Fineman in *Understanding Emotion at Work* (London: Sage, 2003) whilst David Wainwright and Michael Calnan provide a challengingly critical view of the way work stress has become such an important issue in recent times in their *Work Stress: The making of a modern epidemic* (Buckingham: Open University Press, 2002). The variety of forms of mischief that occurs in organisations is reflected upon by Steve Ackroyd and Paul Thompson in *Organisational Misbehaviour* (London: Sage, 1999) in a way which usefully complements the analysis in the present chapter. Humour plays a key part in this, as we have seen, and David Collinson shows us how attempts are increasingly being made in managerial circles to make humour 'work' for the organisation in his article, 'Managing humour' (*Journal of Management Studies*, 39(3): 269–288, 2002). And for more material on the role of sex in work and organisations see Jo Brewis and Steve Linstead's *Sex, Work and Sex Work: Eroticizing organization?* (London: Routledge, 2000).

Further reading

Further reading Work orientations, implicit and psychological contracts

Baldamus, W. (1961) *Efficiency and Effort*, London: Tavistock
Behrend, H. (1957) 'The effort bargain', *International Labor Relations Review*, 10: 503–515
Goldthorpe, J.H., Lockwood, D., Bechhofer, F. and Platt, J. (1968) *The Affluent Worker: Attitudes and behaviour*, Cambridge: Cambridge University Press
Guest, D. (1998) 'Is the psychological contract worth taking seriously?', *Journal of Organizational Behaviour*, 9: 649–664
Herriot, P., Manning, W.E.G. and Kidd, J.M. (1997) 'The content of the psychological contract', *British Journal of Management*, 8(2): 151–162
Kotter, J.P. (1973) 'The psychological contract', *California Management Review*, 15: 91–99
Levinson, H., Price, C., Munden, K. and Solley, C. (1966) *Men, Management and Mental Health*, Cambridge, MA: Harvard University Press
Noon, M. and Blyton, P. (2002) *The Realities of Work*, Basingstoke: Palgrave.
Robinson, S. and Rousseau, D.M. (1994) 'The psychological contract – not the exception but the norm', *Journal of Organisational Behavior*, 15(3): 245–259
Rousseau, D.M. (1995) *Psychological Contracts in Organisations: Understanding written and unwritten agreements*, Thousand Oaks, CA: Sage
Watson, T.J. (2003) *Sociology, Work and Industry*, Chapter 7, London: Routledge

Further reading Emotions and work

Albrow, M. (1997) *Do Organisations have feelings?*, London: Routledge
Damasio, A.R. (2000) *The Feeling of What Happened*, London: Heinemann
Fineman, S. (ed.) (1993) *Emotion in Organizations*, London: Sage
Fineman, S. (2003) *Understanding Emotion at Work*, London: Sage

Harré, R. and Finlay Jones, R. (eds) (1986) *The Social Construction of Emotions*, Oxford: Blackwell

Hochschild, A.R. (1985) *The Managed Heart: The commercialization of human feeling*, Berkeley, CA: University of California Press

Hopfl, H. and Linstead, S. (1993) 'Passion and performance: suffering and the carrying of organizational roles' in S. Fineman (ed.) *Emotion in Organizations*, London: Sage

Muchinsky, P.M. (2000) 'Emotions in the workplace: the neglect of organizational behaviour', *Journal of Organizational Behavior*, 21: 801–805

Putnam, L. and Mumby, D.K. (1993) 'Organizations, emotion and the myth of rationality' in S. Fineman (ed.) *Emotion in Organizations*, London: Sage

Taylor, S. (1998) 'Emotional labour and the new workplace' in P. Thompson and C. Warhurst (eds) *Workplaces of the Future*, London: Macmillan

Taylor, S. and Tylor, M. (2000) 'Emotional labour and sexual difference in the airline industry', *Work, Employment and Society*, 14(1): 77–95

Van Maanen, J. and Kunda, G. (1989) ' "Real feelings": emotional expression and organizational culture', *Research in Organizational Behavior*, 11: 43–103

Wouters, C. (1989) 'The sociology of emotions and flight attendants: Hochschild's "managed heart" ', *Theory, Culture and Society*, 6(1): 95–123

Further reading Work and stress

Cooper, C.L. (2000) *Theories of Organizational Stress*, Oxford: Oxford University Press

Cooper, C.L. and Sutherland, V.J. (1992) 'The stress of the executive lifestyle: trends in the 1990s', *Management Decision*, 30(6): 64–68

Cooper, C.L., Cooper, R.D. and Eaker, L. (1988) *Living With Stress*, Harmondsworth: Penguin

Newton, T., Handy, J. and Fineman, S. (eds) (1995) *Managing Stress: Emotion and power at work*, London: Sage

Wainwright, D. and Calnan, M. (2002) *Work Stress: The making of a modern epidemic*, Buckingham: Open University Press

Further reading Deviance and misbehaviour in organisations

Ackroyd, S. and Thompson, P. (1999) *Organisational Misbehaviour*, London: Sage

Adams, A. (1992) *Bullying at Work*, London: Virago

Collinson, D.L. (1992) *Managing the Shopfloor: Subjectivity, masculinity and workplace culture*, Berlin: de Gruyter

Collinson, D.L. (1994) 'Strategies of resistance: power, knowledge and subjectivity in the workplace' in J. Jermier, W. Nord and D. Knights (eds) *Resistance and Power in the Workplace*, London: Routledge

Dalton, M. (1948) 'The industrial rate buster', *Applied Anthropology*, 7(1): 5–23

Ditton, J. (1977a) *Part-time Crime: An ethnography of fiddling and pilferage*, London: Macmillan

Ditton, J. (1977b) 'Perks, pilferage and the fiddle: the historical structure of invisible wages', *Theory and Society*, 4(1): 39–71

Dubois, P. (1977) *Sabotage in Industry*, Harmondsworth: Penguin

Fine, G.A. (1988) 'Letting off steam: redefining a restaurant's work environment' in M.D. Moore and R.C. Snyder (eds) *Inside Organizations: Understanding the human dimension*, Newbury Park, CA: Sage, 119–128

Henry, S. (1987) *The Hidden Economy: The context and control of borderline crime*, Oxford: Martin Robertson

Jermier, J. (1988) 'Sabotage at work: the rational view', *The Sociology of Organisations*, 6: 101–134

Jermier, J., Knights, D. and Nord, W. (1994) *Resistance and Power in Organisations*, London: Routledge

Lee, D. (2000) 'An analysis of workplace bullying in the UK', *Personnel Review*, 29(5): 593–612

Mars, G. (1982) *Cheats at Work: An anthropology of workplace crime*, London: Counterpoint

Noon, M. and Delbridge, R. (1993) 'News from behind my hand: gossip in organisations', *Organisation Studies*, 14(1): 23–36

Punch, M. (1996) *Dirty Business: Exploring corporate misconduct: Analysis and cases*, London: Sage

Roy, D. (1952) 'Quota restriction and goldbricking in a machine shop', *American Journal of Sociology*, 57(5): 427–442

Roy, D. (1958) 'Banana time: job satisfaction and informal interaction', *Human Organisation*, 18(1): 158–161

Stockdale, M.S. (1996) *Sexual Harassment in the Workplace: Perspectives, frontiers and response strategies*, London: Sage

Thomas, A.M. and Kitzinger, C. (1994) 'It's just something that happens: the invisibility of sexual harassment in the workplace', *Gender, Work and Organisation*, 1(3): 151–161

Further reading Humour in organisations

Barsoux, J.-L. (1993) *Funny Business: Humour, management and business culture*, New York: Cassell

Boland, R.J. and Hoffman, R. (1983) 'Humour in a machine shop: an interpretation of symbolic action' in L.R. Pondy, P. Frost, G. Morgan and T. Dandridge (eds) (1983) *Organizational Symbolism*, Greenwich, CT: JAI Press

Bradney, P. (1957) 'The joking relationship in industry', *Human Relations*, 10(2): 179–187

Collinson, D.L. (1988) 'Engineering humour: masculinity, joking and conflict in shop floor relations', *Organization Studies*, 9(2): 181–199

Collinson, D.L. (2002) 'Managing humour', *Journal of Management Studies*, 39(3): 269–288

Davies, C. (1982) 'Ethnic jokes, moral values and social boundaries', *British Journal of Sociology*, 33(3): 383–403

Fox, S. (1990) 'The ethnography of humour and the problem of social reality', *Sociology*, 24(3): 431–446

Jacobson, H. (1997) *Seriously Funny: From the ridiculous to the sublime*, London: Viking

Linstead, S. (1985) 'Jokers wild: the importance of humour in the maintenance of organisational culture', *Sociological Review*, 33(4): 741–767

Mulkay, M. (1988) *On Humour*, Cambridge: Polity Press

Radcliffe-Brown, A.R. (1940) 'On joking relationships', *Africa*, 13: 195–210

Further reading Sexuality in organisations

Brewis, J. and Linstead, S. (2000) *Sex, Work and Sex Work: Eroticizing organization?*, London: Routledge

Burrell, G. (1992) 'Sex and organisations' in A.J. Mills and P. Tancred (eds) *Gendering Organisational Analysis*, London: Sage

Di Tomaso, N. (1989) 'Sexuality in the workplace: discrimination and harassment' in J. Hearn, D.L. Sheppard, P. Tancred-Sherrif and G. Burrell (eds) *The Sexuality of Organization*, London: Sage

Filby, M. (1992) 'The figures, the personality and the bums: service work and sexuality', *Work, Employment and Society*, 6(1): 23–42

Harlow, E., Hearn, J. and Parkin, W. (1992) 'Sexuality and social work organisations' in P. Carter, T. Jeffs and M. Smith (eds) *Changing Social Work and Welfare*, Buckingham: Open University Press

Hearn, J. and Parkin, W. (2001) *Gender, Sexuality and Violence in Organizations*, London: Sage

Roy, D. (1974) 'Sex in the factory: informal heterosexual relations between supervisors and workgroups' in C.D. Bryant (ed.) *Deviant Behavior*, Chicago, IL: Rand McNally

Managing and motivating

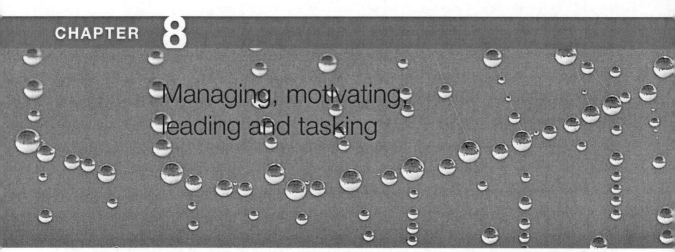

CHAPTER 8

Managing, motivating, leading and tasking

Objectives	Having read this chapter and completed its associated activities, readers should be able to:

- Recognise that those aspects of the organisation of work at the level of basic task performance that are often treated as separate matters – motivation, leadership and job design – are better understood as closely related aspects of managerial task shaping and the winning of employee cooperation.

- See the advantages of considering organisational members' *orientations to work* and the *strategic exchanges* that occur in the context of the employment relationship rather than focus on people's general 'motivation to work'.

- Recognise the advantages of focusing on the managerial manipulation of employees' perceived *implicit contracts* rather than on managerial efforts to 'motivate' employees.

- Understand the extent to which there is negotiation and bargaining within the associated processes of 'motivation', 'leadership' and job design.

- Appreciate the importance of the *indulgency patterns* that arise – the implicit 'give-and-take' practices that can be observed in the relationships between workers and supervisors or managers.

- Appreciate that so-called 'process' theories of motivation like 'equity' and 'expectancy' theories nevertheless contain important insights that fit with the basic *strategic exchange* analysis developed in this chapter.

- Apply the concepts of *direct* and *indirect* managerial control attempts developed in the previous chapter to the *principles of work design* that have influenced the *job design practices* developed over the history of industrial capitalist economies.

- Understand how the application of different types of work design principles at different times can be related to the basic managerial problem of handling contradictions in the basic industrial and organisational system.

● Appreciate the ways in which values, choices and contingent circumstances influence the enactment of specific job designs – and are an element of the more general and strategic organisation-shaping processes that were identified in Chapter 7.

Linking motivation, leadership and job design

The organising and managing of work requires motivating organisational members to behave in certain ways, asking some organisational employees to play a more leading role than others in the workplace and deciding how tasks are to be allocated to people. The issues are always there and have to be tackled. However, it is important to avoid treating matters of motivating, leading and shaping tasks as separate and unconnected matters. This, however, is something that texts which treat 'motivation', 'leadership' and 'job design' as separate and discrete topics might encourage us to do. It is quite normal to find textbooks with separate chapters on 'motivation', 'leadership' and 'job design'. Yet ask any manager trying to direct the activities of an organisational section, department or function where the 'motivating' aspect of their work stops and 'leadership' starts. Even if they accepted the value of these concepts for understanding the work that they do, they would be hard pressed to explain how they differed in practice.

One might similarly ask any manager tackling issues of how tasks in an organisational department are going to be shaped and allocated whether this 'job design' work is simply a matter of the efficient sharing out of work tasks. No, they are likely to reply, a key consideration has to be how effectively different patterns of tasks and roles will 'motivate' or fail to motivate the people undertaking them. To choose whether, on the one hand, to ask employees to tackle the same simple task day in, day out or, on the other hand, to give each individual a variety of challenging tasks to do, requires giving thought to how those employees are likely to react in 'motivational' terms to such arrangements. If 'job designers' find themselves deciding to group people into work teams, it is unlikely to be long before they are talking about the need to design into the teamwork arrangements a role for a team *leader*. In practice, then, those matters that are typically treated as separate issues within orthodox managerial/academic discourses are closely interrelated.

The general meanings of the words that are used in this area would suggest this close interrelationship. When managers 'lead' people, our dictionaries suggest, they are getting people to follow or 'go along with them'. When they 'motivate' them, they are providing 'a stimulus to some kind of action'. These two things are clearly closely interrelated, and both are relevant to the work managers do when they design jobs – when they lay down the patterns of tasks that people are required to undertake. The cluster of tasks that any particular individual is asked to undertake will typically have been designed by managers to get their workers to 'go along with them' and to contain 'stimuli to action'. But managers do not do any of these things in their own departments or sections in isolation from what is going on more generally across the organisation in which they are involved. All of this motivating, leading and patterning of tasks happens in the context of the broader structural and cultural patterns that were looked at in Chapters 6 and 7. And, especially important, as we shall see, is the extent to which the structure and culture of the organisation tends towards the use of *direct* or *indirect* attempts to achieve managerial control. Managerial control is something that will never be completely achieved however hard managers work in *attempting* to achieve it. And the *productive cooperation* that managers are required to pursue will never be complete. Whatever productive cooperation is achieved has to be worked for. It has to be 'won'.

Motivating, leading and job designing are facets of this attempt to 'win cooperation' and they are often indistinguishable from each other in practice. We could say, though, that:

- when people speak of 'motivation' they tend to focus on the *people doing work tasks*;

- when people speak of 'leadership' they tend to focus on the *person trying to influence the carrying out of those tasks*;

- when people speak of 'job design' they tend to focus on the *tasks themselves* and in using the word 'design' are perhaps linking activities at the local level back to the way the organisation as a whole is structured, particularly in terms of either a *direct* or an *indirect* control emphasis.

In Chapter 5 attention was focused in Case 5.2 on Peter Brodie (pp. 177–8) as a manager who was working effectively to win the cooperation of a variety or people upon whom the long-term success of his enterprise depended. The focus there on the individual, however, brings to the fore the 'leadership' aspect of his managerial work. He was thus identified as an effective leader. This 'leadership' effectiveness cannot really be other than temporarily separated from the other aspects of what he was doing in his role as the chief executive of the charity he was shaping and running.

Motivation, leadership and job design need to be regarded as closely interrelated aspects of patterning of activities and understandings across the whole work organisation. And this means remembering that no manager works outside the basic structure and ethos of the organisation that employs them. The present chapter nevertheless tends to concentrate on activities at a more 'local' level within the organisation. It looks at those issues that are traditionally tackled under the traditional headings of motivation, leadership and work design as different facets of the overall processes that occur within task management practices and within the patterns of relationship, rivalry, adjustment and negotiated order that enable productive cooperation to occur to a level that allows the organisation to continue in existence into the future. The three Further Reading guides on leadership (Chapter 5, p. 196), motivation and work design (this chapter pp. 347–8) present material that is made available within the tradition of separating these aspects of managerial work from each other. The chapter itself, however, tries to minimalise this kind of separation.

Earlier, we questioned the value of the social science concept of 'motivation' as a tool for analysing and understanding why people do what they do at work – or anywhere else for that matter. The problems with an emphasis on motives and motivation in understanding human behaviour were discussed in Chapter 3 (pp. 89–90). 'Motivation' was shown to be a concept that is rooted in systems-control thinking about human beings and their behaviour in which the person is seen as 'a little machine-like system in which goals or "motives" operate as a motor "powering" the human entity so that it behaves in a particular way' (p. 86).

The story of Grant Park and his coffee drinking activities was used in Chapter 3 to demonstrate that motives are not usefully seen as things that people 'have' which *precede* behaviour (in the modernist tradition of dualism and linear thinking) (pp. 88–9). Instead, it was argued, 'motives' have to be seen as social rather than purely individual phenomena – often acting as justifications for a piece of behaviour made after the event rather than as causal springs of action or 'triggers' of behaviours. What people do (whether it be to commit a murder or to work hard at a desk all day to please a boss) is an outcome of a multiplicity of factors going way beyond the straightforward fulfilling of motives or the meeting of needs. Whereas systems-control thinking sees human behaviours occurring as individuals who are *motivated* to fulfil *needs* and *wants*, process-relational thinking sees actions taking place 'in the light of interpretations made about the world, to *enact* whatever *projects* individuals who are undertaking *strategically* to shape their lives and to manage *existential challenges*' (Table 3.1, p. 94). Thus, if we want to understand what is 'motivating' a particular individual to behave in a particular way at work we would look at their overall *work orientation* – the meaning that they currently attach to their work (see Chapter 4, pp. 116–24). And this orientation has emerged in the light of their idea of 'who they are' (their identity) and 'where they are going in life' (their personal *strategic shaping*). It is also an aspect of how they are handling life's anxieties and the pressures of their circumstances – matters ranging from how their family is to be fed to ones of values and, say, of conscience about what one 'ought to be doing with one's life'.

From 'worker motivation' to work orientations and strategic exchange

What all of this implies is that we need to stop focusing on people's 'motives' and look at what people are thinking and doing within the broader context of the *strategic exchange* relationships between employing organisations and employees. People going to work in organisations are involved in strategically shaping their lives, and organisations themselves have to be shaped strategically to trade with a whole range of constituencies. Employers and employees come together in an exchange that helps both parties fulfil their respective strategies. And the 'strategy' of the employee can be understood as their basic *orientation to work*. This is something much more subtle, much more complex and much more dynamic than 'motives'.

Activity 8.1

Reread the stories of Ravi Barr (Case 4.1, p. 119) and Sacha and her corporate affairs department (Case 4.2, p. 122):

- to remind yourself of the extent to which people's orientation to work (their overall 'work motivation' as it might be called) varies at different times of their life and in different circumstances;

- to recognise that the efforts of managers and supervisors in the workplace to 'motivate' their staff are only one factor in the resulting 'motivational' state of those staff.

In considering these two stories and what they tell us about the variations that can exist between how people are oriented to (or 'motivated within') their work it readily becomes apparent that we tend to use the notion of motivation in two ways when we look at work behaviour and meaning, as is noted in Table 8.1.

In the story of Ravi Barr in Case 4.1 we notice how a variety of factors in his life experience and his changing notion of identity led to changes in how he was broadly oriented towards work at different times. This could be expressed in terms of how his 'motivation' varied from circumstance to circumstance. The

Table 8.1 Two ways in which we talk about 'motivation' in the work context

Motivation as *the factors leading a person to behave in a certain way at work* (this is similar to the *strategic exchange* notion of a person's orientation to work)	Motivation as *managerial action to influence the people's behaviour at work so they perform as managers require* (in *strategic exchange* terms, this entails managerial manipulation of the implicit contract to get people to behave in a way that leads to productive cooperation)
We say, for example, that a person's 'motivation' has changed when their orientation to work has shifted from one where they sought to maximise their cash return from the employer while showing little interest in the employer's business to one where they concentrate on making a conscientious input to developing the business with a view to building up to a high salary level later in their career	We often say that part of a manager's job is to 'motivate' their staff: find a way of getting them to act in a way that fits with organisational requirements. A manager might observe that the staff are primarily interested in short-term cash reward and prefer to be told exactly what to do. However, the manager decides that it is necessary for these staff to involve themselves in finding new ways of doing the job. The manager might therefore talk of 'motivating my people differently'. This might involve persuading them they will find taking more initiative within their jobs rewarding

term 'orientation' is preferred, however, because it suggests the relevance of a wider variety of factors influencing the way an individual thinks and behaves at work than something as simplistic as a set of 'motives'. It might be reasonable to use the notion of motive to label a simple interest in maximising one's income. However, it is less helpful when it comes to considering such matters as the way in which one expresses one's identity in one's work or the way one develops a working career to fit into a changing set of life priorities or circumstances. We can see the same problem when we look at the staff who work in Sacha Boath's public relations department in Case 4.2. The original 'poor motivation' of Biffy Currie and Sniffy Gerardo, for example, simply cannot be put down to something as simple as 'motives'. Their problems appear to Sacha to be related to problems of identity arising from the loss of their jobs as journalists. Complex problems of marital disharmony and alcoholism were related to this. But their changed work orientations (to a 'positive motivation', as some would put it) seem to have come from changes that they made in their private lives rather than from direct managerial efforts to 'motivate them'. Sacha does claim a part in this change by pointing to her threat to them that they would have to 'ship out' if they did not 'shape up'. For all we know this might have been crucial in getting both men to reconsider what they were doing with their lives, but it can hardly be recognised as a case of a manager 'motivating' a member of staff. Sacha has made a significant managerial intervention, it would seem, but it was an intervention rooted in a subtle consideration of a range of factors influencing the men's lives. It was also risky: the men could have been alienated even more from their work as public relations officers and descended even faster into personal and work troubles.

Trying to influence employees' work orientations is a much more complex matter than simply seeking to 'motivate' them by trying to 'meet their needs' – as much of the standard motivational thinking has it (and to which we will return shortly). One reason for this complexity is the fact, demonstrated in Ravi's case as well as in the case of Smithy (Sacha's third public relations officer), that work orientations are highly influenced by aspects of people's lives outside the workplace. This is not to say that organisational influences are not them-selves of enormous importance. And here, what might seem at first sight like fairly simple changes can have considerable effects. Sacha tells us how Snippy Spedale's approach to her work and to relationships in the office have changed significantly since her desk was moved from a relatively central position in the room. The office rearrangement can be understood as a matter of change in job design – the pattern of tasks and work roles and how these relate to each other is inevitably changed whenever one changes the physical layout of a workplace, however minor this may be. But this has changed the 'reward' side of the perceived implicit contract at the heart of Snippy's work orientation. The pleasure of being at the centre of the office's social life and being able to joke with everybody that entered the office has gone away. And Sacha is thinking about how she can intervene in this. We can infer that she is considering trying to bring something of this back into the informal contract with Snippy when she tells us that she is going to have to 'rethink the office layout'.

Motivating and leading people through the manipulation of implicit contracts

By manipulating Snippy Spedale's work orientation, Sacha is, in orthodox terms, trying to 'remotivate' her. But equally one could say she is attempting this shift in orientation by engaging in some minor job redesign. One might even say she is displaying a degree of subtle 'leadership'. The same might be said of the case of Sparky Learmonth. Sacha recognises that his job has changed – it has become more routine and is thus less intrinsically satisfying for him. But Sparky is happy with his salary and his job security. Such are the complexities and the multiplicity of factors that come into the work orientation of any individual and the implicit contract between them and the employer. Sacha has considered manipulating this by promoting him but, given that this is not feasible, she is talking of finding 'some exciting new project' that will turn him on. Again we can ask whether what is going on here is 'motivation', 'job design' or 'leadership'. It is hard to separate these out. And it is unnecessary. It is more helpful simply to recognise that:

- managerial work involves getting employees to do things that they might not otherwise do;
- to do this managers have to understand the complexities of employees' work orientations;
- any attempt to change these must involve making some adjustment in the individuals' perceived implicit contract – the way employees understand the relationship between what they are 'putting in' to the job and what 'they are taking out' of the employment relationship;
- to change an implicit contract there is bound to be a degree of bargaining, but all negotiations over the 'employment trade' always relate to all the *strategic exchanges* which both the individual and the organisation are making and occur within a relationship involving power differences. The managers, as the employer's agents, with all the organisation's resources behind them, typically have a power advantage over the employees.

Manipulating employees' perceived implicit contract *Concept*

This is at the centre of all motivational, leadership and job design work done by managers. Tasks are shaped and rewards are offered as part of a bargaining process in which managers try to persuade employees to work in the way they want them to work.

All motivational, leadership and work design efforts made by managers attempt to influence employee behaviours by influencing the employee's perception or understanding of the contract that is at the heart of the relationship between the organisation and the worker. How people behave in the workplace is fundamentally

Table 8.2 An 'input–reward' representation of how employees perceive their implicit contract with the employing organisation

Employee input	Employee reward
• physical effort	• money
• mental effort	• job satisfaction
• initiative	• personal 'growth'
• responsibility	• social reward
• impairment – *fatigue, risk of injury etc.*	• security
• compliance – *acceptance of a degree of managerial control*	• power
	• status
	• career potential

influenced by their understanding of the 'employment deal' which, following the analysis provided in Chapter 4 (pp. 115–25), is represented in Table 8.2.

Managers, in 'leading' or getting workers to go along with them, in 'motivating' or giving them incentives to act in a certain way and in shaping their tasks are necessarily involved in complex processes of negotiation. Recognition of this is central to process-relational thinking. It is not just a matter of negotiating with workers what tasks they do or how much they are to be paid for doing those tasks. It is a negotiation over the basic 'realities' of the employment relationship. In the power relationship within which the employment relationship is always set ('if, in the end, you do not do what we ask, you will lose your job') the manager has to establish a pattern of workplace relations and understandings. Within this, the employees have to be persuaded that there is a fair and reasonable return for the efforts and initiatives that they make, the risks to health and mental well-being that they take, and the degree of managerial authority over them that they accept. That return will be a complex mix of monetary, psychological and social rewards. It will be a mix of so much pay, so much security, so much opportunity for career advancement, so much social 'standing' and so on, that makes a fair balance, in the employees' mind, with what is being asked of those employees by the employer.

Activity 8.2

Read the story that Dal Cross tells in Case 8.1 about the foundry yard gang and:

• use as many as possible of the elements or 'headings' in the model of the general 'implicit contract' identified in Table 8.2 to make sense of the yard gang's perceived implicit contract with their employer – the one that prevailed before Dal Cross arrived;

• consider what actions Dal might consider, in terms of manipulating the perceived implicit contract, to change the yard gang's way of working, and stop it being necessary to have a foreman or manager sitting in the office all day turning requests from across the site into direct orders to be given to the 'yardies'.

Dal Cross and the recalcitrant yard gang   Case 8.1

I think I learned everything I know about the management basics from that six months when I was put in charge of the people who do the outdoor work in our foundries. I had only been with the company for about 18 months and was coming towards the end of the management training programme. My final 'attachment', as they called them in those days, was to work with the foundry works manager. This man turned out to be quite different from what I expected. He was a highly qualified metallurgist and he prided himself on being an educated and cultivated individual who, at the same time, had a 'common touch' when it came to his relationships with foundry workers. I'll never forget the words he used when I went to see him to discuss the assignment he was going to give me. He said, 'I can give you a job which, if you succeed with it, will teach you all the basics about managing in this sort of business', and he then used this unforgettable phrase, 'I want you to sort out my recalcitrant yardies'. That night, as you might guess, I looked up the word recalcitrant in my dictionary. It said something like 'not susceptible to control or authority'. What was I taking on?

I had not, in those days, heard of Jamaican 'yardy' gangs and immediately recognised who he was talking about when he pointed out of the window at a couple of men who were slowly – incredibly slowly – sweeping up a section of the factory yard opposite the works manager's office. Their foreman was about to retire and I was to take over from him for a six-month period. The brief was to 'sort things out' and recommend to the works manager what should be done about a permanent replacement for the foreman who, the works manager said, he was 'damned glad to see the back of'. I have to admit that I was rather nervous about taking this on. But I had been complaining to the training manager that I wanted a 'real management assignment' in which I would not only learn about doing management but 'prove myself' as a manager. I'd asked for everything I was going to get, hadn't I?

The foundry site had been developing over 30 to 40 years and it had become a complex jungle of buildings and workshops with all sorts of alleyways leading off the twisting main road that ran through the site. The role of the dozen or so yardmen was to keep these ways clear, clean and safe. They were also responsible for moving materials and 'work in progress' about between buildings on the various motorised trucks and hand-pushed carts that they controlled. The responsibility for scrap handling was also theirs.

The work was very hard and often very dirty. One minute they were shifting foundry sand, the next minute carting heavy castings from the furnace room to the fettling shop and soon after that they were having to sweep floodwater away after a heavy rainstorm or shovel snow or ice off the roadways. The work could be dangerous, especially given the cramped areas they often worked in and the heavy and awkward material they sometimes had to handle. And there was a degree of responsibility with this work. Some of the moulds or patterns that they moved about were very fragile, as were some of the ceramic cores that they handled. One slip with these items and not only was money lost but the production schedule could be completely blown. On top of that, the scrap was often quite valuable and the security people were always anxious that no one with a criminal record or with criminal contacts should be in the gang. Scrap thieving can be quite a lucrative activity around engineering works, you know.

What was obvious to me from the moment I began meeting members of the gang was that they took no initiative whatsoever. They wouldn't even sweep up a broken beer bottle in the middle of the car park without being instructed to do so, I discovered. The foreman had insisted that no work be done unless it was under his instruction. Members of the gang had to do exactly what he told them. If any one of them disobeyed him they would find themselves spending a disproportionate amount of time cleaning lavatories. When I looked at the wages that the blokes got they seemed fairly reasonable to me. They compared well with other manual workers who did not have a skilled trade. It seemed that the relatively dangerous and physically uncomfortable aspects of the job were well compensated for by the fairly high security of employment that the job gave them. The foreman might have been a bossy so-and-so but he made sure that his blokes stayed in work if they went along with him. Nevertheless I was quite puzzled at first that they were willing to put up with the heaviness of the control that he exerted. But after a few days I realised that this was balanced by the space he gave them for 'having a laugh together', as they put it. He allowed them longer tea breaks than any other workers took and he turned a blind eye to their practice of 'taking it easy' for the last half-hour of each working day. I knew that other supervisors across the site resented all of this, both because it undermined their own authority with their workers and because they often found themselves unable to get things moved towards the end of a shift or when the yardies were finishing off their card game during a protracted tea break. But few complained too loudly to the yard foreman because he would 'punish' them by ensuring that their 'breakages' increased for a few days or by saying that he had no truck available to move their goods.

There seemed few satisfactions for the yardies in the tasks that they did but I think they nevertheless enjoyed coming to work. And although, in one sense, their status was low as an unskilled group who had some pretty unpleasant tasks to do, they did carry a certain perverse status among the workforce. This was because of the informal privileges they enjoyed as a result of their foreman's power to protect them from any disciplines that might come from another direction. Nobody, including the works manager, dared question what went on. Too much boat-rocking would follow from upsetting the yardies.

Some of the other supervisors used to call the foreman the 'yard führer' and one of them, who had an Italian background, simply called him 'Il Duce'. This name-calling was obviously more than a matter of people with a knowledge of languages using the German or the Italian word for 'leader'! And if I was going to follow my own beliefs about good leadership in my six months with these men, I was going to have to make some big changes. I had to run things the old way at first, however. If I hadn't, the foundry would have ground to a halt. No man was willing to move from the rest room until he had an instruction from me. When I suggested that they all surely knew 'what needed doing on a Monday morning if they thought about it', they responded that they 'were not paid to think'. That was the foreman's job. But after a couple of days sitting at the old foreman's desk receiving phone calls from around the site asking for a truck here, a lavatory cleaner there, a bin emptied somewhere else and an oil leak cleared up outside the main waxroom – and then despatching the appropriate yardy for that job – I was even more convinced that I had to change things.

The implicit contract between the company and the yard gang members, as Dal Cross understands it, is as complex as one we might find with any group of workers. On the employee 'input' side of the trade there is clearly a high level of physical effort required and the yardies subject themselves to a degree of 'impairment' by getting quite dirty and risking accidents in some of the dangerous conditions they meet. They do not appear to make much input by way of initiative taking, however, and the responsibilities they bear are of a relatively passive kind. They simply have to take care not to damage fragile items that they are moving about. But this is a heavier responsibility than it might at first sound, since damage to some of these goods could harm the overall performance of the foundry as a business operation. We might imagine, though, that the foreman himself would take formal responsibility for such damage, given that he exerts so much direct control over the yard gang's work.

The approach he takes to his job means that anyone working in his gang has to surrender a significant amount of personal autonomy while at work. For the rewards that they receive, these men have to submit to a high level of direction from a 'boss'.

The pay that the yardies received, Dal infers, was not an issue. Taken together with the other rewards, an acceptable balance between the two sides of the effort bargain had been struck. Security of employment was clearly a significant factor on the reward side. There appeared to Dal to be little reward in terms of job satisfaction, personal growth or career potential. But we can imagine that they felt some degree of power through their being identified with the power that the foreman himself had over other supervisors and managers. Dal certainly notes a degree of 'perverse' status coming from certain advantages that the yardies had over other foundry workers. They had a greater opportunity to enjoy leisure at work than any other group, for example. It can be inferred that these lengthy card-playing tea breaks and the winding-down time provided the yardies with a degree of 'social reward' in the workplace. It was a fairly distinct- ive factor going into the mix or balance of 'inputs' and 'outputs' that makes up the implicit contract of this particular group of workers with the employing organisation. It was at the core of their work orientation and is thus something that anybody would need to appreciate – Dal Cross included – who wanted to understand why the yardies thought and behaved in the way they did with regard to their work.

The implicit contract has just been referred to as a trade that goes on between employees and the employing organisation. But, of course, 'the organisation' is not literally a trader itself. The bargain that we say, in a shorthand way, 'the organisation' is making with its employees is in fact made in the organisation's name by the various managers, personnel recruitment staff and supervisors with whom the individual deals at different stages of their entry to and continuing involvement in the organisation. And where there is a manager or supervisor directly involved in shaping the everyday activities of any individual or group of individuals there will necessarily be a degree of day-to-day negotiation or *give and take* about what work is done and how and when it is done. The works manager clearly saw the yard gang as an especially 'recalcitrant' group – clearly thinking of the yardies and the foreman together as a group that had managed to get itself in some ways 'above the law' that applied to other groups under the works manager's authority. However, we could say that all employees – all human beings indeed – are recalcitrant to a degree (see the earlier discussion of this, pp. 2–3). Every manager, schoolteacher or parent knows that the employees, pupils or children formally 'under their control' will never follow every instruction that they are given or submit totally to every rule that is meant to shape their behaviour. There has to be a degree of 'give and take' which allows the person in authority to get 'some of their own way' in return for allowing those subject to that authority to 'get away' with infringing some of the rules which, if followed in every detail, would turn the individual into a puppet or a robot rather than a human being with free will and personal autonomy. Gouldner, in a classic study of factory life (1954), conceptualised as an *indulgency pattern* the tendency he saw for supervisors to 'turn a blind eye' to certain rule-breaking activities. The supervisors did this as part of an implicit understanding that the workers would, reciprocally, indulge the supervisors when they sought compliance over matters that the workers might reasonably refuse to go along with.

Indulgency pattern   *Concept*

The ignoring by supervisors or managers of selected rule infringements by workers in return for those workers conceding to requests that, strictly speaking, they could refuse.

The joiners' shop ritual reported in Chapter 7 (in Table 7.2, p. 286) whereby the joiners always used the first 20 minutes of their shift to take an 'illegal tea break' while the supervisors deliberately kept their backs to the working areas for the same period of time is an example of a ritualised expression of an indulgency pattern. In this case a particularly assertive manual work group is ritually demonstrating that it only cooperates with 'management' on its own terms, and the supervisors are ritually displaying their acceptance of this. A more typical indulgency pattern, however, is one in which a manager ignores their staff taking an extra long lunch break once a week to do their shopping, in return for those employees complying with the occasional short notice request to do some overtime or to cover for another worker who has not turned up for work. The yard foreman clearly indulges his staff by allowing them to take long breaks and to stop working well before the official finishing time. This, we can reasonably infer, is a trade. It is a conceding of free time during working hours in return for the workers allowing the supervisor to have an unusually high level of task control over them.

It is clear that implicit contracts have some very subtle aspects to them. The very fact that they involve a range of formally unstated agreements makes the managerial 'motivational' task quite a subtle and challenging one. The manager is constantly bargaining with the people that in traditional 'organisation behaviour' terms they are said to be 'motivating' or 'leading'. And, given that managers are frequently required to take initiatives to make changes in work behaviour, they face the considerable challenge of having to renegotiate the ongoing work exchange or *contract* with the people whose behaviours they are trying to change. Dal Cross refers to his foundry assignment as a 'change management' one and he uses the analysis of the yard workers' work orientations and perceived implicit contract that we have just reviewed to make the changes he sees as necessary. And the *processes* that he engages in to negotiate these changes are ones where, once again, we see the overlapping of so-called motivational, leadership and job design initiatives.

Activity 8.3

Read Dal Cross's continuing story in Case 8.2 about his managerial experiences with the yard gang in the foundry and:

- using Table 8.2 again (p. 316), analyse the new implicit contract that makes possible Dal's re-organising of the yard gang;

- consider the extent to which Dal has made changes to 'job design' in setting up the modified 'site services' function;

- consider whether you can see a 'theory of leadership' behind Dal's working towards these changes;

- identify the extent to which it might be said that there is now a new 'indulgency pattern' within these 'site services' arrangements.

Leadership in practice and a 'triumph of change management'   Case 8.2

I had talked of 'proving myself' managerially by taking on this assignment with the foundry works manager and I knew that I was either going to fail miserably or that I was going to pull off a triumph of change management. I had been on a change management course and read all the stuff on choosing the 'right leadership style', motivating people, enriching jobs, empowering staff, quality circles and goodness knows what else. As I read through all this stuff again on the Monday evening after my first day with the yard gang, I struggled to make it all add up. I had to fall back on what I believed in about being a manager. When I had been interviewed for the management traineeship in the first place it seemed that I had said very much the right thing when I had argued that managers were going to have to initiate a lot of changes to make businesses successful in an increasingly competitive world. But managers would not be able to – nor should they morally – unilaterally impose these changes on the organisation's employees. The interviewing panel had been wary of my suggestion that this might involve negotiating work organisation changes with trade unions. But they warmed to my theme that managers and their staff had to 'work together' – with those being paid to be managers taking the lead – to find new ways of working that would give benefits to the organisation and the workers alike.

All these fine words came back to me on that Monday night. Although this was rather idealistic sounding, it did feel to me to be the only way I could *realistically* go about tackling the problem of the yard gang. The works manager was simply unwilling to allow the continuation of an operation led by a gang boss who bullied other managers and supervisors into a situation where they could neither question the level of service he gave them nor challenge the way he indulged his staff. What was clear to me was that I could not simply order the yardies to work differently and to start using their own initiative to provide the site with a fast and efficient service that didn't always have to be mediated by a gang boss.

Ever since my early reflections on what being a manager should mean, I knew that my preferred personal style of leadership would have to be one of establishing a relationship of trust with the men and then negotiating with them a new way of working. That Monday night I decided that I would 'give a lead' by proposing a working principle of 'providing a service to the site' and that this would entail treating people in the various foundry departments as 'internal customers'. I was fully aware that I could not simply foist these ideas onto the men as a cynical act of pushing management fads that I had heard about on a course. I was very tempted to use the 'empowerment' word in my discussion, for example. I think the word describes well what I wanted to do. But I thought that the pretentious overtones of this word would not go down well in the foundry context. If I was going to work with them in a trusting relationship I had to be subtle and establish with them that the 'new order' I had in mind would be one in which they would all be better off than under the old regime, in one way or another.

I called a meeting with all the men in their 'winding down' time on the Tuesday evening, promising overtime payment to cover time spent in this or subsequent meetings that might go beyond the end of the shift. I took time to listen to what each of the men felt about the good and the bad aspects of the job and I worked hard to get them to see where, as a bloke, I was 'coming from'. I think this worked out quite well, partly because I think I am quite good at presenting myself as a sincere sort of person. But it was equally because all of this was set within a promise that nobody would 'lose out' if they 'went along with me'. Pay would certainly not suffer and I would look into ways in which an 'improved service to the foundry' might lead to an improved pay level. As I pointed out, the company had a job evaluation scheme which would ensure that if they were to 'increase the thinking or initiative element' of their work then they should move to a higher pay band.

Above all, though, I argued that they would surely be much happier to be 'getting out from under the thumb' of the boss man who had pushed them around for so long. And surely it would be better to get proper job satisfaction from providing a service to people across the foundry that would be genuinely appreciated than to carry on taking whatever satisfaction they had been getting from long tea breaks and card games. Taking my managerial life into my hands – or so it felt at the time – I added to this that whatever pleasure they took in the 'fun time' that they had at work was surely undermined by the disgust that other workers felt at what they were 'getting away with'. A stony silence followed that particular input to the discussions. But I got out of the impasse that I had backed myself into by pointing out that if members of the new 'site services' department were to be given discretion over how they went about providing services then they would also obviously have to be given discretion over when they might need to rest or otherwise recover after carrying out a particularly onerous or exhausting task. All of this, I argued, would have to be part of the trust that would need to exist between the members of the department and whoever would be in charge of it.

I hope all of this doesn't sound too glib. It was all very hard work and I found myself fluctuating between elation and depression as I worked towards the new department that I wanted to establish. Without going into all the details, the 'gang' were now to be a 'team' who would meet each morning to allocate among themselves the areas in which each of them were to work through the day. Sections of the team would be allocated each day to an area of the foundry and the members of that section would themselves agree who would do what task – lavatory cleaning and bin clearing included – as the need for it arose within any given area of the site. I got the jobs upgraded and this was helped by a deal I did with the security department whereby the 'site services staff' carried out certain routine security tasks as part of their work. I also got the works manager to agree that it might be possible to appoint a team leader from within the group when I came to the end of my six months. I told the team that this was simply a possibility but that if any of them was interested in future promotion in the company they might like to talk to me about this idea. I felt it was important that the yard workers should have the incentive of personal development and a career available to them, just like elsewhere in the organisation. Site services, and everybody in it, were on the 'up and up', I was proud to say.

The new implicit contract does not involve any less physical effort or risk of impairment than the old one. The major changes are with regard to the increased degree of initiative that the men are being asked to show in organising their own work schedules and task allocations. This can be seen as an increased 'input'. Alongside this there is what might be seen as a reduced input: the removal of the old requirement to surrender a high degree of personal autonomy by submitting themselves to a foreman's tight and direct control. It is sometimes argued by managers in situations like this that the only change in reward that this requires is one that automatically follows from the workers being freed to take charge of their own working practices: the reward of increased job satisfaction. Such people argue that 'empowering' workers by giving them increased freedom to choose how to work is a reward in itself. However, it is far from unusual for employees to reject this line of bargaining. They are quite likely to respond in the way the yard workers did and raise the principle of 'being paid to think'. Employees are quite likely to observe that their 'empowerment' involves them taking on tasks that managers or supervisors previously carried out. They argue that taking on such work should be recognised with a higher rate of pay. Dal Cross is well aware of this type of argument, it would seem. Consequently he has sought ways of getting their pay increased: using the company's formal job evaluation scheme, one that incorporates the principle of paying for initiative and responsibility. To ensure that such an upgrading occurs he also adds a security guard dimension to their work. This has the potential tacitly to improve the status element of the reward side of the implicit contract. Dal also explicitly addresses the status issue by suggesting they will be better off without the rather questionable sort of status they gained by getting more leisure-in-work time than other employees.

Dal seems to be very aware that taking away the opportunity to enjoy unofficial social rewards in the extended tea breaks is not going to be easy. He therefore seeks to redefine it as implicitly a little shameful and unfair to other workers. It is not an untainted reward. But he goes even further to deal with this potentially tricky issue. In effect, he suggests his own version of the indulgency pattern that was part of the old regime. We can understand in this way his statement to the yard workers that they would 'obviously have to be given discretion over when they might need to rest or otherwise recover after carrying out a particularly onerous or exhausting task'. This offer is subtly connected to the principle of mutual trust that he speaks of as inherent in their generally increased discretion.

There is a lot of subtle 'motivational' work going on in the meetings of Dal and his staff and he shows considerable rhetorical skill in drawing on discursive resources like 'trust', 'service', 'internal customer' and 'team' to paint a very positive picture of the new world into which he wants to lead them. He was wary of using the discursive resource of 'empowerment', however. We might see this reluctance to use a possibly pretentious term as a reflection of Dal's skills of persuasion and leadership. He certainly seems to have worked out his own theory of leadership, one that incorporates a belief that one cannot impose changes on employees (or 'foist ideas' or 'management fads' on them). He sees negotiation as an important part of his 'personal style of leadership' and believes this should happen after establishing a trusting relationship with those with whom he is to negotiate. For Dal, this means allowing the men to get to know him personally and 'where he is coming from'. He also mentions taking time to listen to the views of the group before putting his ideas to them. To be a leader is nevertheless still a matter of initiating actions for Dal. He talks of 'giving a lead' by proposing the site service idea. However, that assertion of leadership is balanced with a clear recognition that is occurring within what is an essentially negotiated relationship of exchange – the employment bargain.

Dal is 'motivating' and 'leading' then, but he is also engaging is some significant job design work. By incorporating much of the foreman's old role into the work of the yard gang members themselves he is significantly redesigning the tasks away from the former *direct* control principles towards one in which control is much more *indirect*. Dal is not moving to a situation where the foundry management abandons control over the yard workers. It is asking them to control themselves, in the interests of the employing organisation as well as for their own benefit. He is utilising work design principles of *job enrichment*, *team-working* and the *semi-autonomous work group* (concepts we look at below, pp. 235–8). He does recognise, however, that the group might not satisfactorily work in an entirely 'leaderless' way when he ends his involvement with them in a few months' time. He therefore talks of the possibility of a team leader being appointed. And in talking of this he is making yet another adjustment to the implicit contract with the group – he is putting into the bargain for the first time a possibility of career advancement.

Equity, balance and expectancies in work orientations

Although it is now common for motivational theories that use ideas of equity or expectancy to be referred to as 'process theories' they go only a part of the way towards the full process-relational thinking that has been developed over the chapters of *Organising and Managing Work*. Their insights do parallel much of what has been said about orientations to work and implicit contracts however. An early process-oriented contribution to what has variously been referred to as 'balance', 'social comparison' or 'equity' theorising in this area was a classical study of American soldiers (Stouffer *et al.*, 1949). The researchers observed that there was a greater dissatisfaction with promotional opportunities in the Army Corps than in the Military Police. This was in spite of the fact that, objectively, there were better opportunities in the former part of the military than in the latter. The dissatisfactions and the 'de-motivating' influence of these were not the outcomes of what was objectively the case but arose out of the expectations of the people involved with regard to promotional opportunities. A general sense of unfairness had developed in large part as a result of individual soldiers comparing their own prospects with the way that others had been treated. Developments in this kind of thinking were pulled together into an 'equity theory of motivation' by Adams (1963, 1965). This sees people balancing what they put into their work with what they get out of it in the light of what they see other people putting in and taking out in similar situations.

The basic insight of so-called 'equity theory' is a vital one and it is wholly consistent with how the *work orientation* and *implicit contract* concepts have been used here. The central attention given in strategic exchange thinking to how people perceive or understand the contract they make with an employer is the same as in balance and equity thinking. The stress on how this perception involves comparisons with other people is implicit but clear in, for example the earlier reference to employees having to 'be persuaded that there is a fair and reasonable return' for everything that those employees 'put into' their work (p. 00). None of us can decide as to how 'fair or reasonable' we can regard anything that we are asked to do or anything that we are offered without making comparisons with other people and their circumstances.

Activity 8.4

Consider how far matters of 'equity', 'balance' or perceived fairness come into the stories Dal Cross in Case 8.2 (p. 321) and Campbell Toon in Case 1.3 (p. 23) have to tell us about:

- the way Dal first analyses the work orientations and perceived implicit contracts of the yard

gang and, later, enters negotiations with the men;

- Campbell's attempts to increase the productivity of the packaging workers in his part of the factory by 'enriching' their jobs.

When Dal Cross was trying to make sense of the work orientations of the members of the yard gang in his early involvement with them he looked at the balance between what they were 'putting in' and 'getting out' – as far as he could understand it as an observer. He is explicit about the fact that he is talking at this stage about his perception of their perceptions, so to speak, when he says that their wages 'seemed fairly reasonable to me'. In effect he tries to put himself in their position, and makes the sort of comparison with others that he thinks that they would make – with 'other manual workers who did not have a skilled trade'. Some more subtle thinking along these lines is done as he goes on to look at what he calls the 'perverse status' that they enjoy in the foundry. This analysis emerges from his trying to make sense in 'balance' terms of the fact that the yardies get more free time for their own leisure during working hours than do other workers. All of these complexities are later taken into account during the bargaining that he enters into with the gang as he works to move them towards a new implicit contract. He tries to get them to redefine this 'privilege' by effectively suggesting that it is not really a reward at all.

Dal is well aware that worker perceptions of inputs and outputs have an important economic dimension. He appreciates that a pay increase is going to be vital in shifting the exchange relationship. It is interesting that the company's 'job evaluation' scheme that he makes use of is a device similar to that which many employers use to deal openly with matters of comparison and perceived fairness in wages or salaries paid to different groups within an organisation. Job evaluation schemes are used in deciding pay relativities in many work organisations. They use measurements of work 'inputs' and 'outputs' that are believed to be acceptable to everyone as the basis for pay comparisons. Such a scheme could also be a help to Cam Toon if he wishes to try again to redesign the work tasks of the members of his department. He reports how his workers were comparing the new tasks that they were doing with what they believe supervisors do. In principle, a job evaluation scheme would enable their new jobs to be measured, compared to the work that a supervisor typically does in similar areas of the organisation and a 'fair' wage for the new employment trade identified.

> ## Expectancy theories of work motivation   *Concept*
>
> These theories show how work behaviour is influenced (a) by the particular wants and expectations which particular employees, in particular circumstances, bring to the organisation and (b) by the extent to which these are met by the employer.

The concept of *expectancy* has been utilised by various theorists to deal with these matters of employee perception or 'understanding'. The concept has played a central part in the turning away of motivation theorists from the focus on 'needs' towards use of the much more realistic 'wants' and expectations that employees bring to particular jobs. Instead of indulging in generalisations about the needs that human beings generally are said to bring to the workplace, it encourages managers to look at the specific work circumstances of whatever group of employees they are concerned with and at the specific expectations that they bring to their employment relationship with a particular employer. The 'expectancies' referred to by psychologists and motivation theorists like Vroom (1964) or Lawler (1971) correspond to some extent to the 'work orientations' notion that has emerged out of the industrial sociology tradition. We can draw out of expectancy thinking some highly commonsensical guidelines that can be applied to the various facets of work organisation and bear on the input–output bargain at the centre of the employment relationship management – from pay systems and promotional policies to job design and management style. For successful 'motivation' to occur several conditions have to be met.

- Employees must see that the effort they put in will, in fact, cause effective performance. It would be inappropriate for an individual output bonus to be paid to someone operating a machine that had a fixed rate or level of output, for example.

- Employees must see that appropriate performance will lead to their receiving the rewards claimed to be linked to them. Promotion would not be a good motivator, for example, if the individual either sees people being promoted for reasons other than effective performance or if they see cases of such performance failing to lead to promotion.

- The rewards available to employees must be ones in which they are actually interested – or can be persuaded to become interested in. The offer of the rewards of intrinsic job satisfaction (that Campbell Toon offered his staff, for example) or increased job status would be poor motivators for employees who simply wanted a quiet life at work in a secure job with a good level of pay to take home.

- Employees must have both the technical skills and knowledge to do the job.

- Employees must understand the broader implications of the role they are taking on – the sort of relationships they are expected to have with managers themselves and with other people in the organisation for example.

These practical managerial guidelines emerge from what textbooks label 'expectancy theories of motivation'. The theory behind these highly commonsensical recommendations is consistent with strategic exchange thinking and its emphasis on the interpretations and understandings that people bring to their employment. Expectancy thinking's focus is on the employees themselves, as we would expect from work emerging from the psychological tradition of 'motivational' theorising. In this respect, it is a more narrowly focused analysis than the strategic exchange one. Strategic exchange analysis is broader and deeper in its locating of managerial attempts to manipulate the implicit contract within both the social and cultural location and priorities of the employee and the strategic position and priorities of the employing organisation (whose exchanges with employees are just one resource exchange among many.

Strategic exchange analysis and the way it uses the concepts of work orientation and implicit contract is also broader (more fully process-relational we might say) than expectancy theory in its attention to the ongoing processes of negotiation and renegotiation that occur in the relationship between employers and employees. This is a relationship that exists within a political–economic context. And the nature of that context means that significant managerial efforts have to go into the constant handling of the basic tensions and contradictions that characterise the employment relationship in industrial capitalist societies. These tensions are always there in the background of every 'motivational' situation in the work organisation. Sometimes they are more obvious than at other times, however. They could be understood as manifesting themselves, for instance, when one of the two workers with whom Campbell Toon discusses the issue of whether or not 'money is a motivator' in Case 1.3 (p. 23) rejects the language of motivation and contextualises the proposed pay claim with the words, 'there's no way any factory worker is ever going to feel that they are paid enough'. Issues of social class and basic employer–employee conflicts are clearly playing a part here.

Work motivation, then, cannot be considered in isolation from a whole range of other issues that impinge on the negotiated relationship between the employing organisation and its employees. And there is no particular aspect of a manager's job that can be separated out from the rest of what they do as the 'motivational element' of their job. It has been clear throughout this chapter, not least in the reported managerial experiences of Dal Cross and Cam Toon, that to 'motivate' people (getting employees to do what they otherwise would not do) managers lead, build relationships, develop understandings, train people, devise promotional schemes and design jobs. Both Dal and Cam are, for example, engaged in a degree of job redesign work in their attempts to 'motivate' their staff to work more effectively. These were personal initiatives applying to their own departments. But, as was stressed earlier in the chapter, we cannot separate out what any manager does in their own department from the wider cultural and structural arrangements of the organisation as a whole. Each of these managers was attempting a move from a relatively *direct* approach to seeking managerial control to a relatively *indirect* one. In this, we can assume that they felt that such a move was not inconsistent with the broader cultural and structural trends in their companies. Broad considerations of job design are an important element in the strategic shaping of the organisation as a whole.

Direct and indirect control principles of work design

Organisational structures, and the task shaping and task allocation that is part of them, are very much 'emergent' phenomena – outcomes of the balance of managerial initiatives and employee acceptance. Process-relational thinking draws attention to the negotiated, political and emergent aspects of organisations. Organisations, as they emerge out of the processes of cooperation and conflict, rarely resemble their official managerial blueprint or organisation charts when we look at them in action. But this does not mean that managers are not continually working to design – or *re*design – the activities that are carried on in the organisation's name. To understand this, it is useful to look at certain work design principles that have played a part in shaping the practices of organisational managers throughout the history of the modern work organisation.

Work design/redesign principles   *Concept*

General principles about how narrow or broad the tasks associated with jobs should be and the extent to which jobholders should use discretion in carrying out those tasks.

> ### Job design/redesign practices   *Concept*
>
> The shaping of particular jobs, especially with regard to how narrow or broad the tasks associated with those jobs are and the extent to which jobholders exercise discretion in carrying out those tasks.

The terms 'job design' and 'work design' are often used interchangeably but, here, we will use them to represent two different but closely related ideas. The actual task pattern that emerges in any particular part of an organisation (the new version of the yard worker job introduced by Dal Cross in Case 8.2, for example) is referred to here as a matter of *job design* (or redesign). The broad principles that are drawn upon when designing or redesigning jobs are, however, referred to as *work design* principles. The former, then, are matters of actual practice and the latter matters of prescription or intent.

Work design is clearly something closely related to the broader structural and cultural 'design' of the organisation as a whole. It was argued in Chapter 7 that there is a basic choice that managers can make in trying to achieve managerial control through this design – through the shaping of the organisation as a whole. This is a choice between *direct* control attempts and *indirect* ones.

- An organisation leaning towards direct control principles would be a highly centralised one with a tightly bureaucratic structure and culture. There would be an emphasis on tight rules and closely prescribed procedures in which a relatively low level of psychological commitment would be sought from the employees. Because these arrangements imply that management is not putting a lot of trust in employees to do what is required of them of their own accord, a 'low trust' culture emerges in which relationships between employer and employees tend to be adversarial. Differences of interest between parties to the employment relationship thus become manifest and visible at a surface level.

- The organisation leaning more in the indirect control direction would be less centralised and have a loosely bureaucratic structure and culture. Rules would be relatively loose and procedures left flexible because employees would have discretion about how to carry out those tasks. They would, however, apply this discretion in a way that fitted with managerial requirements and the strategic priorities of the organisation because of their high level of psychological commitment to the organisation. This commitment is made possible, in turn, because of a culture of high trust between members of the organisation – one in which common or mutual interests between different parties to the employment relationship are emphasised. Differences of interest between parties to the employment bargain tend to remain below the surface of ongoing activities and are not expressed through overt confrontations.

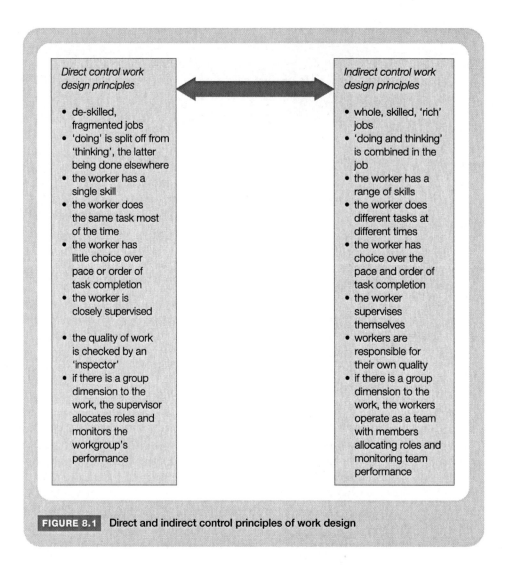

Direct control work design principles

- de-skilled, fragmented jobs
- 'doing' is split off from 'thinking', the latter being done elsewhere
- the worker has a single skill
- the worker does the same task most of the time
- the worker has little choice over pace or order of task completion
- the worker is closely supervised

- the quality of work is checked by an 'inspector'
- if there is a group dimension to the work, the supervisor allocates roles and monitors the workgroup's performance

Indirect control work design principles

- whole, skilled, 'rich' jobs
- 'doing and thinking' is combined in the job
- the worker has a range of skills
- the worker does different tasks at different times
- the worker has choice over the pace and order of task completion
- the worker supervises themselves
- workers are responsible for their own quality
- if there is a group dimension to the work, the workers operate as a team with members allocating roles and monitoring team performance

FIGURE 8.1 Direct and indirect control principles of work design

Within these two basic approaches to what we might call *organisational* design there are two basic sets of *work* design principles and these are outlined in Figure 8.1.

The two sets of work design principles outlined in Figure 8.1 are *ideal types* – constructs created by the social scientist to help make sense of the much more complex and potentially confusing picture that emerges when we go out into organisations to see what is happening 'on the ground' (as we saw with Weber's 'ideal type of bureaucracy' in Chapter 2, pp. 39–40). No actually observable job designs have ever fully followed the descriptions set out as two ends of the continuum in the diagram, and job designs can be found that are close to the basic work design principles set out in the two columns without following every element of the above characterisation. Within teamworking, to take an example from the 'indirect' side, it might be that the team allocates its own roles from day to day but is still subject to external monitoring of the resulting performance. Sometimes teamworking involves a 'team leader' who retains certain of the roles of the supervisor who plays an important role on the 'direct' side.

In practice, the actual job designs we are likely to come across in organisations will fall somewhere along the continuum outlined in Figure 8.1 and may even combine elements from both ends of it. The model is nevertheless valuable because it represents in a clear way the scope of choices open to managers when they embark on designing jobs in particular organisational settings. We might imagine some scheme like this having been in the minds of both Dal Cross and Campbell Toon when they set out to make changes in the designs of jobs for which they had managerial responsibilities. Both, as we noted earlier, were interested in making moves towards more *indirect* ways of controlling the work done in their departments. Each of these two managers were influenced by 'newer' work design ideas that they had come across. Dal tells us how he had been on a 'change management course' and amongst the 'stuff' that he had read was material on 'enriching jobs', 'empowering staff' and 'quality circles'. Cam refers to his 'classes on motivation', where one of the things he learned about was Herzberg's 'job enrichment principles'. Although these men mention different bits of 'management thinking', they do not closely follow any of the texts or manuals on any of these specific techniques. Instead, they pragmatically apply the basic principles that underlie all these specific innovations ('job enrichment', 'empowerment', 'quality circles', for example). These are the basic principles being characterised here as *indirect control* principles. Within these, Dal pragmatically devises his own form of 'teamworking', that in the longer run may or may not have a team leader role within it. Cam speaks of 'rearranging the jobs of my people so that there was more variety in their tasks'. He also tries to give them 'more freedom to choose how to do the work' by removing a level of supervision.

We shall shortly review some of the more significant managerial innovations and fashions that have been put forward in different guises and under different labels over the past half century. But it is more important to see what all of these have in common than to try to look for distinctions between, say, 'job enrichment', 'vertical task integration' and 'empowerment' or between 'semi-autonomous work groups' and 'teams'. Exactly that has been done here by clustering many of the features of these managerial innovations and identifying them as 'indirect control attempts' which, at the level of job design, are used to handle, in effect, the basic contradiction that all managerial work has to deal with. This is the contradiction whereby managers need to control what workers do while, at the same time, recognising that every managerial attempt at control is liable to be challenged. Organisational members, to varying degrees, will demand 'freedom' or autonomy in the workplace. But managers must make sure that this freedom is a freedom to do what, in the end, the managers want them to do. Loose control, in effect, is stronger than tight control. That is the basic principle of indirect control work design thinking.

Modernity, industrialism and the hesitant embracing of direct control work design

There is a powerful irony behind the fact that we typically treat the principles of *indirect* work design principles as managerial innovations, as 'new thinking', or in terms of progressive or enlightened management ideas. This is ironic because, in the larger historical scheme of things, it was the shift in industrialising societies towards *direct* forms of work control that was one of the fundamental innovations of the new industrial capitalist order. One has to take care not to romanticise the pre-industrial past but, generally speaking, the division of labour that operated in pre-industrial societies was a *social (or general) division of labour*.

Social or *general* division of labour	Concept
The allocation of work tasks across society, typically into occupations or trades.	

The key work design principle was an occupational one: the working individual played their part in society as a farmer, brewer or shoemaker and would be expected to develop the cluster of skills that went with their particular craft or trade. They would be able to handle what work design experts later came to call 'whole tasks' – the planting, nurturing and harvesting of a crop or the production of a pair of shoes. In practice there were undoubtedly numerous people who did little more than sweep floors or carry trade workers' tools. However, something along the lines of what we have characterised as indirect work design principles were generally seen as desirable and at the centre of the pre-industrial social order. The rise of industrial capitalism, the growth of the institution of formal employment and the rationalising force of bureaucratisation saw a splitting down of many of the occupational roles within the old social division of labour into de-skilled jobs. There was now to be a *technical (or detailed) division of labour* whereby many work activities in factories and offices were split down so that individuals only did one specialised part of what had previously been the 'whole task' associated with an occupation.

Technical or *detailed* division of labour	Concept
The breaking down of 'whole' occupational roles into specialised and generally unskilled jobs.	

We can envisage the seventeenth or eighteenth century violin maker working on each instrument all the way from the initial woodcarving stage to the varnishing and the adding of the bridge, pegs and strings. But we would find the typical worker in a modern violin factory only able to work the wood cutting machine, glue the front, sides and backs of the instrument together or varnish the violin when it reached the varnish shop. The work would have been de-skilled. Many more violins could be produced at a much higher rate of profit for the employer, but for this to occur, those with the expertise have to take on the role of instructing and monitoring the rest. The managers have to control the workers. Thinking is separated from doing (an important direct control design feature identified earlier in Figure 8.1) and the implications for human beings of this trend were recognised from the start. Adam Smith in his massively influential work *The Wealth of Nations* of 1776, in which the new industrial order was both chronicled and boosted further, provided an analysis of the splitting down of the process of making tacks ('pins' as he called them). This showed that if you fragmented the job of the craft pin maker, who was able to do every stage of pin making, so that each stage of the process became the specialised task of a different worker, a vastly greater number of pins could be produced per day. However, in an industrial order based on this principle, with all the increases of general wealth that would accompany it, these new specialised labourers would be serious 'losers'. 'Those who labour most get least', he observed. What he had in mind was what we might nowadays call the quality of their lives. Someone whose life 'is spent in performing a few simple operations', he observed has 'no occasion' to 'exert understanding' and hence 'becomes as ignorant as it is possible for a human creature to become'.

Smith's reservations about this aspect of modern industrialised labour have come forward and then retreated again at various times ever since he first expressed them. However, the growth of the de-skilling and direct control trend in the nineteenth century was significantly boosted by Charles Babbage (1832). Babbage powerfully demonstrated to employers just how much cheaper de-skilled labour was compared with skilled or craft-based labour. F.W. Taylor in the later part of the nineteenth century codified and systematised these direct control principles of work design and proselytised passionately for their introduction across the workshops of the fast growing industrial enterprises of that time (Taylor, 1911).

Scientific management (Taylorism)   *Concept*

Work design principles that maximise the amount of discretion over task performance given to managerial experts, who calculate and precisely define how each job is to be carried out.

Taylor's so-called called *scientific management* entailed:

- managers and experts systematically or 'scientifically' analysing every work task;
- each job being fragmented to achieve the highest possible technical division of labour, on the basis of this analysis;

- the planning of work being separated from its execution;
- skill requirements and job-learning times being reduced to the minimum;
- materials handling by operators being minimised to avoid distraction from the worker's focal task;
- work performance being closely 'time-studied' and monitored;
- pay being tied directly to individual output to encourage each worker to maximise their efforts;
- the relationships between employers/managers and employees remaining formal and distant.

Although Taylor's principles were rarely followed in their entirety, the basic scientific management approach to work design was widely embraced in the industrial and industrialising world as it moved into the twentieth century. This included communist countries where one might have expected some resistance to what many saw as the de-humanisation of working people. But there was also controversy and resistance to the de-skilling and close control trend. We should perhaps note, however, that although Taylor can be seen as pointing to a way forward for large areas of industrial activity, his thinking was rooted in solving problems of workshops in the late nineteenth century American steel industry where much of the labour was unskilled and the workers unfamiliar with the English language. His system might have been more viable in that context than in others where workers might have expected more than monetary satisfactions from their employment. The same argument may apply to the innovations introduced into the car factories of Henry Ford where the 'robotising' of the worker implicit in Taylorism was extended by the placing of the worker on an assembly line. Ford was very conscious of the costs that could follow from treating workers in this way, however. He therefore departed radically from Taylorism in paying a fixed and relatively high wage and called for the worker to show a long-term loyalty to the employer and live a sober and responsible life fitting for a Ford worker. In this way, there was a shift away from the arm's-length type of employment relationship recommended by Taylor.

Fordism	Concept
A combining of mass production de-skilled job design in the industrial workplace with employment and state welfare policies that develop workers as both fit workers and willing consumers of the products of industry.	

Ford, we might say, set out to manipulate the work orientation of the industrial worker in the more sophisticated way called for by the changing circumstances of the twentieth century. But his innovations also actively influenced the way employment and indeed whole economies and societies were to develop. He recognised that industrial workers could also become the consumers of the products they made. The implicit contract was now to be one which might be expressed by managers as, 'Work hard in our factories in the way we direct you and in return for that you will be well paid and will be able to afford to buy one of the cars you make. And the more cars you buy, the more work there will be – and the better off you will become.' Fordism thus goes way beyond work design. As Fordist work design practices spread in industrialised societies they were supported by the state, whose economic, welfare and educational policies were increasingly aimed at developing a healthy workforce who would also be the consumers of the products and services they produced.

At the same time that Fordism was spreading, attention was beginning to be paid to the arguments of Roethlisberger and Dickson (1939) and Elton Mayo (1933) arising from the research in the Hawthorne plant in Chicago. This research was said to show the importance to them of people's social involvement at work and it was alleged that employees worked more effectively when managers 'showed an interest' in them. These arguments kept alive in some managers' minds an awareness that employees' expectations at work were complex and would not necessarily be straightforwardly satisfied by monetary rewards alone. Such awareness did not detract, however, from general managerial recognition of the immense benefits to employers that Taylorism and Fordism offered by way of both cost efficiency and the tightness of managerial control. A widespread recognition of these benefits meant, and continues to mean, that a powerful de-skilling logic runs through many work design efforts across a multiplicity of different types of employment. As Marxian analysis suggests, the *labour process* in a society based on capitalist principles is one where de-skilling is frequently the option that most effectively enables the employer to exploit the labour power of their employees (Braverman, 1974).

Capitalist labour process   *Concept*

In Marxian analysis this is the process whereby managers design, control and monitor work activities in order to extract surplus value from the labour activity of employees on behalf of the capital-owning class which employs them.

However, de-skilling always has its costs – as observers from Smith onwards had pointed out and as many managers themselves discovered. In some circumstances it was not the most effective way of utilising the efforts of employees (Friedman, 1977, Edwards, 1979).

Continuing doubts about de-skilled and tightly controlled work and the recognition of its inappropriateness to many work and labour market circumstances brings us back to Maslow and the significance we noted earlier of his recognition of the changing expectations that would be coming forward for workers in increasingly affluent sections of fast developing economies. As Cam Toon remembered from his management classes, Herzberg turned the Maslow principle into some specific job design practices: *job enrichment*.

> ## Job enrichment   *Concept*
>
> The expansion of the scope of jobs by such means as the re-integration of maintenance or inspection tasks; an extension of the work cycle; an increased degree of delegation of decision making by job holders.

Herzberg (1966) argued that what were frequently taken to be work incentives or 'motivators' – pay, good working conditions and good relationships with supervisors – were no longer motivators at all. They were, rather, 'hygiene factors' – conditions that had to be fulfilled before motivation would actually happen. And the rewards that would lead to this 'motivation' were ones such as achievement, recognition and, especially, the satisfaction coming from the job itself. Jobs should thus have more variety and responsibility built into them. Job enrichment would see the scope of jobs increased. The argument, in effect, was that managers should 'redesign' jobs along these lines to meet the rising expectations of modern employees.

But what about the social or group dimension of work design? The Hawthorne research referred to earlier (p. 12) had stressed the importance to employees of the social aspects of work and Maslow included 'social needs' in his scheme, albeit at a lower level than the rather idealised 'self-actualisation' notion that Herzberg tried to turn into something practicable. Mayo saw workers being 'tied into' the employing organisation via their location in meaningful groups of fellow workers. Maslow argued that people would look for social needs to be met at work once their lower level needs had been satisfied. However, other advantages of making groups or 'teams' central to work (re)design were stressed by British researchers working with the Tavistock Institute of Human Relations (Rice, 1958, Trist *et al.*, 1963). It was argued that work organisations should be regarded as *socio-technical systems*.

> ## Socio-technical systems   *Concept*
>
> An approach to work design in which the technical and the social/psychological aspects of the overall workplace are given equal weight and are designed at the same time to *take each other into account*.

The Tavistock researchers noted that, typically, the technical aspects of a work enterprise tended to be designed first: the buildings, hardware and the layout of both of these is 'blueprinted' first and a set of social arrangements then designed to slot into it. What would be more effective, the Tavistock writers argue, would be for the technical and the social components of the overall system to be designed simultaneously and for them to take each other into account.

Activity 8.5

Reread the story 'Walt and Roger develop a greenfield site' (Case 7.2, p. 262) and consider the extent to which it could be said that Roger is following socio-technical system principles in suggesting how he and Walt should go about designing both the physical/technical aspects of their new organisation and the social/cultural aspects.

Roger closely follows the principles that socio-technical thinking would suggest appropriate for both organisation and job design. He very effectively persuades Walt that organisation design should consider social and cultural factors, on the one hand, and technical and physical factors on the other hand, *at the same time* – the one taking the other into account. This would mean that when the 'system' is operating these two aspects of it – the 'socio' and the 'technical' – would *fit* with each other. Walt's approach of setting up the 'technical' aspect first and then 'adding people onto it' would lead to real difficulties once the site was operating, Roger persuaded him. At the level of job design, the same principles should be followed according to the Tavistock researchers. In setting up an office or workshop, the technical tasks (together with the desks or machines associated with the tasks) should be grouped together to form a logical 'whole task' that can then be performed by members of the group with minimal supervisory interference. We thus get a *semi-autonomous workgroup* in which a group of people possesses all the necessary skills and all the necessary equipment to manage themselves in, say, the assembly of a motor car. Or, we might see a group of staff take charge, as a team, of producing a company's in-house magazine. Members of the team would share out among themselves and jointly coordinate tasks ranging from the collection of stories to the assembling of the pages on a desktop publishing system.

Teamworking/semi-autonomous workgroups   *Concept*

The grouping of individual jobs to focus work activities on a *whole task*, with team members being fully trained and equipped so that they can be given discretion, as a group, over how the task is completed.

With this example of the 'self-managed' group of staff who produced their company's house magazine we see something that might be labelled 'a semi-autonomous workgroup' or put forward as an example either of 'teamworking' or 'high performance work design'. Labels change in the managerial world as fast as they do in the world of fashion clothing. Something close to what we see modern companies celebrate as highly innovative 'high performance teams' or 'cellular manufacture' might well have been seen in certain craft groups producing goods way back in the middle ages, albeit producing much simpler products or services. A detailed division of labour and tight direct control managerial supervision and surveillance has played a central part in the vast increases in wealth and welfare that industrial capitalism has brought about. But to de-skill and tightly control work task performance is to wield a double-edged sword. It can cut both ways: sometimes helping the managers of employing organisations to fulfil their agenda, sometimes hindering them because of the counterproductive 'de-motivating' or 'alienating' tendencies of de-skilled and directly controlled work.

Dilemmas and choices in shaping work tasks and gaining cooperation

Implicit in our review of changing work design principles and job design practices since the industrial revolution is a recognition that there may be circumstances in which certain work design principles are more successful, from a managerial point of view, than in others. For example, it is very likely that Taylor's scientific management practices would be more viable with the unskilled immigrant workers he came across in the nineteenth-century steel mills than they could ever be with well-educated and articulate workers in a modern aerospace company. Similarly, we are not too surprised to see principles very close to those articulated by Taylor proving satisfactory to the managers of a modern company hiring (and firing) relatively young and transient workers to serve hamburgers to a highly standardised recipe in fixed service format across the world (Ritzer, 1993, Royle, 2000). But we would be surprised to see the motivational and job design practices that prove profitable to the high street hamburger restaurant proving to be managerially successful in, say, a university or a city architect's department. There appear to be 'contingencies' that are relevant to managerial decision making in the job design area. These are the circumstances of the organisation, like its size, technology or environmental situation, which have a better 'fit' with certain types of organisational arrangement and culture than with others.

When we applied the contingency insight to general organisational arrangements earlier, it was emphasised that contingencies do not determine organisational arrangements. Managers take into account their interpretations of contingent circumstances when arguing about and negotiating what patterns of organisation they will work towards. So what are the contingent factors that might be relevant to managerial debate within any given organisation about the work design principles that are to be applied?

Activity 8.6

Review the model in Figure 7.4 'Choice and contingency in organisational shaping' (p. 275) and how this was explained in Chapter 7. How do you think the contingencies represented there might be built upon to bring out circumstantial factors directly relevant to job design issues?

The contingency of *organisational size* might be relevant to job design in that having a large number of employees increases the scope for making people's jobs more specialised, whether this is specialisation of the type that leads to the appointment of a company lawyer, say, or the de-skilling type of specialisation that fragments the job of a pin maker. However, the other two contingencies shown in the model are perhaps more significant – those of technology and environmental stability.

The organisation's *technology* is a key job design factor in two closely related ways. First, it defines the tasks that are to be done and the extent to which those tasks are amenable to fragmentation or de-skilling. The technology of brain surgery, for example, does not lend itself to a detailed division of labour in which a succession of single-skilled individuals take their turn at wielding different types of scalpel for different stages of an operation. The technology of high street hamburger cooking and serving, however, lends itself well to such an approach.

The nature of the *environment* within which the organisation operates is also immensely important. We saw in the last chapter that a fast-changing and highly competitive business environment, one that requires frequent innovative action on the part of employees to enable it to survive, finds an 'organic' or loose structure more appropriate to its situation than a tightly bureaucratic one. This clearly implies a need for job designs that do not involve the sort of tight prescription and standardisation that goes with direct control types of job design. There is a tendency therefore for managers to choose indirect control types of job design where there are environmental pressures requiring high levels of innovation or adaptability on the part of employees. There is an obvious incompatibility between asking people to apply high levels of discretion and innovation in their work and expecting them to take detailed orders from a manager and be continually checked up on by a supervisor.

A concept that is often used in this context is that of *flexibility*. It is frequently argued that a move towards indirect control job designs are necessary if workers are to perform flexibly so that an organisation can quickly change what it is doing to cope with competitive pressures. This, however, is only partly true. There are two types of flexibility that managers of organisations look for: flexibility for long-term adaptability and flexibility for short-term predictability.

Flexibility for long-term adaptability *Concept*	Flexibility for short-term predictability *Concept*
The ability to make rapid and effective innovations through the use of job designs and employment policies that encourage people to use their discretion and work in new ways for the sake of the organisation – as circumstances require.	The ability to make rapid changes through the use of job designs and employment policies that allow staff to be easily recruited and trained or easily laid off – as circumstances require.
This fits with *indirect control* work design principles and high-trust relationships.	This fits with *direct control* work design principles and low-trust relationships.

Sometimes organisations will have a predominant need for just one of these types of flexibility. A consultancy organisation would mainly need flexibility for long-term adaptability, for example, and would therefore tend to follow indirect control work design principles across the firm. An organisation in the sugar beet processing industry, with inevitably seasonal patterns of working, on the other hand, would need flexibility for short-term predictability. It would therefore find it more fitting to adopt predominantly direct control job designs. This would not only suit the seasonal need to hire at one time and fire at another; it would also fit with the generally low levels of skills required to apply the technology. And it would fit with the almost non-existent need to innovate and develop the product.

These two cases are relatively straightforward. But, in many organisations, managers find both types of flexibility are required. Sometimes one type of flexibility is relevant to one area of the organisation and the other to another area. This is a circumstance that will be considered later when we look at issues of how job design issues relate to overall issues of how an organisation is to be 'resourced' with inputs of human skill, knowledge and labour. Researchers on innovations in work design have frequently commented on the tendency for the managerial success of these initiatives at a local level to depend on whether or not they were supported by appropriate human resourcing policies at the level of the wider organisation (Buchanan and Preston, 1992). The possibility of organisations needing *dual human resourcing strategies* to cope with different types of flexibility being required in different parts of an organisation will be looked at in Chapter 10, (pp. 426–8).

Human resourcing policies inevitably have to cope with the fundamental contradiction that work design initiatives are always faced with. They must gain commitment and consent from the same employees that they need to 'exploit'. In recent decades of increasing international competition, we can see various employers desperately seeking new ways to handle this tension in order to stay in business – or rather to find new combinations of established work design principles. This has led to work design and human resourcing practices that incorporate novel mixtures of direct and indirect control principles. The *lean production* practices seen in the car industry are an example of this (Womack, Jones and Roos, 1990). 'Leanness' means that no time, effort, or resources are wasted and high psychological commitment to this ruthlessly tight regime is expected from a workforce that is expected to use its discretion in the spaces where this is allowed, always with the benefit of 'the customer' in mind.

Lean production   *Concept*

The combining, typically within car assembly, of team working with automated technologies. Workers are required both to initiate 'continual improvements' in quality and to ensure that every task is got 'right first time' and completed to a demanding 'just-in-time' schedule.

A similar combining of direct and indirect control work design and human resourcing principles is seen with *business process re-engineering* (BPR) (Hammer and Champy, 1993; see Further Reading on work restructuring and re-engineering, p. 349). BPR has seen organisations across a range of industries restructured to focus on business *processes* (getting a product designed, manufactured and sold, say). This means turning away from an emphasis on business *functions* (where a design function focuses just on design, a manufacturing function focuses on production and a sales function concentrates just on selling, for example). A clear and integrated flow of processes is thus made possible by the use of advanced information technologies. Employees can be *empowered* and given new degrees of freedom to manage themselves in teams. They are no longer trapped in the separate boxes of functional organisation where managers, planners and schedulers have to direct and coordinate people's efforts to ensure that all the separate tasks and operations 'add up' to the provision of a successful product or service. The clearer logic of the basic process flow means that workers can 'make things add up' for themselves, as Roberto Auldearn's managing director put it when explaining the 'embracing of business process reengineering' at Dovecote Components in Case 8.3.

Business process re-engineering (BPR)   *Concept*

The restructuring of an organisation to focus on business processes rather than on business functions. Advanced management control information technologies are used together with team working and employee 'empowerment'.

Activity 8.7

Read Roberto Auldearn's account in Case 8.3 of how Dovecote Components 'embraced' business process re-engineering.

After looking back once again at the model set out in Figure 7.4 (p. 275), note the ways in which a part was played in this exercise in 'organisational shaping' by:

- contextual political, economic and cultural patterns;
- enacted contingencies;
- managerial values, goals and interests;
- managerial argument, negotiation and choice.

Consider the extent to which we are helped to make sense of this story by the notion of a basic contradiction whereby managers have to gain commitment and consent from the employees at the same time as they are required to exploit and manipulate them.

Re-engineering Dovecote Components   Case 8.3

Dovecote Components has been an important employer in this town for a long time. Most people around here just call it 'The Doocot'. For over 20 years now the workforce has been steadily falling as we have increased investment in newer technologies and found a whole lot of ways of making the work less labour intensive. Productivity was steadily rising over this period and, as a management, we felt freer to make changes without having to fight with trade unions over every little detail. Government policies were partly responsible for this, but the unions – indeed the workforce generally – recognised that we were struggling in an increasingly difficult and increasingly international market place. Almost every year would see some redundancies and there was not a great deal of argument about this. I think people regarded these job losses as a sort of unfortunate fact of life and I don't think they affected morale within the company to any real extent. But people did not realise just how difficult things were going to get as we saw the auto companies that bought our components increasingly looking across the whole global economy to source their production.

About five years ago we realised that we needed to make radical changes in the business. We had been developing our technologies incrementally over the years and had introduced at different times a variety of innovations ranging from quality improvement groups to cellular and team working. A lot of our production is now done on a just-in-time basis. Components go out of the door just a few hours before the car plant 200 miles away needs them to stick in its cars. It was becoming clear to us, however, that there were increasing numbers of other suppliers who could get their products to the factories just as promptly. And not only could they supply at significantly lower prices but several of them were much faster than us at developing and improving their products. Our customers were facing increasing global competition just as we were and were constantly looking to improve the quality and functionality of the components they put in their vehicles.

At the first executive meetings where we talked seriously about making radical changes I put forward a plan to set up a completely new 'Research, Design and Manufacturing Innovation' department. This would be a crack team that I would recruit by head hunting from my quite extensive contacts across the engineering world. It would combine product development and the improving of production methods – making sure we designed for ease of manufacture as well as to delight our customers. Immediately I suggested this I was shot down. The first bloke to 'have a go' didn't bother me. As a management accountant, our finance man was right to look critically at my plans and question how we could possibly afford this. But, like every one else, I knew that he personally disliked me and would attack anything I put forward. It was the MD, Jerry Penick, who really put the boot in however. This did bother me. In the first place, he said, 'there is certainly no way we can afford to do that'. And, 'secondly', he went on, 'your whole philosophy is out of date'. That made me wild. I ranted on about how advanced my 'design for manufacturing' ideas were and that I would easily get a job with one of our competitors if he had so little respect for me. In fact I did slam out of the meeting at one point. I think it was when the Manufacturing Director – a blinkered and territorially minded idiot if ever there was one – made it clear that he wasn't keen for me to get involved in manufacturing issues. The MD came and found me puffing a cigar in the directors' lavatory and persuaded me to go back into the meeting and hear his thoughts on 're-engineering the Doocot'.

It turned out that the consultants that Jerry had brought in six months earlier, 'just to look over things' as he told us, had in fact come up with this scheme to 're-engineer' the processes in Doocot 'from top to bottom'. 'We have got to jump out of our functional boxes and our obsession with departmental boundaries,' he said, looking directly at me and then at my manufacturing colleague. 'Everything has got to be stripped down to the basics and everyone will make their contribution to the basic processes of getting ideas quickly and efficiently through from the drawing board to the customer's delivery bay. The bloke on the drawing board will be as interested in that customer's needs as the driver of the delivery wagon will – or as I will.'

At this stage we were all looking at each other a little shocked. Most of us had heard of this 'business re-engineering' thing, but had not really related it to our situation. Molly, our marketing woman, ventured to say that all the re-engineering cases that she had come across had been more exercises in 'blood letting' and 'axing people as well as departments' than improving processes. 'Well', came back Jerry, 'I don't want any talk like that. But the re-engineering exercise will mean taking quite a big axe to our management structures. Levels will be taken out.' He accepted that 'delayering' and 'becoming leaner' would be painful. The consultants, together with a small senior management team, would 'look at everybody's job' and nobody 'whose job doesn't serve our core processes' would survive. This would be hard and it would 'hurt everybody involved', Jerry said. But those who survived would be much better off. It wasn't just that their jobs would be more secure. Their 'prospects with the firm' would also be better. Above all, people would benefit by being 'more empowered'. He explained that, at present, all the efforts that people put in and all the operations across the plant had to be 'made to add up' by managers, supervisors and other 'functionaries'. By taking a lot of these out, people would be given the satisfaction of 'adding it all up' for themselves. And, he added, by 'taking away all the managerial buffers that exist between the workforce and the market place' people will see the need to 'work hard, conscientiously and cooperatively *for the business and not for their department* because they will know that if they don't we all go under'.

The whole thing seemed sensible, if rather terrifying. For six months the 'Re-engineering Action Group' (RAG), comprising four senior managers and four consultants, were to work 'day and night' with Jerry to 'completely reshape the business'. The business was to be more 'focused' than at present and this basically meant making it smaller. 'We have got too big and unwieldy', Jerry argued, 'so we'll cut the less profitable lines and try to stay at a size where a smallish top management team can keep their eyes on everything.' There would be a major investment in ICT, with the savings made on labour costs more than covering the 'costs of the new computer systems'. The 'software and hardware that are available now for management control', he insisted, 'were sophisticated enough now to cover the work of all the people who will be leaving us – and more'.

So, all of this went ahead. I was lucky to be kept on. But both my Finance Director and Manufacturing Director colleagues – and enemies – got the push. I was on the RAG – the action group charged with 'implementing' the re-engineering. At first I felt privileged. But this feeling soon went. I began to realise quite early on that the whole thing was doomed from the start. We had embraced business process re-engineering in a big way. But we had embraced a monster. In principle, I thought, it was wise. It was harsh. But harsh measures were necessary. And all of those who stayed with the business would experience a much higher level of empowerment and involvement with the core processes of the enterprise. They would clearly benefit. But as we all quickly learned, it wasn't to happen like that, and it's so easy to see why, in retrospect.

In one voice, we were saying that people were to be empowered, to be trusted and were to have their 'energies' released to do 'really meaningful work'. But in another voice we were asking people to kneel down to have their heads chopped off. This is where the massive catch in the whole thing lay. On the one hand we were asking people to be empowered, to manage themselves and be committed to the business. The logic of de-layering was one of saying that an empowered and committed workforce could, in many respects, manage things better than managers could. But on the other hand, we were a group of managers and consultants acting as if we were mighty gods who knew better than anyone how things should be done.

As you can imagine, the whole thing was treated with deep suspicion and bitter hostility from the beginning. And that's just among the managers! We RAG members were treated with utter disdain and mistrust as hypocrites and axe wielders. Because nobody would cooperate with us or give us any information we could trust, we simply could not do the work we were meant to do. But how could we back down? Consequently we made lots of cuts and we reorganised the place from top to bottom without really knowing what we were doing. And, yes, the business has survived. But we are running it through a regime of terror with most of the best staff we had having moved out to other jobs. I give the business a couple more years at most. And I shall be out of here well before that. When you see me next time, I'll have flown the Doocot.

These events at Dovecote Components would not have come about if there had not been major changes in the global economy. The most important contextual pressure is the growth of competition from producers of motor components across the world and the combination of this with car manufacturers choosing to 'source' themselves from a global market place. Relevant nationally is the state's role in reducing the ability of trade unions to resist managerial initiatives. And, at the local level, there appears to be a degree of goodwill towards 'The Doocot'. This goodwill might have helped managers make incremental changes which involved loss of employment over the years. Equally, it is possible that a sense of betrayal of this goodwill may have increased the level of resentment towards management when it came to the radical cuts associated with the business process re-engineering initiative.

These contextual matters influenced the particular *contingencies* that Dovecote managers *enacted* (interpreted and acted with regard to). The instability of the increasingly competitive business environment is obviously the major contingent factor. Jerry Penick has also acted on the basis of his view of technological contingencies. He believes that significantly more effective 'management control' hardware and software is now available to the company, and he has views about the contingency of organisational size, arguing that Dovecote is 'too big and unwieldy'.

Although the big decisions about how to handle the company's difficulties have largely been made by Jerry Penick alone, arguments taking place between the senior managers seem to reflect different value positions and interests among them. Roberto himself puts forward a solution that fits with his personal area of expertise and it is a solution that would have increased his personal influence in the company, we can reasonably infer. It was obviously one that clashed with the interests of the Manufacturing Director, an 'enemy' of Roberto who, apparently, was very 'territorial'. This individual was keen to 'fight his corner' as was Roberto's other 'enemy', the Finance Director. It is difficult to separate the values and the personal interests of the protagonists to these arguments. But it would appear that the Marketing Director brought certain values of concern for human beings into the discussions. It would seem that Jerry, in speaking of the inevitability of 'hurting' some people in order to benefit others, has gone through some internal value debate.

It is Jerry's choice, as the most powerful actor within the management team, to adopt business process re-engineering. However, the resistance to the way this was implemented, especially from other managers across the company, turned out to be so great that the initiative was seriously undermined. What Jerry Penick appears not to have realised was that strategic management has to cope with – or 'manage' – the basic contradictions that underlie all employing organisations. The contradiction between the requirement that managers must exploit or 'use' employees as resources and the requirement that they must win commitment and consent from employees as human beings is badly mismanaged here. The Dovecote management is saying that the changes will benefit the 'survivors' of business process re-engineering. People should therefore commit themselves to the changes. But it is making it clear at the same time that, for the moment, every individual is being considered for possible removal from the firm. Roberto expresses this by referring to the company as speaking with two voices. In one voice, he says, it talks of trust and empowerment, but with the other voice it is effectively asking every individual to 'kneel down' to allow the management to cut off their heads, should the 'Re-engineering Action Group' not see them as fitting into the new, re-engineered scheme of things.

Many organisations have in recent years reacted to the sorts of pressure faced by Dovecote Components by adopting business process re-engineering. And, even by the accounts of leading proponents of the practice, many of these have achieved nothing like the dramatic changes expected. Given the radical nature of the initiative and the way it tends to bring to the surface major underlying tensions this is not surprising.

Matters of the basic structure of economies and of global economic change cannot be separated from managerial efforts to 'motivate' and 'lead' people within organisations or from the initiatives they take to design or 'redesign' jobs – whether they involve minor initiatives or larger radical ones like business process re-engineering (see Further reading on Work restructuring and re-engineering, p. 349). Nevertheless, at the level of the individual manager doing the everyday routine managerial tasks that are the responsibility of the majority of managers across the range of work organisations in both the commercial and the public service sectors these bigger issues may not be at the front of their minds. However, one of the purposes of the present book – in the spirit of critical thinking discussed in Chapter 1 – is to enable everyone involved in organisations to be aware of the relevance of these broader factors. And this is vital for thinking in a strategic manner about how any particular organisation relates to its environment. It is to this aspect of the organising and managing of work that Chapter 9 turns.

Summary

In this chapter the following key points have been made:

● What are often seen as separate 'topics' in the study of organisations and their management – 'motivation', 'leadership' and 'job/work design' – can better be seen as closely related to each other and, also, as closely tied into the wider structural and cultural features of the organisation in which they occur and as influenced by the whole way in which modern societies and economies are organised.

● It is more helpful to look at people's general *orientations to work* rather than to consider their 'work motivation'. A focus on orientations allows a wider range of relevant factors to be taken into account and makes us more aware of how people think about their work, and what they are prepared to do, and can change as circumstances change.

- The very notion of a 'theory of motivation' is a questionable and potentially unrealisable one. Such a theory would, in effect, be a theory of 'why people do what they do'. However, useful insights have been developed about the role of perceptions of 'equity' and the role of 'expectancies' in shaping work behaviour under the 'motivation theory' banner. These insights can be incorporated into a process-relational way of thinking.

- There are two main principles of *work design* – direct control and indirect control principles – which can be drawn on when managers engage in specific *job design* work. These two sets of principles, the first of which operates with a logic of de-skilling and the latter with a logic of 'enriching' jobs in skill and responsibility terms, have been applied in different ways at different times across the history of industrialised societies.

- The application of these principles, and how it varies with circumstances and the ways in which managers 'enact' contingent circumstances, can be understood in terms of managerial attempts to cope with the underlying contradictions in the organisation of work and employment in modern societies. Managers need to control and manipulate employees as resources and, at the same time, win a degree of consent and commitment to the enterprise from them as human beings. Problems that can arise with the recently popular managerial initiative of *business process re-engineering* can be understood in terms of managerial struggles to handle these fundamental tensions.

Recommended reading

On the very specific matter of motivation theories and how students relate to them, the Tony Watson study, 'Motivation: that's Maslow, isn't it' (*Management Learning* 27(4): 447–464, 1996; also in C. Grey and E. Antonacopoulu (eds) *Essential Reading in Management Learning*, London: Sage, 2004) can, its author hopes, be entertaining as well as challenging to current teaching and learing practices. And on the broader matter of the trends occurring in the way work is organised and tasks designed, perhaps the most effective way to get an overview is to look at and read selectively from *The Oxford Handbook of Work and Organization* edited by Steve Ackroyd, Rosemary Blatt, Paul Thompson and Pamela Tolbert (Oxford: Oxford University Press, 2004). Also valuable here is David Knights' and Darren McCabe's *Organization and Innovation: Guru schemes and American dreams* (Maidenhead: Open University Press, 2003).

Further reading

Further reading Motivation theories

Adams, J.S. (1963) 'Towards an understanding of inequity', *Journal of Abnormal and Social Psychology*, 67: 422–436

Adams, J.S. (1965) 'Inequity in social exchange' in L. Berkovitz (ed.) *Advances in Experimental Social Psychology, Vol. 2*, New York: Academic Press

Ambrose, M.L. and Kulik, C.T. (1999) 'Old friends, new faces: motivation research in the 1990s', *Journal of Management*, 25(3): 231–292

Carter, P. and Jackson, N. (1993) 'Modernism, postmodernism and motivation, or why expectancy theory failed to live up to expectation' in J. Hassard and M. Parker (eds) *Postmodernism and Organisations*, London: Sage

Maslow, A. (1943) 'A theory of human motivation', *Psychological Review*, 50: 37–96

Maslow, A. (1954) *Motivation and Personality*, New York; Harper and Row

Maslow, A. (1968) *Towards a Psychology of Being*, Princeton, NJ: Van Nostrand

McGregor, D.C. (1960) *The Human Side of Enterprise*, New York: McGraw-Hill

Rauschenberger, J., Schmitt, N. and Hunter, T.E. (1980) 'A test of the need hierarchy concept', *Administrative Science Quarterly*, 25(4): 654–670

Vroom, V.H. (1964) *Work and Motivation*, New York: Wiley

Watson, T.J. (1996) 'Motivation: that's Maslow, isn't it?', *Management Learning*, 27(4): 447–464

Further reading Work design, empowerment and teams

Babbage, C. (1832) *On the Economy of Machinery and Manufacture*, London: Charles Knight

Barker, J.R. (1993) 'Tightening the iron cage: concertive control in self-managing teams', *Administrative Science Quarterly*, 38: 408–437.

Barker, J.R. (1999) *The Discipline of Teamwork*, London: Sage

Becker, B. and Huselid, M. (1998) 'High performance work systems and firm performance: a synthesis of research and managerial implications', *Research in Personnel and Human Resources*, 16(1): 53–101

Belbin, M. (1993) *Team Roles at Work*, Oxford: Butterworth-Heinemann

Benders, J. and Van Hootegem, G. (1999) 'Teams and their context: moving the team discussion beyond existing dichotomies', *Journal of Management Studies*, 36(5): 609–628

Braverman, H. (1974) *Labor and Monopoly Capital*, New York: Monthly Review Press

Buchanan, D.A. (1994) 'Cellular manufacture and the role of teams' in J. Storey (ed.) *New Wave Manufacturing Strategies: Organisational and human resource management dimensions*, London: Paul Chapman, 204–225

Buchanan, D.A. (2000) 'An eager and enduring embrace: the ongoing rediscovery of teamworking as a management idea' in S. Procter and F. Mueller (eds) *Teamworking*, Basingstoke: Macmillan

Buchanan, D. and Preston, D. (1992) 'Life in the cell: supervision and teamwork in a "manufacturing systems engineering" environment', *Human Resource Management Journal*, 2(4): 55–76

Burawoy, M. (1979) *Manufacturing Consent: Changes in the labour process under monopoly capitalism*, Chicago, IL: Chicago University Press

Edwards, R. (1979) *Contested Terrain*, London: Heinemann

Friedman, A.L. (1977) *Industry and Labour*, London: Macmillan

Guzzo, R.A. and Dickson, M.W. (1998) 'Teams in organizations: recent research on performance and effectiveness', *Annual Review of Psychology*, 49: 307–338

Hackman, J.R. and Oldham, G.R. (1980) *Work Redesign*, New York: Addison Wesley

Hampton, M.M. (1999) 'Work groups' in Y. Gabriel (ed.) *Organizations in Depth*, London: Sage, 112–138

Harley, B. (2001) 'Team membership and the experience of work in Britain: an analysis of the WERS98 data', *Work, Employment and Society*, 15(4): 721–742

Herzberg, F. (1966) *Work and the Nature of Man*, Chicago, IL: World Publishing Co.

Marchington, M. (1992) *Managing the Team*, Oxford: Blackwell

Parker, S. and Wall, T. (1998) *Job and Work Design: Organizing work to promote well-being and effectiveness*, London: Sage

Pollert, A. (1988) 'Dismantling flexibility', *Capital and Class*, 34: 42–75

Pollert, A. (ed.) (1991) *Farewell to Flexibility?*, Oxford: Blackwell

Procter, S. and Ackroyd, S. (2001) 'Flexibility' in T. Redman and A. Wilkinson (eds) *Contemporary Human Resource Management*, Harlow: FT Prentice Hall

Procter, S. and Mueller, F. (eds) (2000) *Teamworking*, Basingstoke: Macmillan

Procter, S. and Mueller, F. (2000) 'Teamworking, strategy, structure, systems and culture' in S. Procter and F. Mueller (eds) *Teamworking*, Basingstoke: Macmillan, 3–24

Royle, T. (2000) *Working for McDonald's in Europe: The Unequal Struggle*, London: Routledge

Sinclair, A. (1992) 'The tyranny of team ideology', *Organization Studies*, 13(4): 611–626

Smith, A. (1974) *The Wealth of Nations*, Harmondsworth: Penguin (originally 1776)

Smith, C. and Thompson, P. (1998) 'Re-evaluating the labour process debate', *Economic and Industrial Democracy*, 19(4): 551–577

Taylor, F.W. (1911) *The Principles of Scientific Management*, New York: Harper

Trist, E.L., Higgin, G.W., Murray, H. and Pollock, A.B. (1963) *Organisational Choice*, London: Tavistock

Watson, T.J. (1986) *Management, Organisation and Employment Strategy*, London: Routledge

Watson, T.J. and Rosborough, J. (1999) 'Teamworking and the management of flexibility: local and social-structural tensions in high performance work design initiatives' in S. Procter and F. Mueller (eds) *Teamworking*, Basingstoke: Macmillan

Womack, J.P., Jones, D.J. and Roos, D. (1990) *The Machine that Changed the World*, New York: Rawson

Wood, S. and Albanese, M. (1995) 'Can we speak of high commitment management on the shop floor?', *Journal of Management Studies*, 32(2): 215–247

Further reading Work restructuring and re-engineering

Ackroyd, S., Batt, R., Thompson, P. and Tolbert, P.S. (eds) (2004) *The Oxford Handbook of Work and Organization*, Oxford: Oxford University Press

Buchanan, D.A. (1997) 'The limitations and opportunities of business process re-engineering in a politicised organizational climate', *Human Relations*, 50(1): 51–72

Burke, R. and Cooper, C.L. (2000) *The Organization in Crisis: Downsizing, restructuring and privatisation*, Oxford: Blackwell

Champy, J. (1996) *Reengineering Management: The mandate for new leadership*, New York: Harper Business

Davenport, T. (1993) *Process Innovation: Reengineering work through information technology*, Boston, MA: Harvard Business School Press

Grey, C. and Mitev, N. (1995) 'Reengineering organizations: a critical appraisal', *Personnel Review*, 24(1): 6–18

Grint, K. and Willcocks, L. (1995) 'Business process re-engineering in theory and practice: business Paradise regained?', *New Technology: Work and Employment*, 10(2): 99–108

Hammer, M. and Champy, J. (1993) *Reengineering the Corporation*, London: Nicholas Brealey

Hammer, M. and Stanton, S. (1995) *The Reengineering Revolution: A handbook*, New York: Harper Business Press

Knights, D. and McCabe, D. (2003) *Organization and Innovation: Guru schemes and American dreams*, Maidenhead: Open University Press

Knights, D. and Willmott, H. (eds) (2000) *The Reengineering Revolution: Critical studies of corporate change*, London: Sage

Redman, T. and Wilkinson, A. (2001) 'Downsizing' in T. Redman and A. Wilkinson (eds) *Contemporary Human Resource Management*, Harlow: FT Prentice Hall

Storey, J. (ed.) (1993) *New Wave Manufacturing Strategies*, London: Chapman

Wilkinson, A. and Willmott, H. (eds) (1995) *Making Quality Critical: New perspectives on organizational change*, London: Routledge

Wilkinson, A., Redman, T., Snape, E. and Marchington, M. (1998) *Managing with Total Quality Management: Theory and practice*, Basingstoke, Macmillan

Willmott, H. (1994) Business process re-engineering and human resource management, *Personnel Review*, 23(3): 34–46

Willmott, H. (1995) 'The odd couple?: re-engineering business processes; managing human relations', *New Technology; Work and Employment*, 10(2): 89–98

Working together — team working

WORK GROUPS AND TEAMS

Groups and teams are major features of organisational life. The work organisation and its sub-units are made up of groups of people. Most activities that take place in an organisation require at least some degree of co-ordination through the operation of groups and teamwork. An understanding of the nature of groups is vital if the manager is to influence the behaviour of people in the work situation. The manager needs to recognise the nature of human relationships and be aware of the interactions and operation of work groups and teams.

LEARNING OUTCOMES

After completing this chapter you should be able to:

- explain the meaning and importance of work groups and teams;
- distinguish between groups and teams and between formal and informal groups;
- explain the main reasons for the formation of groups and teams;
- examine factors which influence group cohesiveness and performance;
- analyse the nature of role relationships and role conflict;
- detail the main forms of interactions and team roles;
- evaluate the effectiveness of individual or group or team performance.

To build good teams you need a wide pool of staff with different talents to draw upon ... Good managers should delight in the diversity and excellence of their staff and know that one of their main jobs is to manage the problems that come with any diverse group of talented people. In any group of talented people you will naturally get interpersonal tensions. It is important that you show you respect all the different skills and personalities in your team.

Nic Peeling – frontline manager with QinetiQ
Brilliant Manager: What the Best Managers Know, Do and Say, Pearson Prentice Hall (2005), pp. 129–30

'Groups are an essential part of the structure of an organisation but "teamworking" is no more than a fashionable term used by management to give workers an exaggerated feeling of importance and empowerment. In reality, however, an emphasis on teamworking is only likely to lead to more work, less freedom and even closer control from other team members.' How far do you agree with this comment? What is your experience of teamworking?

THE MEANING AND IMPORTANCE OF GROUPS AND TEAMS

Groups are an essential feature of any organisation. Individuals seldom work in isolation from others. Work is a group-based activity and, if the organisation is to function effectively, it requires collaboration and co-operation amongst its members Although there is no single accepted definition, most people will readily understand what constitutes a group. The essential feature is that its members regard themselves as belonging to the group. A popular definition defines the group in psychological terms as:

> *any number of people who (1) interact with one another; (2) are psychologically aware of one another; and (3) perceive themselves to be a group.*[1]

Another useful way to define a work group is a collection of people who share most, if not all, of the following characteristics:

- a definable membership;
- group consciousness;
- a sense of shared purpose;
- interdependence;
- interaction; and
- ability to act in a unitary manner.[2]

Essential features of work organisations Groups are a characteristic of all social situations and almost everyone in an organisation will be a member of one or more groups. The workings of groups and the influence they exert over their membership are essential features of human behaviour and organisational performance. Members of a group must co-operate in order for work to be carried out and managers themselves will work within these groups. People in groups influence each other in many ways and groups may develop their own hierarchies and leaders. Group pressures can have a major influence on the behaviour of individual members and their work performance.

DIFFERENCES BETWEEN GROUPS AND TEAMS

In common usage and literature – including to some extent in this book – there is a tendency for the terms 'groups' and 'teams' to be used interchangeably. It is not easy to distinguish clearly between a group and a team. *Guzzo and Dickson*, for example, go so far to suggest that it is probably pointless and, in any case, more or less impossible to distinguish groups from teams.[3]

According to *Holpp*, while many people are still paying homage to teams, teamwork, empowerment and self-management, others have become disillusioned. Holpp poses the question, 'What are teams?' It's a simple enough question, but one that's seldom asked. We all think we know intuitively what teams are. Guess again. Here are some questions to help define team configurations.

- Are teams going to be natural work groups or project- and task-orientated?
- Will they be self-managed or directed?
- How many people will be in the teams; who's in charge?
- How will the teams fit into the organisation's structure if it shows only boxes and not circles or other new organisational forms?

Holpp also poses the question, 'Why do you want teams?' If teams are just a convenient way to group under one manager a lot of people who used to work for several downsized supervisors, don't bother. If , however, teams can truly take ownership of work areas and provide the kind of up-close knowledge that's unavailable elsewhere, then full speed ahead.[4]

Teamwork a fashionable term The use of the word 'teams' has become increasingly fashionable in recent years. For example, *Crainer* refers to the use of 'teamworking' as a side-effect of increasing concentration on working across functional divides, one that fits neatly with the trend towards empowerment. However, despite the extensive literature about teams and teamworking, the basic dynamics of teamworking often remain clouded and uncertain.

> *Teams occur when a number of people have a common goal and recognize that their personal success is dependent on the success of others. They are all interdependent. In practice, this means that in most teams people will contribute individual skills many of which will be different. It also means that the full tensions and counter-balance of human behaviour will need to be demonstrated in the team.*[5]

Cane suggests that organisations are sometimes unsure whether they have teams or simply groups of people working together.

> *It is certainly true to say that any group of people who do not know they are a team cannot be one. To become a team, a group of individuals needs to have a strong common purpose and to work towards that purpose rather than individually. They need also to believe that they will achieve more by co-operation than working individually.*[6]

Whereas all teams are, by definition, groups, it does not necessarily follow that all groups are teams.

Belbin points out that, to the extent that teamwork was becoming a fashionable term, it began to replace the more usual reference to groups and every activity was now being described as 'teamwork'. He questions whether it matters if one is talking about groups or teams and maintains that the confusion in vocabulary should be addressed if the principles of good teamwork are to be retained. Belbin suggests there are several factors that characterise the difference between groups and teams (*see* Figure 6.1). The best differentiator is size: groups can be comprised of any number of people, but teams are smaller, with a membership between (ideally) four and six. The quintessential feature of a small well-balanced team is that leadership is shared or rotates, whereas large groups typically throw up solo leaders.[7]

While acknowledging the work of Belbin, it appears that the term 'group' is often used in a more general sense and 'team' in a more specific context. We continue to refer to 'group' or 'team' according to the particular focus of attention and the vocabulary of the quoted authors.

Another possible distinction is based on the development and maturity of the 'group' – for example, in terms of Tuckman's model (discussed later in this chapter under the heading 'Group development and maturity'). Not until a group proceeds beyond the stages of forming, norming and storming and successfully reaches the performing stage does it become a team.

Figure 6.1	Differences between a team and a group

	Team	Group
Size	Limited	Medium or large
Selection	Crucial	Immaterial
Leadership	Shared or rotating	Solo
Perception	Mutual knowledge understanding	Focus on leader
Style	Role spread co-ordination	Convergence conformism
Spirit	Dynamic interaction	Togetherness persecution of opponents

Source: Belbin, R. M., *Beyond the Team*, Butterworth-Heinemann, (2000). Copyright © 2000, reproduced with permission from Elsevier Ltd.

GROUP VALUES AND NORMS

The classical approach to organisation and management tended to ignore the importance of groups and the social factors at work. The ideas of people such as *F. W. Taylor* popularised the concept of the 'rabble hypothesis' and the assumption that people carried out their work, and could be motivated, as solitary individuals unaffected by others. The human relations approach, however (discussed in Chapter 1), gave recognition to the work organisation as a social organisation and to the importance of the group, and group values and norms, in terms of influencing behaviour at work.

One experiment involved the observation of a group of 14 men working in a bank wiring room. It may be remembered that the men formed their own subgroups, or cliques, with natural leaders emerging with the consent of the members. Despite a financial incentive scheme, where workers could receive more money the more work they did, the group decided on 6000 units a day as a fair level of output. This was well below the level they were capable of producing. Group pressures on individual workers were stronger than the financial incentives offered by management.

Informal social relations The group developed its own pattern of informal social relations and codes and practices ('norms') of what constituted proper group behaviour.

- **Not to be a 'rate buster'** – not to produce at too high a rate of output compared with other members or to exceed the production restriction of the group.
- **Not to be a 'chiseller'** – not to shirk production or to produce at too low a rate of output compared with other members of the group.
- **Not to be a 'squealer'** – not to say anything to the supervisor or management that might be harmful to other members of the group.
- **Not to be 'officious'** – people with authority over members of the group, for example inspectors, should not take advantage of their seniority or maintain a social distance from the group.

The group had its own system of sanctions, including sarcasm, damaging completed work, hiding tools, playing tricks on the inspectors and ostracising those members who did not conform with the **group norms**. Threats of physical violence were also made and the group developed a system of punishing offenders by 'binging' which involved striking someone a fairly hard blow on the upper part of the arm. This process of binging also became a recognised method of controlling conflict within the group.

Team performance

According to *Riches*, one way to improve team performance is to establish agreed norms or rules for how the team is to operate and rigorously stick to them. Norms can address the obligations of individual members to the team, how it will assess its performance, how it will work together, what motivation systems will be used, how it will relate to customers and the mechanisms to facilitate an honest exchange about the team norms and behaviour.[8]

A recent study from the *Economic & Social Research Council* draws attention to the importance of social norms among employees and asks if employees are guided not only by monetary incentives but also by peer pressure towards social efficiency for the workers as a group. 'Intuitively, social norms among workers must be important if they work in teams where bonuses are dependent on group, rather than individual effort.'[9] (You may see some similarity here with the bank wiring room experiment discussed above.)

A concept map of group norms is set out in Figure 6.2.

FORMAL AND INFORMAL GROUPS

Groups are deliberately planned and created by management as part of the formal organisation structure. However, groups will also arise from social processes and the informal organisation. The informal organisation arises from the interaction of people working within the organisation and the development of groups with their own relationships and norms of behaviour, irrespective of those defined within the formal structure. This leads to a major distinction between formal and informal groups.

Formal groups

Groups are formed as a consequence of the pattern of organisation structure and arrangements for the division of work, for example the grouping together of common activities into sections. Groups may result from the nature of technology employed and the way in which work is carried out – for example, the bringing together of a number of people to carry out a sequence of operations on an assembly line. Groups may also develop when a number of people of the same level or status within the organisation see themselves as a group – for example, departmental heads of an industrial organisation or chief officers of a local authority. **Formal groups** are created to achieve specific organisational objectives and are concerned with the **co-ordination of work activities**. People are brought together on the basis of defined roles within the structure of the organisation. The nature of the tasks to be undertaken is a predominant feature of the formal group. Goals are identified by management and certain rules, relationships and norms of behaviour established.

Formal groups tend to be relatively permanent, although there may be changes in actual membership. However, temporary formal groups may also be created by management, such as with the use of project teams in a matrix organisation. Formal work groups can be differentiated in a number of ways, such as on the basis of membership, the task to be performed, the nature of technology or position within the organisation structure.

Figure 6.2   Concept map of grop norms

GROUP NORMS

- DEFINITIONS OF NORMS
- EVOLUTION OF NORMS
- CHANGING NORMS
- THE VALUE OF NORMS

Norms are an observable aspect of any group, in or out of the work setting. New group members are alert to signals of acceptance or rejection as they seek to clarify expectations. They find them in formal and informal contacts.

DEFINITION

A group norm is an assumption or expectation held by group members concerning what kind of behaviour is
- right or wrong
- good or bad
- allowed or not allowed
- appropriate or not appropriate.

TYPICAL NORM STATEMENTS
- Around here we always ...
- It doesn't do to ...
- We never ...
- When that happens we ...

IDENTIFYING NORMS

By observation, interview or question you discover
- behaviour which gets reinforced or rewarded
- behaviour which gets discouraged or penalised

EVOLUTION OF NORMS

They may evolve through ...
- modelling behaviour on another 'prestigious' group
- accidental discovery of advantageous behaviour
- witnessing repeated acts
- unintended consequences of formal decisions.

Group norms may evolve over a long period of time. This can lead to them becoming
- rigid
- anachronistic
- irrelevant for current situations.

CHANGING NORMS

A group is often reluctant to change its norms, so for change to take place ...
- get group consensus to change
- generate support for change
- address as many factors as possible which will help the change.

Management's wishes on their own are sometimes not sufficiently strong to have enough influence to change norms.

Individual changes are rarely, if ever, effective in changing the norms of a group.

PROCESS FOR IMPLEMENTING NORM CHANGES (LEWIN'S CHANGE MODEL)

STAGE 1 UNFREEZING
STAGE 2 CHANGING
STAGE 3 REFREEZING

UNFREEZING

Develop an awareness of
- the nature of the change needed
- the methods planned to achieve the change
- the needs of those affected
- the ways that progress will be planned and monitored.

CHANGING
- Defining problems
- Identifying solutions
- Implementing solution

REFREEZING
- Stabilising the situation
- Building and rebuilding relationships
- Consolidating the systems

THE VALUE OF NORMS
- Counteracts anonymity
- Supports small-group identity
- Are legitimate to group members
- May not support organisation's formal goals
- Provides order
- Provides standards
- Influences behaviour
- Embodies the informal 'shadow' organisation

Not necessarily pro- or anti-management

Predictability desirable, avoids chaos

Enables the group to evaluate and control group behaviour

Often implicit

Language, dress, openness/secrecy, competitiveness, productivity

Expresses unwritten sometimes unspoken rules ➝ May encourage 'we–they' attitudes

Source: Training Learning Consultancy Ltd, Bristol, England. Reproduced with permission.

Virtuoso teams *Boynton* and *Fischer* draw attention to **virtuoso teams** that are formed specifically for big change in organisations. They are comprised of individual superstars, or virtuosos, with a single, clear, ambitious mandate and are not to remain together over multiple initiatives or projects.

Virtuoso teams require a special kind of leadership and to be managed in a manner that unleashes the maximum contribution from each individual superstar. Although most organisations rarely form such teams, they are required for radical change opportunities that represent a significant departure from prior practice and/or how an organisation conducts its business. Examples of big changes that called on virtuoso teams are the Manhattan Project, Thomas Edison's inventory factory, and Roald Amundsen's polar expedition.[10]

Informal groups

The formal structure of the organisation, and system of role relationships, rules and procedures, will always be augmented by interpretation and development at the informal level. **Informal groups** are based more on personal relationships and the agreement of the group's members than on defined role relationships. They serve to satisfy psychological and social needs not related necessarily to the tasks to be undertaken. Groups may devise ways of attempting to satisfy members' affiliations and other social motivations lacking in the work situation. Membership of informal groups can cut across the formal structure. They may be comprised of individuals from different parts of the organisation and/or from different levels, both vertically and diagonally, as well as from the same horizontal level. An informal group could also be the same as the formal group or it may be comprised of a part only of the formal group (*see* Figure 6.3)

Members of an informal group may appoint their own leader, who exercises authority by the consent of the members themselves. The informal leader may be chosen as the person who reflects the attitudes and values of the members, helps to resolve conflict, leads the group in satisfying its goals or liaises with management or other people outside the group. The informal leader may often change according to the particular situation facing the group. Although not usually the case, it is possible for the informal leader to be the same person as the formal leader appointed officially by management.

Figure 6.3   **Examples of informal groups within the formal structure of an organisation**

Major functions of informal groups

Lysons suggests four main reasons for the formation of informal groups.

- **The perpetuation of the informal group 'culture'.** Culture in this context means a set of values, norms and beliefs that form a guide to group acceptance and group behaviour. Unless you broadly subscribe to the group culture, you will not belong and be an 'outsider' or 'isolate'.
- **The maintenance of a communication system.** Groups want all the information that affects their welfare, either negatively or positively. If groups are not apprised of policies and motives behind actions, they will seek to tap into formal communication channels and spread information among group members.
- **The implementation of social control.** Conformity to group culture is enforced by such techniques as ridicule, ostracism and violence. This is illustrated, for example, by the enforcement of group norms in the bank wiring room example discussed above.
- **The provision of interest and fun in work life.** Many jobs are monotonous and fail to hold the attention of the workers. Work may also offer few future prospects. Workers may try to compensate by interpersonal relations provided by the group and in such activities as time wasting by talking, gambling, practical joking and drinking.[11]

> *We humans are a gregarious lot. We like to gather together and establish our own social networks, which are often the real key to creativity and innovation in organisations ... But many managers are unaware that seemingly pointless social networking does in fact play a crucial part in the way people interact with each other and get work done.*
>
> Sue Law, *Beyond the Water Cooler*[12]

An example of an informal group

A lack of direction and clear information flow within the formal structure can give rise to uncertainty and suspicion. In the absence of specific knowledge, the grapevine takes on an important role. Rumours start and the informal part of the organisation is highlighted, often with negative results.

A typical example concerned an industrial organisation in a highly competitive market that was experiencing a drop in sales. Two top managers had suddenly lost their jobs without any apparent explanation and there were board meetings seemingly every other day. Although there was no specific information or statements from top management, the general feeling among the staff was that whatever was about to happen was most unlikely to be good news.

At lunchtime, three junior members of staff – one female and two male, each from different departments – were having a chat. With a half smile, the female member said to the others that she could well be seeing a lot more of both or at least one of them before long. She said that she had heard, unofficially, from her manager that the department was about to be awarded a very profitable order. She surmised that other departments, which she had also heard had lost their parts of the same contracts and not had many orders recently, would have to integrate into the successful department with the possible loss of certain jobs. The other two members both believed this and talked about it within their own departments as if it were a fact. The result? Even more uncertainty throughout the organisation, increased gloom and distraction from the task. In fact, no such integration did take place, only a minor restructuring of the organisation with no direct loss of jobs other than through voluntary early retirement. However, it proved very difficult for top management to effectively quash the rumour and restore trust and morale.

Critical reflection

Given the obvious importance of social networks for both the morale and job satisfaction of staff and their levels of work performance, do you think that the main focus in the study of organisational behaviour should be on the operations and effective management of the informal organisation?

REASONS FOR THE FORMATION OF GROUPS OR TEAMS

Individuals will form into groups or teams, both formal and informal, for a number of different reasons.

- **Certain tasks can be performed only through the combined efforts of a number of individuals working together**. The variety of experience and expertise among members provides a synergetic effect that can be applied to the increasingly complex problems of modern organisations.
- **Collusion between members**. Individuals collude to modify formal working arrangements more to their liking – for example, by sharing or rotating unpopular tasks. Membership therefore provides the individual with opportunities for initiative and creativity.
- **Companionship and a source of mutual understanding and support from colleagues**. This can help in solving work problems and militate against stressful or demanding working conditions.
- **Membership provides the individual with a sense of belonging**. It provides a feeling of identity and the chance to acquire role recognition and status within the group or team.
- **Guidelines on generally acceptable behaviour**. It helps to clarify ambiguous situations, such as the extent to which official rules and regulations are expected to be adhered to in practice, the rules of the game and what is seen as the correct actual behaviour. The informal organisation may put pressure on members to resist demands from management on such matters as, for example, higher output or changes in working methods. Allegiance to the group or team can serve as a means of control over individual behaviour and discipline individuals who contravene the norms – for example, the process of 'binging' in the bank wiring room mentioned above.
- **Protection for its membership**. Group or team members collaborate to protect their interests from outside pressures or threats.

Expectations of group membership Individuals have varying expectations of the benefits from group membership, relating to both work performance and social processes. However, working in groups may mean that members spend too much time talking among themselves rather than doing. Groups may also compete against each other in a non-productive manner. It is a question of balance. It is important, therefore, that the manager understands the reasons for the formation of groups and is able to recognise likely advantageous or adverse consequences for the organisation.

GROUP COHESIVENESS AND PERFORMANCE

Social interaction is a natural feature of human behaviour, but ensuring harmonious working relationships and effective teamwork is not an easy task. The manager's main concern is that members of a work group co-operate in order to achieve the results expected of them.

Co-operation among members is likely to be greater in a united, cohesive group. Membership of a cohesive group can be a rewarding experience for the individual, contribute to the promotion of morale and aid the release of creativity and energy. Members of a high-morale group are more likely to think of themselves as a group and work together effectively. Strong and cohesive work groups can, therefore, have beneficial effects for the organisation. There are many factors that affect **group cohesiveness** and performance, that can be summarised under four broad headings, as shown in Figure 6.4.

Membership

Size of the group As a group increases in size, problems arise with communications and co-ordination. Large groups are more difficult to handle and require a higher level of supervision than smaller ones. Absenteeism also tends to be higher in large groups. When a group becomes too large, it may split into smaller units and friction may develop between the subgroups.

It is difficult to put a precise figure on the ideal size of a work group and there are many conflicting studies and reports. Much will depend upon other variables, but it seems to be generally accepted that cohesiveness becomes more difficult to achieve when a group exceeds 10 to12 members.[13] Beyond this size the group tends to split into subgroups. A figure of between five and seven is often quoted as an apparent optimum size for full participation within the group.

Many readers will be familiar with the classic 1957 movie *Twelve Angry Men*, in which one juror persuades the other 11 to change their minds over a murder verdict. This drew attention to a range of intra-group conflicts and the difficulty in groups of more than ten people attempting to reach consensus.

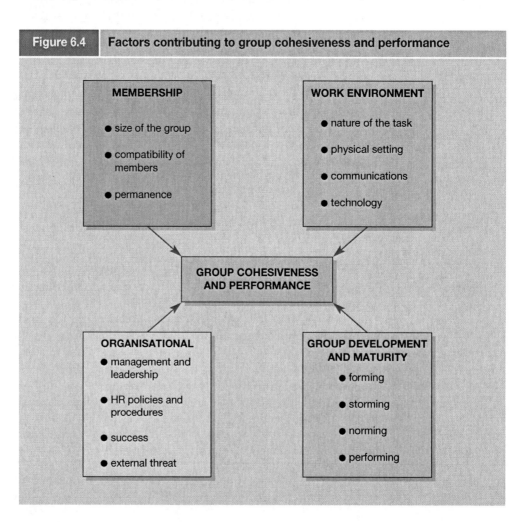

Figure 6.4   Factors contributing to group cohesiveness and performance

Cane asks the question, 'How many people should be in a team?'

> *The answers from different organizations as to what is the perfect number vary from between four and fifteen depending on a whole range of variables. Fifteen is about the maximum number of people anyone can communicate with without having to raise their voice significantly and any less than four has a restriction in the amount of creativity and variety that can be produced. It is interesting to note that these figures range between the maximum and minimum numbers of sports teams – perhaps less of a coincidence than it seems.*[14]

Compatibility of the members

The more homogeneous the group in terms of such features as shared backgrounds, interests, attitudes and values of its members, usually the easier it is to promote cohesiveness. Variations in other individual differences, such as the personality or skills of members, may serve to complement each other and help make for a cohesive group. On the other hand, such differences may be the cause of disruption and conflict. Conflict can also arise in a homogeneous group where members are in competition with each other. Individual incentive payment schemes, for example, may be a source of conflict.

Permanence of group members Group spirit and relationships take time to develop. Cohesiveness is more likely when members of a group are together for a reasonable length of time and changes occur only slowly. A frequent turnover of members is likely to have an adverse effect on morale and the cohesiveness of the group.

Work environment

The nature of the task Where workers are involved in similar work, share a common task or face the same problems, this may assist with cohesiveness. The nature of the task may serve to bring people together when it is necessary for them to communicate and interact regularly with each other in the performance of their duties – for example, members of a research and development team. Even if members of a group normally work at different locations, they may still experience a feeling of cohesiveness if the nature of the task requires frequent communication and interaction – for example, security guards patrolling separate areas who need to check with each other on a regular basis. However, where the task demands a series of relatively separate operations or discrete activities – such as on a machine-paced assembly line – it is more difficult to develop cohesiveness. Individuals may have interactions with colleagues on either side of them, but little opportunity to develop a common group feeling.

Physical setting Where members of a group work in the same location or in close physical proximity to each other, this will generally help cohesiveness. This is not always the case, however. For example, in large, open-plan offices, staff often tend to segregate themselves from colleagues and create barriers by the strategic sitting of such items as filing cabinets, bookcases or indoor plants. The size of the office and the number of staff in it are, of course, important considerations in this case. Isolation from other groups of workers will also tend to build cohesiveness. This often applies, for example, where there is a smaller number of workers on a night shift.

Communications The more easily members can communicate freely with each other, the greater the likelihood of group cohesiveness. Communications are affected by the work environment, the nature of the task and technology. For example, difficulties in communication can arise with production systems where workers are stationed continuously at a particular point with limited freedom of movement. Even when opportunities exist for interaction with colleagues, physical conditions may limit effective communication. For example, the technological layout and high level of noise with some assembly line work can limit contact between workers. Restrictions on opportunities for social interaction can hamper internal group unity.

Technology We can see that the nature of technology and the manner in which work is carried out has an important effect on cohesiveness and relates closely to the nature of the task, physical setting and communications. Where the nature of the work process involves a craft or skill-based 'technology', there is a higher likelihood of group cohesiveness. However, with machine-paced assembly line work, it is more difficult to develop cohesiveness. Technology also has wider implications for the operation and behaviour of groups and therefore is considered more fully later in this chapter.

Organisational factors

Management and leadership The form of management and style of leadership adopted will influence the relationship between the group and the organisation and is a major determinant of group cohesiveness. In general terms, cohesiveness will be affected by such things as the manner in which the manager gives guidance and encouragement to the group, offers help and support, provides opportunities for participation, attempts to resolve conflicts and gives attention to both employee relations and task problems. *McKenna and Maister* draw attention to the importance of the group leader establishing a level of trust among members of the group by helping them understand the behaviours that build trust: 'The job of the group leader is to encourage people to earn the trust of others in their group and then show them how it can translate into greater commitment, greater creativity, greater professional satisfaction, and better performance.'[15]

HR policies and procedures Harmony and cohesiveness within the group are more likely to be achieved if HR policies and procedures are well developed and perceived to be equitable with fair treatment for all members. Attention should be given to the effects that appraisal systems, discipline, promotion and rewards and opportunities for personal development have on members of the group.

Success The more successful the group, the more cohesive it is likely to be; and cohesive groups are more likely to be successful. Success is usually a strong motivational influence on the level of work performance. Success or reward as a positive motivator can be perceived by group members in a number of ways, such as the satisfactory completion of a task through co-operative action, praise from management, a feeling of high status, achievement in competition with other groups and benefits gained, such as high wage payments from a group bonus incentive scheme.

External threat Cohesiveness may be enhanced by members co-operating with one another when faced with a common external threat, such as changes in their method of work or the appointment of a new manager. Even if the threat is subsequently removed, the group may still continue to have a greater degree of cohesiveness than before the threat arose. Conflict between groups will also tend to increase the cohesiveness of each group and the boundaries of the group become drawn more clearly.

Group development and maturity

The degree of cohesiveness is affected also by the manner in which groups progress through the various stages of development and maturity before getting down to the real tasks in hand. This process can take time and is often traumatic for the members. *Bass and Ryterband* identify four distinct stages in group development.

- mutual acceptance and membership;
- communication and decision-making;
- motivation and productivity; and
- control and organisation.[16]

An alternative, more popular, model by *Tuckman* identifies five main successive stages of group development and relationships: **forming**, **storming**, **norming**, **performing**, and **adjourning**.[17]

- **Stage 1: forming**. The initial formation of the group and the bringing together of a number of individuals who identify, tentatively, the purpose of the group, its composition and terms of reference. At this stage, consideration is given to the hierarchical structure of the group, pattern of leadership, individual roles and responsibilities and codes of conduct. There is likely to be considerable anxiety as members attempt to create an impression, test each other and establish their personal identity within the group.
- **Stage 2: storming**. As members of the group get to know each other better, they will put forward their views more openly and forcefully. Disagreements will be expressed and challenges offered on the nature of the task and arrangements made in the earlier stage of development. This may lead to conflict and hostility. The storming stage is important because, if successful, there will be discussions on reforming arrangements for the working and operation of the group and agreement on more meaningful structures and procedures.
- **Stage 3: norming**. As conflict and hostility start to be controlled, members of the group will establish guidelines and standards and develop their own norms of acceptable behaviour. The norming stage is important in establishing the need for members to co-operate in order to plan, agree standards of performance and fulfil the purpose of the group.
- **Stage 4: performing**. When the group has progressed successfully through the three earlier stages of development, it will have created structure and cohesiveness to work effectively as a team. At this stage, the group can concentrate on the attainment of its purpose and performance of the common task is likely to be at its most effective.
- **Stage 5: adjourning**. This refers to the adjourning or disbanding of the group because of, for example, completion of the task, members leaving the organisation or moving on to other tasks. Some members may feel a compelling sense of loss at the end of a major or lengthy group project and their return to independence is characterised by sadness and anxiety. Managers may need to prepare for future group tasks and engendering team effort.

Another writer suggests that new groups go through the following stages.

- the polite stage;
- the 'Why are we here? What are we doing?' stage;
- the power stage, which dominant will emerge?;
- the constructive stage when sharing begins; and
- the unity stage – this often takes weeks, eating together, talking together.[18]

POTENTIAL DISADVANTAGES OF STRONG, COHESIVE GROUPS

Although there are potential disadvantages of cohesive groups (discussed below), they may result in greater interaction between members, mutual help and social satisfaction, lower turnover and absenteeism and, often, higher levels of production.[19]

If the manager is to develop effective work groups, then attention should be given to those factors that influence the creation of group identity and cohesiveness. However, strong and cohesive groups also present potential disadvantages for management. Cohesive groups do not necessarily produce a higher level of output. Performance varies with the extent to which the group accepts or rejects the goals of the organisation. Furthermore, with a very high level of cohesiveness and attention to social activities, there may even be a fall in output. The level of production is likely to conform to a standard acceptable as a norm by the group. It may be remembered, for example, that, in the bank wiring room experiment of the Hawthorne studies, group norms imposed a restriction on the level of output of the workers.

Once a group has become fully developed and created cohesiveness, it is more difficult for the manager successfully to change the attitudes and behaviour of the group. It is important that the manager should attempt to influence the group during the norming stage – when members are establishing guidelines and standards and their own norms of acceptable behaviour. When a group has become fully developed and established its own culture, it is more difficult to change the attitudes and behaviour of its members.

Inter-group conflict Strong, cohesive groups may develop a critical or even hostile attitude towards people outside the group or members of other groups. This can be the case, for example, when group cohesiveness is based on common status, qualifications, technical expertise or professional standing. Group cohesiveness may result in lack of co-operation with, or opposition to, non-members. As a result, resentment and inter-group conflict may arise to the detriment of the organisation as a whole. In order to help prevent, or overcome, unconstructive inter-group conflict, the manager should attempt to stimulate a high level of communication and interaction between the groups and maintain harmony. Rotation of members among different groups should be encouraged.

On the other hand, inter-group rivalry may be deliberately encouraged as a means of building stronger within-group cohesiveness. The idea is that a competitive element may help to promote unity within a group. However, inter-group rivalry and competition need to be handled carefully. The manager should attempt to avoid the development of 'win–lose' situations. Emphasis should be placed on the overall objectives of the organisation and superordinate goals. These are goals over and above the issues at conflict and which, if they are to be achieved, require the co-operation of the competing groups.

CHARACTERISTICS OF AN EFFECTIVE WORK GROUP

The characteristics of an effective work group are not always easy to isolate clearly. The underlying feature is a spirit of co-operation in which members work well together as a united team and with harmonious and supportive relationships. This may be evidenced when members of a group exhibit:

- a belief in shared aims and objectives;
- a sense of commitment to the group;
- acceptance of group values and norms;
- a feeling of mutual trust and dependency;
- full participation by all members and decision-making by consensus;
- a free flow of information and communications;
- the open expression of feelings and disagreements;
- the resolution of conflict by the members themselves; and
- a low level of staff turnover, absenteeism, accidents, errors and complaints.

However, as *Brooks* points out, when teams operate at the higher order of group dynamics, this list is arguably more reflective of 'effective **work teams** rather than work groups and this is how it should be – these are teams not groups'.[20]

The effects of technology Technology is clearly a major influence on the pattern of group operation and behaviour. The work organisation may limit the opportunities for social interaction and the extent to which individuals are able to identify themselves as members of a cohesive work group. This in turn can have possible adverse effects on attitudes to work and the level of job satisfaction. In many assembly line production systems, for example, relationships between individual workers are determined by the nature of the task, the extent to which individual jobs are specified and the time cycle of operations.

ACAS draws attention to technological advances and how new technology enables production to be tailored quickly to customer requirements, often on an individual basis.

> *Mass production techniques, where jobs are broken down into simple tasks, are not suitable for the new customer-focused manufacturing nor the expectations of an educated workforce. Organisations need workers to be more flexible, to co-operate with other workers, supervisors and managers throughout the organisation, to operate sophisticated technology and to be more adaptable. In addition, the sheer complexity of operations in industry, commerce and the services place them beyond the expertise and control of any one individual. In these circumstances some form of teamwork becomes not just desirable but essential.* [21]

The impact of information technology

The impact of information technology demands new patterns of work organisation, and affects the formation and structure of groups. It will influence where and how people interact. Movement away from large-scale centralised organisation to smaller working units can help create an environment in which workers may relate more easily to each other. Improvements in telecommunications mean, for example, that support staff need no longer be located within the main production unit. On the other hand, modern methods of communication mean that individuals may work more on their own, from their own homes, shared offices or hotels or work more with machines rather than other people. [22]

VIRTUAL TEAMS

The combination of increasing globalisation and widespread developments in information communications and technology (ICT) has put greater emphasis on the opportunities for, and need of, **virtual teams**. Instead of face-to-face proximity, virtual teams are a collection of people who are geographically separated, but still work together closely. The primary interaction among members is by some electronic information and communication process. [23] This enables organisations to function away from traditional working hours and the physical availability of staff. Computer-based information systems and increased wireless connectivity further the opportunities for virtual working. By their very nature, virtual teams are likely to be largely self-managed.

According to *Hall*, the virtual team is a potential future compromise between fully fledged teams and well-managed groups.

> *I am watching the rise of this idea with interest but am sceptical that it will actually create a 'third way'. Real teams can only be forged in the crucible of personal interaction: videoconferences and Net communications are still a poor substitute for this. Of course, once a team has formed it can use these media, as members will know each other well, but that's not the important bit. It's the forming, norming and storming that make a team.* [24]

Communication and leadership skills *Parker* highlights that remote working may also have an impact on the social aspects of organisational working, with an increasing feeling of isolation: 'Remote team working is not simply a matter of ensuring staff have access to a laptop and telephone line, and assuming that they will be able to continue with their work. The management and communication skills that this new working culture requires are also key to success.' [25] A similar point is made by Norval, who maintains that many remote workers can feel isolated and that the organisation is ignoring them, which can affect their motivation. Without the visual sense and informal communications within the office, managers need to make a more conscious effort to build rapport and to rethink their management style. [26]

Symons considers one advantage of virtual teamworking using asynchronous media is the clarity and richness of contributions when respondents are removed from the urgency of immediate interaction, and this can be particularly relevant in cross-cultural groups. However, as the leader cannot influence by his or her physical presence and as hierarchies fade on-line, managing dispersed teams requires a range of subtly different leadership skills. It is important to develop mutual trust, a democratic approach of shared control and decision-making and to adopt the role and style of a coach: 'The leader has to establish and maintain "credit" with the group, as "position power" has little or no currency in virtual working.'[27]

Cultural diversity

One reason for the growth in virtual teams is because of increasing globalisation and team members working and living in different countries. This gives rise to potential difficulties of cultural diversity. For example, as *Francesco and Gold* point out: 'The more culturally diverse the members, the more difficult it is to manage a virtual team. Cultural diversity, which will be increasingly common, adds to the complexity of managing virtual teams because different values, customs, and traditions require more leadership under conditions that reduce the ability to use direct leadership.'[28]

According to *Murray*, although virtual working presents some unexpected benefits, if managing diversity in the workplace is a tough task for business leaders, the challenges of keeping executives from different backgrounds working together in various parts of the world is even more difficult. Virtual working does not eradicate the sorts of cultural misunderstandings that can arise in a face-to-face situation: 'Cultural or behavioural differences that can manifest themselves in face-to-face working situations can be exacerbated in virtual team working, particularly when the group has members from different backgrounds.' [29]

Critical reflection   ????

'Personal self-interest and opportunism are natural features of human behaviour and will always take preference over the demands and best interests of the group or teamwork.' How would you present a *counter* point of view? How far are you prepared to put the interest of a work group before your own interests?

ROLE RELATIONSHIPS

In order that the organisation can achieve its goals and objectives, the work of individual members must be linked to coherent patterns of activities and relationships. This is achieved through the 'role structure' of the organisation.

A **role** is the expected pattern of behaviours associated with members occupying a particular position within the structure of the organisation. It also describes how a person perceives their own situation. The concept of 'role' is important to the functioning of groups and for an understanding of group processes and behaviour. It is through role differentiation that the structure of the work group and relationships between its members are established. Some form of structure is necessary for teamwork and co-operation. The concept of roles helps to clarify the structure and define the pattern of complex relationships within the group.

The formal organisational relationships (line, functional, staff or lateral) (discussed later, in Chapter 10) can be seen as forms of role relationships. These individual authority relationships determine the pattern of interaction with other roles.

The role, or roles, that the individual plays within the group is influenced by a combination of:

- **situational factors** such as the requirements of the task, style of leadership, position in the communication network; and
- **personal factors** such as values, attitudes, motivation, ability and personality.

The role that a person plays in one work group may be quite different from the role that person plays in other work groups. However, everyone within a group is expected to behave in a particular manner and fulfil certain role expectations.

A person's role-set In addition to the role relationships with members of their own group – peers, superiors, subordinates – the individual will have a number of role-related relationships with outsiders – for example, members of other work groups, trade union officials, suppliers, consumers. This is a person's **role-set**. The role-set comprises the range of associations or contacts with whom the individual has meaningful interactions in connection with the performance of the role (*see* Figure 6.5)

Role incongruence

An important feature of role relationships is the concept of **role incongruence**. This arises when a member of staff is perceived as having a high and responsible position in one respect but a low standing in another respect. Difficulties with role incongruence can arise from the nature of groupings and formal relationships within the structure of the organisation. There are a number of work-related relationships, such as doctor and nurse, chef and waiter, senior manager and personal assistant, that can give rise to a potential imbalance of authority and responsibility.

Difficulties with role incongruence can also arise in line-staff relationships – for instance, a relatively junior member of the HR department informing a senior departmental manager

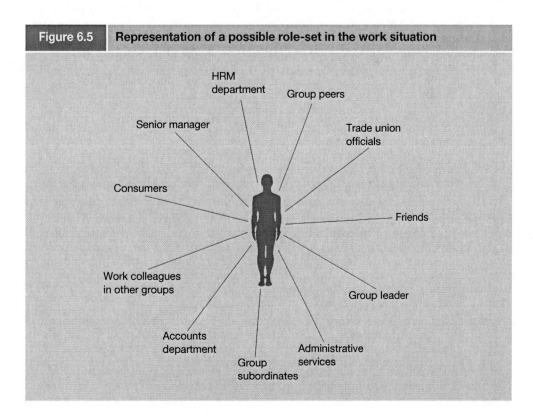

| Figure 6.5 | Representation of a possible role-set in the work situation |

that a certain proposed action is contrary to the policies of the organisation. Another example from the area of staff relationships is where a person establishes him or herself in the role of 'gatekeeper' to the boss[30] – for instance, a comparatively junior personal assistant passes on the manager's instructions to one of the manager's more senior subordinates or a personal assistant attempts to block a more senior member of staff from having access to the manager.

Role expectations

Many **role expectations** are prescribed formally and indicate what people are expected to do and their duties and obligations. Formal role prescriptions provide guidelines for expected behaviours and may be more prevalent in a 'mechanistic' organisation. Examples are written contracts of employment, rules and regulations, standing orders, policy decisions, job descriptions or directives from superiors. Formal role expectations may also be derived clearly from the nature of the task. They may, in part at least, be defined legally – for example, under the Health and Safety at Work Act, or as with the obligations of a company secretary under the Companies Acts, or the responsibilities of a district auditor under the Local Government Acts.

Not all role expectations are prescribed formally, however. There will be certain patterns of behaviour that, although not specified formally, will nonetheless be expected of members. These informal role expectations may be imposed by the group itself or at least communicated to a person by other members of the group. Examples include general conduct, mutual support to co-members, attitudes towards superiors, means of communicating, dress and appearance. Members may not always be consciously aware of these informal expectations, yet they still serve as important determinants of behaviour. Under this heading could be included the concept of a psychological contract, which was discussed in Chapter 1.

Some members may have the opportunity to determine their own role expectations where, for example, formal expectations are specified loosely or only in very general terms. Opportunities for **self-established roles** are more likely in senior positions, but also occur within certain professional, technical or scientific groups, such as senior research staff, or where there is a demand for creativity or artistic flair, such as with head chefs. Opportunities like these may be greater within an 'organic' organisation and will also be influenced by the style of leadership adopted, such as where a *laissez-faire* approach is adopted.

ROLE CONFLICT

Patterns of behaviour result from both the role and the personality. The concept of role focuses attention on aspects of behaviour existing independently of an individual's personality.

Role conflict arises from inadequate or inappropriate role definition and needs to be distinguished from personality clashes. These arise from incompatibility between two or more people as individuals, even though their roles may be defined clearly and understood fully. In practice, the manner in which a person actually behaves may not be consistent with their expected pattern of behaviours. This inconsistency may be a result of role conflict.

Role conflict as a generic term can include:

- **role incompatibility**;
- **role ambiguity**;
- **role overload**; and
- **role underload**.

These are all problem areas associated with the creation of role expectations (*see* Figure 6.6.)

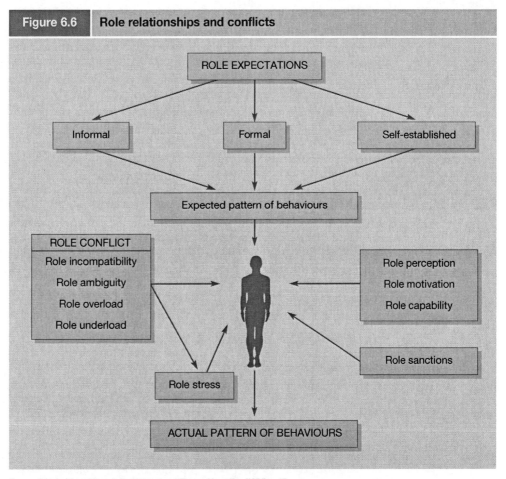

| Figure 6.6 | Role relationships and conflicts |

Source: Adapted from Miner, J. B., *Management Theory*, Macmillan (1971) p. 47.

- **Role incompatibility** arises when a person faces a situation in which simultaneous different or contradictory expectations create inconsistency. Compliance with one set of expectations makes it difficult or impossible to comply with other expectations. The two role expectations are in conflict. A typical example concerns the person 'in the middle', such as the supervisor or section head, who faces opposing expectations from workers and management. Another example might be the situation of a manager who believes in a relaxed, participative style of behaviour more in keeping with a Theory Y approach, but whose superior believes in a Theory X approach and expects the manager to adopt a more formal and directive style of behaviour.
- **Role ambiguity** occurs when there is lack of clarity as to the precise requirements of the role and the person is unsure what to do. The person's own perception of the role may differ from the expectations of others. This implies that insufficient information is available to ensure adequate performance in the role. Role ambiguity may result from a lack of formally prescribed expectations. It is likely to arise in large, diverse groups or at times of constant change. Uncertainty often relates to such matters as the method of performing tasks, the extent of the person's authority and responsibility, standards of work and the evaluation and appraisal of performance.
- **Role overload** is when a person faces too many separate roles or too great a variety of expectations. The person is unable to meet satisfactorily all expectations and some must be neglected in order to satisfy others. This leads to a conflict of priorities. Some writers distinguish between role overload and work overload. Role overload is seen in terms of the total role-set and implies that the person has too many separate roles to handle.

Where there are too many expectations of a single role – that is, a problem of quantity – this is work overload.

- **Role underload** can arise when the prescribed role expectations fall short of the person's own perception of their role. The person may feel that the role is not demanding enough and that he or she has the capacity to undertake a larger or more varied role or an increased number of roles. Role underload may arise, for example, when a new member of staff is first appointed or from the initial effects of empowerment.

Role conflict and matrix organisation Problems of role conflict can often arise from the matrix form of organisation (discussed in Chapter 10) and, for example, from the use of flexible project teams. Where staff are assigned temporarily, and perhaps on a part-time basis, from other groups, this creates a two-way flow of authority and responsibility.

Unless role differentiations are defined clearly, this can result in conflicting expectations from the manager of the person's own functional grouping and the manager of the project team (role incompatibility). It can also lead to uncertainty about the exact requirements of the part the person is expected to play as a member of the project team (role ambiguity). The combinations of expectations from both managers may also result in role overload.

Role stress

Role conflict can result in role stress. As discussed in Chapter 1, although a certain amount of stress may *arguably* be seen as a good thing and, especially at managerial level, helps to bring out a high level of performance, it is also potentially very harmful. Stress is a source of tension, frustration and dissatisfaction. It can lead to difficulties in communication and interpersonal relationships and can affect morale, effectiveness at work and health.

There are various ways in which management might attempt to avoid or reduce role conflict, and the possibilities of role stress.

- Increase specification and clarity of prescribed role expectations – for example, through written statements on objectives and policy, use of manuals and set procedures, introduction of appropriate rules and detailed job descriptions. However, such measures may be resented by staff. They may restrict the opportunity for independent action and personal development, giving rise to even more role conflict.
- Improved recruitment and selection and the careful matching of abilities, motivation, interests and personalities to the demands of a particular role.
- Attention to induction and socialisation programmes, job training and retraining, staff development and career progression plans.
- Medical examinations and health screening to give early indications of potential stress-related problems.
- The creation of new roles or assimilation of existing roles. The reallocation or restructuring of tasks and responsibilities. The clarification of priorities and elimination or downgrading of minor roles.
- Giving advance notice and explanation of what is likely to happen – for example, of an expected, additional heavy workload that must be completed urgently. Where possible and appropriate, provide an opportunity for practice or experience.
- Attention to factors that may help improve group structure and group cohesiveness and help overcome inter-group conflict.
- Review of organisation structure, information flow and communication networks – for example, members of staff being answerable to more than one superior.

Other influences on behaviour

Even if there is an absence of role conflict and role stress, a person's actual behaviour may still be inconsistent with expected pattern of behaviours. *Miner* gives three reasons that may account for this disparity.[31]

- The person does not perceive the job in the way the role prescriptions specify. This is a form of role ambiguity but may arise not because the role prescriptions themselves are unclear, but because the person misunderstands or distorts them.
- Motivation is lacking and the person does not want to behave in the way prescribed.
- The person does not have the capabilities – knowledge, mental ability or physical skills – required to behave in the way the role prescriptions specify.

Application of sanctions

Organisations apply a number of both positive and negative sanctions as inducements for members to contribute and behave in accordance with their prescribed roles. Typical examples are: an increase in salary or wages; promotion; a sideways or downwards move in the organisation structure; the threat of dismissal.

There are also a number of less direct sanctions that may be adopted. These include: the size of office or work area; the allocation of unpopular tasks; giving opportunities for paid overtime work; level of supervision or empowerment; the amount of information given or the extent of consultation; granting or withholding privileges.

Role sanctions may also be applied through the operation of the informal organisation. Members of the group may impose their own sanctions and discipline individuals who contravene the norms of the group or expected standards of behaviour.

THE IMPORTANCE OF TEAMWORK

How people behave and perform as members of a group is as important as their behaviour or performance as individuals. Harmonious working relationships and good teamwork help make for a high level of staff morale and work performance. Effective teamwork is an essential element of modern management practices, such as empowerment, quality circles and total quality management, and how groups manage change. Teamwork is important in any organisation, but may be especially significant in service industries, such as hospitality organisations where there is a direct effect on customer satisfaction.[32]

According to ACAS, teams have been around for as long as anyone can remember and there can be few organisations that have not used the term in one sense or another. In a general sense, people talk of teamwork when they want to emphasise the virtues of co-operation and the need to make use of the various strengths of employees. Using the term more specifically, teamworking involves a reorganisation of the way work is carried out. Teamwork can increase competitiveness by:

- improving productivity;
- improving quality and encouraging innovation;
- taking advantage of the opportunities provided by technological advances;
- improving employee motivation and commitment.[33]

The general movement towards flatter structures of organisation, wider spans of control and reducing layers of middle management, together with increasing empowerment of employees, all involve greater emphasis on the importance of teamworking. 'There's no doubt that effective teamwork is crucial to an organisation's efforts to perform better, faster and more profitably than their competitors.'[34]

Skills of effective teamworking From a recent study of Europe's top companies, *Heller* refers to the need for new managers and new methods and includes as a key strategy for a new breed of managers in a dramatically changed environment: 'making teamworking work – the new, indispensable skill'. Heller refers to the happy teams at Heineken. Part of the cultural strength of Heineken is a realisation that 'the best culture for an organisation is a team culture' and that 'any large organization is a team of teams – and people who have to work together as a team must also think together as a team'.[35] Heller also lists Heineken's manifesto for 'professional team-thinking' (*see* Figure 6.7) and maintains that 'Arguing with any of these 11 points is absurd'.

According to *Guirdham*, the growth of teamwork has led to the increased interest in interface skills at work.

> *More and more tasks of contemporary organisations, particularly those in high technology and service businesses, require teamwork. Taskforces, project teams and committees are key elements in the modern workplace. Teamwork depends not just on technical competence of the individuals composing the team, but on their ability to 'gel'. To work well together, the team members must have more than just team spirit. They also need collaborative skills – they must be able to support one another and to handle conflict in such a way that it becomes constructive rather than destructive.[36]*

A similar point is made by *Ashmos and Nathan*: 'The use of teams has expanded dramatically in response to competitive challenges. In fact, one of the most common skills required by new work practices is the ability to work as a team.'[37]

Figure 6.7	Manifesto for professional team-thinking at Heineken

1 The aim is to reach the best decision, not just a hasty conclusion or an easy consensus. The team leader always has the ultimate responsibility for the quality of the decision taken – and, therefore, for the quality of the team-thinking effort that has led up to the decision.

2 To produce the best professional team-thinking, the team leader must ensure that ego-trips, petty office politics and not-invented-here rigidity are explicitly avoided. There should be competition between ideas – not between individual members of the team.

3 The team-thinking effort must first ensure that the best question to be answered is clearly and completely formulated.

4 The team-thinking process is iterative – not linear. Therefore, the question may have to be altered later and the process repeated.

5 The team leader is responsible for seeing that sufficient alternatives and their predicted consequences have been developed for evaluation by the team.

6 The team leader will thus ask, 'What are our alternatives?' – and not just, 'What is the answer?'

7 The team leader also recognizes that it is wiser to seek and listen to the ideas of the team before expressing his or her own ideas and preferences.

8 In any professional team-thinking effort, more ideas will have to be created than used. But any idea that is rejected will be rejected with courtesy and with a clear explanation as to why it is being rejected. To behave in this way is not naive, it is just decent and smart.

9 A risk/reward equation and a probability of success calculation will be made explicitly before any important decision is taken.

10 Once a decision is made professionally, the team must implement it professionally.

11 When you think, think. When you act, act.

Source: From Robert Heller, *In Search of European Excellence*, Profile Books (1997), p. 231. Reproduced with permission.

INTERACTIONS BETWEEN MEMBERS

Earlier we mentioned that how people behave and perform as members of a group is as important as their behaviour or performance as individuals and drew attention to the importance of effective teamwork. The main focus of attention in this chapter is the actual roles, behaviours and performance of people working in groups or teams. Once again, however, we should be aware of the tendency for the terms 'groups' and 'teams' to be used interchangeably.

If groups are to be successful and perform effectively, there must be a spirit of unity and co-operation. Members of a group must work well together as a team. As *Crainer* reminds us, in most teams people will contribute individual skills, many of which will be different. However, referring to the work of *Obeng*,[38] Crainer points out that it is not enough to have a rag-bag collection of individual skills.

> *The various behaviors of the team members must mesh together in order to achieve objectives. For people to work successfully in teams, you need people to behave in certain ways. You need some people to concentrate on the task at hand (doers). You need some people to provide specialist knowledge (knowers) and some to solve problems as they arise (solvers). You need some people to make sure that it is going as well as it can and that the whole team is contributing fully (checkers). And you need some people to make sure that the team is operating as a cohesive social unit (carers).*[39]

As ACAS points out, 'To remain competitive organisations need to make optimum use of equipment and people if they are to thrive or even survive … In a general sense people talk of teamwork when they want to emphasise the virtues of co-operation and the need to make use of the various strengths of employees.'[40]

In order to understand the functions and processes of a group, it is necessary to understand what happens when people meet, the actions and behaviour of individual members, the parts people play, the patterns of interactions and forces within the group, and influences on individual and group performance. According to Guirdham, for example:

> *Many of the concepts that have helped us understand interactive behaviour in work relationships are also needed for understanding it in groups, including role behaviour, norms and co-operation, competition, conflict and conflict resolution. Most of what there is to understand about group work applies equally to both decision-making groups and teams but there are some further issues particular to the two different kinds of groups. There is, however, no suggestion that teams do not have to solve problems!*[41]

BELBIN'S TEAM-ROLES

One of the most popular and widely used analyses of individual roles within a work group or team is that developed by *Meredith Belbin*. Following years of research and empirical study, Belbin concludes that groups composed entirely of clever people or people with similar personalities display a number of negative results and lack creativity. The most consistently successful groups are comprised of a range of roles undertaken by various members. The constitution of the group itself is an important variable in its success.[42] Initially, Belbin identified eight useful types of contribution – or team-roles.

A **team-role** is described as a pattern of behaviour, characteristic of the way in which one team member interacts with another whose performance serves to facilitate the progress of the team as a whole. In a follow-up publication, Belbin discusses the continual evolution of team-roles, which differ in a few respects from those originally identified and adds a ninth role.[43] Strength of contribution in any one role is commonly associated with particular weaknesses. These are called allowable weaknesses. Members are seldom strong in all nine team-roles. A description of the evolved nine team-roles is given in Table 6.1.

The types of people identified are useful team members and form a comprehensive list. These are the key team-roles and the primary characters for successful teams. Creative teams require a balance of all these roles and comprise members who have characteristics comple-

Table 6.1	Belbin's evolved nine team-roles	
Roles and descriptions	**Team-role contribution**	**Allowable weaknesses**
Plant	Creative, imaginative, unorthodox. Solves difficult problems.	Ignores details. Too preoccupied to communicate effectively.
Resource investigator	Extrovert, enthusiastic, communicative. Explores opportunities. Develops contacts.	Overoptimistic. Loses interest once initial enthusiasm has passed.
Co-ordinator	Mature, confident, a good chairperson. Clarifies goals, promotes decision-making. Delegates personal work.	Can be seen as manipulative. Delegates well.
Shaper	Challenging, dynamic, thrives on pressure. Has the drive and courage to overcome obstacles.	Can provoke others. Hurts people's feelings.
Monitor-evaluator	Sober, strategic and discerning. Sees all options. Judges accurately.	Lacks drive and ability to inspire others. Overly critical.
Team worker	Co-operative, mild, perceptive and diplomatic. Listens, builds, averts friction, calms the waters.	Indecisive in crunch situations. Can be easily influenced.
Implementer	Disciplined, reliable, conservative and efficient. Turns ideas into practical actions.	Somewhat inflexible. Slow to respond to new possibilities.
Completer	Painstaking, conscientious, anxious. Searches out errors and omissions. Delivers on time.	Inclined to worry unduly. Reluctant to delegate. Can be a nit-picker.
Specialist	Single-minded, self-sharing, dedicated. Provides knowledge and skills in rare supply.	Contributes on only a narrow front. Dwells on technicalities. Overlooks the 'big picture'.

(Reprinted with permission from Belbin, R. M., *Team Roles at Work*, Butterworths Division of Reed Elsevier (UK) Ltd/Belbin Associates (1993) p. 23.

mentary to one another. 'No ones's perfect, but a team can be.' Belbin claims that good examples of each type would prove adequate for any challenge, although not all types are necessarily needed. Other members may be welcome for their personal qualities, for example a sense of humour, but experience suggests there is no other team-role that it would be useful to add.

Back-up team-roles and functional roles The most consistently successful teams were 'mixed' with a balance of team-roles. The role that a person undertakes in a group is not fixed and may change according to circumstances. Individuals may have a 'back-up team-role' with which they have some affinity other than their primary team-role. If certain roles were missing, members would call upon their back-up roles.

Team-roles differ from what Belbin calls 'functional-roles'. These are the roles that members of a team perform in terms of the specifically technical demands placed upon them. Team members are typically chosen for functional roles on the basis of experience and not personal characteristics or aptitudes.

Belbin has developed a Self-Perception Inventory, designed to provide members of a group with a simple means of assessing their best team-roles.

The value of Belbin's team-roles inventory

Despite possible doubts about the value of Belbin's Self-Perception Inventory, it remains a popular means of examining and comparing team-roles. For example, in order to explore whether local government managers were distinctively different from the model of private-sector management or not, *Arroba and Wedgwood-Oppenheim* compared samples of the two groups of managers with Belbin's key team-roles. There were noticeable similarities between the two groups, with the noticeable exception of the marked difference between private-sector managers and local government officers in the score for team workers and the team-roles they preferred to adopt. The individual characteristics of managers in the two sectors differed. The data implied that local government officers were committed to organisational objectives and dedicated to task achievement but the low score for team workers suggested that the high commitment to organisational tasks was not supplemented by a concern for interpersonal processes. In local government, the drive and enthusiasm and emphasis on task were exaggerated, while attention to idea generation and productive interpersonal relationships was less marked.[44]

Distribution of team-roles among UK managers

Using Belbin's model, *Fisher et al.* undertook a study of the distribution of team-roles among managers. Over the past 15 years, many layers of management have been removed and the gap left in terms of having people to lead and motivate has increasingly been filled by the creation of multitudes of teams.

The participants in the study were 1441 male and 355 female managers, all with some management experience. All had completed a personality questionnaire and were candidates short-listed for a range of management positions in both the private and public sectors.

The study analysed data supplied by ASE/NFER Publishing Company and results were then compared with the Belbin model. The data broadly agreed with the Belbin model.

The authors conclude that, as much is still unknown about teams, it is reassuring that further support has been found for the popular Belbin team-role model. There are several unresolved problems with teamworking, but these might lie more with practices in staff recruitment than in team theory.[45]

PATTERNS OF COMMUNICATION

The level of interaction among members of a group or team is influenced by the structuring of channels of communication. Laboratory research by *Bavelas*[46] and subsequent studies by other researchers, such as *Leavitt,*[47] have resulted in the design of a series of communication networks. These networks were based on groups of five members engaged in a number of problem-solving tasks. Members were permitted to communicate with each other by written notes only and not everyone was always free to communicate with everyone else.

There are five main types of communication networks – wheel, circle, all-channel, Y and chains (*see* Figure 6.8).

- **The wheel**, also sometimes known as the star, is the most **centralised network**. This network is most efficient for simple tasks, where problems are solved quickly with few mistakes and with few information flows. However, as the problems become more complex and demands on the link person increase, effectiveness suffers. The link person is at the centre of the network and acts as the focus of activities and information flows and the co-ordinator of group tasks. The central person is perceived as leader of the group and experiences a high level of satisfaction. However, for members on the periphery, the wheel is the least satisfying network.
- **The circle** is a more **decentralised network**. Overall, it is less efficient. The group is unorganised, with low leadership predictability. Performance tends to be slow and erratic. However, the circle is quicker than the wheel when it comes to solving complex problems and also copes with change or new tasks efficiently. The circle network is most satisfying for all the members. Decision-making is likely to involve some degree of participation.

Figure 6.8	Communication networks

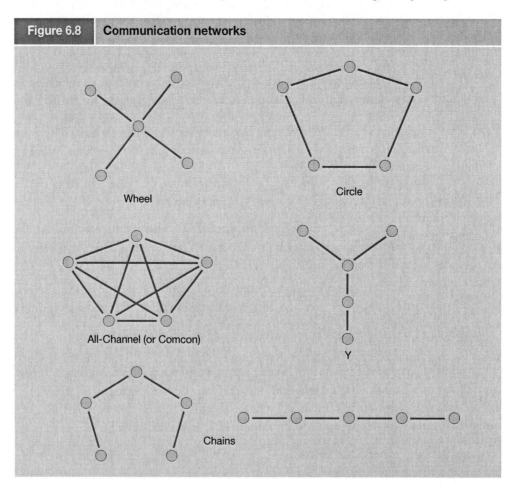

Wheel

Circle

All-Channel (or Comcon)

Y

Chains

- **The all-channel (or comcon) network** is a decentralised network that involves full discussion and participation. This network appears to work best where a high level of interaction is required among all the members in order to solve complex problems. Leadership predictability is very low. There is a fairly high level of satisfaction for members. The all-channel network may not stand up well under pressure, in which case it will either disintegrate or re-form into a wheel network.
- **A 'Y' or chain network** might be appropriate for simple problem-solving tasks that require little interaction between members. These networks are centralised, with information flows along a predetermined channel. Leadership predictability is high to moderate. There is a low to moderate level of satisfaction for members.

The relationship between centralised and decentralised networks and performance of the group is outlined in Figure 6.9.

Implications for the manager Despite the obvious artificiality and limitations of these communication network studies, they do have certain implications for the manager. Knowledge of the findings may be applied to influence the patterns of communication in meetings and committees. They also provide a reasonable representation of the situations that might apply in large organisations. It will be interesting for the manager to observe the patterns of communication adopted by different groups in different situations. The manager can also note how communication networks change over time and how they relate to the performance of the group.

No one network is likely to be effective for a range of given problems. The studies draw attention to the part of the manager's job that is to ensure the most appropriate communication network for the performance of a given task. Problems that require a high level of interaction between members of the group may not be handled efficiently if there are inadequate channels of communication or sharing of information. The choice of a particular communication network may involve trade-offs between the performance of the work group and the satisfaction of its members.

Task and maintenance functions

If the group is to be effective, then, whatever its structure or the pattern of interrela-tionships among members, there are two main sets of functions or processes that must be undertaken: **task functions** and **maintenance functions**.

- **Task functions** are directed towards problem-solving, the accomplishment of the tasks of the group and the achievement of its goals. Most of the task-oriented behaviour will be concerned with 'production' activities or the exchange and evaluation of ideas and information.
- **Maintenance functions** are concerned with the emotional life of the group and directed towards building and maintaining the group as an effective working unit. Most of the maintenance-oriented behaviour will be concerned with relationships among members, giving encouragement and support, maintaining cohesiveness and the resolution of conflict.

Task and maintenance functions may be performed either by the group leader or members. Ultimately, it is the leader's responsibility to ensure that both sets of functions are carried out and the right balance is achieved between them. The appropriate combination of task-oriented behaviour and maintenance-oriented behaviour is essential to the success and continuity of the group.

In addition to these two types of behaviour, members of a group may say or do something in an attempt to satisfy some personal need or goal. The display of behaviour in this way is termed **self-oriented behaviour**. This gives a classification of three main types of functional behaviour that can be exhibited by individual members of a group: **task-oriented, maintenance-oriented** and **self-oriented**.

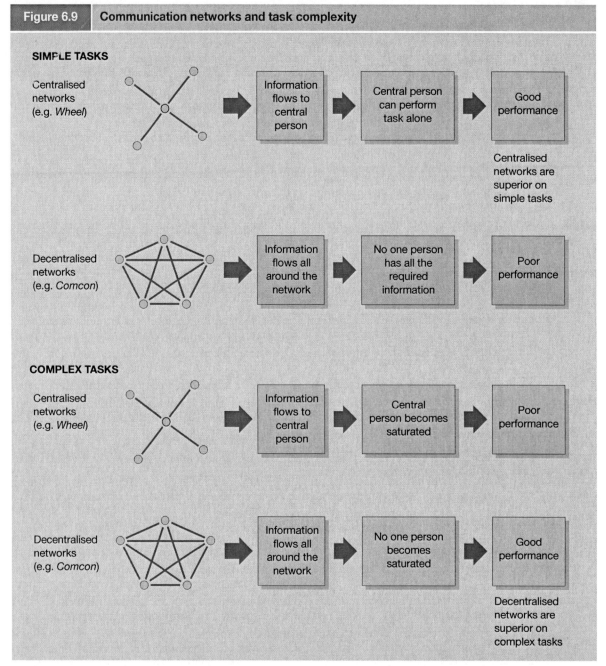

Figure 6.9   Communication networks and task complexity

Source: Greenberg, J. and Baron, R. A., *Behavior in Organizations*, Sixth Edition, Prentice-Hall Inc. (1995), p. 306. Reproduced with permission from Pearson Education, Inc.

Classification of member roles

A popular system for the classification of member roles in the study of group behaviour is that devised originally by *Benne and Sheats*.[48] The description of member roles performed in well-functioning groups, groups them under three broad headings: **group task roles**, **group building and maintenance roles** and **individual roles**.

- **Group task roles**. These assume that the task of the group is to select, define and solve common problems – for example, initiator-contributor, opinion seeker, co-ordinator, evaluator, recorder. Any of the roles may be performed by the various members or the group leader.

- **Group building and maintenance roles**. The analysis of member functions is orientated towards activities that build group-centred attitudes or maintain group-centred behaviour – for example, encourager, gatekeeper, standard setter, group commentator. Contributions may involve a number of roles and members or the leader may perform each of these roles.
- **Individual roles**. These are directed towards the satisfaction of personal needs. Their purpose is not related to either group task or the group functioning – for example, aggressor, blocker, dominator, help-seeker.

In order to help improve the performance of the organisation, it is necessary to understand the nature of human relationships and what goes on when groups of people meet. Working in a group is likely to be both a psychologically rewarding and potentially demanding experience for the individual. Group performance and the satisfaction derived by individuals are influenced by the interactions between members of the group. As an example of this, Figure 6.10 gives an unsolicited commentary from five final-year business studies degree students after completing a group-based assignment.

Figure 6.10	Unsolicited commentary from students after completing a group-based assignment

WHAT WE FEEL WE HAVE LEARNED FROM WORKING IN A GROUP

1 'We learned that we had to listen to everybody's points of view and take these into consideration.'
2 'We found that we had to be prepared to make certain sacrifices and adopted a democratic decision process. However, if an individual felt very strongly about a specific point and persisted with a valid argument then this had to be included.'
3 'We often felt frustrated.'
4 'It was time-consuming and difficult to schedule meetings due to differences in timetables and preferences in working hours.'
5 'We learned that it is good to pool resources because this increased the overall standard of the piece of work. We feel this was only because we all set high personal standards and expected these from our fellow group members. We learned that it is possible to work in other less productive groups where individual levels of achievement may decrease.'
6 'We learned that it is better to work in a smaller and not a larger group, as there is a tendency for individual ideas to be diluted.'
7 'Groups formed on the basis of friendship alone are not as effective as groups formed with work as the major influence. The former tend to be unproductive.'
8 'We found that it was good to get positive response, encouragement and feedback from team members. Likewise, it was demotivating to receive a negative response.'
9 'We learned a lot about our individual personalities.'
10 'We benefited from sharing personal experiences from our industrial placements.'
11 'It is important to separate work and personal relationships.'

Critical reflection ????

'The nature of the hierarchical structure and the inevitable role conflicts, power struggles, politics, and personality clashes means that individuals will usually complete a task more quickly and effectively than a group or team.' To what extent do you think this is fair comment? What has been your own experience?

INDIVIDUAL COMPARED WITH GROUP OR TEAM PERFORMANCE

It is, however, difficult to draw any firm conclusions from a comparison between individual and group or team performance. An example of this can be seen from a consideration of decision-making. Certain groups, such as committees, may be concerned more specifically with decision-making, but all groups must make some decisions. Group decision-making can be costly and time-consuming.

One particular feature of group versus individual performance is the concept of social loafing and the 'Ringelmann effect', which is the tendency for individuals to expend less effort when working as a member of a group than they would as an individual. A German psychologist, *Ringelmann*, compared the results of individual and group performance on a rope-pulling task. Workers were asked to pull as hard as they could on a rope, performing the task first individually and then with others in groups of varying sizes. A meter measured the strength of each pull. Although the total amount of force did increase with the size of the work group, the effort expended by each individual member decreased, with the result that the total group effort was less than the expected sum of the individual contributions.[49] Replications of the Ringelmann effect have generally been supportive of the original findings.[50]

According to *Hall*, there is a danger of elevating teams to the status of a 'silver bullet' – a magic solution to all business problems: 'It is not that I don't think teams work. They clearly do and it would be difficult to run an organisation of any size if you couldn't create and manage a team … The truth is that teams are not always the right answer to a problem. Often a well-briefed and well-managed group of individuals will do a task fine … A further point is that some very skilled individuals are not good team players.'[51]

However, the general feeling appears to be that the collective power of a group outshines individual performance.[52] 'Even though individuals working on their own are capable of phenomenal ingenuity, working together as a team can produce astounding results and a better decision.'[53] *Guirdham* believes that: 'Compared with individuals, groups can make objectively better decisions to which people feel more commitment, while teams can perform functions and carry out projects better and more efficiently. This can only happen, however, if the people have the special skills and abilities needed.'[54]

One might expect, therefore, a higher standard of decision-making to result from group discussion. However, on the one hand, there is the danger of compromise and decisions being made in line with the 'highest common view' and, on the other hand, there is the phenomenon of the so-called risky-shift.

The risky-shift phenomenon This suggests that, instead of the group taking fewer risks and making safer or more conservative decisions, the reverse is often the case. Pressures for conformity means that there is a tendency for groups to make riskier decisions than would individual members of the group on their own. Studies suggest that people working in groups generally advocate riskier alternatives than if they were making an individual decision on the same problem.[55]

Presumably, this is because members do not feel the same sense of responsibility for group decisions or their outcomes: 'A decision which is everyone's is the responsibility of no one.' Other explanations offered for the **risky-shift** phenomenon include:

* the people being inclined to take risks are those who are the most influential in group discussions, rather than the more conservative people;
* risk-taking being regarded as a desirable cultural characteristic that is more likely to be expressed in a social situation, such as group working.[56]

However, groups do appear to work well in the evaluation of ideas and to be more effective than individuals for problem-solving tasks requiring a range of knowledge and expertise. From a review of the research, Shaw suggests that evidence supports the view that groups produce more solutions and better solutions to problems than do individuals.[57]

Groupthink The effectiveness of group behaviour and performance can be adversely affected by the idea of **groupthink**. From an examination of some well-known government policy-making groups, *Janis* concluded that decisions can be characterised by groupthink which he defines as: 'a deterioration of mental efficiency, reality testing, and moral judgment that results from in-group pressures'.[58] Groupthink results in the propensity for the group to just drift along. It is a generalised feature and can be apparent in any organisational situation where groups are relied upon to make important decisions.

Janis identifies a number of specific symptoms of groupthink.

- There is an illusion of invulnerability with excessive optimism and risk-taking.
- The discounting or discrediting of negative feedback that contradicts group consensus results in rationalisation in order to explain away any disagreeable information.
- An unquestioning belief in the inherent morality of the group, which leads members to be convinced of the logical correctness of what it is doing and ignore ethical or moral consequences of decisions.
- The group's desire to maintain consensus can lead to negative stereotyping of opponents or people outside the group and a lack of acceptance of change.
- There is pressure on individual members to conform and reach consensus so that minority or unpopular ideas may be suppressed.
- Each member of the group may impose self-censorship in order to suppress their own objectives or personal doubts or disagreements.
- As a result of self-censorship, there is an illusion of unanimity with a lack of expressed dissent and a false sense of unity.
- In the unlikely event of dissent or contrary information, this will give rise to the emergence of 'mind guards' who act as filters, guarding group leaders, deflecting opposition and applying pressure on deviants.

According to *Hambrick*, 'Groupthink tends to occur when group members have very similar experiences and frame of references, particularly when they have relatively long tenures in the group. A company head who dislikes conflict or who punishes dissenters also creates the conditions for groupthink.'[59]

BRAINSTORMING

A **brainstorming** approach (sometimes now referred to as 'thought showers') involves the group adopting a 'freewheeling' attitude and generating as many ideas as possible – the more wild or apparently far-fetched the better.[60] As an illustrative exercise, a group may be asked to generate as many and varied possible uses as they can for, for example, a house brick or a car fan belt.

There are a number of basic procedures for brainstorming.

- It is based on maximum freedom of expression with a totally informal approach.
- The initial emphasis is on the quantity of ideas generated, not the quality of those ideas.
- No individual ideas are criticised or rejected at this stage, however wild or fanciful they may appear.
- Members are encouraged to elaborate or build on ideas expressed by others and bounce suggestions off one another.
- There is no comment on or evaluation of any particular idea until all ideas have been generated.

Brainstorming is based on encouraging members to suspend judgement, the assumption being that creative thinking is achieved best by encouraging the natural inclinations of group members and the rapid production and free association of ideas. The quantity of ideas will lead to quality of ideas.

An interesting and popular exercise to help illustrate the suspension of initial perceived barriers and the encouragement of creative thinking is given in Figure 6.11 This exercise may also be used to compare individual and group/team-based performance. (Your tutor will provide the (or least one) answer. There may be others that I am is unaware of!)

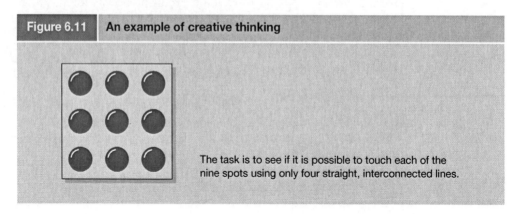

Figure 6.11	An example of creative thinking

The task is to see if it is possible to touch each of the nine spots using only four straight, interconnected lines.

Effectiveness of brainstorming groups One might reasonably expect that members of a brainstorming group would produce more creative problem-solving ideas than if the same members worked alone as individuals. Availability of time is an important factor. Over a longer period of time, the group may produce more ideas through brainstorming than individuals could. Perhaps surprisingly, however, there appears to be doubt about the effectiveness of brainstorming groups over an individual working under the same conditions. Nevertheless, brainstorming still appears to have many advocates and is a popular activity for staff development programmes[61] (*see* Figure 6.12). Despite the rather negative view of nominal group brainstorming, we should recognise the importance of innovation for successful organisational performance.[62]

Aid to creativity

Any procedure which aids the process of creativity should be welcomed and there are a number of potential positive achievements in terms of related structural techniques for stimulating innovation. These include the Delphi technique and quality circles.

The **Delphi technique** is based on multiple anonymous inputs from individual members of the group. Ideas and suggestions are recorded by a central manager and then recirculated to other members for their feedback. The central manager collates the responses and continues the circulation process again until consensus is reached. Although a time-consuming process the Delphi technique helps to overcome the limitations of face-to-face brainstorming and symptoms of groupthink.

BUILDING SUCCESSFUL TEAMS

Whatever the debate about a comparison between individual and group or team performance or self-managed groups, effective teamworking is of increasing importance in modern organisations. This demands that the manager must be aware of, and pay attention to, a number of interrelated factors, including:

- clarification of objectives and available resources;
- organisational processes and the clarification of roles;
- empowerment, decision-making and channels of communication;
- patterns of interaction and attention to both task and maintenance functions;

Figure 6.12	Advantages of brainstorming

BRAINSTORMING

Brainstorming is a problem-solving/solution-finding technique which can be used by individuals, groups or teams. Its full benefit is gained by sharing ideas and possibilities with others.

The first step is to define the problem or situation to which the group or team wants solutions or ideas. Ideally one person should act as scribe and write up ideas on a flipchart. He or she can contribute, but should not comment on others' suggestions. Every idea should be written up, however far-fetched or silly it might seem, without challenge from others.

Everyone should be encouraged to participate.

When all possibilities have been exhausted, suggestions can be examined, clarified, amended, accepted or rejected.

It may be that several options are accepted as possible ways forward. Reverse brainstorming looks at the possibilities and then brainstorms all the *problems* associated with the ideas. This helps give an objective view of ideas or solutions.

If performed correctly, brainstorming is an excellent, non-threatening way to include all members of a team in the problem-solving/decision-making process. It has the added benefit of producing many and various ideas, some of which will be of no value but others which may be of immediate or future benefit. Creativity is contagious and one idea will spark off another. Often, it is one of the most apparently silly ideas that points the way to a solution.

Brainstorming:

- involves everyone;
- focuses the mind;
- encourages creativity;
- meets individual needs for team inclusion;
- encourages communication – listening, information sharing;
- maximises ideas/possible solutions to problems;
- minimises risk of overlooking elements of the problem or issue under question.

Source: Developing Your Staff, Bishop, S. and Taylor, D., Pitman Publishing/Longman Training (1994). Reproduced with permission from Pearson Education Ltd.

- social processes and the informal organisation;
- management systems and style of leadership;
- training and development.

The effectiveness of the team will also be influenced by the tasks to be undertaken, the nature of technology and the organisational environment. Ultimately, however, the performance of the team will be determined very largely by the characteristics of its members. The nature of group personality means that what works well for one team may not work well for an apparently similar team in the organisation.

As *Wilson*, points out, for example, although teamworking, like most management ideas, is very simple, nevertheless this simplicity conceals a great challenge.

The principles of teamworking may be easily understood, but the task of installing it can be quite daunting. Introducing teamworking is not a straightforward grafting job, the simple matter of adding a new idea to those already in place. It is about making a fundamental change in the way people work. Every teamworking application is different. Each organisation, department and individual group is faced with unique problems and in some situations it is more about getting rid of old ways of doing things than injecting new ones.

Wilson, J. 'Building Teams – with Attitude'[63]

A concept map of effective work groups is set out in Figure 6.13.

Figure 6.13   Concept map of effective work groups

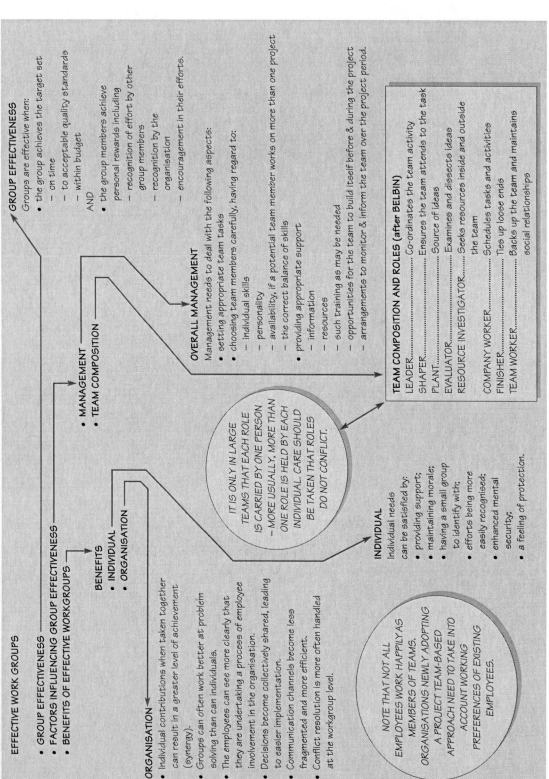

EFFECTIVE WORK GROUPS

- GROUP EFFECTIVENESS
- FACTORS INFLUENCING GROUP EFFECTIVENESS
- BENEFITS OF EFFECTIVE WORKGROUPS

BENEFITS
- INDIVIDUAL
- ORGANISATION

ORGANISATION
- Individual contributions when taken together can result in a greater level of achievement (synergy).
- Groups can often work better at problem solving than can individuals.
- The employees can see more clearly that they are undertaking a process of employee involvement in the organisation.
- Decisions become collectively shared, leading to easier implementation.
- Communication channels become less fragmented and more efficient.
- Conflict resolution is more often handled at the workgroup level.

NOTE THAT NOT ALL EMPLOYEES WORK HAPPILY AS MEMBERS OF TEAMS. ORGANISATIONS NEWLY ADOPTING A PROJECT TEAM-BASED APPROACH NEED TO TAKE INTO ACCOUNT WORKING PREFERENCES OF EXISTING EMPLOYEES.

- MANAGEMENT
- TEAM COMPOSITION

IT IS ONLY IN LARGE TEAMS THAT EACH ROLE IS CARRIED BY ONE PERSON – MORE USUALLY, MORE THAN ONE ROLE IS HELD BY EACH INDIVIDUAL. CARE SHOULD BE TAKEN THAT ROLES DO NOT CONFLICT.

GROUP EFFECTIVENESS

Groups are effective when:
- the group achieves the target set
  - on time
  - to acceptable quality standards
  - within budget

  AND
- the group members achieve personal rewards including
  - recognition of effort by other group members
  - recognition by the organisation
  - encouragement in their efforts.

OVERALL MANAGEMENT

Management needs to deal with the following aspects:
- setting appropriate team tasks
- choosing team members carefully, having regard to:
  - individual skills
  - personality
  - availability, if a potential team member works on more than one project
  - the correct balance of skills
- providing appropriate support
  - information
  - resources
  - such training as may be needed
  - opportunities for the team to build itself before & during the project
  - arrangements to monitor & inform the team over the project period.

TEAM COMPOSITION AND ROLES (after BELBIN)

LEADER..................... Co-ordinates the team activity
SHAPER..................... Ensures the team attends to the task
PLANT...................... Source of ideas
EVALUATOR.................. Examines and dissects ideas
RESOURCE INVESTIGATOR...... Seeks resources inside and outside the team
COMPANY WORKER............. Schedules tasks and activities
FINISHER................... Ties up loose ends
TEAM WORKER................ Backs up the team and maintains social relationships

INDIVIDUAL

Individual needs can be satisfied by:
- providing support;
- maintaining morale;
- having a small group to identify with;
- efforts being more easily recognised;
- enhanced mental security;
- a feeling of protection.

Source: Training Learning Consultancy Ltd, Bristol, England. Reproduced with permission.

Skills for successful teamwork The increasing need for collaboration and teamwork together with recognition for the individual has highlighted the need for attention to social skills and effective relationships between people. If people are not working together they are essentially a collection of individuals. For example, *Douglas* refers to the importance of helping people to master the so-called 'soft' skills.

> *Organisations in most sectors – and especially in ones that are particularly demanding from a scientific or technical point of view – are operating in environments where collaboration, teamwork, and an awareness of the commercial consequences and implications of technical research are as important as scientific and technical skills themselves. Personnel with scientific and technical skills significantly disproportionate to their 'people' skills – by which I primarily mean people management capabilities and the knowledge of how to work with maximum effectiveness as part of a team – are increasingly unlikely to be as much of an asset to their organisation as they ought to be.[64]*

Douglas points out, however, that as we all interact with people to a greater or lesser extent in our everyday lives there is a tendency to assume that people management skills are merely an extension of our natural abilities. In fact, people management skills are the more difficult and rare type of skill, but, to a large extent, they can be learned.

Critical reflection

????

All this discussion about group membership and building successful teams is very interesting and sounds fine in the classroom, but how far do you think it works in practice, does it work when managing groups of workers in a restaurant kitchen; on a production assembly line; in a gay pub; or professionals such as lecturers, doctors or lawyers?

MANAGEMENT IN THE NEWS 6
WINNING TEAMS

Football's example can help companies score

John Kay

Like many lecturers, I have a library of presentation slides. The most frequently used is 15 years old and relates the performance of English soccer league clubs to their expenditure on players. Both wages and transfer fees over a 25-year period are included. The message is that you get what you pay for. There is a strong relationship between cash spent and average league position. There were some outliers, but the outstanding story was Liverpool. Liverpool and Manchester United had invested more than others. But while the performance of Manchester United was exactly what our equations predicted, Liverpool had done much better. Manchester United had assembled a group of outstanding players. Liverpool had assembled an outstanding team.

Is a team more than the sum of its parts? Would another group of equally talented players have had Liverpool's successes?

Source: Neil Tingle/actionplus

→

Management in the news – continued

The story of the 2006 World Cup is that outstanding teams defeated groups of outstanding players. All players in top sides are very good. The reason the countries in the final four were not the ones pundits expected was that their predictions were based on the quality of individual players. But the trophy goes not to the best players, but to the best team.

My slide is popular because references to football bring back to life audiences battered into somnolence by harangues on transformational change. The serious purpose is to illustrate that business success is not simply a matter of acquiring the best people, technology or resources. Businesses create value by establishing a difference between the cost of their input and the effectiveness of their output. The Italian team was more than the sum of its parts, the Brazilian team was not.

The difference between output and value added is relevant to every type of business, but especially important for the professional services company – whether it is a football team or an investment. Goldman Sachs and McKinsey do not simply attract exceptional people – so did Manchester United and Brazil. Like Liverpool and Italy, these businesses achieve more than would be predicted from the quality of the people alone. That makes these companies very profitable. By sharing that excess profitability with their talented employees they keep them in post and maintain their leadership position.

But what are the characteristics that distinguish a great team from a group of great players? Organisational knowledge belongs to the business rather than the individuals who make up the business. My group was impressed by the systematic way in which Liverpool assembled through post-match debriefing and disseminated through pre-match briefing extensive information about other players, clubs and pitches. But their main explanation of Liverpool's relative success came from a simple economic model of the game of football. A player can kick for goal or pass the ball to a better situated player. His choice will depend on the degree to which his incentives relate to the performance of the team, rather than his performance as an individual and on his expectations about whether the next player will shoot or pass in turn. Because an individual's behaviour depends on expectations of the behaviour of others, teams will become locked into particular states. Individuals joining a team will find it best to conform to the local style, so these equilibria are stable.

That is why transformational change cannot be achieved by talking about it and my audiences were right to be more interested in the footballing metaphor than in the guff that had gone before.

Source: FT.com, 10 July 2006 (adapted from source article)

Discussion questions

1 Analyse the commentary on teamwork in this article using the concept map outline of effective work groups given in Figure 6.13. Which features of the model appear to be present and which are missing?

2 Critically evaluate the comments about Liverpool football club in terms of communication patterns. What skills and activities might help managers to achieve effective communication between the members of their teams?

SYNOPSIS

● Work is a group-based activity and individuals seldom work in isolation from others. Groups and teams are an essential feature of all social situations and almost everyone in an organisation will be a member of one or more groups. Members must co-operate with one another for work to be carried out. Harmonious working relationships and good teamwork help make for a high level of staff morale and organisational performance. Whereas all teams are groups, it does not necessarily follow that all groups are teams.

● Groups are formed as a consequence of the pattern of organisation structure and arrangements for the division of work. Formal groups are deliberately planned and created by management as part of the organisation structure and to achieve specific organisational objectives. Informal groups are based on personal relationships and develop irrespective of the formal structure. Informal groups serve to satisfy members' psychological and social needs.

● The manager's main concern is that members co-operate with one another. Factors that affect group cohesiveness can be considered under the broad headings of membership, work environment, organisational and group development and maturity. There are, however, potential disadvantages of strong, cohesive groups and the manager should attempt to prevent unconstructive intergroup conflict.

● The characteristics of an effective work group are not always easy to isolate. The underlying feature is a spirit of co-operation in which members work well together as a united team and with harmonious and supportive relationships. The combination of increasing globalisation and widespread developments in information communications and technology has given greater opportunities for, and need of, virtual teams.

● The concept of 'role' is important to the functioning of groups and for an understanding of group processes and behaviour. It is through role differentiation that the structure of work groups and relationships among members is established. Inadequate or inappropriate role definition can result in role conflict, including role incompatibility, role ambiguity, role overload and role underload. It is important that the manager makes every effort to minimise role conflict and the causes of role stress.

● Members of a group must work well together as a team and there must be a spirit of unity and co-operation. *Belbin* suggests key contributions or team-roles for successful groups. The level of interaction is influenced by the channels of communication. There are five main types of communication networks – wheel, circle, all-channel, Y and chains. Whatever the patterns of interaction, members of a group need to undertake both task and maintenance functions.

● It is difficult to draw firm conclusions from a comparison between individual and group or team performance. However, whatever the debate, building successful teams requires effective leadership with an emphasis on trust, clear communications, full participation and self-management. Although self-regulation is necessary if the potential of teamworking is to be realised, teams will always need some degree of management direction. The task of management is to oversee the development of teams and provide the necessary support and training.

Check your understanding and begin your research with online resources at
www.pearsoned.co.uk/mullins

REVIEW AND DISCUSSION QUESTIONS

1 What is a group? Explain the importance and influence of group values and norms and give practical examples from within your own organisation.

2 How would you distinguish between a 'group' and a 'team'? To what extent do you believe the distinction has practical significance for managers?

3 Distinguish between formal and informal groups and provide your own supporting examples. What functions do groups serve in an organisation?

4 Identify different stages in group development and maturity. What other factors influence the cohesiveness of work groups?

5 What is meant by the role structure of an organisation? Construct a diagram that shows your own role set within a college or work situation.

6 Contrast different types of communication networks. Give examples of a situation in which each type of network is likely to be most appropriate.

7 Distinguish between (a) group task roles, (b) group building and maintenance roles and (c) individual roles. Give your own examples of each of these types of group member roles.

8 Explain what is meant by (a) the risky-shift phenomenon, (b) groupthink and (c) brainstorming. Assess critically the likely standard of individual – compared with group or team – performance.

9 Detail fully the main factors to be considered in a review of effective teamworking.

ASSIGNMENT

Step 1

Obtain or prepare a chart depicting the formal groupings within your organisation or a large department of the organisation.

- Using this chart, identify clearly the informal groups that exist within the formal structure.
- Discuss ways in which these informal groups aid and/or conflict with the work of the organisation/department.
- Explain the extent to which management recognises the influence of the informal groups.

Step 2

Recall your experience of a work group or team with which you are familiar and comment critically on:

- the extent to which members were clear about the goals of the group, what they were expected to achieve and how their performance would be evaluated;
- the diversity of group membership and significances of diversity for the operations and success of the group; and
- what *exactly* made the group effective or fall apart?

Step 3

What conclusions do you draw from this assignment?

CASE STUDY 6

Mumbai's dabbawalahs: a world-class quality service

Those studying organisational behaviour often find themselves reading about the issues faced by global businesses, the managerial excellence of which is supported by cutting-edge technology and major financial investment. The organisation in this case study has neither cutting-edge technology nor major investment and never has had. However, it has become famous in recent years, as the world's business schools have beaten a path to its door to study the extraordinary organisation of Mumbai's dabbawalahs.

Dabbawalahs (or 'tiffinwalahs') runs a service in Mumbai the purpose of which is easy enough to describe. Each working day, they arrange the collection and delivery from Bombay's suburbs of about 175,000 lunches in the traditional tiffin boxes. These meals are prepared by wives or mothers (or sometimes local restaurants) for individual workers in central Mumbai. Obviously, the contents of each box are unique, which is the central appeal of the service. A little later in the day, the dabbawalahs collect the empties and return them to the workers' homes.

The amazing dabbawalahs deliver 175,000 lunchtime tiffin boxes a day in Bombay in a well co-ordinated and highly effective team operation.

In some ways, the design of the system resembles that of a modern international courier service. It is based on local collection of the tiffin boxes, which are then loaded on to local trains for bulk transportation into the centre of Mumbai (special compartments are reserved for the boxes). At each of the central stations, other members of the team unload the boxes for destinations near the station and sort them for hand delivery to the offices and workshops where the individual recipients work. They also load any boxes for delivery further down the line. The train stops for about 20 seconds at these stations, resulting in a turnaround time that would make many of Europe's low-cost airlines look up in surprise. Delivery to the hungry workers is achieved by 12.45 sharp,[65] following which the process is reversed to return the boxes to the homes. The service costs about Rs300–350 per month (about $US6–7) and the dabbawalahs earn about Rs5,000 (about $US115) a month. Customers pay one month's bonus to the organisation for the Diwali festival. This intricate, precisely coordinated operation takes place in a city famous for its bustle, traffic delays and occasional chaos: the dabbawalahs negotiate the traffic on foot and by bicycle at a cracking pace – whatever the weather, the tiffin must get through. The error rate is said to be vanishingly small: one box may go astray every two months.

A team to beat the best

There is no IT support for this daily miracle – no track and trace, no computers, no bar codes, just a handwritten code on each box that allows the dabbawalah to recognise which station the box has to be sent to and unloaded, its ultimate destination and its return address. Many of the dabbawalas have low levels of literacy, but their ability to decode and correctly route the 40 or so boxes that they each carry through the crowded streets is key to the whole system. The very high levels of effectiveness and efficiency achieved in this service have attracted the attention of business schools from many countries. As the dabbawalahs proudly proclaim,[66] the reliability of the system is at six sigma levels (one error in one million), a performance that is comparable to that of the world's leading corporations. Business strategy expert C. K. Prahalad was struck by the performance level of this system as well as by its very low levels of capital-intensiveness:

> That's a good thing by itself because you can dramatically reduce the capital intensity of a business. A lot of the float there is between points of production and consumption can be reduced dramatically around the world.[67]

The interest in this case is not so much in the technical details of the logistics, however, but in the team that makes the service happen. The dabbawalah service is said to have originated in 1890[68], and to have been invented by Indian entrepreneur Mahadeo Havaji Bacche.[69] At the same time, a then much smaller Mumbai was starting to experience a strong growth of daily commuting into the centre. From the outset, the design of the service was much the same as today – the

local trains were hauled by steam engines and the traffic jams on the streets were animal rather than automotive, but the challenge was essentially the same. There has always been strong cultural preference for home cooking among workers in India. In Mumbai, which has always drawn its working population from all over India, 'home cooking' means a kaleidoscope of different regional styles and traditions. Clearly, a service that can bring this diverse range of home-prepared meals reliably to the individual in the workplace is going to be in demand. The service grew to its present levels by the 1950s.

There are about 5000 dabbawalahs in Mumbai today, organised into teams of 20–25 under an experienced group leader. Ragunath Medge is President of Nutan Mumbai Tiffin Box Suppliers Charity Trust (and a regular guest speaker these days at business school conferences). As he explains, those who work for the organisation are mostly shareholders, rather than employees:

> if you have employees, then you have unions and strikes. We are all shareholders in the Trust and thus we share in the earnings.

He explains that the dabbawalahs mainly come from the same region, the Pune district, and that most are related to each other:

> We all come from the region east of the Sahyadri (Western Ghats), and everyone who joins is, is known to us. If an outsider does join in, we initially employ him on a fixed salary, and if in a couple of years he wins our trust, we may make him a shareholder.[70]

These sentiments are echoed in the comments of one of the dabbawalahs in an article published in *The Guardian* in 2002:

> 'It's a very sociable job,' Sapan Mare, a tiffin-wallah since 1970 explained, as we rattled into central Bombay [Mumbai]. 'I like the fact that I meet so many people every day. Between 100 to 110 members of my family are in the tiffin business. I come from a family where four generations have been tiffin-wallahs,' he added proudly.[71]

Mr Medge explains that the job for Trust shareholders lasts for as long as the member is strong enough to do the work. Notes on a blogspot (weblog) of a talk given by Mr Medge provide further detail of the discipline that characterises the dabbawalah team: members are mainly vegetarians and most don't drink alcohol.[72] Drinking at work is against the rules: the first and second offence will result in a fine and the third will result in removal from the service. There is also a dress code for team members, presumably to show pride and confidence in the high standards of the service and also perhaps to secure public co-operation with the smooth daily running of the operation. The organisation sets great store by the integrity and trustworthiness of its members: dabbawalahs just do not have police records.

The future of the service

As any services marketing textbook will confirm, customers often take part in the production of services. In this case, the expertise and hard work of the dabbahwalahs will come to nothing if the meals are not ready for collection on time. Those who prepare the meals in homes and local restaurants can also be seen as part of the team. Sometimes, it is suggested that customers also use the network as an informal communications medium, sending each other little notes in the tiffin boxes.

The city of Mumbai is at the forefront of the huge economic and social changes that are sweeping through India. The dabbawalah system is still a mainstay of the working day in the city, but is starting to experience and respond to change. The growth of fast food is a global phenomenon that has been relatively slow to penetrate the Indian market, but is now starting to make its mark. Mr Medge's operation is still resolutely uncomputerised (what good would gigabytes and parallel processors be in the traffic in Mumbai?), but they do have a website

and are now able to accept orders via the site or by SMS. Their website also seeks to reassert the traditional core values of the organisation in the face of the tide of global fast food.[73] Among the 'top ten reasons for using the Dabbawalahs' services' are the following appeals to the good sense of Mumbai workers:

1 *Home made food is best for health … Outside junk foods may take your life and makes you sick …*
2 *Home made food is cheaper… It's simple maths.*
3 *Do you not love your mother or wife and like to eat food made by her?*

The dabbawalahs have fed thousands of people for more than a century. Their astonishingly effective logistics continue to deliver reliable, low-priced service every working day. As can be seen on their website, they have admirers all around the world – Prince Charles (who invited the two dabbahwalahs quoted in this case to his wedding to Camilla), Richard Branson (of course) and – perhaps paradoxically – the Slow Food movement. For generations, the cohesion, dedication and discipline of this team has been the main guarantee of their legendary service and it seems likely to retain a place in the hearts of Mumbai residents as modernisation proceeds.

Your tasks

1 If a team can be defined as a group of people working towards a common goal, discuss the advantages and disadvantages of the dabbahwalah practice of making team members shareholders rather than employees. Would the same arguments apply to other logistically similar operations?

2 Use the framework in Figure 6.4 to analyse the cohesiveness and performance of the dabbahwalah team. To what extent does the dabbahwalah service display the characteristics of an effective work group?

3 Why has technology played such a small part in the development of the dabbahwalah service so far? Is this likely to change in future? Identify ways in which this might affect the team spirit of the organisation.

Notes and references

1 Schein, E. H. *Organizational Psychology*, Third edition, Prentice Hall (1988), p. 145.
2 Adair, J. *Effective Teambuilding*, Gower (1986).
3 Guzzo, R. A. and Dickson, M. W. 'Teams in Organizations: Recent Research on Performance and Effectiveness', *Annual Review of Psychology*, vol. 47, 1996, pp. 307–38.
4 Holpp, L. 'Teams: It's All in the Planning', *Training & Development*, vol. 51, no. 4, April 1997, pp. 44–7.
5 Crainer, S. *Key Management Ideas: Thinkers That Changed the Management World*, Third edition, Financial Times Prentice Hall (1998), p. 237.
6 Cane, S. *Kaizen Strategies for Winning Through People*, Pitman Publishing (1996), p. 116.

7 Belbin, R. M. *Beyond the Team*, Butterworth-Heinemann (2000).
8 Riches, A. 'Emotionally Intelligent Teams', *Organisational Change & Leadership Development*, www.anneriches.com.au [accessed 11 March 2003].
9 Huck, S., Kubler, D. and Weibull, J. 'Social Norms and Economic Incentives in Firms', Economic & Social Research Council, 5 March 2003.
10 Boyton, A. and Fischer B. *Virtuoso Teams: Lessons From Teams That Changed Their Worlds*, Financial Times Prentice Hall(2005)
11 Lysons, K. 'Organisational Analysis', *Supplement to The British Journal of Administrative Management*, no. 18, March/April 1997.

12 Law, S. 'Beyond the Water Cooler', *Professional Manager*, January 2005, pp. 26–8.

13 See, for example: Jay, A. *Corporation Man*, Penguin (1975). In an amusing historical account of the development of different forms of groups, Jay suggests that ten is the basic size of human groups.

14 Cane, S. *Kaizen Strategies for Winning Through People*, Pitman Publishing (1996), p. 131.

15 McKenna, P. J. and Maister, D. H. 'Building Team Trust', *Consulting to Management*, vol. 13, no. 4, December 2002, pp. 51–3.

16 Bass, B. M. and Ryterband, E. C. *Organizational Psychology*, Second edition, Allyn & Bacon (1979).

17 Tuckman, B. W. 'Development Sequence in Small Groups', *Psychological Bulletin*, vol. 63, 1965, pp. 384–99, and Tuckman, B. W. and Jensen, M. C. 'Stages of Small Group Development Revised', *Group and Organizational Studies*, vol. 2, no. 3, 1977, pp. 419–27.

18 Cited in Green, J. 'Are Your Teams and Groups at Work Successful?', *Administrator*, December 1993, p. 12.

19 Argyle, M. *The Social Psychology of Work*, Second edition, Penguin (1989).

20 Brooks, I. *Organisational Behaviour: Individuals, Groups and Organisation*, Third edition, Financial Times Prentice Hall (2006) p. 99.

21 *Teamwork: Success Through People*, Advisory Booklet, ACAS, April 2003, p. 9.

22 See, for example: Kinsman, F. 'The Virtual Office and The Flexible Organisation', *Administrator*, April 1994, pp. 31–2, and Chowdhury, S. *Management 21c*, Financial Times Prentice Hall (2000).

23 See, for example: Johnson, P., Heimann, V. and O'Neill, K. 'The "Wonderland" of Virtual Teams', *The Journal of Workplace Learning*, vol. 13, no. 1, 2001, pp. 24–30.

24 Hall, P. 'Team Solutions Need Not Be the Organisational Norm', *Professional Manager*, July 2001, p. 45.

25 Parker, C. 'Remote Control – A Case Study', *Manager: The British Journal of Administrative Management*, March/April 2002, p. 30.

26 Norval, D. in conversation with Law, S. 'Beyond the Water Cooler', *Professional Manager*, January 2005, pp. 26–8.

27 Symons, J. 'Taking Virtual Team Control', *Professional Manager*, vol. 12, no. 2, March 2003, p. 37.

28 Francesco, A. M. and Gold, B. A. *International Organizational Behavior*, Second edition, Pearson Prentice Hall (2005), p. 118

29 Murray, S. 'Virtual Teams: Global Harmony is Their Dream', *Financial Times*, 11 May, 2005.

30 See, for example: Lerner, P. M. 'Beware the Gatekeeper', *Amtrak Express*, July/August 1994, pp. 14–17.

31 Miner, J. B. *Management Theory*, Macmillan (1971).

32 See, for example: Mullins, L. J. *Hospitality Management and Organisational Behaviour*, Fourth edition, Longman (2001).

33 'Teamwork: Success Through People', Advisory Booklet, ACAS, April 2003.

34 Lucas, E. 'And the Winner is Everyone', *Professional Manager*, January 2001, p. 10.

35 Heller, R. *In Search of European Excellence*, HarperCollins Business (1997), p. 229.

36 Guirdham, M. *Interactive Behaviour at Work*, Third edition, Financial Times Prentice Hall (2002), p. 12.

37 Ashmos, D. P. and Nathan, M. L. 'Team Sense-Making: A Mental Model for Navigating Uncharted Territories', *Journal of Managerial Issues*, vol. 14, no. 2, Summer 2002, p. 198.

38 Obeng, E. *All Change*, Pitman Publishing (1994).

39 Crainer, S. *Key Management Ideas: Thinkers That Changed the Management World*, Third edition, Financial Times Prentice Hall (1998), p. 238.

40 *Teamwork: Success Through People*, Advisory Booklet, ACAS, April 2003, pp. 6–7.

41 Guirdham, M. *Interactive Behaviour at Work*, Third edition, Financial Times Prentice Hall (2002), p. 463.

42 Belbin, R. M. *Management Teams: Why They Succeed or Fail*, Butterworth-Heinemann (1981).

43 Belbin, R. M. *Team Roles at Work*, Butterworth-Heinemann (1993).

44 Arroba, T. and Wedgwood-Oppenheim, F. 'Do Senior Managers Differ in The Public and Private Sector? An Examination of Team-Role Preferences', *Journal of Managerial Psychology*, vol. 9, no. I, 1994, pp. 13–16.

45 Fisher, S. G., Hunter, T. A. and Macrosson, W. D. K. 'The Distribution of Belbin Team Roles among UK Managers', *Personnel Review*, vol. 29, no. 2, 2000, pp. 124–40.

46 Bavelas, A. 'A Mathematical Model for Group Structures', *Applied Anthropology*, vol. 7, 1948, pp. 19–30, and Bavelas, A. 'Communication Patterns in Task-Oriented Groups', in Lasswell, H. N. and Lerner, D. (eds) *The Policy Sciences*, Stanford University Press (1951).

47 Leavitt, H. J. 'Some Effects of Certain Communication Patterns on Group Performance', *Journal of Abnormal and Social Psychology*, vol. 46, 1951, pp. 38–50. See also: Leavitt, H. J. *Managerial Psychology*, Fourth edition, University of Chicago Press (1978).

48 Benne, K. D. and Sheats, P. 'Functional Roles of Group Members', *Journal of Social Issues*, vol. 4, 1948, pp. 41–9.

49 Kravitz, D. A. and Martin, B. 'Ringelmann Rediscovered: The Original Article', *Journal of Personality and Social Psychology*, May 1986, pp. 936–41.

50 See, for example: Karau, S. J. and Williams, K. D. 'Social Loafing: A Meta-analysis Review and Theoretical Integration', *Journal of Personality and Social Psychology*, October 1993, pp. 681–706.

51 Hall, P. 'Team Solutions Need Not Be the Organisational Norm', *Professional Manager*, July 2001, p. 45.

52 See, for example: Blanchard, K. and Bowles, S. *High Five: None of Us Is As Smart As All of Us*, HarperCollins Business (2001).

53 Stanley, T. J. 'The Challenge of Managing a High-performance Team', *SuperVision*, vol. 63, no. 7, July 2002, pp. 10–12.

54 Guirdham, M. *Interactive Behaviour at Work*, Third edition, Financial Times Prentice Hall (2002), p. 498.

55 Kogan, N. and Wallach, M. A. 'Risk-taking as a Function of the Situation, the Person and the Group', in Newcomb, T. M. (ed.) *New Directions in Psychology III*, Holt, Rinehart and Winston (1967).

56 For a comprehensive review of the 'risky-shift' phenomenon, see, for example: Clarke, R. D. 'Group Induced Shift Towards Risk: A Critical Appraisal', *Psychological Bulletin*, vol. 76, 1971, pp. 251–70. See also: Vecchio, R. P. *Organizational Behavior*, Third edition, Harcourt Brace and Company (1995).

57 Shaw, M. E. *Group Dynamics*, McGraw-Hill (1976).

58 Janis, J. L. *Victims of Groupthink*, Houghton Mifflin (1972) and Janis, J. L. *Groupthink*, Second edition, Houghton Mifflin (1982).

59 Hambrick, D. 'Putting the Team into Top Management', in Pickford, J. (ed.), *Financial Times Mastering Management 2.0*, Financial Times Prentice Hall (2001), p. 289.

60 Osborne, A. F. *Applied Imagination: Principles and Procedures of Creative Thinking*, Scribner's (1963)

61 See, for example: Bishop, S. and Taylor, D. *Developing Your Staff*, Pitman Publishing/Longman Training, (1994).

62 See, for example: Waterman, R. *The Frontiers of Excellence*, Nicholas Brealey (1994).

63 Wilson, J. 'Building Teams – with Attitude', *Professional Manager*, September 1998, p. 13.

64 Douglas, M. 'Why Soft Skills Are an Essential Part of the Hard World of Business', *Manager, The British Journal of Administrative Management*, New Year 2003, pp. 34–5.

65 Harding, L. 'A Bombay Lunchbox', *The Guardian* on-line, June 2002. http://www.guardian.co.uk/elsewhere/ journalist/ story/0,7792,743042,00.html [accessed 4 August 2006].

66 The Dabbawalah website http://www.mydabbawala.com/ [accessed 4 August 2006].

67 Anderson, B. 'Fast Food Delivers Lunchtime Lesson', CNN.com website, 17 August 2004. http://www.cnn.com/ 2004/BUSINESS/08/16/mumbai.dabbawallahs/index.html [accessed 4 August 2006].

68 The Dabbawalah website, http://www.mydabbawala.com/ [accessed 4 August 2006].

69 Harding, L. 'A Bombay Lunchbox', *The Guardian* on-line, 24 June 2002. http://www.guardian.co.uk/elsewhere/ journalist/story/0,7792,743042,00.html [accessed 4 August 2006].

70 The Dabbawalah website, http://www.mydabbawala.com/ [accessed 4 August 2006].

71 Harding, L. 'A Bombay Lunchbox', *The Guardian* on-line 24 June 2002. http://www.guardian.co.uk/elsewhere/ journalist/story/0,7792,743042,00.html [accessed 4 August 2006].

72 Nomad(i) Blogspot of an unknown Indian at http://nomad -i.blogspot.com

73 The Dabbawalah website, http://www.mydabbawala.com/ [accessed 4 August 2006].

HRM as a concept

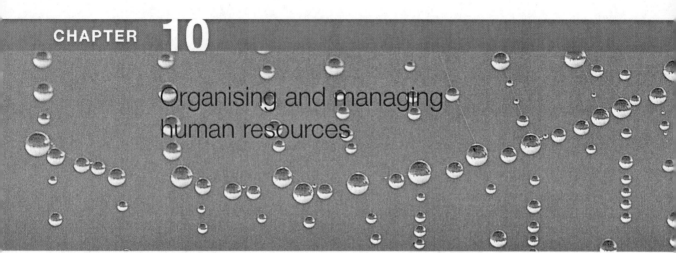

CHAPTER 10

Organising and managing human resources

Objectives   Having read this chapter and completed its associated activities, readers should be able to:

- See the value of regarding the 'human resources' which organisations require for long-term survival not as people but as the efforts and capabilities that an organisation requires to be able to function in both the short and the long term.

- Recognise that human resourcing and employment issues in organisations, while requiring specialist expertise in their management, are nevertheless activities in which all managers are inevitably involved.

- Put into context the alleged 'rise of HRM', noting the considerable ambiguities and conceptual inadequacies associated with the 'HRM' notion.

- Understand the centrality to organisational strategy making of human resourcing issues and appreciate the inadequacy of treating HR strategy as something that follows from or 'serves' the main corporate or business strategy.

- Relate the day-to-day issues of organisational human resourcing to basic dilemmas and tensions that have to be managed when employing people within industrial capitalist societies and economies.

- See how human resource management plays a particularly strategic role in employing organisations because it necessarily applies to employment issues (a) a corporate rather than a sectional focus and (b) a long-term rather than an immediate or short-term focus.

- Appreciate the distinctive tensions and ambiguities facing HR specialists in their relationships with other departments and managers.

- Recognise that the basic choice between *direct* and *indirect* efforts to achieve managerial control identified in Chapter 8 is central to strategic human resourcing choices and relates to the choice between *low commitment* and *high commitment* HR strategies – a choice which is influenced by how problematic employee constituencies are perceived to be for the organisation's future.

- Come to terms with the fact that employees are not unchanging entities, units of labour or 'human resources' that can be selected, recruited controlled and processed, as some HR thinking tends to assume.

Organisational human resources and the employment relationship

Human resourcing and employment issues are utterly central to the existence of work organisations. They not only affect the employment experience of every single member of an organisation, they also pervade every aspect of organisational management. This is not to argue that human resourcing work is more important than finance, production or service delivery, say, as a facet of organisational management. Activities in all of these areas are vital to an organisation's performance and long-term survival. The difference with human resourcing matters is that they tend to arise with regard to every other aspect of managerial work. It is possible for most members of management to leave specialists in these areas to handle the main tasks of marketing, accounting or production. The same is not possible with regard to human resourcing matters however. Most people in managerial positions will have some responsibility for other employees. They thus necessarily get involved in the selection of staff to work in their departments as well as with the training, payment, deployment, appraisal, career development, welfare, grievances, discipline and possible redundancy of these employees. Expert support is likely to be required in all of these areas, and managers with corporate HR responsibilities will almost inevitably impose constraints on local managerial discretion. Human resourcing responsibilities, to varying degrees, will form part of the work of most managers in modern organisations, however. Even where a manager does not have direct responsibility for other employees, they will still be unable to distance themselves entirely from matters of employment relationships – not least because they are employees themselves with an interest in their own rewards, career development and future deployment.

A frequently heard cliché says that 'people management' is a concern of every manager in an organisation. Is this the argument that is being advanced here? It is not – at least not in these terms. In Chapter 1 it was argued that it is unhelpful to frame managerial work in terms of 'managing people'. This was because such a notion is morally questionable and because the expectation that anyone can actually 'manage people' is utterly unrealistic. The recalcitrance or unmanageability of human beings is one of the very factors that make human resourcing issues so central to organisational strategy making. This point will be developed later in this chapter. But in talking of 'human resourcing' or 'human resource management' are we not adopting a position that is even more morally dubious than what is implied in talk of 'people management'? The answer to this question would most certainly be yes – if we were using the term 'human resources' to mean 'human beings'. To speak of people as human resources, let alone to *relate* to people in such a dehumanising way, is surely to adopt a stance little different from that of slave traders and slave owners. To treat people as means to ends instead of treating them as free and autonomous citizens of a democracy would be to abandon some of the key principles that modern societies are allegedly based upon. Yet people's *services* are acquired by employing organisations in industrial capitalist societies and are exploited to serve ends other than those of the employees themselves. In slavery it was people themselves who were bought and sold. Under capitalism it is people's labour – the work that they can do for an organisation – that is bought and sold. In recognition of this, we need a concept of human resources that avoids treating people as 'resources' while recognising that people bring with them into the employment relationship with a work organisation efforts, skills and capacities which are indeed treated as resources and which managers do try to 'manage'.

Human resources	Concept
The efforts, knowledge, capabilities and committed behaviours which people contribute to a work organisation as part of an employment exchange (or a more temporary labour engagement) and which are managerially utilised to complete tasks and enable the organisation to continue its existence into the future.	

A key dimension, then, of the overall managerial task in a work organisation is that which concerns itself with obtaining, developing and from time to time dispensing with 'human resources' in this sense and maintaining the basic pattern of employment relationships which make the utilisation of these resources possible. This takes us towards a notion of *human resource management*.

'HRM': an ambiguous and confusing term?

Before we can develop further a useful notion of *human resource management*, we have to come to terms with the rather messy situation that currently exists whereby the term 'human resource management' is used in a confusing variety of ways. This can cause considerable confusion in the study of human resourcing aspects of organisations and the changing ways in which employment issues are being managed.

The term 'HRM' tends to be used in three ways:

- to refer to an academic area of study which brings together what were previously the separate topic areas of personnel management, industrial relations

Table 10.1 A summary of how much academic writing on HRM tends to contrast an aspired-to 'new' HRM with the 'personnel management' which it rejects	
Key features aspired to for the 'new' HRM	**Alleged characteristics of personnel management rejected by the 'new' HRM**
HRM takes on a strategic emphasis and a strong business or 'bottom-line awareness'	Personnel management is said to have an operational emphasis and simply involve itself in 'servicing' the organisation with a supply of suitable and compliant staff
HRM concentrates on building harmonious and reciprocal relationships with employees	Personnel management is said to concentrate on managing conflicts with employees
With HRM, employment and resourcing issues become the concern of all managers	Personnel management was said to keep employment and resourcing issues as its own specialist concern
HRM specialists work as 'business partners' with other managers (in so far as HR specialists are retained, rather than their expertise being outsourced or 'bought in' from consultants)	Personnel managers are said to relate to other managers sometimes by advising them on employee issues and, at other times, by policing them to ensure compliance with corporate personnel policies and procedures
HRM develops a personal and high commitment relationship between the employer and each individual employee	Personnel management is said to find it acceptable to have either a low commitment arm's-length relationship with each individual employee or to relate to employees 'collectively' through the intermediary of a trade union
HRM is associated with a high-trust organisational culture making significant use of team working and other 'indirect control' devices that make close supervision, detailed procedures and strict hierarchies unnecessary	Personnel management is said to be associated with lower trust relationships with employees, more 'direct' management controls and relatively bureaucratic structures and procedures

and aspects of 'organisational behaviour' such as motivation, leadership and work design;

● to refer to all those aspects of managerial work that deal with employees (sometimes used interchangeably with 'people management');

● to refer to those activities that were once referred to as *personnel management* ones but which are said to justify a re-labelling as 'HRM' when they take on the features identified in the left-hand column of Table 10.1. In this usage, 'HRM' is a new approach to handling human resourcing and employment issues in organisations.

These alleged differences between something called 'HRM' and something called 'personnel management' are ones that have been put forward by academic writers trying to identify possible trends in how human resourcing and employment management issues are dealt with in work organisations (see Storey, 1992, Legge, 1995 and Further Reading on HRM, the academic literature, p. 445). The labelling of these two approaches as 'HRM' on the one hand and as 'personnel management' on the other has been entirely a choice of academics. In the world of personnel management practice, many practitioners were moving in this alleged 'HRM' direction long before academic observers chose to apply the HRM label to such shifts of emphasis. It is important to recognise, however, that the trend within work organisations to replace the 'Personnel' title with 'HR' is not necessarily connected to the alleged move from personnel practices to 'HRM' practices within organisations. Many personnel departments have indeed been renamed as HR departments but this has largely been a matter of adopting a title that is more fashionable and which is felt to sound more hard-headed or businesslike than 'personnel'. It is only marginally connected to the academic distinction between HRM and personnel management.

Unfortunately much academic work jumps back and forth between two uses of the HRM label. Sometimes it uses the term HRM to refer to human resourcing and employment management work generally as we are doing here. At other times it uses the label to refer only to a particular human resourcing and employment management approach – one which we will here be characterising as 'high commitment HRM'. Let us, for now, examine the nature of HRM as a broad phenomenon which occurs in every work organisation, whether it be large or small, socially progressive or reactionary, and whether or not it possesses a formalised 'HR' function.

Human resource management

It was argued in Chapter 2 that systems-control assumptions about work organisations usefully draw attention to patterns of cooperation and how different elements of organisations link to each other. They nevertheless tend to avert attention from all the 'conflicts, arguments, debates, ambiguities and sheer guesswork that characterises the *process* and *relationships* that what we might call "real" managerial practice has to cope with all of the time' (p. 52). Systems-control perspective tends to work with a notion of overall organisational goals, implying through this that organisations are more 'unitary' and have a level of overall consensus about purposes and priorities than has ever been observed in practice. A great deal of HRM writing has a strong unitary flavour of this kind (Watson, 2004, 2006). Process-relational perspective, on the other hand, gives full weight to the multiplicity of goals and priorities that exist within every organisation. It recognises that differences of interest and clashes of individual and group priorities have constantly to be coped with – or managed. It also recognises the centrality of *power* and *micropolitical* activities to the way organisational order is negotiated and it acknowledges the significance of various types of *organisational mischief* to organisational functioning. What is required is a notion of *human resource management* that acknowledges the pluralistic, messy, ambiguous and inevitably conflict-ridden nature of work organisations.

A notion of HRM that is consistent with a process-relational framing of organisational realities would be one that recognises that managerial work involves attempts to achieve as much productive cooperation and unity of purpose as is sensibly possible in any given organisation. It also recognises that this is only ever partially achievable and that HRM work, in every aspect, has to handle ambiguities, tensions and conflicts. It will never find panaceas or 'best practices' that will overcome dissent and turn every organisation into a happy family or a unified team. Instead it will engage in a constant struggle to 'manage conflicts', to persuade, put pressure upon and negotiate with employees – making deals and shaping implicit contracts that will enable work tasks to be performed in a way that helps the organisation continue into the future.

In this spirit we can put forward a formal definition of HRM.

Human resource management   *Concept*

That part of managerial work which is concerned with acquiring, developing and dispensing with the efforts, skills and capabilities of an organisation's workforce and maintaining organisational relationships within which these human resources can be utilised to enable the organisation to continue into the future.

This conception of HRM is essentially strategic in its emphasis on enabling the utilising of employee efforts and capabilities to bring about long-term organisational survival. It incorporates those activities that have always been associated with personnel management, including the recruiting of employees and their training and development. It also acknowledges something that is rarely mentioned in formal definitions of either personnel or human resource management – the fact that a significant element of personnel and HR work has for some decades been the ending of employment relationships with employees, especially through redundancies. The *relational* and *exchange* elements of human resourcing work are acknowledged in the reference to the maintaining of employment relationships. This recognises two important human resourcing tasks: the seeking of compliance, commitment and productive cooperation on the one hand and the handling of conflicts, arguments and employee 'misbehaviours' on the other.

Something that is kept open in the above conception of human resource management is the question of who does this 'HRM work'. The same procedure is being followed here as was followed with regard to 'management' in Chapter 5. Three dimensions of 'management' were identified in Table 5.3 (p. 167): the function of *management* (which has to be carried out regardless of whether a few or many of the organisations employees are directly involved in it); the activity of *managing* (actions taken to achieve the function of managing or shaping the organisation); the formal role of *manager* (which becomes necessary when size or complexity of operations requires a division of labour between managers and others who focus on carrying out direct work tasks). Table 10.2 identifies three equivalent dimensions of HRM.

A whole range of processes and activities are carried out in work organisations to fulfil the strategic function of human resource management, as Table 10.2 shows. All of the human resourcing activities identified in the table are meant to ensure that the organisation has both the human skills and capabilities and the degree of social coherence necessary for its continuation into the

---

Table 10.2 Three dimensions of human resource management

Human resource management as a *function* is that part of managerial work which is concerned with acquiring, developing and dispensing with the efforts, skills and capabilities of an organisation's workforce and maintaining organisational relationships within which these human resources can be utilised to enable the organisation to continue into the future

Human resourcing as an *activity* is the range of actions that fulfil the HRM function:

- monitoring current and likely future staffing requirements to enable some programming of future human resourcing efforts
- collecting and making available for managerial decision making information on employees, employee capabilities and the deployment of both of these
- selecting and recruiting employees
- hiring labour from agencies and sub-contractors (as an alternative to creating an employment relationship with these providers of labour)
- dispensing with employees whose services are no longer required or who are otherwise deemed incapable of fulfilling tasks required of them
- training, and developing employee capabilities
- consulting, communicating and negotiating with representatives of organised labour (trade unions or professional associations) over whatever conditions or details of employment may have become subject to collective bargaining
- communicating and consulting with employees and employee groupings over employment matters without the intermediaries of trade union representatives
- fixing levels of and administering wages, salaries, fringe benefits and other rewards or 'compensation package' elements
- establishing and ensuring compliance with policies on health and safety, sickness and absenteeism, discipline, fair and equal opportunities – both to maintain the health and goodwill of employees themselves and to ensure compliance with legal requirements

Human resourcing (HR) practitioners occupying a *formal role* are employed in a personnel or HR department to ensure that the human resourcing activities necessary for long-term organisational continuation are carried out, directly through their own efforts and indirectly through their involvement (both enabling and constraining) with other managers

---

future. Involved in many of these activities will inevitably be processes of competition, conflict and the wielding of power – all of which can as readily lead to confusion, breakdown and corporate failure as it can help the work organisation 'hold together' and function as a reasonably cooperative enterprise. The challenge faced by those concerned with human resourcing and employment management is enormous, as will be stressed in the consideration of the underlying strategic significance of human resourcing to which we now turn. Once this has been looked at, we will return to the issue of the relationship between human resourcing specialists and other managers with whom they have to work to fulfil the basic HRM function. As Table 10.2 implies – with its reference to there being both an enabling and a constraining role here – this is by no means a straightforward and always harmonious relationship.

The essentially strategic nature of human resourcing

It was argued earlier that human resourcing and employment issues are 'utterly central to the existence of organisations' and that they 'pervade every aspect of organisational management' (p. 403). Subsequently HRM was said to be 'essentially strategic in its emphasis on enabling the utilising of employee efforts and capabilities to bring about long-term organisational survival' (p. 407). One inference that could be drawn from this wording is that we are *analytically* privileging the organisation and its survival over the human beings that are involved in it. Perhaps such a position could be defended on the grounds that it is possible to see an organisation continuing in existence over time in spite of the fact that it has had a complete turnover in the personnel involved in it. However, it is possible to counter this with the recognition that without the human beings that are involved with an organisation at any particular point in time that organisation would not exist at all. We are back to the centrality of human resourcing and employment issues to the existence of the organisation and to three particular aspects of this centrality:

- the centrality of human resourcing issues to *processes* of organisational strategy making;
- the role of human resourcing in handling *tensions and contradictions* that underlie the whole employment relationship in industrial capitalist societies;
- the role of the human resourcing function in maintaining *corporate integration* and capabilities to ensure *long-term* organisational viability.

The centrality of human resourcing issues to processes of organisational strategy making

One frequently hears business leaders and senior managers claim that 'our people are our most important asset'. This wording can readily be criticised as dehumanising employees by treating them as means to ends ('assets' being little different from 'resources'). However, if we generously assume that the word 'people' is simply being used as convenient shorthand for human efforts, skills and capabilities, then perhaps we can acknowledge these words as signalling recognition by those employers that their enterprises are dependent upon the skills and efforts of the people they employ. In fact, we might infer that top managers are coming to recognise that without the people whom they employ – themselves included – the organisation simply would not exist. Yet much of the systems-control thinking that still dominates managerial thinking and a lot of academic writing in this area fails to represent the relationship between general corporate strategies and human resourcing strategies in accordance with this important insight. It treats the human resourcing strategy as something that follows from, supports or serves a main corporate strategy. Malcolm Lossie raises some of the practical issues that can arise from this in Case 10.1.

Activity 10.1

Consider, first, what you think is the most appropriate relationship to exist in an organisation between the shaping of the main corporate or business strategy on the one hand and a human resourcing strategy (in the sense of the general way in which the organisation deals with employment and human resourcing matters) on the other. Consider whether human resourcing strategies are best understood as subordinate to overall corporate strategies, or as equal in significance to them. Then read the conversation with Malcolm Lossie in Case 10.1 and consider whether you are still happy with your original view in the light of what this HR director has to say.

Malcolm Lossie plays it canny   Case 10.1

It took my predecessor as HR director years and years to get a seat on the main board of this company. He fought like mad to get the right even to listen to what the top men were saying about the direction the business should take. But, just before I took over from him, he told me that he rarely found himself able to speak up about HR matters, even when, in his view, they were key to business decisions that were being made.

And is this different for you now?

After three years in the job, I'd say that I am just beginning to make my voice heard. But it is an uphill struggle. And if I get just one thing wrong, I shall lose every bit of the limited credibility that I have built up.

Yet I thought that you were recruited here precisely because you had credibility – in fact I've heard it said that you were headhunted because they knew that HR issues were vitally important to where the company was going. And they apparently thought that you were one of the few people who was good enough.

Yes, that fits with what I was told. But when it comes to it, there is one attitude that dominates. This is the attitude that engineering issues combined with financial considerations are the most important strategically.

Strategic discussions – board level discussions generally – get little beyond that. The board members would prefer it if they could just follow their engineering instincts about strategic directions – you know, pursue those projects that are the most exciting in engineering terms on the assumption that the world will buy the wonderful things that they produce. That's how it once was, I am told. But they have learned that they must temper this approach with recognition of the financial 'realities' that they must work within. Sometimes I think it would be too much to ask of them, that they should treat human resourcing matters alongside engineering and financial matters. I remember so well one occasion when I got quite forceful and pointed out that a decision that they were moving towards would involve a wave of redundancies. This, coming straight on top of an earlier headcount reduction programme, could have a very destructive effect on morale and recruitment to growing areas of the business, I warned. I was immediately shot down by one of the most powerful non-executive directors. 'You can't let the tail wag the dog, young man,' he said, in the most patronising tones I have ever heard. 'If we make the right business decision then it is up to you to make it work in HR terms.' The Chairman was much more gentle but suggested that the board thought that they had recruited in me the best HR man available precisely because some very tricky employment issues were likely to arise from the way they were going to change the business.

So do you accept their definition of the HR role in corporate strategy?

No. I don't.

Sure. But I was looking earlier at your HR mission statement and that is full of stuff about a 'business driven' approach to HR and 'ensuring that the business aims' of the company are 'met through HR policies that are seen as fair, consistent . . .'

Just a minute.

This does sound like the business dog very clearly wagging the HR tail.

Hang on. Get behind the rhetoric. I admit that I am using the language that is preferred along the [directors'] corridor here. I've got to play along with them if I am going to get to where I need to be. It's, you know, 'softly, softly, catchee thief'. I am playing it canny. I know that I have got to talk this language of the 'business coming first' and of the point of HR being to 'help achieve business goals'. But my thinking goes beyond this.

Please go on.

I've got a simple picture in my mind. I see the human resources here as the starting point of our strategic considerations – not as the means of doing whatever suits the shareholders. Now let me make it clear, I am not saying that all the business things we do should be for the sake of the company's employees. But this company is the bundle of brilliant engineering talent that has made it a world leader. The starting point for any strategic discussion has therefore got to be the bundle of core competences that we possess. This is what I am getting my fellow directors to recognise, one by one. As I said to our head of design the other day, 'Where do these brilliant engineering ideas that our future depends on come from in the first place? They come from our human resources.' 'I'd never thought of it like that before,' he replied.

Isn't that a bit abstract though?

It's anything but abstract. It is vital that I get my colleagues to think in this way if I am going to make a proper professional contribution to securing the long-term future of this firm. The danger at the moment is that they are looking at separate projects, one at a time. They are inclined to say to me, 'We're starting to work on such and such – so get recruiting a hundred of these and fifty of those. Oh and we are going to run down x and y, so you can lose the people there. Get the accounting chappies to make sure the costs and savings balance out.' No consideration is given to what projects might come along in the future – or indeed where those projects are going to come from – if we try to operate a hire and fire approach in the labour market we are talking about. This is the market for the world's best engineers. So that's what I am working on: getting them to see the human resources as the starting point for strategic thinking and as the source of the efforts that will provide a future for the business. This is all very practical. It is anything but abstract. I recognise that I will continue to recruit in certain areas and lose people in other areas and that, year on year, I will reduce the overall headcount. But I want to do this within a framework of building a secure core of committed engineering and managerial talent that can innovate and take risks and bring home the bacon for another hundred years.

Malcolm Lossie is giving very hard-headed arguments here for refusing to make human resourcing strategies subservient to general corporate strategy concerns. In effect, he claims that by treating the set of human resources that currently make up the organisation as of equal importance to issues of future corporate performance, a better corporate performance is likely to be achieved in the long run. He recognises that a successful corporate strategy and business performance is not just dependent on the human resources that employees supply in the form of willing and cooperative labour but is also dependent on the human resources of creativity and inventiveness. In this sense, he argues, human resources are the starting point for strategic thinking. They are not

FIGURE 10.1 Systems-control and process-relational ways of framing the relationship between corporate and HR strategy making

something that managerial strategic ingenuity (a 'human resource' itself of course) simply looks to an HR director to supply, like so many nuts and bolts, to help fulfil a corporate strategy. This systems-control view of the relationship between corporate and HR strategy making is a linear one which sees human resource strategy making as a subsidiary or servant of corporate strategy making. It is represented on the left-hand side of Figure 10.1 whereas the more processual sort of relationship that Malcolm encourages us to take is represented on the right-hand side. Here there is a continuous interplay between these two aspects of strategy making and they can be seen as having equal importance.

Human resourcing and the handling of tensions and contradictions underlying the employment relationship

A basic challenge facing the management of every employing organisation is that of managers having to *gain some control over, shape* and *exploit* the human resources of labour, skill and capability brought to them by employees. This is necessary for the enterprise to continue in existence. The challenge is a vast one because these 'resources' can only be obtained and utilised through making exchange relationships with human beings – with people who have minds, wills and identities of their own. To gain access to the *human resources* they want, they have to deal with *human beings*. These human beings will inevitably want to make use of the organisation for their own particular purposes (money income, social status, job interest and all the rest) just as much as the organisation wants to make use of them.

There is thus a basic tension that has to be handled. This is a tension, we might say, between the need for organisational managements to have malleable and controllable human resources of effort, skill and capability continually available to them and the basic recalcitrance or sense of independence inherent in the human beings who are the providers of these resources. This profoundly significant tension, which puts pressure on every aspect of managerial work generally and human resourcing work specifically, is not just one that arises at the level of work organisations. It arises in some key principles of the type of economy and society of which all modern work organisations are components. This is the *industrial capitalist* type of political economy that dominates the twenty-first century world, and at the heart of this way of organising economic and social life is the *employment and rational organisation of free labour*. What we have here is a combination of three principles that are essential elements of *modernity* (Chapter 2, pp. 35–7) and which differentiate modern industrial capitalist societies from, say, feudal or tribal societies. They are:

- The principle of *employment* whereby workers sell some of their capacity to work and apply skills and capabilities to an employer (as opposed, say, to the serf working for a lord as a duty inherent in a feudal type of order or a slave working for the person who owns them).

- The principle of the formally rational *bureaucratic work organisation* whereby work activities are located in a technical division of labour, based on rational calculative 'design work' by expert managers, and a hierarchical control structure (as opposed, say, to people carrying out work along lines traditionally associated with the trade or occupation of which they are a part).

- The principle of *free labour* whereby each citizen has the legal freedom (or 'democratic right') to choose with whom to make an employment contract and to end that exchange relationship whenever it suits them (as opposed, say, to their being tied into a particular work situation by feudal bonds or by an owner–slave property relationship).

These underlying principles of the modern industrialised society have worked together effectively enough to make this type of social and economic order the dominant one in the contemporary world. In systems terms, it is a system that works. (Although we should never forget that while it has 'worked' to give massive increases in human welfare and democratic freedom it has also made possible some of the most systematic tyrannies and murderous wars of all times.) However, there are contradictory tensions within this way of organising society and economy. In the eyes of the most powerful critic of this system, Karl Marx, these contradictions were such that, in the long run, capitalist societies were bound to collapse. History so far, however, has shown that these contradictions have been *managed* to avoid such a collapse and it is possible to see the human resourcing component of the management of industrial capitalist work organisations as functioning to manage these contradictions. It by no means does this on its own. It performs such a role alongside a whole range of general state provisions and initiatives, in education, health and welfare provisions and employment legislation, for example.

The basic contradiction that human resource management helps to 'manage' is that between the principle of *controlling* human activity, which is inherent in the institutions of employment and rational organisation of work, and the principles of *freedom*, *choice* and *autonomy* that are implicit in the institution of free labour. The citizens of industrial capitalist societies are thus given democratic rights, which define them as people who have a right to influence their own destinies and to choose with whom to seek employment. Once in employment, though, they find themselves subject to controls imposed both by bureaucratic rules and by 'bosses' who have authority over them in the managerial hierarchy of the organisation in which they have chosen to work. Members of modern societies are encouraged to be free thinking, mobile, assertive individuals vigorously pursuing their own and their families' interests. At the same time, however, they are encouraged to be loyal and obedient citizens and employees. The continuous tension between these two aspects of modern life is one that, we might say, is 'built in' to the sort of societies in which an increasing proportion of people in the modern world live. And at the 'local' level of each employing work organisation, it is a tension with which managers continually have to deal. They strive to achieve a degree of *control* over employees' activities while at the same time having to accept that they must win employees' *willing consent* to work cooperatively in the way required of them.

This analysis has knowingly and deliberately been provided in terms that derive from the tradition of systems thinking about human social arrangements. There has been an implicit use of a notion of both the industrial capitalist society and the modern work organisation as *systems* whose various components or organising principles can both function well together, keeping the 'system' going, or come into tension with each other threatening the collapse of that system. Further, it could be argued that 'HRM' has been treated here as a subsystem of organisational and societal systems that performs the function of handling disintegrative tendencies and thus avoiding the collapse of the system. An analogy that suggests itself is one of HRM functioning within work organisations in the same way that the regulator or the safety valve on a steam engine avoids a steam driven machine from blowing up. This analogy, for all its crudity, offers a useful insight.

It is in the spirit of trying to develop insights into the deeper or societal implications of human resource management that the basic systems analogy has been used here. It is not being suggested that societies and organisations *are* systems constructed out of sub-systems that sometimes function to achieve system integration and sometimes fail to function and bring about disintegration or disequilibrium. But it is suggested that the use of such mechanistic analogies can help us temporarily to simplify the immense complexities we confront when we try to generalise about large-scale social and economic arrangements – and thus help generate worthwhile insights. We have therefore looked at social orders and organisations for the moment *as if* they were systems. We have to remember that this is simply a device for making sense of the vast complexities of the human initiatives, conflicts, ambiguities, successes and failures in which we have to struggle to see any kind of pattern. It was accepted in Chapter 2 that *systems-control* ways of framing organisations have value in drawing our attention to certain 'system-like' characteristics of organisational life. But the importance was stressed of going beyond systems thinking and looking at the *processes* and ongoing *relationships* that occur within the very limiting 'black box' that systems analysis works with (p. 274). The insight that HRM has a conflict management or a systems integrating *function* needs to be combined with consideration of particular activities, processes and relationships like those in which we saw Malcolm Lossie involving himself earlier in Case 10.1. Similarly Inva Gordon's arguments in Case 10.3 (which we will come to later, pp. 430–3) for adopting more 'indirect control' or high commitment human resourcing measures in the Viewfield call centre organisation can be connected to the notion of HRM 'functioning' to manage more effectively certain potentially disintegrative tensions.

The necessarily corporate and long-term focus of HRM

The managerial function of HRM, to which HR specialists and other managers alike contribute, handles basic work and employment tensions and contradictions in a way that gives human resourcing work a centrally strategic significance. Regardless of who carries it out, human resourcing work plays an important *general* role in ensuring that the organisation is able to continue into the future. It does this by trying to balance the managerial need to gain a certain amount of control over employees with recognition that people do not readily submit themselves to such control. There are, however, two more *specific* strategic human resourcing roles, both clearly related to this more general role, which can perhaps only be performed satisfactorily by a corporate HR department. These are:

- *Maintaining corporate integration.* Meeting the need constantly to monitor and influence the comparative treatment of employees across an organisation of any size or complexity to ensure that there is a sufficiently strong general perception of fair treatment and justice across the organisation to prevent a level of conflict, resentment or legal challenge that might damagingly undermine the level of productive cooperation necessary for the organisation's long-term future or might damage its reputation in the labour markets it draws upon.

- *Human resourcing for the future.* Meeting the need to encourage departmental or functional managers with shorter-term and more specific task responsibilities to look beyond the immediate pressures of their day-to-day situation to consider the pattern of skills, capabilities and commitments that the organisation requires for the longer term.

Activity 10.2

In the light of these two suggested corporate HR roles, consider what particular issues within the range of human resourcing activities (listed in the human resourcing activities section of Table 10.2) might require the existence of a corporate HR department in an organisation of any size. Then read Jack Avoch's justifications in Case 10.2 for retaining a corporate HR department that he put to Jean-Yves, the new Chief Executive at Gollachers.

Jack fights his corner

When Jean-Yves took over as Chief Executive last year, one of his very first meetings was with me. I had this strange feeling as I went up to his office that, as the recently appointed head of HR, I was either going to be given a key role in the company's future or he was going to say goodbye to me. I was right to be anxious. He told me how much he admired what he had heard about my achievements and how he particularly liked the fact that I had seriously reduced the influence of the company's trade unions as well as having got most of the managers 'turned on to HR issues'. It had occurred to him, however, that the next logical step was for the managers across the organisation to take responsibility for the HR in their own areas and for my HR department to be wound up. He put this in terms of 'really empowering managers' and 'making them accountable for their own actions with regard to how they treat people'. He assured me that his mind wasn't made up on the matter but he also put it to me that 'the logic of this is unassailable, isn't it?' He then asked me whether I believed in 'managers' right to manage?' I was rather thrown by this but felt I had to reply that I did. 'So, if this shouldn't be challenged by trade unions and the like, then surely it shouldn't be challenged any more by a corporate HR department.'

I could see the trap I had walked into. When the unions were powerful here, everybody saw a role for a strong personnel or HR department to negotiate with them. They also saw the need to make sure that we didn't get managers making local agreements with their union reps that would lead to comparability claims across the company which would cost the company dear (something that apparently happened several times in the past). What I now needed to do, to fight my corner and defend the people in my HR department, was to persuade Jean-Yves that managers across the organisation simply could not be left to cover every aspect of HR. They would always tend to prioritise local, departmental and immediate issues rather than corporate and long-term ones.

'With the best will in the world', I put it to Jean-Yves, 'you can't expect managers not to give priority to whatever HR issues are most urgent in their own area at any given time. This is the case even if they are very business oriented and strategically aware, as most of our managers are.' I didn't believe what I was saying here, actually, but I knew I would get nowhere if I implied to Jean-Yves that a lot of the managers simply could not be trusted to act in any interest other than that of their own little empire. 'In spite of the unions no longer being the main channel for grievances, this means that it is vital that someone keeps an eye on the whole playing field and ensures that we don't get people in one area being paid more than people in another for similar work.' I told Jean-Yves some stories of recent events that illustrated the problems here. One was the case of a department who organised their own flexi-time arrangements without involving HR. People in three other departments in that building soon decided that they would like to work in this more flexible way, but their managers argued that the work there was different and that they couldn't cope with other than a 9 to 5 arrangement. I pointed out, in the first place, that the manager should not have done that without involving HR. And, in the second place, I observed that if my department had not been there to sort out the rows that blew up, it would have to have been the Chief Executive who would have needed to 'waste her time' dealing with it.

This last bit seemed to make Jean-Yves think. I also told him about a recent industrial tribunal that had given the company a lot of bad publicity and set back one of our recruitment exercises. I said that this arose because a manager had dismissed an employee without reference to HR and that, again, if we weren't there constantly monitoring this kind of thing, there would be a lot more such tribunals. Just one of these 'every now and again' is damaging for the firm I argued. 'And indeed for the chief executive's own reputation,' I dared to add. 'Tell me more,' he went on, looking quite worried now. 'Think of it like this,' I said. 'These things are bound to happen from time to time even if your managers are really sensitive about good employment practice and all the highly complicated employment legislation. But who would have to go into court to speak for the company, if you didn't have a HR director?', I asked him. And I answered my own question before he had time to. 'It would be down to the chief executive again I am afraid.'

I went on to point out the various corporate initiatives I was currently working on. One of these was an improved graduate recruitment programme. Another was a human resource information system which would be centrally run but which would 'considerably help empower managers by making available to them everything from their staff's training records and holiday entitlements to labour turnover figures and salary details. 'Who else but an HR department could do these things?', I asked him. And I asked whether he wanted every manager going out and finding his or her own graduates, for example. Jean-Yves started to fight back by arguing that a number of the things that we did could be 'outsourced' or done by consultants. Our annual staff attitude survey was one he pointed to here. 'But what about our very significant work on monitoring current competencies and future skill needs?', I came back at him. 'Left to their own devices, most of our managers are rather unwilling to divert their staff from current tasks in hand to develop the skills they are going to need in the future. But we currently keep them on their toes on this and press them to what we call "investing in the future through HR development".' You just cannot expect managers, with the departmental and delivery pressures they face every day to look to the long term in this way, without 'being prompted by someone who has this longer-term vision', I insisted.

'Speaking of long-term vision,' Jean-Yves said, standing up and pointing out of his window, 'a lot of restructuring needs to be done across Gollochers.' 'Indeed, I would expect you to be thinking that way,' I commented, feeling my confidence growing by the second. He continued, 'I can see that we are going to be recruiting staff to certain areas at the same time as we are losing people from others – although there might be some scope for redeployment of people if we do this skilfully.' I nodded, and smiled, 'That's not an easy thing to do.'

'Do you think we can do it?', he asked. 'I have done it before', I explained, 'and my staff . . .'. He cut me off, 'I know what you are going to say. No need. I'll come and see you and your people tomorrow and we'll get the job started.'

Jack appears to have been successful in persuading Jean-Yves to retain a corporate HR department and, indeed, to use Jack and his department to help him restructure Gollochers, though Jack had to work hard to 'fight his corner'. Jean-Yves had clear and well thought out reasons for dispensing with the HR department. It was not a matter of his ignoring the importance of the human resourcing function or, it would appear, having received bad reports about Jack himself. On the contrary, he speaks of the good things he had heard about Jack's achievements. And he could be seen as wanting to strengthen the overall human resourcing *function* (as opposed to *department*), rather than diminishing it. Jean-Yves speaks of making managers more involved in HR issues by getting them to 'take responsibility for how they treat people', and he implies that the existence of a formal HR department tends to constrain managers in this respect. It undermines, he suggests, their 'right to manage'. Jack's response to this is a shrewd one. He carefully avoids being too critical of managers but he suggests that 'with the best will in the world' and with all their 'departmental and delivery pressures' managers could not be expected to pay sufficient attention to broad corporate matters or to the long-term human resourcing needs of the business. He talks of the difficulty they are bound to have in looking at 'the whole playing field' or in considering what human resources will be needed for the longer-term future – unless they are prompted by someone like Jack and his colleagues.

Jack uses a variety of illustrations to support his argument for a corporate HR department – an element of the organisation's overall management that can prompt others to think corporately and long term about employment matters. The first one is the pay issue and the implication of his few words here is that dangerous perceptions of unfairness could arise if someone was not 'keeping an eye' on what people in different areas were being paid for work of equivalent value. The specific example of one department independently initiating flexible working times is then used to illustrate the sort of problem that can arise. The negative effects of the company having to defend itself in an industrial tribunal are then pointed out. This damages both the organisation's and the chief executive's reputation, might harm recruitment and can take up a lot of management time, Jack suggests. A corporate HR department would presumably avoid this happening too often and would handle such problems if and when they arose. Jack then turns to the implied inefficiencies and inconsistencies that might arise if each department took on the graduate recruitment work currently done by corporate HR and he stresses how departmental managers would benefit from the sort of human resource information system that can only be run corporately. Jack finally wins his case by letting Jean-Yves work out for himself that the very priority that he has set for himself as chief executive – the 'restructuring' of Gollochers – could not really be achieved without HR help at the corporate level. Jack clearly wants Jean-Yves to recognise that with HR devolved to managers across the various operational areas of the company there would be an enormous problem of managing the recruitment of staff for some areas while people were being dismissed from other parts of the company. All of that could be made more acceptable to a workforce, it is implied, if redeployment of people across the areas is made possible. And the inevitable inference that follows from this is that only a corporate HR department could manage this process. Jack and his corporate HR department survive, having established their indispensability to Jean-Yves as a strategically important unit that can play a key role in supporting the HR aspects of his own strategic work.

Running through the story that Jack Avoch tells is the suggestion that relationships between HR specialists and other managers are not simple or straightforward. Jean-Yves seems to be alluding to certain tensions between the two when he brackets HR departments with trade unions as putting limits on managers' 'right to manage'. And implicit in the corporate HR role that Jack argues for is a notion of HR sometimes *supporting* and *enabling* managers (with the HR information system, for example, or on graduate recruitment) but at other times *constraining* them (on how they pay people, settle their working hours, deal with employment law and training matters for example). While Jack Avoch might want to persuade us that there are likely to be unmanageable problems without a corporate HR department, it is clear that the existence of a formal HR presence can, in itself, create problems.

HR specialists and other managers: tensions and ambiguities

When the three main elements of HRM were identified earlier in Table 10.2, it was recognised that human resourcing activities are likely to be carried out by a mixture of human resourcing specialists and other managers. If we look at the role played by those people who are employed in personnel or HR departments we will see that there are four dimensions to their work:

- They carry out specialised administrative tasks relating to human resourcing (from keeping personnel records to placing job advertisements).

- They work with other managers to support them in the fulfilment of human resourcing activities that affect the departments or functions of those managers. This entails, for example, helping managers select, recruit, develop and reward staff that are needed for the department to carry out its tasks and help the department dispense with the services of employees when they are no longer required. This implies a service or *enabling* relationship between HR and other managers.

- They monitor the activities of managers to ensure that they comply with corporate human resourcing policies and procedures necessary to prevent organisational disintegration. This entails, for example, preventing managers from making decisions that have damaging repercussions for other managers (especially on pay and other rewards where perceptions of unfairness across areas can arise), ensuring that managers comply with employment legislation, negotiated agreements with trade unions and with corporate policies on such matters as equal opportunities, disciplinary procedures, communication and consultation. This implies a 'policing' or *constraining* relationship between HR and other managers.

- They monitor the activities of other managers to ensure that they are acquiring and developing human resources that are necessary for the long-term future, as well as for the present. This implies both an *enabling* and a *constraining* relationship between HR and other managers.

This combination of roles creates considerable problems (see Further Reading on HR and other managers, p. 445). Somehow, HR departments have *both* to serve or enable managers *and* to control and constrain them. This creates a considerable ambiguity in managers' eyes – often confusing them in practice about whether the personnel or HR department is primarily there to help them in their work or to hinder them. The uncomfortable truth is that both of these tend to be the case, from the point of view of managers concentrating on the priorities of their own department and the immediate pressures faced by their department. The result of this is that in many work organisations there is a tense and ambivalent relationship between HR managers and others. On the one hand, the manager is often dependent upon and appreciative of the help that the HR specialists give. But, on the other hand, they come to resent the limits that are put on their actions and decisions by the HR specialists' insistence that the manager complies with certain corporate or legal requirements. This compliance simply makes the manager's day-to-day life more difficult.

On top of these ambiguities are further ones deriving from the history of personnel management. One half of personnel management's historical roots are in a relatively *tender* or *caring* tradition of employee welfare and industrial social work and the other half of its roots are in a relatively *tough* and *controlling* tradition of labour management and collective bargaining with trade unions. The willingness of personnel specialists in recent years to replace the 'Personnel' title with a 'Human Resources' one can partly be understood as an attempt to play down the welfare and caring dimension of this history. Nevertheless, it is unlikely that employee expectations that personnel or HR departments can and should show a caring face towards employees will go away. The caring/controlling set of historical ambiguities with regard to the HR department tends to remain alongside the ambiguities created by the dual role of HR as both a service to and a constraint upon the line or departmental manager.

HR specialists are typically confronted with the considerable challenge of presenting themselves to the workforce generally as a caring department, concerned with justice and the fair treatment of employees while, at the same time, they must present themselves to corporate management as a department concerned with controlling and exploiting the efforts and capabilities of employees. Simultaneously, they have to present themselves to line or departmental managers as providing a supportive, enabling and empowering service while, to corporate management, they promise to monitor, control and constrain managers so that they do not prioritise their departmental interests with regard to employees over corporate and longer-term strategic concerns.

These ambiguities and tensions are bound to have considerable implications for the way strategic human resourcing is carried out in practice. As we shall now see, there are certain circumstances in which employee groups are more problematic to management than they are in others and the extent to which employee constituencies are perceived as problematic for the organisation's future is likely to be a key influence on the type of human resourcing strategy which emerges. Such a perception tends to put pressure on managers to choose relatively *high commitment* human resourcing strategies. Should the workforce be seen, on the other hand, as less of a problem with regard to the organisation's future, then there is less pressure on managers to choose this more complex and potentially costly approach. A *low commitment* human resourcing strategy, in such circumstances, is more likely to be selected. Such processes of HR strategic choice are not simple or straightforward, however. Ambiguity and differences of value, understanding and interest are always present when strategic choices are made.

Choices and constraints in human resource strategy making

It was clearly established in earlier chapters that managerial choices about general strategic direction and about the type of structure, culture and job design that are adopted are influenced by a combination of organisational circumstances (or 'contingencies') and managerial interests, values and preferences. No organisational strategy, structure, culture or pattern of work design comes about as a direct consequence, however, of circumstances or contingencies in the way systems-control oriented 'contingency theory' implies. The state of a national or global economy, the market situation of a particular organisation or its size or technological nature does not *determine* what sort of strategy, culture or structure an organisation has. As our earlier analysis recognised (Chapter 7, pp. 272–82), contingencies such as those of organisational environment, size and technology do have important implications for the way in which any organisation is shaped.

The influence of these factors is always mediated by the way managers interpret and *enact* them, and these interpretations of organisational circumstances are taken into managerial decision-making arguments, discussions and debates. It is in this context of interpretation, argument and micropolitical contest that decisions emerge that lead to actions which, when taken together over a period of time, reveal a strategic pattern. This analysis can now be brought forward from its earlier application to how organisations are 'shaped' to our present concern with how human resourcing strategies emerge.

Human resourcing strategy   *Concept*

The general direction followed by an organisation in how it secures, develops, utilises and, from time to time, dispenses with human resources of effort, skill and capability to enable it to continue into the long term.

The way human resourcing strategy is conceptualised here is fully in accord with the concepts of organisational strategy and strategy making developed in Chapter 9. It attempts to go beyond much of the standard thinking on strategic HRM (Watson, 2004; see also Further Reading on strategic HRM, pp. 446–7) A human resourcing strategy is not looked at as a plan, or as a dimension of a corporate Strategic plan. Instead, it is treated as the general pattern that emerges over time as the managers of an organisation seek to supply the organisation with the human resources – in the sense of human efforts, skills and capabilities – that it needs to go forward into a long-term future. To help us see some patterning in the complex mixture of human resourcing activities and procedures that exists in each employing organisation we can utilise a continuum upon which any particular organisation's human resourcing strategy can be placed. The positions at the ends of this continuum are those of a *low commitment* HR strategy at one end and a *high commitment* HR strategy at the other.

● A *low commitment HR strategy* could be characterised as a 'hire and fire' one, in which labour is acquired at the point when it is immediately needed and the employee is allocated to tasks for which they need very little training, with the employment being terminated as soon as those tasks have been completed. The relationship between employer and employee is very much a calculatingly instrumental one and contact between managers and workers very much at 'arm's-length'.

- A *high commitment HR strategy* can be identified where the employer seeks a much closer relationship with employees and wants them to become psychologically or emotionally involved with the enterprise. The employer is likely to offer employees opportunities for personal and career development within their employment, which is expected to continue over a longer-term period and potentially to cover a variety of different tasks.

It should immediately become apparent that this continuum of HR strategies has a close relationship with the indirect control/direct control continuum that was used in Chapter 7 to consider managerial choices about 'organisational shaping'. It is therefore possible to extend the model that was used in Chapter 7 to incorporate those direct/indirect control options into the choice that is made between high and low commitment human resourcing strategies. This recognises that low commitment human resourcing strategies are typically manifested in large part through the use of direct control management practices and procedures, whereas high commitment strategies are expressed in large part through the use of indirect attempts to achieve managerial control. Figure 10.2 is a version of the model introduced in Chapter 7 (Figure 7.4, p. 275) which has been extended to bring together the notions, on the one hand, of low commitment employment relationships with direct managerial controls and, on the other hand, high commitment employment relationships with indirect management controls.

The basic claim here is that, all things being equal, a low commitment type of human resourcing strategy is likely to be more appropriate to a situation where employees are not a major source of uncertainty for an employer than one where they create strategic uncertainty. An organisation is not likely to require a highly participative and strong commitment set of arrangements if it has a simple technology and a relatively straightforward business environment that allows it to employ easily obtainable and replaceable employees, for example. However, if an organisation's management sees that its future would be uncertain without meeting the much higher demands that are likely to follow from employing a highly skilled or educated workforce to operate a complex technology or deal with an especially tricky business environment – a workforce that is not easy to obtain or replace – it is much more likely to consider a high commitment set of employment conditions and work arrangements. This is necessary to encourage those people both to stay with the organisation and creatively and flexibly apply themselves to undertaking complex tasks. Note, however, that this proposition was made with the qualification 'all things being equal'. They are not equal, of course.

Managerial values and interests also come into the equation, as do the interpretive processes whereby managers decide how problematic the labour force is, in terms of the organisation's future. It is possible for managers to decide that their social values make them prefer higher commitment employment practices

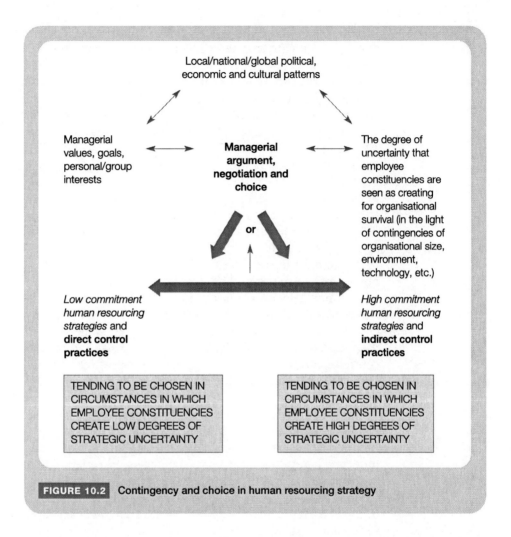

FIGURE 10.2 Contingency and choice in human resourcing strategy

in principle. This, however, would tend to create cost problems – making their labour costs higher than competing employers who were more willing to adopt a simpler hire and fire policy. By the same token, a set of HR strategy makers who disagreed in principle with high commitment practices and indirect management controls, but who employed highly skilled or educated people in a tight labour market would have difficulty retaining staff. In practice, then, there is likely to be interplay between managerial value preferences and perceptions of contingent circumstances making employees more or less strategically problematic (uncertainty creating). And, given that the individuals within any strategy-making management group are likely to vary in their personal interests, values and priorities, we can expect to see strategic choices emerging out of processes of argument and debate. This was very apparent with regard to some human resourcing issues which arose in the Motoline case in Chapter 7 (and to which we will return below). We will also see this kind of process occurring with the case of the Viewfield call centre company, shortly.

Before we do this we must, first, look in more detail at the range of practices and arrangements that tend to be associated with the two ends of the continuum shown in Figure 10.2. Table 10.3 does this by identifying a range of direct–indirect control options that are available with regard to several areas of the organisation and its management that we have considered in earlier chapters – strategy-making practices, culture, structure and work design – together with a number of further areas of organisational management. The table suggests a very inclusive and wide-ranging notion of what human resourcing strategy is about. This is wholly consistent with our conceptualising of human resourcing strategy as the general direction followed by an organisation in how it secures, develops, utilises and dispenses with human resources of effort, skill and capability to enable it to continue into the long term. Such a perspective invites us to see human resourcing strategy as the basic manner or style in which people's work capacities are utilised across every aspect of an organisation. Choices about this manner or style relate to issues ranging from how strategy making is conducted in the organisation down to the way an HR or personnel department is staffed. At the level of strategy making, for example, a low commitment/indirect control approach only utilises the strategic thinking of a minority of those employed as managers – the very senior managers and their specialist strategic advisers. At the opposite end of the continuum, a high commitment/indirect control approach involves many more people in strategic activities – all managers are seen as having relevant competence in this area. And, with regard to the staffing of an HR department, the former approach tends to treat personnel work as something that can only be done by specialists. The latter style, however, takes a broader view of the capacities of both HR and non-HR managers by suggesting both that their work can to some extent be 'integrated' and that both sets of managers, in certain circumstances, can work in the other's area of activity.

Many of the options identified at the high commitment/indirect control end of the continuum should perhaps be seen as *aspirations* rather than as 'options' in the strict sense of the term. A number of these options here have been advocated as generally desirable by the *total quality management* movement (Wilkinson *et al.*, 1998) and the virtues of other practices falling at this end of the continuum have been extolled by those wanting to prescribe 'best practice' in areas ranging from work design and pay systems to human resource development. In spite of all this advocacy, however, managers themselves are likely to be aware that these are aspirations that are never likely to be fully realised in practice. They may wish to move towards a culture where more of the values that people within the organisation hold are 'shared' ones. However, it is unlikely that anyone with any familiarity with the world of work is likely to think that it is realistic to achieve an organisational culture in which everyone holds the same values.

The same point applies to the aspiration in the area of employment relations towards 'mutual' relationships rather than adversarial ones and negotiations in which both sides always 'win'. It is by no means unrealistic to seek some movement in this direction, as trade unions have tended to acknowledge in calling

Table 10.3 General organisational and managerial options and aspirations related to the basic high commitment/low commitment HRM choice		
	General organisational *direct control* options associated with *low commitment HRM* (where human resources tend to create low levels of uncertainty for managers)	General organisational *indirect control* options associated with *high commitment HRM* (where human resources tend to create high levels of uncertainty for managers)
Strategy making	● performed by top management, possibly with the aid of strategy experts	● top management provide 'vision' or 'strategic intent' and develop strategy through interaction with other levels
Culture	● rule based ● emphasis on authority ● task focus ● mistakes punished	● shared values ● emphasis on problem solving ● customer focus ● learning from mistakes
Structure	● layered hierarchy ● top-down influence ● centralisation ● mechanistically bureaucratic (rigid)	● flat hierarchy ● mutual (top-down/bottom-up) influence ● decentralisation/devolution ● organically bureaucratic (flexible)
Work/job design	● de-skilled, fragmented jobs ● doing/thinking split ● individual has single skill ● direct control of individual by supervisor	● whole, enriched jobs ● doing/thinking combined ● individual multi-skilled ● indirect control within semi-autonomous teams
Performance expectations	● objectives met to minimum level ● external controls ● external inspection ● pass quality acceptable	● objectives 'stretch' and develop people ● self controls ● self/peer inspection ● continuous improvement in quality sought
Rewards	● pay may be varied to give individual incentives ● individual pay linked to job evaluation	● pay may be varied to give group performance ● individual pay linked to skills, 'mastery'
Communication	● management seek and give information ● information used for sectional advantage ● business information given on 'need to know' basis	● two-way communication initiated by any party ● information shared for general advantage ● business information widely shared
Employment relations	● adversarial ● collective ● win/lose ● trade unions tolerated as inconvenient constraints ● OR unions used as convenient intermediaries between managers and employees	● mutual ● individual ● win/win ● unions avoided OR unions increasingly by-passed in the hope of their eventual withering away ● OR unions involved in *partnership relations* with employers to give a 'voice' to employees in working towards employment security, innovative work practices, fair rewards and investment in training
Employee development	● training for specific purposes ● emphasis on courses ● appraisal emphasises managerial setting and monitoring of objectives ● focus on job	● training to develop employees' skills and competence ● continuous learning emphasis ● appraisal emphasises negotiated setting and monitoring of objectives ● focus on career
HR/personnel department	● marginal, and restricted to 'welfare' and employment administrative tasks ● reactive and *ad hoc* ● staffed by personnel specialists	● integrated into management, and working as 'partners' with other managers ● proactive and strategic ● staff interchange with the 'line' or other functions

for employers and trade unions to work together in *partnership relations* to the advantage of corporate and employee interests alike. However, the notion that conflicts between the goals and interests of the multiplicity of parties involved in an organisation can ever be totally overcome is utterly unrealistic. In fact, the very existence of trade unions and the institution of collective bargaining recognises differences of interest between employers and employees – interests that these arrangements are intended to manage. And, although trade unions and collective bargaining have become less significant in work organisations in many countries in recent times, they have by no means disappeared. This is recognised in Table 10.3 and the possibility for a continuing trade union role within a high commitment type of HR strategy – one which stresses 'partnership' between employer and employee interests – is included (see Bacon, 2001).

Activity 10.3

The direction in which Mick Moy and Joy Petty were trying to take Motoline (Chapter 7, p. 277) can be understood as one towards a high commitment type of HR strategy. Reread 'Getting on track at Motoline' and:

- use Table 10.3 to note the various ways in which the new management regime was moving towards a high commitment and indirect control approach;

- observe how Mick's personal values and background affected his attitude towards trade unions;

- consider how realistic you think Mick is being in considering what might be characterised as a 'partnership' relationship with trade unions in the new Motoline.

Flexibility and dual human resourcing strategies

We have seen that the basic human resourcing style of an organisation can be understood in terms of whether it leans towards an employment style involving *high commitment relationships* between employer and employees and utilises indirect attempts at managerial control of activities or leans towards an employment style involving *low commitment relationships* utilising direct managerial control practices. It is possible, however, that managers in certain organisational situations might want to apply different human resourcing strategies to different parts of their organisation. Why would they do this? To put it at its simplest, it is done in recognition of the fact that the workers who do certain work tasks can be related to in ways that are less costly than others. In economic terms, the *transaction costs* of going to the market for labour in the lower skilled or more peripheral areas of activity are lower than they would be if that labour were employed or incorporated within the bureaucratic hierarchy of the enterprise (see Rowlinson, 1997 on the application of this type of economic thinking to organisations). In circumstances like these, then, organisations might be found to operate a *dual human resourcing strategy*.

> ### Dual human resourcing strategy   *Concept*
>
> A dual human resourcing strategy exists where an organisation applies (a) a high commitment ('relationship') HR strategy involving a long-term employment relationship to core workers and managers and (b) a low commitment ('transactional') HR strategy to more peripheral suppliers of labour (sometimes involving an employment relationship, sometimes involving a market relationship).

> ### The flexible firm   *Concept*
>
> An organisational pattern in which an organisation seeks some of its human resourcing from a *core workforce* whose members are given employment security, high rewards and skill enhancement opportunities in return for a willingness to adapt and innovate and a *peripheral* workforce whose members are given more specific tasks and less commitment to continuing employment or skill enhancement.

Organisations following a dual HR strategy are adopting features of what has been identified as the *flexible firm* (Atkinson, 1985). The dual HR strategy or 'flexible firm' principle is by no means a new one. It has been used since early industrial times. It even existed during the latter part of the twentieth century when *Fordism* was at its height (Chapter 8) and when it appeared that the standard form of work career for most people was becoming one of lifetime employment with a commercial organisation or a public bureaucracy. Its most obvious presence – as today – was in project-oriented industries like building and civil engineering, where organisations had very different requirements for labour at different stages of the projects they undertook. Thus, one source of 'human resourcing' would be labourers, craft workers and technical experts who would be 'bought in' as required. The other source would be the organisation's own employees who were felt to be necessary to integrate activities over time and give continuity to the organisation's development. Also, many organisations through most of the twentieth century had some elements of this dual human resourcing approach *within* its employed workforce, in the form of a differentiation between 'works' and 'staff'. Here the latter employees generally had superior terms and conditions of employment, and, typically, were expected to be 'closer' to management than the former. A higher degree of commitment was sought from these staff members who, however junior they might be, were, in principle at least, on the bureaucratic career ladder – which 'works' employees were not.

With changing social values, the growth of service work and the reduced significance of differences between manual work and office work, employers have tended to abandon the works–staff distinction and have *harmonised* employment terms and conditions across labour categories. The trend is towards the dual human resourcing principles being applied to those who are, on the one hand, a potentially long-term *employed* group and, on the other hand, a short-time *hired* group. The first exception is where, in terms of the model in Figure 10.2, organisations find themselves with relatively stable markets and simple technologies in which a low commitment direct-control employment strategy is viable (the workforce not being a source of strategic uncertainty for the management). The second exception – where the circumstances will often overlap with those of the first – is in sectors, like certain parts of the hospitality industry, where there are people willing to take on short-term employment. These might be younger people still involved in education or people with family responsibilities who can only manage a partial and perhaps intermittent relationship with employment. Such people are willing to be casually employed because they are only seeking a short-term involvement and this matches the short-term requirement of the employer.

The short-term/long-term distinction is vital to understanding the dual human resourcing approach to achieving flexibility. Managers tend to look for the two different types of flexibility explained in Chapter 8 (p. 339):

- flexibility to meet short-term *adjustment* needs which calls for an ability to bring in and dispense with labour and human expertise as markets fluctuate or as projects begin and end;

- flexibility to meet long-term *adaptability* needs which calls for human commitment and expertise from a core of employees who will willingly and enthusiastically make innovations and actively adapt their practices to ensure that the organisation continues into the long term.

A *transactional* or *market* HR sub-strategy will thus meet the flexibility for short-term adjustment requirement and the *relationship* or *employment* HR sub-strategy will meet the flexibility for long-term adaptability need. And the relative emphasis given to each of the two human resourcing approaches is likely to vary with organisational circumstances. A project-oriented organisation (ship or oil-rig building or civil engineering perhaps) regularly needing to adjust to meet changing demands might give greater emphasis towards a *transactional* (market) approach, for example. An organisation developing and producing high technology consumer products might, on the other hand, use a greater proportion of labour engaged on a *relationship* (employment) basis. In each case, nevertheless, the fact that both types of flexibility are likely to be required in an increasingly competitive economic context means that most organisations will use both means of acquiring human resources of skill, knowledge and labour.

HR strategy making in practice

The strategic options identified earlier in Table 10.3 are based on thinking and practices covered in literatures on HRM, strategic management, labour market analysis, change management, total quality management and various other attempts at giving managerial advice and selling panaceas for managerial inadequacies. What has been avoided here, however, is any labelling of the two basic styles, the 'high commitment' and the 'low commitment' approaches, as 'old' and 'new' or as 'bad practice' and 'best practice'. This would be to play down the relevance of contingent factors – the extent to which different organisational circumstances may fit better with some types of organisational or managerial practice rather than others. Many readers will nevertheless want to apply value judgements to these alternatives, whether this derives from their own notion of what they believe 'works best' or what they feel about the right and wrong way to 'treat people at work'. This is precisely what happens in the managerial 'arguments, negotiations and choices' processes at the centre of the model in Figure 10.2. One manager in a particular organisation may argue, for example, that it is morally wrong to use labour as a short-term means to business ends – because it involves people's identities and their livelihoods and denies them the security that any employee in a modern society should have a right to. He might be persuaded, though, by another manager that such a low commitment employment strategy is the one that is most likely to be successful and to justify this he might point to certain organisational circumstances or contingencies. He might observe that the organisation has a very simple technology, faces very seasonal business demands and enjoys a plentiful supply of job applicants who appear to be happy to accept unskilled work with no long-term future. He is pointing out, in other words, that the employee constituencies in his organisation are not particularly problematic: they do not, in strategic exchange terms, create a great deal of uncertainty for those running the organisation, with regard to its overall strategic direction.

Activity 10.4

Read Inva Gordon's account in Case 10.3 of human resource strategy making at Viewfields and, using Figure 10.2 as an analytical guide, identify the factors that led to a shift in strategic emphasis, noting:

- changing contextual factors at the local or national level;

- the extent to which employees were perceived by the Viewfield management team to be increasingly strategically 'problematic' – in the sense of creating uncertainties for the organisation's continuation and in the light of changing contingencies (i.e. perceived organisational circumstances);

- the interests, values and goals of members of the management group that influenced how they acted with regard to these contingent and contextual factors ('enacted' them);

- how all these things got mixed together in the managerial arguments or negotiations that occurred – considering in particular any of the factors discussed earlier about the tensions that can arise between HR and other managers.

'Viewfields, how can I help you?'   Case 10.3

It was about a year ago I recognised that I was really going to have to assert myself if I was going to do my HR job properly here at Viewfields. Sandy Viewfield had recruited me as a personnel officer when I was only about a year out of university. I know he was impressed with me but he had it mind that I would be a quiet and compliant recruiter of staff who would very efficiently work the human resourcing machine for him – getting people in when he needed them, making sure that no employment laws were broken and getting rid of people when they were no longer wanted. He seemed happy to appoint a woman to the job, given that he believed that 'people work' was particularly 'suitable for a female' (especially since a lot of the staff were women and Sandy found women 'a bit unpredictable and difficult to understand').

Sandy had left a big telecoms company to set up the call centre business. He had risen from an engineering job up to regional manager level and he brought with him several other people with mainly telephone engineering backgrounds. The accountant, Wesley Nigg, came from a telephone systems manufacturing company. He now calls himself the Finance Director and he, together with Sandy, Maddy Dornoch – the Marketing Director – and myself form the senior management group. Sandy uses the word 'strategy' all the time and he likes to think of himself as the great strategist. He talks like this, anyway, always reminding us that he had 'the vision' to set up a business that will stay at the 'cutting edge of call centre technology'. And, yes, by 'technology' he tends to mean the hardware and the computer software that is used. People are just the add-ons that, regretfully, he has to use to work this kit. I am convinced that, in the long run, he thinks that there will be sufficiently intelligent machines available that he won't have to employ operators. For the present, however, he has to have several hundred people working for him on the several dozen accounts that we currently have. As these numbers have grown and as 'personnel problems' have increased in number and frequency he has had to turn to me more and more. It was only after I had proved to him that I was indispensable by rescuing him from what might have been a very damaging court case over a severe harassment affair, did he let me call myself 'HR director' and allow me to play a regular part in senior management meetings. Maddy is in rather a similar position. Sandy is socially unskilled, to put it politely, and he managed to lose several of our best accounts simply by being rude to the people who were bringing him business. That is the main reason he reluctantly decided to get in a marketing expert – or rather let me find someone to take on this role. He didn't like the idea of bringing another woman into the management group. But Maddy was obviously so good that he did the right thing and appointed her. 'Yes, she's clearly the best man for the job.' he commented to me after the interviews, demonstrating his less than sophisticated grasp of HR principles!

I am pleased to have a women colleague in the management group. But it worries me at the same time. We end up with women-versus-men sorts of argument all too often. Sandy and Wesley act like stereotypical engineers and accountants and Maddy and I have to play the 'but people matter' line every time. I am sure that Sandy and Wesley resisted a number of the employment innovations that I have made, with Maddy's full support, more than they would have done had either of us been men. I once accused them of being prejudiced against the managerial arguments that Maddy and I were putting forward just because we were women. This was at a meeting that was turning from the intended company policy review into a seriously unpleasant row. Wesley, however, said that he was resisting our ideas purely on cost grounds. And Sandy said that it was much more a matter of his worrying about our 'general naïvety' about human beings as opposed to any specifically 'female naïvety'.

So what were these issues? They were actually rather fundamental ones about the nature of our business as well as about how we treated our employees. Maddy argued that what we primarily sold to our client companies was a 'human service' – a 'warm and helpful interface between their businesses and the people who wanted to deal with those businesses over the telephone'. I argued that we needed to think about our staff as the key to making this possible. It wasn't the quality of the telephone systems we used that would guarantee us a future, any more than it was the software or the quality of the 'scripts' that Maddy's marketing staff were so good at writing and putting in the operators' hands. It was the ability and the willingness of staff to convince the people who called up that they wanted to please and help them. 'Until you can buy robots that sound like warm and intelligent human beings', I told Sandy that night, 'you are going to have to learn to treat the operators in such a way that they feel committed to the company and are willing to use their initiative to give the callers the quality of service that they – and the client businesses who trust us to represent them – are looking for.'

It was quite fortunate that my mention of robots rather amused Sandy. It might well have angered him if I had spoken less carefully and had seriously implied that he was only capable of relating to machines (which, privately, I sometimes think to be true). In HR work you have got to be subtle and skilled if you are going to get your way. If you start trying to tell managing directors of companies that they are getting it wrong, without being very subtle about it, you are finished – especially if they are men and you are a woman. You've still got to tell them some hard truths, but you tread carefully. You use all the charm and subtlety you can muster to convince them that, unless they listen to you, their business might come unstuck. And we were coming unstuck at Viewfields.

When Viewfields started up it was all very straightforward from Sandy's point of view. He set up the equipment in a rented building on the edge of town and simply advertised in the local paper for staff. There wasn't a lot of competition at that time. Sandy was definitely ahead of the game in the call centre business. He had several big clients and unemployment was high across the region. This meant that he had a plentiful supply of labour, and it was compliant and easily controllable labour too. The technology makes it easy for supervisors to keep a check on the number of calls each operator is handling. It is also easy for them to check that the operators are both following their script and are speaking in a pleasant and helpful manner. Anyone who fell short was simply replaced by the next person in the queue for jobs. The pay was not too bad but there were few rest breaks and there was very limited variety in the work that each person did. Sandy's view was that once a person had 'mastered' a particular script and learned what was expected of them on that client's behalf then time should not be wasted getting them to learn to handle callers on another account. He and Wesley also got very cross if it appeared that operators were going out of their way to be helpful to callers. In fact, it was their harassing a couple of employees who were accused of this that led to the court case that made Sandy and Wesley recognise that they were not the most skilled at handling people issues.

Times have changed a lot since those early days, as reluctant as Sandy and Wesley were to admit it. The labour market is now much tighter and we have to rely a lot on students who do not take readily to supervisors who bully them or to being instructed in every detail of what they are to say to callers. About a year ago our labour turnover and absence levels were becoming so bad that we were struggling to keep the phones manned. Recruitment costs, Wesley said, were unacceptably high and Maddy warned that several clients were threatening to end their contracts if the number of complaints they were receiving about our staff being brusque and offhand did not reduce significantly. 'They are complaining about staff speaking like robots,' Maddy reported – and the irony of this was not lost on Sandy. 'What are we going to do, then?' he asked me. 'What is our HR strategy going to be?'

I explained that we had to take a generally different approach to our staff if the business was going to have a healthy future. Given that we were limited by the standard sort of technology that most call centres use, we could not change things radically – fundamentally upskilling the basic jobs we offer, for example. But we could look for ways of both making people feel less dissatisfied with the work they had to do and also making them feel that the company was one worth staying with and being committed to. The first thing I got accepted was that we would improve some of the basic workplace facilities like the quality of the rest rooms. To my surprise, Wesley said that he could find money to build a small gymnasium for staff to use. Sandy laughed at this, pointing out to us that Wesley had for a long time said that he personally wanted to find a gym to use. But Wesley argued that this kind of thing should be enough to make people prefer to work for Viewfields rather than for any of our rivals, none of which had this kind of facility. I told Wesley that these were just 'hygiene' factors, in motivational terms, and that we had to look for more significant changes relating to the work itself.

When I said that what I had in mind were such things as allowing operators to adapt the basic scripts to suit their personal style, both Sandy and Wesley got very uncomfortable. And when I suggested that we set up development opportunities for staff to learn how to write scripts themselves, by allowing them an hour a week to work with marketing staff, they wanted to end the meeting. Wesley went into a long lecture about unit labour costs, or something of the kind, and Sandy said that it would give us a messy and unmanageable division of labour. 'We can't afford to confuse people about where their place is in the system', he said, 'and it will put supervisors into an impossible position when they are trying to monitor calls – how will they know whether an operator is doing the job properly and efficiently if there isn't a defined script and strictly allocated minutes?' 'Oh, I was envisaging getting rid of a separate supervisor's role and allowing operator teams to allocate one of themselves to the monitoring desk each week, with a view to that individual looking for ways of helping colleagues improve their performance, rather than keeping the old system where supervisors basically used the monitoring equipment to police the operators.'

When I went a step beyond this and suggested that we move to a largely internal promotional system and that we recruit all operators as people who can potentially move upwards, eventually having their own client accounts to manage, Wesley lost his temper and told Sandy that he should never have employed a soft-headed and totally unrealistic 'personnel type' like me. He left the meeting and Maddy and I spent the next two hours working on Sandy. He told us that this sounded like revolutionary talk to him. Yet he was willing to give consideration to what was being said because, he claimed, he 'had enough vision to see that this was as much a marketing development as a soppy HR one'. Without Maddy pointing out that it was a 'hard-headed business case' that was being put to him, I don't think we would have got anywhere with my ideas. But Sandy did invite us to develop these ideas further and he promised that he would try to 'bring Wesley round', if we could persuade them that, not only would these ideas overcome some of the 'people problems' that we currently had, but that they would significantly help the business grow.

After several months of argument I got all of this accepted. In fact, the current HR practices go even further than I originally envisaged. The teams not only choose the person to cover the developmental/monitoring role each week, they also organise their own cover for sick colleagues, altering their own shifts to make sure the work is covered. And it would appear that most of the recruitment that we have done recently has been of people introduced by current employees. Each employee, if they want it, can have an hour's 'personal development time' to work with marketing staff or, if they wish, to work on the self-help and distance learning packages that we have on the computers in the 'development room' that was built as an extension to the staff rest area. I've been especially pleased to see that team members are happy to 'trade' development time within the teams. People who are not career-oriented swap their weekly development allowance for time off with people who do want more than an hour a week to develop their career potential.

All of this was hard fought for, I must stress. The company is a much more morally acceptable place to work in, from my personal point of view. But this has only come about because there was a significant business case to put for changing the HR strategy in this way. Having said that, the business case was not one that was immediately obvious to either Sandy or Wesley. Without the hard work put in by Maddy and me to get the men to think differently, little would have changed. Perhaps if the staffing problems had got really out of hand, they might have shifted their ground. But I have no doubt that any changes that Sandy and Wesley would have been capable of making on their own initiatives would have been nothing more than minimal – and would not have helped Viewfields survive in the long term. Wesley is still sceptical and constantly complains about the salary costs, in spite of the fact that the rate of our business growth and our growing popularity with both clients and employees gives the company the 'leading edge' position that Sandy is so keen to maintain. As Sandy points out to Wesley, the profits that are being made 'fully justify the higher labour costs'. I suppose the four of us operate quite effectively as a management team but I sometimes wonder how much easier it would all be if business arguments were not always mixed up with the tensions that are always there because Maddy and I are women, are younger than the other two and have not got what Sandy calls a 'proper grounding in telecoms technology' or what Wesley refers to as 'a decent financial education'. This is all nonsense of course – but I long ago realised that, in management, you have to deal with the irrational in people as much as with the rational. Perhaps it all adds to the fun of the job. But I think, as I said to Maddy the other day, that the real reward that I get from seeing our HR strategy in practice is when I hear an operator say to a caller 'how can I help you?' and I get the impression that they really mean it.

The final statement that Inva Gordon makes about the sincerity of an operator's offer of help to callers is perhaps rather revealing about her personal values – something also implied by her reference to Viewfields as a more 'morally acceptable place to work'. She brings ethical and caring concerns to her work. Yet we can also imagine Sandy Viewfield, or even Wesley Nigg, taking pleasure in hearing operator's speaking to callers in a seemingly sincere manner, but Sandy and Wesley, we might guess, would be far less concerned than Inva about whether the operators were *actually* sincere in what they said (whether they were engaging in *deep* rather than *surface acting* – see Chapter 4, p. 132). What would matter to them would be that the operators' performances were likely to be 'good for the business'. In spite of the considerable difference of priority and value between the members of Viewfield's strategic management team, a distinctive change had occurred in the HR strategy. This had come about in the light of both varying values among these four individuals and the changing circumstances, or contingencies, faced by the organisation. The 'managerial argument, negotiation and choice' put at the centre of Figure 10.2 was influenced, as the model suggests, by:

- national and local economic and cultural factors – the changing levels of unemployment for example;
- managerial values, goals and interests – these varying from Sandy's ambitions to run a 'leading edge company' and Inva's ethical concerns to Wesley's interest in having a gym available for his own use and the attitudes each of them had towards age and gender;
- the managerially perceived increase in uncertainty being created for the organisation's future by employee constituencies – reflected in absence, labour turnover, recruitment costs and, above all, in the poor level of work performance that was losing Viewfields business. The key contingency behind this was the one of the changing business environment – a higher level of competition in both the main call centre market and in the local labour market.

The managerial choice that emerged from this decision-making *garbage can* (Chapter 6, pp. 215–21) involved shifting along the continuum shown in

Figure 10.2 in the direction of a *high commitment human resourcing strategy* accompanied by a related shift in the direction of indirect control practices (team working, emphasis on promotions within an internal labour market, etc.). There was no question of a radical shift to a wholly different type of employment practice or a sudden embracing of HR 'best practices'. Instead there was a pragmatic shift in managerial approach resulting from a combination of *choice* and *circumstance*, a combination that took its particular form as a result of processes of argument, challenge and debate and as a result of the specific mix of knowledge, insight, ignorance and prejudice to be found within the group of managers making the shift. The changed contingencies affecting the organisation meant that the main employee constituency was being experienced by managers as more problematic than it was before. The newer human resourcing strategy made a better fit with the organisation's circumstances – a higher commitment and indirect control type of strategy was more appropriate to a situation in which employees were becoming a greater source of strategic uncertainty than they had previously been.

This improved 'fit' between organisational circumstances and human resourcing strategy did not come about automatically – it was chosen by the company's managers. But it was a choice that emerged only after considerable argument, debate and conflict over values. It was also made in an atmosphere of interpersonal tension and in the light of differences of gender, age and occupational background among the group of managers making the strategic choice. Also playing a part in this was a tension between Inva as an HR specialist, on the one side, and Sandy and Wesley on the other. Sandy and Wesley were suspicious of the proposals being developed by Inva, seeing them as naïve and as perhaps too people oriented or 'caring'. Maddy's support for this was respected but it too was taken less seriously than it might have been, early on, probably because of her gender, work background and relative youth. Inva and Maddy, however, would no doubt have argued that they were the more business and strategically oriented ones, in the long-term sense, because they could see the necessity of adopting a higher HR strategy if the organisation was going to perform well into the long term.

Human resource decision making does not just occur with regard to the sort of strategic matters that Inva Gordon and her colleagues were tackling. Decisions are made from day to day about which potential employee to recruit, which employees to allocate to which task, which employee to promote, discipline or dismiss. Operational decisions and choices like these are made every day, and they are just as liable to be influenced by ambiguity and differences of interest as are the more strategic types of decision that we have just been looking at.

Selection, choice and discrimination in human resourcing

Human resourcing involves ensuring that work organisations have the necessary human skills, knowledge and capabilities that can be turned into work efforts which will enable the organisation to continue into the future. In practice, this means that decisions regularly have to be made about specific human individuals and about how they are to be treated within a potential or an actual employment relationship. Human resourcing decisions about recruitment and selection, allocation of tasks and rewards, promotions, dismissals and redundancies are routinely made in employing organisations, typically through the combined efforts of human resourcing or personnel specialists and managers who have a more direct authority relationship with the employee. The concern is with getting the 'right person' for a post, a reward, a punishment or a redundancy notice.

Selecting the 'right person' in all of these areas of human resourcing work is, generally speaking, a matter of achieving a decision that is right in two senses. First, the decision needs to be 'right' in the sense that the person selected is the most appropriate one to do a particular job, say, or to go on a particular training course. Second, the decision needs to be 'right' in that it is seen to be broadly fair and acceptable to whatever individuals, groups or authorities that might take an interest in that decision. At the simpler level, this second criterion means that neither the individual employee themselves nor any other employee or manager is likely to be left with a grievance that might lead them to behave in an organisationally disruptive way following the decision. At a more complex level, it means that the decision should neither contribute to a general atmosphere of injustice or low trust within the organisation nor lead to legal actions against the organisation because the employer can be shown to have unfairly treated or discriminated against an employee in a manner which has been deemed to be illegal in that society – with regard, say, to that employee's gender or race.

For these various reasons, there is considerable pressure on human resourcing decision makers to make the 'right decision'. A 'wrong decision' can be very costly in a financial sense as well as highly damaging to an organisation's general performance or public reputation. Personnel specialists have therefore been increasingly pressured to find ways of making managers feel confident that they are making the best possible choices when they make selection decisions about employees – when they discriminate between one person and another as a potential employee or a candidate for reallocation, promotion, reward, punishment or dismissal. Discrimination between one person and another is at the heart of all of these processes. And discrimination means making human judgements that always and inevitably have an ethical dimension to them. To treat one person one way and another person another way inevitably raises questions of justice, fairness, right and wrong. This is something that often makes managers feel uncomfortable – as does the ambiguity and unpredictability inevitably accompanying decisions about human beings and how they are going to behave in the future.

It is perhaps instructive that the term 'discrimination' is widely applied in the employment context only to what might be termed socially unacceptable choices. The notion that there could be a non-discriminatory selection is clearly nonsense (to choose or select is, by definition, to discriminate). Yet it is almost as if managers are trying to convince themselves that they are not discriminating at all and a lot of personnel or human resourcing practice over the years has appeared to support such a possibility. Attempts have thus been made to develop a *rationalistic and bureaucratic personnel management technology* that not only removes ethical uneasiness from personnel decision making but also plays down the ambiguity and unpredictability that is inevitably associated with judgements made by some human beings about others. Managers have wanted to be equipped with an efficient and neutral set of procedures and technologies which can measure and calculate an employee's, or a potential employee's, appropriateness for treatment of one kind or another (recruitment, promotion, etc.).

It would be foolish to criticise managers, inside and outside HR departments, for trying to devise procedures that enable the best possible person to be chosen for any particular role or treatment or for trying to make that choice in a way that will be deemed to be legal and regarded as generally fair by all concerned. However, there is a considerable danger of managers having too much faith in the ethical neutrality and the predictive powers of human resourcing or personnel techniques and procedures. As we will shortly hear Francesca Carrbridge argue with regard to selection decisions generally, 'At the end of the day a manager must recognise that a choice of one person rather than another involves basic human judgement, intuition and trusting to good fortune. You've got to keep these basic human judgements under control with personnel procedures that try to keep things fair and balanced. But all the selection techniques, personality tests and equal opportunity procedures in the world cannot replace simple human guesswork, a trust in one's "gut feel" and the subjective feeling that you are being as fair as possible when you choose Mrs X rather than Mr Y.'

Activity 10.5

Read what Francesca Carrbridge has to say in Case 10.4 about the difference between her approach to employment decision making and that of her predecessor, Dag Dunearn, and try to identify the different sets of assumptions, or styles of 'framing' reality, which each of them tends adopt with regard to:

- the nature of work organisations;

- the nature of human beings.

To do this, it should be helpful to draw on the distinction between systems-control and process-relational thinking that has been used throughout previous chapters and is summarised in Table 1.4 (p. 30), having been introduced, with regard to work organisations in Chapter 2, p. 30, and with regard to human beings in Chapter 3, p. 94.

Francesca dismantles the people-processing sausage machine

I noticed, Francesca, that you very much played down the importance of the personality tests that your staff had carried out when it came to the final discussions at the end of today's appointment process.

Yes, I prefer to pay as little attention as possible to personality test results.

Which raises the question of why you use these tests, doesn't it?

Of course it does. When I first came into HR work, I used to argue vehemently against their use. I felt that they were a form of pseudo-science that managers might use as a sort of crutch. I feared that test results and 'advice from psychologists' might discourage managers from standing on their own two feet and making basic human judgements that they would have to stand by and cope with once the decision had been made. I didn't want to let managers believe that there is such a thing as the 'right person', let alone someone with the 'right personality' for any particular post. I did a psychology degree myself and was very aware of how poor a predictor of future job performance research shows these things to be. I did my degree dissertation on this at university and what struck me most strongly was not just the poor predictive power of these tests but the point that several writers made about how a person's job performance is much more likely to be influenced by how they are treated once they are in a job than by so-called personality attributes that they bring to the job. That's a pretty powerful thought, isn't it?

Yes, it is. Perhaps we can come back to it.

I just want to stress the importance of managers realising that a selection decision involves a fallible human choice – it is not the outcome of a magic personnel technique. I want them to take responsibility for their decisions. This is really important because it is often how they subsequently deal with the person once they are appointed that makes that appointment a successful or an unsuccessful one.

I see. But you still haven't explained why as HR director here you spend time and money on occupational testing, something you appear to be against on principle.

I don't oppose all kinds of occupational testing. I'm very happy to use tests which check that people actually have the aptitudes that we are looking for in certain employees. I wouldn't employ an assembly worker who has to manipulate tiny electronic parts who could not pass a standard manual dexterity test any more than I'd take on an office trainee who could not pass a basic literacy test, a sales worker who could not pass a verbal reasoning test or someone to work in our pay office here who failed a numeracy test.

Your problem is with personality tests, then?

It is. Or rather it was. What I recognised after a while was that managers in selection processes did not generally come to rely on test results to anything like the extent that I feared. The tendency that I have observed across many organisations, and years of experience, is that they only take notice of what the testers say when it tends to confirm what their own judgement is telling them. Contrary indications are just ignored.

So why bother with them?

I decided after fighting several battles, especially with a couple of chief executives I worked with, that it wasn't worth it. To put it simply, it appears to make a lot of senior managers feel better if they think that something sort of 'scientific' has gone on somewhere within the selection process. I think it plays a sort of symbolic role for a lot of managers – it is a talisman that makes them feel better about the rather chancy thing they are doing when they are making a decision to appoint, say, someone on £50,000 a year whose later underperformance could cause major difficulties. Recruitment and selection – let alone promotion and deployment decisions – involve a great deal of guesswork. They are very much a gamble, much of the time. And managers are often queasy about this. They feel better if certain procedures have been followed that appear to have something rational or objective about them. I've come to live with this – as long as it does not involve managers denying their responsibility for the decisions they have made, as I just explained. I've therefore become tolerant of the practice of using some personality testing. I'd much prefer to save time and money and drop them though.

Is cost the only problem you have with these tests now?

Oh, I still don't like them. But I admit my predecessor here put me off them. I think I associate testing with his general way of doing HR, or personnel, work.

This is the man you replaced?

Dag Dunearn was a testing maniac. I used to have major battles with him, as his deputy. He used all sorts of tests, some that are relatively uncontroversial as well as some of the more marginal ones, like graphology, to screen out certain applicants for jobs – rejecting them before the managers whose area the job was in had even got to see their applications. Imagine that: you don't even get to have your application put in front of a departmental manager, let alone get an interview, because some charlatan retained by a personnel manager says your handwriting indicates that you are an unreliable person.

But your problems with his approach went further than this?

Indeed. We just didn't see the world in the same way, let alone how you should do personnel work. In the end, the other top managers decided he had to go. He was simply too inflexible, bureaucratic and officious. So I got his job and I think I am well respected. I do put limits on managers' freedom to manoeuvre – over matters like equal opportunities and other areas where employment legislation affects us. And I am fairly bureaucratic in areas where you need to be bureaucratic – over things like accurate employee records and managers following proper procedures in areas like health and safety, discipline, induction, appraisal and all that. But managers generally understand why these things have to be done and realise that I am happy to see all sorts of innovation and experimentation occurring as long as the basic and necessary procedures are followed.

How was it before you took over then?

Dag took what I call a sausage machine approach to HR. He saw the organisation as a big system that ran on sausages. The job of the personnel department, as it was called then, was to act as a sausage machine, producing sausages of the right size and the right type at the right time for each job that had to be done. I don't think he could tell the difference between sausage making and people processing. He would make sure that the organisation contained the right proportion of sausages with black skins and the designated number of disabled sausages, as well as maintaining what he deemed was a correct balance between male and female sausages – if you'll excuse the analogy here. He believed there was a formula for choosing the 'right' person for every job. Every person, just like a sausage, had a fixed set of properties and the job of personnel was to calculate what sort of characteristics were required for every job in the organisation – and then the right sausage would be served up for that post. Do you follow me?

I'm not sure – you are stretching the analogy a bit. Give me an example.

Well, what I had in mind was the way that, whenever there was a vacancy, no action would be taken by the personnel department even to advertise it until the manager concerned had produced a meticulous job description, accompanied by a detailed person specification which would set out in detail exactly what sort of person (I nearly said sausage) that they wanted the personnel department to find for them.

And the problem with this?

Dag saw the organisation's job structure as a much more fixed thing than it is in practice. Managers often said to me that they would be happy to consider a variety of different candidates, with various different strengths, for appointment to an area where there was a vacancy. If they found someone generally useful, then they could adapt the job to fit the person. This went totally against Dag's view of organisations as machines that require human cogs to make them run. He saw his job as getting exactly the right human cog for every little piece of the organisational machine. I remember an argument I had with him over this. He told me that I misunderstood professional personnel management – the basis of which was to make sure that round pegs were found for round holes and square pegs for square holes. It was totally ridiculous, in his view, to go changing the shapes of the 'organisational holes' to make sure that whatever pegs you might chance upon would fit into them. It seems like quite a good idea to me, however.

He was rather mechanistic, you are saying?

Yes, and it was very counterproductive. The business was increasingly requiring flexible and adaptive workers who would themselves influence the jobs they would do once recruited. And Dag was standing in the way of this. His efforts over equal opportunities were equally counterproductive. On several occasions, for example, he held up important selection or promotion interviews for months, until he could get a list of candidates that he deemed to have a reasonable race and gender balance.

The means were getting in the way of the ends for which they were devised, you could say.

Exactly.

And you avoid this happening?

As far as I can. I am passionately concerned about fairness and equal opportunities. But if I were to get obsessed with setting up checks and controls in these areas, like Dag did, it would take us back to a situation where working towards gender and ethnic diversity would simply have a bad name with managers. And they would do everything they could to get round equal opportunity measures wherever they could. My approach is to get managers to believe in the spirit and principle of fairness and equality. It may sound idealistic but I prefer to see the organisation as a sort of moral community – a place in which people can more or less trust each other. That's what I work towards anyway. People are not fixed quantities or objects, like sausages, and I think that if they are encouraged to work together in a good atmosphere they will both develop themselves, as individuals, and change the organisation so that it can cope better with all the changes that are being thrown at it.

So you are much more open and flexible about processes like selection and recruitment?

Indeed, but not only that. Management is not just a technical matter, in my view. When you go through an interviewing process, for example, you are both trying to get to know the candidates, as human beings, and enabling them to get to know you as an employer with a certain culture and set of cultural values. The process is a sort of negotiation between the potential employee and the potential employer. You, as a recruiter, cannot really know what any of these people is really going to be like if you take them on. And they cannot be too sure of just what it is going to be like working for you. So there is a process of weighing each other up. This involves a great deal of ambiguity and awareness that some people are simply more skilled at presenting themselves to a prospective employer than others (from the completing of the application form to what they both mention and avoid mentioning in an interview). And what this all adds up to is that managers have to deploy the basic human skills of eliciting helpful responses from people and judging the likelihood of one person being a better bet for the organisation than another.

That's how you get the right people for the organisation?

No. The 'right person', as you put it, would be the one who you could guarantee would do the job as required. That is just not possible. It is, as I've just said, a matter of who is 'the better bet'. As I was stressing earlier, some of the most important determinants of how well someone does the job (whatever the job turns out to be like, once they start doing it) are ones that arise after the appointment of the individual. How a person is treated once recruited is surely just as important as the recruitment and selection process that brought them into the organisation. On various occasions I have seen what looked like the perfect appointment turning out to be a disaster because the person's abilities were either misused or under used, once appointed. And by the same token, I've seen some potentially high-risk appointments turning out to be great successes because the managers involved worked hard to use the recruits' talents to the best effect. I want managers to recognise all of this and not see HR as a source of administrative and psychological black magic that can find them the 'right person' for every job.

You want managers to make their own judgements and take on their own risks?

Yes, supported by whatever expertise we have to offer in HR. At the end of the day a manager must recognise that a choice of one person rather than another involves basic human judgement, intuition and trusting to good fortune. You've got to keep these basic human judgements under control with personnel procedures that try to keep things fair and balanced. But all the selection techniques, personality tests and equal opportunity procedures in the world cannot replace simple human guesswork, a trust in one's 'gut feel' and the subjective feeling that you are being as fair as possible when you choose Mrs X rather than Mr Y.

It is apparent from what Francesca Carrbridge says that she is sensitive to the tensions we identified earlier as typically, if not inevitably, existing between HR and other managers. She manages those tensions by allowing managers flexibility and the chance to innovate, as long as they conform with the basic principles that she lays down to fulfil the HR role of maintaining the organisational workforce as a whole (equal opportunities, compliance with legislation, induction and appraisal procedures, etc.). Her predecessor, Dag Dunearn, on the other hand, exacerbated those tensions by dictating to managers and treating them in an inflexible and officious way. This led to his downfall, it would appear, which Francesca relates to his view of the nature of work organisations. She talks of his view of the organisation as a big machine that requires appropriate employees in the same way that a machine requires cogs. This fits with what we have called a systems-control way of 'framing' organisations. It sees the structure of jobs in the organisation as something that is pre-decided in the organisational design – thus making it possible for the personnel department to ask a departmental manager for a precise 'job description' accompanied by a clear 'person specification'. The candidate who fits that specification – with this 'fit' being measured wherever possible by the use of neutral and objective tests – is judged to be the 'right person for the job'. This suggests that Dag sees human beings, and not just organisations, in systems-control terms. Each human being 'has' a particular personality or an otherwise similarly fixed set of characteristics – ones that they will carry forward into their subsequent appointment or promotion, regardless of the circumstances in which they find themselves after that appointment.

Francesca scorns this 'sausage machine' approach to HR. Her analogy is a little forced at times but it gives a clear indication of what she has tried to move away from in her regime. She sees the organisation more as a human community, she explains, in which human and fallible judgements are made about employees and prospective employees. The organisation is a much more ambiguous place and every decision has its moral implications, she suggests. The selecting of people is part of a *process*, which continues long after the actual appointment decision is made. It is not part of a sausage-making system. Managers have to take responsibility for their judgements, not just acknowledging the fallibility of their choice making but accepting responsibility for making the appointment a success after it has been made. All of this suggests a process-relational way of 'framing' both organisations and people. The organisation is seen as a more flexible and negotiable set of arrangements than a

FIGURE 10.3   The people-processing sausage machine

systems-control approach would point to. This makes it possible for managers to consider selecting a generally appropriate candidate for an appointment and for the task structure and way of working to be modified once that person becomes involved in it. But Francesca not only avoids regarding the organisation as a fixed entity. She also sees human beings as adaptable – and not as a fixed set of attributes or personality characteristics. How they behave in the organisation is a matter of the processes that they become involved in and the set of relationships in which they play a part.

A process-relational framing of the 'people processing' aspect of human resourcing is one that locates choices over such matters as recruitment, promotion, appraisal or deployment within the employment relationship between employees and the employing organisation. The organisation does not itself, in any direct sense, employ people, of course. Managers do this in the organisation's name, and managers are fallible human beings working within bounded rationality and with their judgements shaped by personal beliefs and prejudices as well as by personal and group interests. In effect, the HR selection processes in which managers engage are bargaining processes (see Newell, 2004 and Further Reading on 'people processing' aspects of HRM, p. 447) – albeit bargaining processes in which the parties are rarely equals. They are processes within which an implicit contract is created between employer and employee, an often vague and ambiguous contract that is subject to all sorts of change when the individual finds themselves in the post for which they were selected. Also, their *orientation to work* becomes subject to changes both within and outside the work setting (Chapter 4, pp. 115–24). Bargaining is also quite likely to go on between the managers taking part in the selection process themselves. Most HR decisions are made within the sort of 'garbage can' process we examined earlier (Chapter 6, pp. 215–21) with a variety of different managerial and personal views and interests coming into play and contributing to the overall *negotiated order* (Chapter 2, pp. 59–65) of the organisation. And, just as any selection decision is influenced by how the managerial selectors operate, it will clearly also be influenced by how the employee or respective employee presents themselves. A shrewd candidate for a job, a promotion or a posting will tell credible and appealing stories about themselves and who they are and what they can do, drawing on appropriate *discursive resources* to impress selectors. We saw his very clearly with Mike Kilrock in Case 3.4 (p. 103), and his drawing on discourses of *leadership, entrepreneurship* and *professionalism* to win himself a promotion in his funeral directing organisation.

We do not know how successful Mike Kilrock was in his bid for promotion. Whenever a candidate for selection presents themselves to selectors, they take a risk. They cannot know how their presentation of self and the story they construct about themselves will be received. In the same way, the managers who choose or reject such a candidate cannot know with any certainty that the outcome will be the best one that they could have made. They too are taking a risk.

'At the end of the day', to borrow Francesca Carrbridge's expression from Case 10.4 in the present chapter, managerial skills are very much ones of making basic human judgements, shrewd guesses and bargains that will contribute to a greater or a lesser extent to the long-term performance of the organisation that employs them. This analysis applies to human resourcing and other aspects of organisational and managerial work alike.

Summary

In this chapter the following key points have been made:

- It is both unrealistic and morally dubious to regard human beings themselves as 'human resources'. It is more appropriate to treat *human resources* as the human efforts, skills and capabilities that an organisation requires to be able to operate into the long term.

- Human resourcing issues affect every employee in a work organisation – managers and non-managers alike. And, within management, involvement in human resourcing matters is necessarily a concern of both human resourcing specialists and non-HR managers.

- Human Resource Management (HRM) is a term that is used in a confusing variety of ways. It was largely developed as a concept by academic observers trying to detect significant changes in employment practices. Particular confusion has been caused by academic writers' attempts to differentiate 'HRM' from 'personnel management'. Such a differentiation is only very loosely connected to a trend among practitioners to re-label personnel departments as Human Resources (HR) departments.

- Human resource strategy making is central to broader practices of strategy making in employing organisations and the common tendency to see it as following from – or serving – the main business strategy of an organisation can be misleading. It is more helpful to see it as *both* following from and contributing to the main process of corporate strategy making.

- The human resourcing function of modern work organisations can be understood, in part, as helping to cope with some basic tensions or contradictions inherent in industrial capitalist ways of organising economies and societies. In particular, it has to handle the difficulties caused by the fact that although people are taught to think of themselves as free choice-making citizens in such societies, they are nevertheless subjected to supervisory and managerial control at work. Managerial ways have to be found of both allowing a certain amount of discretion to employees and finding ways of exerting a degree of control over them. The involvement of HR functions in both the 'care' and the 'control' of employees and their concern with both 'welfare' and 'efficiency' reflects this.

- The HR role in organisations is a particularly strategic one because it tends to take on responsibilities for maintaining integration of the workforce at a corporate level and for looking at longer-term employment issues that departmental managers are less likely to be concerned with. This contributes to the tensions and conflicts that often arise between HR specialists and other managers.

- Human resourcing strategies vary from organisation to organisation with some being closer to a *high commitment* pattern of arrangements and practices and others closer to a *low commitment* pattern. The pattern emerging in any particular organisation will be the outcome of various managerial preferences and values on the one hand and certain managerially interpreted contingent or circumstantial factors on the other. All things being equal, a high commitment type of employment strategy will tend to be adopted when managers perceive the employee constituencies to be strategically problematic, in the sense of creating uncertainties for long-term continuation. This might result, for example, from a highly skilled or educated level of workforce being required to operate a relatively complex technology. This would lead employees to place high demands on the employer in terms of both intrinsic and extrinsic rewards. When employee constituencies are much less problematic, on the other hand, and are less able to make strong demands on the employer, for example, there are cost and efficiency pressures on managers to adopt a *low commitment* type of HR strategy.

- The *high* or *low commitment* HR strategic option is closely related to a whole set of other options: ones in areas ranging from job design and pay systems to strategy-making procedures and cultural patterns. In all of these areas an *indirect control* approach will be associated with a *high commitment* HR strategy and direct control approach associated with a *low commitment* HR strategy.

● In certain circumstances, organisations may adopt a dual human resourcing strategy, applying different types of strategy to different parts of the overall workforce.

● Human resourcing decisions involving the selection of individuals in areas such as recruitment, promotion, reward, deployment and dismissal are made every day in work organisations. There has been a tendency for a rational and calculative *personnel technology* to be applied to these choices. This involves strongly bureaucratic procedures and the heavy use of such devices as psychological tests. Such a technology is intended to help select individuals in a way that will be deemed efficient, acceptable and fair. However, it tends to become restrictive and counterproductive. Its use can be associated with a systems-control way of thinking about work organisations and people. A more realistic process-relational way of thinking indicates that selection and discrimination processes are highly ambiguous and are dependent on basic human processes of judgement, guesswork, chance taking, debate and negotiation. Selection and HR choice processes in general are better seen as parts of broader and more continuous processes of bargaining and adjustment in which both organisational arrangements and human beings themselves change and adapt within the ongoing negotiated order of the organisation.

Recommended reading

A rigorous critique of how HRM tends to be studied, together with a research-based case study which illustrates an alternative and more 'critical' approach to the subject tying in closely with the material in the present Chapter 10 is to be found in Tony Watson, 'Human resource management and critical social science analysis' (*Journal of Management Studies*, 41(3): 447–467, 2004). But to get an appreciation of the various different facets of contemporary HR or employment management practices it is helpful to read selectively from edited texts such as those by Tom Redman and Adrian Wilkinson, *Contemporary Human Resource Management* (Harlow: FT Prentice Hall, 2003) or John Leopold, Lynette Harris and Tony Watson, *The Strategic Management of Human Resources* (London: FT Prentice Hall, 2005) or Peter Boxall, John Purcell and Patrick Wright (eds), *The Oxford Handbook of Human Resource Management* (Oxford: Oxford University Press, 2006). For those with a special interest in the strategic aspects of HR then Peter Boxall and John Purcell's *Strategy and Human Resource Management* (Basingstoke: Palgrave, 2003) is recommended. And for those wanting to understand trends in employment relations (or 'industrial relations') Peter Ackers and Adrian Wilkinson's *Understanding Work and Employment* (Oxford: Oxford University Press, 2003) is suggested.

Further reading

Further reading HRM, the academic literature

Beech, N. (1998), 'Literature review: rhetoric and discourse in HRM', *Management Learning*, 29(1): 110–113

Beer, M., Spector, B., Lawrence, P.R., Mill, Q.D. and Walton, R.E. (1984) *Managing Human Assets*, Boston, MA: Harvard Business School Press

Guest, D. (1989) 'Personnel and HRM: can you tell the difference?', *Personnel Management*, January: 48–51

Guest, D. (1990) 'Human resource management and the American Dream', *Journal of Management Studies*, 27(4): 377–397

Hart, T.J. (1993) 'HRM – time to exorcize the militant tendency', *Employee Relations*, 15(3): 29–36

Kamoche, K. (2001) *Understanding Human Resource Management*, Buckingham: Open University Press

Legge, K. (2004) *Human Resource Management: Rhetorics and realities*, Basingstoke: Palgrave

Mabey, C., Skinner, D. and Clark, T. (eds) (1998) *Experiencing Human Resource Management*, London: Sage

Marchington, M. and Grugulis, I. (2000). ' "Best practice" human resource management: perfect opportunity or dangerous illusion?', *International Journal of Human Resource Management*, 11(4): 905–925

Noon, M. (1992) 'HRM: A map, model or theory?' in P. Blyton and P. Turnbull (eds) *Reassessing Human Resource Management*, London: Sage

Redman, T. and Wilkinson, A. (eds) *Contemporary Human Resource Management*, Harlow: FT Prentice Hall

Steyaert, C. and Janssens, M. (1999) 'Human and inhuman resource management: saving the subject of HRM', *Organization*, 6(2): 181–198

Storey, J. (1992) *Developments in the Management of Human Resources*, Oxford: Basil Blackwell

Storey, J. (ed.) (2001) *Human Resource Management: A critical text, 2nd edition*, London: Thomson Learning

Watson, T.J. (1995) 'In search of HRM: beyond the rhetoric and reality distinction or the dog that didn't bark', *Personnel Review*, 24(4): 6–16

Watson, T.J. (2004) 'Human resource management and critical social science analysis', *Journal of Management Studies*, 41(3): 447–467

Watson, T.J. and Watson, D.H. (1999) 'Human resourcing in practice: managing employment issues in the university', *Journal of Management Studies*, 36(4): 483–504

Further reading HR and other managers

Caldwell, R. (2003) 'The changing roles of personnel managers: old ambiguities, new uncertainties', *Journal of Management Studies*, 40(4): 983–1004

Gennard, J. and Kelly, J. (1994) 'Human resource management: the views of personnel directors', *Human Resource Management Journal*, 5(1): 15–32

Guest, D. and King, Z. (2004) 'Power, innovation and problem-solving: the personnel manager's three steps to heaven', *Journal of Management Studies*, 41(3): 401–423

Legge, K. (1993) 'The role of personnel specialists: centrality or marginalization?' in J. Clark (ed.) *Human Resource Management and Technical Change*, London: Sage, 20–42

Purcell, J. (2001) 'Personnel and human resource managers: power, prestige and potential', *Human Resource Management Journal*, 11(3): 3–4

Torrington, D. (1998) 'Crisis and opportunity in HRM: the challenge for the personnel function' in P. Sparrow and M. Marchington (eds) *Human Resource Management: The new agenda*, London: FT Pitman

Torrington, D. and Hall, L. (1996) 'Chasing the rainbow: how seeking status through strategy misses the point for the personnel function', *Employee Relations*, 18(6): 79–96

Tyson, S. and Fell, A. (1986) *Evaluating the Personnel Function*, London: Hutchinson

Watson, D.H. (1988) *Managers of Discontent: Trade union officers and industrial relations managers*, London: Routledge

Watson, T.J. (1977) *The Personnel Managers*, London: Routledge

Watson, T.J (2001) 'Speaking professionally – occupational anxiety and discursive ingenuity among human resourcing specialists' in S. Whitehead and M. Dent (eds) *Managing Professional Identities*, London: Routledge

Further reading Strategic HRM

Boxall, P. (1996) 'The strategic HRM debate and the resource-based view of the firm', *Human Resource Management Journal*, 6(3): 59–75

Devanna, M.A., Fombrun, C.J. and Tichy, N.M. (1984) 'A framework for strategic human resource management' in C. Fombrun, N.M. Tichy and M.A. Devanna (eds) *Strategic Human Resource Management*, Chichester: Wiley

Fombrun, C., Tichy, N.M. and Devanna, M.A. (eds) (1984) *Strategic Human Resource Management*, New York: Wiley

Gratton, L., Hope Hailey, V., Stiles P. and Truss, C. (1999) *Strategic Human Resource Management*, Oxford: Oxford University Press

Jacques, R. (1999) 'Developing a tactical approach to engaging with "strategic" HRM', *Organization*, 6(2): 199–222

Kamoche, K. (1994) 'A critique and a proposed reformulation of strategic human resource management', *Human Resource Management Journal*, 4(4): 29–47

Kamoche, K. (1996) 'Strategic human resource management within resource capability view of the firm', *Journal of Management Studies*, 33(2): 213–233

Mabey, C., Salaman, G. and Storey, J. (1998) *Strategic Human Resource Management, 2nd edition*, Oxford: Blackwell

Procter, S.J., Rowlinson, M., McArdle, L., Hassard, J. and Forrester, P. (1994) 'Flexibility, politics and strategy: in defence of the model of the flexible firm', *Work, Employment and Society*, 8(2): 221–242

Purcell, J. (1995) 'Corporate strategy and its link with human resource management strategy' in J. Storey (ed.) *Human Resource Management: A critical text*, London: Routledge

Sánchez-Runde, C. (2001) 'Strategic human resource management and the new employment relationships: a research review and agenda' in J. Gual and

J.E. Ricart (eds) *Strategy, Organization and the Changing Nature of Work*, Cheltenham: Elgar

Schuler, R.S., Jackson, S.E. and Storey, J. (2001) 'HRM and its link with strategic management' in J. Storey (ed.), *Human Resource Management: A critical text, 2nd edition*, London: Thomson Learning

Watson, T.J. (2004) 'Organisations, strategies and human resourcing' in J. Leopold, L. Harris and T.J. Watson (eds) *The Strategic Management of Human Resources*, London: FT Prentice Hall, 6–33

Further reading 'People processing' aspects of HRM

Anderson, N. and Ostroff, C. (1997) 'Selection as socialization' in N. Anderson and P. Herriot (eds) *International Handbook of Selection and Assessment*, Chichester: Wiley

Campbell, J. and Knapp, D. (eds) (2001) *Exploring the Limits in Personnel Selection and Classification*, Mahwah, NJ: Lawrence Erlbaum Associates

Cooper D. and Robertson, I.T. (1995) *The Psychology of Personnel Selection*, London: Routledge

Dipboye, R. (1992) *Selection Interviews: Process perspectives*, Cincinnati, OH: South Western

Judge, T.A. and Cable, D.M. (1997) 'Applicant personality, organizational culture and organization attraction', *Personnel Psychology*, 50: 359–394

McDaniel, M.A., Whetzel, D.L., Schmidt, F.L. and Maurer, S.D. (1994) 'The validity of the employment interviews: a comprehensive review and meta analysis', *Journal of Applied Psychology*, 79: 599–616

Newell, S. (2004) 'Assessment, selection and evaluation' in J. Leopold, L. Harris and T.J. Watson (eds) *The Strategic Management of Human Resources*, London: FT Prentice Hall, 140–177

Newell, S. and Shackleton, V. (2001) 'Selection and assessment as an interactive decision–action process' in T. Redman and A. Wilkinson (eds) *Contemporary Human Resource Management*, Harlow: FT Prentice Hall

Newton, T. and Findlay, P. (1996) 'Playing God? The performance of appraisal', *Human Resource Management Journal*, 6(3): 42–58

Silverman, D. and Jones, J. (1976) *Organisational Work: The language of grading and the grading of language*, London: Macmillan

Townley, B. (1989) 'Selection and appraisal: reconstituting social relations?' in J. Storey (ed.) *New Perspectives on HRM*, London: Routledge

Townley, B. (1993) 'Performance appraisal and the emergence of management', *Journal of Management Studies*, 3(2): 221–238

Semester 2

Processes and practices

Entering the workplace: selection and assessment

Chapter 3

SELECTION AND ASSESSMENT

Sue Newell

Introduction: selection from a decision-making perspective

A given topic can always be viewed from a number of different perspectives. Traditionally, selection and assessment have been viewed from a psychometric perspective. They are treated as representing a measurement problem. There are clearly individual differences (both physical and psychological), which mean that certain people will be more suited to some jobs than others. From a psychometric perspective then, selection and assessment are concerned with finding methods to measure these individual differences more accurately so that individuals and jobs can be appropriately matched.

In this chapter, while not ignoring this psychometric tradition, we will adopt a rather different perspective, which can help us to explore some issues in selection and assessment that may be underemphasised by the traditional perspective. We will view selection and assessment from a decision-making perspective (Brunsson 1982, 1989), where a decision is a conscious choice between at least two alternative actions. We will also consider decisions that are made in respect of both selection and development, both of which involve making decisions based on the assessment of individuals. Thus, in terms of selection, a representative (or group of representatives) of the recruiting organisation chooses between a number of candidates in order to select the individual who best fits the requirements of a particular job for which there is a vacancy. These decisions are made on the basis of some kind of assessment of the relative suitability of a group of potential individuals who might fill the vacancy.

While selection involves decisions about who will best fit a particular job vacancy, the same or similar processes of assessment are also increasingly used within organisations to make developmental decisions related to the promotion potential of internal employees. Thus, it is recognised that it is necessary to prepare current employees for taking on more senior roles within the organisation, so that leadership crises are averted. However, it is also recognised that not all existing employees will be suitable for these more senior roles. Assessment methods are therefore used to identify the developmental potential of existing employees. The result is that choices are made about who will be groomed and developed and for which senior jobs.

The emphasis in the selection literature has typically been on the decision made by the recruiting organisation. However, it is also the case that candidates are making decisions – to apply (or not) for a particular job vacancy, to turn up (or not) to an interview, or to take (or decline) an offered job. In terms of assessment for developmental purposes there has always been more recognition that the candidate is making decisions as well as the assessors. Indeed, with the increasing emphasis on self-direction, assessment exercises are used as much to provide the individual with evidence to make career path choices as they are for the organisation to make promotion decisions. In this chapter we will consider the selection and assessment decision-making processes from the perspective of both the organisation and the candidates.

The decision-making perspective has been dominated by normative research, which prescribes how decisions should be made (Brunsson 1982, 1989). This assumes that the desire is to make decisions as 'rational' as possible. The prescription for making decisions rational is to follow a sequence of specified steps: understand the situation and identify the problem(s); generate potential solutions to the problem(s); systematically evaluate each solution; select the best solution; monitor and evaluate the results; identify the problem(s) etc. This rational, decision-making model has also implicitly underpinned selection and assessment research. Thus, in selection or development decisions, the objective has been to make this decision as objective and rational as possible in order to select the 'right' or 'best' person for the job. It is possible therefore to look at the steps prescribed in the rational, decision-making process and apply them to the literature on selection and assessment. Here we critically apply this rational model to the selection and assessment decision-making processes. In so doing, we also identify the limitations of this rational model and suggest an alternative way of viewing these processes that may bear more relation to what actually happens in practice.

This chapter does not deal with recruitment and election in general.[1] Recruitment and selection involves making predictions about future behaviour so that decisions can be made about who will be most suitable for a particular job. It can be viewed as a process by which the organisation tries accurately to match the individual to the job and can be compared to completing a jigsaw puzzle. Recruitment and selection is a process of selecting the correct jigsaw piece (the 'right' individual) from the incorrect pieces (the 'wrong' individuals) to fit into a particular hole in a jigsaw puzzle (Newell and Shackleton 2001).

Selection and assessment as a rational decision-making process

Each of the steps in the rational decision-making model can be applied to the steps in selection and assessment.

UNDERSTAND THE SITUATION AND IDENTIFY THE PROBLEM(S): ORGANISATIONAL REVIEW AND JOB ANALYSIS

The first step typically identified in the selection process is to undertake a review of the situation to determine that a recruitment need actually exists. Even if an individual has left a job, this should not automatically mean that a job vacancy is presumed. It is necessary to establish that there are not alternative and more effective ways of filling the gap left by the departing employee. For example, this may be a chance for reassigning these tasks to other employees and in so doing provide opportunities for employee development. Alternatively,

---

[1] Several different recruitment methods can be used (internal and external) including advertising in newspapers and trade journals, placing notices in job centres, employing agents, attending careers fairs and posting job advertisements on the internet. Survey evidence shows, however, that the most significant single recruitment method is word of mouth. Decisions about which method or combination of methods to use have to be based on the budget available, the number of applicants considered necessary and the current size of the labour market concerned (Taylor 2002, p.209). The documentation used in the recruitment exercise has a wider impact in that it conveys images of the organisation, its products and its overall philosophy. Legal issues have to be borne in mind when recruiting, particularly in the design and wording of adverts and in on-line channels (Taylor 2002). Furthermore, if the recruitment process generates insufficient applications, or too many unsuitable ones, it will prove expensive (Marchington and Wilkinson 2005). However, the purpose of this chapter is not to dwell on the subject of recruitment. This is well covered in other texts – e.g., Torrington *et al.* 2002; Beardwell *et al.*; Marchington and Wilkinson 2005 – and there is extensive guidance provided by ACAS on their website and in their guidebooks.

the tasks may be automated so that human resources are no longer required. Prior to developmental assessment, the rational model would prescribe succession planning be undertaken to identify the predicted gaps at senior levels for which people need to be groomed.

Once the situation has been reviewed to ensure that a job vacancy or succession gap actually exists, the next step is to conduct a thorough analysis of the particular job. Job analysis is used to gather information about a job in order to determine the key tasks and role requirements and so specify the kind of person most likely to be successful in that job. A problem with traditional job analysis is that it collects information about the job as it currently exists on the assumption that it will be similar in the future (Schneider and Konz 1989). Unfortunately, given the dynamic environment in which organisations operate, this is increasingly an unwarranted assumption. As a result, there is a need to develop new methods of job analysis which can identify the key tasks and the associated knowledge, skills and abilities (KSAs) that are required for jobs that are changing (Hough and Oswald 2000). Unfortunately, this aspect of the selection process has not been adequately scrutinised by scholars, so that job analysis techniques that are used are often problematic (Robertson and Smith 2001). One of the few examples to date of collecting data that is more future-oriented is provided by Landis *et al.* (1998). They begin with a traditional job analysis, collecting relevant information about the target jobs as they currently exist and then use panel discussion groups to develop a comprehensive list of tasks and KSAs. Then subject-matter expert groups are involved to identify how these tasks and KSAs are likely to change in the future.

The traditional person specification has given way to a focus on competencies (Boam and Sparrow 1992). Competencies are behavioural indicators that have been identified as relevant to a particular context. Roberts (1997, p.6) defines competence as 'all work-related personal attributes, knowledge, experience and skills and values that a person draws on to perform their work well'. There are a number of different approaches to identifying competencies, but they have a common focus on specifying 'outputs'. These are 'couched in terms of what an individual achieves and produces from a situation by managing it effectively' (Sparrow and Bognanno 1993, p.51). For example, Alldredge and Nilan (2000) describe the global leadership competency framework that was developed and used by 3M for assessment, development and succession.

Example: **The competencies needed for a diversity consultant**

Diversity consultants should:

- Understand the concept of diversity as it impacts four inter-related layers of the organization – individual, group and work team, interpersonal and organisational.

- Understand the client's business.

- Be able to connect diversity back to work processes and work design.

- Understand what drives their own personal biases and biases regarding individual differences.

- Understand systemic issues of discrimination, and apply an expansive definition of diversity.

- Discern the differences in the concepts of equal opportunity and affirmative action and diversity and inclusion.

- Understand both people and business issues and be prepared to confront difficult issues.

- Demonstrate constant renewal of technical knowledge and skills in the diversity area.

Source: Frase-Blunt 2004

The advantage of using a competency framework is that the focus is on actual behaviour – what a person can do or needs to be able to do – and there is no need to make inferences about personal qualities that might underpin this. Theoretically, this should allow for the fact that different individuals can achieve the same output, but using a rather different approach because of different knowledge, skills and abilities. Unfortunately, while this is true in theory, in practice competency approaches are often used in ways which specify process criteria as well as output or task criteria. In other words, the person is assessed not simply in terms of whether they successfully completed the task but also in terms of dimensions that are 'normally' expected to underpin successful task completion. This means there is a presumption of 'the right way' to complete a task, and the individual will be assessed against this 'right way', as well as against the task output itself.

Nevertheless, whether a job analysis (traditional or future-oriented) or competency analysis is undertaken, the goal is to describe the particular job, identify the task requirements and specify the kind of person most likely to fulfill these requirements.

GATHER INFORMATION AND MATERIALS TO HELP SOLVE THE PROBLEM: IDENTIFY APPROPRIATE ASSESSMENT METHODS

Once the job analysis has been completed, the next step is to identify methods that will allow individuals to be assessed and compared on the various KSAs or competencies identified as crucial for job success. Much effort has been devoted to this step from the psychometric perspective. The reason for this is that traditional assessment methods – unstructured interviews and references – have been shown to be very poor at measuring these important individual differences. The development of newer methods of assessment is considered in more detail below.

GENERATE POTENTIAL SOLUTIONS TO THE PROBLEM: RECRUITMENT

Once this initial phase has been completed and there is a clear idea about the kind of person wanted and the methods to be used to assess individuals, the next step is to attract a pool of applicants from which the 'right' person can be chosen. Where assessment is used for developmental purposes, recruitment will be internal and typically based on information gathered during appraisals as to which individuals are 'ready' and have the potential to be developed. Where an organisation is selecting for a particular job vacancy, recruitment can be internal or external. Internal recruitment, often involving promotion, may often be the better option since this reduces information uncertainty as candidates can be directly observed in the workplace over an extended period; the internal recruit will also already have firm-specific knowledge (Staffsud 2003). Moreover, external recruitment is expensive (Merrick 1997) and often does not produce the quality of candidates required (Fish and Mackim 2004). Nevertheless, companies will often need to recruit externally.

Matthews and Redman (1998) found that, despite such a large amount being spent on recruitment advertising, recruiters were not making the most effective use of it, because generally the advertisements were not well tailored to managerial requirements. In particular, they argue that recruitment advertisements need to be more specifically targeted to the group they are trying to attract. They advocate that this targeting should be done on the basis of market research to identify what the potential applicant is looking for in a recruitment advertisement. With regard to the content of advertisements they suggest that many do not contain enough information to attract the initial interest, especially of the casual job seeker.

For example, they found that one in five advertisements gave no details of salary level and job location, which have been shown to be key to gaining attention. Once attracted, potential applicants then seek further information from the advertisement to decide whether to apply. However, 59 per cent of the advertisements gave no information on minimum qualifications, which is useful to help applicants self-screen. At the same time, 71 per cent did give information on personal attributes required, despite this being condemned by prescriptive models of 'good' adverts (Redmond 1989).

Increasingly, companies are using the internet for advertising job vacancy information. This has the advantage of reaching a global audience, at least of potential recruits with access to this technology. Similarly, applicants are using the internet to submit their CVs, thus potentially speeding up the process of applying. A key advantage of such electronic applications is that CVs can be coded (e.g., in terms of the applicants' competencies) and stored electronically so that they can be easily searched, both for current job vacancies and for jobs in the future. This search can be done on a global basis provided that a company has a shared electronic database for storing and retrieving applicant information. Beyond recruitment, firms are also using the internet for actual selection, for example using computer-based testing that can be done virtually (Anderson 2003). For example, Bingham *et al.* (2002) describe how the Washington State Department of Personnel has introduced online application submissions and instant online screening and testing processes which score and identify candidates suitable for different positions. This has cut down the recruitment and selection process from several weeks to a few hours. The use of the internet for both recruitment and selection is likely to increase as accessibility and familiarity with this medium grow (Batram 2000, 2004).

SYSTEMATICALLY EVALUATE EACH SOLUTION: ASSESSMENT METHODS APPLIED TO CANDIDATES

Once a pool of recruits has been attracted, the assessment methods are applied in order to evaluate each individual against the KSAs or competencies identified as important for job success. For selection, presuming that there are more applicants than vacancies, a first step will be to pre-select those applicants who look potentially suitable. This is done typically on the basis of the application form and/or CV that has been sent in. Despite the widespread use of such pre-screening methods, research evidence suggests that they are not designed or used systematically (Keenan 1995). New methods of pre-screening are now being introduced, for example, as already indicated, pre-selection is often also done using online testing to screen potential applicants (Mooney 2002; Konradt *et al.* 2003). Other methods are also being introduced to get more direct detail about a candidate's background, for example using telephone interviews. Telephone interviews, however, can be costly, especially if there are large numbers of applicants to be contacted. Bauer *et al.* (2004) compared three types of selection screening methods – face-to-face interviews, telephone interviews and interactive voice response (IVR) screening (non-interpersonal screening). They found that although the IVR screening was rated lower on certain variables such as interpersonal treatment and openness, this method was no different in terms of structural fairness. Given the significantly lower costs of IVR screening they suggest that companies should evaluate which types of screening methods fit the recruitment strategy for a particular type of employee. From this initial screening, a smaller number of applicants will be assessed more fully, using whatever is considered to be the appropriate assessment method(s). The different methods of assessment are considered more fully later in the chapter.

SELECT 'BEST' SOLUTION: SELECTION OR DEVELOPMENT DECISION

This step in the decision-making cycle is seen to be the logical outcome of the previous steps. Once each candidate has been measured using the particular assessment methods, the data can be evaluated in a logical manner in order to select the 'best' candidate. Each candidate can be rated against the person specification or competency profile. The candidate who has all the specified essential characteristics and the most desirable characteristics should be selected for the job. Where assessment is used for developmental purposes the decision is more about which candidates are suitable for which senior positions within the organisation. Nevertheless, there is the same assumption that this can be done rationally and logically on the basis of the data accumulated from the assessment exercises.

MONITOR AND EVALUATE RESULTS: VALIDATION

Ratings of employee potential estimated during the selection or developmental assessment process can be compared with subsequent performance on the job. This provides the measure of validity. High correlations between the selection or development ratings (referred to as the predictor) and performance ratings (referred to as the criterion) would indicate that the decisions made during the assessment process were valid (and hence rational). Low correlations would indicate that decisions were not valid. Evidence of the criterion-related validity of traditional methods used to make selection decisions, i.e., the unstructured interview and references, suggests that neither of these methods results in valid predictions.

One particular problem with such validity studies is that the criteria against which the selection or development decisions are compared (i.e., measures of job performance) may themselves be inaccurate (Campbell 1990). The most typical criterion used is supervisory ratings, but research has demonstrated that these may vary widely in terms of accuracy. For example, Sundvik and Lindeman (1998) found that accuracy was dependent on the opportunity the supervisor had to observe the subordinate, especially in terms of the length of the supervisor–subordinate relationship. They also found that female supervisors are more accurate at rating than are males. More recently, Kacmar et al. (2003) similarly reported that job-performance ratings by supervisors were affected by communication frequency although they also found that this was moderated by the relationship between the supervisor and the subordinate.

From the rational, decision-making perspective, however, the key issue is to identify where selection or development decisions have been made that have not been good (i.e., where validity is poor) and to take this as the starting point for repeating the decision-making cycle in order to improve validity.

IDENTIFY PROBLEM

And so the cycle repeats itself!

The selection and assessment decision-making process in practice

While the rational, decision-making model can be applied to the selection and assessment process, and indeed underpins much of the literature on improving the validity of such decisions, research evidence suggests that, in practice, the decision process is often far removed from this ideal. This is true for decisions of all kinds, not just selection and development decisions. Thus, research has demonstrated that such rational decision making does not equate with reality. Rather, empirical research gives mostly examples of irrational decisions when compared to the normative standard (Cyert and March 1963; March and Olsen 1976; Nisbett and Ross 1980; Buchanan and Huczynski 2004). This is the case even where the decision is taken by a group rather than an individual. Indeed, Janis (1972) demonstrated how groups making extremely important strategic decisions failed to adopt the rational, normative approach. Janis used the term 'groupthink' to refer to the fact that, within the decision-making groups he observed, disturbing information was suppressed, immense and unjustified risks taken, and individuals censored their own concerns. The result was an illusion of unanimity for the decision taken, despite individual group members not really agreeing. The concept of groupthink has been used to explain more recent decision fiascos, suggesting that the political nature of decision making is still very evident (e.g., Yetiv 2003).

Given that research evidence does not support a rational, decision-making process in practice, other models have been developed which attempt to mirror reality rather than idealism. Simon (1960) introduced the concept of bounded rationality, which acknowledged the fact that decision makers, in practice, were under pressure to make decisions so that they did not have time to search exhaustively for all possible solutions. He coined the term 'satisficing' to describe how the search for solutions was not exhaustive, but continued only until a satisfactory solution had been found. Another model of decision making that has attracted attention recently has been the intuitive, decision-making model (e.g., Agor 1989; Behling and Eckel 1991). This assumes that managers make decisions by relying on past experiences and their general sense of the situation. Intuition is essentially an unconscious process created out of distilled experience. When managers face complex decisions and cannot get accurate information, they tend to rely on hunches, intuitions and general experiences. As Bazerman (1994) concludes: 'Most significant decisions are made by judgement, rather than by a defined prescriptive model.' Such intuition, however, is not really acceptable in cultures where rational analysis is the approved way of making decisions, such as North America and the UK. So intuition is often disguised or hidden. For example, one of the executives in the study by Agor (1986) commented: 'Sometimes one must dress up a gut decision in "data clothes" to make it acceptable or palatable, but this fine-tuning is usually after the fact of the decision.'

A final, non-rational model of the decision-making process is the garbage can model developed by Cohen *et al.* (1972). They described decision-making processes in terms of a 'garbage can', rather than a rational process. This model suggests that decisions have a random and haphazard element to them – that is, decisions are sometimes made from the random interaction of problems, solutions, choice situations and participants, rather than from intentions, plans and consistent decisions. Various kinds of problems, solutions and energy ('garbage') are dumped into a garbage can by participants. The decision process may then just as well start with the solution as the problem.

These models of decision making acknowledge the limits or 'bounds' to rational decision making, including:

1. Perceptual limitations and biases.
2. Limited availability of information.
3. Prediction is an art not a science so it is not possible to evaluate options as rationally as proposed.
4. Organisational goals constrain decisions.
5. Conflicting goals of different stakeholders mean that interpersonal conflicts, personal biases and power struggles are an inherent part of the decision process.

The irrationality of the selection and assessment decision-making process

The irrationality of decision-making processes has been confirmed in studies focusing on selection and assessment decisions. A brief look at the steps in the decision-making cycle and evidence of what happens at each stage highlights the continued 'irrationality' of the selection process in practice.

UNDERSTAND THE SITUATION AND IDENTIFY THE PROBLEM

The idea that someone leaving an organisation should be used as an opportunity to rationally consider whether or not a replacement is 'really needed', ignores the political realities of organisations (Pfeffer 1981; Contu and Willmott 2003). Power within organisations is at least partly a function of resources that are controlled, including human resources. While individuals are recruited to work for a particular company, in reality they are recruited to particular departments or divisions. A department is unlikely to admit voluntarily that they do not need to replace a particular person since that will diminish their 'empire'. The department may actually be more likely to argue that they 'need' two people to replace the one leaver! Someone leaving may be an opportunity for a renegotiation of resources within the organisation, but this needs to be understood as an inherently political process. 'Need' is not something that can be established as fact, but is socially constructed through a process of negotiation and sense making until a 'workable version of reality' is produced (Weick 1990).

GATHER INFORMATION AND MATERIAL TO HELP SOLVE THE PROBLEM

Despite the extensive effort put into developing new, more valid methods to measure and assess individuals during the selection process, evidence suggests that unstructured interviews and references remain the most dominant methods (Shackleton and Newell 1991; Keenan 1995). This can be related to the human fallacy of us each believing that we are a 'good judge of people', despite evidence to the contrary (see section below on person perception errors). Later in this chapter we will also consider another reason for the continued use of the interview – that is, that selection is not simply about 'valid' selection, but also about commitment and motivation to follow up the decision with behaviours that encourage the individual selected to integrate into the organisation. A recruiter who feels that they have personally selected the candidate is much more likely to feel committed and motivated to helping achieve that integration. Similarly, the selected candidate may well be more committed to the organisation because unstructured interviews are more likely to provide the opportunity to negotiate a 'mutually agreeable psychological contract' (Dipboye 1997).

GENERATE POTENTIAL SOLUTIONS

While the rational model of selection suggests that the recruitment stage is about generating the widest search possible in order to ensure the 'best' pool of applicants, evidence suggests that, in reality, the alternatives considered are often less than exhaustive. For example, some organisations only go to Oxford and Cambridge universities to recruit graduates. While these universities may well have some of the brightest graduates, there will certainly be bright graduates at other universities. Other evidence suggests that the so-called 'old boy network' is still actively used across organisations (Coe 1992; O'Higgins 2002). In other words, it is very often personal contacts, one's social capital (Adler and Kwon 2002) that lead to job opportunities rather than systematic recruitment and selection procedures.

SYSTEMATICALLY EVALUATE EACH SOLUTION

The evidence suggests that assessors, whatever method they are using, do not systematically use the evidence that is collected. For example, the evidence about assessment centres, reviewed below, suggests that assessors are unable to distinguish between different aspects of behaviour within a given exercise, but instead give ratings based on their overall assessment of the candidate's performance on that particular exercise. Research on interviews suggests that decisions are often made very quickly and are subjective, unreliable and vulnerable to bias (Janz 1989; Arvey and Faley 1992; Dipboye 1992).

SELECT BEST SOLUTION

A truly rational decision process would have assessors numerically rate each candidate on each dimension or competency; give the different dimensions or competencies specific weightings depending on their relative importance for the job in question; and then total the score for each candidate, taking into account the relative weightings. The candidate with the highest total would be selected. This can be described as the actuarial method as it is based purely on a numerical calculation of the collected data (although the ratings themselves are subjective). In practice, however, the decision is much more likely to be based on a process of clinical judgement. The ratings may be numerical but these will be evaluated subjectively by the assessors and weightings will be assigned to justify decisions rather than to make the decisions. So leadership skills become more important than numerical skills, if this allows the favoured candidate to come out top! As Beach (1990, p.xiii) states: 'most decisions are made quickly and simply on the basis of "fittingness", and only in particular circumstances are they made on the basis of anything like the weighing and balancing of gains and losses that is prescribed by classical decision theory'.

MONITOR AND EVALUATE RESULTS

In practice it seems that very few organisations carry out a systematic evaluation of their selection process (or indeed any other human resource practice). Moreover, where validity studies have been conducted, they demonstrate low levels of validity even when using methods that can potentially provide reasonable or good levels of validity (see below). These results confirm that selection methods are not used in the prescribed way and that efforts to improve validity have had rather limited impact on actual practice.

The conclusion drawn from such research is that the prescriptive, rational, decision-making process does not typically equate with what happens in practice and that methods of selection actually used by practitioners are often not high on criterion-related validity, despite the fact that evidence now demonstrates that criterion-related validity can be significantly improved using the newer, more structured and systematic approaches (Ryan and Tippins 2004). Exactly the same points could be made with reference to decisions made during developmental assessment processes. The response from those researching and writing about selection and assessment has been to attempt to improve the validity of the methods used to measure individual differences. In other words, the focus has been on trying to find ways of improving the extent to which the rational, normative, decision-making model is actually followed.

Improving the validity of selection and assessment decisions

In particular, attention has focused on introducing methods which provide a better basis on which to make rational decisions. Considerable progress has been made here, which demonstrates how the validity of the selection and assessment decision-making process can be improved (Robertson and Smith 2001).

STRUCTURED INTERVIEWS

The interview is the most common selection tool used within organisations across many countries (DiMilia *et al.* 1994; Shackleton and Newell 1994). Early research demonstrated that the traditional unstructured interview had very low validity (e.g., Mayfield 1964; Ulrich and Trumbo 1965). Given the ubiquity of the interview, effort has been devoted to improving its validity, primarily by increasing the structure of the interview, so that at least all candidates are asked the same sorts of questions (if not the identical questions) and all interviewers use the same dimensions to assess candidates. Research looking at the validity of structured interviews suggests that they can indeed improve validity (McDaniel *et al.* 1994).

There are two main varieties of structured interviews – behavioural and situational interviews. In a behavioural interview, hypothetical situations are posed to the candidate (the same questions to each candidate) and the candidate is asked to say how they would react to this situation. In a situational interview, candidates are asked to identify where they have experienced certain job-relevant situations and to report how they responded to these situations.

Example: **Situational and behavioural interviews: examples of interview questions for a head teacher of an inner-city secondary school**

An example of a situational interview question: You are working in your office when your secretary tells you that there is a gentleman to see you. You invite him into your office, and he tells you that he is a parent of one of your pupils. He says that he wants his daughter to leave school and start work immediately. The daughter is one of your brightest pupils and you know that she is working hard to go to medical school next year. You start to explain this to the parent but he clearly does not place any value on higher education. What would you do?

An example of a behavioural interview question: Can you give me some examples of when you have had to deal with parents who do not value higher education for their children; how have you managed this situation?

Both types of structured interview have been found to be effective. For example, Barclay (2001) uses empirical data from UK organisations to illustrate the advantages of behavioural interviews. Advantages included the ability to gather better information which leads to improved selection decisions, improved consistency between interviewers, and the increased ability for candidates to demonstrate their skills. Similarly, Sue-Chan and Latham (2004) examined the validity of the situational interview and demonstrated its power in predicting both academic and team-playing behaviour of professionals and managers. However, there is some evidence that for complex jobs behavioural interviews are more effective than situational interviews (Heffcut *et al.* 2004). Structuring interviews can therefore potentially improve the quality of decisions made, although there appears to be a ceiling on this, beyond which increasing structure does not improve validity (Heffcutt and Arthur 1994).

BIOGRAPHICAL MEASURES

Biographical measures, or biodata, attempt to capture directly the past behaviour of a person and use this as the basis for predicting future behaviour. Since they are based on actual behaviour, the idea is that they are less prone to misinterpretation, resistance and distortion (Stricker and Rock 1998). Research has indeed demonstrated that biographical measures can produce good levels of predictive validity (e.g., Mumford and Stokes 1992; Stokes *et al.* 1993; Hesketh 1999; Oswald *et al.* 2004). Nevertheless, there remain a number of concerns about the appropriate item content and about test construction methods (Mael 1991). For example, in terms of content many biographical measures contain questions which are indistinguishable from items on an attitude scale (e.g., What is your attitude towards working mothers?); or items that call for subjective judgements (e.g., How punctual are you?); or items that are not under the control of the assessee and so are dubious on ethical grounds (e.g., How many sisters and brothers have you got?). In terms of test construction, a key problem is that because most measures are empirically keyed to predict particular criteria, they cannot be used in different settings. Nevertheless, more recently, research has demonstrated that a biodata form can be designed to predict performance in a variety of organisational settings (Carlson *et al.* 1999).

PSYCHOMETRIC TESTS

Essentially, there are two kinds of tests used for selection or developmental assessment – cognitive and personality tests. Cognitive tests, especially tests of general intelligence, have typically been found to have high predictive validity across a wide range of jobs (Hunter and Hunter 1984), but it is debatable how much additional information they provide since there are other ways of estimating ability, especially from academic qualifications. For example, McManus *et al.* (2003) Showed that 'A'-level score was a good predictor of success in medical training and subsequent career progress, but that a test of ability added no additional predictive validity.

Personality tests have typically been found to have a low validity for predicting job performance (Ghiselli 1973; Schmitt *et al.* 1984). However, more recently, evidence has been established to suggest that personality measures can be valid predictors of job performance (e.g., Day and Silverman 1989; Robertson and Kinder 1993; Salgado 1996). One reason for the early pessimism was that there was no generally accepted model of personality. More recently, the so-called 'Big 5' have emerged, around which there is substantial agreement (the 'Big 5' personality traits are openness, conscientiousness, extraversion, agreeableness and neuroticism). Research using the Big 5 model has shown that measurement of these five traits can help to predict job performance. For example, Barrick and Mount (1991) found that conscientiousness is a valid predictor for all occupational groups and all criterion types. And Hough *et al.* (1990) found that neuroticism is negatively related to general performance measures. Moreover, researchers have begun to consider more thoughtfully the relationship between particular aspects of personality and particular aspects of performance that might logically be related; not assuming that a measure of personality will be related to just any criterion measure. For example, Tett *et al.* (2003) demonstrated that using broad measures of personality obscured potentially useful linkages between specific aspects of personality and performance. Thus they advocate focusing on specific personality traits and specific measures of performance in order to improve predictive validity.

ASSESSMENT OR DEVELOPMENT CENTRES

Assessment or development centres make use of a variety of exercises over a period of time (typically two days) to assess a small group of candidates on a number of dimensions (often defined in terms of competencies) that are deemed relevant to the particular job and organisation. Ratings are made by a small group of trained assessors who observe the candidates on the different exercises. Exercises might include: a group decision-making exercise, a presentation, a role play, an in-basket test, psychometric tests and interviews. In the UK, the use of assessment centres is increasing more rapidly than any other selection procedure, with 65 per cent of large firms (over 1,000 employees) using them (Industrial Relations Service 1997). Research evidence using meta-analysis demonstrates that they can have a relatively high level of predictive validity (Hough and Oswald 2000) and are seen as fair and thorough by candidates (Macan *et al.* 1994; Salgado 1999).

Despite this good predictive validity, research has demonstrated that assessment and development centres do not have good construct validity (Goldstein *et al.* 1998). In particular, research has demonstrated that within each exercise, ratings across the different dimensions are not clearly differentiated, while correlation of a given dimension across exercises is low (Kauffman *et al.* 1993; Joyce *et al.* 1994; McCredie and Shackleton 1994). One suggested reason for this is that the information-processing load on assessors is too high, so that they selectively attend to only certain behaviours, misinterpret key behaviours, and/or confuse categorisation of behaviours by dimensions (Thornton 1992; Fleenor 1996). Schema-driven theory suggests that this occurs because people use established schemata to interpret and evaluate the observed behaviour of others (Zedeck 1986; Fiske and Taylor 1991). Schemata refer to the mental representations that an individual has built up over time to structure and cluster their understanding of perceived phenomena. Any new input will be interpreted on the basis of the assumptions which underpin these schemata. Traditionally, the recommended way to overcome this problem has been to separate the steps of observation and classification – recording behaviours longhand while observing, classifying behaviours according to the defined dimensions for the exercise, and only then rating the individual on each dimension (Bray and Grant 1966; Boyle *et al.* 1995). While this does help to overcome some of the perceptual problems of assessors, the requirement to write detailed notes of the observation can be a distraction and means that the assessor might miss some behavioural information. Similarly, the suggestion by Kolk *et al.* (2002) of having each assessor rate only one exercise and one dimension per exercise is likely to be practically difficult to implement.

Hennessy *et al.* (1998), in an attempt to overcome this problem, experimented with the use of a behavioural coding method of assessment. This provides a list of key behaviours for each of the dimensions rated and requires observers to code the frequency of behaviours as they occur. They are not required actually to note the behaviours per se, but only tally the frequency of the specified behaviours. This has the advantage that information-processing demands are reduced and also limits the extent to which personal schemata will direct the observation. The results of their research demonstrated that this behavioural coding method was as accurate as the traditional method of assessment and reduced differences between raters in their judgements. They suggest that its simplicity in comparison with the traditional method, and its theoretical basis in schema-driven theory, may make this a preferred method for overcoming the construct validity problem of assessment or development centres.

On the basis of reviewing a number of studies which have attempted to improve the construct validity of assessment and development centres, Lievens (1998) makes a number of practical recommendations. For example, in terms of:

1. Dimensions: use only a small number of conceptually distinct dimensions and define these in a concrete and job-related way.
2. Assessors: ensure assessors are trained, especially in relation to understanding the dimensions and categorisation schemes used.
3. Situational exercises: develop exercises which generate a large amount of dimension-related behaviour and avoid exercises which elicit behaviours potentially relevant to many dimensions.
4. Systematic observation, evaluation and integration procedures: provide assessors with an observation aid (a checklist), which operationalises each dimension with 6–12 key behaviours.

While an assessment centre can be improved by observing these types of recommendations, organisations should also think very carefully about using such a method, given the expense of doing so and the fact that other methods may provide as good predictions much more cost-effectively (Robertson and Smith 2001).

The rhetoric versus the reality of the selection and assessment decision-making process

These newer assessment methods appear to offer significant benefits since they can improve objectivity and criterion-related validity. However, as seen, research into actual practice suggests that, in reality, selection and development decisions continue to be dominated by more subjective approaches (Anderson 2003). Moreover, even where so-called 'objective' approaches are used, their interpretation remains highly subjective. That is, the fact that a structured interview or an assessment centre has the potential to reach high levels of validity does not mean that it will be used in ways to guarantee this. For example, DiMilia and Gorodecki (1997) evaluated the reliability and use of a commercially available structured interviewing system. They found that, in practice, the reliability achieved was much lower than considered in the literature to be an acceptable level. This was because there was a lack of role clarity for interviewers, interviewers had different expectations of the job specification and there was inconsistency in the application of the rating system. They conclude that: '. . . whilst an interviewing system can have a number of features described in the literature as necessary conditions for better validity, the actual result of the system is in the hands of the user' (DiMilia and Gorodecki 1997, p.198).

Similarly, while psychometric tests can potentially add valid information to the selection or development decision, it is also clear that this will only occur if tests are used appropriately (Newell and Shackleton 1993). Rees (1996) identifies a number of common misunderstandings among test users which suggest that tests are not always used in a valid and ethical way. For example, a frequent misconception is that it is acceptable to use a poor test to structure a subsequent interview. Rees concludes that such misunderstandings may, over time, undermine the case of those attempting to use psychometric tests 'effectively and appropriately in the occupational setting'. He argues that there are too many test users who are unable to recognise technically poor test material and so use such tests inappropriately to help them make decisions that affect both individuals and organisations.

These observations are not confined to selection decision methods. Other attempts to improve the rationality of decision making, for example by introducing cost–benefit analysis, computer-based information systems or other decision support systems, demonstrate that, in practice, these solutions are not used in the prescribed way (e.g., Ackerman *et al.* 1974; Argyris 1977). Essentially, the normative model of the selection and assessment decision-making process does not equate to reality because selection and assessment is a process that inherently depends on an interaction between two or more parties. Such interpersonal *interactions* involve two (or more) parties who are simultaneously providing input (which the other is evaluating) and evaluating the other. Such interactions are inherently subjective, involving processes of impression management and interpretation.

IMPRESSION MANAGEMENT

Decisions made about candidates during selection and assessment depend on the concrete experiences that are provided. These experiences of the 'target person' (i.e., the candidate) may be indirect (e.g., information from an application form or a personality test) or direct (e.g., behaviour exhibited during an interview). The newer methods of assessment attempt to ensure that the event provides assessors with an accurate reflection of the person being assessed. This assumes that the candidate is passively responding to the various assessment experiences. In reality, of course, candidates are actively attempting to create a certain image of themselves. This is especially the case in the 'high stakes' selection situation. Candidates will attempt to create and maintain a particular impression of themselves which coincides with what they believe the assessor is looking for. Thus, to some extent at least, the assessor only sees what the target person wants them to see. This is referred to as 'impression management' (Rosenfeld *et al.* 1995). Arnold *et al.* (1997) identify a variety of techniques that can be used to convey a particular impression. For example, ingratiation ('I have always wanted to work for this firm'), selective description of events (candidate ignoring details of failed examinations they have taken), positive descriptions of self ('I am a very hard-working person'). For example, Griffin *et al.* (2004) demonstrated that faking was a real issue when personality measures are used for selection, with job applicants responding significantly differently to students on a conscientiousness measure. While it might be obvious to appreciate that candidates are engaging in impression management tactics, it is also the case that assessors are simultaneously attempting to 'create an impression' because they want to attract or retain the 'best' candidates.

INTERPRETATION

The assessor has to make sense of the data that is accumulated about the candidate and this sense-making process is inherently subjective. At the same time, the candidate is also trying to 'make sense' of the situation – what would it be like to work for this company, or what would my colleagues be like, or what are my implied career opportunities? For both parties, there is a stimulus ('evidence' from the candidate to the assessor and vice versa) and a response (a job offer or an acceptance of a job offer). However, the key to understanding this is that between these two observable phenomena are the unobservable processes of perception.

Perception, by definition, is a subjective process by which individuals attend to, organise and so interpret their sensory input in order to give meaning to their environment. Subjective processes, including selective attention, personal judgement and interpretation, will therefore affect the decision. Behaviour is based on the world as it is perceived and a number of factors operate to shape and sometimes distort perception, including personal characteristics, motives, interests, past experiences, and expectations. This will result in biases, such as:

1. **Selective attention** – as we cannot attend to everything, we only attend to some things, but this is not random. Rather, what we attend to is chosen according to our interests, background, experience and attitudes. This allows us to draw conclusions from an ambiguous situation.

2. **Halo/horn effect** – we tend to draw a general impression about an individual on the basis of a single characteristic, such as intelligence.

3. **Contrast effects** – evaluations of a person's characteristics can be affected by comparisons with other people recently encountered. So, in an interview situation, if someone has just been interviewed who was judged very poor, the next candidate may be more positively evaluated in contrast. Conversely, following a very good candidate, an average candidate may be rated poorly.

4. **Projection** – there is a tendency to attribute one's own characteristics to other people. So if I want challenge and responsibility in a job, I assume that others want the same.

5. **Stereotyping** – this involves judging someone on the basis of one's perceptions of the group to which that person belongs.

6. **Heuristics** – these are judgemental shortcuts in decision making. Two common heuristics are availability and representativeness. The availability heuristic is the tendency for people to base their judgements on information that is readily available to them. For example, if there is an internal and an external candidate, the internal candidate may be preferred simply because more information is readily available about them ('better the devil you know!'). The representative heuristic is the tendency to assess the likelihood of an occurrence by drawing analogies and seeing identical situations where they do not exist. So, for example, if four graduates from the same college had all been recruited but none had been very satisfactory, then another applicant from this college might be rejected on the assumption that they also would not be good.

It is just these sorts of impression management problems and perceptual biases that 'new' assessment methods have attempted to overcome. They structure and standardise the information gained during the assessment process, so that decisions are less likely to be biased by these perceptual shortcuts that we use in our everyday judgements of other people, to a greater or lesser extent. To the extent that these new assessment methods can reduce these biases, they can improve validity. The research evidence presented earlier suggests that this is indeed the case. However, as we have also seen, while newer, more valid assessment methods have been developed, and can improve the validity of selection and development decisions, in practice they are often not used in quite the 'rational' way anticipated. Human subjectivity and the political reality of organisations mean that the normative decision model can never be an entirely realistic account of decision-making in practice (Anderson 2003).

Unfounded assumptions: selection as an interactive process

While human perception and organisational politics limit the extent to which a selection or development decision can ever be entirely rational, there is an even more fundamental problem with the normative decision model. The normative approach makes the assumption of a 'right' or 'best' person for the job and assumes that there is one key decision, i.e., to select or reject the candidate, which is the crucial point. The important issue is to select the 'right' person and then this will solve the organisational problem because this person will be able successfully to carry out the particular tasks where there is currently a vacancy (although this may be only after training has been given). However, this ignores the fact that successful performance on a job is rarely, if ever, dependent solely on a particular individual. The individual job exists within a complex network of structures, processes and relationships, which will affect and interact with the actions of the particular individual employee. So a potentially very competent recruit can be thwarted in their ability to perform to a high standard by a whole multitude of events – a lack of adequate resources, poor training, an unhelpful supervisor, colleagues who are not supportive, etc. On the other hand, a barely competent recruit can perform to a high standard if they are exposed to a supportive or benign situation.

In other words, it is not helpful to look at the selection decision itself in isolation from the stream of events that occur both before and after this. Vaughan (1996, 1997) made a similar point in analysing the Challenger space shuttle disaster. She points out that the explosion should not be viewed as the unfortunate result of one bad decision to launch on that day in January 1986. Rather, it was the outcome of an accumulation of many launch decisions over the course of the shuttle programme. Thus instead of focusing on single decisions, she advocates the analysis of cycles of decisions or networks of decisions. This is equally the case in terms of analysing selection or development decisions. Thus, whether a decision to select (or reject) can be described as 'good' or 'bad' is the result of a network of interacting decisions. These decisions are made by both the individual and the organisational representatives, over a period of time, starting well before the actual advertisement of a job. For example, individuals will form an impression of a particular company based on what they know about its products and services or what they know about the organisation itself. These impressions may be formed either on the basis of direct experience (e.g., good or bad experience of service as a customer) or indirect experience (e.g., reading something good or bad about the company in the press). These impressions will influence how an individual responds to a recruitment advertisement. So a potentially ideal candidate may not even apply if they have formed a negative impression. Moreover, decisions made subsequent to the selection decision, will have a considerable impact on the extent to which the recruit performs the job effectively. Particularly important in this respect is the socialisation experience of the new recruit (Anderson and Ostroff 1997). This suggests the need to see selection as an interactive process in which the expectations of both parties are intertwined in a process of continuous exchange, which does not begin and end at the point of the selection decision (Shintaku 2004). Again, exactly the same points can be made with reference to development decisions. Whether the 'right' career path is chosen for and by a particular individual on the basis of evidence from a development centre will depend on a host of decisions made prior and subsequent to this choice.

What this analysis implies is that the normative, rational model of decision making isolates the decision from subsequent action, including subsequent decisions (Brunsson 1982, 1989). Brunsson argues that the normative decision-making perspective fails to recognise that a decision is not an end product but simply a step towards action of some kind. In the case of selection, this equals the effective deployment of human resources. More importantly, Brunsson points out that rational decisions are not always good bases for appropriate and successful actions: 'Since decision processes aim at action, they should not be designed solely according to such decision-internal criteria as the norms of rationality; they should be adapted to external criteria of action' (1982, p.32). The selection or development decision per se is only one episode in the successful integration of the individual in the organisation. Successful integration is more likely to occur where there are positive expectations, motivation and commitment from both parties (Scholarios et al. 2003). Thus, the stronger the expectation, motivation and commitment expressed in a decision, the more power that decision exerts as a basis for action. However, Brunnson argues that to achieve such expectation, motivation and commitment breaks all the rules for rational decision making:

1. Few alternatives should be considered: while the rational model assumes that many (all) alternatives should be considered, from a decision–action perspective parsimony is more appropriate. Considering multiple alternatives generates uncertainty and this reduces commitment and motivation.
2. Only positive consequences of the chosen decision should be analysed: the rational model advocates considering all consequences of a decision, both positive and negative. From a decision–action perspective it may be more sensible to search for consequences in only one direction since this reduces inconsistency which can stimulate doubt.
3. Objectives should not be pre-defined: the rational model assumes that objectives should be pre-defined so that all alternatives can be considered against these objectives. For producing action, a better strategy may be to start from the consequences and invent the objectives afterwards (Lindblom 1959).

This action-oriented perspective can help to explain some of the research findings on the selection and assessment decision process, which suggest that it remains less rational than prescribed best practice would advocate. Examples of this are given below.

1. Continued use of unstructured interviews – the belief that 'I am a good judge of character' allows the interviewer to be confident in their decision and so increases commitment and motivation to make the chosen individual 'fit'.
2. Continued use of subjective (clinical) rather than objective (actuarial) choice criteria – again this empowers the assessor to believe that they were influential in the decision and so makes them more committed to ensuring the decision translates into effective action, i.e., successful integration of the chosen candidate within the organisation.
3. Less than exhaustive search of alternatives – making decisions quickly makes life more comfortable for managers. It allows them to use heuristics or 'shortcuts' to solving problems. Pre-defined recipes for successful selection decisions can increase confidence in the decision and so raise expectations of subsequent success by the candidate.
4. Little systematic evaluation of selection decision – while academic research has focused on establishing the predictive validity of selection decisions, in practice few organisations systematically monitor the success of their decisions. Again, from an action perspective this is sensible since it allows those involved to be confident in their decision-making qualities and so more confident about and committed to the decisions they make. It also reduces the possibility of cognitive dissonance (Festinger 1957). Cognitive dissonance is the uncomfortable feeling that occurs when people hold inconsistent or conflicting beliefs – I made the decision to hire this person, I am good at making these kinds of decisions, this person is not a good employee. Cognitive dissonance can be avoided if systematic evaluation of selection decisions is avoided.
5. Overemphasis of negative data – research has demonstrated that negative information about a candidate is given more weight than positive information. Many of the newer assessment methods are aimed at reducing this effect. However, from a decision–action perspective this is entirely rational. Negative information raises doubts about the suitability of a candidate and so will undermine confidence that the person can be successful. So if there are two candidates, and from an objective evaluation of the evidence, candidate A is 'better', having more of the essential and desirable characteristics than candidate B, then rationally that candidate should be selected. However, if there is also one piece of negative information

about candidate A (for example a question mark over their willingness to collaborate), while there is nothing negative about candidate B, then from an action–decision perspective, candidate B would be preferable. If candidate A were selected there would remain doubts, which might undermine motivation and commitment to the decision.

In each case, the decision–action criteria improve the positive expectations of those involved over the purely rational decision criteria. This is important since expectations can become self-fulfilling prophecies. For example, Eden and Shani (1982) informed the instructors of a command course for the Israeli Defence Forces that one-third of the 105 soldiers on the course had high potential, one-third had normal potential and the rest were of unknown potential. In reality, the soldiers had been randomly assigned to one of these three groups. However, at the end of the 15-week course, those trainees who were given the high potential label scored significantly higher on objective achievement tests and exhibited more positive attitudes to the course and the instructors, than did the rest.

Interactive action-oriented perspective, fairness and justice

One particular problem in selection and development decisions has been the issue of 'fair' discrimination. Thus, while selection is based on making discriminations between people, the objective has been to make these discriminations on the basis of relevant criteria, i.e., ability to do the job effectively, rather than irrelevant criteria like sex, ethnicity and disability. One of the key benefits of the psychometric perspective is that it presents a very rational and objective view of the whole process. It assumes that the 'best' person for the job can be clearly specified in advance, with selection and assessment processes essentially presented as a set of 'rational' choices based on objective evidence gained about the candidates from the various selection methods deployed. This allowed companies to defend against claims of unfair discrimination. Essentially, the traditional approach may be considered to have a high level of procedural justice (Lind and Tyler 1988) since it theoretically treats everyone the same. In this chapter, we have argued that this semblance of rationality is actually a myth. Moreover, it could be argued that the psychometric perspective actually increases the opportunity for distributive injustice (Singer 1993), because its starting premise is that there is one 'best' way to do the job. This 'best' way is likely to be a reflection of the way previous job incumbents have done the job. So if the previous job incumbents have all been white males who have adopted fairly autocratic management styles, worked long hours, relied on a lot of electronic communication, etc., then the assumption will be that these are the characteristics to look for in a replacement. This may perpetuate the status quo and thus the segregation that exists within organisations, although the process may look procedurally 'fair' (Truxillo et al. 2004).

Adopting the interactive, action-oriented perspective provides the opportunity to break through this barrier by recognising that people can do jobs in very different ways but equally effectively. The problem with this perspective, however, is that it acknowledges the subjectivity of the selection process and so could be used as a vehicle to increase unfair discrimination even more. This is entirely true but it will depend on the motives of those involved. If there is a belief in equal opportunities, or, perhaps even better, in the advantages of diversity in the workforce, then this perspective can help to increase these opportunities. The psychometric perspective simply hides behind a façade of objectivity so that it remains easy to perpetuate discrimination even while presenting the whole process as fair. The interactive action-oriented perspective does not have this façade to hide behind so that any continuation of segregated workforces must, by implication, be the result of prejudice and unfair discrimination.

Conclusion

Understanding the selection and assessment process from a decision-making perspective highlights issues that are otherwise not brought into focus. In this chapter, this perspective has been used to contrast the traditional psychometric perspective with its implicit acceptance of the normative rational decision-making model, with an interactive decision–action perspective. The decision–action perspective leads us to recognise both that the process of selection and assessment can never be entirely rational and objective and that the decision per se (to accept or reject) is not necessarily the crucial point in the process. Rather, it is a stage in the ultimate goal of achieving the effective integration and socialisation of an individual within the organisation. Effective integration is clearly unlikely if an entirely unsuitable person is chosen for a job. However, the assumption that there is a fixed type of person for a particular job and that the only goal of selection and assessment is to ensure accurate measurement in order to be able to identify this right type, is inappropriate. It is inappropriate both because of its assumptions about individual differences and our ability to assess these accurately in a selection or development situation and because it ignores the criteria for translating the decision into action. Successful performance on the job is dependent on motivation as well as ability. Ability is dependent not only on fixed characteristics, but also on opportunities for training and development that are provided. An 'ideal' person selected for a job but then given no training or development opportunities is more likely to fail than a moderately suitable person who is given such opportunities.

More importantly, in terms of motivation, success or failure will depend on both the individual's own self-beliefs and on the beliefs of those around them. If these significant others have been involved in the selection and assessment process and believe that the person selected is 'the best', then they will be committed to ensuring they are successful, regardless of whether or not they are best according to some objective, rational decision criteria. An entirely rational, actuarial evaluation of data collected during an assessment centre that results in the selection of a person that those involved do not 'like' or do not think is 'best' (for whatever reason), is unlikely to translate into active commitment aimed at helping that individual succeed. As seen, such commitment is more likely to follow a selection decision process that is less than entirely rational, but that allows those involved to believe that they have chosen someone who will be successful. Similarly, motivation is likely to be high if the selection or development experience results in positive but realistic expectations on the part of those assessed. Self-efficacy beliefs, an individual's belief that they are capable of performing the task they have been selected for (Bandura 1977) will be high, and these beliefs have been shown to be important in influencing the persistence and effort that someone will put into ensuring success (Gist 1987).

An action–decision perspective can help to identify those selection and assessment processes that can generate such high levels of self- and other belief and expectation that lead, in turn, to high levels of commitment and motivation. Of course, measurement of individual differences will remain important in selection and development decisions. However, the recognition that accurate measurement per se is not enough (even if it were possible), can help us focus on the ultimate goal of successful person–organisation fit, rather than just valid and rational decisions that might not readily translate into action. The decision–action perspective, therefore, complements the more traditional psychometric perspective and can help to ensure not only that decisions are made on the basis of reasonably good individual assessment but also that those decisions get translated into successful organisational performance.

CASE STUDY 3.1

ASSESSMENT AT NEWSCO, PHARMCO, RETAILCO AND SCIENCECO

SUE NEWELL, VIV SHACKLETON[*] AND MAXINE ROBERTSON[†]

Taking a decision–action perspective suggests that processes involved in selection and assessment should differ depending on the particular context and, in particular, on the intended action outcome. In order to demonstrate this diversity, we consider three separate cases in the following section. Each had a different objective and so a different design.

Newsco

Introduction

The first example of the application of the assessment techniques we have talked about in this chapter concerns Newsco, a large and successful company in the business of selling news and information. It is a truly international company, operating as it does in most countries of the world. It divides the world up into three zones. We are concerned here with the European part of the operation.

The brief

The company decided to assess the top 50 or so of its managers in this region. The stated purpose was assessment for development. That is to say, the managers would go through a development centre (an assessment-type centre designed with development in mind) in order for them to assess what sort of development they needed. 'Development' is a word that is frequently misunderstood. Here, it does not necessarily mean promotion or acquiring new responsibilities. It means training in techniques or skills, or acquiring new information, that would help them in their present or future roles. The traditional 'sheep dip' approach to management development, training and learning, where everyone receives the same training, regardless of need, is often not appropriate at any level in an organisation. It can be particularly inappropriate for senior people where the opportunity-cost of having them away from their desks on a course is very high. This organisation wanted to target training only on those who needed it, in the areas they most needed.

The role of those participating in the development centre was mostly that of 'country manager', the people who headed up the business in each country, although there were also specialists of various kinds.

The design

The start of the process of designing the development centre was an assessment of competencies, just as we described in the section on the traditional approach to assessment in this chapter. This involved interviewing people in the organisation to establish what the competencies were, both for the present job and for the ways in which the jobs might develop. The interviews were based on in-depth reviews of the role in question and how the organisation might develop. Two other kinds of interview were also used, the repertory

---

[*] Co-author on 'Newsco', 'Pharmco' and 'Retialco'.
[†] Co-author on 'Scienceco'.

grid technique and the critical incident technique. The repertory grid technique asks the interviewee to think of a number of people known to them who do, or have done, the job and to compare the way that they perform that role. From this information, the interviewer can work out the key skills, knowledge, abilities or competencies that effective job holders need and which differentiate the effective from the less effective. The critical incident technique asks interviewees to think of times in the job when they or their team were particularly successful or unsuccessful. The interviewee is encouraged to say what it was that made this particular incident successful or unsuccessful. From this evidence, the experienced interviewer can work out some of the competencies needed in the job.

Some of the competencies in this case were:

- Managing change
  - Continually challenging the status quo.
  - Generating innovative ideas and solutions.
  - Driving change through and overcoming resistance.

- Thinking for the future
  - Anticipating future trends and identifying new opportunities.
  - Thinking strategically.
  - Retaining a global perspective.

- Working with customers
  - Building partnerships with customers by knowing their business.
  - Consulting with customers to understand needs and provide the best service.
  - Promoting a positive image of the company.

Exercises were then designed to provide the opportunity to assess these and the other competencies. Exercises included:

- A role play with a customer, where the customer had a serious complaint about the level of service and support they were receiving.
- A competitor analysis, where participants were given information about three competitors and asked to do a SWOT (strengths, weaknesses, opportunities and threats) analysis of their own organisation and the competition.
- Giving a presentation on issues of their own choosing from their own country business to the top management from the head office.
- A group discussion on a strategic issue facing the whole organisation.
- Some psychometric tests.

The workshop

Each development centre lasted two days. Managers from all corners of Europe and North Africa arrived, eight at a time, for the programme. There were external consultants and managers from head office running the programme and assessing the participants on the competencies. A crucial element of the two days was a one-to-one feedback, lasting around an hour, conducted by the external consultant with each of the participants. The purpose of this meeting was to review the performance of the participant on each of the exercises and competencies, and to get their agreement on the accuracy of the assessment. Most importantly, it was also an opportunity to discuss what the participant proposed to do about developing the strengths and remedying the weaknesses exposed by the programme.

The outputs

Following the workshop, the consultant wrote a report on the participant, summarising their performance and outlining a development plan. In effect, the report summarised and formalised the one-to-one discussion at the end of the centre. The report was sent to the participant and to their human resources manager. Participants themselves only showed it to their line manager or others in the organisation if they so wished. It was a confidential report and the recommendations were to be implemented by the participant in the manner most likely to achieve the development proposed. Development methods included secondments, job shadowing, training courses, self-directed learning, distance learning, job changes, and even withdrawal from the organisation if this was what the participant wanted.

After the development centre, there was no follow-up to check that the participants at the workshop had done any development after the event, and no attempt to evaluate the benefits of the programme. It was sufficient for the participants to say that the workshop had been useful and enjoyable. The feedback was essentially positive. This is not to say that the development centre was anodyne. There was some indication of how they could do even better. It pointed out that, where the participant had demonstrated excellent skills, they might coach others in these skills or seek opportunities to use them even more. Where there were skills that needed improving, suggestions were made on how this might be accomplished. But the whole development centre, and the feedback in particular, was geared to reinforcing, motivating and encouraging, rather than assessing and measuring. The participants were generally very positive about the event, after some initial reservations. They pointed out the many considerable advantages of the programme, including the opportunity to meet others in similar roles, to reflect on their own progress in the organisation, to think about themselves for a change, rather than the job in hand, and to consider how they might change or reinforce certain aspects of their own behaviour. In summary, the opportunity to reflect and learn was very motivating and satisfying for them.

Pharmco

Introduction

The second case concerns a long-established German corporation, Pharmco. Its early beginnings were in the traditional 'smokestack' industries of iron and steel, but since the Second World War it has moved into pharmaceutical manufacture and retail, along with the manufacture of medical and other technical equipment and a number of other businesses. In the more recent past, it has also started to expand beyond its national border and acquire and develop businesses in other European countries, including Britain, France and Spain. It is still predominantly a German company, however, with 90 per cent of its manufacturing and retail business conducted within the country.

The brief

We met up with the company at the point when it was thinking of investing in the development of its young managers to groom them for more senior appointments. In typical German style, it placed great emphasis on the importance of formal, high-quality education. It planned to offer the chance for some of the young managers to broaden their education and experience outside their technical and functional expertise and into a general management education. They would offer the opportunity to enrol in a part-time MBA at a prestigious international business school for those who were assessed as having the potential to profit from it. But who would benefit?

The design

The method they chose to select those who would be offered the opportunity was an assessment centre. Germany, like Britain and America, has a long tradition of using assessment centres, right back from the days of officer selection in the Second World War. Here, however, there was the additional complication of having to design an assessment centre for candidates from a number of different European countries. Although the language of the centre would be English, the exercises would be taken by people from four or five different countries. Whereas Newsco was a very international group, and consideration was given to designing exercises that would not favour one culture rather than another, here the cultural fairness issue was considered even more carefully by the designers. This is because this centre was seen as more akin to a traditional assessment centre, where fairness of treatment and equal opportunity to display skills are paramount.

Once again, the first issue was what knowledge, skills and abilities should be assessed. And again, the favoured means of acquiring that knowledge was a competency analysis. Methods adopted to decide on the required competencies were very similar to those already described for Newsco. Competencies included:

- Cross-cultural sensitivity
  - Demonstrating curiosity and open-mindedness about other national cultures.
  - Acting to promote mutual understanding of other cultures.
  - Demonstrating sensitivity when working with people from other cultures.

- Leadership
  - Focusing a group on generating a range of new ideas and possibilities.
  - Demonstrating confidence and a sense of responsibility.
  - Developing subordinates by making demands on them.

- Orientation to the task
  - Agreeing clear and realistic actions.
  - Prioritising.
  - Taking decisions.
  - Reviewing progress towards achieving the task.

Participants were nominated by their line managers and by human resource professionals in their separate companies, in whichever country they worked. Participants were assessed at the centre by both company managers and by outside consultants, using competency-based rating scales.

Exercises were designed with the multi-cultural audience in mind. They included one on cultural sensitivity, where participants discussed their perception of their own culture and the German culture, as they had experienced it. They had to meet to discuss what recommendations they would make to improve cross-cultural working and how they would know if their recommendations were effective.

When designing assessment centre exercises, it is important to keep these and other cultural dimensions in mind. So, for example, it is important to make sure that exercises have many routes to success for a participant. An example of this need to provide many routes to success (and failure) in a multi-cultural environment is provided by an exercise used in this case. The exercise involved a customer service manager who was new to the post, and a subordinate, a customer service team leader, who had been in post for a long time. This was a role play exercise. An 'actor', a manager who had been in that post in the past, played the team leader. The participant played the superior, the customer service manager. There was some written material on the team leader, such as previous performance appraisal reports and statistical data on the subordinate's performance, available to the new boss. The issues were that the team leader was very good with customers, being liked and respected by them, but not good at developing the team, in part because they spent so much time with customers. In addition, they were not good at organising the work of the team since they were too busy doing the work themselves. The exercise could be done in a number of ways. It could be done from a relationships-building point of view, where, for example, the new boss could coach or mentor the old hand into new ways of working. Or it could be done from a very task-focused point of view, such as saying that this style and level of performance is not acceptable and you should be working in a different way and here are some targets and a timetable to achieve a different level of achievement. Or it could be successfully tackled in ways between those two extremes, such as helping the individual to explore alternative ways of doing the job over the next month and coming back to discuss progress after that time interval. What was important was that the individual was guided to seeing that the job involved two sets of customers, internal and external, and that it was important for the team leader to give attention to both. How participants achieved that aim was up to them.

Retailco

Introduction

The third case is a British-based retailer, Retailco. Like many large retailers in Britain, it was finding organic growth within Britain hard to achieve. It was already market leader, with the market dominated by about five players. Growth in its main market was less than 5 per cent a year, with it achieving this or a little more, year by year. This was likely to be the case for the foreseeable future. It was innovative in expanding in other businesses, but its main core business was unlikely to grow substantially.

An obvious route for a company in this position is growth by acquisition. While this was an option, a few big players dominated the market, so, realistically, a major acquisition in its home market was unlikely. Another route was expansion into other markets, which it was pursuing. A third route was expanding overseas, and it is this route which concerns us here.

Recently, the markets of eastern Europe have opened up considerably. Our case organisation saw this as an opportunity. In four or five countries in that part of the world, it acquired small businesses in its market sector, or, in some cases, developed those businesses from scratch.

The brief

However, this presented the organisation with a difficulty from a human resources point of view. It was completely new to the issue of recruiting and employing a non-British workforce. To start with, it sent experienced, specialist managers from Britain and recruited skilled and semi-skilled workers locally. But this was only a stopgap measure. For the longer term it needed to develop indigenous managers. In Britain, it had a well-designed and long-standing assessment centre for the selection of graduates who would become the senior managers of the future. This selection centre was regularly revised and checked for criterion validity. But could this centre be used for the assessment and selection of foreign graduates?

The design

The answer was a firm 'no'. The exercises and tests were not appropriate for candidates from outside Britain. It was not just the obvious differences, such as use of the English language or measurements in miles and gallons rather than kilometres and litres. It was the nature of the exercises themselves. Topics for group discussion, such as use of drugs by young people, have different meanings and importance for people from other cultures. Exercises dealing with the design of supermarkets are unlikely to work as well in countries less familiar with them. Tests not only have to have local norms and validation studies, but may not be as appropriate in countries where the whole concept of testing is unfamiliar and even disapproved of.

There was also the issue of whether the competencies were the same for graduates being selected for a post within their own country and for a well-established, brand name company in its local market, compared to a start-up enterprise for a company which was small and unknown in its local market. Obviously, the competencies were different. A competency analysis, similar to that described in the first two cases, was conducted. This revealed that being able to be independent of much day-to-day support was important. These managers would be big fish in small ponds, the opposite of new recruits in Britain. So they needed considerable confidence to back their own judgements and to act independently, when they were hundreds or thousands of miles from their head office in England. Similarly, the capacity for innovation and entrepreneurialism was much more important in eastern Europe than it was in the home country. In effect, these managers would be in charge of their own business in a more fundamental way than they would be if running a store in Britain. Finally, a capacity for cultural awareness was important. The candidates would be groomed for the role of international manager. They would spend time in Britain, getting to know the business. They would spend time in their home country, learning about and, hopefully, expanding the business there. But this organisation had big expansion plans. It was considered likely that the European managers would often be transferred to foreign postings outside their home market. So it was important for them to have not just the capacity to work in English, the international business language, but to be able to have some cultural sensitivity and awareness to be able to relate to, and work with, people from a wide range of different cultures. This was not a fundamental requirement for most of the British graduates being recruited in the organisation's home country.

So the whole assessment process was redesigned. Out went those stalwarts of the assessment centre, psychometric tests, since appropriate norms of sufficient sample size were not available. In addition, there were doubts about their acceptability in cultures unfamiliar with such things.

Exercises which could assess the required competencies, such as cultural sensitivity, entrepreneurialism and independence, were designed. An exercise designed for the cultural issue was a group discussion, which involved candidates describing how they saw their own culture and the cultures represented in the group. Observers were trained to look for behaviours which indicated that a candidate was open-minded towards different views of their own culture, and aware of the ways in which their own culture could be viewed. Defensiveness about others' negative perceptions of one's own culture was a contraindication.

This approach is very much in the psychometric tradition: job analysis, followed by description of the job in competency terms, then design of exercises to assess that competency. What is different from the usual approach to the design of selection centres, though, is the cross-cultural dimension. This brings enormous challenges, as described in the case of Pharmco. Once again, the exercises were designed so that there was more than one route to success. How candidates tackled the exercise was much less important than the outcome.

Even here, though, the rational decision-making model was not adopted to the full. Candidates were expected to gain an 'acceptable' score on all competencies, but this was not always adhered to. Rules were 'broken' when a candidate was seen to perform exceptionally well in one or two exercises. There was no attempt to base decisions on a statistical or mathematical calculation of marks (sometimes called the actuarial method) whereby scores given for each competency are summed or weighted in some way. The decision was much more an intuitive feel (sometimes called the clinical approach) for what final grade a candidate should be given based on an impression of the suite of marks. In the early centres the assessors were a mix of expatriates and indigenous managers. The power and influence in contentious decisions about a certain candidate tended to lie with the expatriate. As the company became more established in the foreign market, and more and more expatriates became replaced with indigenous managers, the power shifted. So, even in this more traditional example, the rational, decision-making model is found not to explain all purposes and outcomes.

ScienceCo

Introduction

The final case is of a medium-sized, science and technology-based consultancy company, located in the UK. It was established, in 1986, by a founder and two senior consultants. This 'Group of 3' had previously worked together in a large global consultancy but had become increasingly dissatisfied with what they saw as the 'stifling bureaucracy'. As a result the 'Group of 3' had decided to start their own business. Since 1986, ScienceCo has grown from a small entrepreneurial business, employing a handful of scientific consultants specialising in engineering and communications, to a medium-sized company employing about 200 people (75 per cent consultants, with the rest being technical and administrative support staff) and incorporating other scientific disciplines such as bio-technology, applied sciences and information systems. It operates today on a global basis.

At the time of its inception, the founder – himself a leading, internationally respected scientist – wished to create a consultancy environment that would not only develop solutions in response to client problems, but also stimulate invention and innovation more freely among its employees. The workforce consists of highly educated scientists and technologists, who rely primarily on their expertise and knowledge, rather than equipment or systems, to provide inventions and innovative solutions for manufacturing, engineering and pharmaceutical companies around the world.

The brief

A major issue for management has always been attracting and, just as importantly, retaining a highly skilled, expert workforce of international standing, in order for the firm to grow and successfully compete on a global basis. To a significant extent this has been achieved. Generally far more candidates apply for positions with the firm than there are posts, and turnover rates are only around 6 per cent. Developing and sustaining an appropriate organisational environment in which expert consultants are highly motivated, and perform optimally, has always been considered to be the most important strategic issue. For many years, the firm did not employ a dedicated human resources (HR) manager. However, two years ago, based on predicted project work, and management discussions around the requirements of floating on the stock market, the management team decided to recruit an HR manager. The remit of this HR manager was to increase the expert workforce by 15 per cent (a figure that was projected to continue annually) in order to meet market demand, to develop a more formalised recruitment and selection process, and to develop ways of motivating consultants and maintaining high retention rates across the firm.

The design

In the past, consultants had typically been recruited, informally, by word of mouth, drawing upon consultants' global personal networks of colleagues and contacts. However, according to the HR manager, 'this only works if the person you happen to want to get hold off is on the end of the phone at the time, and able to remember who you should talk to – we miss on opportunities to get great people because we don't have any formal systems to contact them with'. In order to formalise the recruitment process, the HR manager contracted two international recruitment agencies. Once provided with a person specification and a brief that described very broadly the type of work carried out by the firm, they provided shortlists of candidates on an ongoing basis. In terms of the selection process, the founder had always insisted that candidates take an AH6 intelligence test and Cattell's 16PF personality test because, as he put it, 'it is important to use our own scientific knowledge in the science of selecting others'. However, given that the majority of candidates short-listed by the agencies generally had a PhD in a scientific discipline, it was virtually impossible for any candidate to fail the AH6 intelligence test. It was also difficult to 'fail' to qualify on the 16PF because Science Co did not actually have an 'ideal' personality profile for any job, other than 'openness' and a 'willingness to experiment'. Indeed, a major group norm was that diversity should be encouraged and so a mix of personality types should be welcomed. The 16PF was used, therefore, simply because consultants were curious to see what sort of personality profile candidates had. Thus, almost all candidates who had been shortlisted qualified on the basis of these tests and proceeded to an initial short interview with the HR manager and the relevant divisional manager.

During this preliminary interview, the HR manager stated that candidates were expected to demonstrate a strong understanding of their own, and more importantly other disciplines, because of the need to work in inter-disciplinary teams sharing knowledge. They were also expected to be 'almost naturally innovative', have a strong commercial awareness, be fluent in English, and be prepared to adopt the role of a consultant. This role involves marketing their own, and more generally, the firm's abilities and expertise. It is therefore a relatively unique set of characteristics which are sought in candidates. The HR manager stated: 'It's quite a unique mix we are looking for. All the way through the selection process, we give out big indicators to say the sort of organisation we are. It's quite aggressive maybe, and I'm sure interviewees will pick up quite a lot of arrogance on the part of the company. But the messages we are giving out are more about confidence in what we do and how we do it rather than us thinking we are better than anyone else.'

The majority of candidates were rejected at this initial interview stage and only approximately 25 per cent (typically equating to four candidates) progressed to a second interview. While the management team were not overly concerned about the high numbers of rejections (seeing it as a reflection of their high standards), the HR manager found it extremely frustrating. The second interview focused on assessing the candidate's ability to market to clients, their overall level of expertise, and their ability to work within inter-disciplinary project teams. This second interview was a panel interview involving any number of consultants from several divisions who wished to be involved in 'quizzing' the applicant in some depth on their knowledge of their own, and other, science- or technology-based fields. Panel members were randomly drawn from across the firm, based on availability at the time of the interview. If the panel agreed on a candidate, then the candidate would be recommended for appointment to the MD.

Typically 16 candidates were interviewed for each post, and for each of those interviewed, approximately 10 CVs would have been received from the recruitment agencies. While the selection process was described as 'rigorous' by the HR manager, he emphasised that the interviews focused primarily on the candidates' ability to 'fit in' to the ScienceCo way of working – 'You get a CV, and the person has a PhD, and they've worked for a pretty high-powered research agency, and that's brilliant. You've got to see them, but you know that there is a pretty strong chance that the moment you meet them you're going to know what they're not – they're not one of us.' However, beyond a willingness and ability to share knowledge and collaborate across different science and technology-based fields, it wasn't at all clear what 'fitting in' actually meant. Yet, even though 'fitting in' was a movable feast, anyone on the panel had a right to veto any candidate that did not 'fit in' – another major source of frustration to the HR manager who commented 'with criteria as loose as this I don't know how we can ever say yes to anyone'. As a result, the HR manager had attempted to formalise the recruitment process further by asking divisional managers to nominate a consultant within their division to act as an HR liaison and to sit on all relevant panels. However, despite numerous promptings, a list of nominated liaisons had yet to appear.

Questions

1. Compare the four cases according to how far they conform to the rational decision-making perspective (i.e., the psychometric tradition) or to the interactive action-oriented perspective described in this chapter.

2. On the surface, the case of Newsco illustrates the design of a fairly standard assessment for development workshop in the psychometric tradition. What evidence is there to suggest that assessment is not the sole purpose? What other purposes might the centre serve?

3. In what ways is Pharmco an example of an assessment centre, a development centre, or a mix of the two?

4. Why is it important to consider the national/cultural dimension in the design of centres?

5. Why might the rejection of such high numbers of candidates at ScienceCo actually be an important positive aspect of their recruitment and selection process?

References

Ackerman, B., Ross-Ackerman, S., Sawyer, J. and Henderson, D. (1974) *The Uncertain Research for Environmental Quality,* New York: Free Press.

Adler, P. and S-W. Kwon (2002) 'Social capital: prospects for a new concept', *Academy of Management Review,* Vol.27, No.1, pp.17–40.

Agor, W. (1986) 'The logic of intuition: how top executives make important decisions', *Organizational Dynamics,* Winter, pp.5–15.

Agor, W. (1989) *Intuition in Organizations,* Newbury Park, CA: Sage.

Alldredge, M. and Nilan, K. (2000) '3M's leadership competency model: an internally developed solution', *Human Resource Management,* Vol.39, Nos2–3, pp.133–46.

*Anderson, N. (2003) 'Applicant and recruiter reactions to new technology in selection: a critical review and agenda for future research', *International Journal of Selection and Assessment,* Vol.11, Nos2–3, pp.121–37.

Anderson, N. and Ostroff, C. (1997) 'Selection as socialization', in N. Anderson and P. Herriot (eds) *International Handbook of Selection and Assessment,* Chichester: Wiley.

Argyris, C. (1977) 'Organizational learning and management information systems', *Accounting, Organizations and Society,* Vol.2, pp.113–23.

Arnold, J., Cooper, C. and Robertson, I. (1997) *Work Psychology: Understanding Human Behaviour in the Workplace,* London: FT/Pitman Publishing.

Arvey, R.D. and Faley, R.H. (1992) *Fairness in Selecting Employees* (2nd edn), Reading, MA: Addison-Wesley.

Bandura, A. (1977) 'Self-efficacy: toward a unifying theory of behavioural change', *Psychological Review,* Vol.84, No.2, pp.191–215.

*Barclay, J. (2001) 'Improving selection interviews with structure: organizations' use of behavioural interviews', *Personnel Review,* Vol.30, Nos1–2, pp.81–103.

Barrick, M. and Mount, M. (1991) 'The big five personality dimensions and job performance: A meta-analysis', *Personnel Psychology,* Vol.44, pp.1–26.

Batram, D. (2000) 'Internet recruitment and selection: kissing frogs to find princes', *International Journal of Selection and Assessment,* Vol.8, No.4, pp.261–74.

Batram, D. (2004) 'Assessment in organizations', *Applied Psychology: An International Review,* Vol.53, No.2, pp.237–50.

Bauer, T., Truxillo, D., Paronto, M., Weekley, J. and Campion, M. (2004) 'Applicant reactions to different selection technology: Face-to-Face, Interactive Voice Response, and Computer-Assisted Telephone Screening Interviews', *International Journal of Selection and Assessment,* Vol.12, Nos1–2, pp.135–48.

Bazerman, M. (1994) *Judgement in Managerial Decision-making* (3rd edn), New York: Wiley.

Beach, L. (1990) *Image Theory: Decision Making in Personal and Organizational Contexts*, Chichester: Wiley.

Beardwell, I., Holden, L. and Claydon, T. (2004) *Human Resource Management*, London: FT/Prentice Hall.

Behling, O. and Eckel, N. (1991) 'Making sense out of intuition', *Academy of Management Executive*, Vol.5, pp.46–54.

Bingham, B., Ilg, S. and Davidson, N. (2002) 'Great candidates fast: online job application and electronic processing', *Public Personnel Management*, Vol.31, No.1, pp.53–64.

Boam, R. and Sparrow, P. (1992) *Designing and Achieving Competency: A Competency-Based Approach to Managing People and Organizations*, London: McGraw-Hill.

Boyle, S., Fullerton, J. and Wood, R. (1995) 'Do assessment/development centres use optimal evaluation procedures?', *International Journal of Selection and Assessment*, Vol.3, pp.132–40.

Bray, D. and Grant, D. (1966) 'The assessment centre in the measurement of potential for business management', *Psychological Monographs*, Vol.80, No.17 (Whole No.625).

Brunsson, N. (1982) 'The irrationality of action and action rationality: decisions, ideologies and organizational actions', *Journal of Management Studies*, Vol.19, No.1, pp.29–44.

Brunsson, N. (1989) *The Organization of Hypocrisy, Talk, Decisions and Actions in Organizations*, Chichester: Wiley, pp.242.

Buchanan, D. and Huczynski, A. (2004) 'Images of influence', *Journal of Management Inquiry*, Vol.13, No.4, pp.312–24.

Campbell, J.P. (1990) 'Modeling the performance prediction problem in industrial and organizational psychology', in M.D. Dunnette and L.M. Hough (eds) *Handbook of Industrial and Organizational Psychology* (2nd edn), Vol.1, Palo Alto, CA: Consulting Psychologists Press.

Carlson, K., Scullen, S., Schimdt, F., Rothstein, H. and Erwin, F. (1999), 'Generalisable biographical data validity can be achieved without multi-organizational development and keying', *Personnel Psychology*, Vol.52, pp.731–55.

Coe, T. (1992) *The Key to the Men's Club: Opening the Doors to Women in Management*, Corby: IM Foundation.

Cohen, M., March, J. and Olsen, J. (1972) 'A garbage can model of organizational choice', *Administrative Science Quarterly*, Vol.17, No.1, pp.1–25.

Contu, A. and Willmott, H. (2003) 'Re-embedding situatedness: the importance of power relations in learning theory', *Organization Science*, Vol.13, No.3, pp.283–97.

Cyert, R. and March, J. (1963) *A Behavioural Theory of the Firm*, Englewood Cliffs, NJ: Prentice-Hall.

Day, D. and Silverman, S. (1989) 'Personality and job performance: evidence of incremental validity', *Personnel Psychology*, Vol.42, pp.25–36.

DiMilia, L. and Gorodecki, M. (1997) 'Some factors explaining the reliability of a structured interview at a work site', *International Journal of Selection and Assessment*, Vol.5, No.4, pp.193–9.

DiMilia, L., Smith, P. and Brown, D. (1994) 'Management selection in Australia: a comparison with British and French findings', *International Journal of Selection and Assessment*, Vol.2, pp.80–90.

Dipboye, R. (1992) 'Selection interviews: Process perspectives', Cincinnati, OH: South-Western.

Dipboye, R. (1997) 'Structured selection interviews: Why do they work? Why are they under-utilized?', in N. Anderson and P. Herriot (eds), *International Handbook of Selection and Assessment*, Chichester: Wiley.

Eden, D. and Shani, A. (1982) 'Pygmalion goes to boot camp: Expectancy, leadership and trainee performance', *Journal of Applied Psychology*, Vol.67, No.2, pp.194–9.

Festinger, L. (1957) *A Theory of Cognitive Dissonance*, New York: Harper Row.

*Fish, A. and Mackim, R. (2004) 'Perceptions of executive search and advertised recruitment attributes and service quality', *Personnel Review*, Vol.33, No.1, pp.30–55.

Fiske, S. and Taylor, S. (1991) *Social Cognition*, New York: McGraw-Hill.

Fleenor, J. (1996) 'Constructs and developmental assessment centres: Further troubling empirical findings', *Journal of Business and Psychology*, Vol.10, pp.319–33.

Frase-Blunt, M. (2004), 'Selecting a diversity consultant', *HR Magazine*, Vol.49, No.6, pp.147–53.

Ghiselli, E. (1973) 'The validity of aptitude tests in personnel selection', *Personnel Psychology*, Vol.26, pp.461–77.

Gist, M. (1987) 'Self-efficacy: implications for organizational behaviour and human resource management', *Academy of Management Review*, Vol.12, pp.472–85.

Goldstein, H., Yusko, K., Braverman, F., Smith, D. and Chung, B. (1998), 'The role of cognitive ability in the subgroup differences and incremental validity of assessment centre exercises', *Personnel Psychology*, Vol.51, pp.357–74.

Griffin, B., Hesketh, B. and Grayson, D. (2004), 'Applicants faking good: evidence of item bias in the NEO PI-R', *Personality and Individual Differences*, Vol.36, No.7, pp.1545–54.

Heffcut, A.I. and Arthur, W. (1994) 'Hunter and Hunter (1984) revisited: interview validity and entry level jobs', *Journal of Applied Psychology*, Vol.79, pp.184–90.

Heffcut, A.I., Roth, P., Conway, J. and Klehe, U.-C. (2004) 'The impact of job complexity and study design on situational and behaviour description interview validity', *International Journal of Selection and Assessment*, Vol.12, No.3, pp.262–73.

Hennessy, J., Mabey, B. and Warr, P. (1998) 'Assessment centre observation procedures: an experimental comparison of traditional, checklist and coding methods', *International Journal of Selection and Assessment*, Vol.6, No.4, pp.222–31.

Hesketh, B. (1999) 'Introduction' to the International Journal of Selection and Assessment special issue on biodata, *International Journal of Selection and Assessment*, Vol.7, No.2, pp.55–6.

Hofstede, G. (1984) *Culture's Consequences: International Differences in Work-related Values*, London: Sage.

Hough, L., Eaton, N., Dunnette, M., Kamp, J. and McCloy, R. (1990) 'Criterion-related validities of personality constructs and the effect of response distortion on those validities', *Journal of Applied Psychology*, Vol.75, pp.581–5.

Hough, L. and Oswald, F. (2000) 'Personnel selection: Looking toward the future–remembering the past', *Annual Review of Psychology*, Vol.51, pp.631–64.

Hunter, J. and Hunter, R. (1984) 'Validity and utility of alternative predictors of job performance', *Psychological Bulletin*, Vol.96, pp.72–98.

Industrial Relations Service (1997) 'The state of selection: an IRS survey', *Employee Development Bulletin*, Vol.85, pp.8–18.

Janis, I. (1972) *Victims of Groupthink*, Boston, MA: Houghton-Mifflin.

Janz, T. (1989) 'The patterned behaviour description interview: the best prophet of the future is the past', in R.D. Eder and G.R. Ferris (eds) *The Employment Interview: Theory and Practice*, London: Sage.

Joyce, L., Thayer, P. and Pond, S. (1994) 'Managerial functions: An alternative to traditional assessment centre dimensions?', *Personnel Psychology*, Vol.47, pp.109–21.

Kacmar, M., Witt, L., Ziznuska, S. and Gully, S. (2003) 'The interactive effect of leader-member exchange and communication frequency on performance ratings', *Journal of Applied Psychology*, Vol.88, No.4, pp.764–72.

Kauffman, J., Jex, S., Love, K. and Libkuman, T. (1993) 'The construct validity of assessment centre performance dimensions', *International Journal of Selection and Assessment*, Vol.1, pp.213–23.

Keenan, T. (1995) 'Graduate recruitment in Britain: A survey of selection methods used by organizations', *Journal of Organizational Behaviour*, Vol.16, pp.303–17.

Kolk, N., Born, M. and van der Flier, H. (2002), 'Impact of common variance on construct validity of assessment centre dimension judgements', *Human Performance*, Vol.15, No.4, pp.325–38.

Konradt, U., Hertel, G. and Joder, K. (2003), 'Web-based assessment of call-centre agents: Development and validation of a computerized instrument', *International Journal of Selection and Assessment*, Vol.11, Nos 2–3, pp.184–94.

Landis, R., Fogli, L. and Goldberg, E. (1998) 'Future-oriented job analysis: a description of the process and its organizational implications', *International Journal of Selection and Assessment*, Vol.6, No.3, pp.192–7.

Landy, F., Shankster-Cawley, L. and Moran, S. (1995) 'Advancing personnel selection and placement methods', in A. Howard (ed.) *The Changing Nature of Work*, San Francisco, CA: Jossey-Bass.

Lievens, F. (1998) 'Factors which improve the construct validity of assessment centres: a review', *International Journal of Selection and Assessment*, Vol.6, No.3, pp.141–52.

Lind, E. and Tyler, T. (1988) *The Social Psychology of Procedural Justice*, New York: Plenum.

Lindblom, C.E. (1959) 'The science of "muddling through"', *Public Administration Review*, Vol.19, pp.79–88.

Macan, T.H., Avedon, M.J., Paese, M. and Smith, D.E. (1994) 'The effects of applicants' reactions to cognitive ability tests and an assessment centre', *Personnel Psychology*, Vol.47, No.4, pp.715–38.

Mael, F. (1991) 'A conceptual rationale for the domain and attributes of biodata items', *Personnel Psychology*, Vol.44, pp.763–92.

March, J. and Olsen, J. (1976) *Ambiguity and Choice in Organizations*, Bergen: Universitetsforlaget.

Marchington, M. and Wilkinson, A. (2005) *Human Resource Management at Work*, London: CIPD.

Matthews, B. and Redman, T. (1998) 'Managerial recruitment advertisements – just how market-orientated are they?', *International Journal of Selection and Assessment*, Vol.6, No.4, pp.240–8.

Mayfield, E.C. (1964) 'The selection interview: A re-evaluation of published research', *Personnel Psychology*, Vol.17, pp.239–60.

McCredie, H. and Shackleton, V.J. (1994) 'The development and interim validation of a dimensions-based senior management assessment centre', *Human Resources Management Journal*, Vol.5, No.1, pp.91–101.

McDaniel, M.A., Whetzel, D.L., Schmidt, F.L. and Maurer, S.D. (1994) 'The validity of the employment interviews: a comprehensive review and meta-analysis', *Journal of Applied Psychology*, Vol.79, pp.599–616.

McManus, I., Smithers, E., Partridge, P., Keeling, A. and Fleming, P. (2003) 'A levels and intelligence as predictors of medical careers in UK doctors: 20 year prospective study', *British Medical Journal*, Vol.327, No.7407, pp.139–43.

Merrick, N. (1997) 'Big thaw shows up on recruitment market', *People Management*, Vol.3, No.2, pp.10–11.

Mooney, J. (2002) 'Pre-employment testing on the internet: put candidates a click away and hire at modem speed', *Public Personnel Management*, Vol.31, No.1, pp.41–52.

Mumford, M. and Stokes, G. (1992) 'Developmental determinants of individual action: Theory and practice in applying background measures', in M. Dunnette and L. Hough (eds) *Handbook of Industrial and Organizational Psychology* (2nd edn), Vol.3, Palo Alto, CA: Consulting Psychologists Press, pp.61–138.

*Newell, S. and Shackleton, V. (1993) 'The use (and abuse) of psychometric tests in British industry and commerce', *Human Resource Management Journal*, Vol.4, No.1, pp.14–23.

Newell, S. and Shackleton, V. (2001) 'Selection and assessment as an interactive decision process', in T. Redman and A. Wilkinson (eds) *Contemporary Human Resource Management*, London: Prentice Hall, pp.24–56.

Nisbett, R. and Ross, L. (1980) *Human Inference*, Englewood Cliffs, NJ: Prentice-Hall.

O'Higgins, E. (2002) 'Non-executive directors on boards in Ireland: co-option, contributions and characteristics', *Corporate Governance: An International Review*, Vol.10, No.1, pp.19–29.

Oswald, F., Schmitt, N., Kim, B., Ramsay, L. and Gillespie, M. (2004), 'Developing a biodata measure and situational judgement inventory as predictors of college student performance', *Journal of Applied Psychology*, Vol.89, No.2, pp.187–206.

Pfeffer, J. (1981) *Power in Organisations*, Marshfield, MA: Pitman.

Redmond, S. (1989) *How to Recruit Good Managers*, London: Kogan Page.

Rees, C. (1996) 'Psychometrics: topical misunderstandings amongst test users', *International Journal of Selection and Assessment*, Vol.4, No.1, pp.44–8.

Roberts, G. (1997) *Recruitment and Selection: A Competency Approach*, London: IPD.

Robertson, I. and Kinder, A. (1993) 'Personality and job competences: the criterion-related validity of some personality variables', *Journal of Occupational and Organizational Psychology*, Vol.66, pp.225–44.

*Robertson, I. and Smith, M. (2001) 'Personnel selection', *Journal of Occupational and Organizational Psychology*, Vol.74, pp.441–72.

Rosenfeld, P., Giacalone, R.A. and Riordan, C.A. (1995) *Impression Management in Organizations,* London: Routledge.

Ryan, A. and Tippins, N. (2004) 'Attracting and selecting: what psychological research tells us', *Human Resource Management,* Vol.43, No.4, pp.305–19.

Salgado, J. (1996) 'Personality and job competences: a comment on Robertson and Kinder's (1993) study', *Journal of Occupational and Organizational Psychology,* Vol.69, pp.373–5.

Salgado, J. (1999), 'Personnel selection methods', in C. Cooper and I.T. Robertson (eds) *International Review of Industrial and Organizational Psychology,* New York: Wiley.

Schmitt, N., Gooding, R., Noe, R. and Kirsch, M. (1984) 'Meta-analyses of validity studies published between 1964 and 1982, and the investigation of study characteristics', *Personnel Psychology,* Vol.37, pp.407–22.

Schneider, B. and Konz, A. (1989) 'Strategic job analysis', *Human Resource Management,* Vol.28, pp.51–63.

Scholarios, D., Lockyer, C. and Johnson, H. (2003) 'Anticipatory socialisation: the effects of recruitment and selection on career expectations', *Career Development International,* Vol.8, No.4, pp.182–98.

Shackleton, V. and Newell, S. (1991) 'Management selection: a comparative survey of methods used in top British and French companies', *Journal of Occupational Psychology,* Vol.64, pp.23–6.

Shackleton, V. and Newell, S. (1994) 'European selection methods: a comparison of five countries', *International Journal of Selection and Assessment,* Vol.2, pp.91–102.

Shintaku, R. (2004), 'Invited reaction: understanding the experience of college graduates during their first year of employment', *Human Resource Development Quarterly,* Vol.15, No.1, pp.25–30.

Simon, H. (1960) *The New Science of Management Decision,* New York: Harper Row.

Singer, M. (1993) *Fairness in Personnel Selection,* Aldershot: Avebury.

Sparrow, P. and Bognanno, M. (1993) 'Competency requirement forecasting: issues for international selection and assessment', *International Journal of Selection and Assessment,* Vol.1, No.1, pp.50–8.

Staffsud, A. (2003) 'Recruitment policy versus recruitment process: espoused theory versus theory-in-use', *Academy of Management Proceedings,* pG1, 6p.

Stokes, G., Hogan, J. and Snell, A. (1993) 'Comparability of incumbent and applicant samples for the development of biodata keys: the influence of social desirability', *Personnel Psychology,* Vol.46, pp.739–62.

Stricker, L. and Rock, D. (1998) 'Assessing leadership potential with a biographical measure of personality traits', *International Journal of Selection and Assessment,* Vol.6, No.3, pp.164–84.

Sue-Chan, C. and Latham, P. (2004) 'The situational interview as a predictor of academic and team performance: a study of the mediating effects of cognitive ability and emotional intelligence', *International Journal of Selection and Assessment,* Vol.12, No.4, pp.312–21.

Sundvik, L. and Lindeman, M. (1998) 'Performance rating accuracy: convergence between supervisor assessment and sales productivity', *International Journal of Selection and Assessment,* Vol.6, No.1, pp.9–15.

*Taylor, S. (2002) *Employee Resourcing,* London: CIPD.

Tett, R., Steele, J. and Beauregard, R. (2003) 'Broad and narrow measures on both sides of the personality–job performance relationship', *Journal of Organizational Behaviour,* Vol.24, No.3, pp.335–57.

Thornton, G. (1992) *Assessment Centres in Human Resource Management,* Reading, MA: Addison Wesley.

Torrington, D., Hall, L. and Taylor, S. (2005) *Human Resource Management,* London: FT/Prentice Hall.

Trompenaars, F. (1993) *Riding the Waves of Culture: Understanding Cultural Diversity in Business,* London: Nicholas Brealey.

Truxillo, D., Steiner, D. and Gilliland, S. (2004), 'The importance of organizational justice in personnel selection: defining when selection fairness really matters', *International Journal of Selection and Assessment,* Vol.12, Nos 1–2, pp.39–54.

Ulrich, L. and Trumbo, D. (1965) 'The selection interview since 1949', *Psychological Bulletin*, Vol.53, pp.100–16.

Vaughan, D. (1996) *The Challenger Launch Decision: Risky Technology, Culture, and Deviance at NASA*, Chicago, IL: University of Chicago Press.

Vaughan, D. (1997) 'The trickle-down effect: policy decisions, risky work and the Challenger tragedy', *California Management Review*, Vol.39, No.2, pp.80–102.

Weick, K.E. (1990) 'Technology as equivoque: sensemaking in new technologies', in P.S. Goodman, L.S. Sproull and Associates, *Technology and Organisations*, Oxford: Jossey-Bass.

Yetiv, S. (2003) 'Groupthink and the gulf crisis', *British Journal of Political Science*, Vol.33, No.3, pp.419–43.

Zedeck, S. (1986) 'A process analysis of the assessment centre method', in B. Shaw and L. Cummings (eds) *Research in Organizational Behaviour*, Vol.8, pp.259–96, Greenwich, CT: JAI Press.

* Useful reading

Getting on: the development of the human resource

CHAPTER 18

LEARNING AND DEVELOPMENT

THE OBJECTIVES OF THIS CHAPTER ARE TO:

1   Explore four perspectives on the nature of learning and consider the implications that each has for development provision and support

2   Review some of the practical characteristics of learning and development

3   Explain the various methods of addressing learning and development needs

4   Investigate the nature of evaluation in this context

There has been a considerable shift in the way that individual development is understood and characterised. We have moved from identifying training needs to identifying learning needs, the implication being that development is owned by the learner with the need rather than by the trainer seeking to satisfy that need. This also has implications for who identifies the needs and the way that those needs are met. Current thinking suggests that needs are best developed by a partnership between the individual and the organisation, and that the methods of meeting these needs are not limited only to formal courses, but to a wide range of on-the-job development methods and distance/ e-learning approaches. Whilst a partnership approach is considered ideal the phrase 'self-development' is an important one in our development lexicon, indicating the growing emphasis on the individual having ownership of and taking responsibility for their own development. There has also been a shift in the type of skills that are the focus of development activity. Hallier and Butts (1999) for example identify a change from an interest in technical skills to the development of personal skills, self-management and attitudes. Lastly, while the focus on development for the current job remains high, there is greater pressure for development which is also future oriented. These shifts reflect the changes that we have already discussed in terms of global competition, fast and continuous change and the need for individuals to develop their employability in an increasingly uncertain world.

THE NATURE OF LEARNING

For the purpose of this text we consider the result of learning to be changed or new behaviour resulting from new or reinterpreted knowledge that has been derived from an external or internal experience. There are broadly four theoretical approaches or perspectives to understanding the nature of learning, and the training and development that organisations carry out reflect the explicit or implicit acceptance of one or more perspectives. We will look at each perspective, in the evolutionary order in which they became important. There is no right or wrong theory – each has strengths and weaknesses.

The **behaviourist** perspective is the earliest which, reflecting the label, concentrates on changes in observable behaviour. Experiments with animals formed the foundation of this theory, for example the work of Skinner, Watson and Pavlov. Researchers sought to associate rewards with certain behaviours in order to increase the display of that behaviour. The relevance of this for organisations today may be seen for example in telesales training where employees are taught to follow a script and calls are listened to, to ensure that the script is followed. Reward or punishment follows depending on behaviour. Trainers are not interested in what is going on in the heads of employees, they merely want them to follow the routine to be learned. This approach has also been used for a range of interpersonal skills training. One American company, for example plays video sequences to trainees portraying the 'correct' way to carry out, say, a return to work interview. Trainees then practise copying what they have seen and are given cue cards to use when carrying out that particular interpersonal event. The problems with the perspective are that it is overtly manipulative, simplistic and limited. It may produce only temporary changes in behaviour and increase cynicism.

Cognitive approaches are based on an information-processing perspective and are more concerned with what goes on in the learner's head. This is a more technical perspective and maps out the stages of learning such as: expectancy to learn (motivation); attention and perception required; experience is coded (meaning is derived); meaning is stored in long-term memory; meaning is retrieved when needed; learning is applied; feedback is received (which may supply reinforcement). The strengths of this perspective are that it stresses the importance of learner motivation and individual needs, it recognises that the individual has some control over what is learned and it identifies feedback as an important aspect of learning. The weaknesses are that it assumes learning is neutral and unproblematic and it is a purely rational approach that ignores emotion. From this perspective useful development activities would be seen as formal courses offering models and ideas with lots of back-up paperwork. Activities to improve learning motivation are also important, for example helping employees to recognise their own development needs and providing rewards for skills development. Mechanisms for providing feedback to employees are also key.

The third perspective is based on **social learning theory**, in other words learning is a social activity and this is based on our needs as humans to fit in with others. In organisations this happens to some extent naturally as we learn to fit in with things such as dress codes, behaviour in meetings and so on. Fitting in means that we can be accepted as successful in the organisation, but it is not necessary that we internalise and believe in these codes. Organisations often use role models, mentors and peer support, and 'buddies', to intensify our natural will to fit in. The disadvantages of this perspective are that it ignores the role of choice for the individual and it is based, to some extent, on a masquerade.

The **constructivist** perspective is a development of the information-processing perspective, but does not regard learning as a neutral process: it is our perception of our experiences that count; there is no 'objective' view. This perspective accepts that in our dealings with the world we create 'meaning structures' in our heads and these are based on our past experiences and personality. New information and potential learning need to fit with these meaning structures in some way, which means that a similar new experience will be understood differently by different people. We tend to pay attention to things which fit with our meaning structures and ignore or avoid things that don't fit. As humans we are also capable of constructing and reconstructing our meaning structures without any new experiences. These meaning structures are mainly unconscious and therefore we are not aware of the structures which constrain our learning. We are generally unaware of how valid our meanings sets are, and they are deeply held and difficult to change. Making these structures explicit enables us to challenge them and to start to change them. This perspective recognises that learning is a very personal and potentially threatening process. We develop mechanisms to protect ourselves from this threat, and thus protect ourselves from learning. The implication of this is that learning support needs to encourage introspection and reflection, and providing the perspectives of others (for example as in 360-degree feedback, outdoor courses or relocations) may assist in this process.

PRACTICAL CHARACTERISTICS OF LEARNING AND DEVELOPMENT

Learning from experience

A significant amount of work has been done which helps us understand how managers, and others, learn from their experiences. Kolb *et al.* (1984) argue that it is useful to

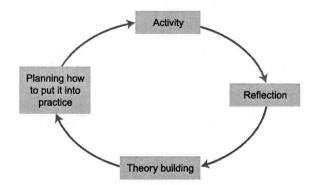

Figure 18.1
The learning
cycle

combine the characteristics of learning, which is usually regarded as passive, with those of problem solving, which is usually regarded as active. From this combination Kolb *et al.* developed a four-stage learning cycle, which was further developed by Honey and Mumford (1989).

The four stages, based on the work of both groups of researchers, are shown in Figure 18.1.

WINDOW ON PRACTICE

Gwen is a management trainer in a large organisation running a number of in-house management courses. She has just moved into this position from her role as section leader in the research department; the move was seen as a career development activity in order to strengthen her managerial skills.

Gwen is working with her manager to learn from her experiences. Here is an extract from her learning diary based on the learning cycle:

Activity – I've had a go at running three sessions on my own now, doing the input and handling the questions.

Reflection – I find the input much easier than handling questions. When I'm asked a question and answer it I have the feeling that they're not convinced by my reply and I feel awkward that we seem to finish the session hanging in mid-air. I would like to be able to encourage more open discussion.

Theory building – If I give an answer to a question it closes off debate by the fact that I have 'pronounced' what is 'right'. If I want them to discuss I have to avoid giving my views at first.

Planning practice – When I am asked a question rather than answering it I will say to the group: 'What does anyone think about that?' or 'What do you think?' (to the individual who asked) or 'What are the possibilities here?' I will keep encouraging them to respond to each other and reinforce where necessary, or help them change tack by asking another question.

Each of these four stages of the learning cycle is critical to effective learning, but few people are strong at each stage and it is helpful to understand where our strengths and weaknesses lie. Honey and Mumford designed a questionnaire to achieve this which identified individuals' learning styles as 'activist', 'reflector', 'theorist' and 'pragmatist', and explain that:

- **Activists** learn best from 'having a go', and trying something out without necessarily preparing. They would be enthusiastic about role-play exercises and keen to take risks in the real environment.

- **Reflectors** are much better at listening and observing. They are effective at reflecting on their own and others' experiences and good at analysing what happened and why.

- **Theorists'** strengths are in building a concept or a theory on the basis of their analysis. They are good at integrating different pieces of information, and building models of the way things operate. They may choose to start their learning by reading around a topic.

- **Pragmatists** are keen to *use* whatever they learn and will always work out how they can apply it in a real situation. They will plan how to put it into practice. They will value information/ideas they are given only if they can see how to relate them to practical tasks they need to do.

Understanding how individuals learn from experience underpins all learning, but is particularly relevant in encouraging self-development activities. Understanding our strengths and weaknesses enables us to choose learning activities which suit our style, and gives us the opportunity to decide to strengthen a particularly weak learning stage of our learning cycle. While Honey and Mumford adopt this dual approach, Kolb firmly maintains that learners *must* become deeply competent at all stages of the cycle. There has been considerable attention to the issue of matching and mismatching styles with development activities: *see*, for example, Hayes and Allinson (1996), who also consider the matching and mismatching of trainer learning style with learner learning style.

ACTIVITY 18.1

1 If you have not already done so obtain the Honey and Mumford questionnaire and work out your learning style(s).

2 Select your weakest style and try to identify two different learning activities which fit with this style, but that you would normally avoid.

3 Seek opportunities for trying out these learning activities. If you practise these activities on a regular basis this should help you strengthen the style you are working on.

4 Log your experiences and in particular what you have learned about these 'new' learning activities.

Learner type	Planned learning score	Emergent learning score
Sage	High	High
Warrior	High	Low
Adventurer	Low	High
Sleeper	Low	Low

Table 18.1
Planned and emergent learning

Source: Adapted from D. Megginson (1994) 'Planned and emergent learning: A framework and a method', *Executive Development*, Vol. 7, No. 6, pp. 29–32.

Planned and emergent learning

From a different, but compatible, perspective, David Megginson characterises learners by the extent to which they plan the direction of their learning and implement this (planned learning), and the extent to which they are able to learn from opportunistic learning experiences (emergent learning). Megginson (1994) suggests that strengths and weaknesses in these two areas will influence the way individuals react to self-development. These two characteristics are not mutually exclusive, and Megginson combines them to identify four learning types, as shown in Table 18.1.

Warriors are those who are strong at planning what they want to learn and how, but are less strong at learning from experiences they had not anticipated. They have a clear focus on what they want to learn and pursue this persistently. On the other hand *Adventurers* respond to and learn from opportunities that come along unexpectedly, they are curious and flexible. However, they tend not to plan and create opportunities for themselves. *Sages* are strong on both characteristics, and *Sleepers* display little of either characteristic at present. To be most effective in self-development activities learners need to make maximum use of both planned and emergent learning. For a further explanation of this model also *see* Megginson and Whitaker (1996).

ACTIVITY 18.2

Consider your development over the past year: do you feel that your strengths are in planning your learning or in learning opportunistically?

Choose your weaker approach, and identify how you could strengthen this.

Learning curves

The idea of the learning curve has been promulgated for some time, and was developed in relation to technical skills development. The general idea was that we tend to learn a new task more rapidly at first, so that the learning curve is steep, and then gradually plateau after we have had significant experience. A slightly different shape of learning is more relevant to personal skills development: the curve is less likely to be smooth, or it

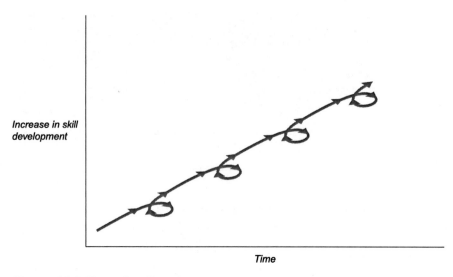

Increase in skill development

Time

Figure 18.2 The reality of learning progress

may not even be curved. Ideally our learning would be incremental, improving bit by bit all the time; in reality, however, learning is usually characterised by a mix of improvements and setbacks. Although, with persistence, our skills gradually increase, in the short term we may experience dips. These dips are demotivating but they are a necessary part of learning. Developing personal skills usually requires us to try out a new way of doing things. This is risky because, although the skills we are developing may be quite personal to us, we usually have to experiment with new ways of doing things in public. Understanding that sometimes things get worse before they get better helps to carry us through the dips. Figure 18.2 shows the reality of learning progress.

Identifying learning and training needs

The 'systematic training cycle' was developed to help organisations move away from ad hoc non-evaluated training, and replace it with an orderly sequence of training activities, but this approach has been less prominent of late. Harrison (2005) contests that such a cycle is not necessarily the most appropriate to use as it falls far short of the messy world of practice, and does not focus adequately on learning. Sloman (2001) argues that it may have fitted the 1960s mood for rationality and efficiency, but it is somewhat mechanical and fits less well with our faster pace of continuous change. In spite of this the cycle does retain some value, and we describe an adaptation of such a model to make it more applicable to today's environment. The model is set within an external environment and within an organisation strategy and an HR development strategy. Even if some of these elements are not made explicit, they will exist implicitly. Note that the boundary lines are dotted, not continuous. This indicates that the boundaries are permeable and overlapping. The internal part of the model reflects a systematic approach to learning and to training. Learning needs may be identified by the individual, by the organisation or in partnership, and this applies to each of the following steps in the circle. This dual involvement is probably the biggest change from traditional models where the

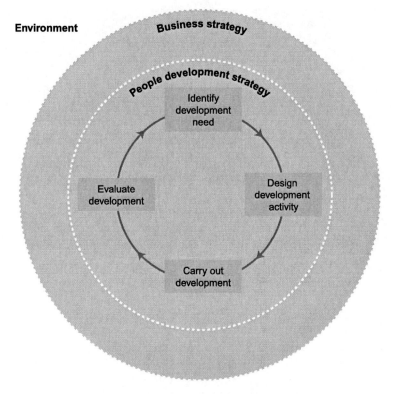

Figure 18.3 A systematic model of learning and training

steps were owned by the organisation, usually the trainers, and the individual was considered to be the subject of the exercise rather than a participant in it, or the owner of it. The model that we offer does not exclude this approach where appropriate, but is intended to be viewed in a more flexible way. The model is shown in Figure 18.3.

There are various approaches to analysing needs, the two most traditional being a problem-centred approach and matching the individual's competency profile with that for the job that person is filling. The problem-centred approach focuses on any performance problems or difficulties, and explores whether these are due to a lack of skills and, if so, which. The profile comparison approach takes a much broader view and is perhaps most useful when an individual, or group of individuals, are new to a job. This latter approach is also useful because strategic priorities change and new skills are required of employees, as the nature of their job changes, even though they are still officially in the same role with the same job title. When a gap has been identified, by whatever method, the development required needs to be phrased in terms of a learning objective, before the next stage of the cycle, planning and designing the development, can be undertaken. For example, when a gap or need has been identified around team leadership, appropriate learning objectives may be that learners, by the end of the development, will be able 'to ask appropriate questions at the outset of a team activity to ascertain relevant skills and experience, and to check understanding of the task' or 'to review a team activity by involving all members in that review'.

ACTIVITY 18.3

Write learning objectives for the following individuals who are experiencing problems in their performance:

1 Tina, who always dominates meetings, and neglects the contribution of others.

2 Brian, who has never carried out a selection interview before, and is very unsure of how to go about this.

3 Mark, who feels he has lots of contributions to make at meetings, but never actually says anything.

4 Sara, who can never get to meetings on time.

The planning and design of learning will be influenced by the learning objectives and also by the HR development strategy, which for example may contain a vision of who should be involved in training and development activities, and the emphasis on approaches such as self-development and e-learning. Once planning and design have been specified the course, or coaching or e-learning activity, can commence, and should be subject to ongoing monitoring and evaluated at an appropriate time in the future to assess how behaviour and performance have changed.

METHODS OF LEARNING AND DEVELOPMENT

Off-job methods: education and training courses

Educational courses undertaken during a career are frequently done on a part-time basis leading to a diploma or master's degree with a management or business label, and/or qualification for a professional body. It is considered that such courses provide value for both the employer and the participant – and MBA study is a popular route. For advantages of such a course for the employee *see*, for example, Baruch and Leeming (2001). An alternative approach to qualification is the NVQ route which we discussed in the previous chapter, which is more closely tied to on-job experiences and not concerned with 'education'.

In addition there are consultancy courses. Varying from a half-day to several weeks in length, they are run by consultants or professional bodies for all comers. They have the advantage that they bring together people from varying occupational backgrounds and are not, therefore, as introspective as in-house courses and are popular for topical issues. They are, however, often relatively expensive and superficial, despite their value as sources of industrial folklore, by which we mean the swapping of experiences among course members.

The most valuable courses of this type are those that concentrate on specific skills or knowledge, such as developing time management, interviewing or disciplinary skills, or being introduced to a new national initiative. This short-course approach is probably the only way for individuals to come to terms with some new development, such as a change in legislation, because they need not only to find an interpretation of the development, but also to share views and reactions with fellow employees to ensure that their own feelings are not idiosyncratic or perverse.

In-house courses are often similar in nature to the consultancy courses, and are sometimes run with the benefit of some external expertise. In-house courses can be particularly useful if the training needs to relate to specific organisational procedures and structures, or if it is geared to encouraging employees to work more effectively together in the organisational environment. The drawbacks of in-house courses are that they suffer from a lack of breadth of content, and there is no possibility of learning from people in other organisations.

Alternatively, there are outdoor-type courses (sometimes known as Outward Bound, after the organisation that pioneered them). Outdoor courses attempt to develop skills involved in working with and through others, and aim to increase self-awareness and self-confidence through a variety of experiences, including outdoor physical challenges. Courses like these continue to be increasingly used, and their differential value is assumed to hinge on their separation from the political, organisational environment. A natural, challenging and different environment is assumed to encourage individuals to forsake political strategising, act as their raw selves and be more open to new ideas. Burleston and Grint (1996), based on ethnographic research into outdoor programmes, found that while most participants did gain from the experience, the idea of providing a de-politicised environment is a naive hope rather than a reality. Ibbetson and Newell (1999) did find, however, that non-competitive outdoor programmes were more effective in meeting teambuilding objectives than competitive programmes. More recently learning experiences based on drama have increasingly been used; in these participants are engaged in improvisation through role play and exercises. For a fascinating insight into the variety of forms this may take *see* Monks *et al.* (2001). There are other forms of simulation in addition to role play, such as games and computer simulations; for a good discussion of definitions and outcomes of such approaches *see* Feinstein *et al.* (2002).

One of the major concerns with these different types of off-job courses and activities is the difficulty of ensuring transfer of learning back to the workplace. As part of their research on the contribution of off-job courses to managers Longenecker and Ariss (2002) asked managers what helped them retain what they had learned and transfer it to the workplace. Developing goals/plans for implementing new skills was most frequently identified. In addition managers said that it helped to review materials immediately after the programme; be actively involved in the learning itself; make a report to peers/superiors on what they had learned; review material and development plans with their mentor/manager; and include development goals in performance reviews. It is generally agreed that a supportive climate helps transfer (for example line manager interest and involvement, and development having a high priority in the organisation). Santos and Stewart (2003), for example, found that transfer was more likely if reward such as promotion or pay was attached to developmental behaviour change, and also where there was a helpful management climate in terms of pre- and post-course briefings and activities. Currently there are number of more creative approaches where experiential job-related activities are included on courses, as shown in the Window on practice.

WINDOW ON PRACTICE

Experiential activities

Brockett (2006) explains how EDF Energy aims to improve customer service via experiential course activities for engineers, dispatch and call-centre workers. During the course participants play the roles of guests at a sixtieth birthday party. Cake, music and decorations accompany this. Half-way though the party there is a surprise power cut represented by a blackout and audio recording of family members becoming distressed and stumbling about in the dark. The aim was to let course members experience what their customers experience when they have a power cut so that they can better understand the effect that it has on people's lives. Performance improvements followed in terms of repair times, accuracy of estimated repair times and increase in commendations letters from the public. This suggests that an experience, especially in the shoes of the customer, can have a powerful impact on employee perceptions and behaviours.

Phillips (2006) provides an example of BUPA care staff in a retirement home. As part of a 'Personal Best' programme aimed at improving customer service staff took the role of residents so as to see life through their customers' eyes. So, for example, they were fed puréed food and were hoisted in a mechanical sling from a chair into a bed. As a result staff behaviour towards residents has changed, for example explaining the hoisting procedure to residents and doing it more slowly.

Sources: Brockett, J. (2006) 'Energy firm gets party vibe', *People Management*, Vol. 12, No. 10, 18 May, p. 12; Phillips, L. (2006) 'BUPA Stars', *People Management*, Vol. 12, No. 22, 9 November, pp. 30–2.

In relation to MBAs Martin and Pate (2001) found, surprisingly, that a poor transfer climate did not affect transfer, but willingness to apply what was learned was related to the individual's positive feelings about the company and his or her intended continuance there.

While courses are no longer viewed as the key means of developing staff, they still have an important role to play, and in Interactive skill 4, in the Focus on skills at the end of Part 4, we therefore explore presentation as well as coaching skills.

Learning on the job

Manager coaching and other internal and external coaching

The line manager's role in learning and development has increased with the devolution of HR tasks. Coaching is an informal approach to individual development based on a close relationship between the individual and one other person either internal or external to the organisation. The coach is often the immediate manager, who is experienced in the task, but there is increasing use of external coaches, especially for more senior managers, or specially trained internal coaches, and 'coaching' has become very much a professional occupation with its own code of ethical practice. We will look at this in more detail, but first we explore the coaching role of the line manager.

The manager as coach helps trainees to develop by giving them the opportunity to perform an increasing range of tasks, and by helping them to learn from their experiences. Managers work to improve the trainee's performance by asking searching questions, actively listening, discussion, exhortation, encouragement, understanding, counselling and providing information and honest feedback. The manager coach is usually in a position to create development opportunities for the trainee when this is appropriate. For example, a line manager can delegate attendance at a meeting, or allow a trainee to deputise, where this is appropriate to the individual's development needs. Alternatively a line manager can create the opportunity for a trainee to join a working party or can arrange a brief secondment to another department. Coaches can share 'inside' information with the individual they are coaching to help them understand the political context in which they are working. For example, they are able to explain who will have most influence on a decision that will be made, or future plans for restructuring within a department.

Skilled coaches can adapt their style to suit the individual they are coaching, from highly directive at one end of the scale to non-directive at the other. The needed style may change over time, as the trainee gains more confidence and experience. A useful text on the practical skills of coaching is Pemberton (2006). In an exploratory study Carroll and Gillen (2001) found a variety of barriers to line manager acceptance of a teaching/coaching role, in particular lack of interpersonal competence, lack of time, performance pressures, and a feeling that the teaching role was not valued and was the role of the HR department. This same article also provides some excellent material on what makes an effective coach. The CIPD (2006) found that competing business pressures and lack of internal skills and experience were the greatest barriers to coaching, and IDS (2006a) suggests that in view of the emphasis in coaching on honest self-reflection, there will be barriers in organisations where the culture is not one of openness and honesty. They also point out that coaching has been seen as a remedial tool but that it probably has more to offer as a development opportunity for turning good performers into excellent ones.

There has been an increasing trend to broaden the concept of coaching in terms of both content and who carries out the coaching. Many organisations are now providing or arranging intensive training for designated internal coaches who operate broadly in the organisation, just in a coaching role. This is quite different from the basic training line managers are likely to receive. External executive coaching is often provided by consultancies and specialist coaching organisations. IDS (2006a) provides an excellent range of case studies demonstrating the different ways in which organisations are using coaching. Various forms of coaching may include career coaching, performance coaching, skills coaching, business coaching and life coaching. Given the increasing professionalisation of coaching it is not surprising that the quality of the coaching experience is receiving attention. Supervision of practice is increasingly being used in a way that is similar to supervision for counsellors, which involves regular meetings with a more experienced practitioner to explore their client relationships and reflect on practice. A CIPD study carried out by the Bath Consultancy Group (Arney 2006) found that nearly half the coaches received regular supervision, and that it was a fast growing practice.

Such individual supervision is carried out with a mind to client confidentiality; however there is also a growing trend for group supervision of coaches and also for organisations wanting to collect common themes discussed in coaching sessions as these can be used to inform organisational thinking (Arney 2006). Both these approaches put client confidentiality at greater risk.

WINDOW ON PRACTICE

Group supervision at PricewaterhouseCoopers

Group supervision has been used for internal coaches for some time and involves sessions of three hours every month led by an external facilitator with experience of coaching supervision and a background in psychology or psychotherapy.

Coaches present a case with the emphasis on the work of the coach and the coaching relationship rather than the individual client. In order to protect confidentiality real names are not disclosed. It is an opportunity for an individual coach to get reactions from others about their own practice, and also to reflect on approaches that others take. So the aim is to encourage constant learning and reflection, through making one's work open to scrutiny.

Source: Summarised from E. Arney (2006) 'Insider's Guide', *People Management*, Vol. 12, No. 23, 23 November, pp. 40–2.

WINDOW ON PRACTICE

Coaching at the Medical Research Council (MRC) and Unilever

Hall (2006) reports on the arrangement that external coaching company 'Laughing Phoenix' has made with the (MRC) which involves coaching the 30 most senior HR professionals. One of the conditions of the agreement was that the company would feed back recurring themes to the MRC so that they could align coaching with the wider business picture. Unilever has contacted internal coaches regularly to 'harvest some of the intelligence they had gathered from their clients', again keen to pick up recurring themes, helping the organisation know which areas to tackle and help the coaches understand the context of their work .

Source: Hall, L. (2006) 'Inside Job', *People Management*, Vol. 12, No. 16, 10 August, pp. 34–6.

The emphasis on coaching is underlined by the recently released CIPD journal, *Coaching at Work*, and the development of the institute's coaching standards. The number of organisations aiming to develop a coaching culture reached 80 per cent in the 2006 CIPD survey, with 79 per cent already using some coaching activities, and Lehane (2005) provides some guidance on getting started on this. Useful ideas for developing a coaching culture include making coaching part of conversations, day to day; shifting the power to the learner; integrating external and internal coaching resources; the focus on continuous improvement in coaching activities making this a valued and natural part of a manager's job; and shifting the emphasis from individual coaching to team coaching (Clutterbuck and Megginson 2005). Concerns for quality are being addressed, for example by a kitemarking scheme for coaching and mentoring qualifications, launched by the European Coaching and Mentoring Council (*see* **www. emccouncil.org**), and the British Psychological Society now has a specialist interest group focused on coaching.

Mentoring

Mentoring offers a wide range of advantages for the development of the mentee or protégé, coaching as described above being just one of the possible benefits of the relationship. The mentor may occasionally be the individual's immediate manager, but usually it is a more senior manager in the same or a different function. Kram (1983) identifies two broad functions of mentoring, the first of which is the career function, including those aspects of the relationship that primarily enhance career advancement, such as exposure and visibility and sponsorship. The second is the psychosocial function, which includes those aspects of the relationship that primarily enhance a sense of competence, clarity of identity and effectiveness in the managerial role. More recently Fowler and O'Gorman (2005) on the basis of research with both mentors and mentees, describe eight individual mentoring functions which are: personal and emotional guidance; coaching; advocacy; career development facilitation; role modelling; strategies and systems advice; learning facilitation; and friendship, whilst Arnold (1997) found that the most common advantages of mentoring were perceived as role modelling and counselling. There is evidence that mentoring does benefit both parties (*see*, for example, Johnson *et al.* 1999), and Broadbridge (1999) suggests that mentors can gain through recognition from peers, increased job satisfaction, rejuvenation, admiration and self-satisfaction. The drawbacks to mentoring that were revealed in Broadbridge's research include the risk of over-reliance, the danger of picking up bad habits, the fact that the protégé may be alienated from other sources of expertise and the sense of loss experienced when a mentor leaves. In addition, the difficulty of dealing with conflicting views in such an unequal relationship was identified. Perceived benefits, however, considerably outweighed any drawbacks. Megginson (2000) identifies the issue of dysfunctional mentoring, and the danger of assuming that mentoring is unquestionably good.

Managers are also seen as responsible for developing talent, and while a mentor/ protégé relationship might not naturally occur, mentorship may be encouraged or formalised. For example, there are systems where all new graduates are attached to a mentor as soon as they join the organisation. The difficulties of establishing a formal programme include the potential mismatch of individuals, unreal expectations on both sides and the time and effort involved.

WINDOW ON PRACTICE

Mentoring at Fifteen

Liam Black, Director of Fifteen (Jamie Oliver's project to turn disadvantaged youngsters into cooks) initiated a structured programme to turn six members of staff into qualified mentors able to support the more vulnerable youngsters to aid retention. The staff are from different companies run by Olliver and are not directly working with the youngsters. The six are working towards a Certificate in Workplace Mentoring from the Oxford School of Coaching and Mentoring (accredited by John Brookes University), which is suitably tailored to their work-based needs. The programme is a six-month blended learning package and the mentors will work with the youngsters setting goals, developing coping strategies and building their often non-existent self-esteem.

Cottee, P. (2006) 'Oliver's Army', *People Management*, Vol. 12, No. 19, 28 September, pp. 44–5.

WINDOW ON PRACTICE

Tony Stott and Jenny Sweeney (1999) report on a structured mentoring scheme with a difference at Shell. While Shell runs a very flexible mentoring scheme appropriate for many different types of employee and purposes, it recognises the importance of the design of the scheme and good administration. The authors suggest that there are five critical elements in a good scheme:

- **A database.** Although the scheme is based on natural selection, that is, a mutual decision between a potential mentor and a new recruit, the database appears to be critical, in order to track the flow of mentees and the availability of mentors. Copies of mentor biographies are available for new recruits to read.

- **Mentor support.** Mentors are trained in their role and in recognising the limits of their abilities. There is also a support mechanism for mentors, and mentors meet to share their experiences.

- **Training.** Both mentors and mentees are trained, and this forms a key part of the induction programme for new recruits, with information on reasons for using mentoring, roles and expectations.

- **Resource materials.** These include websites for mentors. Guidance booklets for mentees are also produced.

- **Evaluation.** Shell found that a non-bureaucratic scheme, which gives ownership to the participants, was appreciated.

Source: Summarised from T. Stott and J. Sweeney (1999) 'More than a match', *People Management*, June, pp. 45–8.

Peer relationships

Although mentor-protégé relationships have been shown to be related to high levels of career success, not all developing individuals have access to such a relationship, and even formal schemes are often reserved for specific groups such as new graduate entrants. Supportive peer relationships at work are potentially more widely available to the individual and offer a number of benefits for the development of both parties. The benefits that are available depend on the nature of the peer relationship, and Kram and Isabella (1985) have identified three groups of peer relationships, which are differentiated by their primary development functions. These can be expressed on a continuum from 'information peer', based primarily on information sharing, through 'collegial peer', based on career strategising, giving job-related feedback and friendship, to 'special peer', based on emotional support, personal feedback, friendship and confirmation. Most of us benefit from one or a number of peer relationships at work but often we do not readily appreciate their contribution towards our development. Peer relationships most often develop on an informal basis and provide mutual support. Some organisations, however, formally appoint an existing employee to provide such support to a new member of staff through their first 12–18 months in the organisation. These relationships may, of course, continue beyond the initial period. The name for the appointed employee will vary from organisation to organisation, and sometimes the word 'buddy', 'coach' or 'mentor' is used – which can be confusing! Cromer (1989) discusses the advantages of peer relationships organised on a formal basis and the skills and qualities sought in peer providers, which include accessibility, empathy, organisational experience and proven task skills.

ACTIVITY 18.4

Consider each significant peer relationship that you have at work. Where does each fit on the continuum of relationships described above, and what contributions does it make towards your development?

If you are in full-time education consider the contribution that each of your relationships (whether at university, home or work) has to your development.

Self-development

Natural learning is learning that takes place on the job and results from an individual's everyday experience of the tasks to be undertaken. Natural learning is even more difficult to investigate than coaching, mentoring or peer relationships, and yet the way in which we learn from everyday experiences, and our level of awareness of this, is very important for our development. To some extent self-development may be seen as a conscious effort to gain the most from natural learning in a job, and to use the learning cycle as a framework. Self-development can be focused in specific skills development, but often extends to attitude development and personal growth.

ACTIVITY 18.5

The video *Groundhog Day* can be viewed as a journey of self-development. Watch the video and answer the following questions:

- How did Phil's attitudes change and how was this reflected in his behaviour?
- What do you think Phil learned?
- How did he learn it?
- Why is personal development so difficult?

The emphasis in self-development is that each individual is responsible for, and can plan, his or her own development, although he or she may need to seek help when working on some issues. Self-development involves individuals in analysing their strengths, weaknesses and the way in which they learn, primarily by means of questionnaires and feedback from others. This analysis may initially begin on a self-development course, or with the help of a facilitator, but would then be continued by the individual back on the job. From this analysis individuals, perhaps with some help at first, plan their development goals and the way in which they will achieve them, primarily through development opportunities within the job. When individuals consciously work on self-development they use the learning cycle in a more explicit way than in natural learning. They are also in a better position to seek appropriate opportunities and help, in their learning, from their manager.

Many of the activities included in self-development are based on observation, collecting further feedback about the way they operate, experimenting with different approaches and in particular reviewing what has happened, why and what they have learned. Self-development, however, is not a quick fix as it requires a long-term approach and careful planning and, as Stansfield (1996) suggests, attention needs to be paid to the 'scaffolding' which supports the self-development process. To this end she suggests that extensive briefing and explanation of the theoretical underpinning of the self-development are both important. In addition she suggests direct skill development concerning the role, importance and nature of peer feedback, and further support in tracking personal learning needs to ensure a more rigorous learning journey. Woodall (2000) also notes difficulties around the support structure for self-development, and identifies confusion in terminology as unhelpful. Confusion in terminology is also raised by Antonacopoulou (2000), who highlights a much neglected influence on self-development − that the individuals themselves have to be capable of taking on this responsibility.

Self-development groups

Typically, in self-development groups a group of individuals is involved in a series of meetings where they jointly discuss their personal development, organisational issues and/or individual work problems. Groups may begin operating with a leader who is a process expert, not a content expert, and who therefore acts as a facilitator rather than, but not to the complete exclusion of, a source of information. The group itself is the primary source of information and may operate without outside help as its members' process skills develop. The content and timings of the meetings can be very flexible, although meetings will require a significant level of energy and commitment if they are to operate well.

Self-development groups can be devised in a variety of contexts. They can be part of a formal educational course, for example a Diploma in Management Studies, where a group of managers from different organisations come together to support their development; they may constitute the whole of a self-development 'course'; or they can be an informal support group within an organisation. However the group originates, it is important that the members understand what every member hopes to get out of the group, the role of the facilitator (if there is one), the processes and rules that the group will operate by and how they agree to interact.

Learning logs

Learning logs are a mechanism for learning retrospectively as they encourage a disciplined approach to learning from opportunistic events. The log may be focused around one particular activity and is usually designed to encourage the writer to explain what happened, how he or she has reflected on this, what conclusions he or she has made and what future learning actions he or she wishes to make. Alternatively logs can be used in the form of a daily or weekly diary.

ACTIVITY 18.6

Identify a management skills area that you need to develop. (You may find it particularly helpful to choose an interpersonal area, for example, assertiveness, influencing others, presentation, being more sociable, contributing to meetings, helping others.)

Keep a learning diary over the next few weeks, logging anything that is relevant to your development area. Use the framework which Gwen used in a previous example (see Window on practice box at the beginning of this chapter).

At the end of the period review what you have learned in your development area and also what you have learned about the learning cycle.

Learning contracts

There is increasing use of learning contracts, sometimes used within more formalised self-development groups; on other management courses; as part of a mentoring or coaching relationship; or in working towards a competency-based qualification. These contracts are a formal commitment by the learner to work towards a specified learning goal, with an identification of how the goal might be achieved. They thus promote a proactive approach to learning. Boak (1991) has produced a very helpful guide to the use of such contracts and suggests that they should include:

- an overall development goal;
- specific objectives in terms of skills and knowledge;
- activities to be undertaken;
- resources required;
- a method of assessment of learning.

The value that individuals gain from learning contracts is dependent on their choosing to participate, their identification of the relevant goal and the importance and value they ascribe to achieving it. Only with commitment will a learning contract be effective, because ultimately it is down to the individual learner manager to make it happen.

WINDOW ON PRACTICE

David wanted to improve his influencing skills and has sent the following draft learning contract to his manager for discussion:

Goal

To improve my influencing skills with both peers and more senior managers.

Specific objectives

- To prepare for influencing situations.
- To try to understand better the perspective of the other.
- To identify the interpersonal skills required – probably active listening, reflecting, summarising, stating my needs, collaboration (but maybe more).
- To be able to identify that I have had more influence in decisions made.

Activities

- Watch a recommended video on influencing skills.
- Re-read my notes from the interpersonal skills course I attended.
- Watch how others in my department go about influencing.
- Ask other people (supportive ones) how they go about it.
- Identify possible influencing situations in advance, and plan for what I want and what might happen.
- Reflect back on what happened, and work out how to do better next time.
- Ask for feedback.

Resources

- Video.
- Notes.
- The support of others.

Assessment

- I could ask for feedback from colleagues and my manager.

- My own assessment may be helpful.

- Make a log over time of decisions made and my originally preferred outcome.

e-learning and blended learning

As technology enables interesting and interactive presentation of distance learning materials, there is evidence of considerable enthusiasm on the part of organisations to pursue this approach to development, and take advantage of the opportunities it presents. CIPD (2003) reports that one of the most significant changes in training over the last five years is the increased use of e-learning, although it is still most heavily used by IT staff. However, by 2006 only a quarter of respondents to the Learning and Development CIPD survey said that it had significantly altered learning and training offerings. E-learning can be defined as 'learning that is delivered, enabled or mediated by electronic technology' (Sloman and Rolph 2003, p. 1). While e-learning has been characterised as requiring high investment in terms of hardware, software and design time, it has also been characterised as cost effective in the long run, with the ability to provide speedy and flexible training. IDS (2006b) identifies the main advantages of e-learning as flexible access across time and place, flexible use of content; consistent delivery; sustainable and easy to update; value for money and of the moment, being particularly useful for the launch of new products. Hammond (2001), for example, describes the case of Cisio which is constantly launching new IT-based products. The company has moved from 90 per cent classroom-based training for its sales representatives to 80 per cent online training so that the large numbers of representatives can experience training immediately the product is launched. Channel Four (Cooper 2001) has a strategy to replace much of its classroom teaching activity with interactive learning, and the London Emergency Services are using virtual reality training to prepare employees for emergency events. Prickett (1997) reports how Hendon Police Training College uses virtual reality to prepare officers to deal with siege and hostage situations. Sloman and Rolph (2003) found that e-learning has been implemented in a variety of ways, from being introduced as a sweeping ambitious change to small incremental changes to the organisation's approach to training, and from a mandatory change to an offer to volunteers. They also report that key barriers are the computer literacy of employees and access to the appropriate equipment.

However enthusiasm from the organisation is not sufficient, and there has been much evidence of employees being unwilling to use e-learning. There was much initial euphoria about what e-learning could contribute, but increasingly it has been recognised that motivating learners is critical and most organisations now have much more realistic expectations of what e-learning can achieve, and often have to improve and re-launch e-learning solutions before they bed in, as for example in Hilton Hotels (Smethurst 2006). The support provided may well be critical, as may the way that such methods are introduced and used.

WINDOW ON PRACTICE

E-learning for leadership development at Barclays

In order to focus more on leadership abilities in promotion decisions Barclays wanted to provide leadership development which was available to all, regardless of age, gender, grade and geographical location. They produced a leadership development portal called 'Take the Lead', which could be used on a voluntary basis. Shortly after the initial launch the offering was re-launched making it more interactive and engaging and accessible, with dedicated 'learning laptops' that could be borrowed. An incentive was also offered in the form of a qualification in conjunction with Nottingham University Business School. Before this they had found that take-up in the UK was lower than elsewhere, with e-learning not being regarded as a first-choice approach to learning. To encourage use of the website news articles were published every two weeks, and managers in the appropriate grades were specifically targeted with 'teaser' postcards asking, for example, whether they were serious about their development. In addition testaments were given by managers of different levels of authority. Target managers also received brochures about the re-launch, their line managers received information packs, and e-learning featured in the in-house magazine. Email reminders were sent to participants who had not logged on to the portal for some months and learning logs were automatically produced when an individual completed a module with the suggestion that he or she should discuss with his or her manager how best to utilise these newly developed skills in his or her job. 'Take the Lead' is gradually becoming a more blended approach. Modules can be completed in any order according to job needs and good use is made of Barclays case studies.

Source: Summarised from IDS (2006b) *E-Learning*, HR Studies, No. 818, London: IDS.

E-learning covers a wide variety of approaches from using CD-roms to the company intranet and the Internet. More sophisticated approaches do not confine e-learning to interactive learning at a distance. Increasingly, synchronous learning is used where all participants log on at the same time, with a tutor or facilitator being available. Individuals can progress through material alone or network with others to complete a task and use chat rooms and have a dialogue with the tutor. Videoconferencing can also be used to bring participants together at the same time. For example, some MBAs have been delivered via videoconferencing rather than classroom-based teaching, and further details of this are provided in Cases 18.1 and 18.2 on this book's companion website at **www.pearsoned.co.uk/torrington**. The concept of blended learning also has had much appeal recently, but this term can be interpreted in different ways. Some use it to indicate the blending of e-learning with face-to-face learning experiences, while others use it more broadly to indicate 'a range of ways that e-learning can be delivered when combined with multiple additional routes that support and facilitate learning' (Sloman and Rolph 2003, p. 6).

WINDOW ON PRACTICE

Hills and Francis (1999) suggest that computer-based learning is a solitary activity, and that social contact and interaction were a necessary ingredient in learning. They assessed the use of their local computer-based training centres in Lloyds TSB, and found that some were used much more than others. The extent of use was not related to geographical accessibility, but instead to the support provided by the centre administrator, before, during and after learning sessions, and also the support of local managers.

Blended learning is increasingly used to indicate a blend of any approaches to learning, and there is evidence that learning and training now involve a much wider range of activities (CIPD 2006), while Pickard (2006) reports on the blended learning approach at the Department for Work and Pensions which integrates self-managed learning, coaching and e-learning.

WINDOW ON PRACTICE

Julie Scumming at AXA

Clarke (2006) recounts a very inventive learning experience at AXA, highly job based and involving a variety of activities. The exercise started with a Christmas card from a fictitious employee Julie Scumming. Posters followed announcing her arrival and then her fictitious husband entered the offices, shouting. After this there were diary entries on the intranet from both Julie and from her boss which staff began to follow, and picked up the story that Julie was a devout Christian and who felt she was being discriminated against and bullied by her boss and peers. Dummy tabloid articles were circulated, a stand-up row in the canteen was performed by actors. Sticky notes were put on computers saying not to get 'stuck like Julie', and an Advent calendar counted down the days to the main event which was a tribunal hearing for managers. When the tribunal panel retired to consider their verdict actors acted out scenes which had led up to the tribunal. Meanwhile employees could log on to discussion forums to express their views about the case, and there was a poll about the anticipated results. Involvement in all of this was voluntary but many staff participated. The objective was to raise awareness about discrimination issues. Responses to questionnaires after the event demonstrated that managers were more aware of religious discrimination issues.

Source: Clarke, E. (2006) 'Julie Diligent', *People Management*, Vol. 12, No. 14, 13 July, pp. 32–43.

EVALUATION OF TRAINING AND DEVELOPMENT

One of the most nebulous and unsatisfactory aspects of the training job is evaluating its effectiveness, yet it is becoming more necessary to demonstrate value for money. Whilst Campbell (2006) estimates that employer, public and individual spend on workforce training and development in the UK nears £30 billion each year, Phelps (2002) suggests there is no satisfactory return on investment calculation to prove its value, and that we remain unsure whether training breeds success or success breeds training. Evaluation is straightforward when the output of the training is clear to see, such as reducing the number of dispatch errors in a warehouse or increasing someone's typing speed. It is more difficult to evaluate the success of a management training course or a programme of social skills development, but the fact that it is difficult is not enough to prevent it being done.

A familiar method of evaluation is the post-course questionnaire, which course members complete on the final day by answering vague questions that require them to assess aspects of the course using only such general terms as 'good', 'very good' or 'outstanding'. The drawbacks with such questionnaires are, first, that there is a powerful halo effect, as the course will have been, at the very least, a welcome break from routine and there will probably have been some attractive fringe benefits such as staying in a comfortable hotel and enjoying rich food. Second, the questionnaire tends to evaluate the course and not the learning, so that the person attending the course is assessing the quality of the tutors and the visual aids, instead of being directed to examine what has been learned.

Hamblin (1974), in a much-quoted work, identified five levels of evaluation: (1) evaluating the training, as in the post-course questionnaire above; (2) evaluating the learning, in terms of how the trainee now behaves; (3) evaluating changes in job performance; (4) evaluating changes in organisation performance; and (5) evaluating changes in the wider contribution that the organisation now makes. Perhaps the most well-referenced approach to evaluation is Kilpatrick (1959) who suggested four levels of evaluation, somewhat similar to Hamblin: (1) reaction level; (2) learning level (have the learning objectives been met?); (3) behaviour (how has the individual's behaviour changed back in the job?); and (4) results and impact on the bottom line (what is the impact of training on performance?).

WINDOW ON PRACTICE

Demonstrating the value of learning, training and development

The CIPD Learning and Development Survey (CIPD 2006) found that nine in ten respondents used some form of evaluation in an effort to identify the value of learning, training and development activities. Of these:

- 98 per cent evaluate to Kilpatrick level 1
- 73 per cent to Kilpatrick level 2
- 62 per cent to Kilpatrick level 3
- 36 per cent to Kilpatrick level 4
- and only 18 per cent look at the full return on their investment.

Source: CIPD (2006) *Learning and Development: Annual Survey Report 2006*. London: CIPD.

Bramley (1996) suggests that performance effectiveness can be measured at individual, team and organisational levels, and that changes in behaviour, knowledge, skills and attitudes need to be considered. He makes the worthwhile point – as do others – that the criteria for evaluation need to be built into development activities from the very beginning, and not tagged on at the end. Lingham and his co-researchers (2006) provide a good example of how this can be done in practice. They describe an action research project where evaluation was built in from the outset and involved collaboration between organisational leaders, trainers, participants and evaluators. A four-phase approach was used:

- Phase 1: Design of training programme (organisational leaders, trainers and evaluators agree design and methods to obtain feedback from participants after the initial runs of the training programme).
- Phase 2: Launch and evaluation of initial programme (training conducted and agreed methods used to collect participants' views).
- Phase 3: Feedback and design of evaluation instrument (organisational leaders, trainers and evaluators meet to review feedback and field notes and adapt the training programme where necessary. A survey instrument designed for evaluation of future iterations of the programme).
- Phase 4: Ongoing training and evaluation (training programme conducted with new design/content, evaluation survey used and results fed back into Phase 3. (adapted from Lingham *et al.* 2006)

Problems with evaluation persist and in the 2006 CIPD survey 80 per cent of respondents reported that their training activities are delivering greater value to the business than they are able to demonstrate. There is always a need, however, to assess value for money, and this is generally worked out on a payback basis, which focuses attention on the short term. Lee (1996) suggests a 'pay-forward' approach to assessing value for money and this concept appears to be more consistent with the nature of training and development strategy and interventions than a payback approach, as the outcome may only be observed in the long term.

While organisations may desire a measure of the impact of training on the organisation, in practice this appears to be rarely achieved. Sadler-Smith *et al.*, for example, found in their study (1999) that the reasons for evaluating training were more often operational than strategic, and they state that evaluation information was used 'mostly for feedback to individuals, and to inform the training process, and less for return on investment decisions' (p. 369).

SUMMARY PROPOSITIONS

18.1 There are four perspectives on learning: behaviourist, cognitive, social and constructivist. Each has different implications for the approach taken to training and development.

18.2 The emphasis has moved from training to learning, with individuals taking ownership of their own learning needs. To be effective learners we need to understand the nature of learning and our own strengths and weaknesses.

18.3   The emphasis on formal development programmes is declining in favour of greater interest in approaches to on-the-job development, such as coaching, mentoring, peer relationships and self-development.

18.4   There has been an upsurge of interest in e-learning. However, the extent to which employees take advantage of such opportunities will be affected by the context and the support available. E-learning is increasingly being blended with other forms of learning.

18.5   Evaluation of development is critical but difficult. It is most effective when built into the design of the development activity rather than tagged on at the end.

GENERAL DISCUSSION TOPICS

1 If learning is an individual process, why is so much training done in groups? What are the implications of moving towards more individualised learning?

2 Discuss the view that the role of the trainer/facilitator is critically important in the effectiveness of a training programme.

FURTHER READING

Hawkins, P. and Schwenk, G. (2006) *Coaching Supervision – Maximising the potential of Coaching, A Change Agenda*. London: CIPD.
This is a full report of the research carried out by the Bath Consultancy Group, and is a fascinating read providing an assessment of current practice, with examples of good practice and guidelines for managers.

Jarvis, J. and Lane, D. (2006) *The Case for Coaching: Making evidence based decisions on coaching*. London: CIPD.
A combined approach from academics and professionals makes this well-researched book both interesting and informative, and includes coaching by a range of different practitioners.

Passmore, J. (ed.) (2006) *Excellence in Coaching: The Industry Guide*. London: Kogan Page.
A combination of contributions from both academics and practitioners provides expertise in a range of areas relevant to coaching.

Reynolds, J., Caley, L. and Mason, R. (2002) *How do People Learn? A Research report*. London: CIPD.
This research report covers the background context to learning in today's organisations and considers the four theoretical perspectives on learning. The report also covers practical aspects of learning and e-learning. This report has been summarised by Jennifer Schramm (2002) in *The change agenda: How do people learn?* London: CIPD.

Tulip, S. (2006) 'Lighting the Way', *People Management*, Vol. 12, No. 18, 14 September, p. 44.
This is a very useful summary of coaching trends.

Thorne, K. (2003) *Blended Learning*. London: Kogan Page.
A useful, broadly based handbook which explains how to get the best out of combining innovative and technological advances offered by e-learning with the best of traditional approaches to learning. Thorne considers the high-level support required for such approaches and the involvement of

stakeholders, and also provides practical design solutions. A range of case studies shows, in particular, the various ways in which different approaches to learning can be combined.

REFERENCES

Antonacopoulou, E. (2000) 'Employee development through self-development in three retail banks', *Personnel Review*, Vol. 29, No. 4.

Arney, E. (2006) 'Insider's Guide', *People Management*, Vol. 12, No. 23, 23 November, pp. 40–42.

Arnold, J. (1997) 'Mentoring in early career', *Human Resource Management Journal*, Vol. 7, No. 4, pp. 61–70.

Baruch, Y. and Leeming, A. (2001) 'The added value of MBA studies – graduates' perceptions', *Personnel Review*, Vol. 30, No. 5, pp. 589–601.

Bee, F. and Bee, R. (1994) *Training Needs Analysis and Evaluation*. London: IPM.

Boak, G. (1991) *Developing Managerial Competencies. The management learning contract approach*. London: Pitman.

Bramley, P. (1996) *Evaluating Training*. London: IPD.

Broadbridge, A. (1999) 'Mentoring in retailing: a tool for success?', *Personnel Review*, Vol. 28, No. 4.

Brockett, J. (2006) 'Energy firm gets party vibe', *People Management*, Vol. 12, No. 10, 18 May, p. 12.

Burleston, L. and Grint, K. (1996) 'The deracination of politics: outdoor management development', *Management Learning*, Vol. 27, No. 2, pp. 187–202.

Campbell, M. (2006) 'Demonstrating the value of learning, training and development', in *Latest Trends in Learning, Training and Development: Reflections on the 2006 Learning and Development Survey*. London: CIPD.

Canning, R. (1996) 'Enhancing the quality of learning in human resource development', *Journal of European Industrial Training*, Vol. 20, No. 2, pp. 3–10.

Carroll, S. and Gillen, D. (2001) 'Exploring the teaching function of the managerial role', *Journal of Management Development*, Vol. 21, No. 5, pp. 330–42.

CIPD (2003) *Training and Development 2003: Survey Report*. London: CIPD.

CIPD (2006) *Learning and Development: Annual Survey 2006*. London: CIPD.

Clarke, E. (2006) 'Julie Diligent', *People Management*, Vol. 12, No. 14, 13 July, pp. 32–43.

Clutterbuck, D. and Megginson, D. (2005) *Making coaching work: Creating a Coaching Culture*. London: CIPD.

Cooper, C. (2001) 'Connect Four', *People Management*, February.

Cottee, P. (2006) 'Oliver's Army', *People Management*, Vol. 12, No. 19, 28 September, pp. 44–45.

Cromer, D.R. (1989) 'Peers as providers', *Personnel Administrator*, Vol. 34, Pt 5, pp. 84–6.

Feinstein, A., Mann, S. and Corsum, D. (2002) 'Charting the experiential territory – Clarifying definitions and uses of computer simulations, games and role plays', *Personnel Review*, Vol. 21, No. 10, pp. 732–44.

Fowler, J. and O'Gorman, J. (2005) 'Mentoring functions: A Contemporary view of the perceptions of mentees and mentors', *British Journal of Management*, Vol. 16, pp. 51–7.

Hall, L. (2006) 'Inside Job', *People Management*, Vol. 12, No. 16, 10 August, pp. 34–6.

Hallier, J. and Butts, S. (1999) 'Employers' discovery of training: self-development, employability and the rhetoric of partnership', *Employee Relations*, Vol. 21, No. 1.

Hamblin, A.C. (1974) *Evaluation and Control of Training*. Maidenhead: McGraw-Hill.

Hammond, D. (2001) 'Reality Bytes', *People Management*, January.

Harrison, R. (1997) *Employee Development*. London: IPD.

Harrison, R. (2005) *Learning and Development*. London: IPD.

Hayes, J. and Allinson, C.W. (1996) 'The implications of learning styles for training and development: a discussion of the matching hypothesis', *British Journal of Management*, Vol. 7, pp. 63–73.

Hills, H. and Francis, P. (1999) 'Interaction Learning', *People Management*, July.

Honey, P. and Mumford, A. (1989) *A Manual of Learning Opportunities*. Maidenhead: Peter Honey.

Ibbetson, A. and Newell, S. (1999) 'A comparison of a competitive and non-competitive outdoor management development programmes', *Personnel Review*, Vol. 28, No. 1/2.

IDS (2006a) *Coaching in the Workplace*. HR Studies No. 831, October. London: IDS.

IDS (2006b) *E-Learning*. HR Studies, No. 818. London: IDS.

Johnson, S., Geory, G. and Griego, O. (1999) 'The Mentoring Model theory: dimensions in mentoring protocols', *Career Development International*, Vol. 4, No. 7.

Kilpatrick, D. (1959) 'Techniques for evaluating training programmes', *Journal of the American Society of Training Directors*, Vol. 13.

Kolb, D.A., Rubin, I.M. and McIntyre, J.M. (1984) *Organization Psychology*, 4th edn. Englewood Cliffs, NJ: Prentice-Hall.

Kram, K.E. (1983) 'Phases of the mentor relationship', *Academy of Management Journal*, Vol. 26, No. 4.

Kram, K.E. and Isabella, L.A. (1985) 'Mentoring alternatives: the role of peer relationships in career development', *Academy of Management Journal*, Vol. 28, No. 1.

Lee, R. (1996) 'The pay-forward view of training', *People Management*, pp. 30–2.

Lehane, S. (2005) 'Whistle while you work', *People Management*, Vol. 11, No. 25, 29 December, pp. 32–3.

Lingham, T., Richley, B. and Rezania, D. (2006) 'An evaluation system for training programs: a case study using a four-phase approach', *Career Development International*, Vol. 11, No. 4, pp. 334–51.

Longenecker, C. and Ariss, S. (2002) 'Creating competitive advantage through effective management education', *Personnel Review*, Vol. 21, No. 9, pp. 640–54.

Martin, G. and Pate, J. (2001) 'Company-based education programmes: what's the pay off for employers?', *Human Resource Management Journal*, Vol. 11, No. 4, pp. 55–73.

Megginson, D. (1994) 'Planned and Emergent Learning: A framework and a method', *Executive Development*, Vol. 7, No. 6, pp. 29–32.

Megginson, D. (2000) 'Current issues in mentoring', *Career Development International*, Vol. 5, No. 4/5.

Megginson, D. and Whitaker, V. (1996) *Cultivating Self-development*. London: IPD.

Monks, K., Barker, P. and Mhanachain, A. (2001) 'Drama as an opportunity for learning and development', *Personnel Review*, Vol. 20, No. 5, pp. 414–23.

Mumford, A. (1994) *How Managers Develop Managers*. Aldershot: Gower.

O'Hara, S., Webber, T. and Murphy, W. (2001) 'The joy of sets', *People Management*, 8 Feb., pp. 30–4.

Paauwe, J. and Williams, R. (2001) 'Seven key issues for management development', *Journal of Management Development*, Vol. 20, No. 2, pp. 90–105.

Pemberton, C. (2006) *Coaching to Solutions: A Manager's toolkit for Performance delivery*. Oxford: Butterworth-Heinemann.

Phelps, M. (2002) 'Blind faith', *People Management*, Vol. 8, No. 9, 2 May, p. 51.

Phillips, L. (2006) 'BUPA Stars', *People Management*, Vol. 12, No. 22, 9 November, pp. 30–2.

Pickard, J. (2006) 'Suits Ewe', *People Management*, Vol. 12, No. 12, 15 June, pp. 36–7.

Prickett, R. (1997) 'Screen savers', *People Management*, 26 June, pp. 36–8.

Sadler-Smith, E., Down, S. and Field, J. (1999) 'Adding value to HRD: evaluation, Investors in People and small firm training', *Human Resource Development International*, Vol. 2, No. 4, pp. 369–90.

Sadler-Smith, E., Down, S. and Lean, J. (2000) '"Modern" learning methods: rhetoric and reality', *Personnel Review*, Vol. 29, No. 4.

Santos, A. and Stewart, M. (2003) 'Employee perceptions and their influence on training effectiveness', *Human Resource Management Journal*, Vol. 13, No. 1, pp. 27–45.

Sloman, M. (2001) 'Hardier laurels, please', *People Management*, Vol. 7, No. 25, 27 December, p. 39.

Sloman, M. and Rolph, J. (2003) *E-learning: The learning curve – The change agenda*. London: CIPD.

Smethurst, S. (2006) 'Staying Power', *People Management*, Vol. 12, No. 7, 6 April, pp. 34–6.

Stansfield, L. (1996) 'Is self-development the key to the future?', *Management Learning*, Vol. 27, No. 4, pp. 429–45.

Stott, T. and Sweeney, J. (1999) 'More than a match', *People Management*, June, pp. 45–8.

Woodall, J. (2000) 'Corporate support for work-based management development', *Human Resource Management Journal*, Vol. 10, No. 1, pp. 18–32.

An extensive range of additional materials, including multiple choice questions, answers to questions and links to useful websites can be found on the Human Resource Management Companion Website at www.pearsoned.co.uk/torrington.

Just desserts — rewarding
and performing

Chapter 13

Reward and performance management

Alan J. Ryan and Julia Pointon

Objectives

- To present the historical and theoretical foundations of reward and performance management strategies.

- To consider and evaluate the issues concerned in designing performance management and reward systems.

- To critically assess the objectives of various reward systems.

- To analyse theories of motivation in the context of performance management.

- To consider the psychological contract in the context of the employment relationship.

- To discuss the interactive links between current trends in human resource management and performance management.

Introduction

This chapter demonstrates the level to which human resource management has developed existing theoretical and practical issues surrounding the management of labour performance within modern organisations. A central element of these debates is the management of reward structures, strategies and systems. In this chapter we introduce the concept of reward(s) as a core function in the development of a strategic role for HR functionaries and offer some explanation of the objectives of current links to performance management.

The often heard comment across many organisations runs along the lines of 'There's only one reason we come here – the money'. Unsurprisingly, these comments reflect the nature of the employment relationship as a reward/effort bargain (Chapters 11 and 12). Whether openly, covertly, personally or collectively, we all become involved in the resolution of this bargain at some time during our working life. This chapter discusses how management have attempted to resolve their problem of converting the labour potential, obtained by their transactions in the labour market, into the labour performance they desire; i.e., securing the required effort levels without rewarding at levels detrimental to the generation of sufficient profit. In this sense we view reward as a core function for HR managers and rewards as composed of more than the mere 'notes' in the pay packet.

The development of reward systems

As a separate management concern the issue of reward systems is fairly recent, indeed reward management has often been viewed as the 'poor relation' of HRM concerned with 'systems, figures and procedures'. During the development of a 'factory'-based economy, owners found that they were unable to control the 'effort' side of the bargain effectively. Workers, who were previously self-controlled and motivated in many respects by subsistence, worked in small 'cottage' industries within which the product of their labour was owned by the producers (workers themselves; notably in regard to the skilled artisans) and they worked as hard as necessary in order to meet their subsistence needs. As Anthony suggests, 'A great deal of the ideology of work is directed at getting men [sic] to take work seriously when they know that it is a joke' (1977: 5). Owners found that getting workers to keep regular hours and to commit the effort owners considered to constitute 'a fair day's work' was problematic. In response to this dilemma they employed the 'butty' system of reward management. Under this system owners committed a specific level of investment to a selected group of workers (normally skilled artisans) who then hired labour on 'spot contracts' by the day. The major problem for the owners with this system was that these 'subcontractors' had control over the effort/reward bargain and were able to enrich themselves at the expense of the owners. The owners enjoyed little or no control over the process of production so the system was economically inefficient and failed to deliver the returns (rents/profits) required or more importantly that were possible from the process of industrialisation.

From this group of 'favoured' workers, along with the introduction of some university graduates there grew a new management cadre. This was a slow process, as Gospel notes that generally, in UK industry, this group (management, technical and clerical) amounted to only 8.6 per cent of the workforce in most manufacturing organisations (1992: 17), within which development was uneven and patchy. These changes did little to address the problems associated with the effort/reward bargain, meaning productivity was below optimum levels. In part the problem was generated by the fact that 'the managers' brain was still under the workers' cap', more precisely that these managers rarely possessed the skills or knowledge of the production process held by the workers. This led to lower than optimum levels of production and reduced profits, a system F.W. Taylor described as 'Systematic Soldiering'. This activity was engaged in by workers, according to Taylor, 'with the deliberate object of keeping their employers ignorant of how fast work can be done' (Taylor, 1964). From his observations Taylor took the view that workers acting in this manner were merely behaving as 'economically rational actors' desiring their own best interests. It was clear therefore that management needed to take the reins of the production process and assert their right to determine the outcome of the wage/effort bargain. Taylor, as the so-called 'father of Scientific Management', developed a system of measuring work which assisted the process of reclaiming managerial rights. Jobs were broken down into specific elements which could then be timed and rated, whilst in the process, returning the determination of the speed of work to management and allowing for the development of pay systems which reflected, however crudely, performance. This scientific system devised by Taylor became the basis of countless pay systems operating effectively alongside the routinisation and deskilling of work which is often associated with Scientific Management within the literature (see, for example, Braverman, 1974; Burawoy, 1985; Hill, 1981; Littler, 1982, 1985; Thompson, 1983; and Wood, 1982). Whilst this allowed management to reassert their control over the level of outputs, to relocate the managers' brain under their own hats and hence the determination of the wage/effort bargain, it did generate problems in relation to managerial attempts to convince workers to take work seriously. In straightforward terms we can suggest that the 'Measured-Work' techniques advocated by adherents of Taylorism further separated conception from execution and led to feelings of alienation. Alienation can be defined as 'various social or psychological evils which are characterised by a harmful separation, disruption or fragmentation which sunders things that properly belong together' (Wood, 2000); in our terms that means the separation of workers from that which they produce. Blauner (1964) argued that such an objective state is created as an offshoot of the subjective feelings of separation which workers experience under modern production systems. These feelings and their outcomes can be briefly outlined in the following manner:

- Powerlessness – the inability to exert control over work processes.
- Meaninglessness – the lack of a sense of purpose as employees only concentrated on a narrowly defined and repetitive task and therefore could not relate their role to the overall production process and end product.
- 'Self-estrangement' – the failure to become involved in work as a mode of self-expression.
- Isolation – the lack of sense of belonging.   *Source*: Adapted from Blauner (1964)

Although Scientific Management originated at the beginning of the twentieth century, its legacy has lived on in many areas. Similar experiences have been reported in the design of work in service industries and call centres (Ritzer, 1997, 2000; Taylor and Bain, 1999; Taylor and Bain, 1999; Callaghan and Thompson, 2001). The solution to this problem has been sought, following Taylor's notion of man as an economic actor (see below), by the introduction of various performance and reward systems and mechanisms, the core objectives of which were originally to operationalise effective control over the wage/effort bargain and later with current systems to alleviate the feelings of alienation and generate commitment to organisational goals.

Design and debates

Whilst this section discusses reward systems in a manner which appears to offer a chronological explanation, we should note that the development of 'new' systems does not indicate the total removal of other mechanisms; indeed in many organisations we find that both 'old' and 'new' pay systems operate in tandem, delivering control on different levels for various groups of workers.

In terms of the types of reward mechanism applied we can note the application of a number of different mechanisms based on 'time worked'. Time rates are mechanisms whereby reward is related to the number of hours worked and are often applied to manual workers in the form of hourly rates and non-manual workers by the application of monthly or annual salaries. A criticism of these mechanisms is that they are often related to historic rather than current value, and can result in discrimination, demarcation disputes and a sense of injustice.

Time-related mechanisms are often based on the notion of a pay spine in which groups of skills are banded. Although widely applied in their heyday, basic versions of these instruments are poor in terms of relating wage to current effort; often rewarding effort which has been applied externally (gaining a recognised skill) and are inappropriate to current tasks. The advantages of these systems are that management can control wage costs by limiting the access to various grades on the spine, can limit the range of the grade (say, 4 per cent top to bottom) and can demonstrate they are fair in relation to agreed procedures. The problems created are not necessarily with the pay spine system *per se* but with the manner in which skills relating to specific grades are defined; solutions must then address the structure, strategy and rationale of the reward system rather than the application of such mechanisms.

Conboy (1976) noted that the key advantage of these instruments is that both parties have a clear idea of the 'wage' element of the bargain. For management the problem is that these mechanisms do not give any clear indication of the 'effort' element of the bargain. This led to time rate instruments being complicated by the addition of 'performance' elements, often in the

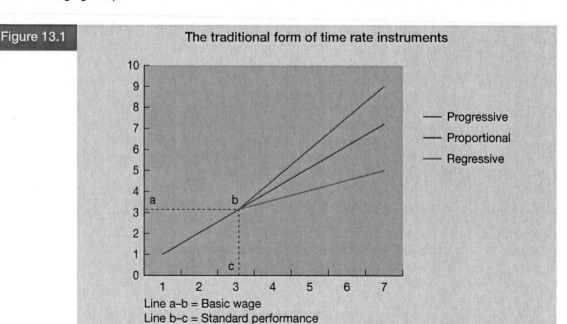

Figure 13.1   The traditional form of time rate instruments

Line a–b = Basic wage
Line b–c = Standard performance

form of 'piece-rates' or other complex 'bonus' calculations in an attempt to determine acceptable effort levels (e.g. Predetermined Motion Time Systems and Measured-Day-Work). The traditional form of such schemes can be demonstrated using the diagram shown in Figure 13.1.

Many schemes give guaranteed basic earnings which are then supplemented in ways which we can class as proportional (wages increase in direct relationship to output), progressive (wages increase more than output) or regressive (wages increase at a slower rate than output).

An important element in this discussion regards the manner in which the 'base' element is decided. We have become familiar with the notion of a National Minimum Wage, which sets the minimum rate for specified groups; outwith this scheme, organisations need some mechanisms by which to assign values to various roles within the organisation. Traditional mechanisms (and in a slightly modified manner 'new pay' systems) have related to job evaluation schemes. A job evaluation scheme operates by allocating values to each of a series of elements (e.g. skill or responsibility) and then measuring each 'job' in order to arrive at an agreed 'score'. The scores are then placed on the pay spine in relation to accepted criteria. These criteria will be formed by the interaction of two sets of relativities. Scores will need to reflect 'external relativities', by which we mean the situation that appears to hold in relation to external markets and environmental conditions, and 'internal relativities', meaning an appearance of fairness in relation to other jobs/roles within the organisation. In the basic form these schemes introduce us to the notion of reward packages under which different elements can be rewarded in various ways. However, these schemes fell out of favour in some respects because they are seen to 'pay-the-job' rather than 'pay-the-worker', and as such were difficult to relate to individual performance.

This is clearly the simplest form of wage payment system, easily understood by both parties; it allows the development of 'overtime' payments for work completed in addition to the contracted hours in any given period and formed the basis of the creation of systems classed as payment by results (PBR).

We can conclude then that such payment by results systems, whilst originally crude, developed alongside the more extensive division of labour achieved by the increasing use and application of technology, ergonomics (pseudo-scientific work measurement) and mechanical production methods. These early techniques can be easily applied to such divided work because of four basic characteristics of such work (adapted from Conboy, 1976):

- short job cycles;
- high manual content (which, using sophisticated ergonomic processes, can be measured);
- batch production (with repeated orders/processes);
- no marked fluctuations in required outputs.

The simplistic assumptions underlying these and other PBR systems are twofold. Firstly, workers are motivated to increase performance (work harder) by money, and secondly, any increases in output will result in equivalent increases in wages. The schemes are intended to be self-financing and designed to reduce 'wasteful activity' in that they can be used to redesign the labour process. Whilst such schemes now enjoy less popularity than they have in previous decades, there is still evidence that they are used in relation to specific groups of workers.

Stop & think   *To what extent do you think such wage systems reflect management's inability to clearly determine the 'effort' of the bargain?*

Table 13.1 shows that while there has been an overall decline in the application of PBR techniques, the decline is not as marked as some proponents of 'new pay' (see below) would argue. The heart of this debate suggests that such schemes can be seen as various techniques designed to act upon worker motivation and as such provide incentives for an individual to reassess the wage/effort bargain.

Table 13.1 Percentage of employees receiving PBR

Class of worker	1993	1995	1997
Manual	29.6	28	24
Non-manual	13.9	14.5	12
All	19.4	19.3	16.1

Source: New Earnings Surveys (1993–1997).

In order to assess the effectiveness, validity and reliability of such arguments we need to consider the underlying assumptions in a little more detail.

Motivation as a mechanism

Early in the new millennium, Miner (2003: 29) concluded that motivation continues to hold a significant position in the eyes of scholars. 'If one wishes to create a highly valid theory, which is also constructed with the purpose of enhanced usefulness in practice in mind, it would be best to look to motivation theories . . . for an appropriate model.'

But, what is 'motivation' and how do we understand it in the context of work? At a very basic level it is characterised by a certain level of willingness on the part of the employee to increase their effort, to the extent that this exertion also satisfies a predefined need or desire they hold. It is therefore all about individual behaviours directed towards realising a goal, it is about 'motives' and 'needs'. In slightly more detail, work motivation is often considered as a set of energetic forces that originate both within as well as beyond an individual's being, to initiate work-related behaviour and to determine its form, direction, intensity, and duration (Pinder, 1998: 11). Thus, motivation can be understood as a psychological process resulting from the interaction between the individual and the environment. Understanding work motivation in this way draws attention to the fact that it will probably vary from individual to individual and over time. In addition, because it is based on needs and motives that alter over time, and on an interaction with the environment, which will also change, the dynamic process is subject to constant reconfiguration.

To summarise, motivation can be regarded as:

- an individual phenomenon – people are unique, and this means that motivation theories usually allow for uniqueness to be reflected in individual behaviour;
- intentional and results in behaviours that are the result of conscious choices;
- a multifaceted concept, which involves (a) factors that arouse people to action (b) choice of behaviour and (c) choices abut the persistency and intensity of behaviour;
- valid as a theory because it helps predict behaviour by explaining what prompts the behaviour of people, which means that it has very little concern with simply describing or categorising behaviour.

Since the level of employee motivation influences productivity, organisations generally and managers and line managers in particular need to understand what motivates employees to reach peak performance. It is not an easy task to increase employee motivation because employees respond in different ways to their jobs and their organisation's practices. Factors that affect work motivation include individual differences, job characteristics and organisational practices. Individual differences are the personal needs, values, attitudes, interests and abilities that people bring to their jobs. Job characteristics are the aspects of the position that determine its limitations and challenges. Organisational practices are the rules, human resources policies, managerial practices, and rewards systems of an organisation. An understanding of work motivation is important in the context of performance management and the development of reward strategies for a number of reasons:

First, it enables organisations to 'humanise' work for employees so that work is inherently more satisfying, the assumption being that organisations have a responsibility to try to provide work that is meaningful, satisfying and as enjoyable as possible.

Second, an appropriate understanding of work motivation allows organisations to make the jobs more satisfying for employees within the company. The underlying assumption is clearly that if employees are happier at work then they will be more productive.

Third, such an understanding enables management to control the behaviour of subordinates more effectively and therefore enables management to 'pull the right strings' in order to achieve organisational goals.

Stop & think

To what extent and why do you agree with the suggestion that organisations have a responsibility to try to provide work that is meaningful, satisfying and as enjoyable as possible?

The theory of motivation has a long history and continues to evolve as we understand more about employees and work. Essentially, there are two main approaches to motivation theory: content and process theories.

Content theory of motivation

Content (or need) theories of motivation focus on factors internal to the individual that energise and direct behaviour. In general, such theories regard motivation as the product of internal drives that compel an individual to act or move (hence, 'motivate') toward the satisfaction of individual needs. Major content theories of motivation are Maslow's hierarchy of needs, Alderfer's ERG theory, Herzberg's motivator-hygiene theory, and McClelland's learned needs or three-needs theory.

Key features from each of the main theories will be considered in the next part of this chapter.

Maslow's hierarchy of needs

This is probably one of the best known. He first presented the five-tier hierarchy in 1942 to a psychoanalytic society and published it in 1954 in *Motivation and Personality* (New York: Harper and Row). His theory identifies five levels of needs (see Figure 13.2), which are best seen as a hierarchy with the most basic need emerging first and the most sophisticated need last. People move up the hierarchy one level at a time. Gratified needs lose their strength and the next level of needs is activated. As basic or lower-level needs are satisfied, higher-level needs become operative. A satisfied need is not a motivator. The most powerful employee need is the one that has not been satisfied.

- *Level I* – Physiological needs are the most basic human needs. They include food, water, and comfort. The organisation helps to satisfy employees' physiological needs by providing a financial reward – pay!

- *Level II* – Safety needs are the desires for security and stability, to feel safe from harm. The organisation helps to satisfy employees' safety needs by benefits.

- *Level III* – Social needs are the desires for affiliation. They include friendship and belonging. The organisation helps to satisfy employees' social needs through sports teams, parties and celebrations. The supervisor can help fulfil social needs by showing direct care and concern for employees.

- *Level IV* – Esteem needs are the desires for self-respect and respect or recognition from others. The organisation helps to satisfy employees' esteem needs by matching the skills and abilities of the employee to the job. The supervisor can help fulfil esteem needs by showing workers that their work is appreciated.

- *Level V* – Self-actualisation needs are the desires for self-fulfilment and the realisation of the individual's full potential. The supervisor can help fulfil self-actualisation needs by assigning tasks that challenge employees' minds while drawing on their aptitude and training.

The theory, especially in relation to reward and performance management, has an uncomplicated appeal because its message is clear – find out what motivates your employees at each of the levels and, more importantly still, at which level each employee is operating, and develop a reward strategy accordingly. However, evaluations have revealed a number of significant flaws that suggest that 'needs' do not always group together in the ways predicted. From this follows the proposition that the theories are unable to predict when a particular need will be manifest because there is no clear relationship between needs and behaviour, so that, for example, the

Figure 13.2

Maslow's hierarchy of needs

Source: http://ollie.dcccd.edu.

same behaviour could reflect different needs, and different needs the same behaviour. This criticism is further developed as we note that 'needs' are generally imprecisely defined in part due to the notion of need as a biological phenomenon being problematic. Applications of the hierarchy of needs to management and the workplace are obvious. According to the implications of the hierarchy, individuals must have their lower level needs met by, for example, safe working conditions, adequate pay to take care of one's self and one's family, and job security before they will be motivated by increased job responsibilities, status, and challenging work assignments. Despite the ease of application of this theory to a work setting, it has received little research support and therefore is not very useful in practice.

Despite these limitations, Maslow's thinking remains influential and continues to influence management deliberations in respect of job design, pay and reward structures. Huczynski and Buchanan (2001: 242) highlight this stating: 'Many subsequent management fashions, such as job enrichment, total quality management, business process re-engineering, self-managing teams, the "new leadership" and employee empowerment incorporated his ideas in the search for practical motivational methods'.

 Stop & think   *To what extent do you consider the achievement of self-actualisation to be a realistic possibility?*

Alderfer's ERG theory

The ERG theory is an extension of Maslow's hierarchy of needs. Alderfer suggested that needs could be classified into three categories, rather than five. These three types of needs are Existence, Relatedness, and Growth. Existence needs are similar to Maslow's physiological and safety needs categories. Relatedness needs involve interpersonal relationships and are comparable to aspects of Maslow's belongingness and esteem needs. Growth needs are those related to the attainment of one's potential and are associated with Maslow's esteem and self-actualisation needs.

The ERG theory differs from the hierarchy of needs in that it does not suggest that lower-level needs must be completely satisfied before upper-level needs become motivational. ERG theory also suggests that if an individual is continually unable to meet upper-level needs that the person will regress and lower-level needs become the major determinants of their motivation. The ERG theory's implications for managers are similar to those for the needs hierarchy: managers should focus on meeting employees' existence, relatedness, and growth needs, though without necessarily applying the proviso that, say, job-safety concerns necessarily take precedence over challenging and fulfilling job requirements.

Herzberg's motivator–hygiene theory

Frederick Herzberg developed the motivator–hygiene theory. This theory is closely related to Maslow's hierarchy of needs but relates more specifically to how individuals are motivated in the workplace. Based on his research, Herzberg identified two factors central to our understanding of motivation:

1 *Motivators*. These were such things as 'a sense of achievement', 'an opportunity for personal growth', 'the sense of having done a job well', 'having responsibility', and 'achieving recognition for your work'.
2 *Hygiene* factors. These included such things as money, working conditions, job security, company policies, the quality of supervision and interpersonal relationships at work.

Herzberg argued that meeting the lower-level needs (hygiene factors) of individuals would not motivate them to exert effort, but would only prevent them from being dissatisfied. Only if higher-level needs (motivators) were met would individuals be motivated. For Herzberg therefore, the opposite of satisfaction is not dissatisfaction, it is merely no satisfaction and equally, the opposite of dissatisfaction is not necessarily satisfaction, simply no dissatisfaction. The implication for managers of the motivator–hygiene theory is that meeting employees lower-level needs by improving pay, benefits, safety, and other job-contextual factors will prevent employees from becoming actively dissatisfied but will probably not motivate them to exert additional effort toward achieving peak performance. To motivate workers, managers must focus on changing the intrinsic nature and content of jobs themselves by 'enriching' them to increase employees' autonomy and their opportunities to take on additional responsibility, gain recognition, and develop their skills and careers.

Bassett Jones and Lloyd (2004) undertook research to determine if Herzberg's two factor theory of motivation was still relevant. The results, derived from a survey of over 3200 responses, indicated that money and recognition do not appear to be primary sources of motivation. In line with Herzberg's predictions, factors associated with intrinsic satisfaction play a more important part. They concluded that, despite the criticism, Herzberg's two-factor theory still has utility nearly 50 years after it was first developed.

McClelland's learned needs theory

McClelland's theory suggests that individuals learn needs from their culture. The three primary needs are first, the need for affiliation (n Aff), characterised as a desire to establish social relationships with others. Second, the need for power (n Pow) reflects a desire to control one's environment and influence others. Finally the need for achievement (n Ach) is associated with a desire to take responsibility, set challenging goals, and obtain performance feedback. The main point of the learned needs theory is that when one of these needs is strong in a person, it has the potential to motivate behaviour that leads to its satisfaction. The implication for managers is they should develop an understanding of whether and to what degree their employees have one or more of these needs, and the extent to which their jobs can be structured to satisfy them.

Criticisms of content theories

There are two observations of content or needs theories that are worth highlighting.

First, at the heart of these theories lies the suggestion that there is a single factor – money, social needs or psychological growth that motivates behavior. The implication is that if managers can identify the key motivational factor and reinforce it, then an employee will 'naturally' be motivated. The reality is that for most employees motivation will be a messy and complicated relationship between a number of factors that are difficult to separate out or identify individually.

Second, content theories also assume that the task of any reward and performance management system is to identify standard motivational strategies that can be applied in any context (e.g. all jobs can be rationalised, redesigned or enriched). But as it is difficult to predict when certain needs become important, we can argue that the application of 'standardised' solutions is neither possible or desirable. It is clear that as the different needs are very difficult to isolate, define or describe and further, that any suggestion that needs have a biological origin is problematic, performance management involves issues to which there is no 'off the shelf' one-size-fits-all response.

Process theories of motivation

Process (or cognitive) theories of motivation focus on conscious human decision making as a process which helps explain motivation. The process theories are concerned with determining how individual behaviour is energised, directed, and maintained. Process theories of motivation are based on early cognitive theories, which hold that behaviour is the result of conscious decision-making processes. The major process theories of motivation are expectancy theory, equity theory, goal-setting theory and reinforcement theory.

Vroom's expectancy theory

In the early 1960s, Victor Vroom applied concepts of behavioural research conducted in the 1930s by Kurt Lewin and Edward Tolman directly to work motivation. Vroom suggested that individuals choose work behaviours they believe will result in the achievement of specific outcomes they value. In deciding how much effort to put into work behaviour, individuals are likely to consider:

- Valence, which is the extent to which the expected outcome is attractive or unattractive.
- Instrumentality, or the degree to which they believe that a given level of performance will result in the certain achievement of the outcome or desired rewards.
- Expectancy, meaning the degree to which the employee believes that putting in effort will lead to a given level of performance – Is the type of effort appropriate to achieving the goal?

All three of these factors, often referred to as 'VIE', are considered to influence motivation in a combined manner. Thus, for an individual to be highly motivated, all three of the components of the expectancy model must be present. If even one of these is zero (e.g., instrumentality and valence are high, but expectancy is completely absent), the employee will not be motivated. Managers therefore need to attempt to ensure that their employees believe that increased effort will improve performance and that performance will lead to valued rewards.

In the late 1960s, Porter and Lawler published an extension of the Vroom expectancy model, which is known as the Porter–Lawler expectancy model or simply the Porter–Lawler model. Although the basic premise of the Porter–Lawler model is the same as for Vroom's model, the Porter–Lawler model is more complex in a number of ways. It suggests that increased effort does not automatically lead to improved performance because individuals may not possess the necessary abilities needed to achieve high levels of performance, or because they may have an inadequate or vague perception of how to perform necessary tasks. Without an understanding of how to direct effort effectively, individuals may exert considerable effort without a corresponding increase in performance.

There are criticisms of expectancy theory that argue that the theory attempts to predict a choice of effort. However, because no clear specification of the meaning of effort exists, the variables cannot be measured adequately. As a process theory, it does not specify the outcomes relevant to a particular individual situation and therefore offers little guidance to the human resource manager seeking to design a performance management and reward system as there is an implicit assumption that all motivation is conscious. The employee is assumed to consciously calculate the pleasure or pain that he/she expects to attain or avoid and then a choice is made.

Equity theory

The equity theory of motivation is based on the principle that since there are no absolute criteria for fairness, employees generally assess fairness by making comparisons with others in similar situations. Therefore, motivation to put effort into a task will be influenced by perception of whether the rewards are fair in comparison to those received by others. To assess fairness an employee is likely to make a comparison between the level of inputs and outputs they are making compared to the level of input and output they consider the comparator to be making. Inputs are often multiple and consist of things an employee may bring to the task – education, previous experience, effort. Outputs are the rewards for the inputs – salary, performance related pay, praise. Inputs are essentially costs while the outputs are the benefits. If, following the subjective comparison, a feeling of inequity prevails, it can give rise to tensions and feelings of psychological discomfort. This may result in a desire to 'do something about it' and take action designed to lessen the tension being experienced. Adams (1965) suggests that there are six basic options available to an employee (adapted from Rollinson, 2002: 235):

- Modify inputs.
- Seek to modify outputs.
- Modify perception of self.

- Modify perception of comparator.
- Change comparator.
- Leave the situation.

Adams (1963) suggests that adopting one or a combination of the options may result in a feeling of restored balance or equity resulting in the employee accepting the situation.

This theory is straightforward and easy to understand, however, it can not cover every contingency. For example, some employees are far more sensitive to perceptions of inequity than others. There is some evidence to suggest that even where inequity is perceived to exist, employees have some tolerance providing the reasons for the inequity are explained and justified.

This has two major implications for managers when designing performance management and reward schemes.

First, it is important to be aware that employees will make comparisons; further, because comparisons are subjective, care must be taken to relate similar jobs in terms of the wage/effort bargain; and if managers wish to avoid inaccurate conclusions about equity it is necessary to be open concerning the basis on which the rewards are made. Generally speaking, it is important for managers to be aware of what employees perceive to be fair and equitable and to recognise that this will vary from group to group. By taking adequate consideration of the employee's perceptions, by providing an adequate explanation of any changes in work process or design and by ensuring policies etc. are applied consistently and in an unbiased manner, employees are more likely to believe the organisation is trying to reduce any perceived inequality and that they are being treated fairly in comparison with the treatment received by others. For the human resource manager equity theory illustrates how important it is to provide a performance management and reward system in which the outcomes are perceived by individuals to be relevant and acknowledge the truth that different employees value different things.

Second, it is clear that human resource managers need to (re)design current compensations systems in order to avoid the performance destroying effects of perceived inequities which result from employee perceptions that the wage/effort bargain provides insufficient rewards and that these redesigned systems need to avoid over-rewarding performance as this does not necessarily result in higher productivity or improved performance.

Goal setting theory

This approach to motivation by Locke and Latham (1984) is based on a simple premise: performance is caused by an employee's intention to perform. What follows is clear: an employee with higher goals will do better than an employee with lower goals. If an employee knows precisely what they want to do, or are expected to do, that employee will perform better than someone whose goals or intentions are vague. In other words there is a positive relationship between goal precision, difficulty and performance. This, however, does not hold for extremely difficult goals which are beyond an employee's ability. Using this prism we can argue that specific goals lead to higher performance than general or vague 'do your best' goals. Specific goals seem to create a precise intention, which in turn aids individual employees in shaping their behaviour with the same precision. Further, the theory proposes that knowledge of results (feedback) is essential if the full performance benefits of setting more difficult goals are to be achieved. Hence feedback offered in an appropriate manner can have a motivating effect on the employee. It is suggested that the beneficial effects of goal setting depend in part on the employee's goal commitment, that is their determination to succeed and unwillingness to abandon or reduce it.

These four principles establish the core of goal setting theory and make it one of the more consistently supported theories of motivation. Locke *et al.* (1981) suggests that financial incentives can enhance performance by raising the level of the goal or by increasing an employee's commitment to a goal which can be achieved where the employee is involved in establishing the required performance. We can therefore argue that, in the workplace, the value of goal setting is enhanced by the provision of adequate, timely feedback.

Goal-based theories of motivation emphasise the importance of feedback in order to:

- increase the employee's feeling of achievement;
- increase the sense of personal responsibility for the work;
- reduce uncertainty;
- refine performance.

However, many systems do not systematically provide for line managers to communicate feedback on performance to those employees for which they have responsibility. This may be for many reasons such as leadership style, protection of power bases or the information system not providing data for management functions. Often employees are provided with feedback 'by exception', typically when performance has fallen below a certain acceptable level and managers are themselves under pressure to improve performance. However, managers have to maintain a careful balance in providing feedback – too little, too late can be demotivating but too much and too frequently can be 'stifling' and perceived as indicative of a lack of trust or respect.

Reinforcement theory

This theory can be traced to the work of the pioneering behaviourist B.F. Skinner. It is considered a motivation theory as well as a learning theory. Reinforcement theory posits that motivated behaviour occurs as a result of 'reinforcers', which are outcomes resulting from the behaviour that makes it more likely the behaviour will occur again. Behaviour that is reinforced in a positive manner is likely to continue, but behaviour that is not rewarded or behaviour that is punished is not likely to be repeated. Reinforcement theory suggests to managers that they can improve employees' performance by a process of behaviour modification in which they reinforce desired behaviours and punish undesired behaviours.

Criticisms of process theories

A key criticism of process theories is that they tend to assume an overly rational view of human decision making. For example, decision making is often habitual or unconscious rather than conscious and rational. Furthermore, when making choices people do not have complete knowledge of the possible results of their behavioural options, and are not normally aware of the full range of options available to them. Another weak assumption of process theories is that individuals have a comprehensive and consistent scale of values with which they might evaluate the value of the various outcomes they are able to identify. Ultimately process theories do not consider why an individual values or does not value particular outcomes, only how the motivation develops.

New motivational techniques

During the last two decades, there has been a shift in organisations towards more team- and group-based work and towards an increased use of mentoring and coaching as strategies designed to enhance levels of employee motivation and performance. This section considers research studies into the design of work for autonomous work teams, the effects of group goal setting which is an extension of individual goal setting research, the role of mentoring and the use of non-financial rewards.

Two studies in particular have examined the effect of job characteristics or work design on the affective and behavioural responses of autonomous work teams. Cordery, Mueller and Smith (1991) conducted a study comparing semi-autonomous work teams and traditionally organised work groups. They found that semi-autonomous teams reported higher levels of freedom in their work, a characteristic associated with intrinsic job satisfaction as well as experiencing extrinsic satisfaction and organisational commitment. Cordery *et al.* (1991) concluded that employees in autonomous work groups report more favourable work attitudes and levels of motivation.

In 1993, Jin examined the effect of work group formation in China, that is how the members of the work groups were selected. Jin found that work groups which had formed voluntarily reported higher levels of work motivation, higher cooperative intentions, better interpersonal relations, greater work satisfaction, had fewer disciplinary problems and produced higher quantity and quality output.

The increased use of teams has resulted in an increase in the need to establish team-based goals – or group goals. A study conducted by Crown and Rosse (1995) found that when group members received individual goals, the group performed less well and were less motivated than when employees received group goals. Group-oriented goals were associated with more cooperative strategies better performance and better reported level of motivation. Individual goals were associated with more competitive strategies that interfered with the group's ability to perform and reduced levels of motivation.

Both studies concluded the use of autonomous work teams and work groups had a positive impact on both levels of employee motivation and performance. One interesting point is that although Cordery *et al.* (1991) also found work groups report more favourable work attitudes their research also revealed higher levels of turnover and absenteeism for semi-autonomous teams. So, while they concluded that employees in autonomous groups were more motivated, they also cautioned that the turnover and absence data may have illustrated some of the pressures associated with autonomous work groups, and which may ultimately become de-motivating.

The current work on mentoring is equally positive. Research results from a study conducted by Orpen in 1997 indicated the better the relationship between mentors and mentees in the mentoring programme, the more mentees were motivated to work hard and felt committed to their organisation. More specifically, it found that mentees who were in a close working relationship with their mentors, were more motivated and committed than those who were physically distant from their mentors. In addition, mentees were more motivated and committed when their mentors on the programme liked and respected them, and enjoyed interacting with them. The study found that when mentees performed poorly or were unmotivated it was frequently due to situational factors beyond the control of either party. Among the more pervasive negative factors that fell into this category were breakdowns in machinery, lack of consumer demand, non-cooperation from colleagues, weak marketing, outdated equipment, inappropriate organisational structure, and lack of training.

What such factors serve to demonstrate yet again is the multifaceted nature of motivation. They illustrate how interaction with the environment and associated difficulties make it sometimes impossible for employees to perform really well, even when they are strongly motivated as individuals and are committed to the organisation.

Non-financial rewards

The extent to which money is a motivator to improved performance remains a bit of an unresolved debate. It has traditionally been held that employees are likely to 'over-report' the importance of pay in any employee survey. However, recent research (Rynes *et al.*, 2004) suggested the opposite was actually true. They reviewed evidence showing the discrepancies between what people say and do with respect to pay and concluded that although pay is not equally important in all situations or to all individuals it is such an important general motivator that many managers underestimate its importance. Although now a little dated, previous research also demonstrates how non-financial motivators have always been identified as significant, see Table 13.2.

Non-financial motivations

According to research by Woodruffe (2006: 29) non-financial factors, such as those he identified in the following list, remain the most important motivators of employee performance.

- *Advancement* – People value the extent to which they perceive that their job is giving them the opportunity for career advancement.

Table 13.2

Year	Most important motivational factor
1946	Appreciation
1980	Interesting work
1986	Interesting work
1992	Good wages
1997	Good wages, full appreciation of work done

Source: Kovach, K.A. (1987) 'What motivates employees? Workers and supervisors give different answers', *Business Horizons*, Sept–Oct, 58–65; Wiley, C. (1997) 'What motivates employees according to over 40 years of motivation surveys', *International Journal of Manpower*, 18, 3: 263–280.

- *Autonomy* – Most people like to be able to get 'on a roll' as far as work is concerned and a degree of real autonomy, where someone can really get 'into' their job, is likely to be welcome.

- *Civilised treatment* – Too many organisations treat people in a brusque, even uncivilised, way. The problem often arises because a line manager responsible for the people in question is working under great stress and, in effect, 'kicks downwards'. This can easily wipe out a great deal of effort by a human resources department in recruiting and motivating the right person.

- *Employer commitment* – People like to feel that their employers are genuinely committed to them and to their careers.

- *Environment* – A pleasant working environment is always essential: stress can be caused by an unpleasant environment.

- *Exposure to senior people* – Most employees like to feel that they are being noticed by an organisation's senior people and that they could approach these people if necessary for advice and guidance.

- *Praise is awarded when praise is due* – One of the classic signs of poor management occurs when staff are given *negative* feedback for what is perceived as poor performance, but never given *positive* feedback. The emotional benefits of praise can be enormous.

- *Support is available* – Employees like to feel that there is someone available to whom they can turn for advice if they need it.

- *Challenge* – Employees like to feel challenged, given that they believe they have the tools and skills to respond to the challenge successfully. Sometimes employees can respond with surprising resilience, energy and commitment to even a really demanding challenge.

- *Trust* – As social animals, humans will habitually, and often for very good reasons, withhold trust until they believe that extending this is justified. Employees know this, so the bestowal of trust is quite rightly regarded as extremely important. Employees, who feel trusted, are more likely to feel a useful and important part of an organisation and therefore are more likely to be loyal.

- *Reliable organisation* – People want to be proud of their jobs and of the organisations for which they work.

- *Assignments* – Every employee, no matter which rung they occupy in the corporate hierarchy, wants to feel important and valued, and there is no better way of helping an employee feel this than by giving him or her some genuinely significant assignments on which to work. The work–life balance is respected – employees know they are going to have to work hard, but an employer who shows sensitivity to work–life balance issues is very likely to outsource one who doesn't.

Box 13.1 Sara Lee Corporation

Chicago-based Sara Lee Corporation is a global manufacturer of brand-name products for consumers throughout the world. Sara Lee has operations in 58 countries, market-branded products in nearly 200 nations and 137,000 employees worldwide.

The Sara Lee Corporation needed to improve levels of employee motivation fast! Managers focused on 'recognition' as the key to raising employee motivation and developed an employee nomination scheme.

Using an online 'Nomination Wizard', every employee could nominate anyone they considered worthy of recognition. The online system asks a series of questions in order to determine the appropriate level of recognition and after approval from the appropriate people the awards, which can be given daily, are presented. Successful employees receive a certificate with an online code that allows them to browse and select a gift from their eligible level of achievement.

For Sara Lee Foods' managers and employees the question was not whether or not to recognise, but when and how. 'You have to find time to recognise', commented a leading manager. 'People certainly appreciate their salaries, but I see people stay and thrive as a group when they understand the vision and the challenges, and when they're appreciated. Appreciation is a critical part of the work experience.

In the experience of a 'recognised' employee 'To be recognised formally gave me extra motivation and made me wonder what I could do to keep the momentum going'.

Source: Case Studies, Melcrum Publishing Ltd (2006).

Box 13.2 Harley-Davidson

Harley-Davidson has been producing motorbikes, parts and accessories, MotorClothes and other merchandise since 1903. There are now 1300 Harley-Davidson dealerships in 60 countries worldwide and its corporate headquarters are based in Wisconsin, USA. The company employs 9000 people across the globe.

Over the past four years Harley-Davidson have witnessed unprecedented growth. Because the attention to growth had effectively forced the HR function to focus almost solely on recruiting, other critical HR practices were not prioritised.

This, in turn, was creating a potentially difficult situation and the HR function recognised that it had to more effectively manage the motivation and performance of its employees.

An emerging tool, called the 'Accenture Human Capital Development Framework', provided critical guidance in this effort. The Framework is a diagnostic approach to assessing human capital capabilities and the processes that motivate them, and then linking human capital assets and approaches to business performance outcomes.

It helps organisations do more than look at levels of spending to get a sense of their human capital development strengths; it also highlights how complete the underlying practices are, how effectively they support employees, and how aligned they are with the organisation's competitive strategy and mission. The framework demonstrates the link between different elements at four distinct levels, or tiers and so recognises the inherent complexity of employee motivation and performance.

- *Tier 1*: Business results – the financial measures of organisational success, such as capital efficiency, revenue growth, return on invested capital and total return to shareholders.
- *Tier 2*: Key performance drivers – the intermediate organisational outcomes, such as customer satisfaction and innovation, that are typically captured on a balanced scorecard.
- *Tier 3*: Human capital capabilities – or the most immediate and visible people-related qualities that human capital processes produce, such as workforce performance, employee engagement and workforce adaptability.

- *Tier 4*: Human capital processes – the specific practices and activities such as performance appraisal, workforce planning and learning management that organisations undertake to develop their human capital capabilities.

Harley-Davidson's 10-week implementation of the Framework began in January 2004. Factual, financial and HR data were collected through interviews with nine business and HR executives (including the CEO and vice president of HR) and a representative sample of five HR executives and 69 employees.

Compelling findings

The results of the Framework confirmed that the organisation was performing above the average in seven of the 13 human capital processes, but executives weren't surprised to learn that there was room for improvement in the remaining six processes:

1 career development;
2 workforce planning;
3 rewards and recognition;
4 employee relations;
5 human capital strategy; and
6 human capital infrastructure.

Subsequent attention to these areas helped the organisation improve employee motivation and performance levels and supported its ongoing success.

Source: Scott, H., Cheese, P. and Cantrell, S. (2006) 'Harley-Davidson'. *Strategic HR Review*, Jan/Feb 2006, 5, 2: 28–31.

New day, new way, new pay?

This discussion indicates that early PBR mechanisms, discussed above, were in some respects aiming at the wrong target. By concentrating simplistically on the cash nexus they avoided more complex motivators which determine the effort side of the bargain. The realisation amongst managers and academics that the application of greater levels of effort could be achieved more effectively by the application of methods other than money led to the development of a wider discussion.

By the 1980s it had become clear that the traditional (old pay) systems were not effectively delivering in terms of key organisational goals. The developing HRM rhetoric and the more apparent interest in business performance led HR managers to reassess the role of reward management in the delivery of organisational efficiency. As White and Drucker (2000) note, these developments have been accompanied by broader economic and social changes which challenged the belief in traditional personnel practices. Within this process of change, reward management underwent a metamorphosis of major proportions in that it was no longer simply about rewarding people for previous attainment but became linked to future performance. According to Armstrong (2002), reward is now 'about how people are rewarded in accordance with their value to the organisation' (2002: 3) and as such can no longer be seen as the mere administration of set procedures and policies. From this perspective the development of HRM has led to an evaluation of reward systems in an attempt to link them more effectively to organisational strategies (fitting in with notions of strategic HRM). Reward strategies then, are viewed as a key organisational contribution and a central element in the work of HR functionaries.

As we can note from the models and maps of HRM (see Chapter 1), reward systems are seen as one of the four key policy choices (Beer *et al.*, 1984) out of which organisations can aim to develop commitment, competence, congruence and cost-effectiveness, while Storey

(1992) indicates reward management as one of the points of difference between personnel and HRM. The older mechanisms, including graded spines based on job evaluation, are in part considered inappropriate in modern business. Rewards, or more precisely reward strategies, are seen as techniques which organisations can apply in order to secure various behaviours and values. Millward *et al.* (2000) note that in 1990 the major influence which determined pay settlements in organisations where collective bargaining was not dominant was individual employee performance (2000: 207); by 1998 the focus had shifted, with the main influence in this group of respondents being economic factors and more recognition of limits set by higher authority (2000: 211). These changes have not resulted in reward systems which are any easier for workers to understand or are less complex than their predecessors. That reward management developed in a manner which encouraged this occupation of a position of central importance has various causes. As we noted above, control of costs is at the heart of managerial responsibilities and, within that, control of labour costs is fundamental to organisational performance. Further, we have suggested that reward systems form part of the employees' notion of organisational justice and as such underlie a sense of loyalty. This simple statement needs unpacking in terms of the manner in which policy and practice have developed as a result of these changes.

In the 1990s, US writers (Lawler, 1990; Schuster and Zingheim, 1992) offered concepts they labelled 'new pay' as a prism through which we can view these changes. The central idea is intended to signify the realisation that reward strategies have to relate to organisational culture, values, aims and strategies, which in turn must take into account the challenges of a modern economy. As Schuster and Zingheim (1992) note, the rudimentary elements of 'new pay' include an acknowledgement that employees form a core ingredient in the recipe for organisational success. They suggest that the change cannot be one of rhetoric (from reward to compensation) alone but must also be demonstrated in the design of 'total compensation' packages which consistently reward required actions and attitudes. They indicate that a key element in such a total compensation package is variable pay, suggesting that pay remains a crucial mechanism for sending messages to employees in regard to the managerially desired effort levels. In this light, reward strategy needs to be integrated with wider organisational and managerial processes rather than being viewed as a 'bolt-on' optional extra. This whole package approach means that all elements (base, variable and indirect rewards) need to support each rather than compete for supremacy. Base pay remains the foundation of the policy and should be set in line with organisational and societal norms in order to ensure 'felt justice' across the organisation. Alongside this element however, the organisation may develop variable elements which do not become permanent, remaining subject to criteria related to either individual or organisational performance. These variable elements can therefore go down as well as up, addressing the issue of wage rigidity which adds damaging costs in periods of downturn. There are a number of means by which this variable element can be determined but they are often grouped under the generic term performance-related pay (PRP), indicating that the measurement of such performance may be based on the individual, the team or the organisation.

In this section we begin with consideration of the organisational element commonly called performance management and link this to a discussion of modern job evaluation schemes, profit-related pay and modern managerial practice. The underlying idea in the introduction of variable/contingent elements was that employees would identify more readily with organisational goals where part of their compensation package was linked to performance/profit. In simple terms, when the organisation did well they would share in the gain and therefore would also share the suffering in bad times. This may work where employees can be encouraged to swap a percentage of their base pay for this variable element but many organisations introduced these schemes as additional to existing compensation levels (see Kellaway, 1993). Current research (Freeman, 2001) looking at these schemes indicates two main findings:

- They have some positive impact on performance.
- Employees can view the rewards as unrelated to individual performance.

The second point is reason enough to move towards systems which apparently reward individual performance more directly. This has been achieved by the introduction of schemes that are based on modern job evaluation, and grading schemes within which the compensation increases the variable/contingent element rather than the base as in the past. Such contingency pay can be based upon:

- competence;
- skills;
- length of service;
- contribution and/or
- performance.

Each of these elements can be included in the development of job evaluation schemes, which are designed to influence employees' perceptions of distributive justice.

Modern job evaluation schemes

Modern organisations base such grading schemes on notions of competencies. Competency can be defined as:

> an underlying characteristic of an individual which is causally related to effective or superior performance in a job.   (Mitrani *et al.*, 1993: 5)
>
> The characteristic set of knowledge, skills, abilities, motivations and procedures that individuals working in specific jobs should possess to allow them to perform their work to minimum standards.   (Cornelius, 2001: 366)

From these comments, we can suggest a list of competencies adapted from Gooch and Cornelius (2001) which includes:

- leadership;
- communication skills;
- presentation skills;
- interpersonal skills;
- workflow management;
- adaptability;
- customer service.

Competence-based payment (CBP) schemes have grown alongside the interest in variable compensation and are often part of modern job evaluations schemes. HR functionaries have expended significant time and energy in the development of 'competence frameworks' which link pay to the achievement of specific behaviours, attitudes and the attainment of required competencies. These schemes are popular with both parties, in part due to the fact that it is clear what is valued by the organisation and hence what will receive increased reward. This differs from traditional 'pay-by-skill' in that it is applied across the organisation to all workers (rather than just the traditional skills) and the required 'competencies' are somewhat broader than the definition of 'skill(s)'. This breadth of definition allows the application and adaptation of traditional job evaluation schemes by taking into account current changes in the organisation of work and the utilisation of new technology. Thus job evaluation techniques were rescued from decline by becoming more flexible, broader in coverage and applicable to modern multi-skilled workers (Pritchard and Murlis, 1992).

Hastings and Dixon (1995) suggest that CBP systems can take three major forms in which the attainment of indicated competencies is:

- the basis for progression within scales;
- the basis upon which the scales are founded;
- the basis both for progression and for the scale.

A second system, which is adopted within modern organisations, is based on employee input and relates to the acquisition of new skills. Within a modern job evaluation scheme development of firm-related skills can be used as a mechanism which allows individuals to move beyond 'bars within grades'. Therefore a grade may contain five or six spine points with a bar after three which limits progression and can only be passed following the acquisition of clearly identified skills.

A length of service approach relates the contingent element to time served. As Daniels (2006: 236) notes it is 'still very popular in the voluntary and public sector'. The basis upon which such an element is included into calculations within job evaluation schemes relates to the idea that longer service equals more experience. Such experience may be seen to allow the individual the possession of more organisational knowledge and hence value to the organisation. However, following recent age discrimination legislation, this has to be objectively justified.

Contribution, as a contingent element of a reward package, is designed to evaluate employee competencies and performance in a more holistic manner. It attempts to measure, albeit subjectively, the overall value of the employee in the pursuit of organisational objectives. In this manner it can be linked to the authentication of a cohesive in-house culture and hence support programmes of cultural change.

Many modern job evaluation schemes continue to use pseudo-scientific mechanisms to measure and reward performance. Such measurement is normally made with reference to defined organisational objectives. Objectives are agreed between the parties and often form part of the appraisal scheme (see below).

Whichever system is applied, a main advantage lies in the ability of organisations to set their own 'characteristic set of knowledge, skills, abilities and motivations'. From such a development, they can develop job families, which allow equality issues to be addressed across various functions. The use of job families, based on broad role profiles, allows a series of job descriptions to be aligned within a single framework, hence financial rewards can be linked to individual performance against a set of organisationally specific competencies.

In recent debates much attention has turned to discussion of a contract which is unwritten and yet seen as being as important as any written terms and conditions. The psychological contract is seen to underpin all reward and performance management systems in that it conceptualises the wage/effort bargain for a new generation of workers and owners. In the following section we consider the formation of the contract and identify the 'agreed' terms (if such they can be called) forming the basis from which human resource managers seek to develop performance norms, organisational values and note the psychological contract as a mechanism in the continuing strategy to encourage 'men [sic] to take work seriously when they know that it is a joke' (Anthony, 1977: 5).

The psychological contract

Defining the psychological contract

As with many aspects of human resource management – such as motivation and performance – the psychological contract is somewhat elusive and challenging to define (for a discussion of this, see Guest, 1998a). However, it is generally accepted that it is concerned with an individual's subjective beliefs, shaped by the organisation, regarding the terms of an exchange relationship between the individual employee and the organisation (Rousseau, 1995). As it is subjective, unwritten and often not discussed or negotiated, it goes beyond any formal contract of employment. The psychological contract is promise based, and over time assumes the form of a mental schema or model, which like most schema is relatively stable and durable. (For a more detailed analysis on how the psychological contract is formed see Rousseau, 2001.) A major feature of psychological contracts is the concept of mutuality – that there is a common and agreed understanding of promises and obligations the respective parties have made to each other about work, pay, loyalty, commitment, flexibility, security and career advancement.

Research undertaken by Herriot *et al.*, (1997) sought to explore the content of the psychological contract in the UK. They researched the perceived obligations of two parties to the psychological contract by identifying the critical incidents of 184 employees and 184 managers representing the organisation. From the results they inferred seven categories of employee obligation and twelve categories of organisation obligation.

In relation to employee obligations, they make reference to both concrete and abstract inputs the organisation hopes/expects the employee will bring to the organisation. At the first level these involve an expectation that the employee will work the hours contracted and consistently do a good job in terms of quality and quantity. The organisation will desire that their employees deal honestly with clients and with the organisation and remain loyal by staying with the organisation, guarding its reputation and putting its interests first, including treating the property which belongs to the organisation in a careful way. Employees will be expected to dress and behave correctly with customers and colleagues and show commitment to the organisation by being willing to go beyond their own job description, especially in emergency. It is possible to suggest that many of these expectations reflect the common law terms implied in the contract of employment and as such it is the 'manifestation' of the required behaviours more than the existence of a psychological contract which is used to manage 'norms' within the organisation.

On the other side of the contract we can note the obligations placed on the organisation in terms of the expectations each employee has of the deal. Most employees would want the organisation to provide adequate induction and training and then ensure fairness of selection, appraisal, promotion and redundancy procedures. While recent legislation has centred on the notion of work–life balance, it is argued that an element of this agreement is an employee expectation that the organisation will allow time off to meet personal and family needs irrespective of legal requirements. It has long been held that workers ought to have the right to participate in the making of the decisions which affect their working lives (see Adams, 1986; Bean, 1994; Freeman and Rogers, 1999); the debate relating to the psychological contract suggests that employees further expect organisations to consult and communicate on the matters which affect them. With the increasingly high levels of 'knowledge' workers it is accepted that organisations ought to engage in a policy of minimum interference with employees in terms of how they do their job and to recognise or reward for special contribution or long service. Organisations are generally depended upon to act in a personally and socially responsible and supportive way towards employees, which includes the provision of a safe and congenial work environment. We have already noted that in relation to reward and performance management systems there is a need to act with fairness and consistency; the expectation goes further in that the application of rules and disciplinary procedures must be seen to be equitable. This perceived justice should extend to market values and be consistently awarded across the organisation, indicating the link therefore to a consistency in the administration of the benefit systems. The final element that many workers expect their employer to provide is security in terms of the organisation trying hard to provide what job security is feasible within the current economic climate.

1 *Write down your expectations of your employer and what you consider to be their expectations of you.*

2 *Reflect on which aspects can be described as formal and which could be considered as unwritten.*

3 *Consider how you reached this 'psychological contract' – did you, for example, negotiate and agree it or have you assumed aspects?*

4 *To what extent are both parties, i.e. you and your employer, aware of the existence and the content of the contract; to what extent do you share the same expectations?*

5 *What might be the issues for you and for the employer if there is a mismatch of expectations?*

6 *Finally, consider with whom you have the contract – a named individual within the organisation or do you have multiple contracts with different agents within the organisation?*

Previous decades have seen many organisations forced, by increased competition and the globalisation of business, to seek to remain competitive by cutting costs and increasing efficiency. This has, in part, given rise to the restructuring endemic in UK and US organisations under the various guises of business process re-engineering, downsizing and rightsizing, all of which apply performance-related pay systems aimed at increasing productivity. The restructuring has also given rise to redundancies, had the significant impact of reducing job security of those who remained, removed many of the middle-level management grades and consequently reduced possible promotion opportunities for junior employees.

While long-term job security, promotion and career progression were perceived by many employees, whose psychological contract was possibly formed many years earlier, to be the 'key' obligations which were owed by the organisation in return for their loyalty and commitment, modern organisations (and in some respects the 'modern' employee) are learning to live without such elements in the psychological contract. The consequences have been predictable; employees feel angry at the apparent unilateral breaking of the psychological contract and at the same time insecure, having lost trust in the organisation. Commitment is reduced, with motivation, morale and performance being adversely affected. This is potentially dangerous for the organisation, as lean organisations need effort and commitment in order to get work done and at the same time a willingness to take risks in the pursuit of innovation. It is suggested (Rousseau, 2001; Guest and Conway, 2002) that negative change in the employment relationship may adversely affect the state of the psychological contract.

Sparrow (1996) claims that the psychological contract underpins the work relationship and provides a basis for capturing complex organisational phenomena by acting in a similar manner to that of Herzberg's hygiene factors. Good psychological contracts may not always result in superior performance, or indeed in satisfied employees; but poor psychological contracts tend to act as demotivators, which can be reflected in lower levels of employee commitment, higher levels of absenteeism and turnover, and reduced performance. Herriott and Pemberton (1995: 58) suggest that the captains of industry have set in motion a revolution in the nature of the employment relationship, the like of which they never imagined. For they have shattered the old psychological contract and failed to negotiate a new one.

It has long been accepted that two forms of psychological contract, termed relational and transactional, operate in the employment relationship (Table 13.3). The former refers to 'a long-term relationship based on trust and mutual respect. The employee offers loyalty, conformity to requirements, commitment to their employer's goals and trust in their employer not to abuse their goodwill' (Arnold *et al.*, 1998: 388). In return, the organisation supposedly offered security of employment, promotion prospects, training and development and some flexibility about the demands made on the employees if they were in difficulty.

Table 13.3 Relational and transactional contracts

	Transactional	Relational
Primary focus	Concerned about economic factors	Concerned about people
Time frame	Closed ended and short term	Open ended and indefinite
Stability of the relationship	Static, rarely changing	Dynamic and frequently changing
Scope of relationship	Narrow	Broad and pervasive
Tangibility of terms	Well defined	Highly subjective

However, as a result of the changes outlined above it is suggested that some employers have had difficulty in maintaining their side of the bargain. As a result, the old relational contracts have been violated and have been replaced by new, more transactional contracts, which are imposed rather than negotiated and based on a short-term economic exchange. As Arnold *et al.* (1998: 388) suggest, 'the employee offers longer hours, broader skills, tolerance of change and ambiguity . . . In return the employer offers (to some) high pay, rewards for high performance and simply a job'.

If the psychological contract is changing as current research appears to suggest, what are the organisational implications for managing the psychological contract in the future? The psychological contract needs careful management; although it is unwritten it remains a highly influential aspect of the employment relationship. In flatter, delayered organisations with limited opportunities for career progression and the absence of any guarantee of a job for life, attaining and maintaining employee commitment becomes increasingly more challenging for management. To manage the psychological contract in the future, organisations need to offer 'realistic job previews' to new entrants, recognise the impact of change on those remaining and 'invest in the survivors'. Further, there is a need to change the management style and to push towards cross-functional teamwork, design tasks and structures to allow employees to feel a sense of accomplishment and develop their skills to increase their own 'employability security'. Such activities are intended to create a new kind of commitment through the creation of meaning and values between employees, not just from a top-down mission statement, to be attentive to the need to balance work and other aspects of life and to be continuous in communication with employees. (For further reading, see the work of Jean Hiltrop.)

Guzzo and Noonan (1994) take the perspective that psychological contracts can have both transactional and relational elements. Employers may have to demonstrate to employees that they can keep to a sound and fair transactional deal before attempting to develop a relational contract based on trust and commitment. Furthermore, as Herriot *et al.* (1997: 161) suggest: 'Organisations may be in danger of underestimating the fundamentally transactional nature of the employment relationship for many of their employees'. The essential point is to recognise that all psychological contracts are different. It is important for the organisation to appreciate the complexities of transactional and relational contracts and to recognise that psychological contracts will have elements of all dimensions and that contracts are individual, subjective and dynamic. The significance of the psychological contract in relation to performance management is that it highlights how easy it is for organisations to assume that employees seek primarily monetary rewards; this is not necessarily the case. The evidence suggests that effective performance management and reward structures in organisations must attend to the quality of the relationships employees experience while at work which are an integral aspect of the psychological contract. The message appears simple: improved performance is affected by more than money.

HRM and performance management

We can see that the key issue related to the determination of the wage/effort bargain is not simply a matter of setting a wage relative to the level of effort and letting things 'tick along'. From the dawn of the industrial era, managers have sought to control the effort side of the agreement by utilising their power to determine the wage. Performance management (or more accurately forms of performance-related pay) has formed a key activity for managers and management in the quest to increase the benefits gained by the application of labour power. There have been various mechanisms applied in order to secure this advantage which were based on the 'current fad' or understanding of the labour process (for a discussion of the influence of the emergence of SHRM, see Schuler and Jackson, 1999). The choice of which management system to adopt has been driven by the answer proposed to the basic question 'what motivates workers to perform at higher levels?' and more often than not can be located within the various schools of thought outlined above. We can see the development of reward management along the lines suggested by Etzioni (1975) in terms of coercive (work harder or lose your job), remunerative (work harder and receive more money) and normative (work harder to achieve agreed organisational goals). Current trends in the management of worker performance fail to be considered in the area of normative managerial practices, but are fraught with difficulty in an era where emotional labour and the knowledge worker hold such a central place in organisational success. These developments need to be considered alongside the evolution of an ambiguous employment relationship (the breakdown of the psychological contract) and the rise of insecurity of modern organisations (reflected in the growth of 'butterfly workers'). As Fisher notes, 'Insecurity is a common phenomenon in organisations' (1999: 167), be it the feelings of insecurity within line managers who have not previously been responsible for the range of issues they now enjoy or that of the HR manager attempting to demonstrate they have put in place all the necessary procedures required to measure performance and show their organisational worth in a modern competitive environment. HR managers, lost in a landscape where memory no longer serves the function of creating security (Schama, 1995), argue that they can apply the techniques presented within expectancy and/or goal-setting theory to the development of procedures which will secure competitive advantage for the organisation. Such procedures are borne within the all-encompassing 'HRM mantra' which declares, for self-assurance as much as public consumption, that the HR function is a strategic player in the organisation network, bringing new understanding to the application of personnel practices and organisational changes.

We can suggest from Figure 13.3 that the HRM mantra, which can be considered as the 'self-reassuring' chant of HR managers, indicates the importance of HR procedures in the success of the organisation and note how a number of these link into our discussion of reward systems and performance management. The notions of 'productivity through our people', customer focus, strong(er) leadership, flatter structures and cohesive cultures all suggest a management framework which seeks to improve individual and organisational performance in ways that can be measured, a concentration on competence (inputs) alongside attention to attainment (outcomes).

These elements turn attention to the fact that in modern organisations it is the quality and behaviours of the employees that generate, as much as other inputs, competitive advantage. While much of the business strategy literature since the 1980s has concentrated on the 'setting and achievement' of organisational goals, what has often been lost is the role of human resources in the attainment of competitive advantage (a trend addressed by the application of the ideas associated with the resource-based view of the firm in recent years; see Chapter 2 on strategic HRM in this edition). However, a set of key questions still remain: 'what motivates workers to perform at higher levels?', 'how do we manage this motivation to the best effect?' and 'how do we measure resulting performance levels?'

Some attempt has been made to answer the first of these questions in the preceding sections using the theoretical constructs offered by Maslow, Herzberg, Taylor, Vroom and Locke.

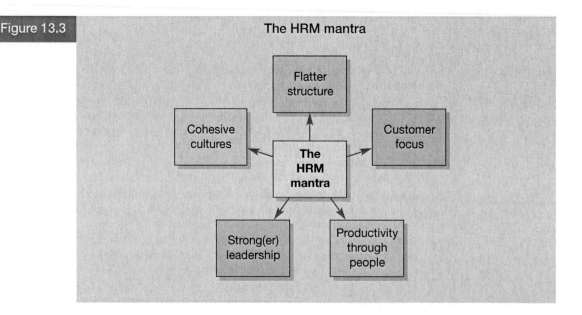

Figure 13.3   The HRM mantra

These, as our discussion of the psychological contract suggested, leave us with some confusion and inconsistencies which present management with as many questions as answers. The recent developments in this area, as suggested above, involve two themes:

- the performance management process, and
- contingent pay.

As Lowry (2002) argues, the management of employee performance is usually seen as a necessary function of the managerial cadre. Centrally, it links a number of themes, including the extent to which the organisation has identified strategic goals reflecting the needs of the business and the degree to which these are communicated to and shared by each employee. We can further note that general definitions suggest that performance management involves a formal and systematic review of the progress towards achieving these goals. In response to the problems this creates, theorists have developed the idea of a performance management cycle within which the elements of the process can be identified, investigated and implemented by HR managers in the attempt to create organisational advantage. The cycle consists of five elements which provide a framework within which we can audit the delivery of strategic objectives with a view to developing continuous improvement. These elements are presented as a common link between organisational and individual performance, which underlies the development of a committed, motivated, loyal workforce. In simple terms, it is suggested that the cycle indicates a system within which performance objectives are set, outcomes are then measured, results are fed back, rewards are linked to outcomes and changes are made before new objectives are set for which the outcomes can be measured. We now consider each of these elements individually.

Setting objectives

There is any amount of prescriptive advice which indicates that the objectives need to be achievable and linked to organisational objectives. Where the purpose of setting such objectives is to direct, monitor, motivate and audit individual performance they must fulfil both of these criteria, otherwise the process will result in the opposite effects being secured. The application of expectancy and goal-setting theories implies that this is best achieved where the individual has an important role in the determination of the objectives for the period concerned. As suggested in the discussion above, this will encourage the selection of appropriate goals which are specific, attainable and owned by the individual. The process, as a management tool, is established on the basis that organisational objectives can be broken down and translated into individual goals, the attainment of which can then be effectively measured.

In recent debates we find that organisations are said to make frequent use of the acronym SMART to assist in establishing effective objectives:

S – Specific or Stretching
M – Measurable
A – Agreed or Achievable
R – Realistic
T – Time bound

There are, however, difficulties in setting objectives for some jobs, e.g. doctors, lecturers and lower levels in the organisation hierarchy, as they may not have the opportunity to improve their performance or demonstrate merit, and may be unable to identify or relate to organisational goals.

Measuring the outcomes

Where the objectives relate to numbers, increased sales or an increased production of widgets, for example, the measurement appears unproblematic. However, not all of us are sales representatives or widget-makers; indeed, in the current economic climate such crude measures may be inappropriate and in some respects a return to 'old pay' notions of piecework. The growth of 'knowledge' workers has been accompanied by a change to competence-based approaches to measurement which centre on the three stages of competence development (know-what, know-why and know-how; see Raub, 2001). Therefore the outcomes can be measured in relation to the individual's success in deploying, integrating and improving their competence in the identified field of activity. This allows the organisation to refocus on the development of competitive advantage through the application of 'core knowledge', including tangible and intangible assets. It allows the application of 'just enough discipline' to establish a relevant 'core knowledge' base which is defined by strategic business drivers and monitored to maintain balance (see Klien, 1998).

The outcomes are often measured by the application of appraisal schemes. The purpose of performance planning, review and appraisal needs to be made clear if employees at all levels in the organisation are to play an active part in the process. It is possible that some employees and line managers may meet performance appraisal schemes with distrust, suspicion and fear, but an integrated and effective process can lead to increased organisational performance and employee motivation. It is important for employees to be genuinely involved in the design of an appraisal scheme, the evaluation of performance, and the objective-setting process. An appraisal scheme should be set up in an atmosphere of openness, with agreement between management, employees and employee representatives on the design of the scheme (Grayson, 1984: 177). Employees need to have a clear understanding of the purpose of the process (evaluative or developmental).

From this we can suggest that the key principles in the design of a performance appraisal scheme are that it should be congruent with the organisation's competitive strategy. It needs to provide direction for continuous improvement activities and identify both tendencies and progress in performance. Manifestly, it needs to facilitate the understanding of cause and effect relationships regarding performance while remaining intelligible to those employees to which it applies. It ought to be dynamic, covering all of the company's business processes, and provide real-time information about all aspects of performance. A scheme that does not include employees' attitudes is unlikely to allow performance to be compared against benchmarks because it will not be composed of effective performance measures. Finally, we can note that a performance appraisal system should provide a perspective of past, present and future performance which is visible to both employees and management.

On the basis of seven case studies, IDS produced the following list of factors which were typically appraised (IDS, 1992):

- job knowledge and abilities (ability to perform all aspects of the job);
- adaptability/flexibility (ability to cope with change; multi-skilling for craft workers);
- productivity (individual work output);
- quality of work (attention to detail; consistent quality);
- attitude to work (commitment; motivation; enthusiasm);
- interaction with others (communication skills; teamworking ability);
- originality of thought/initiative (problem-solving);
- perception (ability to correctly interpret job requirements);
- judgement, use of resources (setting priorities; ability to plan and organise work);
- attendance and time keeping (number of and reasons for absence; punctuality);
- safety awareness (awareness of health and safety standards);
- need for supervision (leadership; ability to develop others);
- performance against targets (extent to which previously set targets have been achieved).

From this we can suggest that assessment of these factors is achieved by a mixture of 'subjective' and 'objective' measures, almost always carried out by the employee's immediate superior. The most commonly used measures will therefore relate to the individual's attitude to work as well as the quality of their work and their attendance and time keeping. These will be assessed alongside their knowledge of the job and productivity, while more subjective measures involving a judgement of their ability to interact with others will be included in a good scheme in order to develop an insight into the effectiveness of recruitment procedures. In terms of 'rating' or 'scoring' individual employees, a number of 'target areas' can be identified for assessment.

Accountabilities

Accountabilities define the responsibilities of a certain job and the results that jobholders are expected to achieve. The employee's actual output in terms of measurable productivity, timeliness and quality may be directly assessed as part of the appraisal scheme. This presupposes the employee's job role is open to such quantitative assessment.

Skills acquisition

Employees may be assessed on their acquisition of new skills required to further improve their performance in the job or the continued development of essential skills. Jones the Bootmaker, a footwear company in the Midlands, have recently developed a new performance appraisal scheme in which they specifically appraise managers on the job they are currently required to do rather than place undue emphasis on developing skills and competences for future positions. Andrew White, company representative, stated 'We found that the previous scheme was appraising managers on competences beyond their current job role, which in some cases led to demotivation' (White, November 2002).

Self-assessment

This approach is mainly concerned with the identification of self-development needs by the actual employee. Margerison (1976) has suggested that self-assessment is the only way to give a complete picture of the performance of the employee and to avoid a 'criticise–defend' scenario. It does, however, require the employee to have a detailed and informed understanding of both the current and future needs of the job role and the organisational needs against which they can accurately assess their current performance and so their future development needs.

Paired comparisons

This is a comparative method of performance assessment in which a superior assesses the performance of pairs of individuals, until each employee has been judged relative to each other employee, or until every possible combination of employees has been considered. A rating scale is then devised to show the number of times an individual employee was judged as 'better' (Roberts, 2001: 542).

Ranking

This is another comparative measure of assessment in which employees are assessed against pre-set and documented measures of effectiveness and placed in a hierarchy from best to worst. At Cummins Engines the appraisal system is based on a 10:80:10 ranking scheme. Those employees ranked in the top 10 per cent are identified for promotion and special development. Those identified within the next 80 per cent are maintained within the organisation and the remaining 10 per cent are effectively 'managed out' of the organisation. In Cummins the appraisal scheme is very open and there are no secrets over how it operates in practice!

Rating scale

This is considered to be an 'absolute' method of performance assessment. The method, according to Roberts (2001: 542), lists a number of factors such as job-related qualities or behaviours or can include certain personality traits. Individual employees are then rated on the extent to which they possess these factors. The rating scale can be numerically, alphabetically or graphically represented on a continuum, i.e. from 'very high' to 'very low'. However, when scoring is involved it can get ugly. The attraction of rating systems – the school-report model that ranks you as a team player from one to five, or rates your customer focus from A to E is that the feedback is easy to gather and produces lots of data that can be aggregated and turned into bar charts. In this respect the HR department is happy because they have made a 'fuzzy' process look scientific, and someone from client services is proud because they got a 4 on knowledge leadership and their colleague only got a 3. But a number may not offer much insight on how to improve. For that you need thoughtful, qualitative comments – harder to gather, but much more helpful.

Behaviourally anchored rating scale (BARS)

This is an attempt to assess actual performance and behaviour, so, for example, it is concerned not with whether an employee has 'initiative', but with specifically identifying what he or she actually does that demonstrates initiative – or the lack of it!

The development of a BARS approach typically involves the following stages:

- Meetings are held with superiors and/or outside consultants to identify several key aspects or categories of performance in particular jobs.
- The same or other sources of information are used to provide examples of good, average and poor performance for each category of performance in an individual's job.
- A number of such categories or anchors are generated (frequently 6–9 per job) and each is ascribed a value, for instance 1–7, or 'average', 'above average', etc. Essentially these define the 'most efficient' through to the 'least efficient' behaviour and performance for the job.
- Appraisers use this format to evaluate the expected behaviour of individual employees holding the jobs concerned.

The underlying job analysis is critical to the success of this approach and many proponents argue that the employee and their superiors should be actively involved in the process to ensure it is relatively realistic.

Development plan approach

In some organisations the link between personal development and the business strategy is weak but is crucial to effective performance management. Effective development plans consider the future skills, knowledge and experiences that will be required by the employee to enable them to do their current job effectively. The identification of needs should also be linked to what the employee may require in the future – needs identification must therefore be closely linked to organisational succession and business plans. The plan may be in the style of an essay or a controlled report which asks for responses to certain headings or sections.

360-degree appraisals

This approach to performance management has grown in popularity and when undertaken correctly is effective, reasonably inexpensive, widely applicable and clearly focused on individual performance.

The idea behind 360-degree feedback is that employees benefit from feedback gathered from a wide range of sources. Characteristically this includes peers, superiors, subordinates and customers; essentially it is designed to obtain comments from 'all directions', above, below and to the side of the employee concerned. It is intended to give a more complete and comprehensive picture of the individual's performance and contribution.

The process typically follows a procedure in which competences have been established and defined and employees are then requested to nominate up to six significant others who cover the range of suitable respondents. Those giving feedback are then asked to use a rating scale or comment on each of the dimensions. For example, Roberts (2001: 543) suggests managers might be assessed by their employees on 'softer' people issues such as communication and support, and their peers on issues such as teamwork. Indicators of both internal and external customer satisfaction may be used, and suppliers and subcontractors may also be asked to give feedback on the individual manager's performance and demonstration of competences.

Possible issues with performance appraisal

Whatever approach to performance appraisal is used, there will inevitably be issues and concerns. In essence, to assess an employee's performance necessarily involves some form of assessment against predetermined standards or behaviours. In both situations there will be an element of human judgement which, as we know, suffers from problems of reliability, validity and bias. Kinnie and Lowe (1990: 47) state that 'appraisers may find it difficult to identify and measure, the distinct contribution of each individual'; this can be because the appraiser does not really know the appraisee or because, as suggested by Howell and Cameron (1996: 28), employees are constantly moving from one project to another.

There may also be many external factors beyond the control of the individual employee which affect their performance, such as resources, processes, technology, corporate and HR strategy, working environment, external business context and management. Equally, the appraisal might be skewed because if there is a long time span between appraisals, managers may place greater importance on more recent performance, called the 'recency effect', thereby possibly ignoring incidents that had occurred earlier.

Role of line manager

Line managers/supervisors may lack the required technical skills and people management skills to be able to conduct an effective appraisal. In addition, a lack of time and resources may hinder line managers in providing comprehensive and effective performance reviews and objective-setting. Managers may perceive the appraisal process as a bureaucratic nuisance and form-filling exercise.

Demotivation consequences

An appraisal outcome that labels an employee as simply 'average', or determines that he or she is not a 'high flier', may lead to demotivation. To state the general principle: when one person begins to make a judgement on another, unless that judgement is favourable, reaction and resistance begin to set in (Margerison, 1976: 32).

Interpretation 'spin'

Roberts' (2001: 545) suggestion of the 'cascading' approach, of progressive levels of management setting objectives for the level below and consequently being assessed themselves by the attainment of these objectives can result in the manipulation and 'fudging' of standards. Further, there is a tendency to retain 'understanding' in the language rather than 'cascade' this to lower levels. Managers attempt to maintain their 'hierarchical' authority by using the interpretation of the 'spin' to reinforce relationships of power within the organisation; by so doing they lessen the effectiveness of the communication mechanisms and therefore of the process.

Conflicting roles

Newton and Findlay (2000: 129) make reference to the writings of McGregor, who draws attention to the issues of the conflicting roles of the appraiser as both disciplinary 'judge' and helpful 'counsellor', suggesting the modern emphasis of appraisal is on the manager as a leader who strives to assist employees achieve both their own and the company's objectives – acting as a sort of mentor or counsellor concerned with the personal growth and development of the employee. At the same time the manager is charged with identifying (and hopefully agreeing) strict targets for achievement and performance. This can involve identifying areas where previous performance has been less than satisfactory – leaving the manager in the role of judge. There are obvious tensions between the two roles.

Much of the literature suggests that this tension can, in part, be overcome by the employee taking an active role in the process. But that is assuming the employee wants to be involved and really wants to take responsibility for improving themselves by taking an 'active role' in the process – and they may not. For example, they may see the whole appraisal process as an attempt to control and manipulate them. Newton and Findlay (2000: 130) suggest employees may view this as a way of removing the responsibility for their development from the organisation, and placing it on their shoulders. In an era in which the notion of 'employability security' as distinct from 'job security' characterises the employment relationship, it is interesting to consider where the responsibility for investing in development lies – with the organisation, or increasingly as seems likely, directly with the employee. The interesting thing is that even as the appraisal process continues to be utilised as part of a spreading audit culture, some companies are already looking to cast it aside – or if they keep appraisals, making them, as Freeserve does, a process whereby employees solicit feedback rather than having it thrust upon them. It will be interesting to monitor how far this marks a turning of the tide against performance management appraisals.

Current trends

The interest in appraisals and other PBR systems draws on the long-standing tradition to divide reward packages between base and contingent elements. The changes in the mechanisms used to identify and quantify these contingent elements currently focus on the notion of rewarding the person rather than the role and links into the notion of 'new pay' which increases the emphasis on the motivational qualities of PBR systems. By linking pay to achievement, whether such achievement relates to production targets, attainment of competencies or objectives set within an appraisal meeting, organisations are seeking to quantify and reward individual contribution to the attainment of business goals or strategic aims. Individuals, whether pay is determined by position on a spine determined by job evaluation or otherwise, may receive increments based on length of service alongside performance elements; these 'service awards' reward experience and loyalty. However, such awards can be withheld where performance fails to meet the desired targets and are useful once 'poor' performance is identified as signals to other workers. Armstrong (2002) lists 15 features of performance management which were identified as being used by organisations in the 1998 CIPD survey. The results suggest that the most common of these (identified by over 60 per cent of the respondents) were objective-setting and review, annual appraisal and personal development plans (2002: 387). At the bottom of the ladder, despite all the discussion in various HR texts, with under 15 per cent acknowledgement were the balanced scorecard (5 per cent) peer appraisal (9 per cent), 360-degree feedback (11 per cent) and rolling appraisals (12 per cent). The results showed that organisations viewed performance management as integral to the employment relationship, thus an important part of managerial activity despite (as noted by 60 per cent of the respondents) being bureaucratic and time-consuming (2002: 388). In contrasting the results of the 1998 survey to those of the 1991 survey, Armstrong suggests a move from performance management 'systems' to a more holistic performance management 'process'. This process, it is suggested, focuses on inputs/outputs, development, flexibility and a shift of ownership towards the users and away from the HR function. Interestingly, taking the results into account, Armstrong suggests that the process also involves an increase in the application of 360-degree feedback (2002: 389).

The development of a process within which performance is related to both input and output is in part the result of the application of an objective-based approach located in the work of Kaplan and Norton (1992). The so-called balanced scorecard, although acknowledged as a feature by only 5 per cent of the respondents in the CIPD survey, underlies much of the discussion relating to the development of a strategic role for the HR function. In this approach there are four stages which start with a vision of the future, whether in the form of a vision statement *per se* or in terms of an answer to the question 'where do we want to be in *x* years?' From this we can identify how the organisation will be different if the targets are achieved in terms of four key areas (*Financial, Customer, Internal* and *Innovation/Learning*) which will determine the success of the organisation in a competitive environment. Reward strategies will impact on all of these areas to a greater or lesser extent by identifying as performance targets those elements which are critical to the successful acquisition of the vision for the future. The scorecard method can be used to identify specific instruments/measurements which can be used to set interim targets and therefore individual performance objectives. These may be competencies (can do), knowledge indicators (know-what) and/or commitment levels (know-why); critical elements in the attainment of these objectives are a strong psychological contract based on open communication, active participation and high-trust employment relationships. Research in 2003 (The Work Foundation, 2003) indicates that where employers are seeking to promote this type of performance management they will allow their employees to identify their own training needs (86 per cent), run regular team briefings (75 per cent), allow and encourage the development of transferable skills (73 per cent), tie reward to service by offering long-service awards (67 per cent) and operate a system of in-house brainstorming sessions or focus groups (66 per cent). The report suggests that employers are acknowledging that performance management ties broader HR policies into the attainment of the strategic goals of the organisation and that this objective can be achieved by the development of a strong psychological contract. Despite these moves, we can suggest that poor levels of goal attainment within organisations can be the fault of bad management of individual employee performance. A recent study by the consultants Mercer (2003) of 3500 employees concluded that a mere 20 per cent believe that their good performance will be rewarded while some 33 per cent feel their organisation operates in such a way that there is an inadequate link between pay and performance. From these results Gilbert notes that:

> Linking pay to performance requires a robust performance appraisal process and the active support of line managers . . . our results indicate that many managers lack either the training or the support to conduct the process. (Gilbert, P. on mercerhr.com, 2003)

The Mercer survey also noted that while firms may be good at appraising individuals, many are weak on providing effective feedback and offer this as a cause for their finding that performance management systems are rarely effective. We have suggested that in part their effectiveness rests on two foundation stones, high levels of motivation and a strong psychological contract; however, research by the CIPD (2003) notes that while most workers are 'happy in their work', fewer than 30 per cent trust their senior managers to look after their interests, indicating a psychological contract which is far from 'strong'. In order to address these problems and develop high-commitment management (HCM) policies, employers are introducing greater flexibility in terms of the employment relationship. These moves include the introduction of flexible benefits, competency-based pay, merit pay and broadbanding (IRS, 2002). The survey upon which these conclusions are based indicated that more than 60 per cent of the respondents used elements of merit-based pay, while over half operated market-related pay systems, suggesting some confusion and cross-over between internal (individual performance based) and external (market equity based) rationales for the development and implementation of reward strategies. This confusion brings into sharp focus the role of HR as a function in the development and implementation of strategic objectives. HR can measure the contribution it makes and/or impact it has against any number of measures; however, a recent IRS survey found that over half of their sample used business objectives or performance indicators, suggesting a continued link to performance management as a key role for HR practitioners (IRS, 2003). The same survey noted that 64 per cent stated that the HR department maintained sole responsibility for pay determination, with only 4 per cent suggesting this was the sole prerogative of line managers.

Stop & think

The report also notes that the typical week for an HR manager entails one day on strategy, two days on supporting line managers and two days on catching up on paperwork. Linked to the above relating to reward management, do you think the findings of the IRS survey indicate that in the area of reward management HRM is still a case of 'systems, figures and procedures'?

Taking the above results into account, how do you think organisations can convince their staff that performance will be rewarded?

Devise a mechanism by which an organisation you know could effectively get the message that 'performance equals higher rewards' across to their employees. What behaviours would they seek to encourage?

Performance management as a control mechanism

We started by noting that reward management systems can be seen as managerial attempts to gain control over the 'effort' side of the wage/effort bargain which mirrors their unilateral control of the wage side. A fundamental element of performance management is the development of control in relation to employee behaviours, motivation and loyalty. In modern parlance, performance management is a mechanism to control values rather than simply actions. With all the monitoring, discussion, measurement, evaluation and goal-setting, some performance management techniques give the impression that they are effective in controlling actions but often miss the target of securing control over effort levels because they do not develop powerful value systems. It is possible for these systems to have some effect on employee behaviours, to bring them into accord with organisation targets, while never really addressing the problem of underlying values. If, as Grint indicates, the traditional view is that 'good management is really concerned with good boundary management' (1997: 10), then performance management may offer a good traditional style in that it manages the boundary between acceptable and unacceptable performance; whether it moves beyond this to offer higher levels of commitment is debatable – we have suggested above that the process only secures that which it measures. There are more serious questions to be answered with regard to those items it cannot or does not attempt to measure. Without the link to the development and implementation of a system of organisational values it is arguable that performance management, whether seen as a process or a system, lacks the attainment of a self-generated goal. Linking performance, by the use of cafeteria reward systems, to individual choice may actually achieve the opposite by reducing the opportunity to link rewards to organisational values. However, by linking the attainment of performance levels which are sufficient to secure the desired reward the organisation could communicate to the employees that the organisation is changing by moving the goalposts to suit the new desirable set of values. In simple terms, we are suggesting that in order to achieve control over the effort side of the bargain, organisations need to acknowledge and apply management systems to the unarticulated links between:

Values – Behaviours – Performance – Growth

The argument here is that growth and performance are inextricably linked to behaviours which are founded upon personal and organisational values. Performance management is effective, therefore, only to the extent to which it can shape these values, irrespective of the measure to which it can change behaviours, as values are said to set the parameters within which people make decisions. Organisations must define, cascade and supervise their own values as they cannot be effectively imposed or imported; no amount of wall-mounted plaques, posters, credit-card-sized personal reminders or mugs can impose a set of values. Values must be lived and the performance management process should be designed to allow organisations to control the creation of the organisational language upon which values are based if it is to deliver control to the extent required within modern organisations.

Some difficulties

Do rewards work? At first sight this seems a simple, if not a simplistic question. The received wisdom has long been that the use of tools, variously described as incentive plans, bonus schemes, merit-based pay, or performance-related pay, is central to the development of improved performance. In part this is based on the accepted wisdom that 'the idea of dangling money and other goodies in front of people will "motivate" them to work harder' (Kohn, 1998: 27). Kohn (1998) goes on to argue that many compensation schemes assign more importance to money than is warranted and confuse compensation with reward. In an earlier argument, he went further to suggest that 'any incentive or pay-for-performance systems tends to make people less enthusiastic about their work' (Kohn, 1993a: 346). This, he suggests, is in part because people reason that if they need to be paid additional amounts to perform some task (or at some level) then what they are doing cannot be that interesting/valuable. Thus, such reward mechanisms merely encourage people to 'get the reward' and hence be less creative. Kohn sees the basic effect of contingency-based payment systems as 'destructive when tied to interesting or complicated task' (Kohn, 1993b: 348) in that they weaken intrinsic motivation. In an article responding to Kohn, Appelbaum (1993) notes most research indicates that 'Attempts to improve performance by manipulating compensation packages has proven to be counterproductive' (Kohn, 1993b: 369). In the same article Kozlowski offers an alternative view arguing that whilst 'elephants cannot fly and fish cannot walk, Kohn's argument that incentive plans cannot work defies the laws of nature' (Kohn 1993b: 371). He suggests that such plans encourage entrepreneurial spirit and focus minds on shareholder value. From this perspective therefore, incentive plans which include large elements of contingency-based pay, can be highly effective when employed in the appropriate circumstances. Alternatively Pfeffer (1998) includes as the fifth of his six 'myths about pay' that 'individual incentive pay improves performance' (1998: 125). This he links with the sixth myth which is that money is the primary reason people work. Pfeffer (1998) suggests that these myths undermine the ability of managers to recognise the real problem with performance and leads them to adopt ineffective solutions. In an era where productivity through effective labour management (including teamworking), customer focus (notably looking at the long term), strong decisive leadership, flatter hierarchies, and developing a cohesive culture have become central to HR thinking, contingency-based compensation, which encourages individualism, short-term focus, leaving leadership to the reward system, conflict-ridden hierarchies and cultural difference, is counterproductive. Pfeffer (1998) suggests that people work for meaning in their lives and indeed to have fun. He concludes that 'companies that ignore this fact are essentially bribing their employees and will pay the price in a lack of loyalty and commitment' (1998: 123). Perhaps we can see here a re-statement of the idea that 'A great deal of the ideology of work is directed at getting men [sic] to take work seriously when they know that it is a joke' (Anthony 1977: 5). As Pfeffer concludes 'Pay cannot substitute for a working environment high on trust, fun, and meaningful work' (1998: 128).

Conclusion

In this chapter we have discussed the notion of reward as an integral part of the managerial function which results from the definition of the employment relationship as a wage/effort bargain; as such, it was seen to operate in a contested relationship within which each party sought to determine the level of effort which constituted a 'fair day's work'. We argued that management have adopted various forms of reward system in order to communicate to the employees the required effort levels and to evaluate the levels of effort exerted. These have often been complex, confusing and ultimately failed to deliver the ultimate goal because they often restrict innovation and reward past achievements. It ought to be obvious that motivation occupies a central place in the rationale for the choices made by managers and hence attempts to understand the effectiveness of any particular reward system. In the application of this understanding of motivation, organisational policies have swayed between 'paying for numbers' and 'paying for skills', while always proving ineffective in the longer term because, we can suggest, they failed to convince people to take work seriously. However, it has also been argued that the idea that waving cash before people will motivate them, whilst an oft quoted 'wisdom' in modern society, is an oversimplification (see Kohn, 1998). Indeed, compensation managers need to take on board Slater's argument that 'The idea that everybody wants money is propaganda circulated by wealth addicts to make themselves feel better about their addiction' (1980: 25). Such an analysis would place the psychological contract in a more central position in the struggle for higher performance.

The issues surrounding the seriousness of work have recently been addressed by the development of the debates linked to the creation and maintenance of a contract in the mind. The psychological contract has been a rich source of ideas for the development of modern reward processes in that it goes beyond mere behaviours to consider the creation of values and understanding. Despite this attention, through which organisations have elaborated the existence of mutual obligations and duties, the psychological contract is seen to be a difficult tool to apply in the development of reward systems. Irrespective of these reservations, organisations have developed a performance management process which relies on the interaction between behaviours and values. These have included cafeteria pay systems, merit-based pay, team-based pay, management by objectives, 360-degree and other appraisal systems, designed to gain control of the effort side and return the levels of productivity purchased in the labour market.

HR practitioners have applied themselves to the development of systems of reward which are closely integrated with other organisational aims and reflect the strategic role played by reward in the achievement of these objectives. We argued that recent surveys suggest that all is not as it might appear from a glance at the literature. The employment relationship, and specifically the wage/effort or reward element, is still disputed territory within which neither side secures all their objectives. The Chartered Institute of Personnel and Development (CIPD) has a very useful website to refer to (www.cipd.co.uk).

Summary

- Reward strategies need to be viewed in the light of the employment relationship as an economic exchange. Employers need to exercise control over both sides of the wage/effort bargain to the greatest possible extent and in this light reward management attempts to enlarge the area of managerial control.

- These strategies have developed over the years since the industrial revolution through various phases and periods in response to the changing use and nature of technology. The basic nature of such schemes, however, continues to be that of payment by or for performance, whether such performance be pieces made, hours worked, merit achieved or compliance with organisational norms.

- Reward schemes attempt to generate a motivated workforce which is committed and loyal to the organisation.

- Motivation theory has evolved from a simple assumption based on notions of a rational economic perspective of employees – i.e. being motivated primarily by money – towards a more sophisticated human relations perspective which takes cognisance of the numerous and divergent 'needs' employees have. This more complex, though realistic assessment of what motivates employees requires managers to develop strategies which enable employees to realise an ever-greater sense of personal achievement and satisfaction in exchange for their contribution to the organisation.

- The psychological contract, seen in terms of transactional and relational elements, is increasingly being acknowledged as a significant aspect of the employment relationship. In the context of delayering, downsizing, limited career progression, the inability to offer a job for life, organisations need to change work patterns to ensure a sense of personal achievement, enhance employability security and engender relationship values in an effort to maintain a healthy psychological contract which will stimulate commitment and loyalty.

- Current debates surround the difficulties inherent in the motivation and management of knowledge workers, the control of emotional labour and the desire to secure additional profits via the application of reward strategies.

- The development of 'new pay' highlights an increased interest in the rules that are applied to the receipt of 'contingent' elements within reward packages.

QUESTIONS

1 Does the concept of employment relationships as economic exchange significantly add to our understanding of reward strategies?

2 To what extent is it possible for managers to convince workers 'to take work seriously when they know that it is a joke' (Anthony, 1977: 5) through the application of reward strategies?

3 How would you depict the evaluation of motivation theory?

4 Critically assess the extent to which money is the primary motivator for all employees.

5 In what way does the psychological contract influence the employment relationship?

EXERCISES

1 Prepare a short report to the HR director in which you make three recommendations for improving performance using modern reward management techniques.

2 Write a short article for an in-house magazine which indicates the effects of poor performance on the attainment of organisational goals and how the use of a performance management system benefits all employees.

3 Prepare a short report to the HR director in which you make three recommendations for improving the morale among the workforce based on sound principles of motivational theory.

4 Debate with colleagues the proposition that 'the psychological contract is a confused and irrelevant concept in the context of the employment relationship'.

CASE STUDY

Widgets Are Us

Widgets Are Us is part of a major multinational company which located at a site in the UK in 1990. They manufacture widgets for the electronics industry which are then branded by their various customers. The company is non-union and in order to retain this status operates a 'workers' forum' for consultations; they do not negotiate in relation to reward packages or levels. The main site has three separate units each producing different sizes of widget for various markets.

Units One and Two consist of four production lines each of which runs a continuous assembly process operating seven days a week and 24 hours a day. The bulk of the workforce is female, part-time and/or agency temporary workers, the latter group comprising some 40 per cent of the staff in each Unit. Each line is divided into six 'areas' within which five workers comprise a 'team' with one designated a 'team leader'. They are paid a base rate with additions for each piece produced by the line during each shift; team leaders are paid at a rate which is 5 per cent above the rest of the team to reflect their responsibility for the team. The base rate is in line with the National Minimum Wage and the line is paid an additional 4p for each item passed by quality control as satisfactory. The quality control operatives are placed mid-way along the line to verify quality prior to the widgets being vacuum packed for dispatch and are paid on a monthly basis at a higher base rate with no incentive element. As staff members they enjoy a choice of additional benefits drawn from the company 'cafeteria' reward system which is not available to other line workers. The widgets are mass produced to agreed specifications for each customer and the line may make widgets with slightly different specifications during each shift (on occasions as many as three different specifications during any one shift). Each line has a line manager who has the responsibility of ensuring that the materials are available for each specification as and when necessary and there are two assistant production managers responsible for two lines each who direct the flow of work to ensure orders are met by priority rather than on a 'first come first served' basis. The team leaders are responsible for ensuring that their teams are up to numbers and report any deficiencies to the line manager. It is the line manager's role to secure authority from the assistant production manager to approach the 'in-house' agency in order to cover any shortfall in the required number of workers.

Each Unit has a goods in/out department which is staffed by a regular crew of 15 workers. These workers are predominately male, semi-skilled, higher earners who are employed on the same basis as the quality control workers. Their main role is to offload materials and transport them to the lines, as and when requested, to collect completed work and load it for distribution. The Units run a JIT system under which there is little or no storage of materials beyond a single day's requirements and vehicles are loaded during the shift for dispatch that evening; all distribution takes place on an overnight basis. The minimum number of drivers are directly employed, with any shortfall covered by contracts with local distribution organisations.

➤

Case study continued

Each Unit therefore has a total three shift workforce of 200 production and distribution workers split into three shifts over a seven-day rota. No shift allowances are paid and overtime payments are not attracted for any hours below 40 whichever day they are worked; where over 40 hours are worked the overtime rate is time and a half whatever day worked. Production workers, excluding team leaders, are allowed 20 days' holiday a year, attract only statutory sick pay and are excluded from the company staff benefits. Temporary workers are treated as employees of the agency and their payment is left to the agency, which also deducts NI contributions and tax.

The third Unit is somewhat more specialised and produces bespoke widgets on a one-off basis primarily for export. It also includes an R&D section dedicated to advances in both widgets and their production. The Unit employs 20 semi-skilled production workers on the standard staff contracts and 10 specialist engineers paid an annual salary in line with local terms and conditions, which, as the area is depressed, are significantly below national averages.

Staff jobs are rewarded in a different manner in that they receive an annual salary with the additional option of picking benefits from the 'cafeteria' package based on the outcome of their appraisal. Only 'staff' are appraised and the merit element ranges between 1 and 5 per cent of their annual salary; they cannot take this value in cash and must select from the benefits cafeteria. These rules apply to team leaders, quality control operatives, warehouse operatives, line managers, assistant production managers, secretarial and administrative staff and office managers. Higher grades, including the engineers, negotiate their own packages on appointment and are then subject to the appraisal rules.

The organisation has a number of problems which the HR department need to address:

1. Units One and Two have high (up to 10 per cent per day) absence rates amongst the production workers.
2. They have a more serious problem with the weekends when the absence rate can be as high as 20 per cent.
3. Each has a turnover rate above the national average for the industry and they find temporary workers difficult to keep.
4. Unit Three has a higher than average turnover rate amongst the engineers.
5. Staff posts are fairly stable across the units but they find quality control workers are difficult to appoint from existing 'in-house' staff, possibly due to the lack of an incentive scheme which can result in their earnings being lower than those of the line operatives.

Questions

1 As an HR manager, how could you change the reward system to address each of these problems?

2 What measures would you take to strengthen the psychological contract?

References and further reading

Adams, J.S. (1963) 'Toward an understanding of inequality', *Journal of Abnormal and Social Psychology*, 67: 422–436.

Adams, J. (1965) 'Inequity in social exchange', in Berkowitz, L. (ed.) *Advances in Experimental Social Psychology*, 2. New York: Academic Press.

Adams, R.J. (1986) 'Two policy approaches to labour-management decision making at the level of the enterprise', in Craig Riddel, W.W. (ed.) *Labour–Management Cooperation in Canada*. Toronto: University of Toronto Press.

Anthony, P.D. (1977) *The Ideology of Work*. London: Tavistock Publications.

Appelbaum, E. (1993) 'Rethinking rewards', *Harvard Business Review*, Nov–Dec.

Armstrong, M. (1996) 'How group efforts can pay dividends', *People Management*, 25 January: 22–27.

Armstrong, M. (2002) *Employee Reward*. London: CIPD.

Arnold, J., Cooper, C. and Robertson, I. (1998) *Work Psychology: Understanding Human Behaviour in the Workplace*, 3rd edn. Harlow: Financial Times.

Austin, J. and Bobko, P. (1985) 'Goal setting theory', *Journal of Occupational Psychology*, 58: 289–308.

Bassett Jones, N. and Lloyd, G. (2004) 'Does Herzberg's Motivation theory have staying power?' *The Journal of Management Development*, 24, 10: 929–944.

Bean, R. (1994) *Comparative Industrial Relations*. London: Routledge.

Beer, M., Walton, R.E. and Spector, B.A. (1984) *Managing Human Assets*. New York: Free Press.

Blau, G. (1994) 'Testing the effect of level and importance of pay referents on pay level satisfaction', *Human Relations*, 47, 10: 1251–1268.

Blauner, R. (1964) *Alienation and Freedom: The Factory Worker and His Industry*. Chicago, Ill.: Chicago Press.

Bowey, A.M., Thorpe, R. and Hellier, P. (1986) *Payment Systems and Productivity*. Basingstoke: Macmillan.

Braverman, H. (1974) *Labour and Monopoly Capital: The Degradation of Work in the Twentieth Century*. London: Monthly Review Press.

Burawoy, M. (1985) *The Politics of Production*. London: Verso.

Callaghan, G. and Thompson, P. (2001) 'Edwards revisited: technical control and call centres', *Economic and Industrial Democracy*, 22, 1: 13–37.

Chadha Y. (2006) *Recognizing employees' efforts at Sara Lee Foods*. London: Melcrum Publishing Ltd.

CIPD (2003) *Pressure of Work and the Psychological Contract*. London: CIPD.

Conboy, B. (1976) *Pay at Work*. London: Arrow Books.

Cordery, J.L., Mueller, W.S. and Smith, L.M. (1991) 'Attitudinal and behavioral effects of autonomous group working: A longitudinal field study', *Academy of Management Journal*, 34: 464–476.

Cornelius, N. (2001) *Human Resource Management*, 2nd edn. London: Thomson Learning.

Crown, D.F. and Rosse, J.G. (1995) 'Yours, mine, and ours: Facilitating group productivity through the integration of individual and group goals', *Organizational Behavior and Human Decision Processes*, 64, 2: 138–150.

Daniels, K. (2006) *Employee Relations in an Organisational Context*. London: CIPD.

Dulebohn, J.H. and Martocchio, J.J. (1998) 'Employee perceptions of the fairness of work group incentive pay plans', *Journal of Management*, 24, 4: 469–488.

Earley, P., Connolly, T. and Ekergren, G. (1989) 'Goals, strategy development and task performance', *Journal of Applied Psychology*, 74: 24–33.

Etzioni, A. (1975) *A Comparative Analysis of Complex Organisations*. New York: Free Press.

Fisher, C. (1999) 'Performance management and performing management', in Leopold, J. *et al.* (eds) *Strategic Human Resourcing*. Harlow: FT/Pitman.

Folger, R., Konovsky, M.A. and Cropanzano, R. (1992) 'A due process metaphor for performance appraisal', in Straw, B.M. and Cummings, L.L. (eds) *Research on Organizational Behaviour*, pp. 129–177.

Freeman, R. (2001) 'Upping the stakes', *People Management*, February: 25–29.

Freeman, R.B. and Rogers, J. (1999) *What Workers Want*. Cornell, NY: Russell Sage Foundation.

Gooch, L. and Cornelius, N. (2001) 'Performance management: strategy, systems and rewards', in Cornelius, N. (ed.) *Human Resource Management*. London: Thomson Learning.

Gospel, H. (1992) *Markets, Firms, and the Management of Labour in Modern Britain*. Cambridge: Cambridge University Press.

Grayson, D. (1984) 'Shape of payment systems to come', *Employment Gazette*, April: 175–181.

Greenberg, J. (1987) 'A taxonomy of organizational justice theories', *Academy of Management Review*, 3, 3: 61–77.

Grint, K. (1997) *Fuzzy Management: Contemporary Ideas and Practices at Work*. Oxford: Oxford University Press.

Guest, D. (1998a) 'Is the psychological contract worth taking seriously?', *Journal of Organizational Behaviour*, 19: 649–664.

Guest, D. (1998b) 'On meaning, metaphor and the psychological contract: a response to Rousseau', *Journal of Organizational Behaviour*, 19: 673–677.

Guest, D. and Conway, N. (2002) 'Communicating the psychological contract: an employer perspective', *Human Resource Management Journal*, 12: 22–38.

Guzzo, R. and Noonan K.A. (1994) 'Human resources practices as communications and the psychological contract', *Human Resource Management*, 33, 3: 447–462.

Hackman, J. and Lawler, E. (1971) 'Employee reactions to job characteristics', *Journal of Applied Psychology Monograph*, 55: 259–286.

Hackman, J. and Oldman, G. (1980) *Work Redesign*. Reading, Mass: Addison-Wesley.

Hastings, S. and Dixon, L. (1995) *Competency: An Introduction*. Oxford: Trade Union Research Unit.

Herriot, P., Manning, W. and Kidd, J. (1997) 'The content of the psychological contract', *British Journal of Management*, 8, 2: 151–162.

Herriot, P. and Pemberton, C. (1995) *New Deals*. Chichester: John Wiley.

Herzberg, F. (1966) *Work and the Nature of Man*. Cleveland, Ohio: World Publishing.

Hill, S. (1981) *Competition and Control at Work*. London: Heinemann.

Howell, K. and Cameron, E. (1996) 'The benefits of an outsider's opinion', *People Management*, August: 28–30.

Huczynski, A. and Buchanan, D. (2001) *Organisational Behaviour: An Introductory Text*, 4th edn. Harlow: Prentice Hall.

IDS (1992) 'PRP grows as tax relief doubles', *IDS Study 520*, December.

IRS (2002) *IRS HR Essentials: Employment Facts, Research and Analysis*. Issue 02, December.

IRS (2003) *Employment Review 773*, May.

Jin, P. (1993) 'Work motivation and productivity in voluntary formed teams: A field study in China', *Organizational Behavior and Human Decision Processes*, 54: 133–135.

Kaplan, R.S and Norton, D.P. (1992) 'The balanced scorecard: measures that drive performance', *Harvard Business Review*, January–February: 71–79.

Kellaway, L.G. (1993) 'Nice little earner (profit-related pay)', *Financial Times*, 23 April, p. 14.

Kinnie, N. and Lowe, D. (1990) 'Performance related pay on the shopfloor', *People Management*, November: 45–49.

Klien, D.A. (1998) *The Strategic Management of Intellectual Capital*. Woburn: Butterworth-Heinemann.

Kohn, A. (1993a) 'Why Incentive Plans Cannot Work', *Harvard Business Review*, Sept–Oct.

Kohn, A. (1993b) 'Rethinking Rewards', *Harvard Business Review*, Nov–Dec.

Kohn, A. (1998) 'Challenging Behaviorist dogma: Myths about Money and Motivation', *Compensation and Benefits Review*, 30, 2: 27–33.

Kovach, K.A. (1987) 'What motivates employees? Workers and supervisors give different answers', *Business Horizons*, Sept–Oct: 58–65.

Kozlowski, A. (1993), in Kohn, A. 'Rethinking Rewards', *Harvard Business Review*, Nov–Dec.

Lawler, E.E. (1990) *Strategic Pay*. San Francisco, Calif.: Jossey Bass.

Lee, C., Law, K.S. and Bobko, P. (1999) 'The importance of justice perceptions on pay effectiveness', *Journal of Management*, 25, 6: 851–873.

Leventhal, G.S. (1976) 'Fairness in social relationships', in Thibaut, J. *et al. Contemporary Topics in Social Psychology*. Morristown, NJ: General Learning Press.

Lind, E.A. and Tyler, T. (1988) *The Social Psychology of Procedural Justice*. New York: Plenum.

Littler, C. (1982) *The Development of the Labour Process in Capitalist Societies*. London: Heinemann.

Littler, C. (ed.) (1985) *The Experience of Work*. Aldershot: Gower.

Locke, E. and Latham, G. (1984) *Goal Setting*. Englewood Cliffs, NJ: Prentice Hall.

Locke, E., Shaw, K., Saari, L. and Latham, G. (1981) 'Goal setting and task performance 1969–1980', *Psychological Bulletin*, 90: 125–152.

Lowry, D. (2002) 'Performance management', in Leopold, J. (ed.) *Human Resources in Organisations*. Harlow: FT/Prentice Hall.

Makin, J., Cooper, C. and Cox, J. (1996) *Organizations and the Psychological Contract*. Oxford: Blackwell.

Margerison, C. (1976) 'A constructive approach to appraisal', *Personnel Management*, July: 30–33.

McFarlin, D.B. and Sweeny, P.D. (1992) 'The psychological contract, organisational commitment and job satisfaction of temporary staff', *Leadership and Organisational Development Journal*, 21, 2: 84–91.

McGregor, D. (1957) 'An uneasy look at performance', *Harvard Business Review*, 35: 89–94.

Mercer Consultants (2003) 'Mind the productivity gap', in *IRS HR Essentials*, May.

Millward, N., Bryson, A. and Forth, J. (2000) *All Change at Work*. London: Routledge.

Miner, J.B. (2003) 'The rated importance, scientific validity, and practical usefulness of organizational behavior theories: a quantitative review', *Academy of Management Learning Education*, 9, 2: 250–268.

Mitrani, A., Dalziel, M. and Fitt, D. (1993) *Competency Based Human Resource Management*. London: Kogan Page.

Newton, T. and Findlay, P. (2000) 'Playing God? The performance appraisal', Chapter 8 in Mabey, C., Salaman, G. and Storey, J. (eds) *Strategic Human Resource Management: A Reader*. London: Sage in association with The Open University.

O'Doherty, D. (2001) 'Job design: signs, symbols and resignations', in Beardwell, I. and Holden, L. (eds) *Human Resource Management*, 3rd edn. Harlow: FT/Prentice Hall.

Orpen, C. (1997) 'The effects of formal mentoring on employee work motivation, organizational commitment and job performance', *The Learning Organization*, 4, 2. Research paper.

Pfeffer, J. (1998) 'Six dangerous myths about pay', *Harvard Business Review*, May–June.

Pinder, C. (1998) *Work Motivation in Organizational Behaviour*. Upper Saddle River, NJ: Prentice Hall.

Pritchard, D. and Murlis, H. (1992) *Jobs, Roles and People*. London: Nicholas Brealey.

Raub, S.P. (2001) 'Towards a knowledge-based framework of competence development', in Sanchez, R. *Knowledge Management and Organizational Competence*. Oxford: OUP.

Ritzer, G. (1997) *The McDonaldization Thesis*. London: Sage.

Ritzer, G. (2000) *The McDonaldization of Society*. London: Sage.

Robbins, S.P. (2002) *Organizational Behaviour*, New Delhi: Prentice Hall.

Roberts, I. (2001) 'Reward and performance management', in Beardwell, I. and Holden, L. (eds) *Human Resource Management*, 3rd edn. Harlow: FT/Prentice Hall.

Rollinson, D. (2002) *Organisational Behaviour and Analysis: An Integrated Approach*, 2nd edn. Harlow: Financial Times Prentice Hall.

Rosenfield, R. and Wilson, D. (1999) *Managing Organizational Behaviour: Text, Readings and Cases*, 2nd edn. London: McGraw-Hill.

Rousseau, D. (1995) *Psychological Contracts in Organizations*. Thousand Oaks, Calif.: Sage.

Rousseau, D. (1998) 'The problem of the psychological contract', *Journal of Organisational Behaviour*, 19: 665–671.

Rousseau, D. (2001) 'Schema, promise and mutuality: the building blocks of the psychological contract', *Journal of Occupational and Organisational Psychology*, 74: 511–541.

Rynes, L., Gerhart, B. and Minette, A. (2004) The importance of pay in employee motivation: Discrepancies between what people say and what they do. *Human Resource Management*, 43, 4: 381–394.

Schama, S. (1995) *Landscape and Memory*. London: HarperCollins.

Schuler, R.S. and Jackson, S.E. (1999) *Strategic Human Resource Management*. Oxford: Blackwell.

Schuster, J.R. and Zingheim, P. (1992) *The New Pay*. New York: Lexington Books.

Scott, H., Cheese, P. and Cantrell, S. (2006) 'Harley-Davidson', *Strategic HR Review*. Jan/Feb 5, 2: 28–31.

Shamir, B. (1991) 'Meaning, self and motivation in organizations', *Organizational Studies*, 12, 3: 405–424.

Slater, P. (1980) *Wealth Addiction*. New York: Dutton.

Sparrow, P. (1996) 'Transitions in the psychological contract', *Human Resource Management Journal*, 6, 4: 75–92.

Storey, J. (1992) *Developments in the Management of Human Resources*. Oxford: Blackwell.

Taylor, F.W. (1964) *Scientific Management*. New York: Harper & Row.

Taylor, P. and Bain, P. (1999) 'An assembly line in the head', *Industrial Relations Journal*, 30, 2: 101–117.

Taylor, P. and Bain, P. (2001) 'Trade unions, workers' rights and the frontier of control in UK call centres', *Economic and Industrial Democracy*, 22, 1: 39–66.

The Work Foundation (2003) 'Unwritten rules', in *IRS HR Essentials*. Issue 07, May.

Thompson, P. (1983) *The Nature of Work*. London: Macmillan.

Vroom, V.H. (1964) *Work and Motivation*. New York: John Wiley.

White, A. (2002) Interview with author at Jones the Bootmaker Ltd.

White, G. and Drucker, J. (2000) *Reward Management: A Critical Text*. London: Routledge.

Wiley, C. (1997) 'What motivates employees according to over 40 years of motivation surveys', *International Journal of Manpower*, 18, 3: 263–280.

Wilson, F. (1999) *Organisational Behaviour: A Critical Introduction*. Oxford: Oxford University Press.

Wood, A.W. (2000) 'Alienation', in *Concise Routledge Encyclopedia of Philosophy*. London: Routledge.

Wood, S. (ed.) (1982) *The Degradation of Work?* London: Hutchinson.

Woodruffe, C. (2006) 'Employee engagement', *British Journal of Administrative Mananagement*, Jan, 50: 28–29.

 For multiple-choice questions, exercises and annotated weblinks specific to this chapter visit the book's website at **www.pearsoned.co.uk/beardwell**

Employment relations — control, conflict and commitment

Chapter 7

INDUSTRIAL RELATIONS

Nick Bacon

Introduction

The terms 'industrial relations' and more recently 'employee relations' are used to indicate those areas of the employment relationship in which managers deal with the representatives of employees rather than managing employees directly as individuals (Edwards 1995). Where employees seek collective representation they generally join trade unions and the reaction of managers to this potential challenge to management authority provides valuable insights into the nature of employment. As the membership of trade unions has declined over the past two decades a critical debate has developed around the nature of employment relations in non-union workplaces. The purpose of this chapter is to chart the changes in the collective regulation of labour and consider the implications of the increasing number of workers who are not represented by trade unions.

Management frames of reference and management style

The suggestion that employees may need some form of collective protection from employers provokes a strong response in many managers. Behind this response are a set of assumptions about the right to manage (frequently termed the management prerogative) and the correct power balance in the employment relationship. These assumptions held by managers are the mixture of a complex blend of experiences, pre-dispositions, learned behaviour and prejudice. They combine to create management frames of reference (Fox 1966, 1974) that capture the often deeply held assumptions of managers towards a labour force. Three separate frames of reference can be identified: unitarism, pluralism and radical. Each of these differs in their beliefs about the nature of organisations, the role of conflict and the task of managing employees. Managers holding a unitarist frame of reference believe the natural state of organisations is one of harmony and cooperation. All employees are thought to be in the same team, pulling together for the common goal of organisational success. The employee relations task of management is to prevent conflict arising from misunderstandings that result if they fail to adequately communicate organisational goals to employees. Any remaining conflicts are attributed to mischief created by troublemakers. A pluralist frame of reference recognises that organisations contain a variety of sectional groups who legitimately seek to express divergent interests. The resulting conflict is inevitable and the task of managers is to establish a system of structures and procedures in which conflict is institutionalised and a negotiated order is established. The radical critique of pluralism is not, strictly speaking, a frame of reference for understanding management views of the employment relationship. It draws upon Marxism and explains workplace conflict within a broader historical and social context and places a stress upon the unequal power struggle of opposing social classes.

There are no simple methods to assess the frame of reference held by managers – indeed, they usually hold a complex set of ideas rather than falling neatly into a single and possibly over-simplistic frame of reference. However, insights into management attitudes can be gained through their responses to questions about trade unions. From comparable questions posed to managers at the start of the 1980s and 1990s, Poole and Mansfield (1993) suggested the underlying pluralistic preferences of British managers were remarkably consistent. Another question posed more recently indicated a majority of workplace managers do not have a single frame of reference. In the 1998 *Workplace Employee Relations Survey* (WERS 98) most managers (54 per cent) were 'neutral' about union membership, whereas 29 per cent were 'in favour' with 17 per cent 'not in favour' (Cully *et al.* 1999, p. 87). However, when managers are asked more directly whether they prefer to manage employees directly or through unions then unitarist preferences emerge. For example, 72 per cent of managers agreed with the statement 'we would rather consult directly with employees than with unions', whereas only 13 per cent disagreed (ibid., p.88). Consequently, management approaches to industrial relations are often characterised as a mixing and matching between unitarism and pluralism in the 'time-honoured' British fashion (Edwards *et al.* 1998). Many managers accept such a view on the grounds that it merely reflects the reality of managing employees who may at times need representation. The evidence suggests, however, that managers can deter or encourage employees from joining trade unions. In the 1998 *Workplace Employee Relations Survey* pro-union management attitudes were significantly associated with union presence in the workplace (Cully *et al.* 1998, p.19).

Frames of references are also important because they underlie the management style adopted in organisations towards the workforce. Many authors have attempted to classify management styles (Fox 1974; Purcell and Sisson 1983; Storey and Bacon 1993; Purcell and Ahlstrand 1994) and as the resulting models have become increasingly complex Some now doubt the usefulness of producing yet more typologies (Kitay and Marchington 1996). The most recent typologies attempt to highlight the interaction between HRM and industrial relations. The central question raised is the extent to which HRM and industrial relations are alternative or complementary systems for managing employees. If they are alternatives then HRM may provide a 'unitarist' alternative to managing with unions (Bacon 2003). Whether managers recognise trade unions indicates the extent to which a 'collective' approach to managing employees is preferred and it does capture a key factor in distinguishing between management approaches. In addition, the extent to which managers invest in and develop employees indicates the extent to which they stress 'individualism'. In Figure 7.1 Purcell and Ahlstrand (1994) use the dimensions of 'collectivism' and 'individualism' to identify six different management styles of employee relations.

Individualism and collectivism have recently become popular terms in employee relations. In comparison with the traditional management frames of reference–unitarism and pluralism–these concepts have 'common sense' meanings and appear grounded in everyday management vocabularies and thinking about employee relations. Individualism in employment relations is traditionally used to denote non-unionism and/or a HRM-style investment approach to employees (Purcell 1987; Marchington and Parker 1990; Storey and Sisson 1993). Correspondingly, collectivism in industrial relations in the 1970s is counter-posed with individualism and HRM in the 1990s (Storey and Sisson 1993). The 'collectivism' dimension includes a unitarist position where trade unions are not recognised, an adversarial position of conflict with unions and a cooperative position of partnership with unions. The 'individualism' dimension includes a cost minimisation approach to employees, a 'paternalist' position of care for employee welfare and an employee development scenario.

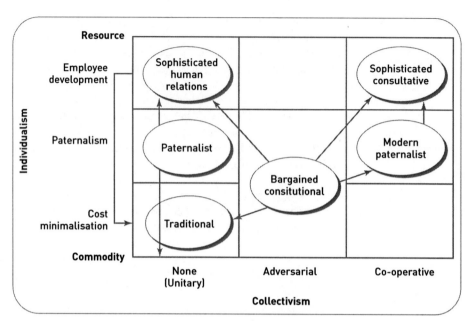

Figure 7.1 Movements in management style in employee relations
Source: Storey and Sisson, 1993, adapted from Purcell and Ahlstrand, 1994

Initial studies of the adoption of HRM policies in unionised workplaces (Storey 1992) suggested little fit between HRM and industrial relations as managers attempted to bypass industrial relations processes and deal directly with employees. This comes as no great surprise as personnel management in the UK is commonly described as pragmatic and largely opportunistic (Sisson and Marginson 1995). In seeking the appropriate recipe for managing employees during the 1980s many managers saw an opportunity to reduce the influence of unions. This involved a secular (if disputed) shift towards unitarism as managers reasserted their prerogative over employees at work. Initially, in the 1980s this appeared in an aggressive form of 'macho-management' as senior executives, often in state-owned industries, attacked unions and the customs and practices entrenched in many workplaces (Purcell 1982). However, most companies did not derecognise unions and commentators noted that 'the lack of clarity about how industrial relations fits with the new initiatives will sooner or later have to be addressed' (Storey and Sisson 1993, p.27). In short, the main issue on the employee relations agenda appeared to be how to combine the individual and collective approaches in a complementary fashion.

Employee views on work

A widespread criticism of management during the 1960s and 1970s, a point which still holds today, is that employees may not feel everyone shares the same goals in their workplace and they may reject a unitarist perspective. In many, if not most, workplaces employees talk of 'us' and describe managers as 'them', believing there are two sides with partially conflicting interests (Clegg 1979). Thus, many employees subscribe to a pluralist perspective and feel workers and managers are on different sides with separate interests, rather than feeling that working for an organisation is like playing for a football team where all groups supporting a club are on the same side and pursuing a common goal (Ramsey 1975).

Where employees feel they have different interests from managers they often join trade unions. Trade unions have approximately 320 million members world-wide which amounts

Table 7.1 What reasons do employees give for joining unions?	
Support if I had a problem at work	72%
Improved pay and conditions	36%
Because I believe in trade unions	16%
Free legal advice	15%
Most people at work are members	14%

Source: Waddington and Whitston 1997, p.521 (www.blackwell-synergy.com)

to between one fifth and one quarter of the global labour force (Visser 2003). Significant variation exists between countries. For instance, Russia, Ukraine and Belarus (58 per cent) and China (42 per cent) have high rates of union membership; around one quarter (26 per cent) of European workers are union members, whereas a smaller proportion of workers in North America (13 per cent) and Asia (10 per cent) belong to unions.

Employees may choose to join trade unions for a wide range of reasons (Schnabel 2003, p.19). They may feel dissatisfied with their work situation (termed the frustration-aggression thesis), joining a union may bring benefits such as higher wages that outweigh the costs of membership (a rational choice explanation), or they may be encouraged to join by the traditions and opinions of their work group (an interactionist explanation). In a survey of almost 11,000 union members in the UK conducted by Waddington and Whitston (1997) employees revealed they continued to join unions for collective protection and to improve their terms and conditions (Table 7.1). Some studies suggest that HRM initiatives introduced over the past 20 years have had little impact on workers' perceptions of 'them' and 'us' (Kelly and Kelly 1991; D'Art and Turner 1999).

The decline of collective regulation

In a majority of countries union membership has fallen over the past twenty years, especially in Europe and North America. The decline in the numbers of union members suggests employment relations have been transformed and we have witnessed 'the end of institutional industrial relations' (Purcell 1993). In the UK, for example, the *Workplace Industrial Relations Surveys* (WIRS) since 1990 record fundamental changes with industrial relations no longer characterised by adversarial collective bargaining at workplace level (Millward *et al.* 1992). Figure 7.2 illustrates this change as captured by these surveys in terms of changes to union presence (the presence of one or more union members in a workplace), union membership density (percentage of employees who are union members), union recognition for negotiating pay and conditions of employment, coverage of collective bargaining (the proportion of employees in workplaces with recognised unions covered by collective bargaining) and joint consultative committees.

The decline in union recognition in the UK since the 1980s is mainly due to the failure of unions to organise workers and gain recognition for collective bargaining in new firms and workplaces (Machin 2000). Responding to heightened competitive pressures managers have proved reluctant to recognise unions for fear of higher wages, and unions have found it difficult to recruit the growing numbers of female and service sector workers. As the number of large manufacturing plants and manual workers declined the traditional habitat for the UK's system of industrial relations based on adversarial collective bargaining began to disappear (Millward *et al.* 1992).

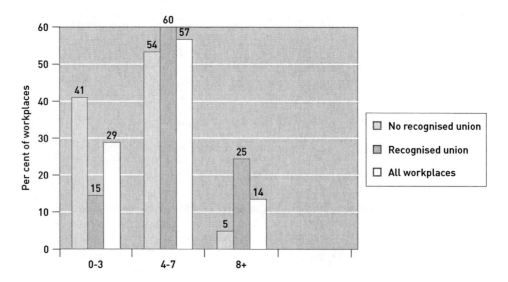

Figure 7.2 Number of high commitment management practices, by trade union recognition.
Source: Cully *et al.* 1999

Table 7.2 The decline of collective regulation in the workplace industrial relations surveys*				
	1980	1984	1990	1998
Union presence	73%	73%	64%	54%
Union membership density	65%	58%	47%	36%
Union recognition	65%	65%	53%	42%
Coverage of collective bargaining	–	70%	54%	41%
Joint consultative committees	34%	34%	29%	29%

Source: Workplace Industrial Relations Surveys; see Cully *et al.* 1999

*Figures related to percentages of workplaces

Trade union influence appears even lower than current levels of union recognition indicate when we consider the scope and depth of joint consultation and bargaining. It is difficult to assess the extent to which managers rely upon collective agreements with trade unions in workplaces. One study comparing collective agreements at the start and end of the 1980s outlined a relative stability in procedural agreements covering how issues are handled between management and labour (Dunn and Wright 1994). A rather different picture emerged from case studies at plant level, indicating managers were increasingly exercising their prerogative to make important changes, particularly in working methods (Geary 1995). Data from the 1998 *Workplace Employee Relations Surveys* indicates a deeper 'hollowing out' of collective agreements. In workplaces where union representatives are present only a 'modest' level of joint regulation occurs. No negotiations occurred over any issues in one half of the workplaces with worker representatives present (Cully *et al.* 1999, p.110). In a further 13 per cent of workplaces negotiations only occurred on non-pay issues, in 17 per cent negotiations only covered pay, and in 22 per cent negotiations occurred over pay and one other issue. Managers in many workplaces appear to regard certain HR issues as 'off limits' to union representatives and do not even involve unions in providing information. In 53 per cent of workplaces with union representatives, representatives played no role at all in performance appraisals, in 52 per cent no role in recruitment, in 46 per cent no role in payment systems, and in 43 per cent no role in training. This evidence suggests that in many cases trade union influence has 'withered on the vine' and where union representatives remain in place this resembles a unionised approach to industrial relations which in fact is little more than a 'hollow shell' (Hyman 1997). Given these findings traditional debates on the most appropriate levels for collective bargaining (at the workplace, corporate or industry levels) and the balance between collective bargaining and joint consultation are giving way to the broader question of whether and on what terms trade unions are involved in any degree of joint workplace governance. The central role played by collective industrial relations has certainly declined but what types of non-union workplaces have emerged?

Non-union workplaces

According to one estimate the majority of UK workplaces had become non-union by 1995 (Cully and Woodland 1996). In the classic account by Fox (1974) it was necessary for managers to enforce management prerogative by coercive power to justify a unitarist ideology and non-union status. Managers have often used a wide-ranging web of defences against unionisation that in their more extreme variants in the United States could combine 'sweet stuff' to make management policies more acceptable to employees, 'fear stuff' to discourage union joining and 'evil stuff' to demonise unions (Roy 1980). A unitarist ideology can therefore include a variety of different management techniques. Returning to Figure 7.1 we can see that Purcell and Ahlstrand (1994) classify three non-union management styles in terms of whether an organisation recognises and develops individual employees. Companies adopting a 'sophisticated human relations' approach invest in staff development and use a wide range of human resource management policies to substitute for the services unions provide for members (a union substitution approach). Other non-union companies adopt a 'paternalist' approach and seek the loyalty and commitment of staff through consideration for employee welfare. Finally, some organisations maintain a 'bleak house' strategy of cost minimisation and avoid union recruitment.

Several key commentators in the late 1980s identified the non-union sector as the most likely location for the development of HRM in the UK, foreseeing a growth in the 'sophisticated human relations' approach (Sisson 1989). As some HRM models, but not all, are fundamentally unitarist, a non-union environment appeared well suited to the demands of developing committed and flexible employees as demonstrated by several large non-union US multinationals such as IBM, Hewlett Packard and Mars (Foulkes 1980; Kochan *et al.* 1986). For example, IBM had combined corporate success, a positive employee relations climate of low conflict, low labour turnover and long service, with good pay and conditions. In addition, the company provided procedures to fulfil many of the functions met by unions, including a complex array of alternative procedures (a no-redundancy policy, single status, equal opportunities policies, merit pay and performance assessments), a strong emphasis on internal communications and a grievance system.

Empirical support for the apparent link between sophisticated HRM and non-unionism was also provided by several case studies in the UK outlining a union-substitution approach. In the case of 'Comco' explored by Cressey *et al.* (1985) employees identified strongly with the company and enjoyed 'greater benefits' and 'less disciplinary pressure'. Most employees working at an IBM plant in the UK studied by Dickson *et al.* (1988) were positively attached to the individualistic ethos of the company and perceived little need for union protection. Scott (1994) outlined a 'golden handcuffs' approach whereby employees in a chocolate works received good terms and conditions in return for accepting a high rate of effort and strict rules. Despite this evidence, initial studies indicated that non-union companies with a sophisticated approach to managing employees may remain the exception. A study of high-tech companies in the southeast of England where we might expect companies to reproduce the IBM non-union model uncovered little evidence of sophisticated HRM, with companies either opportunistically avoiding unions or adopting the style of 'benevolent autocracies' (McLoughlin and Gourlay 1994). Furthermore, the assumed benefits of a 'sophisticated human relations' approach have more recently come under closer scrutiny. Blyton and Turnbull (1994) suggest that Marks and Spencer, so often held up as an exemplar non-union company, simultaneously pursued a 'union substitution' strategy in retail outlets while forcing suppliers into a cost-minimisation approach. In another case study, a steel plant had widely publicised the introduction of an HRM approach and subsequently derecognised trade unions. However, employee gains proved illusory, with managerial strategy geared towards attitudinal compliance, work intensification and the suppression of any counterbalancing trade union activity (Bacon 1999).

As almost one half of workplaces are effectively union-free a 'representation gap' (Towers 1997) may have developed where managers operate without any independent employee voice. Three in five workplaces have no worker representatives at all (either union or non-union representatives), and this increases to nine out of ten workplaces where unions are not present (Cully *et al.* 1999, p.95). The absence of representation is important because if dissatisfied workers cannot express their grievances then their only option may be to leave the organisation (Hirschman 1971). In the absence of union recognition managers can provide employee voice through direct channels by communicating with workers in team briefings and problem solving, and there is evidence managers are more responsive to these communications than in listening to unions (Bryson 2004). However, as we will see below many organisations fail to provide either union or direct channels for employee voice.

HRM: A union or non-union phenomena?

The evidence from the latest UK workplace survey (WERS98) confirms the finding of the 1990 survey (WIRS3, see Sisson 1993, p.206) that sophisticated HRM practices are to be found alongside union recognition mainly in larger workplaces and those in the public sector. In short, these surveys indicate 'an active and strong union presence is compatible with the broad suite of high commitment management practices' (Cully *et al.* 1999, p.111). Furthermore, higher union density (the proportion of employees who are trade union members) is also associated with greater joint regulation and more high commitment management (HCM) practices. Figure 7.2 indicates that of the workplaces with no recognised unions, 41 per cent had between nought and three HCM practices, 54 per cent four to seven HCM practices, and 5 per cent for eight or more. This compares unfavourably with 25 per cent of workplaces with recognised unions reporting eight or more high commitment management practices.

However, only 4 per cent of workplaces in the workplace survey combine a majority of the workforce in unions, collective negotiations over issues and at least one half of the measured list of high commitment work practices in place. There is, nevertheless, evidence from the

1998 *Workplace Employee Relations Survey* that the combination of union recognition and HCM practices has a powerful effect on workplace performance. In the words of the WERS98 team 'workplaces with a recognised union and a majority of the HCM practices . . . did better than the average, and better than workplaces without recognition and a minority of these practices' (Cully *et al.* 1999, p.135). Sceptics of the impact of trade unions may still like to believe that adopting a wide range of HCM practices in a non-union environment may lead to higher performance still, but the fact that WERS98 could find so few such organisations casts some doubt upon this belief. Managers continuing to recognise unions are seeking new approaches to industrial relations involving 'partnership agreements'.

Partnership and the 'New Unionism'

The election of 'New Labour' in the UK in 1997 has resulted in a new public policy environment. The government's Employment Relations Act 1999 and 'Fairness at Work' programme have introduced new rights for trade unions and individual employees (Undy 1999; Wood and Godard 1999). In sum, this legislative programme involves a statutory route for union recognition, an extension of rights for individual employees, a national minimum wage and closer engagement with the social policies of the European Union. A central aim of this legislative programme is to 'replace the notion of conflict between employers and employees with the promotion of partnership in the longer term' (DTI 1998). The influence of a European approach was already felt as legislation obliged companies to establish a European works council if they employed over 1,000 employees in Europe and a minimum of 150 employees in at least two member states. The partial Europeanisation of British industrial relations shows no sign of slowing. The European Union Directive for informing and consulting employees will be phased in from 2005 providing rights for employees to be informed about the economic situation of their employer's business, employment prospects and substantial changes in work organisation or employment contracts. In sum, these changes now make it commonplace to call for less destructive conflict and more cooperation to improve organisational productivity.

The issue of the respective balance between cooperation and conflict in union – management relations is a long-standing tension in employee relations. As the employment relationship encapsulates both shared and contrary interests the relationship between management and unions will contain elements of conflict and cooperation. As management and unions have begun to use the word 'partnership' it has become a contested term that appears inherently ambiguous and at times has no agreed meaning (Ackers and Payne 1998; Undy 1999). As Undy (1999, p.318) has pointed out 'What one party, or commentator, means by "partnership" is not necessarily shared by others'. As with so many terms in the area of employment relations, key pressure groups such as the TUC, the CBI and the Institute of Directors (IoD) have sought to provide 'widely differing interpretations' of partnership (Undy 1999, p.318), defining the term for their own ends. The Institute of Personnel and Development, for example, explains that partnership 'has more to do with an approach to the relationship between employers and employees, individually and in groups, than it has to do with trade unions' (IPD 1997, p.8). Partnership can therefore be defined in both unitarist and pluralist terms. Rather unsurprisingly, the definition favoured by the TUC is pluralistic, with the stress placed on respecting union influence, whereas the Institute of Directors prefers a unitarist definition, whereby employees identify with the employer and trade unions are compliant to the wishes of management.

The Involvement and Participation Association, an independent pressure group, developed an influential definition of partnership with leading companies and trade union leaders. This approach was endorsed by leading figures including representatives from J Sainsbury plc, the Boddington Group, the Post Office and the leaders of several trade unions (Involvement and Participation Association 1992). This definition requires managers to declare security of employment as a key corporate objective; 'gainsharing' the results of success, and recognise the legitimacy of the employees' right to be informed, consulted and represented. In return, trade unions are required to renounce rigid job demarcations and commit to flexible working, give sympathetic consideration to the Continental model of representation of the whole workforce by means of election of representatives to new works councils, and recognise and then co-promote employee involvement methods. Case 7.2 invites you to consider the extent to which you feel companies and unions are able to sign-up to a partnership agenda.

Given the lack of a general consensus on the meaning of industrial relations partnerships, it may be surprising that the term has acquired such a topical currency. A principal reason the concept has taken hold is that it offers an industrial relations solution to the low competitiveness of much of UK industry. In this respect, partnership is no different from previous legislative changes that have sought to improve organisational performance through changes in industrial relations. Influential US literature suggests that in some companies managers may be able to forge a strategic linkage between industrial relations and HRM initiatives to create 'mutual gains enterprises' (Appelbaum and Batt 1994; Kochan and Osterman 1994). In such enterprises important changes are introduced in the reorganisation of work to enhance productivity, to the mutual benefit of employees, unions and management acting in coalition.

The signing of partnership agreements is of potential importance (IRS 1997) although to date there is little evidence they have become widespread beyond around forty companies. If partnerships are to become further established in UK industrial relations then managers and unions must find a workable balance between a number of key tensions beyond the above-mentioned disputes as to the meaning of the concept. The first tension is that workable partnership agreements appear to require a strategic and long-term commitment by managers to working closely with unions in the tradition of companies labelled 'sophisticated moderns' by Fox (1974). If managers are simply behaving in a short-term, contradictory or opportunistic manner then genuine industrial relations partnerships are unlikely to endure. For example, at the Royal Mail several partnership initiatives have struggled, primarily because some managers in the company are not firmly behind the partnership approach (see Bacon and Storey 1996, 2000).

The second tension, not unconnected to the first, is to what extent management and unions are able to commit fully to a single strategy of cooperative industrial relations. If partnerships do not secure the types of compliant trade unionism required in the CBI's definition of partnership then management commitment to such agreements may prove half-hearted. Similarly, at the same time as the TUC is supporting partnership agreements it is also pursuing an organising and campaigning approach to membership growth (Heery 1998). It may prove difficult for unions to convince a company to sign a meaningful partnership agreement in one plant while actively recruiting union members against the wishes of the same or a similar company in another plant.

The third tension is whether partnership agreements form part of a longer term strategy to marginalise trade unions rather than an alternative. Many observers critical of the cooperative relationships between managers and unions that are central to partnership agreements have highlighted continued employer attacks on unions (Claydon 1989, 1996; Smith and Morton 1993; Gall and McKay 1994; Kelly 1996). Although partnerships are frequently presented as a step change away from attempts to de-recognise trade unions this may not be the case. Evidence on this matter is not yet conclusive. Whereas one recent review of partnership agreements in six organisations reported 'none gave serious consideration to ending recognition' (IDS 1998, p.4), a study of management attempts to restructure industrial relations in ten organisations (Bacon and Storey 2000) revealed de-recognition had been more seriously explored. In the latter study, the new agreements signed with trade unions did not appear to reflect long-term commitments to working with trade unions nor sophisticated moves towards derecognition. Managers appeared to display unitarist preferences. However, for pragmatic reasons – for instance, the desire to maintain the trust of employees – they were willing to involve unions in joint regulation albeit within parameters managers attempted to control. In many workplaces union representatives feel they have no option but to accept management terms and union support for partnership resembles a resigned compliance. For example, in the case of United Distillers trade unions either signed the partnership agreement on offer or faced '*de facto* de-recognition' (Marks *et al.* 1998, p.222). The statutory provisions for union recognition contained in the Employment Relations Act 1999 did mark an increase in union recognition agreements suggesting trade unions may have turned a corner in their decline (Gall 2004) with employers showing greater approval of unions (Oxenbridge *et al.* 2003). However, according to Oxenbridge *et al.* (2003) this involved employers seeking union assistance in implementing organisational change and did not restrain the rate at which employers were excluding unions from bargaining over issues such as pay.

Finally, it is not yet clear whether partnership agreements will deliver greater returns for managers and trade unions. If returns are not forthcoming for either party then enthusiasm for the partnership approach may wane. Kelly (1996) has argued that, *a priori*, a union strategy of moderation is inferior in many respects to a militant stance. Union moderation is associated by Kelly with: eroding the willingness and capacity of union members to resist employers; inhibiting the growth of workplace union organisation; generating apathy among union members; involving union 'give' and management 'take'; and resulting in attempts to drive down terms and conditions of employment and failing to genuinely represent member grievances. The key differences between militant and moderate union positions are highlighted in Case study 7.3.

The extent to which Kelly is correct, and neither unions nor employees will benefit from partnership agreements, is an interesting question. Kelly (2004) compared similar UK companies with and without partnership agreements and found that partnership firms shed jobs at a faster rate than non-partnership firms in industries marked by employment decline. In contrast, partnership firms in expanding sectors created jobs at a faster rate than non-partnership firms. Partnership appeared to have no impact on wage settlements or union density. The number of partnership agreements signed between unions and management remains low overall and this may reflect the extent to which such agreements deliver job security and higher wages for employees and the flexibility that managers seek. Gains for employees from partnership appear to be particularly elusive. In a study of 54 companies, Guest and Peccei (2001, p.207) discovered that the balance of advantage from partnership at work 'is skewed towards management' and was associated with positive estimates of employment relations, quality and productivity.

Conclusions

In this chapter we have argued that managers in the majority of workplaces no longer appear to support or utilise collective industrial relations in their employee management strategies. Sisson and Storey (2000, p. x) have recently restated that 'managing the employment relationship will demand both an individual and a collective perspective' in forthcoming years. However, recent evidence suggests that managers in few workplaces have sought to balance an individual and collective approach to employee management. Figure 7.3 presents a summary drawing upon the findings from WERS98 of the current pattern of employee relations. The predominant employee relations style in the British workplace is not to manage both individualism and collectivism, it is to manage neither. Considering all the workplaces who fall into the bottom left hand quadrant of the dotted lines, approximately seven in ten (68 per cent) operate fewer than one-half of 15 high-commitment management practices and do not involve trade unions in negotiations on matters other than pay. Fifty-two per cent of workplaces in this quadrant do not recognise trade unions.

Approximately 14 per cent of workplaces could be described as pursuing an HRM approach but only 5 per cent appeared to combine individualism with either a union exclusion or partnership approach. The majority of workplaces appear to be marginalising unions, and although they remain present significant negotiations do not occur. It is tempting to classify organisations falling into the four corner boxes as having an apparently settled employee relations strategy that is unlikely to change in the near future. The numerous workplaces which fall into the 'Bleak House' classification (approximately 22 per cent) are focused upon cost reduction and will resist any attempts at unionisation. In such 'Bleak House' workplaces employees report lower levels of job satisfaction, organisational commitment, trust in management and experience unfair treatment (Guest and

Figure 7.3 New patterns of employee relations

Conway 1999). The small number of organisations which negotiate with unions but eschew developing employees ('industrial relations traditional') may be resigned to dealing with unions in the absence of a more sophisticated approach to managing employees. A few genuine examples of partnership may flourish in the current political climate but the overall number of such workplaces remains small. Companies adopting non-union HRM are likely to feel they have permanently resolved the union issue.

This leaves approximately 69 per cent of organisations (in the shaded areas of Figure 7.2) who currently operate with an opportunistic mixture of labour management policies. Organisations currently occupying these different positions face somewhat different dilemmas. Those currently using HRM policies to substitute for negotiating with unions but still recognising unions ('union substitution') may at some point in the future sign partnership deals with trade unions to share more decision-making and/or further erode union influence. Companies with 'strong traditional unionism' may further develop HR policies either to substitute for unions or develop a partnership approach. From an industrial relations perspective the most significant developments may occur within the 'weakening unionism' category. Although trade unions in these workplaces are involved in fewer negotiations managers have not developed high commitment management practices to replace the services unions provide for members in terms of voicing collective grievances and seeking to improve terms and conditions. It would appear to be in this category of workplaces that trade unions may target recruitment to increase union density and exert greater influence. The Employment Relations Act 1999 encourages union recruitment and organising efforts as it provides a statutory recognition procedure. As so few organisations appear to have resolved the issue of managing employees through individual or collective means they are likely to face continued pressure from individual employees for increased training and more satisfying work and from employee representatives for a greater say in workplace governance.

CASE STUDY 7.1

UNION RECOGNITION IN THE PRIVATE SECTOR

NICK BACON

Below is a list of the largest private sector employers in the UK taken from *Labour Research*. Which do you think: do not recognise trade unions; recognise and negotiate with trade unions; or recognise trade unions but only for the purposes of consultation or to represent individual employees? Explain your decisions.

Tesco	153,800	Retail – supermarkets
J Sainsbury	150,700	Retail – supermarkets
BT	125,800	Telecommunications
Lloyds-TSB	82,000	Banking and finance
Whitbread	80,000	Food and drink
Boots Co.	75,000	Retail and pharmaceuticals
Asda Group	73,700	Retail – supermarkets
Safeway Group	70,400	Retail – supermarkets
Kingfisher	69,600	Retail
Bass	67,500	Brewing and leisure
National Westminster	66,000	Banking and finance
Rentokil Initial	65,000	Business services
Barclays	60,800	Banking and finance
Granada Group	58,000	Leisure
Marks & Spencer	54,900	Retail
General Electric Co.	52,300	Electronics
HSBC Holding (Midland Bank)	50,000	Banking and finance
British Airways	47,700	Banking and finance
Allied Domecq	46,500	Food and drink
Somerfield	45,700	Retail – supermarket
Burton Group	43,700	Retail
British Steel	43,400	Steel manufacturers
Ladbroke Group	42,000	Leisure
John Lewis Partnership	41,100	Retail – department stores
BMW-Rover Group	39,000	Motor manufacture
Scottish & Newcastle	39,000	Brewing and leisure
British Aerospace	38,500	Aerospace and engineering
MacDonald's Restaurants	36,700	Food retail
Halifax	36,000	Banking and finance
Ford	35,900	Motor manufacturing
Compass Group	35,700	Catering
Co-operative Wholesale Society	35,000	Banking, insurance, retail
OCS Group	35,000	Cleaning
Sears	32,600	Retail
Rolls Royce	31,200	Aerospace and engineering
Rank Organisation	30,300	Leisure and films
Greenhalls Group	30,100	Brewing, food, hotels
WH Smith	30,000	Retail
Royal & Sun Alliance	27,800	Insurance
Securicor Group	27,500	Security services
Wm Morrison Supermarkets	27,000	Retail – supermarkets
Unigate	27,000	Food manufacture
Lucas Varity	26,800	Engineering
BTR	26,600	Industrial conglomerate
Kwik Save Group	26,000	Retail

CASE STUDY 7.2

THE PRINCIPLES AND PRACTICES OF PARTNERSHIP WITH TRADE UNIONS

NICK BACON

As explained in Chapter 7, one option for managers and trade unions is to establish a partnership agreement. However, successful agreements depend upon a serious commitment to the principles and practices of partnership. Thinking of the last organisation you worked for, an organisation you know well or your own personal 'frame of reference', to what extent do you agree or disagree with the following statements? Your answers indicate whether organisations could be committed to a partnership agreement. (Circle one number for each statement.)

	Agree	Neutral	Disagree
Personnel managers worry about trade unions, most other senior managers would rather they disappear	1	2	3
Trade unions don't have a useful function in organisations	1	2	3
All managers should share all information, however sensitive, with unions	1	2	3
Managers can get employees to work hard without making concessions to unions	1	2	3
Job security is a myth in today's world	1	2	3
To attract top managers organisations have to offer extra incentives, such as private health insurance, that are too expensive to give to all employees	1	2	3
Companies should train all employees to a high level even though some will leave	1	2	3

CASE STUDY 7.3

MILITANCY OR MODERATION?

NICK BACON

In Chapter 7 we outlined Kelly's (1996) argument that trade unions would benefit from a militant rather than a moderate stance. Reading through the following statements, indicate the extent to which you believe trade unions should adopt a moderate and militant stance. Explain your choices.

Trade unions should:

Union militancy		Union moderation
Make ambitious demands	or	Make moderate demands
Offer few concessions	or	Offer many concessions
Rely on members' activity	or	Rely on managers' goodwill
Rely on collective bargaining	or	Rely on consultation
Frequently threaten industrial action	or	Rarely threaten industrial action
Believe in a basic conflict of interests	or	Believe a basic common interest

CASE STUDY 7.4

THE CHALLENGE FOR UNION AND EMPLOYER PARTNERSHIP: THE EUROTUNNEL EXPERIENCE

PAUL J. GOLLAN

How will the impending law on information and consultation affect a union–management partnership? Eurotunnel's experience could spell problems and opportunities for both unions and employer.

Recent developments at Eurotunnel could have serious implications for the future of the partnership approach in the UK and of the likely success of the European Information and Consultation Directive.

The story of employee relations at this company shows that putting in place a consultation mechanism does not in itself necessarily give employees an effective 'voice'.

Eurotunnel has a 99-year lease to operate the Channel Tunnel link between Britain and France, running freight trains and maintaining the infrastructure. It consists of two legal entities for the UK and France and employs 3,400 staff, about 1,400 of them based in Britain on UK contracts.

To harmonise the workforce, it set up a company council for UK-contracted employees in December 1992, broadly similar to the French comité d'entreprise. Until June 2000, Eurotunnel (UK) recognised only the company council for consultation. This had one representative and one deputy elected from each of eight constituencies including: Technical Engineering, Shuttle Services, Tourist Division, Train Crew, Freight Division, Corporate (Administration), Technical Railway and the Call Centre.

With the introduction of the Employment Relations Act in 1999, the company signed a recognition and partnership agreement with the Transport and General Workers Union (TGWU) to cover all non-managerial staff. This conferred negotiation rights, confirmed the acceptance of the existing consultation framework and established a joint management – trade union forum. As a result, there are two representation structures: a modified company council with eight representatives meeting six times a year and representing all employees and the joint trade union forum representing union members at Eurotunnel covering all issues of concern, with sole negotiating rights over UK pay and conditions.

▶

The then director of HR indicated that the impetus for change was the threat of industrial action by train drivers in late 1999. This was considered important due to the company's £6.5 billion debt and the perishable nature of service delivery, as industrial action could potentially cost millions of pounds a day in lost revenue. It was felt by management that the legislation could be a catalyst for a number of diverse union arrangements within Eurotunnel, leading the company to opt for a single union agreement with the TGWU rather than a traditional rail union.

The author has conducted research at the company for five years using employee surveys, interviews and focus groups. Employees were surveyed before union recognition from December 1999 to January 2000, and 18 months after union recognition in December 2002, to find out their attitudes towards the company council and the trade union.

Over this period, the TGWU had some success in recruiting members and increasing its presence with some 35 per cent of employees in the second survey indicating they were a trade union member compared to only 12 per cent in the first survey. More than half of respondents in the second survey suggested they had an active union presence in their workplace compared to only 6 per cent from the first survey.

However, the second survey revealed the lack of progress the union had made with many employees suggesting that the trade union had not met their expectations. In the first survey there had been strong support for trade unions in all sections of Eurotunnel with the majority of workers suggesting that a trade union would improve their position over pay and benefits, work conditions, health and safety and employee grievances. For example, in relation to pay and benefits, just over 70 per cent of respondents suggested that trade unions would improve their position. There was a similar finding regarding work conditions, with three-quarters of employees suggesting that trade unions would improve their position over work conditions.

But in the second survey, less than a third of respondents suggested that the union was effective or very effective in representing general employee interests. Furthermore, when asked if the trade union had improved their position on pay and benefits, only around one in ten respondents agreed. This attitude was also reflected with other issues, such as work conditions, health and safety, training, individual grievances and job security.

While the TGWU ambitions and aims were understood and supported, it could be argued that this highlights the risks for trade unions when employees' expectations are unrealistic, which could potentially undermine the impact of unions and their effectiveness in the bargaining process. The vast majority of all respondents suggested that the company council should retain a consultation role even though they wanted union recognition. This view increased in the second survey. However, this is not a vote for the existing company council to replace unions, because nearly two-thirds of employees in both surveys stated that the company council was not effective in representing general employee interests either.

These findings would suggest that the previous company council (before recognition) could not be seen as a substitute for union representation, due to employees' perception of the limited role it played in the bargaining and decision-making processes. In general, it would seem that its prime focus was on information about performance or 'business' issues (improving quality, productivity, customer service and/or sales) rather than issues based on meeting workers' expectations. Managers also saw the company council as a means to communicate the benefits of change and to encourage the need for such change.

The research findings also seem to indicate that while the majority of employees were in favour of union recognition, they are not yet convinced that union representation alone will achieve greater benefits for them. Some employees at Eurotunnel would like the company council to be given greater powers to play an important part in representing the workforce, with its role ranging from an information channel on some issues to a genuine negotiating body on others.

The challenge for the union at Eurotunnel is that increased trade union membership and presence has not made the majority of employees more positive about union effectiveness – one could term this 'seduction without love'. The lack of belief in its ability to achieve traditional union objectives on pay, fairness, protection in disciplinary action, support in making a complaint and changes in employees' immediate workplace. Some respondents suggested they were best able to deal with such issues as individuals. The Eurotunnel employees' perception of a lack of effective union voice could undermine the union's influence on management. This could be seen as the challenge for partnership.

Given the devolution of decision-making in many organisations and the greater focus on employee commitment and effective organisational change, these findings are of particular interest. They suggest that if employers wish to encourage an alignment of interests between employee behaviour and organisational goals, they need to place greater emphasis on giving employees a real voice.

These findings are particularly important given the provisions of the European directive on information and consultation. The directive encourages a more formalised approach, expanding on existing information and consultation rights within enterprises.

The developments at Eurotunnel may signal difficulties for trade unions and employers in satisfying the requirements of the legislation. While the draft legislation and regulations reject a 'one-size-fits-all' approach, arrangements need to meet certain requirements. In particular, they set out processes that force employers to establish an information and consultation framework when a valid request has been initiated by 10 per cent of employees in a firm. If there are existing arrangements, 40 per cent or more must endorse the request in a ballot. If existing arrangements do not satisfy the directive's requirements, the employer must seek to reach a negotiated agreement with 'genuine employee representatives'.

Importantly for trade unions, these existing agreements must cover all the employees in a firm and cannot have been unilaterally imposed by management without discussion with employees and a chance for them to voice disapproval. In other words, 'sweetheart' deals with unions over the heads of employees are threatened.

Also important are the issues on which management must provide information and consult under the directive. They include the economic situation of the enterprise, the structure of and potential threat to employment, and, most significantly, 'decisions likely to lead to substantial changes in work organisation or in contractual relations', on which consultation must take place 'with a view to reaching agreement'. Consultation is defined as enabling information and consultation representatives (elected by all employees and not limited to trade union representatives) to put forward their views and to 'obtain a reasoned opinion from the employer'.

In my view, issues concerning 'contractual relations' may include rewards, such as performance related pay or career structures and procedures etc. 'Changes in work organisation' may also affect workplace restructuring such as teamwork systems. Consultation 'with a view to reaching agreement on decisions within the scope of the management's powers' may be little different to traditional trade union activities of collective bargaining. In addition, they do not provide any automatic participatory rights to union representatives who must stand for election alongside other non-union representatives. Potentially such arrangements may operate with, against, or in the absence of, union structures, threatening the traditional role of unions in collective bargaining.

Experience tells us that any representative structures within firms need to have full support of the majority of employees and to be seen as organic to the workplace rather then an imposed arrangement between management and trade unions. Without such a bottom-up approach, the legitimacy and respect for such arrangements will diminish, creating obstacles for developing meaningful dialogue and trust between management, staff and unions.

The clear message from this research and the requirements under the information and consultation directive is that a mechanism for communication between management and employees at the workplace may not be enough. Voice, the right to be heard and have a true say over workplace issues and at times an acknowledgement of differing interests may be essential for achieving greater employee satisfaction and commitment. These results would suggest that while trade unions may provide greater voice than non-union arrangements, the strength of voice is dependent on the legitimacy and effectiveness of trade unions in representing employees' interests at the workplace.

And that in turn depends on the union being perceived by the workforce as both representative and able to act independently. If it isn't, it will not meet the needs of either employees or management and could run the risk of being supplanted under the provisions of the new directive.

Questions

1. Why was the company council not a 'substitute' for union representation?

2. Can union–management partnership actually succeed? Why?

3. In what way/why could the process of union recognition be handled differently?

4. What can management do to increase union effectiveness?

5. Why could Eurotunnel employees' perception of a lack of effective union voice undermine the union's influence on management?

6. In what way could the new information and consultation legislation affect the union–employer partnership at Eurotunnel?

References

Ackers, P. and Payne, J. (1998) 'British trade unions and social partnership: rhetoric, reality and strategy', *International Journal of Human Resource Management,* Vol.9, pp.529–50.

Appelbaum, R. and Batt, R. (1994) *The New American Workplace,* Ithaca, NY: ILR Press.

*Bacon, N. (1999) 'Union derecognition and the new human relations: a steel industry case study', *Work, Employment and Society,* Vol.13, No.1, pp.1–17.

Bacon, N. (2003) 'Human resource management and industrial relations', in P. Ackers and A. Wilkinson (eds) *Understanding Work and Employment,* Oxford: Oxford University Press, pp.71–88.

Bacon, N. and Storey, J. (1996) 'Individualism and collectivism and the changing role of trade unions', in P. Ackers, C. Smith and P. Smith (eds) *The New Workplace and Trade Unionism,* London: Routledge, pp.1–40.

*Bacon, N. and Storey, J. (2000) 'New employee relations strategies: towards individualism or partnership', *British Journal of Industrial Relations,* Vol.38, No.3, pp.407–28.

Blyton, P. and Turnbull, P. (1994) *The Dynamics of Employee Relations,* Houndmills: Macmillan.

Bryson, A. (2004) 'Managerial responsiveness to union and nonunion worker voice in Britain', *Industrial Relations,* Vol.43, No.1, pp.213–42.

Claydon, T. (1989) 'Union de-recognition in Britain in the 1980s', *British Journal of Industrial Relations,* Vol.27, pp.214–23.

Clegg, H. (1979) *The System of Industrial Relations in Great Britain,* Oxford: Blackwell.

Cressey, P., Eldridge, J. and MacInnes, J. (1985) *Just Managing: Authority and Democracy in Industry,* Milton Keynes: Open University Press.

Cully, M. and Woodland, S. (1996) 'Trade Union membership and recognition: an analysis of data from the 1995 Labour Force Survey', *Labour Market Trends,* May, London: HMSO, pp.215–25.

Cully, M., Woodland, S., O'Reilly, A., Dix, G., Millward, N., Bryson, A. and Forth, J. (1998) *The 1998 Workplaces Employee Relations Survey: First Findings,* London: Department of Trade and Industry.

Cully, M., Woodland, S., O'Reilly, A. and Dix, G. (1999) *Britain at Work,* London: Routledge.

D'Art, D. and Turner, T. (1999) 'An attitudinal revolution in Irish industrial relations: the end of "them and us"?', *British Journal of Industrial Relations,* Vol.37, No.1, pp.101–16.

Dickson, T., McLachlan, M.V., Prior, P. and Swales, K. (1988). 'Big Blue and the Union: IBM, individualism and trade union strategy', *Work, Employment and Society,* Vol.2, pp.506–20.

DTI (1998) 'Fairness at Work', White Paper, London: HMSO.

Dunn, S. and Wright, M. (1994) 'Maintaining the "status quo": An analysis of the contents of British collective agreements 1979-1990', *British Journal of Industrial Relations,* Vol.32, pp.23–46.

Edwards, P. (1990). 'The politics of conflict and consent', *Journal of Economic Behaviour and Organization,* Vol.13, pp.41–61.

Edwards, P. (1995) 'The employment relationship', in P. Edwards (ed.) *Industrial Relations,* Oxford: Blackwell, pp.3–26.

Edwards, P., Hau, M., Hyman, R., Marginson, P., Sisson, K., Waddington, J. and Winchester, D. (1998) 'Great Britain: from partial collectivism to neo-liberalism to where?', in A. Ferner and R. Hyman (eds) *Changing Industrial Relations in Europe,* Oxford: Blackwell, pp.1–54.

Flanders, A. (1970) *Management and Unions: The Theory and Reform of Industrial Relations,* London: Faber.

Foulkes, F. K. (1980) *Personnel Policies in Large Non-union Companies,* Englewood Cliffs, NJ: Prentice Hall.

Fox, A. (1966) *Industrial Sociology and Industrial Relations,* Royal Commission Research Paper No.3, London: HMSO.

Fox, A. (1974) *Beyond Contract: Work, Power and Trust Relations,* London: Faber and Faber.

Freeman, R.B. and Medoff, J.L. (1984) *What Do Unions Do?,* New York: Basic Books.

Gall, G. (2004) 'Trade union recognition in Britain, 1995–2002: turning a corner?', *Industrial Relations Journal,* Vol.35, No.3, forthcoming.

Gall, G. and McKay, S. (1994) 'Trade union de-recognition in Britain 1988–94', *British Journal of Industrial Relations,* Vol.32, pp.433–48.

Geary, J. (1995) 'Work practices: the structure of work', in P. Edwards (ed.) *Industrial Relations,* Oxford: Blackwell, pp.368–96.

Guest, D. (1987) 'Human resource management and industrial relations', *Journal of Management Studies,* Vol.24, No.5, pp.503–21.

Guest, D. (1989) 'Human resource management: its implications for industrial relations and trade unions', in J. Storey (ed.) *New Perspectives on Human Resource Management: a critical text,* London: Routledge, pp.41–55.

Guest, D. (1990) 'Human resource management and the American Dream', *Journal of Management Studies,* Vol.27, No.4, pp.378–97.

Guest, D. (1995) 'Human resource management, trade unions and industrial relations', in J. Storey (ed.) *Human Resource Management: A Critical Text,* London: Routledge, pp.110–41.

*Guest, D. and Conway, N. (1999) 'Peering into the black hole: the downside of the new employment relations in the UK', *British Journal of Industrial Relations,* Vol.37, No.3, pp.367–89.

Guest, D. and Hoque, K. (1994) 'The Good, The Bad and the Ugly: employment relations in new non-union workplaces', *Human Resource Management Journal*, Vol.5, pp.1–14.

*Guest, D.E. and Peccei, R. (2001) 'Partnership at work: mutuality and the balance of advantage', *British Journal of Industrial Relations*, Vol.39, No.2, pp.207–36.

Heery, E. (1996) 'The new new unionism', in I. Beardwell (ed.) *Contemporary Industrial Relations*, Oxford: Oxford University Press, pp.175–202.

Heery, E. (1998) 'The re-launch of the Trades Union Congress', *British Journal of Industrial Relations*, Vol.36, pp.339–60.

Hirschman, A. (1971) *Exit, Voice and Loyalty*, Cambridge, MA.: Harvard University Press.

Hyman, R. (1987) 'Strategy or structure? capital, labour and control', *Work, Employment and Society*, Vol.1, No.1, pp.25–55.

Hyman, R. (1997) 'The future of employee representation', *British Journal of Industrial Relations*, Vol.35, No.3, pp.309–36.

IDS (1998) *Partnership Agreements. IDS Study 656, October*, London: IDS.

Institute of Directors (1994) Evidence presented to the Employment Committee Enquiry, *The Future of Trade Unions*, HMSO, HC 676-II, London: HMSO.

Involvement and Participation Association (1992) *Towards Industrial Partnership: A New Approach to Management Union Relations*, London: IPA.

IPD (1997) *Employment Relations into the Twenty-first Century*, London: Institute of Personnel and Development.

IRS (1997) Partnership at work: a survey, *Employment Trends*, Vol.645, December, pp.3–24.

Kelly, J. (1996). 'Union militancy and social partnership', in P. Ackers, C. Smith and P. Smith (eds) *The New Workplace and Trade Unionism*, London: Routledge, pp.41–76.

Kelly, J. (2004) 'Social partnership agreements in Britain: labour cooperation and compliance', *Industrial Relations*, Vol.43, No.1, pp.267–92.

Kelly, J. and C. Kelly (1991) 'Them and us: social psychology and the "new industrial relations"', *British Journal of Industrial Relations*, Vol.29, No.1, pp.25–48.

Kitay, J. and Marchington, M. (1996) 'A review and critique of workplace industrial relations typologies', *Human Relations*, Vol.49, No.10, pp.1263–90.

Kochan, T. and Osterman, P. (1994) *The Mutual Gains Enterprise*, Cambridge, MA: Harvard Business School Press.

Kochan, T., Katz, H. and McKersie, B. (1986) *The Transformation of American Industrial Relations*, New York: Basic Books.

Machin, S. (2000) 'Union decline in Britain', *British Journal of Industrial Relations*, Vol.38, No.4, pp.631–45.

Marchington, M. and Parker, P. (1990) *Changing Patterns of Employee Relations*, Hemel Hempstead: Harvester Wheatsheaf.

*Marks, A., Findlay, P., Hine, J., McKinlay, A. and Thompson, P. (1998) 'The politics of partnership? innovation in employment relations in the Scottish spirits industry', *British Journal of Industrial Relations*, Vol.36, No.2, pp.209–26.

McLoughlin, I. and Gourlay, S. (1994) *Enterprise Without Unions: Industrial Relations in the Non-Union Firm*, Milton Keynes: Open University Press.

Millward, N., Stevens, M., Smart, D. and Hawes, W.R. (1992) *Workplace Industrial Relations in Transition*, Dartmouth: Aldershot.

Monks, J. (1998) 'Trade unions, enterprise and the future', in P. Sparrow and M. Marchington (eds) *Human Resource Management: The New Agenda*, London: Pitman, pp.171–9.

Oxenbridge, S., Brown, W., Deakin, S. and Pratten, C. (2003) 'Initial responses to the Statutory Recognition Provisions of the Employment Relations Act 1999', *British Journal of Industrial Relations*, Vol.41, No.2, pp.315–34,

Poole, M. and Mansfield, R. (1993) 'Patterns of continuity and change in managerial attitudes and behaviour in industrial relations 1980–90', *British Journal of Industrial Relations*, Vol.31, No.1, pp.11–36.

Purcell, J. (1982) 'Macho managers and the new industrial relations', *Employee Relations*, Vol.4, No.1, pp.3–5.

Purcell, J. (1993) 'The end of institutional industrial relations', *Political Quarterly,* Vol.64, pp.6–23.

Purcell, J. (1987). 'Mapping management styles in employee relations', *Journal of Management Studies,* Vol.24, No.5, pp.533–48.

Purcell, J. (1991) 'The rediscovery of management prerogative: the management of labour relations in the 1980s', *Oxford Review of Economic Policy,* Vol.7, No.1, pp.33–43.

Purcell, J. (1993) 'The end of institutional industrial relations', *Political Quarterly,* Vol.64, No.1, pp.6–23.

Purcell, J. and Ahlstrand, B. (1994) *Human Resource Management in the Multi-Divisional Company,* Oxford: Oxford University Press.

Purcell, J. and Sisson, K. (1983) 'Strategies and practice in the management of industrial relations', in G. Bain (ed.) *Industrial Relations in Britain,* Oxford: Blackwell.

Ramsey, H. (1975) 'Firms and football teams', *British Journal of Industrial Relations,* Vol.13, No.3, pp.396–400.

Roy, D. (1980) 'Fear stuff, sweet stuff and evil stuff: management's defences against unionization in the south', in T. Nichols (ed.) *Capital and Labour: A Marxist Primer,* Glasgow: Fontana, pp.395–415.

Schnabel, C. (2003) 'Determinants of trade union membership', in J.T. Addison and C. Schnabel (eds) *International Handbook of Trade Unions,* Cheltenham: Edward Elgar, pp.13–43.

Scott, A. (1994) *Willing Slaves?,* Cambridge: Cambridge University Press.

Sisson, K. (1989) 'Personnel management in transition?', in K. Sisson (ed.) *Personnel Management in Britain,* Oxford: Blackwell.

Sisson, K. (1993) 'In search of HRM', *British Journal of Industrial Relations,* Vol.31, No.2, pp.201–10.

Sisson, K. (1994) *Personnel Management,* Oxford: Blackwell.

Sisson, K. (1995) 'Human resource management and the personnel function', in J. Storey (ed.) *Human Resource Management: A Critical Text,* London: Routledge, pp.87–109.

Sisson, K. and Marginson, P. (1995) 'Management: systems, structures and strategy', in P. Edwards (ed.) *Industrial Relations,* Oxford: Blackwell, 89–122.

*Sisson, K. and Storey, J. (2000) *The Realities of Human Resource Management,* Buckingham: Open University Press.

Smith, P. and Morton, G. (1993) 'Union exclusion and decollectivization of industrial relations in contemporary Britain', *British Journal of Industrial Relations,* Vol.31, No.1, pp.97–114.

Storey, J. (1989) *New Perspectives on Human Resource Management,* London: Routledge.

Storey, J. (1992) *Developments in the Management of Human Resources,* Oxford: Blackwell.

Storey, J. (1995) *Human Resource Management: A Critical Text,* London: Routledge.

Storey, J. and Bacon, N. (1993) 'Individualism and collectivism: into the 1990s', *International Journal of Human Resource Management,* Vol.4, No.3, pp.665–84.

Storey, J. and Sisson, K. (1993) *Managing Human Resources and Industrial Relations,* Milton Keynes: Open University Press.

Storey, J., Bacon, N., Edmonds, J. and Wyatt, P. (1993) 'The "new agenda" and human resource management: a roundtable discussion with John Edmonds', *Human Resource Management Journal,* Vol.4, No.1, pp.63–70.

Towers, B. (1997) *The Representation Gap,* Oxford: Oxford University Press.

TUC (1993) Evidence presented to the Employment Committee Enquiry, *The Future of Trade Unions,* HMSO, HC 676-II, London: HMSO.

Undy, R. (1999) 'Annual review article: New Labour's "Industrial Relations Settlement": the Third Way?', *British Journal of Industrial Relations,* Vol.37, No.2, pp.315–36.

Visser, J. (2003) 'Unions and unionism around the world', in J.T. Addison and C. Schnabel (eds) *International Handbook of Trade Unions,* Cheltenham: Edward Elgar: 366–414.

Waddington, J. and Whitston, C. (1997) 'Why do people join unions in a period of membership decline?', *British Journal of Industrial Relations,* Vol.35, No.4, pp.515–46.

Wood, S. (1997) *Statutory Union Recognition,* London: Institute of Personnel and Development.

Wood, S. and Godard, J. (1999) 'The statutory union recognition procedure in the Employment Relations Bill: a comparative analysis', *British Journal of Industrial Relations,* Vol.37, pp.203–44.

* Useful reading

Employee wellbeing

CHAPTER **12**

Health, safety and welfare

Objectives

By the end of this chapter you will be able to:

- explain what is meant by the terms 'safety', 'hazard', 'risk', 'welfare' and 'health'
- explain the key points in the main legislation relating to health, safety and welfare at work
- explain the reasons for managing employee health, safety and well-being
- explain the role of various people and groups in health and safety and welfare at work
- describe the Health and Safety Executive's approach to stress management
- explain the main health and safety issues in an international context.

In Chapter 1 we traced the history of people management and considered several approaches to welfare. Some people who adopted the 'hard' human resource management approach tried originally to distance themselves from all these welfare approaches, as they felt that these approaches showed a lack of business awareness. However, reducing accidents and improving occupational ill-health is important for organisations today and many organisations are taking an increasing interest in areas such as managing absenteeism. Health in particular is also coming under government scrutiny as they want to improve the productivity of the workforce. According to the CIPD (2007a), 'a comprehensive review of the nation's health is to be launched by the Department of Work and Pensions, in an attempt to identify improvements that could help the working population.' In the same document, John Hutton, who was Minister for Work and Pensions, is quoted as saying, 'The UK has one of the best health and safety records anywhere in the world . . . but 30 million working days are still lost every year due to occupational ill-health and injury, leading to lower quality of life and economic prospects for many people and reducing the productivity of the workforce.'

Many organisations have already realised the importance to their success of a healthy and productive workforce and are increasingly seeking to adopt a more proactive approach. Health, safety and welfare have also come under the spotlight as a result of recent legislation banning smoking in public places, including the workplace, and also because increased penalties have been introduced for breaches in safety that result in death under the Corporate Manslaughter and Homicide Act 2007. There is clearly a case to be made for organisations to have some interest in the health, safety and welfare of their workforces.

Definitions

Safety

We define safety as absence from danger and avoidance of injury.

According to this definition, we should expect employers to do everything in their power to keep employees away from danger and free of injury while at work. This does not sound like a great deal to expect from an employer, but there is often a conflict in the employer's mind between increased production, which sometimes may involve some risk taking, and the necessity to keep employees safe and uninjured, which may cost money. Legislation has developed over a number of years to protect workers, and was initially designed to protect those who were weak and particularly vulnerable to exploitation from any employers who, tempted by the lure of increased production, might put their employees at risk of injury. Nowadays, with increasingly flexible patterns of work being available, many employees may work from home, or even from their car, for all or part of their working week, so employers will also have to consider the health and safety issues arising from this.

Hazard

A hazard is something that could cause harm to someone. Employers who are being proactive about health and safety therefore have to try to identify potential hazards before they actually do cause any harm. Stranks (2007) says that a hazard can further be defined in three areas as follows:

- exposure to harm
- something with the potential to do harm – this can include substances or machines, methods of work and other aspects of work organisation
- the result of departure from the normal situation, which has the potential to cause death, injury, damage or loss.

Risk

The term risk relates to the chances of the hazard actually resulting in harm being done to someone. Once the employer has identified a potential hazard then they have to estimate the chances or risk of someone being harmed by it.

We shall discuss the idea of risk assessment later in this chapter. The emphasis in health and safety today is on the prevention of accidents if possible by eliminating anything that could be a hazard and by predicting the level of risk in various situations. It is not, of course, always possible to eliminate all hazards or minimise all risks in a workplace, but employers are expected to predict potentially dangerous situations and then do something about them to ensure they become less dangerous.

The emphasis in modern health and safety is to encourage those who own, manage or work in organisations to take responsibility for health and safety in them. For this to happen, both the workforce and safety representatives also need to be involved, risks need to be assessed and action needs to be taken to reduce these where possible.

Welfare

Welfare can be defined as 'well-being', and health and safety are both aspects of welfare as they are both important to the employee's well-being. In the past many employers merely reacted to issues about health and safety without appreciating the benefits that adopting a more proactive approach could bring them. Many still operate in this way. However, some more progressive employers are adopting a much more proactive approach to health and safety and welfare to prevent problems arising in the first place.

Health

Did you know?

In 2004 a senior pilot was forced to resign and two senior cabin crew were dismissed by Ryanair after the two off-duty crew members travelled on a full plane from Gerona to Dublin. Since there were no seats available for them, they sat in the rear toilets of the plane for both take-off and landing. The captain had allowed them to do this even though it contravened aviation regulations and was obviously potentially hazardous.

Here the concern is for good health. We define good health as being physically and mentally well with body and mind in excellent working order.

This goes further than safety in that the employer is no longer just expected not to do anything to injure his or her employees, but should seek to promote activities that encourage the good health of the employees. We shall return to a discussion of health promotion activities later in this chapter.

Safety

According to the Health and Safety Executive's (HSE's) *Health and Safety Executive Statistics* (HSC, 2006a) there were 212 workers fatally injured at work during 2005–6, which is a 5 per cent decrease compared with 2004–5 when the final figure was 223. Accidents that required people to be absent from work for three or more days rose slightly to 146,076 and a further 328,000 accidents at work were reported. In all, 30 million working days were lost at work which averaged to 1.3 days per worker. According to the HSE (2006a), 24 million of these were due to work-related ill-health and 6 million were lost because of injuries at work.

ACTIVITY 12.1

Sometimes employers are reluctant to spend money on safety improvements as they don't feel this is justified. There are, however, costs associated with accidents. What are the possible costs to the employer of accidents at work?

Discussion of Activity 12.1

Obviously, depending on the severity of the injury, there are costs to the injured person in terms of pain and suffering, and possible loss of earnings. There are also costs to the employer, and your list is likely to include at least some of the following:

- cost of lost time and production due to absence caused by injury
- cost of lost time and production due to dealing with the injury
- cost of replacement worker or of training the replacement
- cost of replacing broken machinery or unsafe machinery or equipment
- cost of compensation to injured employee
- higher insurance premiums if the organisation's accident record is not good
- cost involved in carrying out a full investigation into the causes of the accident
- cost of paying fines or even facing imprisonment if the employer was to blame for the accident
- cost of poor morale within the workforce
- cost of people not being willing to work for the organisation because of its poor reputation for safety.

You may have found some other costs involved in accidents as well. Employers should be aware of the hidden costs of accidents; if they carried out a cost–benefit analysis they would probably be amazed at how much accidents were costing them and be more prepared to spend money on accident prevention. In their studies of accidents, the Health and Safety Executive (1995) identified one organisation where the costs of accidents amounted to as much as 37 per cent of profits. This organisation did not have a particularly bad record on health and safety, nor had it suffered any major disasters, fatalities or prosecutions.

We believe that health and safety is an important area of concern for all HRM practitioners, since it is in the organisation's interest to pursue any initiatives that will provide benefits and services which the employees will want and value but that will also fit with the strategic needs of the organisation by enhancing levels of employee performance.

Employers can check for themselves the actual costs both of accidents and work-related incidents in their organisations by using the accident and incident calculators provided by the Health and Safety Executive. They allow employers the choice of two different ways to calculate the annual costs of accidents in their organisation and also of using an interactive tool to calculate costs of other work-related incidents. Now there is really no excuse for employer ignorance of the cost of accidents or work-related incidents in their organisations.

If you would like to see how easy it is for employers to calculate the costs of accidents and work-based incidents by examining these tools for yourself, go to **www.hse.gov.uk/costs/accidentcost_calc/accident_costs_intro.asp** (accessed 20.04.07).

Legislation

Much of the early development of legislation to protect employees at work was closely linked to the historical development of people management. The more enlightened employers were concerned to improve working conditions for their employees and appointed industrial welfare workers to help with this. Less enlightened employers were compelled to pay some attention to the protection of selected groups of employees, and as early as 1840 legislation designed to limit the hours that children worked was passed. In more recent times several new Acts have been passed and regulations issued to protect employees.

The Health and Safety at Work Act 1974 (HASAWA)

In Great Britain the foundation for the system of regulating health and safety at work was introduced by the Health and Safety at Work Act 1974. Although this was a long time ago, HASAWA is still very important today and forms the foundation for much of the later legislation. According to XpertHR (2004) one of the fundamental principles underpinning the Health and Safety at Work Act is that 'those who create risk from work activity are responsible for protecting workers and the public from its consequences.'

Before HASAWA, the legislation that could be used to protect employees at work was patchy and applied to vulnerable groups such as women or children, or to particular industries where there were thought to be high risks. The vast majority of the working population before 1974 were not actually protected by any health or safety legislation. The Health and Safety at Work Act 1974 set up some new bodies and reinforced the power of others. The roles of the following will be discussed later in this chapter:

- the Health and Safety Commission (HSC)
- the Health and Safety Executive (HSE)
- the enforcing authorities.

HASAWA was the first piece of legislation designed to protect everyone at work, and also to protect others who were not at work, such as customers or even passers-by. It is estimated that it brought an extra 3 million people under the scope of protective safety legislation for the first time.

The main aim of the Act was to provide a comprehensive system of law which would raise standards of safety and health for all persons at work and also protect members of the public who might be affected by their actions.

More than 30 years after the Health and Safety at Work Act 1974 became law it still forms the foundation of health and safety legislation in the UK, so it is important to understand some of the fundamental principles that underpin this important piece of legislation.

ACTIVITY 12.2

Both employers and employees have responsibilities under HASAWA. List what you would expect to be the duties of employers and employees with regard to health and safety.

Duties of employers	Duties of employees

Compare your lists with the following duties summarised from the Health and Safety at Work Act 1974.

Discussion of Activity 12.2

Your list probably included some indication that employers were to take responsibility for having a safe workplace with safe equipment that would not injure anyone, and you also probably thought that employees too should take care not to harm anyone at work. There are no specific rules about lighting or temperature in the way that there are in the earlier Acts. Instead the Act is trying to involve people and make everyone take some responsibility for his or her actions. This approach is therefore moving towards a human resource management approach, and health and safety is not just in the domain of the human resource specialist but is shared with others. Sometimes the human resource specialist does have some aspects of health and safety included in his or her job description, and he or she may, for example, be expected to chair the safety committee if there is one.

The responsibilities of employers under the Health and Safety at Work Act

Employers have a basic duty of care to their employees to ensure their health, safety and welfare. As well as this rather general duty, they have five other duties. These are:

- to ensure that the workplace itself is safe; that equipment has been maintained correctly and work is safely organised
- that accidents do not occur because of incorrect handling, storage or transportation within the workplace
- that there is training, supervision and information relating to health and safety
- that the workplace itself is maintained adequately and that there are safe ways to get into and out of the buildings
- that welfare provisions are adequate.

All of these duties are expressed in quite general terms and there is nothing in the Act to specify, for example, how much training or information should be given. The words 'so far as is reasonably practicable' are used frequently within HASAWA. The exact meaning of this phrase will be discussed later in this chapter. The employer also has a further specific duty to produce a safety policy statement and we shall also discuss later in the chapter what this involves.

As we said earlier, HASAWA was designed to gain involvement in health and safety from as many sources as possible, so the responsibility was not just one way. Employees also have responsibilities.

The responsibilities of employees under the Health and Safety at Work Act

As you might expect, there are fewer responsibilities for the employees than for the employers. They have three main areas of responsibility under HASAWA in relation to health and safety. These are:

- to take responsibility for their own health and safety, and for any health and safety problems which might be caused to colleagues by their actions or in some cases their failure to act
- not to recklessly interfere with or misuse any machinery, equipment or processes
- to cooperate with employers about health and safety initiatives.

Although they may not seem very onerous responsibilities, they are important since employees who do not follow these guidelines could be disciplined or even face prosecution themselves if an accident occurred for which they were responsible. They should cooperate about health and safety issues, such as wearing protective clothing, if the employer provides it. Since they must take responsibility for their own health and safety and that of others, they must also not do anything to interfere with safety guards, as this could result in injuries to themselves or to other people.

> **Pause for thought 12.1** The phrase 'as far as is reasonably practicable' is used several times in HASAWA. What factors do you think should be considered in determining whether or not something is 'reasonably practicable'?

This phrase means that circumstances, risks and cost need to be considered when an employer is endeavouring to make the workplace safe for employees. It would be very difficult to make anywhere completely safe and eliminate all accidents. Accidents are by definition something that you cannot predict; nevertheless, many situations do occur where it is possible to predict that someone could be injured if improvements are not made, and employers should try to anticipate the likelihood of these types of accident and take steps to prevent them from occurring. 'Reasonably practicable' means that a calculation must be made in which the risk is compared with the sacrifices, cost and level of effort needed to avert that risk. If there is a very slim chance that a comparatively minor accident might occur, but this chance could be eliminated by spending thousands of pounds on new equipment and also by disrupting the workforce, it might not be considered to be reasonably practicable to do so. If, however, the risk was of a serious injury or possibly death, then it would be reasonable to take every step and spend any amount of money to eliminate this risk. The term 'as far as is reasonably practicable' therefore means that the employer should do as much as they can to try to eliminate risks but that they need to review the balance between the risk and the amount of effort required to eliminate that risk.

Control of Substances Hazardous to Health Regulations (COSHH) 1988

This is another far-reaching piece of legislation comprising 19 regulations and 4 approved codes of practice which came into effect on 1 October 1989 and which have subsequently been revised in 1999, 2002 and 2003. Apart from some minor changes to tidy up the 1999 regulations, as these amendments relate to fairly specialised areas they do not alter the main thrust of this legislation and are too detailed to include in an introductory HRM textbook.

COSHH is designed to protect anyone who works with substances that could be hazardous to health. The regulations apply to all workplaces and include all substances with the exception of asbestos, lead, materials that produce ionising radiations and substances underground, which all have their own separate legislation. The legislation basically applies to any other substances that can cause harm by being inhaled, ingested, coming into contact with the skin, or being injected or introduced into the body, so they do cover a very wide range of substances.

COSHH regulations require all employers to carry out an assessment of risks to their employees from substances that are identified in the workplace as being potentially hazardous to either their employees or others who might be affected. Any risks that are identified must then be controlled. This emphasis on assessing risk and then doing something about it is a very different approach to that of HASAWA.

While it would be easy to assume that these regulations would not have much effect on ordinary workplaces, this is not in fact the case, as many of the substances identified as potentially hazardous will be found in any workplace – e.g. fluid for photocopiers or cleaning products – so in reality all workplaces are affected. The main areas that employers should focus on are:

- assessing the risk of substances used and identifying the required precautions
- introducing appropriate measures to control or prevent the risk
- ensuring the correct use of the control measures, and that equipment is regularly maintained
- conducting health surveillance to monitor health of employees where there is a known identifiable risk
- informing and training employees about risks that may arise from their work, and informing them of the necessary precautions to take.

The Framework Directive

The European Union Framework Directive has broad objectives which were implemented in EU member states by 31 December 1992. This established in general terms the European Commission's approach to health and safety. The main objectives of the directive were to introduce measures to encourage improvements in safety and health of workers at work. In order to do this it contains general principles concerning the prevention of occupational risks, the protection of health and safety, the elimination of risk and accident factors, as well as informing, consultation and providing balanced participation in accordance with national laws.

The British response to the EU directive was made in the Management of Health and Safety at Work Regulations 1992, which were accompanied by an approved Code of Practice which came into effect on 1 January 1993. Five further sets of regulations were also implemented in Britain on 1 January 1993 and all these have become known as the 'six-pack'. The 'six-pack' comprised:

- Management of Health and Safety at Work Regulations 1992
- Workplace (Health, Safety and Welfare) Regulations 1992
- Provision and Use of Work Equipment Regulations 1992

- Personal Protective Equipment at Work Regulations 1992
- Health and Safety (Display Screen Equipment) Regulations 1992
- Manual Handling Operations Regulations 1992.

Legislation becomes out of date and does not always meet the requirements of modern organisations, so amendments are often necessary. All of the original 'six-pack' regulations have recently been amended and updated so the new dates and any significant changes will be included with the regulations as they are discussed. The Provision and Use of Work Equipment was amended in 1998 and the Management of Health and Safety at Work Regulations in 1999. The remaining four regulations were also amended later under the Health and Safety (Miscellaneous Amendments) Regulations 2002.

The Management of Health and Safety at Work Regulations 1999 (MHSWR)

This is the law in the UK that implemented the Framework Directive. The HASAWA covered some parts of the directive but there were also new things that employers needed to do, such as carrying out certain detailed procedures, assessing risks, implementing certain safety measures and communicating with staff on health and safety. According to Stranks (2007), 'these regulations do not stand alone – all other modern health and safety legislation such as the Workplace (Health, Safety and Welfare) Regulations 1992 and the Provision and Use of Work Equipment Regulations 1998, must be read in conjunction with the general duties under the MHSWR.' This is therefore a very important piece of legislation which has the following key features.

It states that employers shall:

- carry out assessment of health and safety risks to both employees and the public (this may be done in writing or on computer)
- monitor and review protective and preventive measures
- appoint a competent person or persons to be responsible for protective and preventive measures
- establish emergency procedures
- give comprehensible and relevant information and training to employees (the training can be provided by a suitable training provider other than the employer)
- cooperate with any other employers who may share the same work site.

Also, employees shall:

- use equipment in the way in which they have been trained to use it
- report any dangerous situations or any problem areas that they spot in the arrangements that the employer has made for health and safety.

These regulations are intended for use in cases of criminal action against an employer, and may not be used in any civil cases as evidence of negligence.

Pause for thought 12.2 To what extent do you feel that the Management of Health and Safety at Work Regulations 1999 differ from the HASAWA 1974?

These regulations are more forceful than HASAWA and specify that employers 'shall' do certain things, whereas HASAWA only expected employers to carry out its provisions 'so far as it is reasonably practicable' to do so.

The new regulations also mean that employers have a legal duty to predict what could go wrong, before it actually happens, and to take preventive action to avoid it happening. They must record the preventive action that they have taken. This is referred to as risk assessment and is the same principle as under COSHH, but it is now applied more widely. This will be discussed more fully later in the chapter.

The new regulations require employers to be proactive and actively manage activities aimed at protecting the health and safety of their employees. This is more in line than previous legislative measures with the human resource approach of being proactive and actively managing human resources.

Workplace (Health, Safety and Welfare) Regulations 1992, amended by the Health and Safety (Miscellaneous Amendments) Regulations 2002

This law is intended to rationalise older pieces of legislation and provide clearer ruling as to exactly what facilities the employer should provide for the employee. As stated earlier it is important that it is read in conjunction with the Management of Health and Safety at Work Regulations (MHSWR) 1999.

Employers shall:

- provide a good working environment with appropriate temperature, ventilation and level of lighting
- carry out maintenance and be responsible for keeping the workplace clean.

The 2002 amendments include further guidance for employers about achieving this, primarily in relation to rest rooms and rest areas. The amendments specify that there should be sufficient seats (with backs) and tables for the number of people likely to use them at any one time.

The 2002 amendment regulations state that employers must ensure they meet the needs of any disabled workers by also providing suitable rest areas for them. Other equipment and facilities, such as workstations, passageways, doors, and washroom facilities, should also be designed to meet the specific needs of disabled workers.

Provision and Use of Work Equipment Regulations 1998, amended by the Health and Safety (Miscellaneous Amendments) Regulations 2002

This law aims to bring together many older laws governing equipment used at work.

Employers shall:

- consider when they purchase new equipment the working condition of the equipment and risks that it may pose to employees
- ensure the provision of appropriate levels of lighting and warnings about the safe use of the equipment
- ensure that the equipment is suitable for the use to which it will be put

- provide adequate information and training
- provide adequate protection from any potentially dangerous parts of the equipment or machinery.

Personal Protective Equipment at Work Regulations 1992, amended by the Health and Safety (Miscellaneous Amendments) Regulations 2002

These regulations replace part of more than 20 old pieces of legislation which were concerned with provision of protective equipment for employees. They aim to ensure suitable provision of protective equipment such as head protection, high visibility clothing or safety harnesses. Employers must ensure the equipment is appropriate for the likely type of risks, the specific working conditions in the workplace and the duration for which it is likely to be worn. In addition, they should consider the ergonomic requirements of the job, state of health of the person employed and any particular characteristics of their workstation that might affect the use of the personal protective equipment. Particular attention should also be paid to ensuring that the equipment provided is hygienic and compatible with any additional personal protective equipment that the worker may need to wear simultaneously.

Employers shall:

- ensure that equipment used is suitable for the job to be done
- adequately maintain, clean and replace equipment as necessary
- store it safely when it is not in use
- ensure correct use of the equipment
- inform and train employees in the correct use of the equipment.

Health and Safety (Display Screen Equipment) Regulations 1992, amended by the Health and Safety (Miscellaneous Amendments) Regulations 2002

This law implements the EU's Visual Display Unit Directive and specifies minimum levels of health and safety for people who spend a large part of their time at work working in front of computer screens or who are about to become employed in that capacity. It is primarily aimed at the prevention of damage to their upper limbs, and to prevent eye strain, fatigue and stress.

Employers shall:

- assess the risks and reduce any that are found
- ensure that workstations meet at least the minimum requirements
- ensure that the work is planned to include breaks and changes of activity
- arrange for employees to have their eyes tested regularly at time limits designated by the optician appointed by the employer and provide spectacles if necessary
- provide appropriate training for users or those about to become users of visual display units.

Eyesight tests should be completed as soon as possible after any request, or in the case of someone who is about to start work, before he or she becomes a computer user.

Manual Handling Operations Regulations 1992, amended by the Health and Safety (Miscellaneous Amendments) Regulations 2002

This aims to reduce the levels of injury and ill-health associated with manual handling of loads at work.

Employers shall:

- ensure, as far as is practicable, that employees do not need to use risky techniques when handling loads
- assess whether any risks are inherent in the manual handling that has to be done
- take necessary steps to reduce risks by introducing mechanical help, ensuring loads are lighter and assessing the capabilities of the individual
- ensure the provision of information to all employees
- if employees sometimes work on another employer's premises, liaise closely with the other employer.

When trying to determine whether each specific manual handling activity involves any risk, employers should pay particular attention to the following:

- the physical suitability of the employee for safely completing the particular form of manual handling required
- what the person is wearing and its suitability for the job
- the amount of knowledge and training that the person has received
- the results of any risk assessments that have already been completed that relate to the job
- whether the employee has been identified as being one of a group of employees who are particularly at risk
- the results of any health surveillance that has been undertaken.

This legislation is far reaching in its scope although its effects will vary from one organisation to another, depending on the nature of the work undertaken.

Reporting of Injuries, Diseases and Dangerous Occurrences Regulations (RIDDOR) 1995

RIDDOR requires employers to report certain work-related accidents, diseases and dangerous occurrences to the enforcing authorities so that they can identify risks and investigate serious accidents. The following briefly describes some of the circumstances in which reporting should occur:

- The death or major injury of an employee, or of a self-employed person working in the organisation, or of a member of the public must all be reported to the enforcing authorities immediately and this must be followed within 10 days by a completed accident report. Reportable major injuries include fractures, amputation, dislocation, loss of sight.
- If an employee or self-employed person working on your premises suffers an accident or injury which requires that person to be absent from work for at least three days, then a completed accident form must be sent to the enforcing authorities.

- Some work-related diseases, such as occupational dermatitis, skin cancer or occupational asthma have also to be reported on a disease report form to the enforcing authority, as do infections such as hepatitis, tetanus or tuberculosis.
- There may be instances where something occurs which does not actually result in a reportable injury but which could have done. For example, the collapse of a lift or an explosion in a closed vessel are likely to constitute a dangerous occurrence, even if no one is injured. Any dangerous occurrence has to be reported immediately by telephone to the enforcing authorities. An accident report form should also be completed within 10 days of the dangerous occurrence. (Details of where to find more information are given in 'Further study' at the end of the chapter.)

The enforcing authority will be the environmental health department of the local authority if the type of the business is an office, retail or wholesale, warehousing, hotel or catering, sports or leisure, a residential home or place of worship. Accidents or dangerous occurrences which happen in any other type of business will need to be reported to the area office of the Health and Safety Executive. Nowadays accidents and dangerous occurrences can even be reported using the Internet. Have a look at the websites at the end of this chapter for more details of how to do this.

The Working Time Regulations 1998

We discussed the Working Time Regulations 1998 briefly in Chapter 4, but have also included them here, since the hours people work can have a big impact on both their health and safety in the workplace.

It is often claimed that the UK is the 'long hours capital' of Europe and that working such long hours adversely affects workers' health. In some organisations there is a culture of 'presenteeism', where people are expected to arrive early for work and leave late, forgoing home and social life. While some workers thrive in a long hours culture and live to work, such a culture is likely to hide a great deal of inefficiency and result in increased levels of stress and ill-health for many other workers. These regulations attempt to control the hours worked and control the way the hours are organised. They also establish minimum holiday levels for employees in the UK, although it is frequently claimed that a large number of UK employees actually fail to take all the holiday they are entitled to, either because they are too busy or are too frightened to be away from work for their whole holiday entitlement.

Although the regulations emanate from the Working Time Directive, adopted by the EU Council of Ministers in 1993, and therefore apply to all EU countries, there is some flexibility available for countries to implement European directives in their own way. Other European countries, for example France with its 35-hour working week, have implemented the directive differently. The main features for adult workers in the UK were outlined in Chapter 4.

Although the 48-hour working week means workers in the UK still work much longer hours than their counterparts in France, it is nevertheless considerably better than the

> **Did you know?**
>
> Death from overwork is so common in Japan that they even have a special word for it, *Karoshi*. The first documented case of Karoshi occurred in Japan in 1969 but there have been many cases since. In Japan the spouses of those who have died from Karoshi have won claims for compensation from the companies concerned and each year between 20 and 60 claims for compensation are brought. This is still probably a gross underestimate of the real number of cases of Karoshi in Japan.
>
> (*Source*: Nishiyama and Johnson, 1977)

expectation in countries such as Japan. In Japan it has been documented that many workers regularly work for over 100 hours per week, for many weeks, or even years at a time and that this frequently leads, not surprisingly, to ill-health or even death. Since we work increasingly in a global economy, where people are constantly accessible via mobile phones or email, these long-hour work practices are spreading to the USA and the UK.

Statutory holiday entitlement in the UK increased to 4.8 weeks from 1 October 2007 and from 1 October 2009 to 5.6 weeks. This right applies to all workers and not just employees. (The distinction between workers and employees will be discussed in Chapter 13.) Having rights to increased holiday is not of much use if workers do not take it. According to XpertHR (2006), 'As the Working Time Regulations are essentially a health and safety measure, [employers] should take steps to ensure that workers take the holidays to which they are entitled.' Here there is a role for both HR managers and line managers to ensure that good management practices are carried out and that a culture is built that should discourage a culture of presenteeism.

Legislation about smoking

Four related pieces of legislation have been introduced in Scotland, Wales, Northern Ireland and England prohibiting smoking in public places, including workplaces, and similar legislation has been introduced throughout the rest of Europe.

The Smoking, Health and Social Care (Scotland) Act 2005 was the first to come into effect and resulted in a ban on smoking in public places, including workplaces from March 2006. A similar ban on smoking in public places came into effect in Wales from 2 April 2007, in Northern Ireland from 30 April 2007 and in England from 1 July 2007. These related pieces of legislation are designed to protect workers who may previously have been affected by passive smoking and also to promote positive health improvements by encouraging smokers to stop.

The Corporate Manslaughter and Corporate Homicide Act 2007

The Corporate Manslaughter and Corporate Homicide Act 2007 makes corporate manslaughter a criminal offence from April 2008. This has also increased the interest in health safety and welfare as companies found guilty could face an unlimited fine if they are found to have caused death through gross negligence or failures in their safety systems. People working for some organisations such as Crown bodies, previously exempt from prosecution, will now be covered by this legislation. While this is to be welcomed, Richard Jones (2007) argues that it does not go far enough and that there are still too many exemptions. He goes on to say that 'HR needs to actively engage workers in helping keep workplaces safe, and should regularly consult them on health and safety issues.' Safety should certainly be of concern to all managers including HR managers and line managers.

Most of the legislation discussed here, with the exception of the anti-smoking legislation, has focused primarily on safety although clearly health and welfare are also closely linked to this.

The people and organisations involved in health, safety and welfare

We have already discussed at length the roles of employers and employees and have mentioned briefly others such as the Health and Safety Executive. But there are other health, safety and welfare roles currently undertaken by the Health and Safety Commission and local authorities. What do these organisations actually do? How are they organised?

The Health and Safety Commission (HSC)

The Commission was set up under the Health and Safety at Work Act 1974 and is a quango responsible for carrying out the policy of the Act and for providing advice to local authorities and others about how to implement the provisions of the Act. It is largely independent and acts on behalf of the Crown, but reports to Parliament primarily through the Secretary of State for Work and Pensions. It has a chairman and nine other members drawn from bodies representing employers, employees and local authorities, who are appointed by the Secretary of State for Transport, Local Government and the Regions.

In 1999 John Prescott, who was the Deputy Prime Minister at that time, announced a new impetus for health and safety called Revitalising Health and Safety. He said that the Health and Safety at Work Act 1974 had done its job as evidenced by the fact that the 'number of deaths at work today is a quarter of the 1971 level'. However, he wanted a strategic appraisal of the health and safety framework in order to build on the work of the previous 25 years and to establish a new agenda for the first 25 years of the new century (Prescott, 2000).

The HSC, after consulting widely about ways of revitalising health and safety produced targets for health and safety in Great Britain and a Strategy Statement and Action Plan. The HSC (2000) said that targets for health and safety in Great Britain are needed because:

> Health and safety is central to sustainable development and securing a better quality of life for all.
>
> - Raising workplace standards will promote better public health and *social progress which recognises the needs of everyone.*
> - Reducing the £18 billion bill for health and safety failures will contribute to *maintaining high and stable levels of economic growth and employment.*
> - Controlling harmful substances in the workplace will help to *protect our environment.*

The Health and Safety Executive (HSE)

The Health and Safety Executive (HSE) consists of three people who advise and assist the HSC. The executive also has a staff of approximately 4,000 to help carry out all its responsibilities in relation to its day-to-day functions. The HSE consists of policy advisers, inspectors and experts in medicine, science and technology. They are responsible for making provision for enforcing the legislation, for dealing with daily administration and conducting research, and for identifying the range of information necessary to enable the HSC to remain properly informed.

Guidance

This fulfils three main purposes:

1 To help people to understand the law by explaining it in a clear way.
2 To ensure they then comply with the law.
3 To provide rather more specialist advice.

Approved codes of practice

These give examples of good practice and help employers and workers understand what they should do to comply with the legislation. Failure to comply with a code of practice would not in itself mean that the individual or organisation would be prosecuted but, in any legal proceeding brought against them, failure to comply with an approved code of practice would be used as part of the evidence against them.

Regulations

Regulations can be made under HASAWA 1974 to identify specific risks in specific situations and the actions that need to be taken.

As well as enforcing health and safety legislation the, HSC and HSE have also been given the following tasks by the Government:

- Modernise and simplify the regulatory framework.
- Provide appropriate information and advice.
- Promote risk assessment and technical knowledge.
- Operate statutory schemes. (HSC, 2001)

Local authorities (LA)

Local authorities also have responsibility for enforcement of health and safety in approximately 194,000 workplaces. Under HASAWA, the Secretary of State for Work and Pensions (DWP) can make regulations for local authorities to take on responsibility for certain activities and to ensure that there is no duplication of effort between them and the Health and Safety Executive. The local authority inspectors, normally known as environmental health officers, are responsible for health and safety mainly in the services sector, while the HSE tends to concentrate on the more hazard-prone industries. There is a liaison committee which ensures consistency of approach between the HSE and local authorities. The HSE publishes a wide range of material each year explaining its role and the practical implications of legislation. The Health and Safety Executive can provide guidance, approved codes of practice and regulations.

The Gangmasters Licensing Authority (GLA)

Not all workers are lucky enough to work in well organised and regulated workplaces even in the UK. The death of 18 Chinese cockle pickers in Morecambe Bay, Lancashire, in 2004 drew attention to the world of unscrupulous operators who employ migrant workers, sometimes illegally, to work in low-skilled jobs. The Gangmasters Licensing Authority was formed to license genuine workforce organisers and providers of migrant workers and has the power to revoke licences where poor practice has occurred. Initially legislation targeted the agricultural sector where gangmasters and migrant workers primarily worked. However, it is claimed by MPs and trade unions that 'legislation to regulate gangmasters in the agricultural sector could be pushing unscrupulous operators into providing workers for care homes instead' (CIPD, 2007c). The Labour MP Jim Sheridan who was responsible for legislation creating the GLA has been pushing for a new bill to extend the GLA's scope to other sectors. Sheridan said, 'We believe the GLA's remit could be rolled out universally sector by sector. There are really important health and safety issues here. We don't want workers to be abused or intimidated, but we don't want them in skilled jobs either if they are not qualified' (CIPD, 2007c).

Changes to the organisations involved in health and safety

In 2004 Bill Callaghan, chair of the HSE, in the foreword to *A strategy for workplace health and safety in Great Britain to 2010 and beyond* (HSE, 2004) said, 'This strategy is to promote our vision, which is to see health and safety as a cornerstone of a civilized society and with that, to achieve a record of workplace health and safety that leads the world. This strategy builds on success and takes forward the Revitalising Health and Safety Statement of 2000.'

The HSC and HSE's continuing aims (2007) are to:

- Protect people by providing information and advice, promoting and assisting a goal-setting system of regulation, undertaking and encouraging research and enforcing the law where necessary.
- Influence organisations to embrace high standards of health and safety and to recognise the social and economic benefits.
- Work with business to prevent catastrophic failures in major hazard industry.
- Seek to optimise the use of resources to deliver our mission and vision.

HSC and HSE's new aims are to:

- Develop new ways to establish and maintain an effective health and safety culture in a changing economy, so that all employers take their responsibilities seriously, the workforce is fully involved and risks are properly managed.
- Do more to address the new and emerging health issues.
- Achieve higher levels of recognition and respect for health and safety as an integral part of a modern, competitive business and public sector and as a contribution to social justice and inclusion.
- Exemplify best public sector practice in managing our resources.

The world of work has changed dramatically over the years and there is now a much more diverse workforce working in increasingly flexible ways. These new aims are intended to address this. New health and safety issues arise as people work from home, or while on the move and the risks to their health and safety also need to be assessed. There are also fewer large organisations and more small ones. According to the HSE (2007), '90% of the 3.5 million or so businesses employ fewer than 10 people but nearly half of the workforce are employed in large organisations.'

There are still rather too many bodies involved in health and safety and this in itself can be confusing as there can be an overlap of responsibilities. To make sure that *A strategy for workplace health and safety in Great Britain to 2010 and beyond* is achieved the main factor that needs to change according to the HSE is the way that the organisations concerned with health and safety work together. HSE feel there is 'a perception that there is no coherent direction to the overall health and safety system. HSC, HSE and LA cannot/should not do it all. There is agreement that boundaries need to be set.' A consultation document written in 2007 sets out proposals for a new organisation where all three former organisations work together and where boundaries are removed.

The enforcing authorities

We shall now discuss how the current inspection of workplaces and investigation of accidents is shared between HSE inspectors and local authority enforcement officers. Basically the HSE inspectors cover work conducted primarily in factories, building sites, mines, fairgrounds, quarries, railways, chemical plants, offshore and nuclear installations, schools or hospitals. The local authority enforcement officers cover retailing, some warehouses, most offices, hotels, catering, consumer services, sports and leisure activities and places of worship. Both have similar powers of enforcement. These include a right to:

- enter employers' premises
- carry out inspections/investigations
- take equipment or materials on to premises
- take measurements, photographs or recordings
- carry out tests on articles or substances
- examine books and documents
- issue improvement notices
- issue prohibition notices.

The last two points are very important and we shall consider each in turn. However, sometimes when an enforcing inspector finds a breach of the law which is relatively minor he or she may feel that improvement notices and prohibition notices are not appropriate.

Informal methods

In the case of a minor breach in legislation the inspector may choose to use informal methods and may simply give the employer or contractor advice about what they should do to comply with the law, and explain the reasons.

Improvement notices

If the inspector feels that an organisation is contravening one of the relevant provisions of legislation then he or she can issue an improvement notice which will specify that improvements must be made within a specified time limit to bring the equipment or process up to the required standard of safety.

Prohibition notices

If when the inspector visits he or she feels that there is serious danger or risk of injury to employees, he or she can issue a prohibition notice which will stop work activity immediately until the risk has been dealt with. In some circumstances a deferred prohibition order may be issued: this would occur, for example, if it would be difficult to stop a process in mid-cycle or if there was no immediate risk of injury. The Health and Safety Commission's Enforcement Policy Statement (2002) states the approach which both the Health and Safety Executive and local authorities should take in relation to law enforcement. The overall aims of the HSC are to protect the health, safety and welfare of employees and to safeguard others such as members of the public who may be exposed to risk from the workplace or activity.

> ### Did you know?
> In 2005/06 1,012 offences resulted in prosecution by the HSE and the local authorities prosecuted 332 offences.
> (See www.hse.gov.uk/statistics for latest figures.)

Normally in England and Wales most prosecutions would go to a magistrates' court but more serious cases are referred to the Crown Courts. Under the Scottish judicial system the majority of cases go to a sheriff court or before a jury. Organisations and individuals can face prosecution, and prison sentences and unlimited fines can also be given by the Crown Courts.

Any accidents at work that result in death are treated as manslaughter. The police are involved in these cases and have overall responsibility for them. However, there had been general dissatisfaction that the system was not tough enough and that employers were on occasions shirking their responsibilities with regard to health and safety and frequently escaping prosecution even when an employee had died as a result of the company's actions or inactions. The Corporate Manslaughter and Corporate Homicide Act (2007) is intended to create a criminal offence of corporate manslaughter for the first time. According to Baker (2007), 'The law is likely to lead to more prosecutions for deaths resulting from an organisation's acts or omissions, and may lead to higher fines. It will certainly lead to greater scrutiny by the courts of the way in which companies organise themselves internally in terms of health and safety.' This should make it easier to examine the conduct of senior managers, and a company can be found guilty of corporate manslaughter if it can be proved that the way they managed and organised their activities led to a death and that this amounted to a gross breach of its duty of care to the employee.

In 2002 the HSC (HSC, 2002) revised its Enforcement Policy Statement and set out the criteria for whether or not particular incidents or complaints should be investigated. This Policy Statement stresses four main things:

1 *The principle of proportionality.* This means that the severity of the action taken should be in proportion to the level of risk and the seriousness of the breach of law.
2 *Targeting.* The people/organisations who cause the most serious risks or who have failed to control hazards in the workplace adequately should be the ones to be targeted by the inspectors.
3 *Consistent.* For people to have faith in the system and the inspectors they need to feel that they will be treated in a consistently fair way.

4 *Transparent.* Every action taken should be clear, with explanations given for any action that is taken.

Prosecution

If the case is very serious then the inspector may also need to initiate a prosecution. Any decision about whether or not to prosecute will be taken after considering the HSC's Enforcement Policy Statement.

Safety representatives

As we said earlier, there is a duty for employers to consult with and involve safety representatives in the workplace. In October 1978 the Safety Representatives and Safety Committees Regulations came into effect. These regulations form part of the Health and Safety at Work Act, and within a year over 100,000 safety representatives were in post. The regulations provide that any recognised trade union can appoint safety representatives, and they recommend that in general the people who are appointed should have worked for that employer for at least two years so that they have a reasonable range of experience from which to draw. In some trade unions the shop stewards take on the role of safety representatives, while in others the safety representative is a separate post. The people to fill these positions are, however, selected by the trade union, not by the management. Organisations where there are no recognised trade unions can still appoint safety representatives, and they are normally elected by the workforce.

The safety representative's main function is to represent the employee in consultation with the employer on issues relating to health and safety in the workplace, and they can investigate hazards or potential hazards as well as carrying out inspections of the workplace. They are entitled to paid time off to perform their duties and for training to enable them to carry out their duties effectively, and they may also require some facilities such as the use of a telephone, a filing cabinet and a room to conduct interviews. If two or more safety representatives make a written request to management for a safety committee to be established, then the employer is legally obliged to do so.

The Management of Health and Safety at Work Regulations 1992 (MHSWR) as amended in 1999 add to the Safety Representatives and Safety Committees Regulations 1977 and specify that every employer shall consult safety representatives in good time with regard to:

- the introduction of any measure at the workplace which may substantially affect health or safety of the workforce
- arrangements for appointing or nominating a 'competent person' who is able to assist the employer to carry out risk assessment exercises and help him or her in carrying out duties in relation to health and safety
- the health and safety information that the employer is supposed to provide to employees
- the planning and organisation of health and safety training
- the health and safety consequences of the introduction of new technology at work.

There are, as you can see, a wide range of duties performed by safety representatives. Safety representatives usually receive excellent training from trades unions for this demanding role and those who take on these roles can also choose to take the training further and use it as part of a professional qualification in health and safety.

Safety officer or safety adviser

None of the legislation actually specifies the need for a safety officer but, as the law has grown in complexity, many organisations have felt that it is necessary to appoint a person to specialise in this area of work. This is a management appointment and must not be confused with the trade union/employee-appointed safety representative. Safety officers are sometimes appointed to advise senior management without being part of any other department and report directly to the board, but in many organisations they form part of the human resource management department. Smaller organisations may not wish to appoint a full-time safety officer and may instead call on the expertise provided by independent consultants to act as safety advisers. It is important that anyone appointed as safety officer or safety adviser has the status and level of competence to provide authoritative advice to management and the workforce on aspects of health and safety.

A competent person

This has a specific meaning in terms of health and safety as the Framework Directive (Article 7), which is discussed later, says that employers must designate 'a competent person' who has practical and theoretical knowledge of particular equipment and who is able to identify any problems that may occur with it. The provision of this directive is reflected in Regulation 6 of the Management of Health and Safety at Work Regulations 1992 and clearly refers to a management nominee, although not necessarily to the safety officer but to someone who because of his or her knowledge and experience of particular machinery, plant or equipment is able to identify problems or defects in it. That person needs to be competent not just to do the job but to carry out risk assessment for health and safety for employees and the public, and must monitor and review protective and preventive measures. A safety officer may fulfil this role but is not likely to be the only designated competent person, as she or he is unlikely to have the required level of knowledge or experience for all machinery.

Safety committees

Safety committees have to be established, as we said earlier, if two or more safety representatives request the organisation to do so, but many organisations do not wait for this request, and it is good practice to set up a safety committee in any case. The main objective of a safety committee is to promote cooperation between employers and employees in instigating, developing and carrying out measures to ensure the health and safety at work of employees. They are likely to provide some or all of the following functions:

- study figures and trends for accidents and notifiable diseases
- examine safety audit reports
- consider reports and factual information provided by inspectors
- consider the reports of safety representatives
- assist in development of safety rules and safe systems of work

- monitor the effectiveness of safety training in the workplace
- monitor the effectiveness of the safety and health communication in the workplace
- encourage publicity for health and safety programmes in the workplace
- provide a link with the appropriate inspectorates.

Membership of the health and safety committee

The membership of the committee should be agreed between management and the employees. The committee should normally include equal numbers of people from management and the workforce and should have representation from different areas of the workforce and different grades of management. People such as the organisation's doctor, nurse or safety officer should also be invited to attend as ex officio members. It is a good idea for the person who chairs the committee to have sufficient status within the organisation that they can authorise money to be spent on necessary aspects of health and safety without having to refer all such decisions to higher authority. A senior member of the management team would fulfil this role well, although in many organisations the chair of the safety committee may also alternate between management and the workforce.

Health and safety arrangements

Safety policy statement

You will remember that under HASAWA one of the duties of an employer is to provide a safety policy statement to show each person's responsibilities and the arrangements they have made to carry out the policy. The safety policy applies to all organisations that employ more than five employees. This is supposed to be a document that can be used to show in a practical way how the arrangements for health and safety are to be carried out in the workplace, and it should be designed to have a genuine effect on health and safety working practices. This means that it should be clearly written and should be easily available to any employee, and a copy should preferably be given to each employee. It does not mean that it is a secret document, as some organisations in our experience seem to think, kept locked in a filing cabinet well away from the gaze of employees. In order to encourage awareness of health and safety and produce an effective safety policy document, it is also advisable that a range of people should be involved in its design and that key decision makers have been involved fully in these discussions. In some organisations a person will be chosen to champion the policy and targets for improvements in specific areas of health and safety may also be set. Arrangements should also be made to review the health and safety policy regularly, at least annually, since what is important is whether the policy is having an effect on health and safety in the workplace, rather than how well written it is.

The HSE recommends that the following two issues should be addressed in a safety policy statement.

- Who has responsibility for health and safety?
- What are the arrangements made for health and safety?

Responsibility for health and safety

The safety policy should show management's approach to health and safety and who is actually responsible for specific tasks. The safety policy is basically concerned with people, their duties and their accountability. It should include a management chart showing the chain of command in respect of health and safety, with a clear statement that the ultimate responsibility for health and safety rests with the board or chief executive or equivalent. The safety policy document should carry at the end the signature of the person with the ultimate responsibility for health and safety at work. There should be a clearly defined role for the safety adviser, if such a position exists, and clear explanation of his/her relationship to senior management and line management. This part of the document should also indicate the role of those appointed as 'competent persons' to assist the employer in implementing the safety policy.

According to David Morris (2001), Head of the HSE's Strategy and Management Branch:

> In principle, small firms will have much the same policy statements as larger firms, and their risk assessments will cover much the same ground. But there are differences. The policy statement is likely to show that there is less scope for delegation in a small firm, where many responsibilities are exercised directly by the owner. Equally, small firms may have relatively few, or simple, hazards, meaning that risk assessment will be less complex.

The practical arrangements

This section should establish systems and procedures and the practical arrangements for their implementation. It should also show the system for monitoring safety and for publishing results. The section of the safety policy covering arrangements should be a practical section that is regularly reviewed and updated.

The HSE (2003), in a booklet, *Stating Your Business*, suggests that small organisations organise their arrangements for managing health and safety under the sections listed below.

- health and safety risks arising from our work activities
- consultation with employees
- safe plant and equipment
- safe handling and use of substances
- information, instruction and supervision
- competency for tasks and training
- accidents, first aid and work-related ill-health
- monitoring
- emergency procedures – fire and evacuation
- key areas of risk.

Health and safety risks arising from work activities

This means that the arrangements for carrying out risk assessments, the results of the risk assessments and the actions taken will all need to be shown, although the findings and resulting actions will need to be shown in a separate document. Risk assessments will be discussed in more detail later in the chapter.

Consultation with employees

We have already discussed the fact that if there is a recognised trade union which has appointed safety representatives then by law they must be consulted about any changes likely to affect the health and safety of their members. If there is not a recognised trade union then the employers must consult their employees directly or through a works council.

Safe plant and equipment

This requirement is taken directly from HASAWA and means that employers must keep vehicles, machinery and equipment in good working order. In the safety policy, the names of people responsible for this should be stated, as should arrangements to deal with problems. Those responsible for checking that new machinery and equipment meets the required standards should also be listed here. Records of maintenance and service history of vehicles should be kept, perhaps separately in a log book.

Safe handling and use of substances

This section relates to those responsible for identifying substances that need a COSHH assessment. Once again the names of people with responsibilities should be listed here. This includes the names of those carrying out the assessments, those responsible for ensuring that any actions needed are taken, those who have to tell employees about the results of the assessments as well as the names of those people who have responsibility for checking the safety of new substances prior to purchase. There should also be an indication as to the frequency of assessments.

Information, instruction and supervision

This should show where health and safety law posters are displayed or where leaflets relating to health and safety are kept. It should also detail where health and safety advice can be obtained and the names of those responsible for supervising the work of trainees or young employees.

Competency for tasks and training

The names of people who provide induction training and job-specific training should be listed here. Some jobs may pose particular risks, for example the risk of back injury to workers involved in the manual handling of heavy or awkwardly shaped goods. Both the jobs and the training needed should also be identified. Training records should be kept for all health and safety training as well as other training and the safety policy should indicate where the records are stored and by whom.

Accidents, first aid and work-related ill-health

In this section any health surveillance required for certain jobs, such as work with flour, asbestos or some chemicals, needs to be identified. This should mean any problems in a worker's health caused by the job will be identified at an early stage so that action can be taken to prevent their health becoming worse. It shows who is responsible for health surveillance and where records are kept.

The locations of first aid boxes need to be shown and first aiders should be listed. Records of all accidents, however trivial, and instances of work-related ill-health should be recorded in the accident book and the location of this book should also be given in the health and safety policy.

Monitoring

It is very important that the policy is used and that good practices are checked regularly. Those who have responsibility for checking that working conditions are safe and that safe practices are being followed should be listed here, as should those who are responsible for carrying out investigations of accidents or investigating work-related causes of sickness absence.

Emergency procedures – fire and evacuation

Obviously it is important that there are adequate safety procedures in place in case there is a need to evacuate the building in an emergency. In this section it is important to state who checks the escape routes and the frequency of these checks. Safety equipment such as fire extinguishers have to be maintained and checked, alarms need to be tested, emergency evacuation drills need to be carried out and records of these must be kept.

Key areas of risk

These will vary depending on the organisation and the type of work undertaken, but might include risks relating to particularly dangerous substances such as asbestos, or to stress or potential violence to staff from members of the public. Each organisation will need to carry out its own risk assessments relating to the areas of risk which are identified.

People need to be aware of their responsibilities as, if something goes wrong and a serious accident occurs, the relevant enforcement officers will want to know who was responsible. These enforcement officers would carry out a full investigation and would also want to examine the safety policy document. If a supervisor did not know that he or she was responsible for checking that a protective guard was in place, then the employer would have to be able to prove that he or she had informed the supervisor of his or her responsibilities and had also trained him or her adequately in the fulfilment of these responsibilities. Many tasks will of course be delegated to different levels of management and employees do, as we have seen, have some responsibility for their own actions. Senior management cannot, however, abdicate their ultimate responsibility for overall safety within the organisation, and must try to ensure the health and safety of their employees and others affected by their employees' actions. Those who carry the ultimate responsibility for this, such as the board of directors, could face prosecution and possibly a large fine or even a spell in prison for individual directors if their organisation is found to be at fault. Similarly, others with specific responsibilities such as safety officers, human resource managers, line managers or training officers could be charged and convicted of an offence.

First consider the following case study and identify the health, safety and welfare issues that you think occur here then complete Activity 12.3.

CASE STUDY 12.1 Health and safety

The Sheffley Company employs nearly 330 employees and specialises in the production of steel castings. The organisation has a director, Mr Jones, whose great-grandfather founded the business. There is a new production manager, Mr Tandy; an import and export manager, Ms Jeffries; and an administration manager, Mrs Groves. Mr Tandy has eight line managers reporting to him, who have a total of 280 employees working for them. Mrs Groves has a payroll manager, a canteen manager and a personnel officer reporting to her and Ms Jeffries runs the purchasing, goods inward and goods outward departments, and the warehouse and export sections.

The work involved in the production of steel castings is hazardous and the company has not had a good record with regard to health and safety. It is not only in the production areas that there have been problems – the offices also have suffered rather a large number of accidents which have required employees to have more than three days off work to recover. The office staff are expected to regularly work long hours and work whatever hours are necessary to complete the job. Several are absent with serious long-term illnesses including the payroll manager and of course this puts additional pressure on those who remain. Mrs Groves is beginning to show signs of the strain from doing her own job and that of the absent payroll officer and is suffering from regular headaches and feelings of anxiety.

The new production manager decides that something must be done about the record on health, safety and welfare. He decides a punitive approach will work best and in the weekly meeting with the production supervisors he informs them that from next week any employee who does not wear the protective equipment provided will be dismissed. The safety equipment comprises safety boots, safety goggles and overalls.

During the lead-up to the introduction of the safety equipment, notices are put up to explain the disciplinary penalty for non-compliance with the regulation, but information about the use and location of some of the equipment is not provided. Neither the safety representatives nor the safety committee have the opportunity to inspect the new protective equipment or to advise employees on its suitability.

The employees prove to be reluctant to wear the protective goggles which, they complain, pinch their skin and impair their vision. The production manager realises that the enforcement of safety is going to be problematic, and at the next week's meeting informs the supervisors that they do not have to be too rigid in their enforcement of the rules.

Two serious accidents occur just a month later in the production area and a further serious accident occurs in the offices. In the first incident molten metal splashes on to the foot of an employee, causing serious burns. In a separate accident a few days later an employee slips, splashing molten metal close to his eyes. Luckily his sight is saved, but he suffers severe burns and scarring. The accident record in the offices is also unsatisfactory, and one employee is injured when chemicals used in the photocopier spill on her leg, causing a severe itchy rash to develop. She has been having problems at home but has felt she must keep working although her mind has not been on her work all the time. Other employees in the wages office complain of backaches and headaches which they say are caused by poor lighting, uncomfortable chairs and badly adjusted screens on their visual display units.

You should be able to identify some of the many issues raised here about health, safety and the welfare of the employees such as the exact nature of the employer and employee responsibilities. The employer in this case, and indeed anyone involved in this area of work, also needs to comply with legislation, so, based on your reading of the chapter so far, you should also be able to identify the key legislation infringed by both the employer and the employees. A full discussion of this case study can be found if you go to our website at **www.pearsoned.co.uk/foothook**.

ACTIVITY 12.3

Design a safety policy statement for Sheffley Company. Remember that this should be a practical document that can be used by people in the organisation. Use the sections and main headings that we have given earlier (see pages 382–384).

Risk assessment

The idea of assessing and controlling risks was introduced to Britain with the Control of Substances Hazardous to Health Regulations 1988, when employers had to assess the risk of harm to people from certain substances being used at work. This was developed further in the 'six-pack' regulations in 1992. The 1992 Code of Practice for the Management of Health and Safety at Work made it a legal duty for employers to assess and record health and safety risks, and to appoint a 'competent person', i.e. a person who has been suitably trained, and who is allowed adequate time and facilities, to perform this role and assist in this and other safety tasks.

Every organisation has to carry out its own risk assessment, and strategies for this should be devised by management after consultation with all interested groups in the workforce.

According to the HSE in the booklet *Five Steps to Risk Assessment* (2006), the five main steps involved in assessing risks and hazards in the workplace are:

1 Identify the hazards.
2 Decide who might be harmed and how.
3 Evaluate the risks and decide on precautions.
4 Record your findings and implement them.
5 Review your assessment and update if necessary.

Assessments do not have to be carried out by health and safety experts and small organisations may choose to undertake the initial assessment of risk by themselves: alternatively, they may prefer to employ a consultant.

Steps 1 and 2 Identify the hazards and decide who may be harmed by them

Most organisations should be able to carry out the first two steps quite easily and identify sources of risk and then identify those who may be harmed by the risks. Many of the risks will probably be well known to you already such as the risk of slipping in areas where the floor may sometimes be wet, but sometimes even obvious hazards such as this are ignored. Identifying hazards involves looking and talking to people in the area being assessed. It also involves identifying which groups of workers are likely to suffer harm and the type of injury that they are likely to suffer.

● Step 3 Evaluate the risks and decide on precautions

Once you have identified the hazards and those likely to be affected by them then you must do something about them. Remember under the Health and Safety at Work Act 1974 you have to do everything that is 'reasonably practicable' to protect people from harm.

Pause for thought 12.3 If the floor is sometimes wet due to cleaning or spillages, what could you do as a precaution?

It is best to try to get rid of the risk if it is possible but if not then ways to minimise the risk should be tried. What could you do to prevent accidents in the case of a wet floor that was slippery in your college/university or workplace?

Your answers should follow the following order if possible. Complete them in the grid below.

Order for trying to control risks	Your response to each of these where there is a wet and slippery floor
1 Try to find a way of doing the job that carries less risk	
2 Ensure people don't come into contact with the hazard	
3 Minimise exposure to the hazard	
4 Issue personal protective clothing	
5 Provide adequate facilities to deal properly with people who have suffered in some way because they come into contact with the problem	

Go to **www.pearsoned.uk/foothook** now to check your answers to this exercise.

● Step 4 Record your findings and implement them

Small organisations with five employees or fewer do not have to record their findings but it would be good practice to do so anyway. Workers need to know what is happening as far as minimising risks is concerned and it also helps to involve them more in health and safety. According to the HSE (2006b) employers need to show that:

- a proper check was made;
- you asked who might be affected;
- you dealt with all significant hazards, taking into account the number of people who could be involved;
- the precautions are reasonable, and the remaining risk low; and
- you involved your staff or their representatives in the process.

Although it would be excellent if you could tackle all hazards immediately this will probably not be practicable so you need to plan an order of priority. Which are the most dangerous hazards? Which are quick and easy to solve? Are there any temporary solutions that could be used while a longer term solution is being organised? How will you monitor your solutions are working? Who is due to take action on each point and by when?

Step 5 Review your risk assessment and update if necessary

All workplaces are subject to constant change so something that works well at first may, due to changing circumstances or work patterns, no longer be so effective. Therefore the risk assessment needs to be monitored on a regular basis. For some organisations where there is a great deal of change this may involve reviewing risk assessments on a monthly or perhaps even weekly basis, while for other organisations an annual review may be more appropriate unless some unexpected change makes it more urgent to review risks.

Welfare

As described in Chapter 1, the main focus of people management has changed over the years. One of the earliest roles for HR specialists included that of the welfare officer (Fowler, 1994). The focus of this role was on the well-being of employees and it sometimes meant taking a paternalistic viewpoint, i.e. adopting a moral stance and telling people what was best for them. The modern HR function has changed and become more complex, adopting a more strategic and integrated approach to human resource management, a theme taken up in a number of chapters. Individual well-being, however, is still a factor which has an obvious impact on employees' ability to function at high levels and add value to their organisation. Employees who cannot concentrate at work or who may even stay away from work because of physical or psychological health problems obviously cannot contribute to their full potential, which has a negative impact on the goal of high-performance working (Income Data Services, 2002). In this context, the Engineering Employers' Federation (EEF, 2001) identifies effective stress management as 'a key part of a positive, proactive human resources policy'.

There is evidence then that a concern for employee welfare is nowadays an important aspect of human resource management. Even if the aforementioned paternalistic elements are not acceptable in our modern culture, employers are expected to care about their employees, and responsibility for this may be held by line managers as well as human resource and other specialists. There is a range of business and legal reasons for saying that an employer has not just an obligation but also a right to be involved in employee welfare.

The Health and Safety Executive (HSE) has also been focusing on ways to draw all employers' attention to the benefits to be gained from a more proactive approach. It has launched a series of initiatives called Revitalising Health and Safety because organisations are increasingly operating in new ways with increasingly flexible ways of working. The HSE has been consulting with and involving employers to demonstrate the business case for improved health and safety measures.

The role of the employer in employee well-being

One area of debate on the subject of welfare is whether this is a personal and private matter. We have already said that there is a business case for employer involvement in the health and safety of their workforce but should an employer also have a right to enquire into other aspects of the well-being of employees that involve their private lives? If so how far should this go?

Pause for thought 12.4 Before you read on, take a few minutes to think about your position on this issue. Make a list of arguments for saying that employers should be concerned about the personal welfare of their employees, and a list of reasons why they should not.

Go to our website at **www.pearsoned.co.uk/foothook** for further discussion and to check your arguments with ours.

Did you know?

In November 1994, John Walker, a senior social worker with Northumberland County Council, won his case in a high court, claiming that the employer had been negligent in its handling of this employee's stress. Mr Walker had returned to work after suffering a nervous breakdown. After his return to work the employer failed to make adjustments in his workload, and Mr Walker was dismissed on ill-health grounds after he had a second nervous breakdown. The fact that Mr Walker had suffered a first nervous breakdown meant that it could reasonably have been foreseen that the workload was a potential hazard for this employee. Mr Walker received an out of court settlement of £175,000.

(*Source:* Midgley, 1997, p. 36)

If an employee's personal problems result in falling standards at work, or even in an event that could be construed as misconduct, this could result in formal disciplinary action. On the whole, managers prefer to handle such issues in an informal manner to preserve good working relationships, and regard formal discipline as an action to be taken if the informal approach fails. This approach is encouraged by the ACAS guidelines on discipline (2004). You will find a fuller discussion of this in Chapter 13. It should suffice to make the point here that the proper use of counselling may obviate the need to embark on formal disciplinary action. According to the Inland Revenue Service (2007) at least one in five employers do provide employee assistance programmes (EAPs) though most are actually funded by the employer and are provided on their behalf by external suppliers. Typically about 10 per cent of the workforce use the EAP in any year but the popularity of EAPs has increased with employers after a legal case in 2002, when it was argued that just having an EAP provided sufficient defence for an employer against stress compensation claims. This was subsequently modified in a 2007 case so that it is not now possible just to rely on this as a defence in stress management cases. Typically the EAP service provided involves help with counselling, often by providing access to telephone helplines and to specialist advisers. Since corporate manslaughter is now a criminal offence employers should certainly be diligent in their responsibilities regarding any health, safety or welfare issues that could result in death and should of course take their responsibilities for all health, safety and welfare issues equally seriously.

Finally, we can justify an employer's interest in the well-being of employees with reference to the basic need to develop good working relationships, on the part of individual employees, individual managers, and from a corporate point of view. Abraham Maslow (1954) was one of the first writers to describe motivation in terms of human needs, and these concepts have often been applied to the workplace. One of the needs that Maslow identified is the social need for relationships, and indeed the importance of relationships has been reinforced by the inclusion of this factor in the HSE's list of aspects of stress management. A number of surveys on motivation have identified the importance of good relationships at work, and specifically the relationship between supervisor and subordinate. It is not inappropriate to care about the people we work with. Much has also been written about corporate image, and many employers wish to be recognised as 'good employers', especially since corporate image can affect an organisation's ability to attract and retain good employees and can therefore have a major impact on the success of the organisation.

The reasons for employers to be involved with employees' problems can be summarised as follows:

- to address problems with productivity, standards of work, attendance and turnover
- to meet legal obligations to ensure the health, safety and welfare of employees
- to avoid the development of disciplinary problems
- to maintain good employee relations.

Types of problem and their sources

There can be an infinite range of personal problems faced by workers which could affect their work. Many will arise from sources outside the organisation, such as family breakdown, alcoholism, drug abuse, care duties or bereavement, while others might be the result of bullying, working conditions, excessive workload or some form of discrimination in the workplace. The HR department needs to be clear about each of these issues and have policies and procedures in place to deal with issues such as alcoholism or drug abuse and should certainly also have effective policies to prevent unfair discrimination or bullying within work. It is not within the scope of this textbook to deal with all these specific issues but one area which has caused a lot of concern recently is the area of stress, which we shall focus on next. As you saw in the case of *Walker* v. *Northumberland County Council*, there can be serious repercussions for both the employee and the organisation if an employer fails to deal with stress in an appropriate way.

Stress and stress management

Stress is one major area of concern, and can be regarded as an umbrella term for a range of problems. Stress is manifested when people are dealing with so many pressures that their normal behaviour patterns become affected. Hans Selye (1956 and 1974), a noted writer on stress, used the terms 'eustress' and 'distress' to explain that stress is not always a negative concept. Sometimes people are stimulated by having to deal with a number of issues; this can be exciting and motivating. When it becomes too much and one cannot cope and at the same time continue to behave within the range of one's normal behaviour patterns, this is what Selye refers to as distress. This is what we normally mean when we refer to stress these days (Le Fevre *et al.*, 2003).

What are the causes of stress? There are a wide range of factors that cause stress both in personal relationships and in work relationships (see Figure 12.1); these factors are referred to as stressors. Holmes and Rahe (1967) identified a number of life events as being sources of stress. Ranked at number one as a source of stress was the death of one's spouse, and other factors identified included divorce, taking on a high mortgage and taking a holiday.

Figure 12.1   Some causes of stress

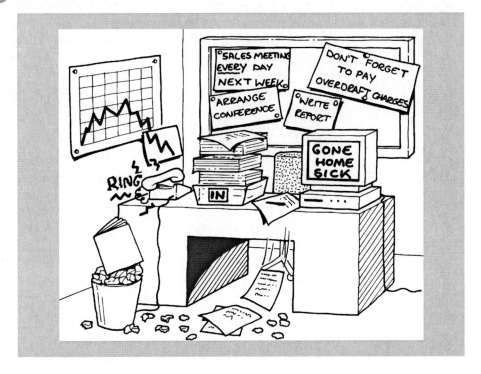

It is also recognised that circumstances at work such as poor relationships, especially with one's manager or supervisor, and overwork or underemployment can contribute to stress. The case of John Walker mentioned earlier is an example of too high a workload combined with the demanding nature of the work contributing to stress.

The symptoms of stress include the behavioural changes we previously identified that might alert you to the fact that a colleague is under pressure. If not dealt with, the end result can be physical or mental illness leading to mental breakdown.

The Health and Safety Executive (HSE) has played a major role in the development of guidelines for employers on various aspects of stress management. The duty of care addressed in the Health and Safety at Work Act 1974 applies to employees' physical and mental well-being, and since these can be affected by stress caused by workplace factors, the duty of care constitutes an obvious legal obligation to pay attention to stress management. The Management of Health and Safety at Work Regulations 1999 also impose a duty on employers to conduct a risk audit on potential hazards in the workplace, which also applies in this area as the effects of stress can be regarded as a hazard.

The main focus of the Health and Safety Executive has been on the development of standards for employers to achieve in terms of stress management, and after a series of consultation and pilot exercises, the HSE (2005) launched an official set of standards.

Organisations can use these standards to measure their achievements in terms of stress management. The stress management standards are not legally enforceable on organisations, but the HSE may use them as evidence that an organisation is not fulfilling its duty with regard to stress management. The HSE has already issued an improvement order against one organisation for failing to manage stress adequately: West Dorset Hospitals NHS Trust in 2003 (reported by Hayden-Smith and Simms, 2003), though Income Data Services (2004) report that the Trust has since remedied the situation with suitable interventions.

The standards address six areas of work that should be audited. These are laid out with a brief description of what each entails in Table 12.1. The basic idea is to ascertain what percentages of staff feel that they are able to cope with any work situations in these six areas. According to the International Stress Management Organisation (2004), 'the target is for all organisations to match the performance of the top 20% of employers that are successfully minimalising work-related stress.' Organisations must also be able to show that they have systems in place locally to respond to any individual concerns and should be carrying out risk assessments for stress. As Quinn (2004) points out, the identification of stress factors

Table 12.1   HSE stress management standards

Area of work	The standard	Desirable outcomes that organisations should be working towards
Demands This is about demands caused by the workload, work pattern or the work environment.	Employees should be able to indicate that they can cope with the demands of their job. There should also be systems in place to help deal with individual concerns.	The organisation should ensure hours of work are reasonable and that demands made on the workers are not excessive. There should be a matching of people's skills to their jobs. There should be systems set up to address concerns that workers may have so that these can be resolved.
Control This is about how much influence an individual has about their job.	Employees should be able to indicate that they get a say in the way they do their work. There should also be systems in place to respond to individual concerns.	Individuals should have control over their pace of work wherever possible. They should get opportunities to use their skills and initiative in their work. They should be encouraged to develop new skills so they can undertake new or more challenging work. The employees should also have a say about when breaks should be taken and be consulted about their work patterns.
Support This concerns the support mechanisms, or lack of them, from colleagues, line managers, and others such as HR staff. It is also about levels of employee awareness about support.	Employees should be able to indicate that they receive adequate support and information from colleagues and superiors. There should also be evidence of systems in place to adequately address employee concerns.	There should be policies and procedures in place to adequately support staff and there should also be systems in place to enable and encourage managers to support staff. Since support is also sometimes provided by colleagues there should be systems in place to encourage employees to support others. Employees should know how to access resources necessary to do their job and should also get regular and constructive feedback.

Table 12.1   Continued

Area of work	The standard	Desirable outcomes that organisations should be working towards
Relationships This is about encouraging positive behaviour so that conflict is avoided and about creating ways to deal with unacceptable behaviour.	Employees should be able to indicate that they are not subjected to unacceptable behaviour at work such as bullying or harassment and that there are systems in place to deal with these issues.	The organisation should promote positive behaviour to ensure fairness and avoid conflict and employees share information about their work. The organisation should have policies in place to prevent or resolve unacceptable behaviour and employees should be able to report unacceptable behaviour.
Role This concerns the extent to which people understand their role and whether the organisation ensures the individual does not have conflicting roles.	Employees should be able to indicate that they understand their role and responsibilities and there should be systems in place to address individual concerns.	The organisation should try to ensure as far as possible that the different requirements it places on employees are compatible and clear and that the individual understands them. If they have concerns about role conflict or about their role then they should be able to raise them.
Change How much change are employees expected to cope with, and how well prepared are they when they do have to deal with change? Are the arrangements for information sharing and consultation adequate?	Employees should be able to show that the organisation consults with them frequently when undergoing organisational change and that there are systems in place to respond to any concerns they may have.	The organisation should be consulting adequately and providing opportunities for individuals to contribute to and influence the changes. This information needs to be timely and sufficient for employees to understand the reasons for the changes and the likely impact on their jobs. Employees also need to be aware of the timetable for changes and have suitable access to support during the change period.

Source: Adapted from HSE (2005) *Tackling Stress – The Management Standards Approach.*

through such an audit makes the eventuality of stress foreseeable, so employers would be obligated to take some action in such an instance.

> **Pause for thought 12.5** Consider any organisation in which you have worked. To what extent to you think that organisation has considered each of the stress management standards?
>
> What is your evidence for this?
>
> How does this compare with the views of others in your class about organisations in which they have worked? Did job roles seem clear and unambiguous? Were you made aware of structures to support you?

As you can see from these standards there are a great many implications for HR departments to ensure that they have not only policies in place but also that they have designed jobs well to ensure there is no role incompatibility or work overload, that individuals understand their roles through induction and subsequent training and that there are support systems in place for those who may be experiencing problems. Management also need training to ensure they respond in an appropriate way to those suffering from stress. This means that they need to recognise that just increasing workloads and hoping that the person can cope is not a satisfactory way to manage but that there is a need for proper analyses of the job and the workload, and to match these to the person's capabilities.

An additional factor to do with employer obligations is that employment tribunals hearing cases of unfair dismissal would expect employers to have conducted a full investigation of the circumstances surrounding an incident of alleged misconduct or incompetence. The investigation should have shown whether this may have arisen as a result of personal problems or stress, particularly in the case of a person who previously had a good work record. Employers would be expected to take any such extenuating circumstances into consideration. You can read more about this in Chapter 14. The point about legal obligations could be summarised in the statement that employers have a duty of care.

The Chartered Institute of Personnel and Development in conjunction with the HSE (2007b) have sponsored a research project to develop a competencies framework for stress management. This aims to identify and develop the behaviour needed by managers for reducing and preventing stress at work and this is part of ongoing research in this area.

Organisational policy and procedures

Policy statements and procedures provide guidelines for all employees. They let managers know how to handle problems, and inform everyone about the help, assistance and support they can expect to receive including the things in the stress management standards. There is a dual role for policies as far as situations requiring counselling are concerned. First, there is a need for policies relating directly to the provision of counselling and, second, an organisation should have policies dealing with workplace behaviour or events that have been identified as causing distress. For instance, in a *Guardian* Careers Section article, Professor Cary Cooper was quoted as saying that bullying probably accounted for a third to a half of all stress-related illness (Venning, 1995).

> **Did you know?**
>
> Some occupational groups and industry groups are more prone to stress than others. According to the HSE, groups that suffer particularly high levels of stress include teachers and nurses, professional and managerial groups, particularly those in the public sector.
> (*Source*: HSE, 2007)

Policies on bullying and sexual/racial harassment can help to eliminate these unwanted behaviours and promote a less stressful working environment. Many organisations such as banks and retail outlets, where staff handle cash and at the same time have direct contact with the public, have recognised that specialised counselling is necessary to deal with the trauma their employees can suffer after an episode involving violence or a threat of violence. This is true when they have either been directly threatened or witnessed an incident. Employers will obviously have to decide which issues are most important for their organisations, and this may involve surveying employees to discover which issues are of concern to them, and which solutions the employees would most like to take advantage of. The package of welfare policies, procedures and benefits an employer offers to employees is often referred to as an 'employee assistance programme'.

Policies should also address the following issues:

- who will be involved in providing counselling, and what are the parameters of their roles
- what type of services will be offered
- issues of confidentiality. (Seenan, 2004)

Health promotion

So far, we have focused primarily on approaches to safety and welfare in response to legal requirements and as a way for employers to ensure that they motivate their workers. Recent legislation does encourage employers to be proactive about safety and to carry out risk assessments and then take action to reduce or eliminate risks identified. Many good employers take this a stage further and not only promote measures to promote improvements in safety and welfare but also encourage developments to ensure good health among their workforces.

The high cost of absenteeism is a strong financial reason for taking measures to promote and improve health. Many employers have provided health screening services and membership of private health insurance schemes for their managers, and some are extending this provision to the workforce as a whole. Increasingly, organisations are actively trying to promote a healthier lifestyle among their employees. Among the measures that have been tried are:

- help for smokers to quit, with support/self-help groups and psychologists giving advice and support
- a healthy diet, with a wider choice of health foods on the menu at work
- membership of a health club or purchase of multi-gym exercise equipment for employees to use to get fitter
- stress management programmes
- policies and education programmes on HIV/Aids
- policies and education on substance abuse.

In organisations where these programmes have been made available to all the workforce on a long-term basis, there have been benefits to employees' health, with weight reduction and improvements in blood cholesterol and blood pressure levels, and also improvements in absenteeism rates. It is claimed that the cost of the introduction of this type of programme is more than offset by the savings from lower rates of absenteeism. The CIPD (2004) stated that 'a survey of 97 organisations showed that employees who were participating in "wellness" programmes each incurred between £1,335 and £2,910 less per year in healthcare and absenteeism costs than colleagues who were not participating.'

Absence management

While prevention is always better than cure one of the areas that many HR departments are also becoming increasingly interested in, and which can be used in a complementary way to a wellness programme, is absence management. Westminster City Council 'introduced improved absence management procedures which have reduced its absence rate by more than two days per person per annum and saved it £800,000 annually' (Inland Revenue Service, 2007b). They achieved this by using a mixture of approaches such as the introduction of an employee assistance programme and a new absence management programme which involved return to work interviews and earlier and more positive use of the occupational health department and trigger points. This meant that 'once an employee had more than seven cumulative days' sickness absence in any rolling period, then an enhanced sickness management procedure kicks in. And if sickness absence exceeds 20 days in any one episode, then long-term sickness management procedure applies. Further, when more than eight days of sickness have been recorded over the rolling 365-day period the employee's manager will refer the employee to the council's in-house occupational health service.'

The occupational health strategy

While the numbers of accidents in the workplace has dropped steadily, there is now a focus on achieving the same effect for work-related illness. In 2000 one of the priorities of the HSE was to improve this situation and an Occupational Health Strategy was devised to:

1 Stop people from becoming ill because of work.
2 Help those who are absent due to long-term illness to get back into work.
3 Improve work opportunities for those who are not currently in employment because of their ill-health or disability.
4 Use the workplace to encourage people to maintain or improve their health.

This approach is based once again on the idea of partnership between Government, the HSE and employers, workers and trade unions. Targets were set to inspire action and five key programmes were started to complement other Government initiatives, such as the Welfare to Work schemes. The five programmes of work which were established were about:

1 compliance
2 continuous improvement
3 knowledge
4 skills
5 support.

Targets were also set and it is hoped that all interested parties will be involved in working towards their achievement. It is hoped that by 2010 the following targets will be achieved:

- A 20 per cent reduction in the incidence of work-related ill-health.
- A 20 per cent reduction in the ill-health of members of the public that has been caused by work activity.
- A 30 per cent reduction in the numbers of days absence caused by work-related ill-health.
- All who are employed but who are unable to work because of their ill-health or disability should be made aware of opportunities for speedy rehabilitation back into work.
- Everyone who is not employed because of their ill-health or disability should be offered opportunities to prepare for and find work.

It has been estimated that if just three of these targets are achieved, the value to the UK could be huge and worth somewhere between £8.6 and £21.8 billion, although it is obviously very difficult to calculate such figures with any degree of accuracy.

A Partnership Board was established, not only to oversee the implementation and delivery of the strategy but also as a way of drawing on ideas from a range of interested parties. The roles of the Partnership Board are to:

- be strategic
- act as a champion
- use contacts to network and solve problems
- review progress overall
- make sure that sound management practices, such as evaluation, are fully used
- provide regular reports on progress to the HSC.

Failure to take steps to reduce risks in the workplace is likely in the future to lead to higher insurance payments for organisations as insurance companies start to link premiums to the way that organisations manage risks of accidents and ill-health. Smokers generally suffer worse health than non-smokers and the charity Action on Smoking and Health (ASH) claims that 34 million working days are lost in Britain each year, just because of smoking. Some employers are becoming more proactive about their employees' health and are introducing measures such as bonuses to encourage smokers to quit. These can, however, prove controversial as non-smokers may then also want to benefit from bonuses.

International issues in health and safety

Although British health and safety legislation does not apply to workers based outside Britain, employers still have a duty of care towards their employees, no matter where they work. Employees who operate in a global scene need additional knowledge relating to the particular country in which they are working, and this also applies to health and safety. The HR departments in those organisations need to check on health and safety legislation in the countries concerned, and should also carry out a risk assessment of not only the job but also the country, and should evaluate the employee's health. This would help ensure, for example, that they are not sending an asthmatic employee into a very dusty desert environment that would probably make the employee's health worse.

There are also social and ethical responsibilities that large organisations need to take into account when some of their products such as clothing or food is being produced in third world countries for them. Although they produce goods at cheap prices for those in the developed world, this is often at the expense of the workers in that country, by paying people poorly and by allowing them to work in poor health or safety conditions that would not be tolerated in the UK.

Even within Europe we have seen that individual countries can interpret European directives in different ways so the actual health and safety legislation in countries may vary. Attitudes to safety can be different and vary from one culture to another. In cultures where people tend to sue for damages, such as America, people are used to having lots of rules even when they are relaxing, away from work, so on beaches they only swim in the designated areas and obey the lifeguards. In the Greek islands, tourists would seek their own sheltered cove and swim from their own secluded beach so would have to take more responsibility for their own safety. Such differences in cultural expectations do shape attitudes to health and safety, so it is important to take into account the culture of the country and consider this in relation to health and safety. When Disney first opened in Paris some of the instructions on rides such as the requirement 'to exit the ride using your left foot first' jarred a little with Europeans who were used to making such decisions for themselves!

Some employees are sent to work in countries which may be regarded as high risk and where dangers such as kidnapping could occur. Staff need to be briefed as to precautions to take in these countries, as do the local staff, who may actually be more at risk than the ex-pat staff, who probably live in a secure compound and have a driver to transport them safely. Some groups such as humanitarian aid workers are also likely to be at risk, since the nature of their jobs ensure that they are likely to be working in high-risk areas. However, they should still not be exposed to unnecessary risks.

HR departments who have staff working in potentially high-risk countries should carry out risk assessments, relating both to the dangers to health and to potential threats to safety, and should devise suitable emergency plans which can be put in place quickly. They should also devise suitable training programmes, perhaps drawing on local knowledge and expertise, for people undertaking these jobs. The workforce could even be involved in analysing the hazards and designing their own security plans for the compounds in which they live. Training in potential high-risk countries is likely to cover specific issues such as personal safety, office security, compound security, threats to convoys, risk analysis, first aid and emergency evacuation plans.

If this is done the workers are likely to feel and be safer and since health and safety will be perceived as being important, it is likely that they will take more care themselves. Measures such as these can do a great deal to eliminate unnecessary risks, although it is impossible to eliminate all risks completely.

Did you know?

In response to the killings of three UN workers in West Timor on 6 September 2000, humanitarian workers from around the world marched in protest for better protection. They sent a petition to the UN headquarters demanding 'greater pressure from the UN on national governments to guarantee the safety of humanitarian workers, together with internal measures addressing management accountability, risk assessment and more funding for security provision'.

(*Source*: Hammond, D., 2001)

Conclusion

We said at the beginning of this chapter that it is not enough for employers just to be concerned about preventing accidents in order to comply with legislation, although that in itself is a good start. We have shown in this chapter that there has been a change of approach within the law, from mere compliance with minimum legal requirements in the legislation prior to HASAWA to the encouragement of increased involvement of all, and from compliance with legal requirements 'so far as it is reasonably practicable' under HASAWA to placing the duty on managers that they must introduce management systems, implement these systems and monitor the effectiveness of them.

Although the newer legislation is more forceful and hence more prescriptive, in some respects it is more in tune with the human resource management approach, since there is an emphasis on the need for managers to manage, on the development of strategies, procedures and systems for improving health and safety, as well as on a need for monitoring the implementation of these systems. This approach to health and safety should link with the overall business objectives of maximising efficiency and effectiveness by improving morale and reducing costs, and also allows for some scope for individuality and flexibility in how this is to be achieved. It is the approach to health and safety that we would advocate, and it is a very different approach to the purely legalistic one of just being concerned with not breaking the law. This approach to health and safety involves the following features:

- The need to create a culture in which health and safety are seen to be important to the organisation. The safety policy statement will contribute to this if it is effectively written, known about and acted upon. The legal requirements must be complied with and risk assessments carried out, as well as gathering information about health and safety and carrying out a cost–benefit analysis. If there is to be a culture of health and safety awareness, there also need to be campaigns and publicity, and involvement of top management, individuals and teams. There needs to be regular communications and discussion of health and safety and the contribution that improvements will make to the organisation's overall effectiveness, so that all members of the organisation realise that health and safety are important to the way it operates.
- Commitment from the top to the achievement of progressively higher standards as expressed in the mission statement and safety policy. Top management must not only sign the policy documents but also set a good example in relation to health and safety, and emphasise that it is an area of importance to them and to the future of the organisation by showing their interest and by setting up new systems and monitoring the effectiveness of these systems.
- Commitment throughout the organisation, with all parties clear about their own responsibilities for health and safety, the targets they have to meet and the contribution these make to the organisation's objectives. This should be considered as an aspect of performance management, as individuals and teams would be encouraged to take responsibility for their own actions and to agree and work towards targets when making improvements.
- Managers to demonstrate by their example their commitment to the importance of a safer and healthier work environment. They should also find ways to motivate everyone to make a contribution to health and safety improvements. Prizes and awards to individuals and teams can have an important effect.
- Policies and procedures designed to take account of the importance of a safer and healthier environment. There should also be effective systems to monitor their effectiveness.
- Policies to be backed by adequate resources for equipment and training. Provision of good health and safety costs money but the cost of not providing these can be higher, as any cost–benefit analysis is likely to prove.
- The setting of realistic and attainable targets for everyone in the organisation.
- Encouragement of all to take responsibility for their own actions and involvement of all in health and safety.

The approach of the HSE to revitalising health and safety also reinforces these points. They encourage employers to become aware of health and safety issues by emphasising the business case for health and safety. They also encourage managers to be proactive about managing both the health and safety of their workforce. National targets have been set as part of the process to reduce both the number of accidents and the number of days of sickness absence. Involvement and partnership are both approaches which are strongly encouraged and these methods are typical of the HRM approach.

REVIEW QUESTIONS

1 Interview people (friends, family or work colleagues from a range of organisations) about their own responsibilities in relation to health and safety and then about their perceptions of other people's roles in their particular organisation. Try to establish how the roles relating to health and safety differ for managers, other employees, human resource managers, safety officers, safety representatives and someone designated to be a 'competent person'. Are these roles the same in different types of organisation? How do they compare with what we said earlier in the chapter about these roles?

2 Obtain a copy of the safety policy for either your college or your workplace.
   (a) Use this to identify the roles of various people in the organisation in relation to health and safety.
   (b) Use the safety policy to assess whether health and safety are linked to the organisation's strategic objectives.

3 Design a checklist for carrying out a safety inspection in the workplace. Use your checklist to actually carry out an inspection of a designated area either at work or in your college. Write a report about your findings for the safety officer.

4 Write a short report in which you assess the impact of one piece of health and safety legislation on an organisation of your choice.

5 Prepare arguments and then debate the following statements in two teams. Try to persuade the members of the other team to your point of view.

   TEAM A: There is much too much legislation regarding health and safety at work and this is unnecessary as it is in the employers' interests to look after their employees. Legislation merely hinders employers in their ability to run their businesses effectively.
   TEAM B: Legislation is necessary to control employers who would otherwise ignore health and safety issues at the expense of their employees' health, safety and welfare.

SELF-CHECK QUESTIONS

Answer the following multiple-choice and short-answer questions. The correct responses are given on pages 478–479 for you to check your understanding of this chapter.

1 Which of the following was the first piece of legislation designed to protect every-one at work, and also to protect others who were not at work, such as customers or passers-by?
   (a) the Factories Act 1961
   (b) the Offices, Shops and Railways Premises Act 1963
   (c) the Fire Precautions Act 1971

(d) the Health and Safety at Work Act 1974

(e) the Control of Substances Hazardous to Health Regulations 1988.

2 Which of the following pieces of legislation established the Health and Safety Commission?

(a) the Factories Act 1961

(b) the Offices, Shops and Railways Premises Act 1963

(c) the Fire Precautions Act 1971

(d) the Health and Safety at Work Act 1974

(e) the Control of Substances Hazardous to Health Regulations 1988.

3 An improvement notice is issued when:

(a) something is found to be so dangerous that the factory inspectorate feels it necessary to stop work immediately

(b) improvements are required by the factory inspectorate but the employer can decide when these should take place

(c) improvements are required by the factory inspectorate within a specified period to bring the equipment or process up to the required standard

(d) the required improvement has been made by the employer

(e) improvements are required by the safety committee to be made within a specified period.

4 The term 'so far as it is reasonably practicable to do so' means:

(a) that employers must do everything in their power to make the workplace safe

(b) that employers may weigh up the costs of a safety improvement against the risks when deciding whether to make the improvement

(c) that employers must assess the risks of substances used and identify the required precautions to be taken

(d) that employers have a legal duty to predict what may go wrong before it happens

(e) that employers should be proactive and actively manage health and safety issues.

5 The Management of Health and Safety at Work Regulations contain the following legal requirement:

(a) that employers must do the best that they can to make the workplace safe

(b) that employers may weigh up the costs of a safety improvement against the risks when deciding whether to make a safety improvement

(c) that employers must assess the risks of any substances used by employees and identify the required precautions to be taken

(d) that employers should carry out an assessment of health and safety risks to both employees and the public

(e) that employers should carry out an assessment of health and safety risks for their employees only.

6 The term 'six-pack' refers to the following six pieces of legislation:

(a) the Factories Act 1961, the Offices Shops and Railways Premises Act 1963, the Fire Precautions Act 1971, the Health and Safety at Work Act 1974, the Control of Substances Hazardous to Health Regulations 1988, the Manual Handling Operations Regulations 1992

(b) the Factories Act 1961, the Offices Shops and Railways Premises Act 1963, the Fire Precautions Act 1971, the Health and Safety at Work Act 1974, the Control of Substances Hazardous to Health Regulations 1988, the Management of Health and Safety at Work Regulations 1992

→

(c) the Factories Act 1961, the Health and Safety at Work Act 1974, the Control of Substances Hazardous to Health Regulations 1988, the Management of Health and Safety at Work Regulations 1992, Workplace (Health, Safety and Welfare) Regulations 1992, Provision and Use of Work Equipment Regulations 1992

(d) Management of Health and Safety at Work Regulations 1992, Workplace (Health, Safety and Welfare) Regulations 1992, Provision and Use of Work Equipment Regulations 1992, Personal Protective Equipment at Work Regulations 1992, Health and Safety (Display Screen Equipment) Regulations 1992, Manual Handling Operations Regulations 1992

(e) the Health and Safety at Work Act 1974, the Control of Substances Hazardous to Health Regulations 1988, Management of Health and Safety at Work Regulations 1992, Workplace (Health, Safety and Welfare) Regulations 1992, Provision and Use of Work Equipment Regulations 1992, Personal Protective Equipment at Work Regulations 1992.

Refer back to Case study 12.1 (page 385) and answer the following questions.

7 Describe what the role of the safety committee should have been within the Sheffley Company.

8 Imagine that you are a consultant brought in to advise about health and safety at the Sheffley Company. Write a report to the director in which you outline the improvements that should be made in health and safety at Sheffley, and recommend how these improvements should be introduced.

HR IN THE NEWS   FT

Health and safety red tape

Government attempts to reduce the burden of health and safety legislation are having little effect, according to the Federation of Small Businesses.

Almost three-quarters of small companies surveyed by the FSB said the administrative requirements of health and safety legislation were more bureaucratic than five years ago.

A separate FSB report claimed that small companies on average spent seven hours a week dealing with red tape.

The study is part of a federation campaign to push the UK government and the European Commission to deliver on their promises to reduce the regulatory burden.

Tina Sommer, EU affairs chairman for the FSB, said: 'There is no doubt that the volume and complexity of red tape is excessive. Shorter, simpler regulations will enable businesses to follow the rules more easily as well as protect their existing employees.'

(*Financial Times*, 6 October 2007. Reproduced with permission.)

Union hits at labour safety stance

By Andrew Taylor

Failure to introduce tougher laws to punish company directors who do not follow safety rules has cost workers' lives, according to a union report that criticises the 'voluntary approach' adopted by the Health and Safety Executive.

The report by UCATT, the construction union, coincides with voluntary guidance notes for directors due to be published on Monday by the HSE and the Institute of Directors.

The safety body, which is due later this week to publish national injury figures, has reported an 11 per cent rise in the number of employees killed at work during the 12 months to the end of April.

Ministers rejected union calls to make directors personally liable for safety breaches when the corporate manslaughter and homicide bill was passed in July.

Monday's report, commissioned by UCATT from the Centre for Corporate Accountability, says the HSE had revealed that only 44 per cent of companies had appointed a director responsible for safety since it introduced its voluntary guidelines in 2001.

The union's report finds that accident levels fell by 25 per cent on average at companies that had taken 'positive action at director level regarding health and safety'.

Alan Ritchie, UCATT general secretary, said: 'This damning report demonstrates the government's failure to introduce statutory legal duties forcing directors to take responsibility for their companies' health and safety policies is literally costing workers their lives.'

The Health and Safety Commission, which oversees the HSE, reported earlier this summer that 241 lives had been lost at work during the 12 months to the end of April. This compared with a record low of 217 deaths the previous year.

UCATT said the results were particularly poor in the construction industry, where 347 workers had been killed between 2002–03 and 2006–07. Only 13 directors or senior managers had been prosecuted for health and safety breaches during that period, it added.

Judith Hackitt, of the Health and Safety Commission, recognised that some groups 'believe that the approach we are currently taking is by no means strong enough' but said the corporate manslaughter bill would 'make it easier to prosecute companies'.

Miles Templeman, director general of the IoD, said it was 'vital that board members should lead the approach of their organisation to health and safety'.

(FT.com, 29 October 2007. Reproduced with permission.)

Question

1 These two articles show very different attitudes to health and safety. To what extent do you agree with either of these articles? Do you think that there is too much red tape regarding health and safety or that there is too little protection for workers? List the arguments for and against your point of view.

WHAT NEXT?

Do you remember the balanced scorecard that we discussed in Chapter 1? Research conducted by Aberdeen University on 13 offshore oil installations applies the balanced scorecard to occupational health. The article also discusses the results of interviews with UK and Norwegian managers on health and safety performance indicators and the reasons for including occupational health and safety as one measure of performance within the balanced scorecard. What do you think about the idea that measures of occupational health should be included in an assessment of an organisation's performance?

Mearns, K. and J.I. Havold (2003) Occupational health and safety and the balanced scorecard, *The TQM Magazine,* Vol. 15, No. 6, 408–423.

References

Advisory, Conciliation and Arbitration Service (2004) Discipline and Grievances at Work, *The ACAS Advisory Handbook,* ACAS.

Baker, J. (2007) Net closes on corporate killing, *People Management,* Vol. 13, No. 5, 8 March, 22.

Cacanas, Z. (2004) *The Guardian,* 24 July.

Chartered Institute of Personnel and Development (2006) *Occupational Health and Organisational Effectiveness,* CIPD (available at www.cipd.co.uk; accessed 10.09.07).

Chartered Institute of Personnel and Development (2007a) *DWP work-health review launched,* CIPD (www.cipd.co.uk/news; accessed on 17.04.07).

Chartered Institute of Personnel and Development and Health and Safety Executive (2007b) *Managing stress at work: a competency framework for line managers,* CIPD (www.cipd.co.uk/subjects/health/stress/_Instrwkcmptn.htm; accessed 10.09.07).

Chartered Institute of Personnel and Development (2007c) *Gangmaster legislation should be extended,* CIPD, 31 July (www.cipd.co.uk/news/_articles/gangmasterlegislationshouldbe extended.htm; accessed 10.09.07).

Department for the Environment, Transport and the Regions (2000) *Revitalising Health and Safety: Strategy Statement June 2000,* DETR (www.hse.gov.uk/revitalising/strategy.pdf; accessed 10.09.07).

Eagle, M. (2007) *Justice for Corporate Deaths: Royal Assent for Corporate Manslaughter and Corporate Homicide Act* (www.justice.gov.uk/news/newsrelease260707b.htm; accessed 10.09.07).

Engineering Employers' Federation (2001) *Managing Stress at Work,* EEF.

Fowler, A. (1994) Personnel's model army, *Personnel Management,* September, 34–3.

Hammond, D. (2001) Dangerous liaisons, *People Management,* 30 May, 26–7.

Hayden-Smith, J. and R. Simms (2003) Pressure points, *People Management,* 25 September, 17.

Health and Safety Commission (2000) *Revitalising Health and Safety: Strategy Statement,* HSE.

Health and Safety Commission (2001) *Strategic Plan 2001–4,* HSE (www.hse.gov.uk/aboutus/plans/hscplans/plan0104-07.htm; accessed 10.09.07).

Health and Safety Commission (2002) *Enforcement Policy Statement,* HSE (www.hse.gov.uk/pubns/hsc15.pdf; accessed 10.09.07).

Health and Safety Commission (2004a) *Accident Costs: Work Out Yours, Revitalising Health and Safety,* HSE (www.hse.gov.uk/costs/accidentcost_calc/accident_costs_intro.asp; accessed 10.09.07).

Health and Safety Executive (1995) *Be Safe: Save Money. The Costs of Accidents: A Guide for Small Firms,* HSE Books, 4.

Health and Safety Executive (2003) *Stating Your Business. Guidance on Preparing a Health and Safety Policy Document for Small Firms,* HSE, INDG 324 (available at www.hse.gov.uk; accessed 20.07.04).

Health and Safety Executive (2004) *A Strategy for Workplace Health and Safety in Great Britain to 2010 and Beyond,* HSE.

Health and Safety Executive (2005) *Tackling Stress: The Management Standards Approach* (available at www.hse.gov.uk/pubns/indg406.htm; accessed 10.09.07).

Health and Safety Executive (2006a) *HSE Statistics,* HSE (available at www.hse.gov.uk/statistics; accessed 10.09.07).

Health and Safety Executive (2006b) *Five Steps to Risk Assessment,* HSE, INDG 163 rev. 2 (available at www.hse.gov.uk/pubns/indg163.htm; accessed 10.09.07).

Health and Safety Executive (2006c) *HSE Statistic: Occupational Health Bulletin 2005/6,* HSE (available at www.hse.gov.uk/statistics/overall/ohsb0506.htm; accessed 10.09.07).

Health and Safety Executive (2007) *Statistics: Stress-related and psychological disorders,* HSE (available at www.hse.gov.uk/causdis/stress.htm; accessed 10.09.07).

Holmes, T.H. and R.H. Rahe (1967) The social readjustment rating scale, *Journal of Psychosomatic Research,* August, 216.

Incomes Data Services (2002) *IDS Studies Plus: Employee Assistance Programmes,* IDS.

Incomes Data Services (2004) *IDS HR Studies 775: Managing Stress,* IDS.

Inland Revenue Service Employment Review (2007a) *Employee assistance programmes: the IRS report,* IRS 874, 04.06.07.

Inland Revenue Service Employment Review (2007b) *Westminster City council's successful absence management procedure,* IRS 877, 16.07.07.

International Stress Management Association UK (2004) *Working together to reduce stress at work,* International Stress Management Association UK.

Johnson, R. (2001) Security counsel, *People Management,* Vol. 7, No. 11, 31 May.

Jones, R. (2007) Manslaughter Act doesn't go far enough, *Personnel Today,* 6 March.

Le Fevre, M., J. Matheny and G.S. Kolt (2003) Eustress, distress, and interpretation in occupational stress, *Journal of Managerial Psychology,* Vol. 18, No. 7, 726–744.

Maslow, A. (1954) *Motivation and Personality,* 2nd edition, Harper & Row.

Midgley, S. (1997) Pressure points, *People Management,* 10 July, 36–39.

Ministry of Justice (2007) Justice for Corporate Deaths: Royal Assent for Corporate Manslaughter and Corporate Homicide Act, Ministry of Justice (www.justice.gov.uk/news/newsrelease260707b.htm; accessed 12.09.07).

Morris, D. (2001) How to draw up a health and safety policy, *People Management,* Vol. 7, No. 10, 17 May.

Nishiyama, K. and J. Johnson (1997) *Karoshi – Death from Overwork: Occupational Health Consequences of the Japanese Production Management,* 6th Draft for International Journal of Health Services, 4 February (available at www.workhealth.org/whatsnew/lpkarosh.html; accessed 10.09.07).

Quinn, J. (2004) Dodging the draft, *People Management,* 30 June, 17.

Sample, I. (2007) Stressful Jobs Double the Risk of Depression for Young Workers, *The Guardian,* 2 August, 10.

Selye, H. (1956) *The Stress of Life,* McGraw-Hill.

Selye, H. (1974) *Stress without Distress,* Lippincott.

Seenan, G. (2004) No frills – and no travelling toilet class, *The Guardian,* 24 July.

Stranks, J. (2007) The Health and Safety Handbook: a practical guide to health and safety law, management policies and procedures, Kogan Page.

Venning, N. (1995) Taking the bull by the horns, *Guardian Careers Section,* 15 April, 2–3.

XpertHR (2004) *How to comply with general health and safety duties,* XpertHR, 03.09.2004 (www.xperthr.co.uk; accessed 29.07.07).

XpertHR (2006) *How to manage workers' statutory entitlement to paid holiday leave,* XpertHR, 16.03.2006 (www.xperthr.co.uk; accessed 29.07.07).

Further study

Books

Advisory, Conciliation and Arbitration Service (2003) *Health and Employment,* ACAS. This booklet focuses on measures that employers can take to help promote good health in their workforce.

Stranks, J. (2006) *The Health and Safety handbook,* Kogan Page. A book and a CD which give clear practical guidance for managers and others who are interested in health and safety.

Stranks, J. (2007) *Human factors and behavioural safety,* Butterworth-Heinemann. This book examines factors such as human behaviour and human error and their impact on safety.

Articles

HSE publications exist on a wide range of topics, too numerous to include here, from general books to detailed explanations of legislation. Some of its leaflets are also available on the web page listed at the end of this chapter.

Internet

Control Risks Group	**www.crg.com**
Employment Conditions Abroad	**www.eca-international.com**
The Health and Safety Executive	**www.hse.gov.uk**
The International Labour Organization's report on teleworking which includes	
health and safety issues	**www.ilo.org/safework/telework**
The Job Stress Network	**www.workhealth.org**

Site with articles about many work and health issues including stress and *karoshi.*

RIDDOR   **www.riddor.gov.uk**

The site gives information about RIDDOR and has forms which can be downloaded to report accidents and dangerous occurrences, or these can now be reported directly online.

XpertHR   **www.xperthr.co.uk**

An excellent source of articles from various publications.

Where next? The future of work

CHAPTER (34)

THE FUTURE OF WORK

THE OBJECTIVES OF THIS CHAPTER ARE TO:

1   Outline the likely demand for skills in the UK over the next twenty years

2   Introduce the debate about whether the workforce will need to upskill or downskill in the future

3   Set out the major demographic trends in the UK and their consequences for the supply of skills

4   Discuss the major consequences for HR practices arising from a changing workforce profile

5   Debate the merits of the argument that traditional employment practices will change radically in the future in response to environmental trends

6   Put the case for focusing on labour market and regulatory developments as well as developments in product markets when considering the future of work

In a business world that is increasingly seen as being subject to instability and change, managers are right to be interested in likely future developments so that they can prepare effectively and, hopefully, keep one step ahead of their competitors. Business history is littered with examples of big, powerful corporations that have failed to survive because they did not adapt fast enough in the face of unstoppable developments in technology, changes in customer demand or the innovations of competitors. In a global economy governments are also right to be interested in the same developments so that they can put in place measures which will give their organisations the best chance of competing effectively internationally. The trouble is, as Mark Twain famously wrote, 'prediction is difficult, especially when predictions relate to the future'. People have very different ideas about the ways in which our business environment will evolve in future decades, and they can't all be right.

Differences of opinion about the likely future of working life are particularly diverse. On the one hand there is a highly influential school of thought associated (in the UK) with the work of writers such as Charles Handy and Susan Greenfield which predicts a radically different future for work in western industrialised countries. Not only will the nature of the work people do be different from that done by most workers today, the radical view foresees a future in which the very idea of the 'job' will become increasingly outdated. Forms of self-employment and subcontracting will be the norm, as 'knowledge workers' pursue 'portfolio careers', moving from assignment to assignment and retraining regularly in order to make a living. Others agree that the future of work will develop in important ways, but reject the idea that we are heading quickly and inexorably towards radically different working lives. They expect to witness evolution rather than revolution as current trends continue steadily to adjust expectations about work and the demand for and supply of workers. This is the main message that has come out of many recent studies carried out under the auspices of the ESRC's Future of Work research programme (*see* Nolan 2004 and Taylor 2002). A third view stresses the significance of the changes we have witnessed in the past twenty or thirty years and predicts a future for work which, by contrast, is rather more stable than we have become used to. Instead of further transformation, the tendency will be for earlier changes, such as the move from a mixed to a market economy, the feminisation of the workforce, the rise of the service sector, globalisation of business activity, and the rise of employment law, to bed in as western countries enjoy a period of relative economic stability by the standards of recent history. According to this view, the future of work has to a considerable degree 'already happened'. We now need to adjust more fully to the consequences of developments which are clearly permanent and not temporary.

THE FUTURE DEMAND FOR WORKERS

If current trends are maintained we can expect to see continued increases, year on year, in the number of jobs being created by British organisations. In 2006 there were 37.1 million people of working age in the UK, of whom 30.8 million were in work. Around 1.5 million were unemployed and actively seeking work, while a further 7.9 million people of working age were defined as being 'economically inactive' (ONS 2006a). The total number of jobs has grown steadily in recent years to reach its current peak of 26.7 million. The figure decreased during the recessions of the early 1980s and early 1990s, but the long-term trend has been upwards for over sixty years.

Importantly, this increase in the amount of employment in the UK has occurred at a time when many major industries have seen the introduction of labour-saving technologies and when millions of jobs have effectively been 'exported' to developing countries where labour costs are much cheaper. Major industrial restructuring has occurred, yet the demand for labour over the long term has increased steadily. Provided the economy continues to grow, we can thus expect to see further increased demand for people on the part of employers over the coming decade.

But what sort of skills will employers be looking for? Here too long-term trends paint a clear picture which there is every reason to believe will continue for the foreseeable future. The official method used to classify occupations in the UK was changed in 1999, so it is not possible to make a precise comparison of today's figures with those produced by government statisticians before then. Nonetheless an obvious long-term pattern can be seen in the two sets of statistics presented in Tables 34.1 and 34.2. These show a pronounced switch occurring over a long period of time, and continuing strongly in more recent years, away from skilled, semi-skilled and unskilled manual work towards jobs which require higher-level and more specialised skills. The major growth areas have long been in the professional, technical and managerial occupations.

The change in the occupational profile of the UK workforce has largely been driven by the revolutionary shift that has occurred in the nature of our industries during the past thirty years. In 1978, which was the first year that data was collected on employment by sector, seven million people worked in manufacturing and a further one and a half million in the energy, water, farming and fishing industries. These have all hugely declined since then. Manufacturing now employs only three million (12 per cent of all jobs). Agriculture

Table 34.1 Changes in occupations, 1951–1999

Occupation	% in 1951	% in 1999
Higher professionals	1.9	6.4
Lower professionals	4.7	14.9
Employers and proprietors	5.0	3.4
Managers and administrators	5.5	15.7
Clerks	10.7	14.9
Foremen, supervisors and inspectors	2.6	3.1
Skilled manual	24.9	12.7
Semi-skilled manual	31.5	23.0
Unskilled manual	13.1	5.9

Source: *Labour Force Survey* statistics accessed at **www.statistics.gov.uk**.

Table 34.2 Changes in occupations, 2001–2006

Occupation	% in 2001	% in 2006
Managers and senior officials	12.9	14.7
Professional occupations	11.7	12.7
Associate professional and technical occupations	13.2	14.2
Administrative and secretarial	14.9	13.5
Skilled trades	9.5	8.4
Personal services	7.5	8.3
Sales and customer services	8.6	8.6
Process, plant and machine operatives	8.7	7.4
Elementary occupations	13.2	12.1

Source: *Labour Force Survey* statistics accessed at **www.statistics.gov.uk**.

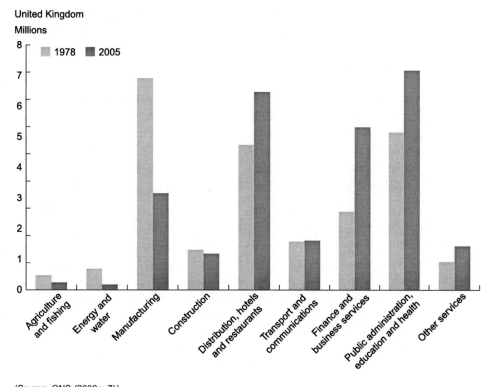

Figure 34.1
Employee jobs:
by industry,
1978 (Quarter
2) and 2005
(Quarter 2)

(Source: ONS (2006a: 7))

and fishing account for just 200,000 jobs; energy and water for fewer still (*see* Figure 34.1). The big growth areas have been in retailing, distribution, hotels and restaurants, finance, business services, public administration, education and health. Employment in the financial services sector has grown especially quickly, more than doubling since 1978.

In the most recent years the biggest growth areas in terms of jobs have been in the public sector. Public sector employment fell during the 1990s. Having peaked at 5.9 million in 1991, it reached a 'low point' of 5.1 million in 1998 before climbing back to 5.9 million again. Over 300,000 new jobs have been created in the NHS since 1998 and over 200,000 in education. The expansion of local and central government has led to the creation of 128,000 jobs, a further 45,000 being created in the police service (ONS 2006a, p. 26). Another major employment trend since the 1970s has been a substantial growth in the proportion of people working in small businesses. The small firms sector now employs 55 per cent of the UK workforce.

ACTIVITY 34.1

Why do you think countries such as the UK have seen so great a transformation in their industrial structure since the 1970s? Why are there so many fewer manufacturing jobs and so many more jobs in the service sector? Why are organisations so much more likely to employ small numbers of people than was the case fifty years ago?

One of the most vigorously contested debates among labour market economists concerns the nature of the skills that employers will be looking for in the future, a debate that has very important implications for government education policy, which, as a result, is itself controversial (*see* Grugulis *et al.* 2004). In recent years a highly influential group has argued that in the future economies such as the UK's will see a speeding up of the trends identified above. Influenced by figures such as Manuel Castells of Berkeley University in California, it has become common for policymakers to believe that a 'new economy' is rapidly developing which will increasingly be dominated by companies which are 'knowledge-intensive' in nature. According to this 'upskilling thesis', lower-skilled jobs will be rarer and rarer in industrialised countries. Because they can be done far more cheaply in developing economies, they will increasingly be exported overseas.

It follows that the governments such as the UK's should prepare the workforce as best it can for the challenges of a 'high-skill, high-wage economy' in which those who do not have a relevant higher education are going to struggle to make a living. Hence we see the rapid expansion of universities, heavy investment in schools and the provision of all manner of schemes designed to equip unemployed people with new skills.

Critics of Castells tend to look to the writings of a very different American academic guru figure – Harry Braverman. His theories derive from a Marxian perspective as well as from observations of the activities of corporations in the 1960s and 1970s. This contrasting 'deskilling thesis' argues that businesses competing in capitalist economies will always look for ways of cutting their labour costs, and that they do this in part by continually reducing the level of skills required by the people they employ. It follows that, far from leading to a demand for higher-level skills and knowledge, the advent of an economy based on information and communication technologies will *over time* reduce such demand.

Both schools draw on widely documented trends to back up their positions. The upskillers draw attention to the fact that the major growth areas in labour demand are in the higher-skilled occupational categories. Demand for graduates is increasing, demand for lower-skilled people is less strong, and is decreasing in some industries. They also draw attention to the emergence of skills shortages in many industries as employers find it steadily harder to recruit people with the abilities and experience they need.

By contrast, the downskillers draw attention to the growth of call-centre-type operations which use technology to reduce the amount of knowledge and expertise required by customer services staff, and to the increasing use of bureaucratic systems which reduce the number of situations in which people have a discretion to make decisions. They also point to the strong growth in industries such as retailing and hotels which are characterised by employment of people who need only be low skilled and who are relatively low paid. They thus forecast a situation in which the workforce is heavily overqualified and in which graduates are increasingly employed in jobs for which no degree is necessary. They also argue that many of the 'skills' that employers say are in short supply are not in fact 'skills' at all, but are merely 'attributes' or 'characteristics'. The target here is an evolving business language that refers to 'communication skills', 'interpersonal skills', 'teamworking skills', 'problem-solving skills' and 'customer-handling skills'. These, it is argued, have nothing whatever to do with a knowledge-based economy and cannot be gained through formal education.

As with all debates that concern the likely future direction of society, it is difficult to reach firm conclusions about this debate. However, in truth what appears to be happening is that we are seeing the emergence of an 'hourglass' occupational structure in the UK in which half of the jobs are of the 'high-skill/high-pay' variety, and the other half are 'low skill/low pay' (Grugulis *et al*. 2004: 6). The metaphor of the hourglass was originally advanced by Nolan (2001). But it has been popularised and expanded in the highly influential article by Goos and Manning (2003) entitled 'McJobs and Macjobs: the growing polarisation of jobs in the UK'. What seems to be happening is the following:

- Increasing numbers of people are being employed in relatively highly paid, secure, professional and managerial occupations in the finance, private services and public sectors.

- Lower-skilled jobs in manufacturing along with many lower-paid clerical and administrative roles are being 'exported' to countries in Eastern Europe and South East Asia where cheaper labour is readily available.

- But, at the same time, the growing number of higher-paid people are using their disposable income to purchase services which cannot be provided from overseas. Hence there is a simultaneous and rapid growth in demand for hairdressers, beauticians, restaurant workers, and people to work in the media, tourist and entertainment-oriented industries.

- There also remains a great demand for, and shortage of, some groups of skilled workers – plumbers, builders, decorators, etc., whose jobs also, by their nature, cannot be so easily exported.

For the foreseeable future, therefore, we are likely to see growth in demand *both* for people who have gained a higher education or who have specialised higher-level skills *and* for people who have strong interpersonal skills (or attributes) to work in the expanding personal services sector. From a public policy point of view, this means that government is broadly correct to put more investment into higher education, but that it is equally important to make available high-quality, specialised forms of vocational education so that the future needs of all industrial sectors are properly provided for. This latter area is one in which the UK has been conspicuously weaker than other European countries for many years.

WINDOW ON PRACTICE

In 2006 the Confederation of British Industry (CBI) published a survey of employers which revealed a lack of basic educational skills among new recruits. According to respondents the big problem in the UK is a lack of basic numerical skills among school leavers, but good reading and writing skills are also in short supply. The problem extends to graduate recruits too. The survey suggests that 23 per cent of employers are unhappy with levels of literacy among their graduates and that 13 per cent are concerned about numeracy levels. The response, according to the CBI, is for one in three employers to provide remedial tuition in reading, writing and arithmetic.

Source: M. Green (2006) 'Employers alarmed at skills shortage', *Financial Times*, 21 August.

THE FUTURE SUPPLY OF WORKERS

The UK population currently stands at 59.8 million. This accounts for 13 per cent of the European Union population, eight per cent of the total European population and just under one per cent of the world's total population. Unlike that of most European countries, the UK population is currently growing (Jeffries 2005). This is for two reasons:

1 Birth rates currently exceed death rates. Each year approximately 700,000 babies are born in the UK, while 615,000 people die – a net gain of 85,000 people.

2 Each year it is estimated that around 150,000 more people migrate into the country than emigrate out of it. Total immigration is now in excess of half a million a year.

The population is therefore growing at a rate of nearly a quarter of a million people each year (ONS 2006b). Official estimates state that the total UK population will reach 65 million by 2050, but this figure will be reached a good deal sooner if current levels of immigration continue. This upward trend in the UK population represents a reversal of the position in the in the 1970s and early 1980s – a period of substantial net emigration and relatively low birth rates.

The birth rate increased substantially after the Second World War and continued at relatively high levels until the late 1960s. Over a million babies were born at the peak in 1964. This created the large 'baby boom' generation who are now in their forties and fifties. From 1964 onwards the UK saw a sharp decline in its birth rate, which reached a low point in 1977 when only 657,000 babies were born (i.e. fewer than the number of deaths). This was due in part to the relatively low number of births in the country in the war years (1939–45), in part to the wide availability of the contraceptive pill and abortion, and partly to changes in social attitudes leading to later marriages. The downward trend was reversed somewhat in the 1980s as the baby boomers had children, but fertility rates remain at relatively low levels historically. As a result of these patterns, we have an ageing population. There are many more people in the UK in their forties and fifties than there are in their twenties and thirties (*see* Figure 34.2).

ACTIVITY 34.2

Why do you think that people, on average, choose to have fewer children than they did a generation ago? Can anything be done to reverse the trend? How far should governments see it as their role to encourage more births?

This will mean that there are many more retired people in the future than there are at present, but at the same time the number of adults of working age is projected to increase rather than decrease. Official estimates state that there will be 40.5 million people who are over school leaving age and below retirement age in 2020 as a result of continued net immigration and the equalisation of male and female state pension ages at 65 from 2010. The average age of this group will increase substantially because there will be a higher proportion of older people in the workforce and because younger people are projected

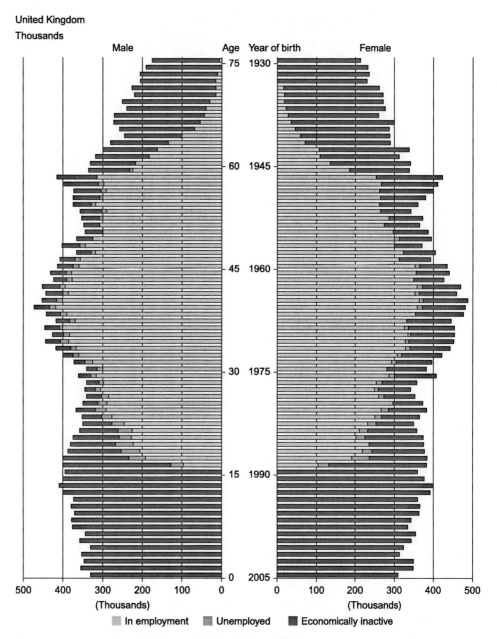

Figure 34.2
Population structure: by age, sex and economic activity, autumn 2005[1]

United Kingdom
Thousands

Male   Age   Year of birth   Female

(Thousands)   (Thousands)

▨ In employment   ▨ Unemployed   ■ Economically inactive

(Source: ONS (2006a) Labour Force Survey.   [1] Not seasonally adjusted)

to choose to stay on in full-time education for longer, on average, than they currently do (Smith *et al.* 2005). We can thus conclude with a degree of confidence both that the supply of labour will increase in the coming two decades and that the profile of the workforce will age significantly.

However, there are important regional differences that it is important to note. The structure, density and growth of the population are by no means likely to be uniform across the whole country. The highest concentrations of older people, for example, are in the resort towns along the south and eastern coasts. Christchurch in Dorset is officially the 'oldest' place in the UK where 33.2 per cent are entitled to draw a state pension. By contrast, pensioners are few and far between in inner London. Tower Hamlets boasts the lowest proportion (only 9.8 per cent), but the numbers are also low in some commuter towns close to London and in cities with large student populations.

The highest concentrations of children are found in Northern Ireland where fertility rates are much higher than elsewhere in the country, while young adults are concentrated in university towns and cities, reflecting the fact that there are now 1.4 million full-time students in the UK. As far as England is concerned, between the 1930s and 2001 the major trend was a movement of people from the north of the country to the south, the southern regions gaining 30,000 people a year on average during this period. Since 2001 there has been an apparent reversal of this long-term trend, the north gaining 35,000 people per year at the expense of the south (Champion 2005). However, as a result of migration and falling fertility rates the populations of Scotland and Wales are both falling. In both countries there are considerably more deaths than births each year and relatively high levels of net emigration.

We can also predict with some certainty that there will be greater diversity among the workforce in terms of ethnicity and national origin as a result of net immigration.

All around the world international migration is increasing. As far as the UK is concerned this means that the long-term trend is towards greater levels of both emigration and immigration (Horsfield 2005). Until the early 1990s the UK had been broadly in balance as far as international migration was concerned for around twenty years. Indeed, for much of the 1970s and during the early 1980s more people left the UK each year than entered it. Since 1993 this trend has changed. Every year there are now substantially more immigrants than emigrants, a gap which widens year on year. People leaving the UK tend to be older on average than the new arrivals. Many leave in order to retire in sunnier climes, while others seek new opportunities in Australasia, the USA, Canada and EU countries. A fair proportion of annual emigration each year involves people who were born overseas returning to their countries of origin, for example following a period studying in a UK university. Historically the main source of immigrants into the UK has been from new Commonwealth countries such as India, Pakistan, Bangladesh and from the Caribbean. However, more recently we have seen a substantial growth in people arriving from other developing countries (such as Somalia) and especially from the countries which joined the European Union in May 2004 (i.e. Poland, Slovakia, Hungary, Cyprus and the Baltic states).

As a result of net immigration the proportion of the UK population which was born overseas increases each year, the vast majority of these people being of working age (Randall and Salt 2005). At the time of the 2001 census just under five million UK residents had been born overseas. This represents 8.3 per cent of the population. This is a great deal higher than was the case at the time of previous censuses. In 1991 the figure was 6.7 per cent, and in 1951 only 4.2 per cent. Here too, however, there is considerable regional variation. Forty-eight per cent of immigrants arriving in the UK settle in London and the south east of England, the largest numbers settling in inner London. The London borough of Brent boasts the highest proportion of foreign-born residents (46.6 per cent). By contrast, the lowest levels (under 3 per cent) are found in the English-Scottish border regions.

If current trends continue the supply of labour across the UK as a whole should be sufficient to meet the growing demand for labour. Chronic skills shortages will be avoided provided government and employers continue to invest in the education and development of people. Importantly, in these respects the UK is a great deal better placed than many of its competitor countries where the population is falling and is ageing at a far faster rate than is the case in Britain. Fertility rates in many southern and eastern European countries have now fallen well below 1.5, meaning that each couple produces on average fewer than 1.5 children. A fertility rate of 2.1 is required to maintain a stable population, yet it is 1.32 in Germany, 1.28 in Italy, 1.27 in Spain and only 1.26 in Poland (United Nations 2005). In the UK immigration allows the maintenance of steady population growth, despite historically low fertility rates (1.66 in 2006). This is in contrast to the position of many countries where immigration rules are more restrictive or where low wages and relatively high unemployment make them less attractive to economic migrants.

The statistics suggest, however, that employers in many regions will continue to face some skills shortages. Provided unemployment remains relatively low, this will tend to push wage rates up beyond the rate of price inflation. The result, as has been the case for the past fifteen years, will be greater pressure on organisations to improve labour productivity by reorganising, merging to achieve economies of scale and outsourcing activities where they can be supplied more efficiently by external providers. It will also be necessary for employers willingly to employ more older people than they have tended to be accustomed to doing. Indeed, in order to meet their demand for labour it is likely that organisations are going to have to target older groups and take steps to make employment attractive to them. There are three distinct groups who have not traditionally found themselves to be in great demand by recruiters:

- people over the age of fifty who are still working,
- people who have taken early retirement/redundancy,
- people who are over the state retirement age.

In the case of the first group, traditional full-time jobs will be sought. The others are more likely to be looking for part-time work or some other form of flexible working. Research strongly suggests that most people have a preference for phased retirement as opposed to full-time work until a retirement day and then leisure (HSBC 2006). Employers who can provide flexibility of this kind will be in a far stronger position to compete for the services of older workers than competitors who do not. Another consequence of an ageing population will be the presence among younger employees of more people with responsibility for caring for elderly relatives. Attracting and retaining them will also require flexible working options.

Aside from flexibility, the other major element that needs to be in place in order to attract and retain older people is a culture which fully respects and values their contribution. A great deal of research has been carried out in recent years looking at attitudes to older workers among managers and younger employees. The conclusion is that people commonly stereotype older workers, just as they tend to stereotype young workers. Older workers tend to be seen as being reliable, stable, mature and experienced, but also as difficult to train, resistant to change, over-cautious, poor with technology, slow and prone to ill health. Organisations which are serious about employing more older people will need to tackle such stereotyping and to ensure that opportunities for development are provided for people of all ages.

However, at the same time, employers need to recognise that people do change as they age and do contribute different qualities than younger colleagues. They thus need to be managed somewhat differently from an HR perspective. It will be necessary, for example, to tailor reward packages to suit the needs of older workers as well as younger ones. Clearly this will include pension arrangements, but may also incorporate other benefits which older employees value more than younger employees such as health insurance.

Organisations often seek a workforce which reflects its core target market. This is particularly true of creative and media industries which need younger employees to ensure that they are in touch with the needs, aspirations and concerns of people in the key 18–30 group. This is a major source of age discrimination in the labour market which is likely, over time, to change. Instead of seeking employees who match their consumers by age, employers will want people of any age who reflect the values and attitudes of more broadly-aged target markets.

The changes to HR practice required as a result of increased numbers of workers from overseas are less profound but equally important. The key here is to make sure that the organisation both gains and retains a reputation for fairness in its labour markets. Once an organisation is perceived to be prone to acting in a discriminatory fashion towards members of ethnic minorities or migrant workers, the reputation is hard to shake off, making it harder to recruit and retain a skilled workforce. In this area perceptions of managers about the fairness of their policies and practices is irrelevant. The perception of the target labour market is all that matters, so we can expect to see organisations in the future 'bending over backwards' to ensure not just that they are committed to equal opportunities and diversity, but that they are seen to be too.

ACTIVITY 34.3

According to the demographers at the United Nations several European countries are going to see substantial falls in their populations over the next forty years due to low fertility rates. It is estimated that the German population will fall from 83 million to 79 million by 2050, and the Italian population from 58 million to 51 million. In Russia the projected fall is from 143 million to 112 million By contrast the British and French populations are projected to increase modestly during this period, while in Turkey the population will increase hugely from 77 million today to 101 million in 2050.

What do you think are the main long-term implications for organisations in these different European countries? What will the effect be on the labour market? What will be the effect on the capacity of public sector organisations to deliver vital public services?

FUTURE CONTRACTUAL ARRANGEMENTS

While there is general agreement among commentators about the nature of the work we will be carrying out in the coming decades and the profile of the workforce that will be employed to carry it out, there is considerable disagreement about the types of contract (both legal and psychological) that will be prevalent. For some years now a diverse group of futurologists have gained considerable influence by predicting substantial changes in this area. The most prominent figure in the UK is Charles Handy, who has published a series of books in which he argues that radical change is in store (*see* Handy 1984, 1989, 1994 and 2001). A broadly similar analysis has been developed by Davidson and Rees Mogg (1997), Rifkin (1995) and Bridges (1995), and more recently by Susan Greenfield (2003a and 2003b). While each of these writers, and others who have advocated the evolution of a similar future for the world of work, justify their conclusion somewhat differently, all predict a switch in the dominant form of work from employment to various forms of self-employment. Moreover, where employment continues, people will be far more likely to work from home (connected to others electronically) and to work for small, highly specialised companies and will neither have nor expect long-term job security.

For Handy the future is one in which portfolio careers will dominate. People will move from employer to employer regularly, often working for two concerns at the same time. There will be periods of self-employment and periods of employment, the conventional working life being likened to that of an actor auditioning for work and moving from production to production on stage, screen and television. There will be periods in between assignments when we will be under-employed, and other periods when we have more than enough work on our plates. Davidson and Rees-Mogg (1997, p. 237) prefer the example of film production companies which assemble a group of talented specialists to work on a project, but when it is over 'the lighting technicians, cameramen, sound engineers and wardrobe specialists will go their separate ways'. Others, including Greenfield (1993, p. 92) go further in arguing that 'the concept of the "job" as we know it may disappear altogether' and that 'firms will perhaps bid for employee time almost on a day-to-day basis'. Insecurity of employment, according to this view, will soon become the norm.

The analysis on which these writers base their predictions is thoughtful and logical and can be persuasive. At root they all argue that greater volatility in the world of employment is inevitable as organisations experience increasing volatility in their product markets. Because employers will no longer operate in markets which are at all stable and predictable, it follows that they will be unable to guarantee any kind of stable employment. For most analysts, increased volatility is seen as being a product of increased competition. Sparrow (2002) uses the term 'hyper-competition' to describe a business environment in which lean, highly productive organisations make use of the latest information and communications technologies to sell their goods and services to anyone, anywhere in a fast-evolving, knowledge-based global economy. In such a world, it is argued, no organisation can be viable if it burdens itself with large numbers of dependent employees expecting to enjoy lengthy, stable careers. Instead organisations will continually be expanding and retracting, forming and dissolving, and hiring different people, with different skill-sets on an 'as needs' basis. Greenfield's conclusion is the same, but for her the change will arise not as a result of increased competition, as she predicts greater cooperation and less competition, but simply because increased technical specialisation will mean that the most efficient and effective enterprises will be those which are small and highly flexible. Rifkin argues that traditional jobs will disappear because technological advances will create a world in which machines do many of the jobs currently performed by people. His future is a world of under-employment in which there are not enough jobs to go round, forcing a large proportion of the workforce either into self-employment or into a working life of short-term employment as and when opportunities arise.

A number of arguments have been advanced in opposition to this radical vision of an employment-free future world of work. Nolan (2004) has led the assault in the UK, drawing on empirical data indicating that in most respects, despite evidence of increased volatility in product markets, traditional, long-term, full-time employment is showing no sign whatever of withering away. Indeed, in some respects the trend is towards greater security, albeit in smaller enterprises. He is contemptuous in his criticisms of those who continue to peddle what he sees as misleading myths:

> Scarcely a week passes without a well-paid visionary heralding the demise of paid work and employment or the growing salience in the new economy of the 'free-worker'. Attention to detail is invariably slight. The great variance in the patterns of work and the consequences of past upheavals in employment are routinely ignored. (Nolan 2004, p. 7)

He goes on to make reference to the real trends that are observable in both the UK and the USA, to many of which we have referred in this and in earlier chapters:

- employment levels (i.e. the number of traditional jobs) are rising and not falling;
- the vast majority of workers continue to be employed in permanent jobs;
- job tenure rates have remained broadly stable for decades;
- around a third of the workforce has been employed (already) for ten years or more by their current employer;
- self-employment has not grown appreciably over the past decade;
- the number of temporary workers has fallen substantially over the past ten years.

While this evidence is very convincing, it is too early to condemn Handy, Rifkin and Greenfield as having been hopelessly wrong in their predictions. It is possible that over the coming few decades they will be proved right. But it is fair to point out that, at least in the case of Handy, the same claims were being made twenty-five years ago about what the world of work would be like today, and in many respects the opposite has turned out to be the case.

One possible reason that the predictions of these futurologists may prove to be inaccurate is their over-reliance on an analysis of what is likely to happen to product markets, ignoring in the process other determinants of employment arrangements such as labour market pressures and the regulatory environment. The evidence suggests that they are right about increasing competition and the need for organisations to become more specialised, flexible and productive, but that they are wrong to ignore other factors in the evolving business environment which serve to push organisations in an opposite direction to that which they would prefer given a free hand. For example, it is very often claimed that in the future, because employers will be unable to guarantee long-term employment, they will instead provide their workers with a capacity for greater 'employability'. People will be recruited and motivated, not with the promise of job security, but with skills development and work experience which will help them to build successful portfolio careers. This is a logical prediction if it is assumed that employers do not have to compete with one another for relatively scarce skills. However, as we have seen throughout this book, in recent years the trend has been towards tighter labour markets in which people increasingly have a choice about where they work and are willing as well as able to switch employers when they become dissatisfied. It is at least arguable that most would-be workers prefer secure employment to employability and portfolio career-building. If so the organisations that will be most successful in attracting and retaining people will be those which maximise job security by offering employment on a permanent basis.

Moreover, in a world in which the quality of staff increasingly provides the key to achieving competitive advantage, it is probable that employers will prefer to nurture high levels of commitment and discretionary effort from their people, rather than hiring and firing them on an as needs basis. In other words, employers may well conclude that a committed, productive workforce is not compatible with highly flexible organisation structures, and that the former is a better route to establishing competitive advantage than the latter.

The potential influence of regulation also needs to be taken into account. In the UK there is general agreement among employers and the political establishment that the best way of securing high levels of employment over the long term is to minimise labour market regulation so as to free businesses of costs which make them less competitive internationally. However, much employment regulation now originates at the European level and would not, for the most part, be on UK statute books were it not for Britain's membership of the European Union. The political establishments of the other larger EU countries have tended to take a different view, believing increased social protection to be necessary as a means of promoting greater security of employment. A perception of insecurity, in their view, tends to reduce people's willingness to spend and to put their savings in riskier types of investment vehicle. The result is less economic growth and a greater propensity to stagnation and recession (European Commission 2000). The outcome, as we have seen in recent years, has been a plethora of new employment legislation aiming to increase security by making it increasingly hard for employers to hire and fire either cheaply or easily. This creates a situation in which any journey on the part of employers towards much more flexible organisational forms is made harder both to embark on and to complete.

Finally it is necessary to point out that some economists are increasingly questioning the commonly held view that the business environment of the future will necessarily be characterised by greater volatility, at least as far as the western industrialised countries are concerned. Indeed already they observe far greater levels of economic stability pertaining in countries such as the UK and the USA that have moved farthest down the road away from manufacturing and towards the establishment of knowledge-based service industries. Kaletsky (2006), for example, argues strongly that manufacturing activities are the major source of volatility and that exporting these overseas, leaving home-based employees to focus on product design and marketing, actually serves to guarantee greater security of employment in a global economy. He gives the title 'platform companies' to organisations like Nokia, Dell and L'Oreal which sell their products internationally, but subcontract the entire manufacturing process to other companies:

> Because the manufacture of physical goods is the most volatile and capital-intensive part of the business process, outsourcing [overseas] does not just transfer jobs and factories – platform companies also outsource to China and other developing countries much of the economic volatility that goes with capital investment, inventory cycles and the unionised factory environment. (p. 21)

Could it be therefore that long-term, stable employment, far from being consigned to the dustbin of history, will actually become more common in the future as organisations increasingly outsource the more volatile elements of their operations and concentrate instead on higher-skilled, value-adding activities? Only time will tell, but an analysis of the major current labour market trends is consistent with this possibility.

WINDOW ON PRACTICE

In recent years the UK government has made major investments in new technology as a means of improving standards of service delivery in the public services and reducing costs. In 2004 the Gershon Report entitled 'Transformational Government' was published. This identified £21 billion of possible annual savings across government that could be gained by greater efficiency generated by IT. To date the government claims to have saved £9.8 billion.

In order to deliver the government's ambitious agenda in this field, there is a need to recruit IT professionals with the experience and knowledge to develop highly complex systems. This task is proving difficult because there are relatively few people with the required skills and many potential competitors for their services. Critics say that the government will continue to be restricted in its ambitions until it accepts, as it has been reluctant to do, that it needs to pay people at or above the market rate for their services, while also creating clear career paths so that IT people, once recruited, can develop careers by moving across the different government departments. Historically IT people have tended to be hired on a subcontracted basis to work on one-off projects. This no longer works effectively as a means of sourcing scarce skills because private sector competitors are able to offer the prospect of longer-term career growth.

Source: R. Newing (2005) 'Technology: Rethink on careers as
IT skills shortages loom', *Financial Times*, 15 June.

SUMMARY PROPOSITIONS

34.1 The likely future direction of employment practices in the UK has attracted a great deal of attention in recent years and has led to several hotly contested debates.

34.2 The occupations which are growing fastest are higher-level professional, technical and managerial jobs in the public and private sectors, and lower-paid jobs in the private services sector.

34.3 The working population in the UK is likely to grow at a slower rate in the future than it has in the recent past. It is also going to age and become more ethnically diverse.

34.4 Labour markets are likely to tighten further, leading to more skills shortages and a demand for skilled workers from overseas.

34.5 A radical vision for the future of work has been advocated by several influential management thinkers in recent years. They predict many fewer jobs, less job stability and more self-employment.

34.6 The radical vision is increasingly being challenged by researchers who maintain that the organisation of work is unlikely to alter radically in the foreseeable future.

GENERAL DISCUSSION TOPICS

1 What are the major trends in your own organisation's future demand for skills? To what extent do you foresee these being harder to source in the future and why?

2 What purpose does a study of current demographic trends serve from the point of view of the HR function in organisations?

3 Why do you think management writers continue to predict a revolution in the way work is organised in industrialised countries, despite the presence of evidence suggesting a continuation of the approaches that are currently prevalent?

FURTHER READING

Robert Taylor, formerly labour affairs editor of the *Financial Times*, has published five excellent papers over the past few years focusing on different aspects of the future of work. These draw on the large range of academic research that has been contributed to the Economic and Social Research Council's Future of Work programme. You can download these papers without charge at **www.leeds.ac.uk/esrcfutureofwork**.

The government's Office of National Statistics (ONS) also has an excellent website which can be used to gain access to a large range of authoritative articles and statistics concerning demographic trends and the demand and supply of skills in the UK. You will find summaries of the most recent trends in their annual publications *Social Trends* and *Labour Market Review*.

REFERENCES

Bridges, W. (1995) *Jobshift: how to prosper in a workplace without jobs*. London: Nicholas Brealey.

Champion, T. (2005) 'Population movement within the UK', in Office of National Statistics, *Focus on People and Migration*. London: HMSO.

Davidson, J.D. and Rees-Mogg, W. (1997) *The Sovereign Individual: The coming economic revolution. How to survive and prosper in it*. Basingstoke: Macmillan.

European Commission (2000) *The Future of Work*. London. Kogan Page.

Goos, M. and Manning, A. (2003) 'McJobs and Macjobs: the growing polarisation of jobs in the UK', in R. Dickens, P. Gregg and J. Wadsworth (eds), *The Labour Market Under New Labour*. Basingstoke: Palgrave.

Green, M. (2006) 'Employers alarmed at skills shortage', *Financial Times*, 21 August.

Greenfield, S. (2003a) *Tomorrow's People*. London: Penguin/Allen Lane.

Greenfield, S. (2003b) 'Flexible Futures', *People Management*, 23 October, pp. 52–3.

Grugulis, I., Warhurst, C. and Keep, E. (2004) 'What's happening to "Skill"?', in C. Warhurst, I. Grugulis and E. Keep (eds), *The Skills That Matter*. Basingstoke: Palgrave.

Handy, C. (1984) *The Future of Work*. Oxford: Blackwell.

Handy, C. (1989) *The Age of Unreason*. London: Business Books.

Handy, C. (1994) *The Empty Raincoat: Making Sense of the Future*. London: Hutchinson.

Handy, C. (2001) *The Elephant and the Flea: Looking Backwards to the Future*. London: Hutchinson.

Horsfield, G. (2005) 'International migration', in Office of National Statistics, *Focus on People and Migration*. London: HMSO.

HSBC (2006) *The Future of Retirement: What the World Wants*. London: HSBC.

Jeffries, J. (2005) 'The UK population: past, present and future', in Office of National Statistics, *Focus on People and Migration*. London: HMSO.

Kaletsky, A. (2006) 'Why the sun is rising over Britain, not Japan', *The Times*, 10 November, p. 21.

Newing, R. (2005) 'Technology: Rethink on careers as IT skills shortages loom', *Financial Times*, 15 June.

Nolan, P. (2001) 'Shaping things to come', *People Management*, 27 December.

Nolan, P. (2004) *Back to the Future of Work*. At **www.leeds.ac.uk/esrcfutureofwork/downloads/events/colloquium_2004/nolan_paper_0904.pdf**.

ONS (2006a) *Labour Market Review 2006*. London: HMSO.

ONS (2006b) *Social Trends 2006*. London: HMSO.

Randall, M. and Salt, J. (2005) 'The foreign-born population', in Office of National Statistics, *Focus on People and Migration*. London: HMSO.

Rifkin, J. (1995) *The End of Work: The decline of the global labour force and the dawn of the post-market era*. New York: Puttnam.

Smith, C., Tomassini, C., Smallwood, S. and Hawkins, M. (2005) 'The changing age structure of the UK population', in Office of National Statistics, *Focus on People and Migration*. London: HMSO.

Sparrow, P. (2002) 'The Future of work', in D. Holman, T. Wall, C. Clegg, P. Sparrow and A. Howard (eds), *The New Workplace: a guide to the human impact of modern working practices*. Chichester: Wiley.

Taylor, R. (2002) *Britain's World of Work – Myths and Realities*. At **www.leeds.ac.uk/esrcfutureofwork**.

United Nations (2005) *World Population Prospects: The 2004 Revision*. New York: United Nations.

INDEX